CCB

Charles Culp Burlingham, c. 1930

CCB

The Life and Century of

CHARLES C. BURLINGHAM

New York's First Citizen

1858 – 1959

GEORGE MARTIN

HILL AND WANG

A division of Farrar, Straus and Giroux

New York

Hill and Wang
A division of Farrar, Straus and Giroux
19 Union Square West, New York 10003

Owing to limitations of space, illustration credits can be found on pages 689–90.

Library of Congress Cataloging-in-Publication Data
Martin, George Whitney.
    CCB : the life and century of Charles C. Burlingham, New York's first citizen,
1858–1959 / George Martin. — 1st ed.
      p. cm.
    Includes bibliographical references and index.
    ISBN-13: 978-0-8090-7317-7
    ISBN-10: 0-8090-7317-X (hardcover : alk. paper)
      1. Burlingham, Charles C. (Charles Culp), 1858–1959.   2. Politicians—New
York (State)—New York—Biography.   3. Social reformers—New York (State)—
New York—Biography.   4. Lawyers—New York (State)—New York—Biography.
5. New York (N.Y.)—Biography.   6. New York (N.Y.)—Politics and government—
1898–1951   7. New York (N.Y.)—Social conditions.   I. Title: C.C.B.   II. Title.

F128.5.B927M37 2005
324.2'092—dc22
[B]   2004054088

Designed by Dorothy Schmiderer Baker
Maps designed by Jeffrey L. Ward

www.fsgbooks.com

1 3 5 7 9 10 8 6 4 2

For New York City,

WHICH HE AND SO MANY OTHERS

HAVE LOVED

CONTENTS

The Burlingham and Hoe family trees can be found on pages 86–87.

Maps of parts of New York City that were important in Burlingham's life can be found on pages 114, 312, and 356.

Illustrations follow page 338.

CCB

PROLOGUE

New York's First Citizen

CHARLES C. BURLINGHAM, though holding no public office, liked to "meddle"— his word—in public affairs, municipal, state, and national. In this he was not unique; there were, and are, many like him in American cities and towns, for we have in this country a tradition of private citizens seeking singly or in voluntary associations to influence community leaders and representatives in government. But historians tend to overlook the impact of these people, whose deeds often are done "behind the scenes," by a phone call, letter, or loan, without publicity sought or expected, and hence go unnoted. Yet frequently the history of any event or period—what happened in New York or on Main Street, U.S.A., or even what life is like today—can be fully understood only when the acts of these private citizens are uncovered.

By profession Burlingham was an admiralty (maritime) lawyer, with a practice in the country's largest city and port. Like many in his era, 1858–1959, he to some degree created himself and the activities for which he is worth remembering—chiefly his efforts to improve the administration of justice, especially the selection of judges in the municipal, state, and federal systems, and his continual drive to cleanse New York City's government of corruption. He had no power, no elective office or constituency at the polls, but he had influence with many who did, presidents and chief justices of the United States, governors of the state, and mayors of the city, most notably Franklin D. Roosevelt and Fiorella La Guardia. Gradually the newspapers discovered his influence at work and, approving his goals, began to celebrate him as "New York's First Citizen," and in the last quarter of his long life he was well known in legal, government, and journalistic circles and also to newspaper readers generally, for he wrote many excellent letters to the papers on public issues.

Today he is mostly forgotten, though appearing often as a name in other men's biographies. Yet his life is worth recalling. He made of it something special, and he had a hand in many important events, some of which can be charted correctly only when his "behind the scenes" role is disclosed—events ranging from the lawsuits that followed the sinking of the *Titanic* through the nomination and election of La Guardia as mayor of New York to the fights between Roosevelt and Robert Moses over the construction of bridges across the city's East River.

To discover his part in such events, I have had to rely greatly on interviews with those who knew him, on unpublished memoirs, and on his very wide and mostly unpublished correspondence. Fortunately, he hated the telephone but liked to write letters; indeed, he should be reckoned one of the country's great letter writers. In those to newspapers he analyzed complicated public issues with remarkable clarity; more privately, he deployed a breezy charm; and even in hasty notes, to which he was much given, he seemed to breathe his thought directly onto the page, so that his familiar voice rang pleasantly in the reader's ear. No doubt his flow of ideas, expressed with such clarity and charm, induced many recipients, though busy and famous, to reply, and these exchanges, because his generation seems to have saved almost anything put on paper, have been preserved in libraries and family collections, and frequently cast light on otherwise obscure events.

Consider, for example, the nomination and election of La Guardia to be mayor of New York in 1933. It has a claim to be the most significant event in the history of our country's efforts to cleanse its cities of municipal corruption, yet it also is a model of attempts at reform in smaller cities and towns across the country. In New York, the politicians and private citizens may be better known, but in their personalities, in their actions and reactions, their counterparts can be found in any city. Thus, to reveal Burlingham's part as a private citizen in this event not only tells his story but suggests the parts played by others across the country in similar events. Without forgoing a particle of his particularity, he can also serve as a representative of the many others who, taken altogether, have wrought a long and bright tradition of American citizenship.

By midsummer 1933 Burlingham, by then commonly called "CCB," was about to turn seventy-five and, unlike most of his contemporaries, was still in good health and practicing law in the city. The firm Burlingham, Veeder, Feary, Clark & Hupper was his; he had created it, guided its growth, took the largest share of its profits, and as the "old man" could do what work he wanted while calling on others to help him. In his already long life he had accomplished much. But when in early August a political crisis in the city brought him a chance to do more, despite age and the summer heat, he seized it. In public affairs, as he one time confessed, "I like to butt in."[1]

This time, however, he entered by invitation, asked to rescue a movement for reform that was failing. Throughout that spring and early summer, political reform groups in the city had sought a candidate whom all could support in the November election of mayor. By uniting behind one man, the reformers hoped to defeat the usually dominant Democratic organization, led by Manhattan's Tammany Hall, the political clubhouse with citywide power. Tammany's corruption recently had been exposed in a series of investigations that had shocked the city and nation. For three years newspapers across the country had trumpeted New York's shame, with headline stories of police and judicial corruption, of graft and bribery in every department of City Hall. The trail of money stolen from the city by Tammany officeholders—even from funds to aid the hundreds of thousands of unemployed in those Depression years—had led to the top, to Mayor Jimmy Walker. After the state's governor, Franklin D. Roosevelt, himself a Democrat, had removed the city's sheriff from office, the mayor, to avoid the same fate, on 1 September 1932 had resigned and promptly sailed for Europe.

CCB had worked for municipal reform in many previous movements, and with success in 1894, 1901, and 1913. But Tammany, after enduring a single term of a reform administration, always had recovered its strength and retaken City Hall. Now, with Tammany's corruption so plain, the chance to elect another reform administration, one that might last longer than four years, seemed excellent. Would-be reformers—Republican, anti-Tammany Democrat, Socialist, businessmen, and Independents— joined groups like the City Club, the Citizens Union, the Chamber of Commerce, or, as had CCB, the newly formed Independent Fusion Committee. These groups, in turn, had united in support of a large Fusion Coordination Committee, on which they all had seats. New York, however, was a Democratic city, and Tammany had a comfortable margin in any election of some 500,000 votes. That margin plainly required the reformers to "fuse," lest by splitting their votes they lose separately. Yet by mid-July this committee, despite many meetings, had not found a candidate, and the September primaries were nearing.

At a lunch on 2 August three reform leaders discussed the need for an inner "Harmony" Committee of a dozen or so to lead its parent group to agreement, and that afternoon one of the three went to Burlingham's office to invite him to act as Harmony chairman. In politics, CCB was an Independent Democrat, and among reformers generally was considered to be the "oldest and wisest sage."[2] Spry at seventy-five, he had useful qualities besides age and wisdom: he never sought office or reward for himself; had a light touch in discussion; stood well with important newspaper editors; and had a skill, in public letters, in articulating issues. If anyone could, he might lead the reformers from quarrel to accord and to a "Fusion" candidate.

The two men most often mentioned for nomination were the Independent Democrat Samuel Seabury and the Republican Fiorello La Guardia. Each was honest, passionate, and at times headstrong. Seabury, one of the three proposing the Harmony Committee, was a New York City lawyer and former judge with a new nationwide reputation as the special prosecutor whose investigations had forced Mayor Walker to resign. He was tall, dignified, white-haired, and a good speaker. Some persons thought him a bit pompous, but to most he seemed the ideal Fusion candidate: who would not vote for the gallant Knight of Reform? But despite all calls, he refused to run. Yet because he seemed so suited to the post, the appeals continued, making it difficult for reformers to agree on a substitute. Seabury held to his decision, continually proposing La Guardia instead.

La Guardia, short, round, and rumpled, was also a good speaker, but in that summer of 1933 he was not popular with any reform group. A Republican congressman for fourteen years, he had won a national reputation for his liberal views, particularly for sponsoring the Norris–La Guardia Act, which forbade injunctions in labor disputes. Because in Congress he always had been a party maverick, many Republicans distrusted him, and in 1932 he had lost his seat in the Democratic landslide that had brought Governor Franklin D. Roosevelt into the presidency. Currently without office, he was eager to run for mayor, but the city's Republican leaders were unenthusiastic, and most of the Republican business community considered him a demagogue. In speeches and articles La Guardia had railed against bankers as the chief cause of the Depression, and had made charges, only partially true but luridly stated, that had angered the bankers and their friends, families, and clients.

Not surprisingly, many members of the City Club and the Chamber of Commerce rejected him as a candidate, turning instead, with Seabury unavailable, to General John F. O'Ryan, a World War I hero. O'Ryan, who had some political experience and now was a banker, was also a leading member of another new group, the City Fusion Party. Politically, he was counted an Independent Democrat, but because he was conservative in his views, he was acceptable to Republicans. But he was immediately wounded as a possible Fusion candidate by an irate Seabury, who proclaimed in headlines that O'Ryan had no chance of defeating Tammany's candidate—whereas La Guardia, born in Manhattan of Italian and Jewish parents, two groups increasingly powerful in the city, could win.

By 2 August, when CCB agreed to lead a Harmony Committee, he was also inclined to favor La Guardia, and for more than demographic reasons. He had met him at a small dinner party and been impressed by the ex-congressman's grasp of the city's problems and possible solutions. But as chairman of the new committee, he did not lobby for him. Calling his committee to meet at the City Bar Association on the night of 3 August, in the midst of the summer's worst heat wave, CCB required it to choose its candidate for mayor. Neither La Guardia nor O'Ryan was present, but in addition to CCB and Seabury there were ten men and two women, with all the important reform groups and the Republican Party represented. The discussion became rancorous, and ultimately CCB ordered Seabury to sit down, a command that brought a startled general silence. In the end, when La Guardia had won by a divided vote, CCB telephoned O'Ryan, told him of the tally, and asked him to withdraw so that the decision might be unanimous. O'Ryan graciously complied. Thus, after midnight, the Harmony Committee had its candidate.

The campaign against Tammany's candidate, John P. O'Brien, began at once. La Guardia's name would appear on the ballot on two lines, the Republican and the Fusion Party. The Republicans set up a campaign office for him, but his main source of support lay in the Fusion campaign committee, which met every weekday for breakfast to plan strategy. The "steadies" of that committee, in CCB's phrase, were CCB; Seabury; William M. Chadbourne, an elderly Republican who lent his apartment for the meetings and provided breakfast; and La Guardia.[3] In the mid-September primary elections Fusion's ticket ran strongly, whereas Tammany's did poorly, revealing a revolt in the Democratic clubs and cohorts that suggested a split vote in November. La Guardia, in a poll taken immediately after the primary, led O'Brien 4 to 1, and reformers' spirits soared.

Then, on 29 September, they crashed. President Roosevelt, in a backhand fashion, entered the race. At his suggestion, "Boss" Ed Flynn of the Bronx Democratic organization announced a new "Recovery Party" with Joseph V. McKee, a banker and Independent Democrat, as its candidate for mayor. Roosevelt wanted a mayor indebted to him for the office so that he and Flynn could have some say in filling the thousands of city jobs open to patronage appointment. Neither O'Brien nor La Guardia owed their nominations to Roosevelt or Flynn, and neither would be likely to grant them any favors. But with McKee they would have leverage, and so they launched their new party, suddenly turning the election into a three-way race.

McKee made a good candidate because in September of the previous year, when Walker had resigned, McKee, as president of the Board of Aldermen, had served four months as acting mayor—four months until, in a special election, the voters could choose a mayor to finish the last year of Walker's term. (Tammany had won that special election, putting O'Brien in office and expecting him to run in November for the next full term.) But McKee, in his brief term, had proved himself a good, honest administrator, and Roosevelt hoped that Republicans disliking La Guardia, and rich Democrats who wanted to vote against Tammany without leaving their party, would support McKee, quickly filling his campaign chest. Despite the efforts of CCB and others, La Guardia's coffers were close to empty, and in mid-October the Fusion campaign, though rich in volunteers, ran out of money. To keep it going, CCB, who was comfortably off but not rich, came to the rescue with a large loan over and above what he already had contributed. If the Fusion campaign ended solvent, he would be repaid in whole or in part; if not, he would count the loan a gift.

By then McKee, not O'Brien, was proving to be La Guardia's chief opponent, and to lessen his appeal to voters Seabury and La Guardia in their speeches continually cast him as a front for Tammany. If McKee won, they warned, though he might be personally honest, Tammany would control the lesser posts and the old corruption would continue. Meanwhile, over the last weeks of the campaign hovered the prospect that Roosevelt would do something—invite McKee to the White House or mention him favorably in a speech—that would bestow on him a highly publicized presidential blessing.

CCB knew Roosevelt well, had supported him steadily in his New York political career and in his campaign for president. But he also had never hesitated to write to him, though usually in a gentle, humorous vein, when he thought Roosevelt was doing wrong. In this election, however, he apparently decided not to challenge the president directly; his disapproval of the McKee maneuver was plain enough in his vigorous support for La Guardia. Where he could, however, he sought to keep himself and his activities in the president's mind.

As the campaign entered its final two weeks, he sent a two-sentence letter to Roosevelt, confident it would be delivered promptly and its idea considered. At the time, the German Jewish physicist Albert Einstein was on his way to the United States to take a post at Princeton's Institute for

Advanced Study, and CCB suggested: "Don't you think it would be a grand gesture if you should invite Professor Einstein to call on you or break bread at the White House? It would seem natural and appropriate for the President to show hospitality to such a great man, and for that reason it could not be treated by official Germany as objectionable."[4] Typically, CCB launched his suggestion in a brief letter, without preaching or seeking credit for himself, while offering the recipient an opportunity to shine. Roosevelt at once saw political advantage in the idea, and by 28 October, ten days before the New York election, had cleared the proposed invitation with the State Department. The following January, Professor and Mrs. Einstein spent the night at the White House and were reported in the newspapers to have admired the president's collection of marine prints.[5]

Meanwhile, in New York, the campaign for mayor ran its course, and the presidential blessing Roosevelt had promised to McKee was withheld—without explanation to either Flynn or McKee. Whether CCB's note to Roosevelt had any part in Roosevelt's betrayal of his candidate is quite speculative. It may have served, however, to remind the president that he liked CCB, perhaps owed him a little something, and perhaps should not interfere so directly in New York City affairs. For CCB, at least, such a way of thinking and acting would be characteristic.

Fusion's final rally for La Guardia was held in Madison Square Garden, five days before the election. When the candidate entered the arena, the crowd stomped and cheered, and when time came for La Guardia's speech, which was to be broadcast, CCB, as chairman, raised a sign for silence and the crowd quieted. La Guardia repeated the theme of his campaign: the destruction of Tammany and its system of crony government, and the promise of a more responsive, more beautiful, more humane city. After the election, when the votes were tallied, La Guardia had 868,122; McKee, 609,053; and Tammany's O'Brien, 586,672. Roosevelt's McKee, thus, was a true "spoiler," keeping La Guardia, who had won only 40 percent of the total vote, from gaining a secure majority. Further, the Fusion ticket, because of McKee, lost many posts to Tammany that it had hoped to win. Still, on New Year's Day, La Guardia was mayor.

CCB's part in the Fusion campaign, though less visible than Seabury's because he did far less stump speaking, had not gone unnoticed. His name was frequently in the newspapers, and soon after the Garden rally Roy Howard, editor and publisher of the *World-Telegram*, stated bluntly in an editorial: "The anti-Tammany movement owed a big debt of gratitude to Charles C. Burlingham."[6]

Also after the election CCB received many private letters of praise and thanks. One came from his friend Learned Hand, a federal judge and New York City voter who had followed the campaign closely: "I cannot let the day pass without some word to you to show my feeling for what you have done to bring about this victory for all we hold best in government. I was not on the inside and can only go on what I have heard, but you were the person who made all this possible, your tact, your skill, your persistence and your courage."[7] CCB replied in his usual offhand style: "Perhaps I ought to have settled down into old age some time ago. The truth is I like messing about in public or quasi-public business. I have especially enjoyed my relations with the crooked Republican county leaders and got a lot of fun out of my talks with [Tammany Boss] Curry, et al."[8]

He was more open to Hand than to others. In the midst of his efforts he had told one acquaintance, "It is unseemly that an old codger like me should be going through all these motions which belong to youth." That was the mask he held up to the public. But in truth, he liked "messing about" in civic affairs. He had been doing it for years.[9]

Nevertheless, CCB did not expect to have any role in La Guardia's administration. In August he had written to one well-wisher that his work would end with balancing the ticket[10]—but always there had been more to do. In late November he wrote to his friend Felix Frankfurter, the Harvard law professor who that year was lecturing in England:

> La Guardia is back [from vacation in Puerto Rico] and is out for the best [men to appoint]. I know a few of the names and they're good, but he has talked only for a moment or two with me. He has seen a lot of Samuel Seabury whose advice, I think, has been excellent. I don't expect to have to do much with La G. I feel that [Adolf A.] Berle [Jr.] will have a lot of influence, and there is a very good and sensible fellow, Paul Windels, one of the counsel for the Port Authority, whom La Guardia knows well and trusts. The future is at least interesting.[11]

CCB's view that he would have little to do with La Guardia's administration soon proved wrong. La Guardia increasingly turned to him for advice, a development CCB enjoyed, and after a few months it became clear to those around the mayor that a special relationship was growing between the old man and the city's chief executive. Often in the morning, La Guardia, who continued to live in his walk-up apartment on the edge of East Harlem, would stop in his official limousine at 860 Park Avenue, pick up CCB, and on the way to City Hall they would discuss the issues of the day. Sometimes a clue to what was said can be found in a note scribbled later, but for the most part their discussions went unrecorded. Every now and again in the late afternoon CCB, who became concerned about La Guardia falling ill from overwork, would stop by City Hall and, in an act no one else would have dared, would hand the mayor his hat, saying, "Come on, Fiorello; it's time to quit. We will ride uptown together." And the mayor would smile, and go. As another of La Guardia's biographers noted, the mayor "would take a scolding" from CCB—"and from no one else in the world."[12]

The older man seemed to fill some sort of psychological need of the younger, but the relationship was not reciprocal. CCB became fond of La Guardia but had no such need of him, and probably his lack of emotional involvement strengthened his hand in dealing with the mayor, who often, especially when tired or distressed, became a bully. La Guardia had a temper, which he frequently lost or as frequently used to cow subordinates and to defeat opposition. Nevertheless, what La Guardia offered New York, what CCB and others valued highly, was extraordinary competence, demonstrated from his first day in office. With La Guardia in City Hall, reform might conduct such a revolution that, by dispossessing Tammany and making its restoration impossible, the city might be cleansed of the corruption that many political scholars considered the greatest blot on American forms of government.[13]

What CCB had to offer the mayor was a lifetime of experience in city affairs, disinterested judgment (for CCB coveted no office or honors), and a very wide range of influence. Influence, not power. Unlike Flynn and President Roosevelt, for instance, CCB could not deliver for La Guardia the Democratic vote in the Bronx, nor could he, in any project, order action to be taken. Yet such was his influence that even when opposing Roosevelt's candidate, he had Roosevelt's ear. Moreover, he could write in that informal style not only to the president of the United States but to the chief justice of the Supreme Court, to the governor of New York, to heads of banks, bar associations, and civic organizations. And most, when he spoke or wrote to them, replied. Similarly, those in lower ranks, aware of CCB's direct access to the top, were quick to respond to his requests for information, and so, through a wide correspondence, he kept himself remarkably well informed.

To many who observed Burlingham in these years he seemed the ideal lawyer-statesman, one who, though not in public office, influenced public affairs for the better. One young Republican who worked closely with him on the La Guardia campaign, Herbert Brownell (later President Eisenhower's attorney general), particularly admired CCB's geniality, enthusiasm, pragmatism, and ability to give young people a feeling of sharing in the work to be done. Brownell marveled at the way CCB could "take people of all kinds, without judgements on them, and do with them what good was possible."[14]

When and how did Burlingham acquire that ability? Answers from those who knew him are surprisingly unclear. Many people assumed that he was born a "patrician" and always had or soon developed the ability to take people as they are, without judgment, because of an innate, aristocratic self-assurance. One of La Guardia's biographers, for instance, said that CCB "carried the caste mark of the American establishment." In fact, he had a simpler background and more complicated personality than most of his legal friends and acquaintances realized, and was more self-constructed than they suspected.[15]

It was not until the Fusion campaign of 1933 and La Guardia's first year in office that journalists "discovered" him as a personality and began with regularity to celebrate him. Possibly the earliest description of him as New York's First Citizen appeared in *The Nation* in September 1933. Its editor and publisher, Oswald Garrison Villard, a strong advocate of Fusion and reform, wrote:

> There would have been no fusion ticket at all if it had not been for a singularly fine, able, fearless and devoted citizen of New York, Charles C. Burlingham. If any man deserves the title of First Citizen of this municipality, it is Mr. Burlingham. If there [is] any good liberal cause which has not had his aid and support, I should like to know what it is . . . Isn't it wicked that when there are Americans of this admirable type we get so damnably few of them into our public life?[16]

Other journals soon picked up the complimentary title, and by the end of the 1930s it was in common use. Eventually some New York papers, particularly the *Times, Herald Tribune*, and *World-Telegram*, started a custom of noting his birthday, 31 August, with an article about him and his activities. He thought the attention premature; soon enough at death. To the editors of the *Times*, following their effusion in 1938, he wrote: "Your piece about me might well have been saved for a later occasion, but it was certainly very nice of you . . . I greatly prefer Youth to Age. Yes, I know—Sophocles, Voltaire, and B. Franklin, but most of us old fellows cumber the ground."[17]

By September 1933 CCB was already ten years past his life expectancy, and perhaps the journalists felt their time for celebration was short. Still, he continued busily alive. At a Harvard commencement in 1934, he defused a potentially ugly political confrontation over President Roosevelt's New Deal. In 1937 he had a leading role in opposing Roosevelt's efforts to dilute the judicial opposition to his programs by increasing the number of judges on the Supreme Court. In 1941, with others, he led a campaign against a Brooklyn-Manhattan bridge proposed by Robert Moses, which would have overwhelmed the southern tip of Manhattan. Outside of municipal politics, he worked hard on church and social causes, and advocated the greater inclusion of women and ethnic minorities on the bench, in the law schools, bar associations, and in his church. Meanwhile, he acted as minister without portfolio to La Guardia, sometimes preserving the mayor from excess and mistake.

All the while the newspapers continued to celebrate him as New York's First Citizen. He thought the publicity and praise overdone. In 1948, after his ninetieth birthday, he thanked a friend for a telegram, describing it as "wasteful but welcome." Then he added: "The 1st Citizen business is the bunk of course, and this is its origin—at a lunch in La G's first campaign for Mayor a silly ass introduced me as 1st cit. It has haunted me ever since. La G. used it to tease me . . . The consequence is a mass of letters, telegrams and cards. I thought I'd answer them all, but I can't, and I am printing a card like a wedding or a death notice."[18]

Yet he continued healthy and active, becoming with each advancing year more extraordinary, and the newspapers continued their annual salutes. Whether he wished it or not, for twenty-five years—he died in 1959, in his 101st year—he was New York's First Citizen.

Part One

AS THE TWIG IS BENT . . .

I

A Boy's View of the Civil War

"I WAS BORN CHEAP," Burlingham would reply when asked how he, New York's First Citizen, came to be born in Plainfield, New Jersey. At the time, 31 August 1858, his father, the Reverend Aaron Hale Burlingham, was pastor at the South Baptist Church on New York's West Twenty-seventh Street, and his parents lived in a small brick house nearby. Yet "I was taken in my mother's womb to Plainfield to be born cheap in the house of my aunt, with the aid of my medical uncle, and I returned to New York City as speedily as practicable."[1] He always regretted the circumstance. When, in 1933, Columbia University gave him an honorary degree and President Nicholas Murray Butler referred to him as a "Son of New Jersey," he squirmed and later told Butler he was "not entitled" to that honor: Plainfield had been a quirk of finance, without loyalty entailed on either side.[2]

In his naming, however, he escaped a discomfort. His father proposed "Theophilus Culp," to honor a close friend of Dutch ancestry. But another friend warned, as CCB told the story, that "all the boys would call me 'teacup.'" So in place of "Theophilus" the name of CCB's paternal grandfather, Charles, was substituted, and he was christened "Charles Culp."[3]

According to CCB, his grandfather Charles Burlingham (1776–1852) "was a weak man," and in old age, which on the frontier could come early, perhaps he was. Born in Smithfield, Rhode Island, as a young man he went west to Saratoga County, New York, and in 1818 farther west to the upper Genesee Valley, to what later became the town of Pike, in Wyoming County. The place was then a wilderness, and he, with his wife and family, followed blazed roads and Indian trails until, at what seemed a likely place, they stopped and began to hack a home from the woods and to farm. His eldest son, Benjamin, eighteen at the time, recalled, "[We] "had plenty of axe and handspike work."[4] The family grew, and the children ultimately numbered seven boys and three girls—another girl dying in infancy.

After fifteen years of combating nature, the grandfather's energies began to fail, and at age fifty-seven he gave his farm to a son, Prentice, who soon turned it over to his brother John. Upon each transfer there was a condition: the holder of the father's farm must maintain the parents as well as the youngest child, the eleven-year-old Aaron (1822–1905).

The combined farms now had ninety acres and two small houses, and because John, with his wife and baby, lived in the larger, he took in with him his brother, Aaron, an arrangement that for Aaron was not wholly satisfactory. Except for the three and a half months of winter when he went to the local district or common school, he was expected to work full-time on the farm, and John was not an easy man. Years later Aaron wrote of him, "John was not flush with money, nor free from littleness in the administration of the double home and in his treatment of the boy. And his wife sympathized with him. Still, they were good people and on the whole meant well."[5] But as a boy and young man, bound by his father's agreement with John, Aaron frequently felt like an indentured servant.

The school was both his refuge and means of escape. Common schools of the time in western New York were an early form of public school, organized locally but, if meeting certain standards, receiving some aid from the state. In the rural counties most children of both sexes, at least until the age of sixteen, attended the brief winter sessions except when needed at home or at work, which was often. Instruction was basic: reading, writing, spelling, arithmetic, geography, and sometimes a little history. Because of the suspicions and prejudices among the many Protestant sects, religion as such was not taught, but the Bible was used as a reader, and pastors of most persuasions visited the schools to conduct prayer meetings and distribute tracts and magazines.[6]

The people of western New York in the forty years before the Civil War were notably alive to religion. The area, then and later, was known as "the burned-over district"—the analogy being, as one writer put it, "between the fires of the forest and those of the spirit." In the intense revivalism of the 1820s and 1830s, everyone read the Bible and was eager to dispute its meaning. New sects formed and after a time were abandoned (Mormonism being the exception). Among those that failed, superstition and credulity often mixed with moral intensity. Thousands, persuaded the world would end on 22 October 1844, had to face the unexpected dawn. Yet by and large the "Yorker Yankees," as they were called, "were extraordinarily wide-awake, well-informed, and ambitious for greater knowledge. Beyond the routine of formal education they were more alert than most other Americans."[7]

Aaron shared in the ferment of this Second Great Awakening and continued in his local common school past sixteen. When eighteen, apparently with John's approval, he went for six weeks to a private school in nearby Castile, a town larger than Pike, and for the remainder of the winter he taught in a village common school there, boarding with local people and giving John the balance of his earnings. For summer, he returned to John's farm, to work without pay. And he did this for two years.

Meanwhile, in 1840, when another religious revival swept western New York, both Aaron and his eldest brother, Benjamin, declared their allegiance to Christ and were baptized by the Reverend James Reid, "uniting" with Reid in the Castile Baptist Church. "I was never a dishonest or immoral young man," Aaron wrote later, "but I came to feel that I was a great sinner, inasmuch as my life was away from God; and I decided to turn over a new leaf and live for the Lord Jesus and for the good of my fellow men." He would be a Baptist preacher.[8]

After a third winter of teaching at a local school, and soon after his twenty-first birthday, on 18 February 1843, Aaron left farm and family at Pike for the Hamilton Literary and Theological Institution at Hamilton, New York, a town of 1,300 people twenty-eight miles south of Utica and 180 east of Castile. He started by horse and wagon, driven by John to the Genesse River Canal, where he boarded a canal boat for Rochester; from there, he went on to Utica by horse-drawn barge on the Erie Canal, built less than two decades earlier. The horses, he noted, "only walked," and the fee was one cent a mile, bunk and board included. Finally, from Utica he rode the stage to Hamilton, where, to save a quarter, he carried his trunk on his back up the long hill to the "university."[9]

The Hamilton Institution then had four buildings, housing a preparatory school for the college (called the Academic Department), the college itself, and the theological school. This collection of schools (which in the spring of 1846 changed its name to Madison, now Colgate, University) had been founded by Baptists in 1819 to train ministers, and by 1843, when Aaron entered, the three schools altogether had a faculty of ten and a student body of 213, most of the latter four or five years younger than Aaron. Nevertheless, he enrolled for the full course—a year of preparatory work, four of college, and two of divinity school.[10] He had seventy-two dollars, earnings from the winter's teaching, which John had allowed him to keep. Years later he recalled:

I ought to have bolted three or four years earlier, yes, five years. I was without money, only the $72, nor had I the promise of any from any source for the undertaking. My brothers, Ben and John, had no conception of the need of an education for the ministry. They discouraged my going to Hamilton as a Utopian scheme—to take an eight [*sic*] years' course of study with $72! They did not give one cent for my education. My church did not offer to help me. My pastor, one of the best of men, a royal preacher and kindly disposed, appreciated my mission and need, but was too timid to press the case upon the church . . . But something impelled me; I was impressed that God in some way would see me through. So gathering together what few little things I could with the ready aid of my dear mother who loved her boy and helped him in whatever his judgement and sense of duty approved, I started out.[11]

Aaron was the first in his family to break away from what he later called "the narrow and unpromising limitations of that backwoods neighborhood." And he did not look back. Somehow, in seven years, taking odd jobs here and there, he put himself through Hamilton's three schools, though "I was prepared for nothing in the course of study . . . I had never seen a Greek or Latin book before. I was too old to commence these studies, but I tugged along as best I could."

On graduating from the divinity school in 1850, his first post as pastor was at the Grant Street Baptist Church, Pittsburgh, from which he soon moved to a church in Oswego, New York, where he stayed two years, during which he married a woman as religious in spirit as he, Emma Lanphear Starr, the daughter of a tanner in Hamilton. She became his companion for life and the mother of his sons, Albert and Charles. And though her family loved and honored her, the better-educated father set its tone and pattern.[12]

He seems never to have returned to Pike or to have introduced his boys to their Burlingham relatives. Some of what he had escaped there is suggested in an obituary of his eldest brother Benjamin, the only family member whose memory Aaron preserved in a family album:

He held fast to what he believed to be right with a grip of iron. Justice and right were words often upon his tongue and he believed that he thoroughly understood their meaning. A different education in youth might have softened some of the asperities of his character which was admired rather for its rugged boldness than for its quiet beauty. He was a man of strongly marked characteristics, having opinions of his own and not loath to defend in any presence and to any extremity that which he believed to be the right.[13]

Aaron had much of Benjamin's contentious steel, but tempered by education and a wider experience of the world. Yet even in late middle age he could preach with a fiery moral certainty that recalled the frontier Protestantism of his youth.

> The man, woman or child who violates the sanctity of the household and brings scandal and shame to the domestic hearth, making the cheek of virtue to blush and filling the air with a moral nausea that sickens and disgusts, is a foul fungus growth on the body of society. Let it be cut off. Aye, not alone does religion and does the church of God say that he who, professing Godliness, so far forgets himself as to be guilty of wanton infidelity to his family, should fall under the censure of his brethren, but also social authority which has its primal seat in the family says that such a sinner should suffer and wither under the scourge of social ostracism as well. The Lord is served by the maintenance of domestic integrity, because the family is of His own founding, and because in the conservation of its purity is involved the weal of humanity in general.[14]

On the other hand, in a lecture he titled "Atmospheres," he revealed a different side of his personality. After stating that he did not intend to talk of oxygen or nitrogen but of men and women, he began to describe how "Individuals and communities create atmospheres of their own, and live in them . . . One snarling man may change the whole air of the shop or field, and make it intolerable. In the presence of some rich men you feel a fullness of blessing coming to you; in the presence of other rich men you feel yourself in a blighting atmosphere."[15]

True riches, for Aaron, lay not in material wealth. He lamented that boys were taken out of school at fourteen or fifteen and put to work, because "in nine cases out of ten" it was the end of any "intellectual growth." And the "esthetic" was equally important to a full Christian life; everything "pertaining to a love of the beautiful . . . is a real thing in our nature." As an example he mentioned the lift in spirit he felt one day when visiting London's grimy tenements and seeing window boxes filled with flowers. Moreover, people needed a good social atmosphere: "When not social we lose enjoyment, virtue, tone and power to do good. Home without the social element is a prison." He extolled families who conversed together, where "the very atmosphere is charged with the sweet breath of congenial spirits." Work, the aim of life, was better done when approached in this spirit, the spirit of "Him in whose glory we hope to find complete and eternal blessedness."

Toward the end of his life, *The Gospel Age* (a Baptist journal) judged Aaron Burlingham to have been a good preacher with "a sharp, incisive style of speech," "originality of thought," and a willingness to deal "with the present truth rather than effete speculations and doctrines." He was not a philosopher; but his thoughts suggest that his home was one in which traditional standards of morality were believed with fervor, yet where people were unafraid of beauty, change, or adventure, a home in which the classical learning of the past was revered even as the new ideas of science were examined and sometimes accepted. Aaron continually admonished his sons to preserve inward integrity but also to look outward, with optimism, to gaze on the world in all its variety, and to find it, for the most part, good.[16]

CCB's earliest recorded memories are of the draft riots that shook New York City for four days during the Civil War. Because volunteers no longer met the needs of the Union army, President Lincoln in the winter of 1863 requested, and Congress passed, a conscription act under which men, beginning in July of that year, would be drafted. The act declared all "able-bodied male citizens" between the ages of twenty and thirty-five and all unmarried men between thirty-five and forty-five liable for military duty, the order of call-up to be decided by a lottery. Those called, however, could escape service by presenting an "acceptable substitute" who would enlist for three years, or by paying three hundred dollars. Because these provisions favored the rich, they angered the poor, who also saw in the act's application to "citizens"—construed as only white men—a discrimination against white labor to the advantage of black, left free to take the white workers' jobs. More than any other Civil War legislation, the Conscription Act brought the federal government into the common citizen's home and workplace.

In New York, on Monday, 13 July 1863, two days after a blindfolded official had drawn from a revolving drum the names of the first 1,200 men to be called, mobs sacked the draft offices. They destroyed the lists of names, smashed the furniture, poured turpentine on the floor, and burned the buildings. One office on Third Avenue near Forty-sixth Street, a block not yet fully built, was attacked at noon, and by evening the building and five or six houses nearby had been destroyed. Another draft office, at Broadway and Twenty-ninth Street and closer to the Burlinghams, by 5 p.m. was in flames along with neighboring buildings. And many houses north of Fourteenth Street were looted.[17]

Initially, the mobs may have been organized and instructed by "Copperheads," members of the Democratic Party who opposed the war, despised

Lincoln, and saw in the Conscription Act a chance to embarrass him and aid the Confederacy. Outside the first draft office to burn, for instance, a well-known Confederate sympathizer, John U. Andrews, addressed the mob. And the timing of the insurrection was well chosen, for much of the state's militia was then in Pennsylvania, at Gettysburg, where the bloody battle had been fought only the week before. Also, the prompt destruction of the tools of war—telegraph lines, shipyards, and railroads—suggested planning. More tenuously, the state's Democratic governor, Horatio Seymour, was characteristically slow to respond, as was also the city's moderate Republican mayor, George Opdyke. But no conspirators have ever been named.[18]

At first, the leaders of the mobs were factory workers, many of them German immigrants who held good jobs and who directed their protests primarily against the draft offices. These men seemed to have intended a one- or two-day strike, but they soon lost any control they had, and by the end of the first day leadership shifted to Irish immigrant longshoremen and day laborers, the least skilled of the city's workforce. These men, miserably paid, housed, and educated, hated abolitionists and the Republican Party and feared that an influx of recently emancipated slaves would take what jobs they had. By late afternoon, increasingly drunk and urged to excess by their women, they were dominated by those with a lust for violence. One such mob attacked the Colored Orphan Asylum on the northern edge of the city, at Fifth Avenue and Forty-third Street, a landmark four-story building housing some 250 children. As the mob in front howled "Burn the niggers' nest," the children were hurried out the back, the large carrying the small, and led to a police station. The mob plundered the building and, despite the efforts of firemen, burned it to the ground; a few hours later, on the city's west side, a waterfront mob hanged a Negro, William Jones, the first of many racial beatings and lynchings.[19]

With many buildings in flames and his own house looted, Mayor Opdyke sought aid for his police from the few units of state militia remaining in the city (mostly staffing armories) and from federal units at the harbor forts guarding the Narrows. The few militia were too ill trained and fearful to be of much help, but the federal troops, though numbering barely a hundred, brought two cannons, bayonets, some sharpshooters, and the discipline to maneuver while under fire. Even so, the police and soldiers were not always able to contain the mobs.

On the second day, Tuesday, despite strong police and troop opposition, a mob broke into the Union Steam Works, an arms factory at Twenty-first Street and Second Avenue, seizing muskets and bullets. As a mob pursued a detachment of soldiers, the troops, alternating ranks and firing directly into the mass of people, retreated in good order. By midnight, buildings in all the northern wards were burning, and the mobs began to build barricades.[20] For four days they controlled many blocks and whole sections of the city, beating, hanging, and shooting all whom they judged responsible for the war or who opposed them. Besides Negroes, abolitionists, and Republicans, their chief victims were the city police, many of whom were Irish. Estimates of the dead ranged from seventy-four to several hundred, with about 125 later identified and probably more not counted because their bodies had been thrown into the Hudson and East Rivers. Not until late Thursday, when federal regiments, with guns and artillery, began to return from Gettysburg, did the mobs start to disperse. In all, the four days of rioting was the most violent civil disorder in the United States of the nineteenth century.[21]

Charley Burlingham, not yet five, could not have understood much of what was happening throughout the four days he was kept indoors. Still, he noticed that guests, common enough in a pastor's home, stayed on, and they, too, never went out. He watched his mother lift a floorboard before the hearth and hide her jewelry. He heard his father, who had gone out early one morning to buy food, report the sight of a Negro hanging from a lamppost. He saw a wounded man carried into the house and later taken out across the roof. In recording his memories CCB added nothing beyond what he had seen. Characteristically, he reported facts, not his feelings.[22]

An exception to this rule was the fire two years later at Barnum's American Museum, "which my brother and I had the great delight of seeing . . . burned to the ground."[23] Neither Albert nor Charley, then eleven and going on seven, had anything against Phineas T. Barnum: CCB meant only to confirm that Barnum once again had presented "the greatest show on earth" as firemen led from the building a collection of animals, sideshow freaks, and a corps de ballet. The museum, five stories high and a half block long, at the corner of Broadway and Ann Street and close to City Hall, was then at the center of the city's civic and cultural life. Broadway, as Edgar Allan Poe had proclaimed in 1845, was "the finest street in the first city of the New World," a sunbathed boulevard of bustle and trade.

> It is the great artery through which flows the best blood of our system . . . The most elegant shops in the City line its sides; the finest buildings are found there, and all fashions exhibit their first gloss upon its sidewalks . . . Wall Street passes its wealth into its broad channel, and all the dealers in intellectual works are here centered, every exhibition of art is found here, and the largest caravansaries in the world border upon it. Its pavement has been trod upon by every distinguished man that has visited our continent.[24]

Set in the midst of this excitement, and a major part of it, Barnum's American Museum partially fulfilled the functions of museums of art and natural history. In addition to the sideshows of curiosities and freaks for which he was most famous, Barnum offered a picture gallery, zoo, aquarium, restaurants, and several large "Lecture Halls," so called not to offend those who from religious scruples would not enter a "Theatre."[25] Everyone knew the museum—admission in 1865 was $.30 for adults, $.15 for children under ten—and when word of the fire passed round the city, a crowd of 40,000 gathered to watch it. Happily for the Burlingham boys, one of their father's parishioners was an official at the Astor House on Broadway, a hotel that was catty-cornered to the museum and close enough to have to drape itself in wet blankets for protection. From a balcony Charley and Albert could see and hear everything: monkeys jabbered, dogs barked, and parrots screeched. The crowd, happy to see the curiosities free of charge, cheered the giantess, the fat lady, the albino girl, and the corps de ballet who, having lost their street clothes to the fire, emerged in costume. Fortunately, the boys could not see the charred bodies of the animals that did not escape, such as the two white whales which had cooked in their tanks.[26] The next day newspapers estimated Barnum's loss at $400,000 and his insurance at $40,000. Within four months he reopened.[27]

On 15 April 1865, Albert's eleventh birthday, the Burlingham family was visiting friends in Brooklyn, and in the early morning the boys, waiting for their mother and father to come down to breakfast, went out on the sidewalk to play. A newsboy delivered the morning paper, which had heavy black borders and a headline LINCOLN ASSASSINATED. The boys were shocked, for theirs was a Republican family—their father had voted for Lincoln and served as an inspector for the U.S. Sanitary Commission—and they ran inside to tell their parents.[28]

The news stunned the city. Shops did not open, and people gathered in crowds awaiting bulletins. As one New Yorker, George Templeton Strong, wrote that night in his diary: "Above all, there is a profound, awe-stricken feeling that we are, as it were, in immediate presence of a fearful, gigantic crime, such as has not been committed in our day and can hardly be matched in history." Soon a plan emerged: Lincoln would be buried in Springfield, Illinois, transported there in his coffin by a train passing slowly through seven of the Northern states, halting for ceremonies in twelve of the larger cities, including New York.[29]

In Philadelphia the coffin was placed in Independence Hall and an estimated 330,000 people passed on either side to gaze on Lincoln. That day a local Episcopal minister, Phillips Brooks, soon to be one of the country's greatest preachers and one with a direct impact on CCB's development, delivered an address on Lincoln that in the coming years became possibly the best known. Characterizing the president as "the Shepherd of the People," Brooks talked of the issues that had shaped his life and views, chiefly the conflict between freedom and slavery. Stressing the inevitability that some slave-holder would want to kill the representative of freedom, he concluded: "I charge this murder where it belongs, on slavery."[30]

From Philadelphia, the funeral train and coffin proceeded to Jersey City, the railroad's terminal on the western bank of the Hudson River. There, in a solemn changing of the guard, dignitaries of New Jersey consigned the closed coffin to their counterparts of New York, who, with soldiers carrying it shoulder-high through silent crowds, accompanied it aboard the ferry *Jersey City*. Thousands then, on either shore, watched the ferry draped in black, with flags at half-mast, cross the Hudson to Manhattan, docking at the foot of Desbrosses Street. New York's Seventh Regiment was waiting, having formed a hollow square to contain the funeral cortege for the march to City Hall. Along the route, a crowd waited, but again, thanks to his father's friend at the Astor House, Charley was at a window overlooking Broadway as the cortege passed by.[31]

Down Broadway came the ranks of officials, dignitaries, and generals, followed by the honor guard, with Colonel Emmons Clark on horseback and his troops surrounding the cortege. The hearse of plate glass, topped by eight plumes of black and white feathers, was draped with the American flag and drawn by six gray horses, each covered with black cloth and led by a groom dressed in mourning. Years later, in describing the procession to his grandson, CCB stressed its silence: "No sound except the drum, the clop of hooves, the women sobbing."[32]

The coffin was put in the rotunda of City Hall, on the second floor, in the space before the door to the Governor's Room and reached by flanking stairways. By noon on that Monday, 24 April 1865, the people began to file past. In two lines they ascended one stairway to the open coffin, paused, and descended the opposite stair. One who that day looked on Lincoln was CCB.[33]

The next afternoon, a grander procession formed at City Hall to accompany the coffin to the Hudson River Railroad terminal at Ninth Avenue and Thirtieth Street, where it would be put on a train for Albany and cities farther west. For this march there were seven divisions of troops and dignitaries, with the honor guard again New York's Seventh Regiment, led by Colonel Clark, marching with arms reversed, gun muzzles to the ground. The funeral cart now was more ornate, a big platform with a dais for the coffin and a canopy of black cloth above. At the foot of each column were three national flags festooned and creped, and at the top, at the canopy's corners, four huge sable plumes, nodding and quivering at every movement. Like a crown atop the canopy's raised center was a small circular Temple of Liberty, unwalled, open, empty. Sixteen gray horses pulled the cart, each led by a groom, horses, and men in black. This procession Charley watched from a sidewalk along the route.[34]

Sometime in the 1930s, he described it to a friend's son, a young boy amazed to discover a man who had been at Lincoln's funeral procession; and sixty years later that boy attempted to recall the account. "Somehow, CCB got himself a place on the curbstone, and then: 'Here comes the so-and-so regiment, led by Col. Somebody-or-other, on his horse, Flibberti-gibbet. But this is no ordinary horse. Oh, no. Let me tell you. This is a very special horse. At the battle of Cedar Creek . . .' My God! The old man knew it all. We were in the mid-1930s, yet there he was, a child of the Civil War!"[35]

As a preacher's son Charles Burlingham was raised on ideas of public duty and sacrifice, and in his earliest memories Lincoln and others who gave their lives in the Civil War represented an ideal of manhood. When grown, he knew if not the men themselves their survivors; for instance, the family of Colonel Robert Gould Shaw, among whom he was to have many friends.[36] And in middle age, in his summer cottage at Black Point, Connecticut, CCB hung on his main study wall, over his desk, a large sepia photograph of Augustus Saint-Gaudens's bronze monument to Shaw. The bas-relief shows the colonel, on horseback, leading his Fifty-fourth Massachusetts Regiment of Negro volunteers down Beacon Street in Boston. The moment represented is 28 May 1863, the day the regiment embarked for South Carolina. On 18 July it took part in the attack on Fort Wagner, where Shaw and many of his men were killed. They were buried together. For many in the North Shaw personified the call to duty and sacrifice articulated by Julia Ward Howe in her immensely popular "Battle Hymn of the Republic":

> In the beauty of the lilies, Christ was born across the sea
> As he died to make men holy, let us die to make men free.[37]

For CCB, the example of living and dying offered by such men as Lincoln and Shaw never staled. Driven deep into his spirit when a boy, it was with him always.

2

A Spirit Open to Stimulus

IN THE SUMMER OF 1865, in Dr. Burlingham's ninth year at his South Baptist Church, on Twenty-fifth Street, he abruptly quit. According to CCB, his father "had a quarrel with one of his deacons and came home one day and told my mother he had resigned. She was much distressed and said, 'What shall we do?' 'Oh,' said my father, 'we will go to Europe.'" He sold his small brick house, in which his equity "was only $2,000," and at a cost of probably no more than fifty dollars booked passage for the family to Liverpool.[1]

They sailed on the *William F. Storer* of the Black Ball Line. The company's ships, broad of beam and blunt of bow, were built for cargo and safety rather than speed, and Black Ball had been the first in the United States (in 1818) to offer scheduled sailings to Liverpool, whether or not the ship had a full complement of passengers or freight. The line's symbol soon became world famous: atop the mainmast a red pennon with a black ball, and sewn on the fore-topsail another huge black ball, visible for miles even with the sail half furled. The *Storer*, a small, full-rigged sailer, carried only a few passengers and required twenty-two days to cross.[2] Albert and Charley, eleven and seven, had the run of the ship but no interest in the sea. For the family, adventure lay ahead, in the sights of England.[3]

From Liverpool they went to London, where Dr. Burlingham had letters of introduction to several Baptist preachers, of whom the best known was Charles Haddon Spurgeon, possibly the most famous Baptist of his day, preaching to crowds every Sunday and Thursday. His theology was Calvinist, but in his sermons he lightened Puritan doctrine with common sense and humor.[4]

Dr. Burlingham evidently impressed Spurgeon and the others on whom he called, for they arranged for him to preach far and wide. In London, CCB later declared, "we stopped at a boarding house in Bloomsbury" and went to "the Tower, Westminster Abbey, St. Paul's, Kew Gardens, Windsor, Eton. We spent several weeks in a little village in Sussex, Cuckfield. We went to Edinburgh, the Trossachs, Melrose Abbey, Abbotsford [Walter Scott's house], and Lochs Lomond and Katrine." On the Isle of Wight they visited Carisbrooke Castle, where in the English Civil War their Puritan forebears had imprisoned Charles I and his family. More than the history, however, at Carisbrooke Castle young Charley was impressed by a donkey said to be sixty years old.[5]

As summer turned to autumn, Dr. Burlingham "received a call" to what was known as the American Chapel in Paris, an English-speaking congregation founded by a Congregationalist in 1834. Ministers of several Protestant denominations had served the church, and the post was offered to Burlingham for the six-month winter season while the present holder, a Presbyterian, was away. A condition of the call, which he accepted, was to conduct services according to Episcopalian usage.[6]

The chapel, on the rue de Berri, was then the only English-speaking Protestant church in Paris, and most of the congregation's Americans were Northerners—Republicans who had supported the Union. Two were New Yorkers, Richard M. Hoe, a businessman, and the journalist-diplomat John Bigelow, who was U.S. minister to France. Possibly they knew of Burlingham by reputation and had suggested him for the post. The family stayed in Paris first at a boardinghouse run by a French journalist and his wife, and the man delighted the boys by giving them tickets to a circus, where they saw a troupe of performing lions. Discovering that the animals were stabled close to their house, they spent hours waiting "for a peek when the door opened." Exotic animals then were rarely seen except in a zoo or circus, and to many people even the common horse was interesting. A perfectly matched pair or a team pulling well together was a pleasurable sight.[7]

From the boardinghouse the family moved to an apartment on the rue de l'Oratoire, where Mrs. Burlingham started weekly receptions for the congregation and its French friends. The boys were sent to a small French school in which the master was memorable for his habit of picking fleas from his hair and cracking them between his nails, but after a few weeks, in a shift probably arranged by Bigelow, they transferred to a larger, Catholic school where Bigelow's two sons were enrolled. Here, when prayers were recited, the Burlinghams, stiff-necked Protestants, refused to bow their heads. The French ignored their rudeness, leaving CCB in later years to "blush" at the memory of it.[8]

As in England, Dr. Burlingham sought to show his boys every sight in Paris or nearby, and besides the monuments of the city they visited

Versailles, Fontainebleau, and Le Havre, where their father had a friend who was U.S. consul. Most exciting, however, was Rouen, which CCB saw "with thrills because of Jeanne d'Arc." In those years, Joan was probably the only French historical figure, other than La Fayette, whom most American Protestants felt they could admire without reservation. She, after all, had fought the English for independence and defied the Catholic hierarchy.[9] Despite such attitudes, Dr. Burlingham arranged for his Baptist family to attend a Sunday mass in the chapel of the Tuileries Palace, a service to be attended by the emperor Napoleon III and his empress Eugénie. For the occasion Mrs. Burlingham bought a hat, whose color CCB called "mauve," but which probably was "magenta," for that was Eugénie's favorite shade of mauve and so named by her, facts known to every Parisian milliner. As the service began, the imperial couple entered quietly and took their seats in an upper box projecting into the chancel.[10]

The sense of an imperial city, a modern Rome with history, monuments, and beauty, excited CCB. Napoleon III in 1865 was at the height of his power, and he and his prefect for the Department of the Seine, the urban planner Baron Georges Haussmann, were transforming Paris from a medieval city of gates, walls, and cramped streets, with wholly inadequate sewers, into the finest city in Europe, with wide boulevards, spacious plazas, and sewers so vast, hygienic, and efficient they became a popular tour. The city's parks were another achievement. The Paris of 1850, with a population of a million, had forty-seven acres of public parks with a few more acres privately owned and sometimes opened to the public—in all, an acre of park for every 5,000 inhabitants, and in 1870, when Haussmann left office, an acre for every 390.

Already by 1866 the light, air, and beauty of Paris were impressive, and from his boyhood experience of it, CCB carried away an idea of what a city could be. When in middle age he built a summer cottage for himself and his family he hung on the wall beside his desk a pictorial map of Paris, circa 1885, that showed all the buildings on every street. And when in the next century similar improvements were started in New York under the leadership of the city's parks commissioner Robert Moses, CCB was often, though not always, an enthusiastic supporter.[11]

Though Napoleon's rebuilding of Paris was not yet completed, its plan, originating with the emperor, was clear, and Napoleon himself went out regularly to inspect its progress. CCB, who liked to tell how he had seen the emperor at mass and reviewing troops on the Champs de Mars, recalled: "One of the most exciting events was to see the Emperor Napoleon III driven through the streets in his victoria at a gallop—four horses with postilions and footmen standing at the back. We joined in the cries of 'Vive l'Empereur!' The Empress and the Prince Imperial were driven in the same way but always alone—doubtless for fear of assassin."*[12]

For CCB, the memories never lost their glamour. By his own admission, as the events receded ever further into the past—sixty, seventy, eighty years—he enjoyed remarking to others that he was "one of the few men alive who had seen Napoleon III." Once, when "boasting" in this fashion to a vestryman of his church in New York, the man "countered by informing me that his father once took him to see the Emperor." Instantly on guard, CCB asked the date of the man's sighting. Learning it was after the emperor's "dethronement," CCB continued boasting.[13]

Then, sometime in the late summer of 1866, the Burlingham family returned to New York, sailing from Glasgow on the Anchor Line. CCB was still too uninterested in ships to record the ship's name, but did note that, because the crossing was by steam rather than sail, it required only twelve days.[14]

Dr. Burlingham probably was already in touch with the Second Baptist Church of St. Louis, Missouri, even before leaving Europe. A friend from Hamilton, J. Osgood Pierce, some years earlier had moved with his family to St. Louis and joined the church, at the time the city's largest Baptist congregation, and when its pastor resigned in June 1866, planning to depart in September, Pierce suggested Burlingham as the replacement.[15] But the Baptist national weekly *The Examiner* raised objections, protesting that Dr. Burlingham, having officiated in Paris with Episcopalian rites, was no longer suited to lead a Baptist church. The St. Louis search committee, after interviewing him, however, saw no ground for objection, and inasmuch as Baptist churches operate independent of any denominational hierarchy, the congregation's decision was final. In November the call was issued formally and the family moved to St. Louis, boarding for the first few weeks as paying guests with the Pierces. CCB, fresh from the beauties of Paris, remembered the architecture of the Pierce house, known locally as "Cracker Castle," as "of an especially hideous type."[16]

St. Louis in the Civil War, like New York, had been a city of divided loyalties, but with a crucial difference: though Missouri was a slaveholding state and St. Louis was geographically close to the Confederacy, the city's political and business leaders had been far more determinedly Republican

---

*In 1858 an attempt had been made to kill the emperor and empress, but the bomb, thrown under their carriage as they drew up to the Opéra, failed to explode.

and pro-Union than their New York counterparts. And as the threat of armed rebellion in St. Louis had increased, its government imposed martial law. Despite the inconvenience and, no doubt, some injustice, civic peace had been preserved. When the war began, the city, with a population of 150,000, had become a Union stronghold, a shelter for some 40,000 refugees, a prison camp for thousands of Southern soldiers, and a hospital for thousands of Northern sick and wounded. By the war's end in 1865, the population had almost doubled, and though the frontier had moved westward, the city retained many qualities of a frontier town. It was dusty, steaming hot in summer, and had many streets still unpaved or merely "thrown" with rocks left for wagon wheels to crush. Herds of cattle, horses, and mules frequently clogged the streets, and soft coal, burned for all uses, including home heating, blackened the air with soot. The drinking water, CCB declared, "was mud."[17]

In the Second Baptist Church, the war had split the congregation. As soon as Lincoln succeeded Buchanan as president, a committee requested that their pastor, Dr. Galusha Anderson, drop the prayer for the health of the president of the United States. Dr. Anderson declined, saying the prayer was traditional and used for all who held the office, regardless of party. Nine days after Southern guns fired on Fort Sumter, Anderson, taking Romans 13 for his text, preached on the duty of obedience to the established government. He closed by asking the congregation to sing "My Country, 'tis of Thee." A sizable number stood silent. Later, during a service, stones crashed through the windows; a deacon of the church was shot; the congregation split; and Dr. Anderson's name appeared on a Confederate list of ten men "most wanted." Even some of his supporters urged him to retreat to Ohio, but he refused.[18]

Dr. Burlingham's job, as set out to him, was threefold: to bring the congregation back together, healing division among neighbors; to unify, if possible, the state's General Association of Baptists, where a similar schism existed; and to lead a reunited congregation in the building of a new church at a new location, a move needed because of the city's steady growth westward from the river but certain to be contentious. In his ten years in St. Louis, Dr. Burlingham succeeded in all three tasks; it was the great work of his life.[19]

The Burlingham family may have found the ten years in St. Louis hard, for there seems to have been little money for anything beyond necessities, and there were few diversions. Emma Burlingham chaperoned a group of young men and women on a boat trip to New Orleans and back, and she took her boys with her; presumably she received a fee, or at least her expenses. Another time, a friend who was a director of the Union Pacific Railroad sent her and the boys to Denver in his private railroad car. CCB recalled the trip happily, for along the way they "had the pleasure of seeing herds of buffalo, prairie dogs and rattle snakes." After a few days in Denver, they went on to Boulder, which was then "wild country," and "we boys rode ponies, picked up opals in the fields, saw Placer mining, and had a glorious time."[20] Mostly, however, Emma Burlingham was the pastor's good wife, entertaining for him, keeping friendships alive in other churches, and frequently attending Baptist conventions, camp meetings, and revivals. Whenever possible, she made short trips with her children, once taking them by riverboat up the Mississippi to St. Paul and back. During the summers, often leaving her husband behind, she would take them East to visit relatives and friends.[21]

While in St. Louis, CCB grew from an uncomplicated boy of eight into a youth of eighteen inclined to be somewhat solitary, preoccupied, and reticent. He continued to be a loving son and loyal brother, and did well at school and in two years at college, for all of which he had good teachers, with classes typically of twelve students or less. But it is notable that in these years, when many persons make lasting friends among their fellows, he did not. Nor, in later years, did he retain acquaintances in the city. In fact, soon after he left St. Louis to enter the sophomore class of Harvard College—entirely his own idea—his father resigned from the Second Baptist Church and took the family back to New York City. Never thereafter did CCB return to St. Louis, or follow its development, or claim an association with it. Even as a boy in St. Louis, thanks to his father's subscription, he daily read the *New York Tribune*.

Yet he learned much in St. Louis, in school and out. His formal education began in a public school there, though in the fall of 1870, when he was twelve, his father transferred him to Smith Academy, run by Washington University in St. Louis (founded in 1853) as a four-year preparatory school. His brother Albert was enrolled there, and for two years the brothers attended the same school. Calculating strictly by age, Albert, older by four years, should have graduated before CCB entered.[22] There is no reason, however, to think that Albert was in any way "slow." Still, an older brother typically will open doors of experience to one younger, but that seems not to have been the case with Albert and Charles. Though they were fond of each other, in CCB's development Albert is rather a blank. After graduating from college he went on to support himself in a succession of jobs and to found a business concerned with printing, the National Roller Company, serving as president for twenty years. Long after his death, when CCB's son was asked what Uncle Albert had been like, after thought he only could muster, "He was a nice man."[23]

CCB's interests matured slowly. When he was ten or eleven he had a gray pony named Beauty; but he always preferred walking to riding, and in his letters the pony appears only once.[24] St. Louis, with its many German immigrants, was a good town for music, and CCB's school and college mate Frank Taussig played the violin in small groups; but CCB was not drawn to music, though as an adult he often sat through concerts in order to enjoy a friend's company. An art in which he did develop an interest, but slowly, for he could not pursue it in St. Louis, was the legitimate theater or, as he called it, "the stage." As a boy, the only theater he ever saw were the Guignols—French puppet shows—in the Paris parks. His parents, like many Americans of the day, considered "the stage" inherently sinful, and did not take their boys to plays. But sometime in the early 1870s he began to read in his father's *New York Tribune* reviews of Henry Irving's productions at the Lyceum, in London. The journalist George W. Smalley, besides writing about war and politics, frequently reported on theater, and his accounts of Irving and Ellen Terry stirred young Charley's curiosity. Then, either at the school or college, CCB began to read plays in earnest.[25]

> Every year Edwin Booth came to Ben DeBar's Opera House with a company and played Shakespeare. Prof. Crunden, as soon as he learned what plays Booth would produce, gathered us boys together and we read the plays Booth had announced, and the students attended at least two or three of these plays—all [the students] but one and *I* was that one—and the reason was that I was the son of a Minister, and it was considered by the Baptists wicked for me to attend a theatre. They made no objection to a circus.[26]

Unlike the theater, however, there was no ban on politics, and when Charles was eighteen and a sophomore in college, he attended two memorable events in St. Louis. The first was the Democratic Party's convention, 27–29 June 1876, to nominate a candidate for president in the November election. The convention, held in the Merchants Exchange, was the first of either major party to meet in a city west of the Mississippi; two weeks earlier the Republicans had nominated Rutherford B. Hayes in Cincinnati.

A question of corruption stirred both conventions. President Ulysses S. Grant, nearing the end of his second term, had lost much of his immense popularity as one scandal after another had scarred his administration, and both parties were demanding reform. Among Democrats the chief contender was New York's governor Samuel J. Tilden, celebrated nationally for his part in exposing Tammany's "Tweed Ring" in New York, and from the gallery CCB heard Tammany's successor to Boss Tweed, "Honest John" Kelly, rail against Tilden.[27] By 28 June, the day of the balloting, summer had seized St. Louis and the weather was sultry. A crowd of 5,000 delegates and observers jammed the exchange. Men took off their coats, loosened their collars, and even so, reported *The New York Times*, "many fainted from the suffocating heat."[28]

Tilden won easily. Preserved among CCB's papers is a tally sheet of the crucial second ballot, on which he recorded how the delegates of the thirty-eight states voted. Despite Tammany's hostility to Tilden, he won all seventy of the New York delegation's votes, and on the initial count he apparently received 469 of the 492 votes needed for the nomination. Before the total was computed officially, however, some delegations began to switch votes to him, so that when the result of the second ballot was announced, Tilden had 508. The delegates then moved promptly to make the vote unanimous, and CCB, to confirm his presence at the historic moment, dated and signed his tally sheet.[29]

The second event to engage CCB started earlier, continued for months, and stemmed from the sordid scandal that overtook President Grant and his administration in May 1875, culminating the following winter and spring in a series of military and civilian, civil and criminal trials known collectively as the Whiskey Ring Trials. Making much use of evidence gathered in congressional hearings, some of these trials were held in Washington and some in St. Louis. The various St. Louis trials extended over several months, and while CCB left no record of when or how often he was present, he stated, "I was at the Whiskey Ring Trials; I was just interested in the scandal." Everyone was, yet not everyone bothered to attend; CCB apparently went to the trials alone, without Albert or a friend.[30]

For several years, it seemed, a ring of politicians, with headquarters in St. Louis, had defrauded the U.S. government of millions of dollars in taxes on distilled whiskey, helped by officials in the U.S. Treasury and, it turned out, the president's personal secretary, Orville E. Babcock. Grant had thundered, "Let no guilty man escape," but few were convicted, and among the acquitted was Babcock—in part because of a deposition sent by the president to Babcock's trial in St. Louis. Many people at the time thought Grant had perjured himself to save a friend; and today historians are convinced of it. But Grant had sworn to the truth of his testimony, taken at the White House, under cross-examination, and before the chief justice of the Supreme Court. For many, then and now, nothing in Grant's career so stained his honor as this act.[31]

Grant's leadership in the Civil War had made him a hero, but his actions during his two terms as president raised profound questions: how can wartime greatness be reconciled with corruption in office? Can a man be a hero in one circumstance and a coward or fool in another? What of the theory that the duties of high office can by themselves raise the holder's competence so that he rises to the occasion? Allowing that party loyalty is needed for effective government, to what extent in the convention hall or at the polls should a voter ignore criminal behavior in order to sustain the party? All these issues attracted CCB's attention, and they were also the very stuff of the classical curriculum by which he was being educated.

At Washington University, he studied mathematics and physics, history, French, German, and, above all, Latin and Greek. By middle age CCB had lost his fluency in Greek, but he always retained considerable Latin, often quoting or even composing tags of verse and phrases. In both languages the substance of the literature, the examination of virtue and morality as displayed in the lives of men and women, stayed with him and, like his religion, did much to shape his character.[32] An often implicit premise of classical Greek and Latin thought is that individuals have some control over their lives, their behavior, their decisions. Impersonal forces in life are recognized to exist and frequently are acknowledged in the form of capricious gods; yet for mortals there always is left some room for choice. Hence, if only in part, each of us is responsible for our own acts.

How to live, how to behave, what sort of person to be—these are apt questions for students with their lives before them. For the ancient Greeks and Romans a main purpose of education was famously stated by the Roman general Aemilius Paullus, who warned: "The difference between foolish men and wise lies in this: The former learn from their own misfortunes, the latter from those of others."[33] The history of men and women, therefore, in whatever form it may be found—myth, drama, biography, epic poetry, philosophy, political science—is what is most important in a school curriculum, or so classicists believe. In classical literature students can see how the drama of life plays out, how curses uttered, like the chickens at night, come home to roost, and how choices have consequences, not only for a person but for the city and state. Further, the ancients being pagan, the contentious issues of current religious faith can be left aside. And then there is the matter of style. The struggle for students when translating to find the one right word, to re-express a phrase or sentence exactly, can do much to improve the quality of their own expression. CCB was to earn a reputation for the moral bite of his conversation and letters and for the clarity and precision with which he expressed his thoughts. He was also admired for his classical terseness. In advising a young man one day he did not say, "Preserve your intellectual independence," but "Don't yelp with the pack." And in writing a suggestion to President Franklin Roosevelt about entertaining Einstein, he packed a bundle of ideas into two sentences.[34]

Moreover, in the ancient histories of Greece and Rome there are few statistics, polls, or government publications. The history lies in the characters of the leaders, and in what they chose to say or do in a crisis. In the mid-nineteenth century these classical examples had meaning for Americans. As everyone knew, George Washington had modeled himself on Cincinnatus, called from the plow in 458 B.C. to save the Roman army from defeat by the Aequi. Elected dictator of the Roman republic, he routed the enemy and then returned to his farm. (In 1876 many people wished Grant had done the same after Appomattox.)[35] Thomas Jefferson's favorite author was Homer; John Adams's Cicero; and Alexander Hamilton's Plutarch, whose *Lives* of great men were written in pairs so the reader could contrast their moral characters. How to live was always the question. Ancient wisdom offered two suggestions, inscribed on the temple of Apollo at Delphi, "Know thyself," and "Nothing in excess." Aristotle later said much the same in recommending a life free of self-deception and self-destruction. That was a goal of a classical education, to which CCB was exposed.[36]

Another classical theme that evidently appealed to CCB was the belief that a man, to achieve a full life, must play a part in the civic and political affairs of his city. In Greece, the idea was most strongly held in the era of its city-states, before Alexander of Macedon overran them; and in Rome, in the six centuries before its republic was subverted by Julius Caesar into the Roman Empire. In the United States, it was strongest in the Republic's early years, gradually losing force as the country's role and power in the world increased and as the classical curriculum gradually was phased out. But CCB always felt it strongly. The men to whom he was drawn, whom he was most eager to assist and to admire, were those with a sense of responsibility for their city and state.

Of course, many students found the classical curriculum difficult, useless, boring. But CCB had mostly good to report of his teachers, and he plainly found his first two years at college stimulating. So much so that when he was eighteen and a sophomore, he asked his father's permission to transfer to a larger university. Perhaps he was beginning to feel too old to live at home; perhaps he was tired of St. Louis, of being the preacher's son and unable to attend the theater; or perhaps he felt himself drawn to the more settled, ordered life he had glimpsed on his summer trips to the East. In any case, his father agreed to the plan, and CCB wrote to several colleges for catalogs.[37]

After reviewing several, he inclined toward Harvard, in part because its catalog had included specimens of examination papers that "looked pretty hard to me, but they attracted me; and I told my father I should like to go to Harvard." The choice agitated his mother, who feared that in Cambridge he might abandon the Baptist church and become a Unitarian. Boston, after all, was the seat of Unitarianism, and Harvard Divinity School the fount of its preachers. "But my father was a very liberal man for a Baptist at that time, and he consented and wrote to President [Charles W.] Eliot [of Harvard]."[38] The following fall, September 1876, CCB entered Harvard.

Of the many friends the Burlinghams had made in Paris in 1865, the most important to them on their return to the United States was the Hoe family, led by Colonel Richard March Hoe (1812–1886). The "colonel," whose title stemmed from a temporary commission in the 1830s in the New York National Guard, was an inventor and leading manufacturer of printing presses, also a man of great charm combined with a gift for hospitality; almost every summer while the Burlinghams were in St. Louis, he invited the family to spend a week or more with him when they came East to escape Missouri's heat. Though he kept a house in lower Manhattan in order to be near his factory, in the mid-1850s the robust and country-loving colonel had bought a farm just three miles northeast of the city at Hunts Point, a broad peninsula projecting from lower Westchester County into Long Island Sound. Ten years later, at the close of the Civil War, when the trip to town had shortened to under an hour, he made the farm his main residence and a second home to his friends.[39]

The colonel called his fifty-six acres Brightside, cultivating the land with fruit, flower, and vegetable gardens and keeping a herd of Jersey cows. At its center he built a large, comfortable house that overlooked the Bronx River to the east and the Sound to the south. Though the area today is in New York's Bronx County and wholly urban, when Hoe first rented and then began to buy parcels of adjoining land, Hunts Point was bucolic. Nearby Edward G. Faile had the finest herd of Devon cattle in the country, and three miles west, at Mount Fordham, Lewis G. Morris bred the best short-horned cattle in New York State. Yet by 1870 Hoe knew that Hunts Point, only three miles north of the Manhattan village of Harlem, in time would be overrun by the city and that his farm's value ultimately would lie in lots for urban development.[40]

By his first wife, who had died in 1841, Hoe had two daughters, Emily and Adeline, who in the 1850s had married brothers, Cyrus and DeWitt Lawrence, who together in the next decade founded a long-lived securities and investment banking firm. During the summers the two Lawrence families and their eleven children were often at Brightside or in rented houses nearby.[41] And by the colonel's second wife (the gregarious man remained a widower only two years), he had three daughters, Annie, Mary, and Fanny, all, in the early years of the Burlingham visits, at home and unmarried. All were older than CCB, the eldest, Annie, by six years and the youngest, Fanny, by three. Annie, who limped from some undiagnosed problem, was the last of the three to marry, living at home until 1886 and becoming for some years CCB's closest friend.[42] Meanwhile, in the mid-1870s Mary wed J. Henry Harper, and Fanny his second cousin John Harper, members of the family that owned Harper & Brothers, publishers since 1817. And in the prolific fashion of the day, the colonel soon had seven Harper grandchildren to add to the Lawrence eleven. Fortunately for the large and growing family, as a son-in-law wrote, Hoe was a man "of exceptionally cheerful temperament and gentle ways," a man who was "devoted to his life-work, but at the same time was essentially domestic." Whether at factory or farm, he was the presiding spirit; and under his sovereignty, by all reports, Brightside was a happy home.[43]

The arrival of the Harpers in the Hoe family reinforced the colonel's natural printer's interest in books, which already extended beyond the mechanics of printing. In 1839 his brother-in-law, Moses W. Dodd, had started a publishing house which, in 1870, Dodd's son and another of the colonel's nephews, with their uncle's backing, expanded into the firm of Dodd, Mead (1839–1987). Another nephew, Robert Hoe III, in the mid-1860s had started a collection of rare books which, at his death in 1909, would be one of the greatest the world had seen. The colonel himself collected books, encouraging his daughters to do the same. He also liked opera, and whistled its tunes. When in Paris he gave his daughter Annie piano lessons with Clara Schumann; when in London his daughter Fanny had singing lessons with Manuel García. At Brightside or wherever the family gathered, the conversation turned as often to books, art, and music as to business.[44]

Nevertheless, everyone recognized that it was the skill and inventiveness of R. Hoe & Company that made the attractions of Brightside possible. By 1860 the colonel was a man of international reputation, with jobs to distribute, prestige to bestow, and the power to move plans and people ahead. Many of his younger male relatives at some time in their lives worked for him, and among the sons of friends whom he employed would be CCB's brother, Albert. Even CCB, though never working for him, for a time used the company's office as a mailing address.[45] Hoe was famous not only because his company was the world's foremost manufacturer of printing presses of all kinds, with factories in New York, Boston, Chicago, and London, but also because he himself was the inventor of many improvements in the art of printing. Undoubtedly his greatest invention was the rotary press, which because of its speed was known popularly as the "Lightning" press or, sometimes, as "Hoe's Last Fast Press."[46]

Before the Lightning's debut in 1847, the speediest newspaper presses had managed only about 2,000 impressions an hour (2,000 pages printed on one side). The typical press, for instance, had its type locked in a frame fixed firmly on a flat surface, typeface up, beneath a cylinder that rolled sheets of paper over it, sheet by sheet. The slow speed limited newspapers to four or six pages and a press run of less than 10,000. To attempt anything more required a battery of presses and pressmen, operating twenty-four hours a day, and was profitless.

The colonel brooded for five years on the problem before the solution hatched one night in a single, complete vision: put the type on the cylinder. This was not easy to do, for if the cylinder turned rapidly, centrifugal force would cause the type to spin off. But the vision included the solution, and on 22 March 1847 the Philadelphia *Public Ledger* issued the first paper by the new method, printing 8,000 impressions an hour. Within the year *La Patrie*, a daily paper published in Paris, bought a Lightning press, and on the night of 13 June 1849, when a riot in Paris nearly ended the country's Second Republic, the paper issued 69,000 copies. Publishers from other European countries came to inspect the marvel, which, surprising to some, had been made in the United States—American machines had only just begun to penetrate Europe. Soon Edward Lloyd of London ordered a similar press for his *Lloyd's Weekly Newspaper*. Hoe sent over his brother Robert and two of the company's best workers to install it, and the first issue of the weekly printed on it—140,000 copies—appeared on 6 July 1856. Lloyd immediately ordered a second press, and when other English orders followed, the colonel in 1862 opened a sales office in London and, not long after, a factory.[47]

Within months of the introduction of the first Lightning press in Philadelphia, R. Hoe & Company had made improvements in it, and by 1850 in New York the *Sun* could print 20,000 impressions an hour, though still only on a single side. In 1875, at the *Tribune*, Hoe introduced a "web" press able to print on both sides of the sheet, using for the first time a continuous roll of paper. This press could produce 12,500 eight-page papers an hour, allowing the *Tribune* to keep its columns "open" until 3 a.m. rather than "locking type" at midnight. By the early 1880s the company offered a press that could print a newspaper of twelve pages, with each paper cut and folded, at a rate of 24,000 copies an hour; and in 1901 a press that could print and fold a 96-page paper at still higher speeds.

Printing and publishing in these years became one of New York City's leading industries. By the 1880s, on and near Park Row (just south of City Hall) and centered on a statue of Benjamin Franklin, "printer," twelve daily newspapers formed the largest collection of press offices in the world, several of them housed in some of the city's biggest, most distinctive buildings. Among these were the offices of the *Times, Sun, Tribune,* and *Staats-Zeitung*; and close by, on Pearl Street, was Harper & Brothers, with its books and magazines. On Park Row in 1890 Joseph Pulitzer, using the new style of steel structure, erected for his *World* the first building in the city to overtop Trinity Church's spire, roughly 310 to 280 feet. In the vaults of these buildings the whirling presses became one of the city's sights. An 1866 guidebook urged a visit to the *Times* to see at work "Hoe's lightning press, that magnificent piece of machinery." Almost forty years later and a decade after the *Herald* moved north to Broadway at Thirty-fourth Street (the intersection there was renamed "Herald Square"), a 1904 *Baedeker's Guide to the United States* recommended a visit to the paper to watch "the powerful Hoe printing presses."

As the guidebooks stressed, underlying the print industry was the epoch's revolution in speed, a quality noticeable also in the creations of Robert Fulton, Eli Whitney, and Robert Morse. The British Privy Council, in renewing a patent on Hoe's press, called it "the greatest step ever made in the art of printing," and an American historian noted, "Perhaps no other single development was so vital to the maturity of American Society."[48] Rather more important, then, than any mechanical ingenuity were the social and political results that flowed from Hoe's inventions. In the more industrialized countries, as their populations had steadily increased, so, too, did the proportion of citizens with some claim to being well informed. Without that surge in the number of books, journals, and newspapers printed and sold at ever cheaper prices, the continual extension in these countries of the right to vote might have slowed or even stopped. Their ability to absorb immigrant workers by the millions, to assimilate them into a shared culture, and to educate huge numbers of children at public expense might have been more difficult or even impossible. Thus the advances in printing, by fostering civic education and participation, helped to sustain the modern democracies.

On the other hand, as many lamented, the Hoe press and its improvements also had consequences that seemed to threaten the quality of life. The speed made possible a vast increase in the number and circulation of "penny dreadful" papers that focused primarily on the lurid details of corruption, crime, and sexual scandal. These papers, led in New York for a number of years by the *Herald*, while offering only a minimum of civic education, peddled what amounted to a new kind of mass entertainment, often at the most vulgar level. In this way, too, Hoe's invention helped to shape the future.[49]

Hoe's position in the world, however, did not cramp his charm or hospitality. The church-poor Burlinghams were as welcome at Brightside as the industrial rich and always included in any family activities. One summer, for instance, in the early 1870s, there was an afternoon party in Tarrytown at the home of the Fletcher Harpers, parents of Hoe's son-in-law J. Henry Harper, at which many branches of the Hoe and Harper families gathered. The colonel and his contingent, including the Burlinghams, drove the twenty or so miles to Tarrytown in a procession of carriages. Everyone could be put up for several nights, for the colonel's brother Robert and family had a house close by, and also that summer his daughter Adeline and her husband, DeWitt Lawrence, had rented a house in nearby Irvington. Some of the Lawrence children came to the party, among them a red-haired Louisa, ten or eleven years old. In later years she liked to tease CCB, by then her husband, by saying that at this party she had fallen in love with him, which required him to confess he'd been a good deal slower to notice her.[50]

Even several years later, when Louisa had reached thirteen and CCB eighteen, he was hardly aware of her. By then he had started at Harvard, and rather than returning to St. Louis for Christmas spent the holiday with the Hoes in New York. That winter the colonel, to be nearer his factory and to his married daughters on Murray Hill, had rented a house on West Twenty-fifth Street, and Charles in his three-week vacation made close friends of Richard Lawrence, eldest son of Cyrus, and of Robert, the only son of DeWitt, and greatly strengthened his friendship with Hoe's daughter Annie. Louisa Lawrence, or "Louie," as she was known in the family, unable to compete with the young men and the mature Annie, still "made no impression on me." Nevertheless, during CCB's three years at Harvard, whenever he was at Brightside Louisa, by luck or design, was often about. Once she tried to send him a photograph of herself, but it went astray in the mail. Once Annie reminded him of Louisa's approaching birthday, but CCB merely sent back congratulations through Annie. Yet ultimately he would say, "I was just a Baptist pup, till I met Louie."[51]

With the Hoes, CCB was introduced to a style of family life that was deeper and broader in its humanism than his own, and less intense in religious fervor, though the colonel and his family were constant in church attendance. On Sundays at Brightside, they and their guests would drive in carriages to St. Ann's Episcopal Church in Morrisania (now part of the Bronx), filling several pews and hearing sermons by the Reverend Huckle, who with his jet black beard impressed CCB as "a gloomy figure." The colonel, a vestryman, passed the plate at service. He also served on the boards of the Home for Incurables and the House of Refuge, a school for juvenile delinquents for which he designed remedial programs based on training courses used in his factory. In addition, for apprentices at his factory he ran a free night school that included a free supper and extra pay for the teachers, who were usually the company's senior draftsmen.[52] Long before Louie took CCB in hand, the colonel, Annie, and Brightside had a part in his education.

Some people at the time may have thought that the friendship between the Hoe and Burlingham families, however understandable in Paris, was remarkable for continuing in the United States. Some may have wondered whether the Reverend Burlingham had not attached himself and his family to Hoe as a likely source of patronage for himself and his boys. Hoe, after all, was rich and famous, and Burlingham neither; Hoe was a worldly Episcopalian, and Burlingham a rather unworldly Baptist. Hoe, though he never would have claimed as much, in his later years was a highly cultivated man, Burlingham less so. What father loving his boys would not have tried to expose them to Hoe?

The friendship between the men appears to have been genuine, however, rooted in similarities of education and point of view. And initially it was they, not their wives or children, who brought the families together, and as the years passed, Burlingham, more than his wife, nurtured the relationship. When Hoe died, in 1886, Burlingham was one of nine pallbearers for the funeral at St. Ann's, but thereafter the friendship between him, his wife, and Hoe's widow lost its vigor.[53]

In some respects the men's friendship reflects an ethos of their era. This was a time, roughly 1830–80, when for many middle-class families in the United States the possibilities of both business and family life greatly expanded. Increasing economic security, whether achieved by luck or hard work, combined with better health and longevity to allow more time for the pleasures of the mind and art. Men and women who in childhood and youth had known mostly hardship began, in middle age, to find life marvelous. The exploration of its possibilities was thrilling. Some people, of course, held back out of fear or prejudice or religious scruple, but two who pushed forward were Hoe and Burlingham.

Each, for example, responded strongly to his visits to England and to France. Burlingham took his boys everywhere, presenting London and Paris to them as grand opportunities to see, learn, and ponder. Hoe, inventing a collapsible chair for his slightly crippled daughter Annie, took her to museums and soon found himself so stimulated he began to collect paintings and books. Though the fathers came to culture late, they were eager to bring their children to it early.[54]

Both men were aided by a lack of any social or cultural pretension. For the colonel and equally for his two younger brothers, despite their success and money, the society of "Old New York," the descendants of the Dutch and English aristocracies, did not exist. Their father, Robert, had come from England in 1802, a carpenter who knew how to construct, repair, and improve printing presses made of wood and, later, of iron; he had married into a family of tradesmen and farmers in Westchester County and with a brother-in-law had opened a two-man shop in New York City to build printing presses. To the extent that he could, he sought to educate his nine children, and from time to time they attended city schools; but much of their learning was taken from work around the house and, for the boys, in their father's shop, which in 1822 had become a sole proprietorship, R. Hoe & Company. When ten years later the forty-eight-year-old father was forced to quit work, fatally ill, the eldest son, Richard, only twenty and not yet the colonel, succeeded to the business; and as his two younger brothers came of age, he took them in as partners.[55]

Like their father, this second generation of Hoes lived in homes close to the shop, which gradually became a factory, in small three-story brick houses that were hard to heat and without plumbing. Water for whatever use had to be fetched in buckets from a pump in the street. The colonel, as he prospered, engaged a maid-of-all-work and with his brothers combined to buy a carriage and hire a coachman. By the late 1840s, with the success of the Lightning press assured, the three brothers left their small brick houses on the Lower East Side, which under the pressure of immigration was becoming a slum, and moved north to the burgeoning Murray Hill area of Manhattan, where newer buildings offered larger rooms, better heating, and plumbing.[56]

Culturally as well as physically the move was from cramped antebellum brick to spacious, Victorian brownstone. Yet the brothers still thought of themselves as workaday mechanics. They were more successful than others perhaps because they were a bit smarter, perhaps more God-fearing and hardworking, but surely because their trust in one another was absolute and because they never lived beyond their means. That last was the family's great fear, the unpardonable sin, and when the colonel announced he had bought a farm at Hunts Point, property that plainly would consume money, not produce it, his brothers were aghast. But by then their continually improved presses were making them richer than they realized, and the colonel, showing the way, soon had lured his brothers into buying country estates.[57]

The history of the second generation in the Harper family was much the same, and in thousands of other American families which, like these, had a small business that blossomed in the mid-nineteenth century. And Aaron Burlingham's experience was like the colonel's, though as a preacher he did not attain wealth; but he experienced the same rise from poverty and hardship to a life physically easier, with greater play for the mind and more open to culture.

In the third generation of these business families, the history changed. The grandchildren had more formal education, and many of them received or expected to inherit large amounts of money. They had more options for careers or for idleness. They entered the family business often in great numbers, though ever less closely related: the original four Harper brothers became, in the second generation, five first cousins, and in the third, eleven distantly connected cousins. And the eleven, not surprisingly, lacked the fraternal trust that had allowed their grandparents to operate without a written or oral agreement on the division of profits. (Until about 1859, the four Harper brothers simply drew from their common fund whatever each needed for personal expenses.)[58] As the expanding businesses required ever greater capital, outlay, and income, the family partnership as a legal structure became increasingly inadequate. To meet the new problems many family companies reorganized as corporations, with all employees, whether or not family, on salary. Profits, after paying expenses, were distributed to shareholders. (Of the Hoe-related companies, Harper Brothers incorporated in 1896, R. Hoe & Company in 1909, and Dodd, Mead, smallest of the three, in 1916.)

Lost with the increasing size and complexity, besides the bond of family, were the old simplicity and democracy of factory and office. Colonel Hoe had walked about his factory whistling arias, and his office door was open to all; he knew his longtime workers by name, and when one was in trouble, he helped. His successor in the next generation, his extremely talented nephew Robert Hoe III, had a more introverted personality and a workforce three or four times larger. Whether or not true, it was said that he ate breakfast every morning "between two seated French poodles," and it was true that he fired two workers for daring to address him in the factory yard and another for riding with him in the office elevator. Yet he did much for the company, as both an inventor and a manager, and rivaled J. Pierpont Morgan as a connoisseur and collector of rare books. (He also kept a mistress in London who, on his death, sued his estate, soiling his name and hers in the newspapers.)[59]

To many of the third and later generations who struggled to keep a family business prosperous and family-owned, life seemed more difficult than it had been for the parents or grandparents. It was harder to be clever, harder to be rich, harder to be virtuous. A few managed brilliantly, but more looked back at what seemed a golden age, when life's prospects in business and family life had opened to a world of marvels waiting to be discovered. Colonel Hoe and Aaron Burlingham had enjoyed that earlier ethos, and CCB shared their optimism, partly by gift of his own nature and partly by his elders' example, which in youth he took to heart. Raised in St. Louis, gateway to the West, as a young man he turned eastward for adventure, seeking it first at Harvard and then in the country's greatest city, all the while displaying the same ability as his father and Colonel Hoe to welcome new experience. As one admirer put it: "He was always a man for the next chapter!"[60]

3

Harvard and Phillips Brooks

IN OLD AGE CCB scattered through his conversation and letters an image of himself and his St. Louis schoolmate Frank Taussig arriving at Harvard in September 1876 like two visored Arthurian knights come out of the West, CCB modestly behind, to joust in the tournament of life against the best of the East. "With Frank Taussig," CCB would say, "I became a member of the Class of '79." He then would pause, sure that those he addressed knew that Taussig was not only the most distinguished member of the class but one of Harvard's intellectual giants, world renowned as a scholar, teacher, and editor who shaped the study of what then was called political economy and today economics.[1] In their transfer from Washington College CCB claimed no glory for himself except by reflection. "Taussig and I," he once wrote, "expected to be examined for admission to sophomore class not only on the subjects required for admission but also for the studies of the freshman year. We reported to the Dean, Charles F. Dunbar, professor of political economy. He was a wise man and sized us up as serious, studious boys, and I remember going to his office and telling him that there was an examination in Latin that afternoon; and he said, 'I wouldn't trouble about that.' And we were admitted to Harvard without any examination at all."[2]

His account is true in fact but not in implication. They were admitted without examination, but that was hardly exceptional. Both he and Taussig had completed sophomore years at Washington, and in entering Harvard as sophomores had agreed to repeat that year.[3] In other ways, too, the poetry of legend, those "serious, studious boys," crumbles into the prose of an ordinary college admission. CCB's letters suggest that he traveled to Cambridge not with Frank Taussig but with his mother, who spent a month in the Boston area visiting friends and settling her son in Cambridge. Charley roomed alone, and in his first letters home and to Annie

Hoe he did not mention Taussig; in fact, in none of his letters that survive from his college days, with thirty of them recording in detail his activities and thoughts, did he mention Taussig. Evidently the friendship, strong fifty years later, in these years was weak.[4]

The elderly are prone to romanticize events of their youth, but with age there may also come a tendency to grow crabbed, rigid, censorious. In CCB's case, with age came an ever-increasing geniality of spirit that his contemporaries found very attractive. He who upon graduation and for the next twenty-five years was one of the least of the Class of '79, gradually thereafter became one of its most popular and admired members. By the mid-1930s he was in many ways its leader. He and others, then, forgot he had not always been the man he had become. Fortunately, a family trunk preserved many of his college letters, and they reveal a youthful personality remarkably different from that of his old age. For CCB, the child was not father to the man but kin more remote—grandfather perhaps, or cousin.

Harvard College in 1876 had a faculty of 42 and an enrollment of 821, of which 222 were sophomores, and it shared with other departments of the university the forty-two-year-old president, Charles W. Eliot, who was determined to transform a provincial college with a few small graduate schools into the equal of the best universities in Europe, with those of Germany as the model. Eliot took office in 1869 and had mostly achieved his aim by 1890, but in 1876 the college rules and curriculum were still in a state of confusing transition. Eliot, for instance, much to CCB's delight, allowed all but freshmen a free choice of courses; yet daily morning chapel continued compulsory (until 1886), though to CCB the requirement was not oppressive.[5]

Physically, the college centered on "the Yard," a broad rectangular space crisscrossed by gravel paths, shaded by American elms, and bordered by eight large buildings housing most of the students, some unmarried faculty, and a few classrooms and administrative offices. Built of red brick or stone in a mixture of Georgian and Federal styles, the four-or-five story buildings individually were undistinguished but in balance well defined the space. The Yard, though not beautiful, had character.

A second, looser cordon of buildings ringed the first. The most important of these for CCB were the Appleton Chapel, gray stone in a style faintly Romanesque, and Gore Hall, a Gothic library modeled on King's College Chapel, Cambridge, England. The library had outgrown its building, and an addition was rising that was structurally revolutionary. For the first time in the United States or Europe, the shelving would be attached to a system of upright iron ribs, rising without break from the foundation to the roof, and into these, adjustable shelves could be secured. This iron skeleton would support the entire building—floors, roof, shelving, and books. The "stacks," with only narrow aisles between them, would hold many more books than the former "alcove" system, in which each subject had an alcove off the main reading room supposedly containing all the relevant books. The new system was designed to meet Eliot's demand for a great library with books available to students: the stacks were to be as "open" as the alcoves.[6]

Beyond this second ring of buildings, but still nearby, were the president's house and Memorial Hall, where students ate and attended public "readings" and lectures by distinguished visitors. "Mem Hall," as students called it, had been erected in the early 1870s to commemorate the 138 Harvard men who had given their lives for the Union in the Civil War. Constructed of red brick laid in black mortar and with decorative lines of black brick that showed the influence of John Ruskin, it was (and is) a vast secular cathedral, its parts bound together and pinned to earth by a large central tower. The "nave" was the dining hall, able to serve more than 500 students at a sitting; the "apse," shaped like a theater, an auditorium seating 1,500; and the "transept," the commemorative hall, with marble tablets, stained glass, and wooden rib vaulting.[7] Also outside the Yard was the law school's small Dane Hall and, a few blocks away, the Lawrence Scientific School and the divinity school; in Boston was the medical school, and in Jamaica Plain the agricultural school.

For Charley, Harvard was the Yard, the library, the chapel, and Mem Hall. The area was flat, and everyone walked or ran between buildings (bicycles were uncommon until the 1890s) with little regard to the gravel paths. Beneath the arching elms the ground was hard and often bare, a surface of scuffed grass, scraggy bush, and dusty shortcuts. Dogs were everywhere. As Charley noted in a letter, "There are a great many swell fellows here, with pugs and terriers" who "are therefore obliged to room outside the college buildings." But the stray dogs knew no boundaries.[8]

Surrounding the college lay the small city of Cambridge, with a population of 52,000, and southward between it and Boston lay the estuary of the Charles River, a tidal wash of muck, bordered by marshes and mud flats. (In 1910 a dam blocked the influx of salt water, created a freshwater basin behind it, and cleared the course of the river.) Boston then was a city of 300,000, the capital of New England and, in the opinion of many, "the Athens of America." It could be reached by taking "a jingling horse-car," or in an hour's walk by crossing on "the breezy West Boston bridge"; and it offered all that a tired, bored, or avid student could not find in the college:

music, art, libraries, taverns, "girlie shows," preachers, and politics, as well as a cultivated society for those with entry to it.[9]

Charley had no use for taverns or "girlie shows," and though his parents had friends on whom he paid periodic calls, he had no web of contacts in Boston such as had Theodore Roosevelt in the Class of 1880. But then the two men, though overlapping at Harvard for three years, hardly attended the same college. Roosevelt lived in rooms outside the Yard, had the services of a landlady, a laundress, and a man to light his fire in the morning; and because of an interest in zoology, kept in his suite a menagerie of snakes, lobsters, and a tortoise. He ate not in Mem Hall but at private clubs, and he regularly attended dinners and dances in Boston and neighboring Brookline. Wishing to court a young lady (who later became his first wife), he had his best horse and two-seater carriage shipped from Long Island.[10] Like Roosevelt, Taussig lived outside the Yard in what CCB later described as "a palatial suite."

But whatever the style in which a student attended Harvard, in the 1870s even going to college was still somewhat unusual. Many of the country's most talented or ambitious young men forwent it, for no degree was necessary to enter business, politics, or a profession. For Aaron Burlingham, not a rich man, who had put himself through college and divinity school, to urge and assist both sons to graduate from a college shows an uncommon belief in formal schooling.[11] And as a survey published in 1878 reported, only Columbia was more expensive than Harvard. At Cambridge, tuition was $150, and in addition, as Professor Dunbar advised CCB's father, the cost of meals at Memorial Hall "is about four dollars and a half ($4.50) per week." Like the tuition and the room rent, the cost of meals had to be paid in three installments, not in advance of the school year but during and after it—in January, April, and the following October. The survey estimated the minimum cost for a year at Harvard at $450.[12]

The college offered 112 scholarships to its students—"from $250 to $300, per year, the others smaller"—assuring about one in seven of some help. But the stipends were not awarded until after the college year was completed and the student's work graded, and then the grants were assigned on the basis of scholarship, not financial need, the greatest amount going to the best scholar who applied "and so on down until the scholarships are exhausted."[13]

Thus, Charley could not apply for his first scholarship until the summer after his sophomore year, and when the moment came, he somehow fumbled the application. In early September 1877, as he started junior year, he had to write his father, "But no it is impossible for me to get one, for they have been assigned ere this . . . Tell me frankly whether without a scholarship you can put me through another year." Acknowledging that the college registrar "is right according to existing regulations," he insisted, "the whole thing is a misunderstanding."[14] In the end, the college ignored his mistake and awarded him $250 toward the expenses of his sophomore year, and in due course an equal sum for the junior and senior years. He never received the highest award, but always one about the average, which then was $235. He worked hard to keep his marks high— "'Grind' is my watch word," he wrote to his father—and in February of his senior year he was elected to Phi Beta Kappa.[15]

In later years, CCB sometimes claimed that "after a year in college I made quite a considerable sum by tutoring," but he may have confused his college years with those at Columbia Law School, when he did prepare three boys for college.[16] In his letters from Harvard, many of which concerned finances, he never mentioned any income from tutoring, any time set aside for it, or the name of any student tutored. Still, in his first month at Cambridge he helped a classmate with a paper, though apparently not for money, and he reported to Annie Hoe: "This fellow had written some fine sentences filled with 'which' and 'as' clauses. *As* is not very swell, you know." And later, again to Annie, he remarked, "Some *very* stupid fellows here. For instance, in history the other day a fellow said that Mary, Duke of Burgundy was the *son* of Maximilian."[17]

After the Christmas holiday spent in New York at the Hoes, he described for Annie the train ride back to Cambridge in a car full of "Harvardites, all rather festive and a few, I am sorry and ashamed to say, rather boozy. I am glad," he continued, "you are not one of those who say: 'Boys will be boys, you know; they are only sowing their wild oats. They will settle down.' Most of them settle down much lower than such people think." Apparently, throughout the seven-hour trip from New York to Boston, he sat alone.[18]

Despite joining the Society of Christian Brethren, a group of evangelical Protestants, he seems to have made no good friend at Harvard that first year. In the spring the prospect of the Harvard-Yale crew race at Springfield excited him, but he planned to go not with a classmate, or with anyone from Harvard or Yale, but with Dick Lawrence. And finding a roommate for the coming year was troublesome. He hoped that someone named Eames would enroll in the college so they might room together, but Eames did not, and for the next two years he roomed alone.[19] Yet in one respect he improved his situation: he moved from the fifth floor of Grays Hall to the second of Matthews. In winter, the lower floor was a degree or two warmer, and in all seasons closer to the only source of water, an outdoor pump.[20]

Some Harvard historians report that students in these years washed rarely. If so, Charley was an exception. He was by nature clean, took pleasure in appearing well dressed, and even when old and blind fretted if he knew his suit was spotted. In college, though dressing simply, he was conscious of clothing, reasonable about it in requests to his parents for money, yet always aware of the worn or inappropriate. One time he lamented to his father that for lack of anything lighter he must wear wool in May. "I have but one pair of pants—a thick pair—my others being seatless, knockakneed etc. etc. What shall I do?" He proposed new trousers: "Mr. R. will make them for very little, and they do fit so much better when made to order. All this ought, I suppose, to be put in a letter to mother, but I didn't know I should say anything about it when I began."[21]

About his studies he always wrote with enthusiasm, and the courses he chose to take were mostly in language and history. Washington College had prepared him well in the grammar, syntax, and parsing of Latin and Greek, but at Harvard he met these languages as literature and found them exciting. "The large classes, the learning and ability of the teachers made a new world for me." In his first year this was especially true of Latin, in which, under the guidance of Professor George Martin Lane, he read a comedy of Plautus, some lyric poems of Catullus, and parts of the *Annals* of Tacitus.[22] Lane was famous for the originality of his thought, for his ability to season ideas with wit, and for asking hard questions relating literature to life, questions for which he admitted no one could have sure answers. He seldom bothered in class to hear recitations on passages assigned for homework, but instead had the students read ahead at sight, asking them to discuss the meaning of the passage and its grammatical points. He called on students randomly, unnerving those expecting him to proceed alphabetically or by seat and row, and in a practice that startled Charley, he sometimes called "on a man a second time in a single second." And on examinations he asked questions on subjects not discussed in class. "Here we have a non marking system," Charley wrote to Annie, "that is, recitations are not marked and everything depends on examinations . . . But take it all in all I like this system better than any other."[23]

Eliot and the faculty, in their efforts to upgrade Harvard's educational standards, had designed a program for mature students, young men, not boys, and under Eliot the average age of those entering the college rose from fourteen to eighteen. The new style of instruction released professors from taking attendance, disciplining unruly boys, and grading daily recitations, and freed them in class to pursue ideas. Those students who could rise to the occasion had the jarring, thrilling experience of being present while a great mind was at work.[24]

In the fall of 1877, for example, Charley took William James's course on philosophy (its subject matter today might be called psychology), which offered a combination of the abstractions of philosophy with a study of how the brain worked. James's great years as a teacher still lay ahead, and in later years CCB could recall little about the course, which had shown him that he did not think or experience life in Jamesian terms. Still, one side of James he did not forget: "Sometimes Dr. James would put his hands to his head and say, 'I can't think today. We had better not go on with the class,' and he would dismiss us." CCB saw that not as a weakness but, rather, "he was unwilling to give anything but his best."[25]

If James's abstractions and science meant little to Charley, the relation of art, literature, and history to life meant much. One course he attended without credit, yet taking careful notes, was Charles Eliot Norton's "History of the Fine Arts of Construction and Design, and Their Relation to Literature." Norton, a friend of Ruskin, believed that art and life were closely connected, and beginning in 1874 he year after year convinced large numbers of Harvard students that the fine arts were frequently the best expression of the spirit of past ages—and worth study. In the 1870s that idea was new; before Norton, Harvard, like most colleges of the day, had no course on fine arts. Like Ruskin, he stressed the social and ethical implications of the arts, which often put him out of step with the optimism of the time. In an era of American social and economic expansion, with "Progress" on the march, Norton continually spoke out against the blights of industry, the rise of monopolies and an uncultured business class, and the evils of the country's growing imperialism. Of the "Gilded Age," the era of corruption which followed the Civil War, he wrote to a friend, "The Democracy has been a disappointment in its incapacity to rise morally in proportion to its rise in material welfare and in power." An undue emphasis on equality, he felt, was making a world that was crass and ugly, lowering standards in literature, churches, amusements, and politics.[26]

When lecturing, Norton often commented on current affairs, not hesitating to anger his students. CCB liked to tell of an episode in the fall of 1876 that infuriated some classmates. The Republican leader James G. Blaine, whose son Emmons was taking Norton's course, was chief spokesman for his party's presidential candidate, Rutherford B. Hayes; and though Blaine's private life was spotless, his public career included a festering scandal that caused Democrats to call him "the Continental Liar from the State of Maine." One day Norton, passing from art to politics, excoriated Blaine, and though by chance the son was not in the room at the time, his friends on his behalf were outraged.[27]

Another Norton story that CCB liked to tell concerned a visit by William James's son Henry and his mother to Norton's house in Cambridge. "He was in his gloomiest state, thinking everything was wrong in America. His daughter Sally took her views from him, and as she saw Mrs. James and Henry to the door, she continued in her father's vein, concluding, 'Isn't it dreadful!' To which Mrs. James replied, 'It would be if it were true, but it isn't.'"[28] Still, the tension inherent in Norton's opposition to much of what others considered Progress stimulated students and forced many, as they examined the arts of the past, to question the quality of art and life in the present. Charley, able to contrast Napoleon III's Paris with St. Louis and New York, agreed with Norton: American cities needed better art, architecture, and urban design.

Although at Harvard Charley pushed eagerly through the intellectual doors the college opened, he held back at the social opportunities. Unlike Taussig, who played the violin and joined an orchestra, Charley had no musical talents; and again, unlike Taussig, he took no part in athletics. Theodore Roosevelt walked, boxed, rowed, and exercised in the gymnasium. CCB walked, but seemingly always alone and never farther than in and out of Boston, which in those days, when everyone walked, was a stroll. His college mate Richard Welling, Class of '80, walked to Worcester with a friend in a day, and on discovering the distance was only forty-four miles, walked an additional six to make the day's total an even fifty. Typically, CCB seems not to have known Welling in college. Yet later in New York, working for civic reform, they became such friends that Welling dedicated his autobiography to him.[29]

Though CCB had joined the Society of Christian Brethren in his first year at the college, in his letters he never mentioned any activity taken under the society's auspices; and his election to Phi Beta Kappa in his last year came too late for it to be a source of friends. While in college, he apparently attended only a single function, a lunch in June 1879, at which Dr. O. W. Holmes presided. Ralph Waldo Emerson, seventy-six and beginning to fail, attended, and "when Mr. Emerson entered the room, everyone instinctively rose."[30]

Nevertheless, in the spring of his junior year CCB joined one club, the Signet, which linked him with others in an activity he enjoyed. Signet members rented "two wretched rooms" in an old building near Harvard

Square and met there periodically on Friday evenings for fellowship and a paper read by a member who afterward led a discussion on his subject. For his evening, CCB planned, and presumably delivered, a paper on Ruskin's theories of political economy, probably those expounded in the books published in the late 1860s, such as *Sesame and Lilies* (1865). Ruskin felt the industrial revolution had promoted greed and squalor, and produced an architecture of astonishing ugliness with strong antihuman implications, and he proposed economic and social programs, such as accident compensation, old-age pensions, and unions for workingmen, that would restore to life some of the humanity that industry had driven out.[31]

The more purely social clubs, such as the Hasty Pudding, the Porcellian, and the "A.D.," Charley ignored, as they seemingly ignored him. Later he inclined to dismiss them as snobbish and would describe a man he disapproved of or disliked as "a Porcellian type," meaning the fellow was a social drone who drank too much and knew too little. "Most of my friends," he declared, "were fine students and became notable scholars and men of affairs."[32]

The implied disparagement of the Porcellian, however, did not always fit. Of its members in CCB's years, the most famous soon would be Theodore Roosevelt. Though on occasion TR drank and smoked (which CCB never did), for all four years at Harvard he taught Sunday school (which CCB never did), published several scholarly works, and in maturity became a noted man of affairs.[33] And even the Porcellian's social and financial standards were not so rigid as CCB liked to pretend. One member of the Class of '77, and later a friend of CCB, was Edward S. Martin, who came to Harvard from Auburn, a small city in upstate New York, and was the tenth of eleven children of a family in financial decline. At Harvard he lived in the Yard, had no manservant to light his fire, and shared a room with others. Along with constant paternal admonitions to spend less money, he had to struggle with a growing deafness that by graduation was almost total. Yet despite his lack of wealth and deafness, Martin was elected to the Porcellian, rowed on a crew, sang songs with his friends, wrote light verse for club and class occasions, and was one of the founders in 1876 of the *Harvard Lampoon*.[34] His one social advantage over CCB was coming to college via Phillips Academy, Andover, and so entering with some friends, though none was elected to the Porcellian. But clubs among the students then were constantly forming, dissolving, and transmuting, and many students belonged to three or four; they were a way of enjoying one's fellows. The energetic TR, for instance, belonged to at least seven, and he and

Welling, with friends, started still another, which met once a week for "literary exercises" and coffee. Among the founding members was Frank Taussig.[35]

Why not CCB? One reason, surely, was that while at Harvard, Brightside and the many branches of the Hoe family continued to be the center of his emotional life—a condition his father encouraged. Two months after Charley entered Harvard, his father had written to "Dear Miss Annie"

> to thank you for having written to Charlie. Your letters do him good. He is an ambitious fellow at present and I want him kept so. A hint and a nudge occasionally from a lady having the influence over him that you have and deserve to have will be of great benefit to him. I believe in Charlie and am glad to think he will come out of College, if his life [be] spared, unharmed by the temptations peculiar to student life. But if you will guard him by a kind word once in a while, his Mother and I will be very thankful to you.[36]

Possibly Annie, six years older than Charley, needed no urging to write, for she cared for him. Their letters while he was in college even suggest that for these years the two may have been, in some platonic way, in love, for each seemed to find in the other's attention something needed. And though both married elsewhere in the 1880s, their friendship continued close until Annie's death in 1886.

Another reason Charley gained little from Harvard's social activities was his eager search among preachers of all sects to find a meaningful basis on which to build his life. In his letters to Annie and his parents, thoughts on religion are frequent, and the events most often reported are sermons heard and services attended. For the first few months at Harvard, in addition to daily chapel with its hymn, prayers, and brief sermon or Bible reading, on Sundays he went to a Baptist church in Cambridge. But he soon abandoned the Cambridge church in favor of services in Boston where he could hear the greatest preachers of the day. He rather liked Dwight Lyman Moody, disliked Ira David Sankey, both evangelists, and found the Unitarian Edward Everett Hale uninspiring. The one to whom he was drawn was the Episcopalian Phillips Brooks (1835–1893), "the best preacher I ever heard." For the thousands in New England who heard Brooks in person or read his sermons, he was the preacher who freed Protestant beliefs from a Calvinistic stress on grace, atonement, and damnation by proposing other doctrines more contemporary and satisfying. Of Brooks CCB would declare, "No one has had a greater influence in my life."[37]

In 1858, the year of CCB's birth, the witty, wise professor of anatomy at Harvard Medical School, Dr. Oliver Wendell Holmes, published in *The Atlantic Monthly* a death notice of New England's form of Calvinism. The obituary, in verse, ostensibly commemorated the hundredth anniversary of the death of Jonathan Edwards, the Congregational preacher who more than any other had constructed that system of belief. Holmes titled his poem "The Deacon's Masterpiece; or, The Wonderful 'One-Hoss Shay': A Logical Story," and he made of the shay's history a parable to show how New England's Calvinism, built by logic to last forever, "ran for a hundred years to the day" and then, in an instant, shattered and died. (In the poem, the centennial celebrated is that of the Lisbon earthquake, 1 November 1755, the event which inspired Voltaire's *Candide*.) Who better to recount this perfect example of Calvinist predestination than the learned son of a Congregational preacher?

> . . . First of November, 'Fifty-five!
> This morning the parson takes a drive.
> Now, small boys, get out of the way!
> Here comes the wonderful one-horse shay . . .

But the shay takes a spill, and when the parson gets up, before him lies:

> The poor old chaise in a heap or mound
> As if it had been to the mill and ground!
> You see, of course, if you're not a dunce,
> How it went to pieces all at once,—
> All at once and nothing first,—
> Just as bubbles do when they burst.[38]

The vernacular idiom, monotonous rhyme, and absurd rhythm all served to state, in a style of humor wholly American, a problem besetting Christians of all kinds, but particularly those Protestants who looked for their instruction and belief directly to the Bible. With the rise of scientific rationalism and the increasing acceptance of Newton's physics—that the earth, for instance, was not the center of the universe but merely one of several planets revolving in a unitary system around the sun—the traditional belief in mankind's special relationship to God had become all but impossible to maintain. Similarly, other tenets of Calvinism had come to seem arbitrary and unreasonable: that God predestined some people to be saved and all others to be damned; that a life of good works counted for naught in the division of the saved from the damned; that after the Fall (from an Eden that seemed increasingly a poetic fiction), all children were born sinful, heirs of Satan; that they continued inherently evil and condemned by God until as adults they were "born again" by an admission of guilt and adherence to Christ as the way to salvation; and that only in Christ's death on the cross, the atonement, was salvation possible—and even then possible, so Calvin's logic demanded, only for those God had predestined.

William Lawrence, a theological student in the 1870s and later an Episcopal bishop, recalled the confusion and distress of these years as people attempted to relate the old creeds to the new thought:

> In the first half of the nineteenth century, and even into the second half, there was no conception of the unity of the universe. As the stars were aloft and separate from all relations to the world, so to a great degree was God from man. The natural man had nothing in common with the spiritual man; there were two classes of men—the sinners and the saints . . . The Atonement was a transaction as separate from man as the proceedings of a judicial court are from the people. Theology had as little relation to life as dogma had to ethics. The members of the Church were the elect; all others were given over to the uncovenanted mercies of God.[39]

Later generations, he suggested, could "have no conception of the dread that from time to time was felt by Christian people at the discovery of truths which might be antagonistic to the Christian faith. When some new and bold statement of science was made, almost the whole Christian world shuddered at its possible result." It was a time when "we moved along week by week, month by month, dropping opinions, prejudices, and what we had thought were essentials of the Creed."[40]

Some Protestants filled the void left by the erosion of the old beliefs by joining the Unitarian Church. The first congregation to adopt Unitarian tenets had been King's Chapel, Boston, in 1785, and by mid-nineteenth century many Congregational churches in New England and elsewhere had joined the movement, enough so that in 1865 a National Conference of Unitarian Churches gathered in Boston. For Unitarians, Jesus was not divine, not Christ born of a virgin, conceived by the Holy Ghost, and a third of the Trinity. God was single, unitary, with the man Jesus his prophet. For Unitarians a child was born by nature good and only later sometimes corrupted by evil; such doctrines as the Fall, the atonement, and the threat of eternal damnation were invalid. Reason and conscience led the way to belief and salvation. Typical of Congregationalists who became Unitarians was Dr. Holmes, who though he admired Brooks greatly and often attended his Episcopal services nevertheless assured him that "my natural Sunday home is King's Chapel."[41] But for more conservative Protestants, particularly for those far from urban and intellectual centers, the Scriptures continued to be the foundation of all law and morality. For these, only the Bible could furnish answers to such questions as the will of God, the origin of man, and the destiny of the soul, and to them Unitarian rationalism was sacrilege.

Still others felt uncomfortable with either extreme, and for those in the middle, among them CCB, Phillips Brooks seemed to mark a trail through the crumbling ruins of the old ideas. By preaching a reworking of God's special relationship to men and women, he offered a way to join Unitarian acceptance of modern rational liberalism to the traditional beliefs in Christ's divinity.

Though Brooks was a minister of the Episcopal Church, many who heard him were unaware of his affiliation or, like CCB, were unconcerned. Brooks did not preach to gain converts for his church. "Preaching," he said, "is the communication of truth by man to men."[42] Standing at a lectern or in a pulpit in his preacher's black robe, Brooks was an impressive figure. He stood six-foot-four, weighed close to three hundred pounds, yet was light of foot and well-proportioned. He spoke very directly in a low and resonant voice and at an astonishing speed, but so clear was his diction that people easily followed him. By the mid-1870s, when CCB began to hear him regularly, Brooks was widely acknowledged to be a great preacher.

Though Holmes, in proclaiming the end of Calvinism, had published his poem a year before the appearance of Darwin's *On the Origin of Species*, as a doctor and professor he probably knew of Darwin's theories, which had begun to circulate. Most of his initial readers, however, almost certainly did not, and they took the poem, with pleasure or dismay, as a response in part to the impact on Christian thought of Newtonian physics. Brooks, preaching several decades after the appearance of Darwin's theories, offered a partial response, at least, to the impact on Christian thought of Darwinian evolutionary theories, which made a literal belief in the biblical stories of creation, and much else, still more difficult to maintain. If Newton had delivered the first great blow to Christian self-esteem and belief, Darwin delivered the second. (Fifty years on, Freud, with whom CCB would have dealings, would deliver a third.) And the young CCB found Brooks's dramatic, poetically intense sermons helpful. In one Brooks stated:

> I cannot but think also that the whole present tendency of physical science, which with its theories of evolution, dwells upon the presence in the world of nature of a continually active formative force, is in the line of Christianity. Christ not merely taught that the divine Power was always at work in the world. He *was* Himself that present active divine power, and so, in some sense, not merely made miracles seem occasionally possible, but made all events seem miraculous, which is not the abolition of the idea of the miraculous any more than the flooding of the world with sunshine is an extinction of the sun.[43]

In 1879, CCB's last year at Harvard, he wrote to Annie Hoe describing how for him the advances in science had made a literal belief in the Bible impossible. One of his classmates had insisted that if Charley "accepted the Bible as an inspired book," which he did, then "I must believe all that is written in it." Charley disagreed.

"Do you remember," he asked Annie, "in Phillips Brooks' sermon on the present and future faith, his statement of the character of the times? Till now, Mr. B. says, rocks and ice have been bound fast together. No one could tell what was firm and what was not. Now as the ice breaks up, we can see what is firm, and we can cling to that." He added, "For my part, I am glad the ice has begun to 'break up' now. It must have done so sooner or later. Why not now?" But that, no doubt, was easier for a young man to maintain than for his elders, and possibly a reason why he wrote these thoughts to Annie rather than to his father.[44]

In his first year at Harvard Charley began going to Boston regularly to hear Brooks, even before the "new" Trinity Church, closely associated with the preacher, was completed. The "old" Trinity, in downtown Boston, had burned in the great fire of 8–9 November 1872, but fortunately plans for a new church were already under way. A few months before the fire, Trinity's congregation, with some hesitation and loss in members, had voted to leave the old church, now isolated in a business district, and to build anew in Back Bay, a residential area of the city created by filling some marshes of the Charles River. The vestry hired Henry Hobson Richardson as architect, and his building, of red stone and brick in Franco-Spanish

Romanesque style, with interior decoration by John LaFarge, became a masterwork of church architecture.

Its interior, though shaped as a cross, is entirely open, a "low" church in style. There are no pillars or side chapels, and all pews have a clear view of the pulpit and altar. The Episcopal church in these years, as to some extent it is still, was uneasily split into "high" and "low" church, with extremists in each wing viewing their opposites with suspicion or even hostility. Those favoring "high" church, sometimes called "anglo-catholics," liked their architecture Gothic, with deep shadows, darkly stained windows, and a strong sense of awe and mystery. In their services they stressed the liturgy and established rites, not the sermon, which could vary in quality with the preacher and lead to heresies. They wanted their ministers, whom they often called "priests," to wear richly colored vestments and to stand physically and symbolically between the congregation and the altar. And the altar, typically of marble, was put on a high pedestal and backed against the east wall so that it dominated the length of the longer axis of the cross.

In Trinity, however, a great circular pulpit dominates, pinned to the northeastern pier of the central tower, where the four limbs of the cross meet. Any minister preaching from the pulpit is visible to all. In Brooks's day the minister might wear a black cassock with white surplice, or, as did Brooks, a "preaching cassock," solid black without surplice. And Trinity's altar (redesigned in 1914) also was typically "low" church, merely a large freestanding wooden table in the middle of the chancel, surrounded on four sides by a communion rail at which the congregation knelt to partake in the Lord's Supper.[45] The area around the altar, the chancel, was not reserved for clergy or even the choir. If the preacher was popular and the congregation overflowing, people sat in the chancel, on the steps and floor.[46] The focus on the pulpit and the sermon harked back to the Puritan tradition in the church as opposed to the anglo-catholic—to the Puritans who, in the English Civil War, had fought for Cromwell and Parliament against Charles I and executive divine right.[47]

That Brooks and Trinity were "low" church made it easier for CCB and other evangelical visitors to feel at home. At a "high" church "mass," with incense, bells ringing at the elevation of the host, and possibly even chanting in Latin, he might have felt out of place and not returned. Brooks, with new ideas, proposed a faith considerably different from that held by Charley's father, yet to the son many of Trinity's ways, including its open interior and great pulpit, were familiar.

The church was consecrated on 9 February 1877, and in the months thereafter Charley began to attend Sunday services regularly, often morning and afternoon. Brooks usually preached twice on Sunday, a new sermon in the morning and one recycled from previous years in the afternoon. In the evening he would repeat the morning sermon in a Boston suburb.[48]

Charley first mentioned Brooks to Annie in March 1877, revealing that he had already heard him several times. On the previous Sunday, 11 March, he had spent the day "visiting four churches" and had heard at least three different preachers, of which the last, in the evening, was Brooks.

> He preached on Nicodemus, and one point in his sermon pleased me very much. Speaking of what a mystery is, he said that it was a perfectly plain result with an unknown cause. We are ourselves mysteries; we know that we live, we feel it, but how we received life we know not.
>
> Applying this to the spiritual life, we know not how we have been born again; we only know that we are spiritually alive. The life can not be without birth in the spiritual as well as in the physical sense. For if we have the life we must have had the birth. That is the proof of conversion.
>
> I don't know whether I have made clear to you what I want to say, but I know it is true all the same.
>
> You must hear Phillips Brooks; he is the best preacher I ever heard.[49]

Brooks drew young people, like Charley and the future Bishop Lawrence, in part because he so emphatically placed truth before orthodoxy. Of the latter he once remarked: "It makes possible an easy transmission of truth, but only by the deadening of truth, as a butcher freezes meat in order to carry it across the sea."[50] According to Lawrence, Brooks believed "Whatever truth is discovered, and from whatever source revealed, it is of God. Man must keep mind and heart ever open to new revelations of God . . . He [Brooks] had no patience with that man or church who was timidly asking of present thought, 'Is it orthodox?' The vital question was, 'Is it true?'"[51] Charley, struggling with the seeming conflict of orthodoxy versus truth, went on Easter morning, 1879, to Trinity to hear Brooks preach. Moved by what he heard, he wrote promptly to Annie:

> Mr. B. in his Easter sermon this morning said, that if we knew what immortality meant and what Christ's love was we could resist *all* temptations. That is certainly a truer interpretation of the command "Be ye perfect" than that so often given "Be as perfect as you can (and be content with it)" . . .

... Annie, I am, I fear, growing heretical. I want to be unorthodox in many things, but I do not want to go further than I ought. Still I do get comfort from some things that I believe. I do not know what God is. I do not know what personal means when applied to him. I am not anthropomorphic enough to think him like myself. Yet he is incomprehensible to me, different from me. I know that my inability to conceive him is no proof against his being. Indeed, although I cannot *prove* his existence (The *a posteriori* argument seems of little worth to me), I believe he exists because I often feel him *in* me. But this faith will not convince others.

I said some things comforted me. They are Christ's life and love. When I cannot understand God, I can understand him [Christ].[52]

CCB's emphasis on Christ followed what Brooks always preached: the absolute centrality of Christ to any faith and understanding of Christianity. As Brooks once said, "I have been led to think of Christianity and to speak of it not as a system of doctrine, but as a personal force ... The personal force is the nature of Jesus, full of humanity, full of divinity, and powerful with a love for man."[53] But of course for many who heard Brooks regularly, the opening of a door to understanding and faith was achieved initially through the force of his preaching. Lawrence recalled a typical Sunday morning at Trinity:

Promptly at halfpast ten all doors are opened, and the waiting crowd surges up the aisles, entering the pews, and up into the chancel, filling the sedalia around the chancel, sitting upon the cushions of the Communion rail and on the chancel steps, and lining the walls wherever there is room to stand. The people have come in all sincerity and reverence to hear the Gospel of Jesus Christ.

The rector and his assistant enter quietly from the side, and kneel for prayer, as do the people. The organ is silent, then with the rustle of movement, the whole congregation stands, and the rector's voice, "The Lord is in His holy temple," is heard. There is something that touches one's humble spirit, as without processional the service begins and the Confession is repeated. Morning Prayer over, the rector retires to the robing room and exchanging his surplice for the preacher's black gown, enters, kneels at the chancel rail, mounts the pulpit steps during the last of the hymn; he looks wonderingly at the people, feeling their needs and hopes; turns the pages of his manuscript over; then again gazes intently at the people. The hymn over and the people seated, the preacher in a quiet voice gives out the text; then in a stronger voice repeats it, so that all may hear; then he and the people with him "are off." There is no other fitting expression: the torrent of thought, imagination, illustration, conviction and passion is let loose: from that moment to the end preacher and people are united in one intense purpose, to give and to receive the message of the Gospel of that day.[54]

After Lawrence published his biography of Brooks in 1930, CCB wrote to him praising the accuracy of his description of a service in Trinity. In his letter CCB recalled one trait of Brooks that Lawrence had not mentioned: "When he had finished his sermon, as we thought, and the silence was intense, he would utter three or four additional sentences, as if perhaps these might be the last words he might ever speak to us. That was the feeling I had—that the message must be driven home."[55] In his sermons Brooks always passionately sought to persuade those who listened to come to decision and to take action. He scorned the mystic who sought "to lose himself in God." The aim in submitting to God was to "be used, to illuminate and help the world." The aim of life should be to do God's work.[56]

After graduating from Harvard, CCB had few opportunities to hear Brooks preach, but when one occurred, he seized it. By chance he was in London on 4 July 1880, when Brooks conducted a service in Westminster Abbey, and CCB heard then, perhaps not for the first time, one of his famous sermons, "The Candle of the Lord." Taking as his text Proverbs 20:27, "The spirit of man is the candle of the Lord," Brooks made of it a metaphor to depict the relationship between God and man or, as one scholar has summarized it, "The soul draws its purpose, its inspiration, and its fire from God."[57] Ten years later, in Trinity Church, New York, when Brooks delivered a series of noonday Lenten lectures to businessmen, CCB attended many of them.

Possibly the most important quality that CCB appreciated in Brooks was his optimism, which permeated every sermon, including one of his last, delivered on Thanksgiving Day, 1892:

It [optimism] is not merely a matter of temperament, nor does it mean that this is a thoroughly good world in which we live, nor is it simply a careless passing over the evils of life, nor is it a way of seeing how everything is going to come out for good. But it is a great belief in a great purpose, underlying the world for good, absolutely certain to fulfil itself somehow. That must have been what God saw when He looked upon the world and called it good."[58]

CCB, by temperament and under the influence of Brooks, shared that hopeful view: attempt great deeds for God, and with his help great deeds may be achieved. With Brooks's theology CCB was less concerned, though not unmindful. A recent biographer of Brooks has concluded that in his maturity, roughly 1873–93, Brooks preached "an overarching moral and aesthetic design to the universe and that this design is to be seen in Jesus Christ." For Brooks, the incarnation—God becoming man in Jesus—was more significant for Christians than the atonement, for it opened a door to humans for greater understanding of God. Conversion, however, was not a "one time experience" preceding faith; it followed faith, and "the commitment constantly had to be renewed." Sanctification, the daily attempt to achieve a life free of sin, "meant movement toward the figure and pattern of Christ, 'his perfect manhood.'" And in his metaphors and analogies he continually sought "ways in which to make theology not the private domain of seminarians, church bureaucrats, and professional academicians, but the property of men and women in the pew." What he accomplished was "a restatement of the Puritan demand for the centrality of Jesus Christ."[59]

Thus Brooks's theology flowed directly from the Bible, as in St. John's Gospel, when an anxious disciple, Thomas, asks his Lord, "How will we know the way?" Jesus replies, "I am the Way, the Truth, and the Life." CCB, writing in 1944 to an Episcopal minister, closely echoed Brooks and St. John in stating, "For most of us it is through Christ that we come to know God as our Father."[60]

Such a definite statement is rare for CCB, for he seldom discussed his theological beliefs, and it is possible that he never gave them much thought. Among the laity, many "low church" Episcopalians did not. The old creed was now simply a battle cry, a banner beneath which each morning men and women of goodwill could gather, form ranks, and march to their work of bringing God into the world.[61] Even about the afterlife CCB said little. In old age he confessed in a letter that for about ten years after his wife's death, he had hoped after his own death to be with her again, but in time belief in this possibility faded. He frequently said, however, that he looked forward to death, that the twenty minutes after its embrace would be life's most interesting.[62]

Still, those who knew CCB best knew his life had a religious basis. At home, he prayed daily, in private but without secrecy, and sometimes in audible anguish. Had his beliefs been purely humanistic he might not have worked as hard and long for his church and such organizations as the Welfare Council. Disappointment would have drained the ardor; other interests might have intervened. Yet he was not always silent about his beliefs. One day, prodded by the persistent questioning of a nephew, he burst out with such force that the words were not forgotten: "Belief in God and trust in his over-ruling power form the basis of my character."[63]

4

Slouching into the Law

THE RELATED QUESTIONS of what young Charles Burlingham might do with his life and how he might support himself after college began to bother him early in his junior year. His father, he knew, hoped he would become a preacher, but in a letter to his mother in January 1878 he mentioned the possibility of practicing law. Musing on the purpose of a college education, he remarked: "It isn't the great amount learnt in a college course, is it, but the ability to continue studying, after graduating, in a systematic and effective way that marks the college bred man. A college graduate can do better work than a green hand at study in Law School, for instance, other things being equal of course."[1]

The following month, again to his mother, in lamenting the sinfulness of work on Sunday he observed, "It is poor policy to get into a habit of working on Sunday if one intends to be a professional man." Since preachers work on Sundays, it would seem he had another profession in mind.[2] Later that spring he wrote to Annie more openly, saying he was "in a quandary" over electing courses for his final year at Harvard. "My choice ought to be made with reference to my future profession or business. If I am to be a lawyer I must study more history, more political economy, less fine arts and language. So the question is ever before my mind. Am I to be a lawyer or not? I cannot dissect my feelings on the subject—or rather I will not. I am impelled, first one way, then another."[3] He confessed he did not feel strongly drawn in any direction. "Ought I enter upon any work unless I feel that work is the very best work for me?" He thanked God he was not rich, for the wherewithal to be idle would only double confusion and delay decision. In closing, he called his letter foolish and urged Annie to burn it.

Yet even "poverty" did not help him to a clear choice. After electing to take natural history, philosophy (Kant, etc.), and forensics (written themes stressing style and argument), he balanced a course he felt was suited to the law, political economy taught by Charles Dunbar, against one he felt was not, on Renaissance art with Charles Eliot Norton.[4] And in March of his senior year he was still writing Annie in an agony of indecision.

> My life is, to an extent, selfish from necessity, more selfish, however, than it need be . . . There are some things which I cannot understand. One of them is, how to reconcile my duty to myself with my duty to my fellow man. How can I tell how far I have a right to try to improve myself! Sometimes self-improvement seems wrong to me. What good can I do the world by reading certain books, by learning certain things. For instance, although one may possibly do good by going into society (this is mere hypothesis), ought one to heed the risk of being hurt oneself, when the odds are so against doing any good?[5]

Finally, he chose the law. According to Burlingham family tradition he told his father that as a lawyer he might earn more than as a preacher and so could do more for the poor. Possibly also he stressed that his father, when young, had felt called to preach the Gospel, and called with such force that no obstacle could bar the goal, whereas he felt no such call. Perhaps he realized that he yet was skeptical, using the stimulation of Brooks's sermons to sort his own beliefs, as if asking of religion: How much of this can I believe? whereas Brooks and Aaron Burlingham blazed with belief.[6]

In any case, Dr. Burlingham gave the decision his blessing, and Charley then faced the questions of where and how to train for the bar. He evidently assumed he would practice in New York City, where his family again was living. Albert, on graduating from Washington University, had returned to New York in the summer of 1877 to work in Colonel Hoe's company, and at the same time Dr. Burlingham had resigned his post in St. Louis and taken one with the First Baptist Church in Paterson, New Jersey. Remaining there only six months (the church apparently defaulted on a mortgage and closed), he moved to the Willoughby Avenue Church, Brooklyn, where he caught a chill and was sick much of the winter. Finally, in October 1879, he accepted the post of district secretary of the American Baptist Missionary Union, with its local headquarters in New York City. For Charley, with Burlinghams, Hoes, Lawrences, and Harpers in the city, New York offered a prospect of future clients and, what he still seemed to want, emotional support.[7]

Another choice for Charley was whether to go to law school. Before 1850, when the country's population totaled roughly 23,500,000, there were nine law schools; by 1879, with the population slightly more than doubled, there were forty. Despite the increase, most men still entered the profession by serving another lawyer as clerk for three or four years, often starting without pay. And then, if the apprentice was recommended by his mentor, he was admitted to practice in the state courts upon motion of a member of the bar or, if the state required it, by some sort of examination (in some states the examination was only an appearance before friends).[8] It may seem strange—it certainly did to many of CCB's friends in later years—that he did not continue at Harvard, where his college degree gave him entry to the law school. After all, Harvard's was the country's oldest university law school (founded in 1817) and, though neither the largest nor considered the best, well-known. But for Charley, besides family and friends in New York, there were other reasons to prefer Columbia.

At Harvard President Eliot in 1870 had started reorganizing the law school by appointing as dean of the three-man faculty Christopher Columbus Langdell, but Langdell's reforms were as yet neither completed nor fully accepted. He had begun by tightening requirements for entry and graduation, while extending the course of study from eighteen months to three years. Columbia's school, on the other hand, offered a degree in two years, a difference Charley probably could not ignore. His father had helped him through five years of college, and on 31 August 1879 Charley turned twenty-one. For law school, surely, two years were better than three.[9]

Further, Langdell had introduced a new method of teaching. Most law faculties then usually lectured on texts that summarized for students the principles of law; and after these were established, a few cases, often hypothetical, were examined to show how a judge might apply or misapply the pertinent principles. Langdell, however, plunged students into reading reports of actual cases and then in class pitted students against each other or the professor to analyze the court's reasoning. Out of this Socratic dialogue the students were expected to dig out for themselves the existing decisive principles. For Langdell, law was not an art but a science which by careful study, as if through a microscope, would reveal its classifications and principles. The idea appealed to Eliot, a chemist, and it fit the scientism of the age.

Harvard's 150 law students at first found the new system of instruction chaotic, and they and several of the faculty resisted its imposition, so that in the spring of Charley's college graduation the law school had an as yet unproved system of teaching and was in considerable turmoil. Conversely, the Columbia school, with 500 students and five professors, though squeezed into a shabby building at 8 Great Jones Street (south of Astor Place), was teaching in the old way, led by Theodore W. Dwight, who had founded the school in 1858 and was considered by many the greatest teacher of law in the United States. Dwight thought as little of Langdell's method as Langdell did of his. Wrote Dwight in 1891: "Law decisions are but a labyrinth. Woe to the man who busies himself with them without a clue (in the form of a legal principle) to guide him."[10] Probably for a mixture of these reasons, Charley chose Columbia.

In later years CCB complained that Dwight and his faculty "spoon-fed" the students, but he never questioned Dwight's skill as a lecturer. In 1932, speaking at the dedication of a Columbia memorial to Dwight, he first assured those gathered of the man's greatness, quoting two giants of the English bar, A. V. Dicey and James Bryce, to show how Dwight's reputation had spanned the ocean. Then, turning to the still controversial "best method of teaching law," he conspicuously refused to prefer one method to the other. "It is not methods," he insisted, "but men, that make a law school." Even Dwight's extraordinary clarity in outlining principles of law, he said, was ultimately misleading to students, as was also, by implication, Langdell's case system. For "after we had left the law school, we discovered that the law is not an exact science, that many things we thought settled were far otherwise."[11]

Throughout sixty-odd years of practice, CCB was always skeptical of the certainty and clarity with which professors set forth their concepts of the law. In the perennial argument over how to teach law—by 1912 Langdell's method was under attack for too often ignoring the nonlegal reasons, often social or economic, underlying a decision[12]—CCB continually spoke for the practicing lawyer, preferring experience and pragmatism to doctrinaire theories. He may even have thought that if only times were different, better than a law school was the older system of apprenticeship, for in clerking in a law office the student more often met the realities of life and of the courtroom where witnesses sometimes lied or, telling the truth, were disbelieved. But he saw that with the rise in the country's population and the increasing complexity of its social, political, and economic institutions, some standardization was needed. The world of his youth, the individual's world of moral causation and free agency, was becoming a corporate world of liability insurance and legislative decisions on who should pay. Changes in legal principles were coming more swiftly than in the past, and requiring of lawyers ever greater specialization. The number of law schools steadily rose, and by 1936 there were 190.

By his own admission, CCB's work at Columbia Law School was perfunctory. He spent much time escorting Annie Hoe to choral and literary events, and on the afternoon of 30 March 1880 accompanied her and Colonel Hoe to the dedication of the Metropolitan Art Museum's new building, formally opened by President Hayes. He was continually at the Hoe and Lawrence houses in the city or at Brightside, while falling gradually in love with Annie's niece, red-haired Louisa Lawrence. Perhaps because he and Louie saw each other so often, no letters between them in these years survive, but in old age he stated that by the summer of 1880, when she was seventeen and he about to be twenty-two, they had become secretly engaged.[13]

To help his father with the law school's annual tuition of $100, he tutored two boys for college, Theodore Dunham for Harvard and Henry de Forest Baldwin for Yale. He could present himself as a tutor for before leaving Harvard he had received from his professors and President Eliot letters recommending him as "a private tutor or teacher in a school," and even had been asked to teach Latin, Greek, and modern languages at Colby Academy, New London, New Hampshire. (The salary offered, $1,200 a year, was attractive, but he declined, for despite a continuing interest in education, he never imagined himself as a teacher.)[14] Perhaps because of the distractions of tutoring, his growing love for Louie, and sociable evenings with Annie, CCB's memories of Columbia Law School are as perfunctory as his work there. No recollection rings with the intellectual excitement he felt at Harvard, but a summer trip to London and Paris in 1880, taken between the law school's first and second year, brought him lasting new friends and experiences.

He sailed on the bark *Constantine*, twenty-eight days to London, with his future brother-in-law Robert Lawrence, Rob's first cousin Henry C. Lawrence, and a brother of Henry Baldwin, Charles. The Baldwin parents, pleased with what CCB had accomplished with Henry, had hired CCB for the summer to tutor this younger son and to show him the sights of London and Paris. He may also have received some pay to keep an eye on the Lawrence boys, though Henry, at age twenty, and Rob, at nineteen, were close to independence. With young Baldwin, however, CCB worked every day on the voyage over, fair weather or foul, and "we had some wonderful storms." Sea travel then was still perilous (in the first six months of 1880 the *Times* reported thirty-three ships "lost").[15]

In London, CCB started a vigorous round of sightseeing. Applying to the dean of Westminster Abbey, his father's acquaintance A. P. Stanley, for permission to visit parts of the abbey closed to the public, he received from the dean, who was ill and soon died, an almost illegible letter. Continually displaying it to guards, CCB led the boys into many rooms not usually seen.[16]

Meanwhile, Rob Lawrence's parents, together with Annie Hoe, arrived in London with their five daughters—Mariella, two years older than Rob, and the four younger, in order: Louie, Fanny, Grace, and Edith. CCB claimed later that his meeting with the family was accidental, though that seems unlikely. In any case, he led his young men to Canterbury, and then on to Rouen and to Paris, where once again the Lawrence family and Annie joined them. She and the Lawrences put up at the Normandie, on the Avenue de l'Opéra, while CCB and the young men stayed at a cheaper hotel. CCB's sightseeing group now swelled to include Louie and her younger sisters, and one day he so exhausted Grace and Edith, only ten and eight, that before one historic building they sank onto a step and burst into tears. The event, in less dramatic guise, would recur, for family members sometimes found CCB's energy a burden.[17]

One Sunday afternoon in Paris, CCB, fulfilling a request of his parents, paid a call at teatime on their friends Dr. and Mrs. Joseph T. Evans, who had been living in Paris for several years. While he was with them, in their apartment near the Arc de Triomphe, their son Joe entered, quite unexpected, "dusty with travel, a rucksack on his back, and easel and staff in his hands. He was just arriving from Oberammergau. I was attracted at once by his beautiful face, with lustrous brown eyes and a light beard."[18] A year older than CCB, Joe Evans had been born physically sound, but as an infant an attack of scarlet fever apparently injured his development, and he grew into a hunchback. By some mystery of nature, however, the handicap had not only brought beauty to his face, especially to his eyes, but also liberated his spirit. He was a man for friendship; and with a handshake and a few remarks he charmed CCB, who promptly invited him to the Hôtel Normandie to meet Annie and the Lawrence family. And "Joe came, he saw, he conquered."[19]

As the summer wore on, the American travelers began to leave for home. The first to depart were members of the DeWitt Lawrence family, taking with them CCB's companion Rob. Next to go was young Charles Baldwin, leaving with CCB only Henry Lawrence and Annie. Soon Henry drops from CCB's memories, leaving only CCB and Annie, and finally they sail on the Inman Line's steamship *City of Berlin*, which needed only seven days to cross and was famous for bearing in its lounge the first electric lights on a transatlantic liner.[20]

Before they sailed, however, they had several weeks with Joe Evans, who showed them a new side of Paris, artistic rather than historic. He was studying at the École des Beaux-Arts in the atelier of Jean-Léon Gérôme, and he introduced his new friends to many of the students and professors.

Later, in New York, through Joe, they met Augustus Saint-Gaudens, George de Forest Brush, and Abbott Thayer, another of Gérôme's students. Evans, who seemed to know every artist of his generation, became president of the Art Students League in New York (1891–93) and a founder of the Society of American Artists. Neither he nor Thayer was destined to be a great painter, but any student of Gérôme—Thomas Eakins was the greatest of the Americans—was well trained in the classical traditions of drawing and color. Though Impressionist painters had begun to exhibit in Paris in the 1860s, Gérôme continued in the older school, specializing in historical subjects such as *The Death of Caesar*. For him and his students, inspiration still lay in the examples of Courbet or Corot.

Thayer, for the earlier part of his life, was an important painter, and as much a naturalist as an artist. He followed a generation of American painters, admirers of Audubon, who produced hunting scenes for patrons' dining rooms—pictures of a brace of partridge or duck, or of trout lying on a mossy background with rod and creel. With Thayer, fin and feather were not flecked in suggestively, but precisely represented. His formal portraits were similarly well drawn and painted in dark colors, and in the mid-1880s, at the request of Annie's friends, Thayer painted her portrait, which, upon her death in 1886, passed to CCB, who, until he died in 1959, hung it in his living room above his favorite chair.[21] The adherence of Evans and Thayer to an academic tradition that by 1913 (the year of the Armory Show in New York) was judged by most critics and patrons to be old-fashioned perhaps inclined CCB, out of loyalty to them, to fall behind the changing styles. In any case, after Evans died in 1898, CCB's interest in art began to slacken. If he went to the 1913 Armory Show, he left no word of it.

His interest in theater, also greatly stimulated by Evans, was more intense and lasting, and on this trip abroad he blossomed into an avid playgoer, who even in old age could recall the plays and actors seen. While in Paris, he went often with Evans to the Comédie-française to see the Molière plays he had studied at Harvard, and among the actors he admired were Gôt, Delaunay, and the Coquelin brothers.[22]

But his greatest enthusiasm he reserved for the English actress Ellen Terry. In London, he had hurried to the Lyceum to see her and Henry Irving in a double bill of *The Merchant of Venice* (shorn of its final act) preceded by the Danish poet Henrik Hertz's one-act curtain-raiser *Iolanthe; or, King René's Daughter*, a story of a blind girl who finds love. As Iolanthe, the blind girl, Terry had been "unspeakably lovely," and possibly the power of her impact on him in that play owed in part to his always strong emotional response to persons in some way crippled—such as Annie and Joe.[23] In CCB's memories that summer was notable. Traveling mostly at his own expense, without parents or elder brother, with young people committed to his care, choosing what they would do and see, he matured. And with the trip completed, he returned to New York secretly engaged to Louie— they had told only Annie—and eager to finish law school.

CCB received his law degree in May 1881 and looked forward to prompt admission to the bar of New York State, which then was one of the few requiring a written examination. Throughout the 1870s the state legislature had continually revised the law on admission, and early in 1881 the judges of the Court of Appeals (the state's highest court), as they had been ordered and empowered to do, issued new rules requiring all applicants for admission to take an examination. And as a prerequisite applicants had to have studied law for three years, either in a school or as a clerk in a lawyer's office.[24]

At the start of 1881, however, there still existed a statutory exemption for the graduates of four law schools—Hamilton College, University of Albany, New York University, and Columbia. In effect, the four law schools, not the court, admitted their candidates to the bar, a system to which many judges and lawyers objected. There was, after all, no check on the quality of the schools, and the financial value of the loophole to them raised a clear conflict of interest. The loophole's importance can be seen in some figures for New York City (then only Manhattan) in 1875. That year the local court, the First Department of the State Supreme Court, admitted 36 men to practice, and the two local law schools, Columbia and New York University, 250. Of the latter, less than half were college graduates (though that year, Columbia adopted some educational requirements for future law classes, including an examination for entrance from which it exempted students with diplomas from "literary colleges").

Many lawyers and judges continually protested this system of privileged admission, and the state legislature finally allowed the exemption for the four schools to expire in early 1882. The last Columbia Law class to enjoy the old privilege therefore would be CCB's of 1881, or so it seemed. In May the law school awarded diplomas to 123 men (of which 47 had not graduated from a college), with perhaps as many as 50, including CCB, intending to practice in New York. Dean Dwight led these men to a session of the general term of the state's First Department of the Supreme Court, but to their dismay the presiding justice, Noah Davis, with his two associates concurring, refused to swear them in, pointing out that the state

Court of Appeals had recently issued rules establishing a board of examiners, and despite Dwight's protest, the judges referred the Columbia graduates to that board for examination.[25] "Nothing daunted," as CCB later told the story, on 15 September "Professor Dwight took us to the General Term in Brooklyn," which was then a separate city and served by the Supreme Court's Second Department, "and Joseph Barnard, P.J. and his colleagues admitted us."[26]

Trouble followed. In the First Department a lawyer prominent in the city bar association brought suit to revoke the license to practice of CCB's classmate Lewis S. Burchard, who, though admitted in the Second Department, was residing and practicing in the First—as was CCB. Throughout the winter of 1881–82 this cloud of uncertainty hovered over CCB's right to practice until finally, in June 1882, the First Department court denied the challenging petition. The judges, in *Matter of Burchard, et al.*, reluctantly ruled that however "irregular" it was for Burchard, having had his application rejected by the First Department, then to apply to the Second; and however "indecorous" for that court to entertain the application, the only question to be considered was whether the Second Department had acted within its powers. And it had.[27] Needless to say, the Class of 1881 followed the case closely, for Burchard had been selected for trial only because he led the class alphabetically; if he lost, so would they all. Dwight argued in defense of his students, and Judge Charles Daniels wrote the decision, which, though favorable to the students, was scorching in its language: "This discrimination [in their favor] is neither just nor fair . . . Discriminations of this nature are not in harmony with the policy of the law, or the institutions of the State. They create invidious distinctions . . ."

Thus, by a back door most lawyers wanted slammed shut, CCB snuck into the New York bar. "It was a shameful performance," he said later. "If the fourth letter in my surname had been "a" or "b" instead of "l," then instead of Burchard "I should have gone down in legal history in disgrace."[28]

In other ways, too, the transition from law student to practicing attorney proved hard for CCB; and for several years signs of distress appear in his letters and were visible to those who cared for him. His first legal position, found for him by his father, was temporary and without pay. In late spring, when CCB, not yet admitted to practice, was unable to find work, Aaron Burlingham had asked an acquaintance, Theodore Hascall, for help. Hascall, a partner in the two-man firm of Strong and Hascall, had a relative, Francis Lynde Stetson, who in the previous year had resigned as the city's assistant corporation counsel and had formed a new firm of four lawyers—Bangs & Stetson. Thinking it might need a clerk, Hascall spoke to Stetson on CCB's behalf. As no other job for CCB seemed likely until he was admitted to the bar, an event now postponed at least until September, he one morning reported to Stetson for work. Meanwhile, as he had done during law school, he lived at home with his parents and brother, Albert, in Mount Vernon, a residential village in Westchester County easily reached from the city.[29]

CCB's situation at Bangs & Stetson was as unsatisfactory as might be expected when one lawyer foists on another a clerk not of the latter's choosing. Stetson asked him to catalog the firm's library and recommended that he read the opinions of Chief Justice Marshall, but otherwise took little notice of him. At summer's end, Stetson suggested that CCB would learn more in a smaller office, in effect dismissing him with advice that CCB later claimed, emotionally and wrongly, was "very bad."[30]

Nevertheless, in the fall, with a reference from Stetson and admission to the bar achieved in the Supreme Court's Second Department (though still challenged in the First), CCB was able to start work for pay as clerk to Theron G. Strong, at the time a single practitioner, for Hascall had left him to join another lawyer. Partnerships then were constantly forming and dissolving, often on no more than a handshake. The agreement did not need to be in writing, did not require recording with the state or city, and incurred no tax. Between honest partners, separating was as easy as coming together.[31] Single practitioners, however, were still a large part of the bar, and no firm in New York City had more than eight partners.*

Strong, in his book *Landmarks of a Lawyer's Lifetime*, estimated that a good partnership could handle "at least one-third more than the combined volume of business of each individual member of that firm practicing separately." But he warned of the difficulties of partnership: the need for true compatibility, not just in skills and business but in moral outlook, for "partners are at each other's mercy, not only with respect to the kind of business undertaken and the method of conducting it and in dealing with clients, but in their relations with each other."[32] And some men, he felt, were not suited to be partners simply by temperament. Strong himself

---

*According to *Hubbell's Legal Directory for Lawyers*, for the year 1873–74 there were roughly 275 lawyers in the city who could be recommended as "prompt, able, and reliable" (though many honored lawyers were not listed). Those named divided as follows: one firm with six partners, one with five, four with four, twenty-six with three, fifty-two with two, and the balance of lawyers—sixty-eight—practicing alone. Throughout the 1880s the proportions remained much the same, except for a large increase in firms of four partners. Those with more continued to be unusual, with eight the largest number.

often had partners, and in 1884 would form a firm with Elihu Root and three others, Root & Strong. But in September 1881, when he hired CCB, he was alone, and paid his new clerk in the range of $8 or $10 a week, barely $500 a year. By comparison, Charles Evans Hughes, the future chief justice of the United States, working for a three-man firm, earned in his first year of practice, 1884–85, nearly $1,500. CCB's small salary infuriated him. Even sixty years later he would describe Strong as a man of "paramount meanness."[33]

CCB's complaint must be discounted. Hughes was the exception, already recognized as brilliant, whereas CCB was quite undistinguished. Worse, his right to practice had been challenged in *Matter of Blanchard.* Further, his wage, for a starting lawyer at that time, was average; moreover, the complaint is constant, raised in every age by every young lawyer whose self-appraisal exceeds the value put on him by others, and in time would be raised against CCB by younger lawyers.[34] To contemporaries, Strong was an able lawyer and pleasant companion. His book, recounting his experience of forty years at the bar, reveals an attractive man, one whose literary bent might have been expected to appeal to CCB. Yet CCB never warmed to him.

Strong's office, at 41 Wall Street, was two blocks east of Trinity Church, whose 280-foot spire (roughly 22 stories) still dominated lower Manhattan, and it was only five minutes' fast walk from the courts near City Hall. Like most legal offices at the time, it was on an upper floor of a five-story building without an elevator and perhaps had a small office for Strong off a larger room that served as a reception area and office for the clerk. As the building had no central heating, this main room, at least, would have had a coal-burning Franklin stove or a potbellied "Baltimore Heater." One of CCB's duties would have been to tend the stove and to sweep up both rooms frequently, for coal dust settled everywhere. But because buildings then did not provide charwomen, and clerks were generally too lazy or too busy to clean, most law offices, as Strong reports, were "filthy."[35]

Telephones had become available in 1877–78 but were still uncommon. They were awkward to use—separate mouth- and earpieces mounted on a varnished board attached to the wall and set in operation by a hand crank—and at first, of course, there was almost no one to call. Another disadvantage was that they were so very public. To overcome static, or perhaps a disbelief in the contraption's powers, the caller often shouted, disrupting his own office and perhaps revealing more to his clerks than he wished. Strong did not acquire his first phone until 1884, after CCB had left him.[36] Typewriters, too, had appeared in 1878 but were equally slow to be adopted;

an experienced hand copyist often could outstrip the early typists. CCB doubtless copied many letters and documents by hand, and Strong, keeping the drafts for his office files, would send the "fair," or final, copies, typically hand delivered by CCB, to clients, lawyers, and the courts. CCB would also have kept current the log of all letters and documents entering or leaving the office, and if Strong had a case coming up at court, CCB would attend the court's trial calendar call, estimate when the case would be reached, and make sure that Strong was on hand to argue it.[37]

Strong's practice was a general one of commercial, personal, and real estate law, and those cases that he took to trial he mostly argued in the state and city courts, located in the "Tweed Courthouse" just north of City Hall. This small building, put up in the late 1860s when Boss Tweed and his Tammany Democrats were in power, is possibly, because of the fraud and graft in its construction, the most expensive public building, per square foot, ever erected, costing four times as much as Great Britain's Houses of Parliament.[38] CCB would have walked or run to it almost daily, up and down William or Nassau Streets, and in delivering letters and papers to other law offices he came to know every nook of Manhattan south of City Hall.

Law clerks then enjoyed a freedom soon lost. In this pre-telephone era, once out of the office, they were beyond recall. No employer could overtake them with a message or check the progress of their rounds, and they had the habit, which everyone understood was part of their apprentice training, of lingering at the courthouse to hear cases argued. On days when great advocates were at trial, clerks frequently were joined by their elders—among them, Strong—who came to listen, criticize, and admire. The pace of legal practice then was slower and the art of advocacy, whose decline Strong later would lament, more fully savored.[39]

CCB tarried often at court to listen and observe—further evidence that Strong was not so "mean" as he reported. He particularly enjoyed hearing two of the greatest lawyers of the day, William M. Evarts (1818–1901) and the younger Joseph Hodges Choate (1832–1917). In 1868 Evarts had defended President Andrew Johnson in his impeachment trial; in 1871 he represented the United States at the Geneva arbitration of Civil War claims against Great Britain; and in 1875 he successfully defended Henry Ward Beecher, the Brooklyn preacher, against charges of adultery, perhaps the most sensational trial of the decade. He also had a leading role in 1870 in founding the Association of the Bar of the City of New York (often called the City Bar Association), which had organized to put Boss Tweed in jail and to break Tammany Hall's grip on the city and state judiciary.[40]

Though Choate was possibly the greater orator and advocate, CCB admired him less than Evarts. Choate was a witty after-dinner speaker and in court was known particularly for his summations to the jury, which were always clear, simple, and easy. And he crowned his career with six brilliant years, 1899–1905, as U.S. ambassador to Britain. Yet to CCB, Choate was "always falling short of greatness," too often lending his prestige to unworthy men and actions. He lacked "the capacity for moral indignation."[41]

Despite the opportunities to hear great lawyers argue in court and to learn the office routine of a successful single practitioner, CCB plainly found his position with Strong frustrating. With college and law degrees in hand, he had stepped forward to take a place in the world, a place his family, friends, and teachers had assured him was waiting, yet the world, he had discovered, was indifferent to his coming. And worst of all, the low wage was delaying marriage to Louie. His unhappiness soon showed itself in another way, though the underlying facts are obscure.

Sometime in the fall of 1881, he wrote a letter to Colonel Hoe that offended the older man. Evidently the colonel either said as much or showed the letter to his daughter Adeline Lawrence, Louie's mother, for Mrs. Lawrence suggested to CCB that he should apologize. On 2 May 1882, on Strong's elegant office stationery, CCB drafted a letter.

> Dear Col. Hoe:
>
> I have heard indirectly from Mrs. Lawrence that you think I ought to ask you for the letter I wrote you last fall. You would do me a great kindness to send it to me, or else destroy it, for although I have never intentionally been disrespectful to you, I am heartily sorry to have appeared so.
>
> I am sorry, too, not to have written you before, instead of waiting for some expression of your feelings directly from you. It was not from any want of respect that I failed to do so. Still it was wrong of me, and I am sorry for it.
>
> Will you kindly remember me to Mrs. Hoe and Annie, and believe me,
>
> Most sincerely and respectfully,
>
> Charles C. Burlingham[42]

Whatever his offense, his apology was accepted, and Hoe continued to welcome him at Brightside and in his town house, even on occasions when neither Louie nor Annie was present. For the colonel, famous for his good humor, to forgive a young man's mistake was in character; but for CCB such a misstep was not. And later that year, this time with Annie, he stumbled again.

One day at Brightside they talked about sexual purity. They had a friend who in some way had sinned sexually, and they discussed the meaning of a pure life and how it should be achieved. In a letter the next day, Annie argued for a "positive" spirit of purity, quoting Phillips Brooks, against a mere "negative" observance of a commandment. Whatever their difference of opinion, her closing sentence was vehement: "I can't *bear* to have you *talk down*, as you did yesterday." He had the formal education, but she had seen more of the world, and would not be put down.[43] To have written a letter that offended the colonel and then to have brought Annie to such an outburst suggests that CCB's spirit was in turmoil.

Continually hoping to leave Strong, he knocked on other doors, but none opened. On 16 February 1883, on bar association stationery and with careful penmanship, he addressed himself to Butler, Stillman, and Hubbard, a firm with seven partners: "Gentlemen: I take the liberty of applying to you for a clerk-ship in your office, thinking my acquaintance with Mr. Stillman a sufficient apology for the bluntness of my application." He offered as his reason for wishing "to leave Mr. Strong's employ" the desire "to get a wider experience than his office affords." But he was not hired.[44]

Nevertheless, he was absorbing the life of the city in which he later was to distinguish himself. In the 1940s and 1950s, young lawyers working with CCB would be startled to think that in 1881, when CCB began with Strong, the Brooklyn Bridge, the first dry route to Long Island, had not yet opened. Manhattan was then still very much a water-bound port. Sailing ships outnumbered steam by almost three to one, and all but a few docked in the narrow East River, where winter ice floes were less troublesome than on the wide Hudson. Piers, poking into the river on wooden piles, lined South Street, and when the bigger ships were in, their bowsprits, often with carved figureheads, reached across the street as if to touch the buildings.[45] In 1856 Walt Whitman had published one of his great poems, "Crossing Brooklyn Ferry," in which he wrote of "the countless crowds of passengers" who crossed from Brooklyn to "mast-hemm'd Manhattan." By 1880 the Union Ferry Company, operating six of the eleven lines to Brooklyn, by day ran ferries every five to ten minutes, by night every fifteen to twenty, and carried annually some forty million passengers. With at least nine lines regularly crossing the Hudson River to New Jersey, one to Staten Island and three to Queens, fog in the harbor, it was said, could make half the city late to work.[46]

By 1880 the elevated railroads, running north-south on several of the city's avenues, were beginning to extend their lines to greater distances, but walking and the horse-drawn omnibus were still the most common forms of travel. Along the waterfront, around the markets, and in the commercial areas on Broadway, horse and wagons were in a continual jam. There were no one-way streets, no painted lanes of traffic, no traffic dividers, no red lights, not even an accepted rule to keep to the right. Carters drove on every side of the street, in every direction, relying on a loud voice and terror to win their way. Most lawyers still walked whenever possible to office, court, or home, for walking was usually faster and pleasanter than the horse-drawn omnibus. Strong, in 1914 recalling the city of 1882, advised young lawyers to "bless the day of elevated roads and subways."[47]

Though CCB may have despaired of advancement so long as he remained with Strong, while there, his future was shaped for the better. In 1882 Strong rented space in his office to another single practitioner, Harrington Putnam, who, after several years as managing clerk at a three-man firm, Hill, Wing & Shoudy, was starting on his own. The next year, when James K. Hill, the firm's senior partner, told his juniors that he planned to retire, the younger partners appealed to Putnam to return and join with them in starting a new firm. Putnam hesitated, and continued to work out of Strong's office.[48]

Meanwhile, the firm of Hill, Wing & Shoudy, with Hill gone, now lost their current managing clerk, and Wing and Shoudy again sought Putnam's help. He recommended for the clerk's job CCB, whose work he had been watching for more than a year, and then, having placed "his" clerk in the firm, Putnam joined its two partners to form Wing, Shoudy & Putnam. Sometime in the spring of 1883, CCB started work there as head clerk, at a weekly salary of fifteen dollars, but now his job was closer to that of associate lawyer than clerk, as the terms today are understood. Most of his work now became legal, with clerical and footwork left to junior clerks.[49]

The firm's office was on the fifth floor of the Liverpool & London & Globe Insurance Company building at 45 William Street, an eight-story fireproof edifice put up in 1879 and much admired. Taller than its neighbors, it offered among other innovations central heating and an elevator. The latter was rider-operated, no one yet having thought to make a job of it. To go up, the rider grasped the cable running through the car and pulled down; to go down, he pulled up. To stop at a floor he seized the moving cable, protecting the palm of his hand with a piece of carpet left in the elevator, and held on, bringing the car to a stop.

The building's upper floors were a roost for small law firms. Shearman & Sterling shared the fifth floor with Wing, Shoudy & Putnam; two flights up was Bangs & Stetson; on the top floor, Page & Taft (Henry W., younger brother of the future president), and somewhere below the fifth, Stearns & Curtis. In 1883, from the west windows of the office CCB could see the spire of Trinity Church, but by 1906, when the firm moved, the view had long been lost.[50]

Like many retired lawyers, Hill kept an office in his former firm and came in to see clients who still sought his advice. CCB recalled, "He sat in a large bare room at a small pine table with a bowler hat tilted back on his head. This he never removed except for ladies or for supremely important clients." He had a gift for terse expression. Once, during a meeting with a deaf client, he jotted on a pad, as the client spoke, a summary of the case the man wished to make. The man, taking the pad, read the outline and smiled his delight. Then "Hill took the pad, wrote 'Won't Wash,' and handed it back to the client, whose smile vanished."[51]

Compared to Hill, James A. Shoudy was bland. Still, he was a meticulous worker, more effective with judges than with juries, especially on appeal, where his careful briefs could make their point. He specialized in commercial cases tried in the state courts, leaving all the maritime cases, tried on the "admiralty side" of the federal courts, to his partner Henry Thomas Wing. The latter, who had started as Hill's clerk in 1869, still had for the old man a respect that CCB likened "almost to awe." Mild-mannered, even diffident, he had a talent for admiralty disputes, seeming to have an instinctive understanding of sailors, of the sea, and of what probably happened in any collision, despite the confusions and contradictions of testimony. But he was cautious, averse to taking responsibility, and inclined to hire outside counsel to argue his cases. To serve that purpose the strong, assertive Putnam had been brought into the partnership, and he began at once to try Wing's cases. "From the time he and I joined up with the firm," CCB recalled, "Mr. Wing never took charge of a new case. Putnam had all the important ones, and I had the chicken feed." In this sudden, unexpected fashion, CCB entered the practice of admiralty law.[52]

His first case, a seaman suing the bark *Exile* for withheld wages, was chicken feed. In July 1884 Wing sent him across the Hudson to the federal district court in Newark, New Jersey, where CCB was to answer for the firm if the case was called before Wing arrived. The case was called, CCB responded, Wing never came (he probably never intended to come), and CCB argued the case.

It was a libel *in rem* (a claim against the ship), with CCB arguing for the ship. A cook, David Mitchell, had joined the English bark in Bordeaux, signing articles in the presence of the British consul and agreeing to a voyage to New York or any other port, "and back to a final port of discharge in the United Kingdom or continent of Europe." Mitchell had left the ship in New York, claiming he had agreed to go only so far. The voyage from Bordeaux had taken six weeks; he was to be paid thirty dollars a month, and upon signing had received twenty dollars in advance. He figured he was owed twenty-two dollars. Because of the signed articles, Mitchell would lose unless he could show some improper action by the ship's captain. He claimed the captain had offered to settle the dispute with fists, but he had declined to fight, saying he had signed on to cook, not to box. But CCB showed that in the verbal skirmish with the captain Mitchell had sustained no injury, and had never again been physically threatened; the judge ruled that the captain's offer of fisticuffs was "harmless bravado." CCB had won.[53] For his competence that July day in Newark, CCB surely owed a debt to Theron Strong; but nowhere in his voluminous recollections does he acknowledge it. Even in old age, despite a greatly increased geniality, he still burned with a young man's unreasonable rage over what he mistakenly deemed ill treatment.

5

Three Women: Louisa Lawrence, Ellen Terry, and Josephine Shaw Lowell

STRENGTHENED BY HIS new position and increased wage, CCB and Louie Lawrence, in the summer of 1883, announced to their parents their intention to marry. "Both families thought it a reckless thing to do, but we didn't."[1] CCB was turning twenty-five and Louie was twenty, but besides love and the new job another reason may have inclined them to push ahead. In October 1882 Louie's mother Adeline Lawrence had died, changing family relationships in a way that Louie may not have liked.

In her family's collective memory Mrs. Lawrence does not loom large. No anecdotes are told of her, no grandchild is named for her, few surviving letters recall her. Because strong or eccentric personalities usually are remembered, she possibly was a bland, conventional person, loving her children and loved by them but without arousing much passion.[2] On her death, however, her eldest daughter, Mariella, who had sat beside her mother's bed and closed her mother's eyes, became mistress of her father's house, both in the city and in Bantam, Connecticut, where DeWitt Lawrence rented a summer cottage. Mellie was only three years older than Louie, and though the sisters seemingly were fond of each other, Louie, who later demonstrated a strong will, may not have liked a household in which Mellie was "Miss Lawrence" and head of the family.[3]

On 29 September 1883, in DeWitt Lawrence's Murray Hill home, Charles C. Burlingham married Louisa W. Lawrence in an Episcopal ceremony conducted by CCB's father. After the wedding the couple retreated to Bantam for "a very short honeymoon,"[4] returning to the city to board for several weeks with a Dr. Pardee on West Thirty-fourth Street.

Annie Hoe had found for the couple a small apartment at 200 East

Twenty-seventh Street, on the eastern slope of Murray Hill, and also, it seems, had persuaded Louie's father to pay its rent for the first year. (She was, after all, the first of his children to marry and doubtless would bear his first grandchild.) Meanwhile, family and friends gave the newlyweds large pieces of furniture—an upholstered chair, a hat rack shaped like a ship's wheel, and a sideboard, all still in use when CCB died seventy-six years later. If custom in the 1880s decreed that wedding presents should be substantial, it also decreed that they should be cherished; marriage was for life, and so, too, were the presents.[5]

CCB and Louie soon moved into their home, on the fifth floor of a building that boasted an elevator, probably as primitive as the one at CCB's office. The apartment had five small rooms, a parlor, to the front, with two windows looking out on the Third Avenue elevated; and behind the parlor, in line off a narrow hall, a tiny bedroom, dining room, bathroom, and kitchen. Despite the small rooms, they had a cook, "a large American country woman" named Marilla, and "I can't remember or imagine," CCB wrote later, "where she slept"—in the kitchen, he thought, or perhaps in the basement.[6]

That first winter of marriage, 1883–84, was a time of constant pleasure and new experience, and CCB reveled in all its aspects. "Were we happy?— Well, Oh, so happy!" He loved Louie passionately. Going to work in the morning, he would walk to the extreme southerly end of the El platform at Twenty-eighth Street, where he could just be seen by her if she leaned out the parlor window, and they would wave "a handkerchief or a kiss."[7]

Their apartment became a haven for unmarried friends—Louie's brother Rob and first cousins Richard and Henry Lawrence, the painter Joe Evans, and the four Taber brothers, introduced to them by Annie, and their sister, Florence (who married the future publisher Henry Holt). Of the brothers, the eldest, Henry, was a mathematician (who in another three years would marry Louie's younger sister, Fanny); then Charles, a businessman; Martin (Mintie), a painter; and Robert, an actor. Mintie and Robert came often to the apartment for Sunday evening, when the Burlinghams offered supper, and after eating they would play parlor games—radical behavior for a time when their elders, observing the Fourth Commandment, held the Sabbath holy, denying to themselves any work or play.[8]

One Sunday evening, CCB recalled, "my Mother, who was a strict Sabbatarian, on her way to evening service came in on us when we were having a gay time; and her long upper lip drawn down chilled us into silence. The shock was increased by Louie calmly knitting on the Sabbath. We urged Mother to stay, but she went off to Church."[9]

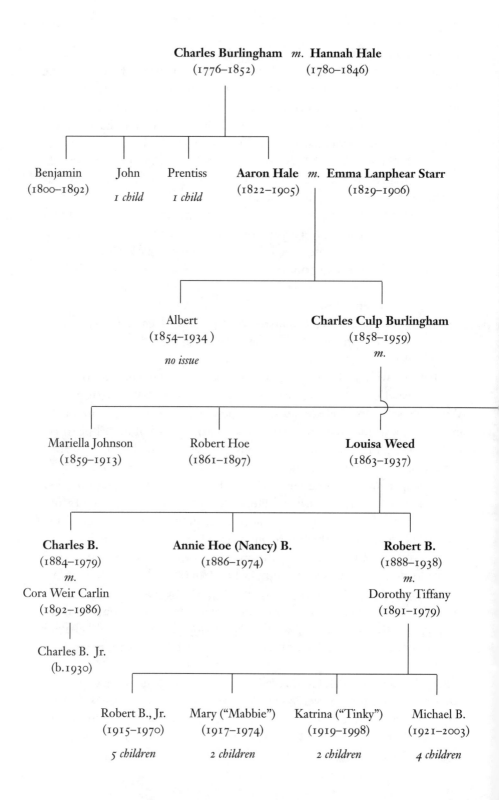

Charles Burlingham *m.* **Hannah Hale**
(1776–1852)   (1780–1846)

Benjamin
(1800–1892)

John
1 child

Prentiss
1 child

Aaron Hale *m.* **Emma Lanphear Starr**
(1822–1905)   (1829–1906)

Albert
(1854–1934)
no issue

Charles Culp Burlingham
(1858–1959)
m.

Mariella Johnson
(1859–1913)

Robert Hoe
(1861–1897)

Louisa Weed
(1863–1937)

Charles B.
(1884–1979)
m.
Cora Weir Carlin
(1892–1986)

Charles B. Jr.
(b.1930)

Annie Hoe (Nancy) B.
(1886–1974)

Robert B.
(1888–1938)
m.
Dorothy Tiffany
(1891–1979)

Robert B., Jr.
(1915–1970)
5 children

Mary ("Mabbie")
(1917–1974)
2 children

Katrina ("Tinky")
(1919–1998)
2 children

Michael B.
(1921–2003)
4 children

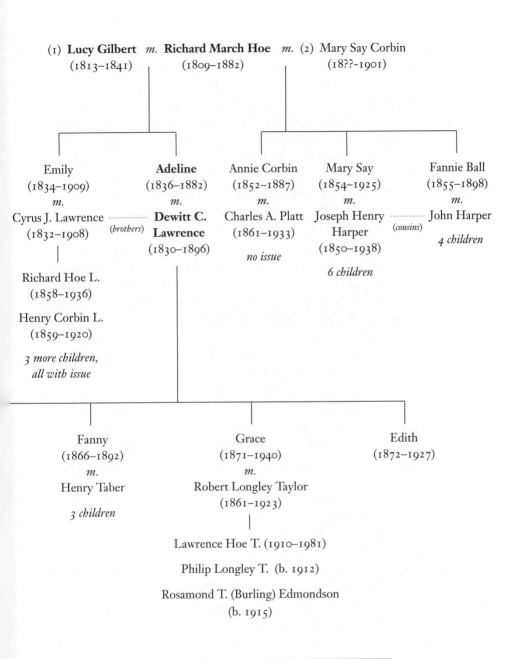

(1) **Lucy Gilbert**   *m.* **Richard March Hoe**   *m.* (2) Mary Say Corbin
(1813–1841)   (1809–1882)   (18??-1901)

Emily   **Adeline**   Annie Corbin   Mary Say   Fannie Ball
(1834–1909)   (1836–1882)   (1852–1887)   (1854–1925)   (1855–1898)
m.   *m.*   *m.*   *m.*   *m.*
Cyrus J. Lawrence ---------- **Dewitt C.**   Charles A. Platt   Joseph Henry -------- John Harper
(1832–1908)   *(brothers)* **Lawrence**   (1861–1933)   Harper   *(cousins)*
                                 (1830–1896)   (1850–1938)   *4 children*
Richard Hoe L.   *no issue*
(1858–1936)   *6 children*

Henry Corbin L.
(1859–1920)

3 more children,
all with issue

Fanny   Grace   Edith
(1866–1892)   (1871–1940)   (1872–1927)
m.   *m.*
Henry Taber   Robert Longley Taylor
                        (1861–1923)
3 children

Lawrence Hoe T. (1910–1981)

Philip Longley T. (b. 1912)

Rosamond T. (Burling) Edmondson
(b. 1915)

The Burlingham & Hoe Families

Mrs. Burlingham might have been still more shocked had she known how often CCB and Louie went to the theater. In the fall of 1883, the English actor-manager Henry Irving brought his Lyceum Theatre company to the United States, with all its spectacular sets, costumes, and fabled leading lady, Ellen Terry. The tour, with eight plays for New York, was exceptionally lavish and stirred tremendous excitement. On opening night, 29 October, Irving appeared (without Terry) in what was perhaps his most famous role: Mathias in *The Bells*, an adaptation of a French melodrama, *Le Juif Polonais*, by Erckmann-Chatrian. The play recounts how a respectable Alsatian mayor, Mathias, having killed a Jew for his money, constantly hears in his mind his victim's sleigh bells. In the last act, though safely at home in bed and still unsuspected of the crime, he has a nightmare in which he is taken before a court where, under hypnosis, he begins to testify against himself. To his family at his bedside, as he dies of terror, he blurts out the truth. One critic has described *The Bells* as "a cathartic experience for middle-class Victorian audiences, who related to a person like themselves (rather than someone rich or poor) being thrust into villainy for his family's sake and then losing out to a guilty conscience. It was a rip-roaring sermon."[10] For that opening night in 1883, CCB and Louie, Joe Evans, Robert Taber, and some six or eight more friends were in the top gallery of the Star Theatre (Broadway and Thirteenth Street), where the seats were fifty cents and unreserved. To secure places, the men waited on the sidewalk until the doors opened and then ran up the stairs to hold seats for the women.[11]

The next night, he, Louie, and some others went with Annie Hoe to Chickering Hall, Fifth Avenue and Eighteenth Street, to hear Matthew Arnold's first American lecture, on "Numbers," a discussion of the influence on ancient and modern nations of the size of population. Arnold's most famous poem, "Dover Beach," expressing anguish at a loss of faith, had been conceived (though completed only later) in the same year as Dr. Holmes's "One-Hoss Shay." In recent years, however, Arnold had turned more to lecturing than poetry, and on the podium he appeared the model of a Victorian speaker, with his long English face, high cheekbones, and trim muttonchop whiskers. That night, however, he spoke too softly, and there were insistent cries of "Louder!" CCB's group had seats "well forward" and could hear, but most of the audience, he thought, "heard nothing."[12]

Arnold finished by 9 p.m., so CCB and some of his friends ran the six blocks to the Star to see and hear what they could of Irving and Terry in W. G. Wills's historical tragedy in blank verse, *Charles I*. Though the play was half over, they bought standing room for a dollar, finding places to the rear of the orchestra at the moment (Act III, the Royal Camp at Newark) when Irving as King Charles (costumed as if painted by Van Dyck) and Terry as Queen Henrietta Maria stood before their tent studying a map—while to the back, hidden from them, lurked the traitor Moray. Terry, CCB never forgot, "was in a black velvet dress, with a plumed hat, and brown gauntlets, bending over the map." He saw her in the role many times, for the play had a vogue, largely because of her and Irving, lasting almost forty years.[13]

That winter, Irving's company played in New York for four weeks, went on tour, and then returned to New York for four weeks. CCB, Louie, and their friends were constantly in the theater. To record their admiration for Terry, Joe Evans made her a small parchment book, beautifully printed and full of his drawings, and one night in the green room the group presented it to her. Soon thereafter Irving's manager, Bram Stoker (later the author of *Dracula*), was directed to admit them free to any performance. There were always seats to be found in some gallery, and as there were then no fire laws for theaters, CCB and others often sat in the aisles of the orchestra.[14]

The next year, when Irving and Terry returned to New York, playing again at the Star Theatre, Stoker assigned CCB and his friends a box, high on the proscenium. From there one night, after a performance of *Twelfth Night*, with Terry as Viola, Charles Taber hurled onto the stage a huge wreath of chrysanthemums bearing a broad gold ribbon on which Evans had painted "To Sweet Ellen Terry, whom the Gods adore."[15] The crash of the wreath on the stage caused a sensation. Two stagehands hurried out to hold it up for the audience to see. When Terry, dressed in her boy's costume for Viola, took her second curtain call, she had put a chrysanthemum in her hat, and "she cocked her eye at us who were the gods of the gallery."

For fifty years, until deafness defeated him, the theater was CCB's joy. For him, Irving's style of production, pictorial realism, carefully conceived, beautifully painted, softly lit, remained the standard by which more modern styles were usually found wanting. And no actress ever matched Terry.[16]

Among playwrights, he prized Shakespeare, going to almost every production staged in New York before World War II. When Sarah Bernhardt played Hamlet in a French prose translation at the Garden Theatre in December 1900, he went and saw a virile young prince, bent on vengeance, not at all indecisive, and certainly not mad. Before following the ghost, Bernhardt's Hamlet crossed himself, startling Protestants in the audience, and equally unusual, her Hamlet died standing. The next morning at his office CCB discovered that his clerk, not yet a lawyer, had also been at the performance, and half a century later the clerk in a letter recalled for him their morning conversation: "You asked me where I had sat, and I told you 7th row, center aisle, in the parquet. Then you roared at me in your fiercest voice: 'What right had you to sit there when I had to sit in the family circle.' And I said, 'You don't know the right people. I went with an actress and she asked for two tickets, got them, and didn't even have to pay.'"[17]*

In the summer of 1907, when Burlingham was in a haberdasher's shop in London, his devotion to the theater had its reward. He saw the salesman's eyes shift—once, twice—from him to another customer. Looking around, he saw Terry holding up a man's blue shirt, turning it this way and that. Though he had not seen her in many years, he knew her instantly. He went over, introduced himself, mentioning a friend he knew they had in common, the sculptor Augustus Saint-Gaudens, who recently had died. Talking of sculptors, he asked her if there were any portraits or busts of Irving, who had died several years before, and she said she had one. "She said I must come and see it. I said, 'When?' 'Anytime,' she replied. 'That means now.' I got a hansom and drove her home. On the way she said, 'Oh, I lent that portrait to [blank].' The shirt she had bought was for her new husband. She called to him to come down as there was an American to meet. We three lunched together."[18]

For many years, CCB kept a drawing of Terry as Portia on his study wall. Joe Evans had drawn it from a photograph and given it to CCB's eldest son on the boy's first birthday. Though in time the boy grew up and claimed his present, even without it as a reminder CCB's enthusiasm for Terry never waned. At the mention of her name, his eyes would sparkle, his voice rise, and, if allowed, he would slip into a story of this goddess on the stage.[19]

At Wing, Shoudy & Putnam, because of the way the three partners apportioned their clients, CCB worked almost exclusively with Harrington Putnam on admiralty suits. According to CCB, Putnam initially knew little or nothing about admiralty practice, but being unmarried, he was able to devote his entire attention to learning and soon became, in CCB's opinion, "a great admiralty lawyer," taking many cases to the U.S. Supreme Court, with CCB "on the brief." Eventually, in November 1909, Putnam would leave the firm for a seat on the New York Supreme Court, and only thereafter did it become "the Burlingham firm."[20]

---

*The clerk, reminiscing about the law firm, wrote: "You were the only really human being among all the partners. When I left, you were the only one for whom I retained a feeling of friendship and affection." There are few bonds as strong as a shared enthusiasm, and one of CCB's most attractive qualities, which increased as he grew older, was his eagerness to share his enthusiasms with anyone on equal terms. People responded.

A big man, Putnam had a dominating personality. CCB worked with him for twenty-six years and, though no more than six years younger, only slowly attained an equality in their relations. Putnam also was dour. The clerk Beardsley doubted that he ever laughed and thought him "about impossible" to know. "The only time I ever saw a gleam of glee in him was when he came into the outer office and announced that General [Piet] Cronjie had defeated one of the English generals in the South African war." And no one but Judge Gailbraith Ward ever slapped him on the back and called him "Put." CCB usually referred to him as "Putnam," or "H.P.," and in return was called "Burlingham."[21]

Like many lawyers of his time, Putnam walked everywhere, and like some he was solitary. His favorite sport—he did not count walking, even long distances, as exercise—was rowing in a single scull around Staten Island. And until marriage, which, according to CCB, "made him a bit more like the rest of us," he ate only once a day and "stuffed himself with bread at that meal." It would take CCB more than ten or twelve years of working with Putnam to feel at ease with him.[22]

Meanwhile, there were family, friends, and Louie, CCB's perpetual haven, to whom he released all his emotions, hope, fear, irritation, anger, and his need of her: "Oh, Louie, my whole heart is throbbing with love for you. Well as I am, my hand is trembling." If they were apart for even a day, he would write, often twice a day, and though the letters sometimes say little, their verbal caresses suggest how she filled his mind. Once, in 1893, having left him only the day before, she wrote him a short factual note ending, "I have nothing to say. Your loving Louie"; and she left two pages of stationery blank. He promptly filled all the empty space with cooings and mailed the letter back.[23] If their separation was longer, his letters not infrequently grew ardent; and about his deeper feelings he was more articulate than she about hers. Even in 1894, the twelfth year of their marriage, toward the end of a letter reciting his parents' activities, books he was reading, and stories he wanted to tell the children, he suddenly broke out with longing:

> I fill up my letter with *things* but you can read between the lines the love of my heart. I feel sobered and sad and lonely, as I always am without my darling. I have lost my life, that is it.
>
> Oh, dear dear Louie, how precious you are to me; and how unchanging and eternal my lover's love is! I am still the warm young lover, and I could write love letters that would make the paper burn.
>
> What a happy, blessed life we have.[24]

His passionate love included his three children, of whom the first, his eldest son, Charles, was born on 8 June 1884. In writing to them, though usually less open in expression, when he did speak of his feelings his words were often so intense, perhaps from being long withheld, as to be quite startling. To Charles, for instance, on the latter's fifty-seventh birthday, 8 June 1941:

> My Beloved Son:
> I have no present for you, but what could I give you that would express my love for you and my gratitude to God for His gift of you to me?
> You can hardly imagine what it meant to us 57 years ago, a warm day like this, in our tiny flat 200 East 27th Street when Dr. Shelton (Dr. Allen away) helped you out into this world. Dr. Shelton's bill was $15, but Dr. Allen, who had a farm in Litchfield, gave us milk from his dairy for a year! . . .
> You were a perfect child, a joy to behold and to be with *et sic fuisti semper.*
>
> Thank you for living . . . [25]

Few fathers, when a child is nearing sixty, can recall such details, or care to. But CCB poured the same energy into his family that he gave to his law practice.

His passion, however, sometimes turned sour. Only two months after the birth of "Young Charles," as the boy was known even as a man, CCB wrote to Annie, who evidently had purred insufficiently over the new baby: "Your letter to Louie and me was not responsive nor did it come out of your heart . . . I suppose you have seen dozens of babies, so one doesn't count with you as it does with us. Goodby from Charlie." Much of the letter is such an angry scrawl it can't be read.[26]

Reflecting on CCB many years later, his niece Rosamond Taylor Edmondson, who knew him well, concluded that though he had wit, which on occasion he could employ brilliantly, he had no sense of humor. He never could see himself as others sometimes did, as excessive or comic in his opinions or emotions. And when his passion, which for the most part he kept concealed, broke through constraint, its unexpected force could unhinge the person at whom it was directed.[27]

As CCB reached the end of his third decade, a lawyer, husband, father, and increasingly a leader in his own and his wife's family, it became clear to those close to him that he had developed an uncommon flow of energy. In his work, he seemed never to turn down an opportunity for lack of time or fatigue; and in family life he eagerly acted the patriarch, with a finger in every pie. Louie might run the house and the children's routine, but all larger decisions, such as the children's schooling or a move to a new apartment, were discussed, and the decision often was his. That energy was a blessing, for him, for his colleagues, and for his family; it allowed him to hold his own against the best in one of the world's largest, most exciting cities. But it also had a dark side, at least for his family, which would become apparent only slowly.

CCB's marriage not only strengthened his ties to the Hoe and Lawrence families but introduced him, through Louie's friends, to another extensive and influential New York family, that of Francis and Sarah Shaw, whose four daughters had married men named Curtis, Minturn, Lowell, and Barlow. The children of these marriages formed a web of first cousins with several of whom Louie had gone to school, and with whom she and CCB had lasting friendships.

Louie's school, "Miss Brackett's," in a house at 9 West Thirty-ninth Street, was unusual for its day. Before the 1880s many of the country's richer families, even those in big cities, typically educated their daughters privately, as did the Hoes with Annie, by tutoring at home, with perhaps a final year in a boarding school; then followed a tour of Europe and perhaps a year or two abroad for the study of art or music. Anna C. Brackett offered parents something different, a small neighborhood school in fashionable Murray Hill, staffed by four women, all trained professionals. She and her three colleagues had studied in St. Louis under the educator and philosopher William T. Harris, superintendent of the St. Louis public school system and later U.S. commissioner of education. Like President Eliot of Harvard, Harris favored German models for education, and he was known nationally for helping to found, at St. Louis in 1873, the country's first permanent kindergarten. His pupil Anna Brackett, adapting many of his ideas to older students, had founded a private school for girls that soon won a reputation for intellectual rigor. Thus, Louie and her classmates probably received as good a secondary education as then was available to women, and in addition, many of them, such as Louie, had some experience of Europe. Yet neither she nor her friends went on to college. The disparity in formal education between CCB and Louie therefore was great and typical of most marriages among their friends.[28]

In the family of Francis and Sarah Shaw, among whose granddaughters Louie found friends, the one boy, Rob, had been sent to boarding school and to Harvard College. Yet the four sisters, at least within the family, were considered the equals of men, and in growing up discussed art, politics, and reform as eagerly and knowingly as their father, who in addition to his philanthropic activities published literary reviews, translations of foreign novels, and articles on education, prison reform, and political economy. As adults, the four daughters, following their parents' example, had active roles in women's and children's causes and in movements for better treatment of the insane and reform of city government.[29]

The parents, Francis and Sarah Shaw, were Bostonians, heirs to a merchant fortune founded on the China trade and invested in Boston real estate. They had come to New York in 1847 seeking a cure for Sarah's bouts of blindness, and having found one under the care of a specialist, Dr. Samuel Mackenzie Elliott, had decided to stay on to be near him. Because Elliott lived and practiced on the north shore of Staten Island, at the time still rural, they bought a large plot on the island's Bard Avenue, in West New Brighton, and built an elegant, comfortable house which they filled with family and friends. Indoors, the house offered a grand staircase and many rooms with attractive vistas, while outdoors there were extensive stables, bridle paths, and a croquet lawn.[30] More family soon settled nearby.

In 1856 the Shaws' eldest child, Anna, married George William Curtis, fast becoming a well-known orator, writer, and advocate of reform. For thirty-five years, 1857–92, he was the political editor of *Harper's Weekly*, and for thirty-nine, author of the "Easy Chair" column for *Harper's Monthly*. His chief crusades were for abolition, women's rights, civic reform—to oust Tammany and Boss Tweed—and civil service reform, which to some extent after the Civil War succeeded abolition as the popular reform movement. Of the three Curtis children, CCB and Louie in later years knew best the second, Lizzie (Elizabeth Burrill Curtis), who became a leader in New York for women's suffrage.[31]

Both the Shaw and Curtis families were Republican in politics, Unitarian in religion, and abolitionist in cause. And in all their affairs they were, or tried to be, high-minded, judging issues predominantly by moral standards. On Sunday mornings, the two families together would walk the mile to the Gothic-style Unitarian church, where, if a minister was lacking, Curtis would read from the best of recent sermons. "I love Frank and Sarah," wrote their houseguest and fellow abolitionist Lydia Maria Child, "partly because they are good-looking, partly because they dress in beautiful colors, and partly because they have many fine qualities." A few years later she added, "They are very free from sham; for which they deserve the more credit, considering they are Bostonians and are rich."[32]

When the New York City draft riots erupted in July 1863, the violence soon spilled from Manhattan to Staten Island, where gangs of Irish immigrants vented their anger about poverty, jobs, and the war chiefly by attacking Negroes and their homes. They beat a black woman to death and destroyed the catering shop of a former butler of the Shaws, a man named Green. Many Negroes fled to the Island's woods, and throughout the week, rumors whispered that the gangs were planning to attack well-known abolitionists and Republicans, with the Shaw and Curtis families likely first targets. The Shaws took refuge with a neighbor; and Curtis, sending his wife and children to relatives in Massachusetts, joined neighbors to plan for mutual defense, though his only weapon "was a large family umbrella." But no attack came, and by the week's end the rioting had ceased.[33]

After the war, in 1869, the Shaws sold their big house to their second daughter, Susannah, and her husband, Robert Minturn. His father owned a shipping line, Grinnell, Minturn and Company, which dispatched a fleet of cargo and passenger ships around the world, including regular packet lines to Liverpool and London, and among the more than fifty ships flying its Swallow Tail house flag was the clipper *Flying Cloud*. Like the Shaw and Curtis families, the Minturns were Republican and abolitionist. In time, their two daughters, May and Edith, went to the Brackett school, and May became a close friend of Louie, and later of CCB. (Subsequently, she strengthened the tie further by marrying his friend Henry Dwight Sedgwick, a lawyer who soon would leave the law to write histories and biographies.) Meanwhile, the Shaws, to continue close to their married children, bought a smaller house overlooking Kill van Kull, the waterway joining upper New York Harbor and Newark Bay. From their veranda the lawn swept down to the water's edge, offering a view of ships in the channel, their signal flags aloft as they passed in and out of the bay.[34]

In this setting, Louie's classmate Carlotta Russell Lowell and her widowed mother, Josephine Shaw Lowell (the Shaws' third daughter), lived until 1874, when, in part to be near Miss Brackett's school, they moved to a brownstone house at 120 East Thirtieth Street in Manhattan, usually returning to Staten Island for holidays and weekends and often inviting Louie and CCB to come out for Sunday afternoon and supper. The ferry, between Whitehall Street and St. George's, was cheap—five cents; the harbor, as yet without the Statue of Liberty (1885), was busy and beautiful, and the walk from St. George's to the house, only five minutes.[35] Sometimes on these Sunday outings CCB, Louie, and the Lowells dined at the Shaws, and sometimes all six of them went to the big house to join the Minturns. If the latter, the meal often included the Curtis and Barlow families—the Shaws' fourth daughter, Ellen, had married Francis Channing Barlow—as well as visitors. And conversation sparkled.[36]

The Shaws' family life was not free of pain, however. Their only son, Robert Gould Shaw, had died in the Civil War. As colonel of the Massachusetts Fifty-fourth Regiment, the first with Negro troops to reach combat, he had led his men on 18 July 1863 against the Confederate Fort Wagner, near Charleston, South Carolina. The attack failed, and the Confederate officer in charge of burying the dead, without ceremony and with intentional disrespect, stripped Shaw of his uniform and threw his body into a trench with his soldiers—most of them black. Later, when the fort was taken and a movement started in the North to disinter Shaw's bones and rebury them with military honors, his parents asked that Rob be left with his men.

Then arose the question of a monument to Colonel Shaw, to be erected in Boston where the regiment had formed, recruiting among others two sons of Frederick Douglass and two younger brothers of William and Henry James. The site proposed was opposite the State House, on Beacon Street, down which Colonel Shaw and the regiment had marched to embark for the front. Though money for the memorial was soon raised, the contract for it was not let until 1883, twenty years after Rob's death, and by then his father had died. Rob's widow and his widowed mother, shown the initial sketch of a typical nineteenth-century equestrian statue, protested: the concept was unsuited to Rob, who had been a colonel, not a general; his troops infantry, not cavalry; his heroism not of that sort. William James, in a memorial speech, best defined it: "In this new Negro-soldier venture, loneliness was certain, ridicule inevitable, failure possible; and Shaw was only twenty-five." The sculptor Saint-Gaudens began a new design, a mounted Shaw with his troops marching alongside him, their column led by two drummers. This bronze relief of life-size figures became what many consider to be the country's greatest memorial sculpture, but it was not finished and unveiled until 1897, thirty-four years after Shaw's death.[37]

For the family, there was also the continuing pain of Josephine Shaw's widowhood. The third of the Shaws' four daughters, she had married Charles Russell Lowell, of the Boston family, in 1863. He had graduated with distinction from Harvard College in 1854, and though initially much influenced by Emerson's ideas of nurturing one's private self, he had found his ideas about life changing under the impact of war. In letters to his friends and fiancée, he spoke eloquently of the need to join thought with action, so that a life might be "useful" to compatriots and country. At the time he had married Josephine, in the Shaws' Unitarian church on Staten Island, he was a colonel in command of the Second Massachusetts Cavalry; twelve months later he died of wounds received in the battle of Cedar Creek. His widow, only twenty-one, was eight months pregnant.[38]

According to CCB, who heard it from the family, when Josephine Lowell was told her child was a girl, she turned her face to the wall. But then she rallied, and for months as she worked her way through the shock of her husband's death, she walked about the Shaws' big house on Bard Avenue with the baby in her arms, nurturing her, loving her, and recalling with her name, Carlotta Russell Lowell, the dead father and husband. For the rest of her life Josephine Lowell wore black, yet beneath her black bonnet, which soon became a familiar sight in New York and which to CCB's eye was "sometimes a little on one side," there was bright brown hair, blue eyes, a winning smile, and a mind with a remarkable gift for words, facts, and administration. Until her death in 1905, she worked to help all those shunted into poverty by the new urban industrial society that emerged after the Civil War.[39] The source of her lifelong dedication to the poor undoubtedly lay in her family's emphasis on civic responsibility, in the examples of sacrifice and duty set for her by her husband and brother, and to some extent in her Unitarian faith, which stressed action and practical goodness.[40] Her brother-in-law George William Curtis once defined his beliefs, to which hers probably were close: "I believe in God—Who is love—that all men are brothers, and that the only essential duty of every man is to be honest, by which I understand his absolute following of his conscience, when duly enlightened. I do *not* believe that God is anxious that men should believe this or that theory of the Godhead or of the Divine Government, but that they should live purely, justly, and lovingly."[41]

CCB, as a Baptist much influenced by Phillips Brooks, knelt in prayer, whereas Unitarians did not; he believed in the divinity of Christ, which Unitarians did not; and he put Christ at the very center of his faith, adhering to one definite theory of the Godhead, the Trinity. Yet in the ethics of daily life and the morality of civic responsibility, he was close to Curtis and Lowell, sharing their belief in the brotherhood of man and the need to "live purely, justly, and lovingly." By temperament and education he was drawn to a life not of contemplation or withdrawal but of action in the workaday world. But neither Curtis, Lowell, nor CCB interpreted the commandment to love his fellows as a command to forgive misdeeds, or sloth, or drunkenness, or a tendency of some to recline forever on the charity of others. Nor did they believe, as some sociologists were beginning to, that any judgment on their fellows was inherently undemocratic. These reformers expected those who received aid to work to help themselves, and those who did not could be dismissed, sometimes in harsh language.[42]

In the words of one biographer, Josephine Shaw Lowell "was not an original thinker, but rather a talented popularizer who was able to marshal effective, forceful, and clear arguments for reforms in charity, labor, and politics." To another, she was "the philosopher of the American charity organization movement." She saw the connections between poverty, unemployment, and corrupt government, and also the inability of traditional methods of public and private care to resolve such problems.[43]

The inadequacy of private individual charity to meet modern needs was a lesson learned in the Civil War, especially in the experience of the U.S. Sanitary Commission, which had tried to improve the care of the Union wounded. At the war's end, the country had some 600,000 widows and orphans, and it also had, because of the war's disruptions and dislocations, a seemingly permanent pool of almost a million unemployed men. Aggravating these problems were the severe economic depression of 1873–77 and the uncontrolled immigration which in only twenty-five years (1865–90) raised New York State's population, despite the war's losses, from 3.9 to 6 million, with many of the newcomers starting poor and needing help.[44]

So effective did Josephine Lowell become with her analyses of problems, exposures of corruption, and suggestions for solutions that in 1876 New York's Governor Tilden—after reading her report on "Adult Able-Bodied Paupers"—appointed her to the State Board of Charities, its first female member. In 1882 she created the Charity Organization Society, which by merger in 1939 became a part of today's Community Service Society. The primary aim of her society was not to furnish material aid to the poor but to act as a bureau of information, registration, and investigation that would match a person's need to the charity best suited to help. "Not alms but a friend" was the motto. In 1884 she published *Public Relief and Private Charity*, in which she outlined a modern scientific approach to poverty that would combine the new concepts and techniques of social science with older Christian traditions of charity. Thus, when Josephine Shaw Lowell entered CCB's life, she was already a potent influence in the councils of city and state.[45]

By the late 1880s Sarah Shaw had left Staten Island to live beside her widowed daughter Josephine on East Thirtieth Street. Another daughter, Ellen Barlow, owned the adjoining brownstone, No. 118, and Mrs. Shaw, moving in with two housekeepers, made it her own. Though the houses remained separate, in back they shared a veranda and a yard with a garden and shade tree, allowing any activity to spill easily from one house to the other. This Shaw-Lowell enclave in Manhattan became a stopping place for family and friends, and Sarah Shaw, who enjoyed company and apparently ran the kitchen for both houses, had the Burlinghams for dinner "two or three times a week."[46]

In the summer, when those with means went to the country to avoid the city's heat and threats of cholera and diphtheria, Josephine Lowell's work often kept her in town, and her mother frequently stayed with her to run the house. Then CCB, alone in the city while Louie had the children in the country, ate dinner at one or the other of the Shaw-Lowell houses "almost every night." One summer, he recalled, young Bob Minturn was there, and in the evenings on the veranda, Minturn would bring out his guitar and they would sing. In all seasons there were outings, or concerts, or a cooling ride on the new Third Avenue elevated railway, down to the Bowery to the Chinese Theatre. CCB cared little for music but enjoyed the company; Sarah and Josephine, "free from sham," chatted with everyone, and a favorite memory of CCB was of "Mrs. Lowell talking to the Chinese."[47]

In these years, CCB often saw Lowell at her work. Her house, like most brownstones, had two rooms on the main floor, a parlor to the front and a dining room to the back. Because the latter faced south, it had the better light, and Lowell had her desk in the dining room. After a meal, or even during it, if seized by an idea, she would go to it and quickly pen a letter. (She kept a record of these, and in the year 1893 she wrote 1,899 letters, most by hand.)[48] Because she stated points clearly and had a reputation of wanting nothing for herself, her letters carried weight. Those she wrote to newspapers typically built their arguments with care, asking readers to lay aside prejudice and think. One such, published first in the *Tribune* and then as a pamphlet, followed the bloody riots in July 1892 during the steelworkers' strike at the Homestead Mills, near Pittsburgh. It set forth in calm language, for consideration by "persons who desire to be fair-minded and to do justice to their fellow-men," the idea that an industrial worker "who by his labor for a series of years helps to build up a great business, be it factory, mine or railroad, thereby acquires a distinct right of property in that business." And Lowell discussed the reasons why, in future, the laws of property might need to include such a property right.[49]

She also wrote many private letters to officials, often setting out facts and making suggestions. The officials usually responded, not only with letters but sometimes with actions taken, for they knew she would pursue the matter. According to Homer Folks, soon to become a leader in American health and welfare movements, "She never missed the distinction between conversation and action . . . The next morning she would ask, 'What have you done about this business?' "[50]

In the next century, that was a characteristic for which CCB would become known: like Lowell, he followed up. As a young colleague once remarked, "He could find in you some nerve to press, and then press, until the job was done."[51] And he surely also learned from observing Lowell the certainty that women could match men in executive and intellectual ability, a lesson that at the time was no small achievement in a man's education. Other lessons absorbed are more difficult to define, but they would include the power of an organizing mind, of honesty and clarity of purpose, and of persistence in the pursuit of goals. He also saw in her, as did Folks, a remarkable willingness to listen, a flexibility of mind that allowed her to draw new facts and ideas of value from any person or event, however unusual. Perhaps of equal significance, and again like Folks, he saw the influence of a leader who asked for no personal reward and had no salary, office, or perquisite that she would not sacrifice to speak truth. Finally, she was intellectually honest, and in expressing her thoughts to others she was not unkind, though often blunt. As Folks noted, "She didn't look for good reasons, but for the real reasons. She didn't soften the blows or cover the issue that had to be raised." In sum, "She didn't soften down."[52]

Neither, in the future, would CCB. When faced with bad reasoning, dubious facts, or shavings of the truth, he would snort, "Nonsense!" And he wanted language, as well as thought, to be honest. He hated euphemisms, even about death, especially the phrase "he passed." Hearing it, he would cry: "State the fact; use the active voice: he died."[53]

Though by nature and upbringing he shared many of these qualities with Lowell, they certainly were strengthened in him by her example, constantly on display. The 1880s and 1890s were turbulent decades in the country's industrialization. Between 1881 and 1894, labor strikes and lockouts, hitherto almost unknown, numbered some 14,000 and involved more than four million workers. Though in the years 1860–90 the country's national wealth had increased from roughly $16 to $78 billion, most of that gain had gone into the pockets of one-third of 1 percent of the population, while workers saw the value of their wages decline, with one result an increase in child labor and "sweatshops." Typically, Wall Street lawyers who represented large corporations knew less about the hardships of those at the bottom of the industrial ladder than did the charity workers who saw them daily. CCB, however, knew more than most about the poor and unemployed, and through Lowell and her activities was kept aware of the country's underlying economic and social problems.[54]

6

The Lawrence and Hoe Families
in the 1880s

As CCB and Louie's ties to the Shaw and Lowell families gained strength, those with the Hoe and Lawrence families weakened, blighted by several deaths, marriages, and the ill health of Louie's father, DeWitt Lawrence. Even before the death of his wife Adeline in 1882, he had begun to behave strangely, and after her death his symptoms increased. Part of his illness was drink, but by 1884 he also was having epileptic fits, was continually angry without reason at his son Rob, and to his children and others seemed at times insane.[1]

DeWitt's youngest brother, Darius, forty-seven and unmarried, was also deep into drink and suffered bouts of depression. On the afternoon of 3 April 1885, while in delirium tremens, he locked himself in a room in their brother Cyrus's house in New York, babbling that the city's poor had risen, were rioting on Wall Street, and had routed soldiers sent to disperse them. Cyrus persuaded him to open the door and rushed him to Hahnemann Hospital, at Fourth Avenue and Sixty-seventh Street. There, while the nurse was out of the room, Darius stropped a razor, slashed all the muscles and arteries on the left side of his face, and, falling on the bed, bled to death. The next day newspapers recounted every detail: the locked door, the imagined riot, the blood on the wall, the pillow, the razor. In its story the *Herald* also proclaimed the evils of drink: "He had squandered the greater part of his property," and the *Times*, on its front page, described him as "the erratic brother" in the family. Happily, DeWitt's problems escaped notice. But within the Lawrence family, the lurid suicide of one brother surely increased fears for the fate of the other.[2]

After five years of worsening troubles, DeWitt went to Paris in the summer of 1887 to seek help from Dr. Jean Martin Charcot's neurological clinic, then considered the world's best. Rob, his second child, followed him, staying in Paris many months. Charcot diagnosed melancholia aggravated by drink, a condition most likely coming on for some time, and recommended rest and treatment.[3] At times DeWitt was violent, needing a special room. But by September Rob sent word to the family that the doctors were reporting an improvement and even suggesting that DeWitt might recover sufficiently to return home.[4]

That good news, however, raised its own dismal problem. Sometime after his wife Adeline's death and before becoming so ill, DeWitt had married a widow, Louisa Colton, who had a son, G. Q. Colton Jr., to whom she and DeWitt soon added a half brother, Charles Lawrence. DeWitt now had two families. To which would he return?[5]

In Paris Rob of necessity had business and medical dealings with the new Mrs. Lawrence, and his reports of her suggested that he found her a decent person. DeWitt, however, had never been as competent as his brother Cyrus in the making and managing of money, and now, with medical expenses and a second family, his financial as well as physical health seemed threatened. The needs of the second wife and child competed with those of Adeline's six children, which still were large.

Mariella, the eldest, who might have been expected to make a home for her father, brother, and three unmarried sisters, was herself sick and in need of help. Diagnosed in 1886 to have Bright's disease, she was fast becoming a recluse with no part in family life. Unmarried, childless, she would live until 1910, but like her mother, would have only a weak hold on family memory. A niece who never knew her recalled that "her name was seldom mentioned," and about her hung a hint of trouble, undefined.[6] At the younger end of the family were Grace and Edith, sixteen and fifteen, with school to finish. Their Uncle Cyrus proposed they join Rob in Paris for the winter of 1887–88, but CCB and Louie, in whose apartment the girls often stayed, suggested instead a New England boarding school; and ultimately they entered Miss Capen's School, in Northampton, Massachusetts.[7] Apparently Cyrus paid the bills in whole or in part out of De Witt's share in the brothers' stock and investment business. For part of the holidays the girls squeezed into CCB and Louie's small apartment, and in the summer they went with Louie and her children to the country.[8]

CCB and Louie, increasingly the leaders of their branch of the Lawrence family, also had a part in the engagement and marriage of Fanny, three years younger than Louie and the sister nearest to her in age. Fanny loved Harry Taber, the eldest of the Taber brothers and a mathematician, a graduate of Yale and Johns Hopkins, and in time a professor of mathematics at Clark University, in Worcester. But besides lacking money, about which he seemed to have little judgment, he was eccentric. More interested in numbers than in people, he treated Fanny in an offhand manner, so offhand that CCB one day remonstrated, angering both Fanny and Taber. The next morning she protested to CCB in person, and Harry sent a letter. CCB drafted a reply to Harry, which he showed to Louie, who thought it "too mild." But Joe Evans advised him that in such matters one did "better to speak than to write," and on reflection, CCB agreed and put the letter aside. Yet eager not to be deprived of self-justification, he wrote to Annie a full description of the affair, ending, "So you see the reward of the kind interferer."[9] For a time, relations between the two couples improved, until in December 1885, only a month before Fanny and Harry were to marry, at a Christmas party in the Burlingham apartment, Harry had no present for Fanny, nothing at all, and again CCB rebuked him, provoking an angry exchange. Still, in the fortnight before the wedding, relations returned to cordial.

The following summer the Taber and Burlingham families both rented cottages in Bantam, Connecticut, and then Harry one day abruptly departed Bantam for his family's home in Stowe, Vermont—without Fanny. He claimed to have found the town of Bantam unattractive. He also may have found that proximity to CCB and Louie brought interference. His marriage survived his sudden, solitary departure, but thereafter the Tabers, living in Worcester, kept apart from the Burlinghams, and this pattern in CCB and Louie's dealings with relatives—interference, anger, rupture—would recur.[10]

Sometime in 1888 DeWitt Lawrence returned to New York and to his second wife and family. His son Rob, perhaps the chief casualty of his father's remarriage, lived much of the winter of 1888–89 with CCB and Louie, who recently had moved from a small fifth-floor walk-up apartment at 142 East Fortieth Street to one larger at Park Avenue and Fifty-sixth Street. Park Avenue then was not fashionable, since the New York Central Railroad's tracks and steam engines ran up the center of it through a sunken, open cut and the avenue was dirty and noisy, but it offered cheap rents.[11]

Rob, though by all reports industrious and competent, was unable to establish himself in New York in any line of work. He had not attended college, which CCB lamented, for Rob had scientific talents and an interest in nature, especially birds. But after trying several jobs in the city he went west, to Washington, and claimed a homestead on Puget Sound, planning to study ornithology with the intent perhaps of becoming a teacher or a practicing scientist. He soon disappeared from family affairs, and in 1897, at thirty-six, unmarried, childless, his potential unrealized, he died. Though no one today is sure, it seems likely that CCB and Louie named their second son, born in 1888, after her brother Robert.[12]

With Mariella ill and Rob in the West, Louie became, by age, health, and temperament, the undisputed head of the truncated Lawrence family, and the situation facing her and her sisters was unhappy from every point of view. Not only was their financial outlook increasingly bleak, as their father turned his attention to his new family, but at his side, only blocks away, was an unwanted stepmother and half brother. By the time DeWitt died in 1896, lines had been drawn, and the first family, led by Louie, to the extent possible ignored the second. The Burlinghams' eldest son, for instance, was amused to know he had a half uncle, Charles Lawrence, who was younger than he; in later years he saw the man in business settings and knew him well enough to greet him on the street. But the families were never intimate.[13]

Unfortunately for all, the expenses of DeWitt's illness and second family drained his resources. Though no one said as much, in Hoe and Lawrence family circles the DeWitt branch was slipping into the vexed position of "poor relations." His brother Cyrus tried to help, at least until DeWitt's death in 1896, but thereafter the lack of contact between his and De Witt's children is remarkable. They were, after all, double first cousins (the brothers had married Hoe sisters), had grown up together, and as adults lived in the same city. Yet there were no friendships.

In the years to come, in Louie's family any memory of Uncle Darius and his suicide was buried in silence; few in later generations even knew of his existence. DeWitt's illness, however, was well known and sometimes caused his descendants to wonder about inherited tendencies to mental instability. CCB's niece, for instance, could ask, Was this the reason Mariella lived alone for so many years, without family visitors? Was this why her Aunt Edith, DeWitt's youngest daughter, in middle age had a nervous breakdown, requiring a stay in an institution? And when two of CCB's three children showed symptoms of mental disorder, some family members suspected the cause was "Lawrence bad blood."[14]

As a counter to the troubles in Louie's family came news from Italy, in March 1886, of Annie Hoe's engagement to Charles A. Platt, a member of a large and well-known New York family. Annie, while with her parents in Paris, had met Platt, who was studying at the École des Beaux-Arts and preparing to become, in another fifteen years, one of America's distinguished architects. Though she was thirty-four, lame, and nine years older than he, her personality had sparked a romance, and when she and her parents went to Florence, Platt followed. There he fell ill of typhoid fever, and in April, while she nursed him to health, they married.[15]

Two months later in Florence, on 7 June, Colonel Hoe had a heart attack and died. CCB, hearing the news, wrote to Rob Lawrence regretting that the seventy-four-year-old colonel "should have died so far from home . . . With what good temper he has lived his life, with how little bitterness." From Annie he received a letter lamenting her father's sacrifices for her and stressing her need for the Burlinghams' love. Annie's sister Mary Harper and her husband sailed at once for Paris to accompany the widow home, leaving Annie and Platt, when well, to follow.[16]

By September 1886 the Platts were at Brightside, and Mrs. Hoe gave an afternoon party to introduce her new son-in-law to the family. For some reason Louie was unable to go, so CCB, sitting that evening at a desk in Brightside, wrote her his impression of Annie's husband: "Well, you want to know what I think of Charley? I am much disappointed in his looks. His features are rather coarse, but he has a sweet smile. But of him I think very well. I like his manner . . . He is not fresh in any way. He looks fully 28, and is quiet and dignified, not free spoken. I should be terribly surprised if he were not *good*, dear. Annie is very happy."[17]

Eight months later, in Paris, Annie died giving birth to twin daughters, who also died. A desolate Platt came back to New York and in his grief called often on CCB and Louie: he "would come up to our apartment, listen at the door to learn if we were alone, and if we were, he came in and we talked about Annie. This went on for several months."[18] Those evenings cannot have been easy for any of them. The previous year CCB and Louie had named their second child, a daughter, Anne Hoe Burlingham, and at the baptism Annie, by proxy, had been a godmother. Though at times CCB had been critical of Annie—just a week after the party at Brightside he had complained to Louie that Annie "was not deep enough in her feelings . . . We must think of her as different from us"—in the years after her death, he never wavered in loyalty, was eager always to talk of her and to acknowledge her influence. In August 1953 he wrote of her that she "had great beauty although her chin projected a little"—it was always necessary to be honest—and, borrowing a line from Wordsworth, concluded, "She was a perfect woman, nobly planned."[19]

With the colonel's death, Brightside, too, began to die. At St. Ann's Episcopal Church, in nearby Morrisania, hundreds attended his funeral in August (before Annie and Platt returned), not only the family in its many branches of Hoe, Harper, Lawrence, Dodd, and Mead but also employees from his factory; representatives of the General Society of Mechanics and Tradesmen, and of his charities, the Home for Incurables and the House of Refuge (for juvenile delinquents); graduates of his school for apprentices; and others who simply had been touched in some way by his constant good humor. So many came that reportedly several hundred had to stand for the service on a grassy slope outside the church. Yet he was buried modestly in the crypt, without a memorial stone in the yard or church wall, until in 1941 a bronze tablet was put in the nave to commemorate the man who was "Twenty years a Vestryman" and "Inventor of the Rotary Printing Press."[20]

Understandably, no one could care for Brightside as much as he who had created it. His family's interests now were elsewhere, and in any case the steady advance of New York City into the Bronx doomed the estate. A manor house on a working farm, with prize fruits and cattle, was already out of place. Developers had plans for Hunts Point, and Brightside lay squarely across the entrance to it. The first assets sold were the books, which went at auction in May 1887, unhappily fetching only the lowest prices. CCB, going out to the house a few months later, wrote Louie, "The place is very queer without the books—with the funny lacish [sic] curtains in the bookcases. It is a place I love very very much, though. I should like to have you there a bit. It is full of Annie."[21] In June the prize cattle went on the block. But the previous winter the herd had been ravaged by an epidemic of "pleuropneumonia," and buyers were cautious. Despite the pedigrees, the average successful bid was only $64 a head, the price of common cattle, and the auction raised only $2,430.[22]

For a time Mrs. Hoe kept the house open, though using it little. Then in 1892 she bought a new town house in the city, at 11 East Seventy-first Street, and gave her attention to it. Brightside thereafter slowly gave up its luster, its trees unpruned, its fields fallow, its rooms empty. Finally, in January 1900, it was sold, according to the newspapers for a tremendous profit. The colonel would have been pleased—except that ten days later the city announced the extension of subway lines into the Bronx, and the ten-day owners reaped the greatest profit.[23] Of the bucolic beauty that was Brightside, no part remains. Hunts Point today is a depressed city slum. The grid of streets and tenements ruthlessly pressed onto the land has obscured any outline of the drained and contoured fields, the winding drive, the terraced gardens. Decades later, CCB recalled the colonel passing the plate at St. Ann's, and how, despite a leg broken in a carriage accident and poorly mended, he "took up the alms, limping gracefully down the aisle with a smile for everybody—and what an engaging smile it was."[24]

Nevertheless, the colonel's fortune, buttressed by the sale of his interest in R. Hoe & Company to his nephew Robert Hoe III, was sufficient to sustain his widow in luxury and, upon her death in 1901, to contribute to the support of his children and grandchildren. Upon his widow's death, the estate was divided into five parts, one for each of his daughters (or if one predeceased the widow, that daughter's share to be divided among her children). For Adeline Lawrence's surviving children, Mariella, Louie, Fanny, Grace, and Edith, the legacy, though small, was a help. Invested with care, the fund might bring in a thousand dollars a year, and as common wisdom then held: the first thousand beyond necessities makes the biggest difference.[25]

Aside from the troubles in the Hoe and Lawrence families, CCB's life in the late 1880s was quiet and happy. He rejoiced in his family: three children born healthy, a competent, loving wife, and parents close by (but not too close) and able to care for themselves. Money for the family still was short, but he was solidifying his position at Wing, Shoudy & Putnam, and from time to time received small improvements in pay. He knew now that, as Putnam's assistant, his legal work for years to come would be mostly in maritime cases tried in federal courts, and so he immersed himself in learning everything he could about federal procedure, court history, and personnel. He had no role in any of the city's great events, but he liked to attend them when he could, and in August 1885 the city staged an event that reportedly drew a million people.

General Ulysses S. Grant, commander of the Union army in the Civil War and the country's eighteenth president, had died, after a long illness, on 23 July. Because he had lived his last four years in New York and become associated with the city, Mayor William R. Grace offered Grant's family a site for a mausoleum at 122nd Street and Riverside Drive—a superb location with vistas across to the Palisades and up and down the Hudson River. Until money could be raised by subscription to build the tomb, the mayor proposed that Grant be buried in a temporary vault on the site, and planned for 9 August a procession (longer and greater than Lincoln's) to accompany the coffin from City Hall to the temporary grave: up Broadway to Fourteenth Street, over to Fifth Avenue and up to Fifty-seventh Street, over to Broadway and up to Seventy-second Street, and then up Riverside Drive. Among the marchers, with many regiments and bands, would be surviving generals of the Union and Confederate armies, and on the reviewing stand President Grover Cleveland. With Louie and Young Charles in the country for the summer, CCB, though cool to Grant, was drawn to the funeral procession by his sense of history.

At the time of his death, Grant's reputation was very mixed. His career offered people much to admire and much to deplore, causing many of his countrymen, in the manner of Plutarch, to sift the good and bad for a residue of moral lessons. Admirable in war, Grant had failed in peace.

There were, of course, vast social and economic forces over which Grant in his eight years as president (1869–77) had no control, such as the exploitation of the West, the increasing dominance of railroads, and the new wealth and scandals of Wall Street. But where he had power, especially in his personal relations with politicians and cabinet officers, he proved inadequate to the needs of the office, often because, out of mistaken loyalty, he would defend and promote those whom he should have dismissed. With the exception of his secretary of state, Hamilton Fish, he drove out of his cabinet the better men, seeming always to prefer the worse. (During his two terms, twenty-five men served in a seven-man cabinet, including five secretaries of war, three of them in one year, five attorney generals, and four each of postmaster general and secretary of the Treasury.) Under no other president has there been such a shuffle of office, and by 1877 his administration had, in the historian C. Vann Woodward's summary, "virtually [come] apart at the seams. Whole departments were demoralized or staffed with raw and inexperienced recruits. The Cabinet was in a turmoil of resignations and appointments, and the President was patently without a policy to his name and losing much popular respect." Meanwhile, a congressional committee was digging out "the disgraceful details of the relations between the White House and the Whiskey Ring."[26]

Even out of office Grant had more public failures. When in 1880 he tried to win the Republican nomination for a third term, he was defeated by James A. Garfield. Four years later the New York brokerage firm of Grant and Ward, in which he and his son were two of the four partners, failed. Besides the financial loss, the bankruptcy brought disgrace, for the firm had committed fraud and Grant could plead innocence only on the grounds of extreme ignorance or stupidity.[27] By then he knew he had cancer of the throat and only a year or so to live.

In an effort to recoup honor and to leave a legacy for his widow, he set about writing his memoirs. Calling on his wartime determination, despite pain and sleepless nights he completed the book four days before dying. His *Personal Memoirs*, frank, modest, charming, ranks with the best of military autobiographies, but at the time of his funeral procession, only excerpts had been published and many people were not ready to forgive him.[28] Perhaps that dubious reputation explains CCB's seeming lack of interest in Grant, for in his account to Louie of the funeral procession he mentions Grant only once, in passing.

His long letter in two parts was written Sunday morning and afternoon at his parents' home in Mount Vernon, the day after the procession, and starts with his thoughts the night before as he and two friends walked down Riverside Drive and saw the preparations for the temporary grave.

> In the darkness made our way to the tomb of Gen. Grant. Brick layers and carpenters working there. A soldier was standing guard. Two police men and a dozen spectators made up the rest of the company. Off in the mist we could see the lights of anchored vessels, and the lights of tows moving slowly up and down the river. It was a sobering sight. Even the profanity of the soldier and the rough play and loud talking of the workmen didn't rob the scene of solemnity. To me it seemed a modern "gravedigger's scene."

They continued down the drive in the darkness and mist and then crossed to upper Broadway where they found "wagons waiting for the morning—men asleep in them or busy making benches for spectators. Booths had been put up all along the road and raised rows of seats." The next morning he and friends watched the procession from a window ledge on Fifth Avenue from which they could see over "the struggling mob beneath."

> Of that I can tell you nothing that will make it real to you. We saw one big boy fall fainting right below us. Across the street a woman fainted and was carried in to the crowd with a bleeding face. At last two mounted policemen came up the street at full speed, and the street-full of men and women and children seemed to run madly against the human walls that rose from there on either side. It was a great sight—Sherman and Joe Johnston and Sheridan and Buckner—that was the sight of the day.
>
> *Afternoon*
>
> I don't think I shall go to the city. Al will mail this for me, dear. It is a lovely, country, free day. I slept till almost 10 o'clock this a.m. I read the paper; began this letter; had dinner; talked with mother and Al and a Mr. Adams, who came in, about the war, and our good Lincoln. Oh, it is a glory to have had him! Mother tells me that father saw men in N.Y. so sick the day Lincoln died that they vomited in the streets. Mr. Adams said he cried himself all day. A man who spoke slightingly of him was thrown off from a ferry boat.[29]

The newspapers in reporting on the procession wrote of Grant in the sentimental, florid style—the fallen warrior—that had become prevalent in speaking of the Civil War, a style unconsciously adopted perhaps to avoid the war's awful reality. But for CCB, Grant could never be a true hero: he had lacked moral character.[30] Still, the country as a whole soon forgave Grant, perhaps out of a need to forgive itself for the debauchery of the Gilded Age, so closely associated with him. As the years passed, Woodward wrote, "the Grant Administration began to seem more and more like something that had happened to Grant and the American people rather than something Grant or the American people had done, more a misfortune than a misdeed. Between the General and the people there grew a bond of bereavement and mutual need for vindication."[31]

The general's tomb, the largest mausoleum in the United States, was dedicated in 1897, with President McKinley and nearly a million spectators on hand for the ceremony. For a quarter of a century, until after World War I, when memories of the Civil War began to retreat before those of wars more recent, Grant's Tomb, high on Riverside Drive, with its views of the Hudson, its marble interior and sunken crypt, was one of the country's most popular tourist sights. CCB on occasion would take out-of-town visitors to see it—for the architecture and for its views of the river. Unpersuaded by the flux of public forgiveness, he did not raise his appraisal of Grant as president. The true hero of the war and presidency was Lincoln.

Marriage to Louie brought CCB closer to the Episcopal church, but with his father a Baptist preacher and his mother ardent for that denomination, he was not yet ready to leave the church of his youth. Yet he regularly attended services with Louie at the Episcopal Church of the Incarnation, on Madison Avenue at Thirty-fifth Street, a small, elegant building in English Gothic style, with exquisite woodwork and stained glass. Its rector was Arthur Brooks, a younger brother of Phillips and a tall, thin scholar much loved by his parishioners. At least once a year he had his brother down from Boston to conduct a service and preach.[32]

In 1882, when a fire damaged the church, the congregation of Temple Emanu-El invited the Episcopalians to use their temple for services, an invitation gratefully accepted, and CCB heard Phillips Brooks preach there. He also read collections of Brooks's sermons as they were published, and he and Annie Hoe frequently sent each other religious articles, though one time she balked at reading Arthur Brooks's sermons.[33]

In the spring of 1886, Louie, but not CCB, was confirmed in Brooks's church, and CCB agreed to have the children, young Charles and Anne

Hoe, whom they called Nancy, baptized by him. The children's sponsors, besides the parents, were Joe Evans, Louie's brother Rob, and her married sister, Fanny Taber, with Louie presumably standing in for Annie, who was in Paris.[34] The next day CCB wrote to his mother, in Chicago:

We had the children christened by Mr. Brooks. Louie has wanted to have them christened, as perhaps you know. I have objected, but not because I thought it could do any harm (for as a service of dedication it seems to me very beautiful and appropriate), but because I thought it not a real baptism; but as Mr. Brooks said, even if I felt that way, there was no reason why I should stand in Louie's way. So I yielded, and on Monday before Rob went [to Chicago], we went to the church to the christening, Rob acting as godfather with me for Charles. I sent a note to father, but too late to reach him in time for him to attend the service.[35]

Evidently, despite the pull of Louie and Phillips Brooks, CCB still felt more comfortable with Baptist ways, and two years later, writing to Louie from his parents' house in Mount Vernon, he reported, "We have had a quiet peaceful day. We went to the Baptist church in a.m. as a matter of course. I have slept an hour and half this p.m. and have read and sat about in true Sunday fashion."[36] Louie, though, was increasingly happy with Arthur Brooks and the Church of the Incarnation; and she and CCB had their third child, Robert, born on 29 February 1888, baptized there while a baby.[37] Yet two years later, on 7 December 1891, having moved to East Thirty-eighth Street, they formally joined St. George's Episcopal Church on Stuyvesant Square, at Sixteenth Street and Second Avenue—considerably farther from home than the Church of the Incarnation.[38] St. George's, one of the city's older and better-known churches, was "low" Episcopal, and the Incarnation was, if not "high," certainly higher. St. George's therefore may have been CCB and Louie's compromise.

St. George's "new" church, rebuilt after a fire in 1865, stood (and still stands) on a plot given it in 1846 by Peter G. Stuyvesant that faced the small park of Stuyvesant Square, its two massive clock towers dominating the area. Like Brooks's Trinity Church in Boston, it was Romanesque, not Gothic, with a large nave without columns and the pulpit visible to all. Preaching was the core of St. George's tradition, and its current rector, William S. Rainsford (1883–1905), was a preacher of the Brooks stamp.[39]

In these years the Puritan strain of the Episcopal church was strong at St. George's. It had not an altar but a freestanding communion table, without a cross or candles. On the wall behind it hung the tablets of the Law, flanked by the Lord's Prayer and the Apostles' Creed, all lit by a skylight at the crown of the apse. So great were considered the perils of Rome and idolatry that not until 1950, in a service held to demonstrate "the wide range of ceremonial used in Episcopal churches to express our common liturgy," were copes and miters worn by the clergy and incense swung in the aisles, clothing and acts common in high-church services. And not until 1976, seventeen years after CCB's death, did the communion table bear candles.[40]

At St. George's CCB found a spiritual home. He took to it with enthusiasm, and from 1914 to his death in 1959 served on its vestry or as a warden. When he joined, the best-known vestryman was J. P. Morgan, who funded the rector's social programs so generously that St. George's often was called "Morgan's Church." Toward the end of CCB's life, to many persons it had become "Burlingham's Church," not because of his financial support, for he was never rich, but because as he worked for it over the years his style and its merged so closely he seemed to personify it: a man and a church—in personal affairs, conservative, but in response to the day's social and economic issues, broadly liberal.[41]

Louie, however, never found a place for herself at St. George's, or perhaps never sought one. In those years a church often was a cause for which married couples worked together; at St. George's, Mr. and Mrs. Henry H. Pike for thirty-five years jointly ran the Sunday school, whose annual enrollment reached 2,000. Louie might have volunteered for any number of undertakings, such as the Girls' Friendly Society, the Nutrition Clinic, or the Women's Industrial Society. But her name, except for an occasional social note in a church bulletin, never appears in the records.[42]

Meanwhile, at Wing, Shoudy & Putnam, CCB as Putnam's assistant continually practiced in admiralty courts where much was different from those of common law. Roughly speaking, and with many curious exceptions, what most people consider the typical subjects of law—real estate, commercial contracts, trusts and estates, highway and rail accidents, as well as most crimes—are governed by state law, and disputes are tried in state courts. But if two ships collide in navigable waters, then, by Article III, section 2, of the Constitution, the controlling law is federal and the case must be tried in a federal court. For its first sixty-three years the U.S. Supreme Court followed the traditional English definition of "navigable waters," meaning on the high seas and waters within the ebb and flow of tide. All of New York Harbor fell within that definition as well as the Hudson River for roughly 140 miles north, to the city of Troy. Then, as the country's interior was settled and commerce began to move on its rivers, lakes, and connecting canals, the Supreme Court in 1852 extended the meaning of "navigable waters" to include any river or lake capable of carrying interstate or international commerce. By 1883, when CCB came to admiralty practice, this wider definition was well settled, and suits in admiralty were as likely to follow collisions on Lake Superior or on the Missouri-Mississippi River as those on the high seas.[43]

The substance and procedures of the law governing admiralty disputes derived mostly from the cases and procedures of the British colonial admiralty courts, which had been succeeded, after the Revolution, by the federal district courts. Historically, maritime courts emerged in medieval England in seaports, independent of each other and of the evolving common-law courts. Sea trade, with its obvious special risks, had long-established rules (compounded from the laws of many nations) for apportioning responsibility for disasters at sea among those involved, chiefly sailors, merchants, and shipowners. In Tudor times, these independent seaport courts gradually were absorbed into a maritime court attached to the Crown's lord high admiral, a court whose law and procedure also owed much to the civil codes of the leading European seagoing nations. The "custom of the sea" always has been a more international, cosmopolitan system of law, less tied to national sovereignty than is land law.

In its American colonies as throughout its empire, England—acting through its High Court of Admiralty in London—commissioned lesser vice admiralty courts in all major seaports. New York's had been established in 1678, fourteen years after the English seized the city and colony, when governor-general Sir Edmund Ambrose appointed Stephen Van Cortlandt, the city's mayor, as judge of the Court of Admiralty of the Province of New York.[44]

After the formation of the United Kingdom of Great Britain by the Act of Union, 1707, all the British vice admiralty courts adopted as a symbol of authority and jurisdiction a silver oar. Carried ceremoniously before the judge as he entered the courtroom, throughout the proceeding it lay in a cradle on the judge's bench, and at the hearing's close a bailiff, walking before the judge, bore it ceremoniously from the room. The size and design of these silver oars, made in each port by local artisans, were roughly similar, twenty-two inches long with an engraving of the British royal arms on one side of the blade and on the other the crowned anchor, seal of the Admiralty Court itself. In the turmoil of the Revolution, however, the silver oars in the colonies disappeared.[45]

Because of the Revolution, New York's colonial Vice Admiralty Court came to an end on 19 December 1775, and in its place the former colony—

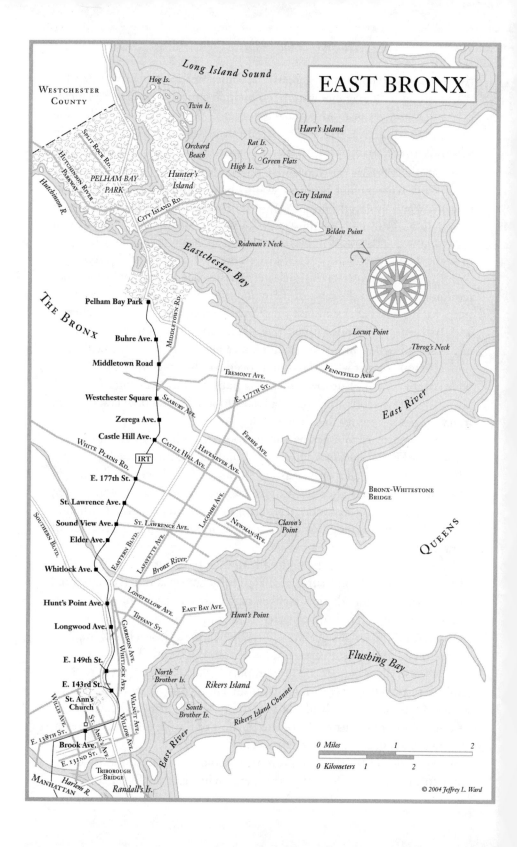

now a sovereign state—established an Admiralty Court of the State of New York, which sat, as had its predecessor, in the City Hall on Wall Street (where now stands Federal Hall). This state court, using the same English precedents as the court it replaced, lasted until the adoption of the United States Constitution in 1789. The first court to be formed under the Constitution (even before the Supreme Court) was the U.S. District Court for New York, whose chief business was to hear admiralty cases. President Washington appointed James Duane the court's justice, and it convened for the first time on 3 November 1789 in the Exchange Building on Broad Street, across from Fraunces Tavern; among the attorneys admitted to practice before it on that day were Alexander Hamilton and Aaron Burr. Because this court was the country's first federal court, sentimental and historically minded lawyers and judges sometimes refer to it as the "Mother Court" of the Republic.[46]

With the expansion of the United States and growth of waterborne commerce on oceans, lakes, and rivers, the number of admiralty cases rapidly increased, so much so that in 1814 Congress divided the New York federal district court into Northern and Southern Districts with a judge for each.[47] The Southern District (still counting itself the "Mother Court," though its judge, by choosing at the split to sit in the Northern District, gave the latter a claim) included New York City, Long Island, Staten Island, and the nine counties bordering the Hudson River up to the southern boundaries of Albany and Rensselaer Counties; and the Northern District had the rest of the state. Yet soon the Southern District's admiralty docket was so busy that Congress, in 1865, again divided the court in two, creating an Eastern District with sole jurisdiction of Long Island and Staten Island, totaling 350 miles of shoreline, and joint jurisdiction with the Southern District of New York Harbor. In all, the Eastern District, sitting in Brooklyn, a city with a population then of 300,000, had exclusive jurisdiction of about a quarter of the harbor's 770 miles of waterfront and over roughly one-quarter of all its foreign commerce.[48]

In 1883 the Southern and Eastern District courts, in which CCB regularly practiced, had but one judge apiece. (A century later so much had business increased, the Southern had twenty-nine and the Eastern fourteen.) The Eastern District's courtroom was in downtown Brooklyn, which CCB could reach easily from his firm's office at 45 William Street, Manhattan, crossing the East River by ferry or by carriage, trolley, or on foot (for a penny) over the Brooklyn Bridge. When the bridge opened on 24 May 1883, with the mayors of Brooklyn and New York leading processions from either side to shake hands in the middle, it was a wonder of the world. The span between its towers was then the world's longest, 1,595.5 feet, with an arch at mean water soaring 133 feet above the river. Its buttressed towers of granite rose 272 feet, only 8 less than Trinity's spire but far more massive. On the city's skyline the bridge's presence was immense.[49]

The Southern District courtroom was on the fourth floor of the Federal Post Office and Courthouse Building, at the south end of City Hall Park, where the new bridge debouched into Manhattan, and opposite the Astor House on Broadway from whose windows CCB as a boy had watched Lincoln's funeral procession and the fire at Barnum's Museum. (In 1875, in a fit of architectural insanity, the city had sold to the federal government for a penny the southern half of City Hall Park as the site for a huge office building, which, in a style called variously neo-Renaissance, French Empire, and high Victorian, rose five tall stories crowded with pillars, pediments, cornices, cupolas, and domes—all of which soon grew dingy and dilapidated. It was noisy, smelly, inefficient, and its back-side loading docks opened almost directly onto the steps of City Hall. Unlike Brooklyn Bridge, the federal building was a structure no one loved, and when in 1939 it was torn down and the site returned to park, everyone rejoiced, not least judges and lawyers.)[50]

In the Eastern District until about 1915 most cases continued to be admiralty suits, with many ferry and tugboat collisions. In the Southern, the balance between admiralty and nonadmiralty shifted sooner, as after the Civil War railroads gradually overtook ships and barges as America's chief carriers of interstate commerce and as New York became the country's financial center, with its stock exchange and its banks attracting business from all over the country; the number of nonmaritime suits in the Southern District Court greatly increased, and it became in some respects the most important court in the country. Fortunately, in the years of CCB's practice, it enjoyed a succession of superior judges, drew into its courtroom many fine lawyers, and continued to have numerous and significant cases in admiralty.[51]

The admiralty bar has never been numerous. And whatever a court's designation—colonial, state, or federal—when sitting "in admiralty," its procedures have differed from those of other courts. Until almost a decade after CCB's death in 1959, a lawyer in an admiralty suit was called a "proctor in admiralty"; the complaint, a "libel"; the plaintiff, the "libelant"; and the defendant, the "respondent." Yet "in admiralty" as in common law, the party that felt injured and sought recompense brought the facts and the alleged perpetrator before a court and argued the case (in admiralty, which offered no right to a jury, almost always to a single judge).

Most of "the admiralty," as CCB called the specialized bar, were remarkably sentimental about the traditions of their practice. Though he at times pretended impatience with its lore, when he found himself in 1883 unexpectedly thrust into it, he tackled it with energy and soon succumbed to its charms. By 1891 he had developed enough of a reputation in the field to be asked to write the chapter on admiralty for a handbook on *Federal Practice in Civil Causes.* His essay brought him little fame, probably less money, and perhaps was undertaken as a form of self-education; and he never referred to it. But at the time the partners of Wing, Shoudy & Putnam surely were pleased by the notice taken of him.[52]

The judges of the Eastern and Southern District Courts before whom he appeared were Charles L. Benedict and Addison Brown. In those early years, admiralty practice "was a rather close preserve," he later recalled; indeed, in the Eastern District, where Judge Benedict had presided since the court's creation in 1865, it was "a family party."[53] The leading admiralty lawyer in New York in the 1880s was the judge's brother, Robert D. Benedict, who regularly argued cases before him. Another brother, B. Lincoln Benedict, known always as "B. Lincoln," was the court clerk and was constantly given references from the bench—legal jobs for which he collected considerable fees.[54] The Benedicts were honest and talented, but their fraternity struck many as inappropriate, and in the Southern District, Judge William G. Choate (1878–81) had forbidden his brother Joseph Hodges Choate or any member of the latter's firm to plead a cause before him.[55]

By the time CCB began practice, Judge Choate had resigned from the bench but was remembered with approval, particularly for the circumstances of his resignation. The salary of a federal district court judge was then $4,000 a year, and members of the New York bar, fearing they might lose the much admired Judge Choate, had vainly petitioned Congress to raise his salary, citing the court's importance. In 1881 Judge Choate resigned, giving as his sole reason the low salary. The *Tribune* published a long editorial on "Our Pauper Judges," proclaiming "the poverty of the Federal judicial salaries is and has been for years a National scandal." It listed the salaries of federal judges, starting with the chief justice of the U.S. Supreme Court, $10,500; associate justices, $10,000; circuit court judges, $6,000; and district judges in urban commercial districts, $4,000, and in rural areas such as the Western District of Arkansas, $3,500. New York paid its state judges on a scale ranging from $6,000 to $17,000. Choate's resignation, urged the *Tribune*, "ought to set Congress thinking." But Congress did nothing.[56]

Choate's place was taken by Addison Brown, a Harvard classmate who had an independent income, and for eighteen years, starting in 1883, CCB argued cases before him. Brown in his term as judge (1881–1901) became probably the greatest American judge of his day for admiralty law, aided in part by an outstanding court clerk, Samuel H. Lyman (1876–1901), who in 1883 took in as an assistant Alexander Gilchrist Jr., who served the court equally well until 1930.[57]

It is difficult to exaggerate the importance to a court of a competent, honest clerk. He can keep not only the judge, or judges, operating efficiently, but also the lawyers, saving them if they will listen from procedural and even substantive mistakes. And since the head clerk and his assistants, more than the judges, deal directly with the public, they have a large part in creating a court's reputation for fairness. In CCB's opinion, Gilchrist was "one of the best public servants our government ever had. He knew everything there was to be known of federal practice and procedure. He forgot nothing. Even before he became clerk or deputy clerk, he was the one to whom the young lawyers always resorted."[58]

Judge Brown knew the worth of Gilchrist, telling him one day, "I will sign any order you will put your initials to in *Ink.*" In handling money, Brown, who had a scientific turn of mind—he was both a mathematician and a botanist—was exact, but neither generous nor self-indulgent. If a letter came to him with postage due, he repaid the pennies a clerk had advanced. If he sent a clerk on an errand needing carfare, he paid, though not a penny more than needed. His battered stovepipe hat proclaimed a New Englander's thrift.[59] He had no social life. His first wife was an invalid who, according to Gilchrist, spent most of her time in bed "writing alleged poetry." His backyard was full of flowers and the top floor of his house full of potted plants. (He wrote a monumental study of North American flora with Dr. Nathaniel L. Britton, director of the New York Botanical Garden.) His routine was to work flat out for several weeks until exhausted, stay at home in bed for a week or two until rested, and then return to court for another bout. The general view of him was that as a judge he was strongest on bankruptcy, extradition, and admiralty. CCB ranked him a "great" judge. He knew that Brown frequently was criticized for dividing the damages in the collision cases, "but he was usually right. He treated these cases somewhat as scientific problems and resolved them by scientific methods rather than by the weight of evidence."[60]

In one respect, however, CCB found the judge lacking. Brown was "a poor judge of men; he hardly knew whether a witness was lying, or even whether he was drunk." Judge Benedict, in the Eastern District Court, knew better: with sailors inclined to bend the truth to preserve a captain and a ship, a judge needed a sixth sense and lots of experience. Judge Benedict "would often decide a case against the heaviest weight of evidence because he could spot a liar as a cat catches a mouse. He asked a few irrelevant questions, not interfering with the lawyers, and then made up his mind."[61]

Early in his career, CCB discovered that for him the trial court, or even the case on appeal, was drama, not drudgery; that for him the practice of law was as much an art as a science. He liked that—the law was human, about people—and he went off to work as eagerly in the morning as he returned home to Louie and the children at night.

7

Breakdown and Rescue

WITH THE BIRTH of their third child, Robert, on 29 February 1888, CCB and Louie completed their family. They were five, loving and happy, but in material circumstances falling behind; his earnings barely kept abreast of life's necessities. Their situation was never dire, and CCB, by temperament, was not inclined to view it so. Nevertheless, during the summer months when Louie took the children out of the city to escape the threat of cholera and diphtheria, his letters to her often turned to money and the lack of it, even for small expenses. One August weekend in 1890 when Louie and the children were at Ashland, Massachusetts, against his heart's desire he stayed in town in order not to borrow ten dollars for the railroad fare.[1]

By then he was no longer on salary at Wing, Shoudy & Putnam but instead received 20 percent of the fee in any case he tried or settled. Putnam continued to keep for himself the larger, more lucrative cases, but there were many smaller ones. In winter, when the courts were open, CCB could earn more than in summer, and on 29 June 1890, estimating that in the past six months he had earned $1,250, he wrote to Louie, "If I can keep this up for the rest of the year, I shall be satisfied."[2]

To economize, he and Louie moved several times to apartments in neighborhoods cheaper than Murray Hill, but in 1891 returned to a small house at 156 East Thirty-eighth Street for which the annual rent was $1,600. At that time, a financial rule of thumb for families of their social class was that no more than a quarter of annual income should go for rent; but of his income rent took more than half.[3] In later years he would insist that there never had been much money in an admiralty practice, and he would protest that he could not understand why anyone should be interested in it. In 1920 he wrote to a corporate lawyer who was recommending a young man eager for employment:

It is in the air; every young lawyer seems to think that his future lies on the sea. I spent the early years of my professional life telling young men to keep out of the Admiralty, as there was no money in it except for a few, and now I find that every other man from the law schools wants to go into the Admiralty.

What is it anyway? Except for collisions, general average and marine insurance, there is nothing special about it. Any lawyer can try a personal injury case or a charter party or carrier case if he has never heard or seen the loud-roaring sea.

Forgive this essay.[4]

The man was not hired. But CCB's oft-stated reasons why the admiralty was a poor choice for young lawyers did not abate the enthusiasm of those seeking a job in his firm. CCB might pretend indifference to the romance of "the loud-roaring sea," but it was real, and many heard it.

Even on a grumpy day, CCB admitted the practice offered some interesting specialties, the first being the ancient law of general average. As stated in the digest of Roman law published in A.D. 534 by the emperor Justinian: "It is provided by the Rhodian Law that if merchandise is thrown overboard to lighten the ship, the loss occasioned for the benefit of all must be made good by the contribution of all." The principle, devised first by merchants and lawyers on the island of Rhodes, seems fair.[5]

Another specialty was the law of collision. Ever since the first admiralty court came into being somewhere in the Mediterranean, its descendants have spent much time on collisions, for in a busy port, however spacious, there will be ten to a hundred a day. Leaving aside the peculiar problems of ships dependent on wind, consider the impossibility of bringing any ship to a full stop. Except when docked, and not always then, a ship is continually in motion because of wind, wave, or current. Any sharp turn for a liner, freighter, or ferry requires a large circle and considerable time to accomplish. When docking, ships frequently damage themselves or the wharves; and in fog they creep about the water's surface, fearful and hooting, often with close calls and scraped sides. Many people find something inherently exciting and dramatic in collisions, and the ramifications of them—damage to ship, to wharf, to cargo, to stevedore, to seaman, to passenger—was a large part of CCB's practice.

Marine insurance, the third special facet of admiralty law, is quite possibly the oldest form of insurance known to man. So risky did seaborne transport of goods seem to the earliest merchants, they started a tradition of insurance and reinsurance of cargoes and ships that has developed into a system unmatched by any other industry. In maritime commerce today, almost every possibility of loss is covered by insurance, which in turn usually is covered by some form of reinsurance, so that the loss ultimately is spread very wide—so wide that one day Learned Hand, a successor to Addison Brown in the Southern District Court and perhaps the greatest admiralty judge of his generation, lifted his head from a tangled record from which he was trying to draw justice and said to his clerk: "I don't know why I do this. Y'know I've decided so many Admiralty cases in my life, and there is so much insurance and reinsurance in shipping, if I had decided every case in exactly the opposite way, it wouldn't have made any difference to anybody."[6] Yet Hand, like CCB, loved the admiralty, and so do most of its lawyers and judges.

Though no court in the United States has records so continuous and old as the Admiralty Court of New York, whose records date back to 1715, it has been served over the years by remarkably few lawyers. (One historian has estimated that for the fifty years 1739–89 80 percent of the admiralty cases in New York were handled by less than twenty-five people, and even in 1995 the Maritime Law Association of the United States, to which nearly all admiralty lawyers and judges in the country belong, had only some 3,200 lawyers and 225 judges and law professors.)[7]

When CCB began in admiralty, everyone knew everyone else, at least by reputation, and, as CCB observed, "it was very friendly. We had no restrictive rules of practice. We would telephone to our opponents and ask them when it would be convenient to take a deposition and would grant and give favors to each other. Instead of seizing a vessel against which we were filing a libel, we would call up the counsel and ask him if he would agree to appear without process. It was a very agreeable practice." Still, it did not pay well, and for those of its practitioners who fell ill or were struck by a personal catastrophe, despite the maritime world's vaunted system of insurance, there was none for its lawyers.[8]

In the fall of 1892, CCB began to feel ill. He had dizzy spells, he several times fainted, and he frequently lost his ability to concentrate. Not knowing how to treat his troubles, he worked all the harder, hoping they would pass, but the spells grew worse. He consulted a doctor, who advised a long rest. "It was the nerves of my stomach that were frazzled." CCB's future and that of his family suddenly was bleak. He had no salary, and without the 20 percent of fees received for his cases tried or settled, he would have no income. His father was not rich, and Louie's father was mentally ill, with a second family to support. Something, of course, could be worked out: loans, a much cheaper house or apartment away from friends, splitting the family with the children going to CCB's parents, or perhaps a move for the family out of the city—though in the country CCB's training in admiralty would be useless. All options were hard: "It was not a pleasant outlook."[9]

While still undecided, he and Louie were rescued by friends, primarily by the Shaw-Lowell family, acting in a three-generation conspiracy whose working ranks were Louie's schoolmates Lizzie Curtis, May Minturn, and Carlotta Russell Lowell.

At CCB's office, in early October, he received a letter from the family's matriarch, Sarah B. Shaw.

> [7 October 1892]
> Friday, 118 East 30th St., NYC
>
> Dear Charley,
>
> This is a letter from your *"Grandmother." So listen*—From what you say of your symptoms, it seems to me that you have what was called when I was young *"Nervous Dyspepsia."* I want very much to have you consult Dr. Reisig. His treatment of our beloved friend was marvelous, and I believe if he had been his doctor from the first, he would be a well man. He is the oldest homeopath in N.Y. and our old Dr. Donovan thought very highly of him.
>
> I enclose his address [Richard Reisig, M.D., 205 West 56th Street]— I would tell him you are a friend of Mr. Curtis, and that one of his family advised you to consult him.
>
> Now, Charley, here is another "pint." You've got to take a rest and your "Grandma" is going to help you to do it, and it is your "bounden duty" to show your love and confidence in her, by taking what she can spare *just as well as not*, and dear Charley I shall feel *dreadfully hurt* if you aren't willing to give me this *real pleasure*.
>
> Don't mind any answer to this note but mind your Grandmother.
>
> Ever affectionately,
> SBS[10]

While CCB was opening Mrs. Shaw's letter and finding her check (amount unknown), her second daughter Susannah, May Minturn's mother, and in CCB's term "une grande dame," called on Louie at home and gave her a check for $1,600, the rent for a year. For the next twelve months, at least, the family could stay in its home, and young Charles continue at his school nearby.[11] Bob Minturn gave CCB a check for $1,000; and independent of the Shaw family another friend who had been watching the situation, Henry Galbraith Ward, a fellow admiralty lawyer, one day said to him, "Burley, you must need a little money. Take this"—a check for $500. That CCB accepted these gifts speaks to the gravity of his illness, for he had an average man's pride, and perhaps a good deal more. Yet at age thirty-four, a lawyer, and father of three, he could not support himself and his family.[12]

Evidently Mrs. Shaw's Dr. Reisig was not helpful. Leaving their children at home with their Uncle Albert in charge and Louie's sisters Grace and Edith in an apartment nearby, and "Cousin" Lizzie, "Aunt" Lotta, May Minturn, "Uncle" Joe Evans, and the Burlingham grandparents dropping by regularly, CCB and Louie went to Philadelphia to see a doctor recommended by May Minturn. The man was a colleague of S. Weir Mitchell, a neurologist internationally known for his development of a "rest cure" for nervous disorders. The Burlinghams put up at the Hotel Bellevue, where the doctor came to make his examination, but "he wasn't greatly interested, made a few suggestions, and we went on to the next stage, Old Point Comfort, Virginia,"[13] where, presumably on the doctor's recommendation, they took a room at the Hygeia, one of the country's oldest resort hotels and popular with Northerners and Southerners alike. Built in 1821 on a point where Chesapeake Bay meets the Atlantic, it was famous for its salubrious sea air. As CCB recalled,

> The huge hotel was almost empty, and we sat or crept about on the vast piazzas and took our meals with a dozen guests in the enormous dining room. One morning who should appear but Carlotta! She had come by train and boat to Norfolk and the Point to bring us comfort and help. And of all days it was her birthday, November 30, to her mother and grandmother the most precious day in the calendar.[14]

In Virginia, CCB's health still did not improve, and he and Louie moved on to Morristown, New Jersey, where he seems to have entered some sort of rest home or sanitarium. "I was put to bed, as I should have been weeks before, and stayed in bed for a long time and got better and better. I acquired a very good technique, and when I began to feel giddy, and knew I was going to faint, I made my way speedily to a bed or couch and fainted without giving much, if any, trouble."[15] Presumably Louie stayed with him in Morristown, for there are no letters between them, but in April they were again apart and corresponding. Louie was back in New York with the children, and CCB on Staten Island, with Mrs. Shaw's eldest and recently widowed daughter, Anna Curtis, Lizzie's mother. "I guess I am a bit better," he reported, "not much—but I *know* that this is the best place for me. I should be worse in town."[16]

In the midst of the letter, he had a relapse. There are dropped words, strange constructions, sudden jumps in thought, and a handwriting at times strangely spaced. As a final page he enclosed a list that he titled "Causes of present discontent": first, "Weather," then "Tum-tum, little food *pigeons*!!! for dinner and tea—mince and hash and etc." Next, a new heading of "*Symptoms*" followed by "Gen. rockiness," and in huge letters, "D R E A M S." Lastly, under the heading "*Remedy*," he suggests "Louie if possible, A child, pony," and closes with "Bob should have a cup, not with *Love the Giver*, but with *Forgive the Lover*!" And as the final word of the list, "*Fidelio*." Louie, with a wife's understanding, may have been able to follow every thought, or she may have found the letter alarming; but clearly he was not ready to return to work.

For much of the summer of 1893 they were apart. Louie took the children to a cottage in Cornish, New Hampshire, across the Connecticut River from Windsor, Vermont, the nearest large town. CCB went with Carlotta Lowell and her mother to a camp at Westport, New York, on the western shore of Lake Champlain, where he stayed for most of July and all of August. He went on picnics, sometimes riding, sometimes in a carriage, and hiked in the mountains. On 30 August he wrote a long letter to his mother, to thank her for a gift of money and to add:

> I saw Dr. James Putnam at the Camp. He is a specialist in nervous diseases. He thinks the time has come for me to take a somewhat different regime. More exercise—steadily increasing walks and rest afterwards. He encouraged me . . .
>
> I want to make a thorough job of this thing. I shall begin to work a bit now—read a little law and get myself in trim. Dr. Putnam says that I shall never know exactly when I am well; that everything will come hard at first; and that it will do me good now to do a little mental work. It was certainly a great thing for me to go where I was thrown on my own resources. If you had seen the things I did you wouldn't have believed anything was the matter with me. I got *confidence*.[17]

But he still was not well. On returning to Louie in Cornish, while driving the carriage one day, he nearly fell out in a faint. So when she and the children returned to New York, he went to Ashfield House, a large hotel in Ashfield, Massachusetts, where he was under the watchful eyes of Anna Curtis and her daughter Lizzie. He wrote Louie on 10 October, recalling that it was Annie Hoe's birthday and confessing that he was even now "not living in the *very* present." The days passed quickly, he played some "gentle" tennis with Lizzie and was homesick. "I count the days and nights when I go to bed."[18] Then, sometime in November, he returned to New York and to work, having been out of the office for a full year. As Dr. Putnam had predicted, CCB never knew exactly when he had recovered fully. The following summer he was still regaining lost weight.[19]

Neither he nor those who loved him ever were sure of the cause or cure of his sickness. In later years, in an offhand way, he would call it "an attack of nervous prostration," sometimes adding, "My illness was more from under care, I fancy, than from over work." He rarely referred to it, but the memory of it remained fresh and was a reason, seldom fully stated, why in the years ahead he steadily refused to be considered for a seat on a court. To any such suggestion, he always replied that he was physically not up to the job.[20] And he claimed to have learned one lesson from his illness: "Never to eat when tired and to rest either before or after dinner." He also had done much thinking and praying. He wrote to his mother, "I feel that this sickness has been a blessing to me. I have sometimes been a little impatient; but I don't think I have ever really repined. I needed it." Just as he hoped he was "a better *son* for being a father," he hoped now to be a better man for having been so mysteriously ill. In his letters, a harshness of tone in judging others now starts to soften, and he seems to have a greater appreciation of friendship and of God's grace in the gift of health.[21]

But what of the debts he owed to those who had helped him? The financial part of it was easily calculated, and CCB and Louie were always meticulous about money. (In their first year of marriage, when Louie's father sent them a check each month for rent, in the last months the rent was slightly reduced, and they promptly passed back the saving to him.)[22] But in the present instance they either considered the debt too great to repay or thought it perhaps impertinent even to try to repay. Better to make of the rescued life a worthy example of the benefactors' ideals. CCB never forgot what others had done for him. In 1934, in a bar association memorial of Henry Galbraith Ward, he recalled, "He was quick to perceive and to relieve the needs of others, and especially of the young"—a trait that, after his illness, CCB made his own.[23]

In the fall of 1890, the partners at Wing, Shoudy & Putnam had changed the letterhead of their office stationery. In the upper left-hand margin, below their three names, they had added a printer's rule, and below that line CCB's name, thus stating to the world that though not a partner, he was associated with the firm.[24] When he fell ill, the partners held his place for him and throughout his absence did not hire a replacement, not even for a short term. They doubtless had to turn away business they otherwise would have accepted, but their loyalty to CCB ensured that his return to work would be as happy for the firm as for him. Whether his percentage of fees increased at this time is not known, but after he returned to work in November 1893, his anxious discussions with Louie about money ceased. They lived modestly on East Thirty-eighth Street, on what he called "the slummish slopes of Murray Hill," his earnings supported his family, and after ten years of practice he began to attract clients.[25]

In the spring of 1894 he had a case that for the first time as chief counsel took him to the Supreme Court. It began when the Franklin Sugar Refining Company sued the Liverpool steam freighter *Silvia*, owned by the Red Cross Line, for damages to goods in transit; in legal terms the suit was "a libel in admiralty." The sugar company had made "a charter party"—a contract—with the Red Cross Line to carry a shipload of sugar in sacks from Matanzas, Cuba, to Philadelphia, New York, or Boston, and as usual it contained these provisions:

> The vessel shall be tight, staunch, strong and in every way fitted for such a voyage, and receive on board, during the aforesaid voyage, the merchandise hereinafter mentioned (the act of God, adverse winds, restraint of princes and ruler, the Queen's enemies, fire, pirates, accidents to machinery or boilers, collisions, errors of navigation and all other dangers and accidents of the seas, rivers and navigation, of whatever nature and kind soever during the said voyage always excepted).[26]

Both the facts and the law seemed to deny any recovery, and CCB, arguing for the sugar company first in the Southern District Court before Judge Brown and then on appeal to the Second Circuit Court, lost in both.[27] The client, however, wanted to continue. So CCB appealed to the Supreme Court.

In the Court's opinion associate justice Horace Gray set out the facts of the case:

> The *Silvia*, with the sugar in her lower hold, sailed from Matanzas for Philadelphia on the morning of February 16, 1894. The compartment

between decks next the forecastle had been fitted up to carry steerage passengers, but on this voyage contained only spare sails and ropes, and a small quantity of stores. This compartment had four round ports on each side, which were about eight or nine feet above the water line when the vessel was deep laden. Each port was eight inches in diameter, furnished with a cover of glass five eighths of an inch thick, set in a brass frame, as well as with an inner cover or dummy of iron. When the ship sailed, the weather was fair, and the glass covers were tightly closed, but the iron covers were left open in order to light the compartment should it become necessary to get anything from it, and the hatches were battened down, but could have been opened in two minutes by knocking out the wedges. In the afternoon of the day of sailing, the ship encountered rough weather, and the glass cover of one of the ports was broken—whether by the force of the seas or by floating timber or wreckage, was wholly a matter of conjecture—and the water came in through the port, and damaged the sugar.[28]

The Harter Act, passed by Congress in 1893, controlled the law of the case, and its third section stated:

If the owner of any vessel transporting merchandise or property to or from any port in the United States of America shall exercise due diligence to make the said vessel in all respects seaworthy and properly manned, equipped and supplied, neither the vessel, her owner or owners, agent or charters, shall become or be held responsible for damage or loss resulting from faults or errors in navigation or in the management of said vessel.[29]

Under this law, CCB had to show that the broken glass port was the result not of a fault or error in the management of the vessel, but rather of the owner, who in some way had failed to make the vessel seaworthy before she sailed from Matanzas. He had to convince the court that the Red Cross Line had sent its steamer to sea in an "unseaworthy" condition in that the iron covers for the glass portholes had not been closed. Only then could the sugar company hold the ship, and ultimately her owner, responsible for the spoiled sugar. Argument was set for 8 March 1895, and CCB, with Putnam assisting, appeared for Franklin Sugar. Opposing him was J. Parker Kirlin, of the New York City firm of Convers and Kirlin, a lawyer whom CCB knew well.

In those days, the Supreme Court had no building of its own (not until 1935), but sat in the Old Senate Chamber, which had become available in

1860 when wings were added to the Capitol to give the ever-expanding House and Senate larger halls. The old chamber, as renovated for the court, was an attractive semicircular room, with a high half-domed ceiling and a large central skylight. The nine justices sat on a dais before a loggia of gray-green marble Ionic columns behind which hung dark red drapes. Below the judges was an open area with tables for counsel, and behind these were more chairs and benches, with red velvet cushions, for spectators. The semicircular wall at the back was white, set off in sections by pilasters faced with the gray-green marble, and at the center of each section was a console supporting the marble bust of a former chief justice.

Besides its architectural features, the room had tradition and history. Here, the Senate had confirmed the treaty providing for the Louisiana Purchase and ratified the treaties ending the 1812 War and the Mexican War. Here, during and after the Civil War, the Supreme Court had decided a series of cases establishing it as the final arbiter on state and federal legislation. Here, during the years of Reconstruction, the Court had held ten federal statutes unconstitutional (as compared with two between 1789 and 1864). And here, in March 1895, the Court, hearing argument in the same week as the *Silvia* case, held the 1894 income tax law, applying a flat 2 percent on all incomes above $4,000, unconstitutional—a decision that led directly to the adoption of the Sixteenth Amendment to the Constitution in 1913.[30]

The justices wore robes of solid black and simple cut, and custom decreed that attorneys in the courtroom should wear formal clothing. By 1893 this meant a "morning suit," typically a long dark coat, gray-striped trousers, waistcoat, stiff collar, and dark cravat. So attired, CCB put forth his client's claim, but his arguments left the Court unconvinced. Justice Gray, writing for a unanimous court, affirmed the decisions of the lower courts to dismiss the libel on the ship.[31]

Following Shoudy's death in August 1894, Wing, Shoudy & Putnam dissolved and a new firm promptly took its place: Wing, Putnam & Burlingham.[32] Staying in the same office at 45 William Street, the three new partners associated with themselves two lawyers whose names were listed on the left-hand margin of the stationery as if full partners. These were Everett Masten and James Forrester, and their names, in that order, were directly beneath CCB's. Nowhere in the list was there a line to proclaim a difference of rank or relationship, but traditionally the senior partners' names come first, and other indications also suggest that Masten and Forrester were junior to the three, with a smaller share of profits.[33]

Masten, the elder of the two and a graduate of Columbia College and Law School, was ten years younger than CCB, had started with the firm as a clerk in 1889, and would stay with it until he retired in 1942. He lived on Staten Island, where he could pursue his beloved canoeing, sailing, and fishing, even as he developed a remarkable skill in drafting and redrafting the documents of maritime trade—insurance contracts, charter parties, and bills of lading. Well liked and recognized as an authority in his niche, he was soft-spoken, quiet, and inclined to keep to himself.[34]

James Forrester's background was quite different. He lacked both college and law school, and sometimes in the mid-1880s had applied to the firm for work of any sort. CCB remembered him as "an overgrown boy, poorly dressed, his yellowish overcoat much too small for him." CCB and Putnam had explained that they had no place for an office boy, "but something about him appealed to Putnam, who stepped into the hall, called him back and engaged him at $7 or $8 a week." It soon transpired that Forrester's father, an estate manager in England, had died penniless, and the boy was supporting his mother and older brother in Brooklyn by working several jobs. He was highly competent, and to retain him the firm raised his pay. Meanwhile, having taught himself German, Forrester earned considerable fees for translating. As the years passed, he secretly attended law school in the evenings, passed the bar examinations, and by the early 1890s worked for the firm full-time as a lawyer. Since he had a flair for accounting, he made himself an expert in bankruptcy actions, and in one long-running case, *In Re Vetterlein*, soon was the only one in the office who knew what it was about. He was less cultured than Masten, had no interests outside the law, and worked incessantly. CCB recalled that Forrester had "round shoulders and a contracted chest. He took no exercise and gave no thought to his health. Finally he had several hemorrhages from the lungs. We sent him off to Saranac, where he spent several months. I never expected to see him again; but breathing the pure air, playing whist and drinking whiskey he recovered." The whiskey, however, soon turned into a curse, and Forrester became an alcoholic. Sometime in late 1910 or early 1911 he left the firm, and in 1915 his name "was stricken from Roll of Attorneys by Appellate Division, First Department." The next year he died.[35]

To these five partners a sixth was added in 1896, Esek Cowen, whose name for four years led all the rest, Cowen, Wing, Putnam & Burlingham. What the partners hoped to gain from Cowen, or on what terms, is unclear. In the years 1865–90 he had developed a practice in Troy and Albany of railroad and patent law, and presumably he brought his clients with him.

But when in January 1900 he died, the firm reverted to Wing, Putnam & Burlingham, and whatever business Cowen had brought apparently evaporated.[36]

For almost a decade thereafter the firm remained the five partners, supported by a small office staff. How they divided their profits is not known. Probably Wing and Putnam took the largest shares, CCB a middling one, and Masten and Forrester the smallest. Wing could claim to have supplied many of the best clients and Putnam to be the outstanding litigator. They were also elders in age and experience, considerations that lawyers are slow to discount. Putnam, however, was the leader, and his plans, his schedule, his decisions ruled. One summer, before returning from England, Putnam fired off his orders, and from the office in New York CCB reported to Louie, "Poor Wing had as bad a time as I. Putnam wrote for him to come home, just as he had got to Nantucket and was starting out on excursion." And Wing came back.[37]

The firm's staff are almost anonymous. There was an elderly man named Aylwin, perhaps a lawyer or a bookkeeper, and a Miss Middleditch, who was probably a typist. By then the typewriter, which when introduced had typed only in capitals, had become more practical, and with increasing use had brought women into the office in place of hand-copying male clerks. And there was an office boy, Ten Eyck Beardsley. Years later and long since a successful lawyer elsewhere, he reviewed for CCB the office at the turn of the century: "Mr. Putnam was a fine man and I think a good lawyer, but I doubt if he ever laughed." Masten "was a fine fellow, too; but I do not recall anything he ever said except when poor Muir [otherwise unknown] was fired for being away one too many Mondays, Masten said he hoped the discharge was not unjust. I liked him for that."[38] Beardsley, smart and energetic, liked CCB's style, and had some affection for him. He recalled a preliminary hearing in a suit against the North German Lloyd Line, in which CCB was "a bit facetious" and the line's attorney, a large, pompous man in flashy attire, grew irritated, an emotion that increased his lisp. "I with you'd thop," he thundered, an explosion that Beardsley and others in the courtroom found very comic.[39] Out of such experiences CCB, looking back, could say, "I have enjoyed the practice of law, and especially admiralty."[40]

Besides admiralty cases, the firm was ready to take almost any kind of work a client offered, mostly decedents' estates, real estate, commercial contracts, and even an occasional criminal action. One odd nonmaritime case that CCB brought to the firm and which generated an unusual amount of publicity was the divorce of the actress Julia Marlowe from

Robert Taber, the youngest of the four Taber brothers (the eldest, Harry, had married Louie's sister Fanny).

Taber's acting career had blossomed in the late 1880s, and he had played increasingly with Julia Marlowe, whose ability, at least in these years, was perhaps less vital than her charming face and personality. In a performance of *Cymbeline* in September 1891, CCB had thought Taber "fine" as Posthumus, but had judged Marlowe "very sweet but not powerful." Nevertheless, the two found success together, and in 1894 they married and formed a company with the intent of playing mostly Shakespeare. One of their productions, which unhappily emphasized a difference in their styles, was *Henry IV, Part 1* in which he played Hotspur and she Prince Hal. Taber as usual was strong and vigorous, even to a fault, whereas Marlowe was appealing but frail. Together, they seemed to throw the play out of balance, a defect increasingly charged against them.[41] So they agreed to separate, and in the fall of 1897 he went to England (where he successfully played Macduff to Johnston Forbes-Robertson's Macbeth and the young prince Alexis to Henry Irving's Peter the Great). Meanwhile, in the United States, Marlowe, too, flourished, leading them to decide on an amicable separation and then, in December 1899, a divorce. For the latter they went to Stowe, Vermont, where his mother lived and where, unlike in New York, Marlowe need not allege adultery, only "intolerable severity."

Marlowe's maid, Mary Daly, testified at the hearing. "She told her story," CCB recalled, "but embroidered it shockingly in order to make assurance doubly sure. The New York City newspapers printed her testimony in full, and Taber was overwhelmed with shame, for the stories that Mary told were absolutely false." And so despite the couple's efforts to avoid unattractive publicity, the *Times* trumpeted on its front page that Taber had abused his wife and "one time he threw her out of their bed and choked her."[42]

Though Queen Victoria, by knighting Henry Irving in 1895—the first actor so honored—had given the profession greater respectability, much of the American public still believed that actors by nature and calling were dissolute if not downright sinful. Asked for their advice, CCB and Joe Evans urged Taber to leave the country, go to London, and join Irving's company, which he did. The divorce, ending so unhappily for a friend, gave CCB little pleasure; and despite his interest in the stage, divorce and theater law were specialties he did not pursue.[43]

To his family life, in all aspects, CCB brought the same intensity and loyalty that he brought to the law. When Louie's father died in 1896, leaving his second wife a widow with a child, there was not much inheritance for

Louie and her five siblings. She and CCB stayed on in their house on the edge of Murray Hill, acting as guardians to Louie's younger sisters, Grace and Edith, who by combining the incomes of their two small trusts managed to afford an apartment nearby. Grace eventually would marry, but Edith remained single and in middle age declined into ill health.[44]

CCB's parents continued to live in Mount Vernon, but in 1895 his father had a stroke that left him partially paralyzed. Though Dr. Burlingham struggled to carry on his work as secretary to the American Baptist Missionary Union, he no longer was able to speak in public, and after 1899 could not work at all. He awaited death with resignation, his faith strong. To a resolution of the Southern New York Baptist Association expressing gratitude for his long service to the church, he replied, "My fourscore line is nearly reached, and my half-century marriage anniversary is near. I have not long to stay. I will wait and pray and try to be patient till the time for crossing the river comes in God's own good time. The Great Pilot will carry us all safely over. We will trust him."[45] But God did not call Aaron Burlingham until 1905, and the long wait grew hard. CCB soon reported to Louie that his father had become "very weepy" and would sit for hours alone in the nearby church. Another time he wrote, "Father and Mother are quite lonely, and I am glad I can be with them, now that Albert is away. It is hard for mother to have company, but now I see that Albert is right and it is better to have people with them than to be alone." He concluded a bit desperately, "We *must* do something." But nothing he and Albert did seemed entirely satisfactory.[46]

When CCB visited his parents, who tired easily in conversation and went early to bed, he had time for reading or for writing letters to Louie and his children. In the summer of 1897, he progressed through a collection of books on the Oxford movement in the Anglican church, reread the sermons and public speeches of Phillips Brooks, and looked forward to works by Arthur Stanley, the deceased dean of Westminster. At the same time, he read Kipling and Dickens, particularly recommending the latter's *Great Expectations* to his thirteen-year-old son, Charles.[47]

CCB's letters to his children were notably adult. Young Charles, at age twelve, received one on a sheet of office stationery on which the letterhead had printed awry. It began: "You see something happened to this sheet, like the Democratic party at Chicago when it got turned askew on the currency question." He went on to explain the debate over silver that was roiling national politics that summer of 1896, ending, "Now, if you will read, mark, and inwardly digest this stupid dry old Daddy's letter, you'll know a good deal about the silver question."[48]

His first letter to his daughter, Nancy, also written in the office and sent to her when she was five and a half, reads in full:

2 August 1891

My dear Nancy:

I have never had a letter from you, but I have never written to you. So why should I expect one. I am going to tell you a story about a little girl and littler boy, whom I saw while I was going away far from my chimney. The little girl was bigger than you, about as big as Margaret Beaman, and the little boy was not so big as you, about like Charlie Perkins. They could not speak English. They had come with their father and mother thousands of miles, across the seas.

Well, when we were waiting for a new engine to take us on, these little children were waiting, too, sitting on some trunks. They looked tired and sad. So I gave them each an orange. And what do you think they did? They did not know how to say "Thank you." But the little girl jumped up from her seat and made me a pretty little curtsey, and put out her hand and shook mine.

The little boy had put his orange in his pocket, without saying or doing anything; but his sister took him by the sleeve and said something to him which I couldn't understand, and then he, too, got up and put out his hand in the same way.

I was very happy to be thanked in so pretty a way.

Now, dear little daughter, will you write me a letter? Mother will help you do it.

I think of you, my children, and of your dear, dear mother all the time. Please tell Charles that I shall write to him very soon.

From your own dear father

Charles C. Burlingham.[49]

Beneath his name CCB drew a large *N*, for Nancy, which he enclosed in a circle, a common way at the time to say "With balloons of love."

It is a formidable letter for a five-and-a-half-year-old, even for one with a mother to help her, and not at all in the "See Nancy run" style that pediatricians sometimes recommend on a theory of allowing children to enjoy the childishness of childhood. CCB longed for his children to be adults so that he could talk with them as equals. His love for them was intense, perhaps too intense, for not all children benefit from such focused attention. With their mother's help, and in their childish way, they responded to his letters. When they did not, he complained: "I should like a letter from my daughter."[50]

His correspondence with Louie never ceased. Day after day he confirmed his love and need of her. In July 1888, only four months after the birth of their third and last child, their Victorian reticence about their sexual relations briefly yields to anxiety. He is with his parents in Mount Vernon and Louie is in Washington, Connecticut, with the children. She feels ill, and fears she is again pregnant. In a long letter on a variety of persons and subjects, he comes back again and again to her fear.

> Louie, dear, I feel very much worried about you . . . If it is, as you fear, a little baby that is troubling you, I shall be so sad to think that I have brought so much more trouble and pain to my dearest love. Oh, Louie, you are my truest love. I am father to you, and husband, and lover. I think of you with my other children, as the dearest child of all. And I think of you as their mother too. You are the smartest loveliest mother . . . I can't keep worrying. All day long I have been thinking of you dear, and wishing myself near you to comfort and rest you.
>
> If you have any doubts whether you are going to have a baby, then you needn't worry, for you would most certainly know it.
>
> If you really believe that you are, then tell me certainly that we may be sadly happy together.
>
> I am not going to say anything more till I hear from you. I wish I were with you.[51]

Whatever was bothering Louie, she was not pregnant; and the number of their children remained three. Their privacy about such matters precludes any certainty about their sexual relations and practices. His parents were fervent Protestants of a church and generation that probably viewed any such talk, even of conception and pregnancy, as sinful. CCB and Louie apparently were more open about such matters, but not greatly so. He writes as if they did not limit intercourse to the procreation of children and as if they knew and practiced the current prophylactic precautions against pregnancies, but whether they did or not seems less important than the fact of their sexual compatibility. He found her physically attractive, and she responded. Their marriage was happy.

8

Taking on Tammany Hall

FOR MANY PEOPLE TODAY, the period 1890–1905 lives most vividly in its cheerful and sentimental songs—"After the Ball," "The Bowery," and the bicycler's "Daisy." New York's Fifth Avenue then was at its most fashionable, adorned by mansions of the rich who summered at Newport or crossed to Europe on ever more luxurious liners. Men's clothing, rejecting the rumpled look of the Civil War era, adopted the careful tailoring—cutaway suits, capes, and knickerbockers—of the portly Prince of Wales, who in 1901 became King Edward VII. And for American women, the magazine illustrator Charles Dana Gibson set the style with his tall "Gibson Girl," who favored broad shoulders, puffed sleeves, and a corseted waist.

Early in this period, the frontier was said to have closed—an event without time or place yet powerfully affecting the American imagination. For more than three hundred years the frontier had been out there, available as an escape, a refuge, a challenge. Now railroads and telegraph connected every city, big or small, while telephones compressed time and distance even more. In the past, the great fortunes typically had been mercantile in origin, based on the speed of clipper ships sailing to Europe and to China, and established by men joining in partnerships, often for a single venture, and then putting their profits into real estate. Now the fortunes were industrial, founded in railroads, oil, and steel, and organized in business corporations that would endure even after their creators died. A sense of possibility and progress hovered and was buoyed by a constant flow of industrial inventions displayed at state and national fairs, of which the two most famous were the World's Columbian Exposition at Chicago in 1893, celebrating the four hundredth anniversary of the discovery of America by Columbus, and, in 1904, the centennial Louisiana Purchase Exposition at St. Louis (with its song "Meet Me in St. Louis, Louis").

There was, however, a less cheery side to American life. In 1888 James

Bryce published *The American Commonwealth*, a study of the country's people and institutions, which for perceptive analysis by a foreigner was second only to Alexis de Tocqueville's *Democracy in America* (1838). In his chapter "The Working of City Governments," Bryce concluded decisively: "There is no denying that the government of cities is the one conspicuous failure of the United States." To his eye, the faults of the federal and state governments were "insignificant compared with the extravagance, corruption, and mismanagement" of most of the nation's municipal governments. New York's was the worst. But no city with more than 200,000 in population had escaped the "poison germs," and some as small as 70,000 were infected.[1]

The chief virus was the political parties' spoils system, "whereby office becomes the reward of party service, and the whole machinery of party government made to serve, as its main object, the getting and keeping of places." The larger the city the more pernicious the system: "For in great cities we find an ignorant multitude, largely composed of recent immigrants, untrained in self-government," and thus easy for local political leaders to organize and control for their own enrichment. Bryce also suggested other reasons for the country's failure with city government, but despite his brilliant analyses and telling examples, his scholarly style limited the book to educated readers.[2]

In 1890, however, Jacob Riis, a police reporter turned lecturer and journalist, published *How the Other Half Lives*, an account of life in the city's tenements. Using studies by health and charity workers and drawing on twelve years' experience on New York's Lower East Side, he wrote in a vivid, popular style and offered thirty-nine photographs, reproduced as halftones and line engravings, that spoke even to the illiterate. Confirming with new evidence many of Bryce's conclusions, Riis carried them to a wider public. He began his final chapter with a question: "What, then, are the bald facts with which we have to deal in New York?" And he started his reply with the assertion: "That we have a tremendous, ever swelling crowd of wage earners which it is our business to house decently." Americans, he assumed, were their "brother's keeper." They owed the country's immigrants better housing than the cramped, unsanitary buildings known as tenements.

Legally, a tenement was a house "occupied by three or more families, living independently and doing their cooking on the premises." In fact, it was usually a narrow five-story building, twelve small rooms to a floor with the ground floor typically a store or saloon. In Riis's worst example of overcrowding, one such building housed 101 adults and 91 children. "The tenements today," he insisted, "are New York, harboring three-fourths of its population." His friend Josephine Shaw Lowell, who in 1894 arbitrated a strike called by tenement garment workers against retail clothing manufacturers, put the immigrants' importance more bluntly: "The laboring classes are the people—all the people. The few people that don't belong to the laboring classes don't amount to anything."[3]

Because of Bryce, Riis, Lowell, and others favoring reform as part of progress, in the early 1890s a movement started in New York, as in other cities, to reform city government. The aim, at least in New York, was to reform it not only politically but also, if possible, in all its social, economic, and educational activities, a movement in which Burlingham for ten years had a modest but significant part. Living on East Thirty-eighth Street, he could see firsthand something of life in the tenements that lay just a few blocks to the east, and he was familiar with the projects of St. George's Church that aimed to help its tenement families. Moreover, dining often with Lowell and her mother, he heard continually of the poor, the tenements, and the problems caused by immigration.

After the Civil War, immigration into the United States, without inspection, regulation, or limit on numbers, overwhelmed New York, the chief port of entry. In all, an estimated twenty million immigrants arrived in the nineteenth century, four-fifths of them after 1860, with the greatest number staying in New York. Poor, mostly uneducated, and offered no assistance by any government, federal, state, or city, they were easily cheated by the unscrupulous. Debarking in Battery Park, at the southern tip of Manhattan, they were processed through Castle Clinton (Ellis Island did not open until January 1892). Unless met by family, they often fell prey to "runners" who led them to boardinghouses charging high for food and lodging. From these, they scattered quickly to sections of the city where living was cheapest: the shantytowns in what after 1858 became Central Park, the tenements of the Lower East Side, or the slightly better housing of the Upper East Side. Regardless of place, they soon heard from neighbors that their best friend was the local district leader of the Democratic Party's organization, Tammany Hall.

Tammany's "boss" in the years 1886–1901 was Richard Croker, who at age five had come from Ireland in 1846 with his parents and lived his first years in the city in a shanty, though later, when his father found a steady job in a livery stable, the family moved to better quarters on Twenty-sixth Street near Third Avenue. As a boy, Croker sporadically attended a primary school, where the teacher traced letters and numbers with a pointed stick in a box of sand. The city's primary schools often had as many as a hundred children to a teacher, and instruction usually was by rote, the memorizing and reciting of prescribed answers. Later, off and on, Croker went to grammar school (grades 4–6), but mostly he educated himself in the streets, where he became a member of the Fourth Avenue Tunnel gang. Soon, by the power of his fists, he became its leader. He worked for a time as a machinist, but discovered he could do better by joining the Democratic Party, whose leaders arranged for him to be an attendant at a municipal court, with an annual salary of $1,200. Working his way up the party ladder, he became the protégé of "Honest John" Kelly, who had remade the party after its defeat in the early 1870s under Boss Tweed. When Kelly died in 1885, Croker succeeded him, and as Tammany's "Boss Croker" he was the most important Democrat in the state, "King of the City." Once when he entered New York harbor on a liner, a police boat greeted him with a twenty-one-gun salute. For his entrance to a banquet in his honor at the Metropolitan Opera House, the band played "Hail to the Chief," a song already long associated with the president of the United States.[4]

Meanwhile, New York's tenement population steadily increased, along with immigration. In the last fifteen years of the century the number of immigrants per year averaged slightly more than 500,000, and by 1903 the figure reached 800,000 and for the next ten years hovered annually at 1 million. By 1890 the city's Tenth Ward had a density of 522 persons per acre (whereas the most crowded acres in Philadelphia had only 118, Chicago 84 [in 1895], and Boston 157 [in 1898]). By 1908 New York was said to have slums more crowded than Calcutta, and on its Lower East Side, below Fourteenth Street, a population larger than Buffalo and Pittsburgh combined. Riis, for one, favored a limit on immigration, for in their numbers the immigrants were simply too many for the available housing, schools, and jobs.[5]

Some succeeded; some failed. One who succeeded, an immigrant of a later generation than Croker, was Robert F. Wagner (1877–1953), who advanced through the city's public schools to City College, graduating in 1898, and then rising in Tammany and posts in the state government, ultimately becoming an outstanding U.S. senator (1926–49). But he never forgot that he rose on the backs of his parents, brothers, and sisters. His parents had come to New York from Germany in 1886 and moved into Yorkville, on the Upper East Side. His father, a dyer, unable to find a job, had served as a janitor to several tenements, earning five dollars a week and a basement apartment for himself, his wife, and their six children. To make ends meet everyone worked except the youngest, Bob, whose tuition, after the first six grades (offered free by the city) was paid by the sacrifices of his brothers and sisters. His parents, after ten years of failure, returned to Germany; the children remained in New York. Asked one day while senator about life as an immigrant boy, Wagner burst out: "I came through it, yes. But that was luck, luck, luck! Think of the others!"[6]

Mostly because of Riis's lectures, books, and articles and the work of Lowell's Charity Organization Society, the problems of tenement housing were addressed. Riis had his vivid stories and examples to stir people, and the society had its statistics and studies. It also had in Lawrence Veiller, who was in charge of its Tenement House Committee, an executive of remarkable persistence and vision. In February 1900 Veiller mounted a Tenement House Exhibit that along with facts, figures, and photographs presented models for better buildings as well as a papier-mâché reproduction of an actual block of tenements. The latter showed how the existing buildings, though conforming to state and city laws, were unsafe and unsanitary. There were few requirements for fireproof construction. The air shafts between buildings were typically only twenty-eight inches wide and closed at both ends, blocking ventilation. Toilets were often one to a building, in the basement or in the yard, and each used daily by up to a hundred people. Even if each floor had a toilet, it would serve three or four families. Usually there was no bathtub, and estimates suggested that 65 percent of the people in the city had no access to a bath. One in ten died of tuberculosis.[7]

The state legislature in Albany, pushed by public anger and Governor Theodore Roosevelt, authorized the appointment of a state commission. Its report led to the Tenement House Law of 1901, which required all new construction to include a wider, open-at-the-sides air shaft between buildings and a toilet in each apartment (to which the builder sometimes added the less expensive tub). Moreover, the entire first floor of each six-story house had to be constructed of fireproof material. Though the city's housing slowly improved, as late as 1939 two million New Yorkers still lived in "old tenements."[8]

The way in which the movement for better housing led from the city to Albany, to the state legislature and governor, was typical of what reformers were discovering: whatever the field of endeavor—housing, health, education, parks, the courts, prisons, charities—the road to improvement led directly to politics. First to Boss Croker and Tammany Hall, for the Democratic Party controlled the city; then to Albany where the Republican party, led by Boss Thomas Platt, controlled the state legislature; and finally to the governor, who was usually, though not always, a Republican. But first, Tammany Hall.

By 1890, under Croker, Tammany was close to the height of its power. It controlled the elections in Manhattan (New York County) and a small part of the Bronx, already incorporated into the city. Soon, when Brooklyn, Queens, and Staten Island joined Manhattan and the Bronx to form the five boroughs of Greater New York, it dominated still more. But already in the 1880s it was one of the largest business organizations in the country, larger than Andrew Carnegie's steel company. If Tammany won elections in Manhattan and the Bronx, it had at its disposal 12,000 jobs with an annual payroll of $12 million.[9]

Founded in 1788, the Tammany Society initially was a patriotic craftsmen's guild or fraternal order, though it soon took political positions and endorsed candidates. Its transformation into a political machine structured as a patriarchal hierarchy is usually set in 1854, with the election of a member, Fernando Wood, as mayor of New York. Although William M. Tweed, Tammany boss from 1863 to 1871, was a Protestant, its leaders increasingly were Irish Catholic immigrants or their descendants, and it operated most efficiently under the leadership of Croker's mentor Kelly (1872–85), Croker (1886–1901), and Charles F. Murphy (1902–24). Of the eighty years from 1854 to 1934, Tammany governed New York for seventy.[10]

The organization's chain of command typically started with a tenement captain who reported to a block or precinct captain, a member of an election district committee, led by the district leader. This man, boss of the district clubhouse, usually held open house twice a week, when party workers—or anyone in the district—could meet their elected and appointed officeholders. The district leader was the workhorse of the Tammany organization, and because in direct contact with the voters below and leaders above, he had great power. If disaffected, on Election Day he could give the appearance of working hard to turn out the vote while in fact doing little. Or, as sometimes happened, by leading a revolt he could win for his own men the offices and salaries he denied to Tammany's candidates.

In turn, the district leader was a member of the assembly district committee, in charge of the larger district from which an assemblyman was elected to the state legislature. And the assembly district leaders formed the county executive committee, headed by a chairman who was nominally the leader of the county's Democratic Party—except that often the most important person did not hold the top office. Croker, for instance, on succeeding Kelly, instead of becoming county chairman took the post of chairman of the finance committee of Tammany Hall, leaving the appearance of leadership to a deputy, John C. Sheehan. But no one doubted who was boss.

On Election Day, Tammany would field a slate of candidates for various municipal and state offices, and the district leaders were expected to turn out the vote and elect the Tammany men by big majorities. Votes sometimes were bought—top price in the 1890s usually was five dollars—but the majorities more often were ensured by "repeaters" who voted "early and often." It was said that a man with a full face of hair could vote at least four times, fooling the election clerk and reform poll-watchers by gradually shaving, first to side-whiskers, full mustache, and trimmed beard, then to mustache alone, and finally clean-shaven. If the clerk and poll-watchers were Tammany-controlled, whether by loyalty, fear, or cynicism, there was no effectual limit. In 1865 in Greenpoint, Brooklyn, where Croker was not even a resident, he voted seventeen times for the Democratic candidate for constable.[11]

Voting was public and brawling at the polls frequent. There was as yet no secret ballot. Voting chits were prepared not by the city but by the political parties and handed to the voters by party stalwarts at the ballot box—allowing the latter a close look at who voted and how. The district leader for the Bowery, "Big Tim" Sullivan, was notorious for his use of repeaters, for his threats of violence, and for all but marching his voters to the polls in groups of ten. When in the 1892 presidential election the Republican Benjamin Harrison defeated the Democrat Grover Cleveland, one of Big Tim's precincts voted 388 for Cleveland and 4 for Harrison. Reporting to Croker, Sullivan promised, "Harrison got one more vote than I expected there, but I'll find that feller!" In Tammany's Bible, the First Commandment was loyalty to the district leader.[12]

In most cases, Tammany gained that loyalty without bribes or threats. The district leader, working through his precinct captains, earned it by his attention to his people, attention that no one else in the city seemed disposed to grant. Though perhaps a drink bought in a saloon, or a sack of coal or turkey at Christmas, or a hunk of ice in the summer may have won votes in the tenements, these favors probably mattered less than personal services. When a child was in trouble at school or with the police, parents went to the precinct captain for help. They were apt also to go to him for a doctor or a lawyer, or for any purpose, personal or commercial. Need a dispensation from the city to start a business? Call first on the precinct captain. Call at any hour. Help was given without regard to creed or color, and from the poor the only payment asked was a vote at the polls.

Croker one day, on a liner crossing from Liverpool to New York, discussed with an English journalist the reason and nature of the spoils system in New York's municipal and state government.

Politics are impossible without the spoils . . . Look the facts in the face. There are in our country and in New York a small number of citizens who might reasonably be expected to respond to the appeal of patriotic and civic motives. They are what you would call the cultured class . . . From them, no doubt, you might expect to meet with such response to your appeals as would enable you to run your State upon high principles and dispense with spoils . . . [But] cultured leisured citizens will not touch political work—no, not with their little fingers. All your high principles will not induce [them] to take more than a fitful interest in an occasional election . . . Do you expect the same lofty motives to be sufficient to interest the masses in politics? . . . And so we need to bribe them with spoils . . . I admit it is not the best way. But think of what New York is and what the people of New York are. One-half, more than one-half, are of foreign birth. We have thousands upon thousands of men who are alien born, who have no ties connecting them with the city or the State. They do not speak our language, they do not know our laws, they are the raw material with which we have to build up the State. How are we to do it? . . . Tammany looks after them for the sake of their vote . . . If we go down into the gutter, it is because there are men in the gutter; and you have to go down where they are if you are to do anything with them.[13]

As much as Bryce, Croker was a political thinker, but in this famous interview, published in 1897 in the London *Review of Reviews*, he was not telling the whole truth about Tammany. While helping poor and ill-housed immigrants and educating them in the ways of democracy, Tammany also preyed on them.

It was not just that Tammany raised the cost of government for everyone, rich and poor alike. Boss Tweed and his colleagues had stolen somewhere between $30 and $200 million out of their dealings with the city. Because of lost and destroyed records the exact amount was never settled, but a state investigating commission in 1877 (in an opinion accepted by Bryce) concluded that "more than one-half of all the present city debts are the direct results of [Tweed's] intentional and corrupt misrule." At the close of 1876 the city's debt totaled $113 million.[14]

Boss Croker and his deputies were less greedy, though most died millionaires many times over. There was also a more personal side to corruption in the sale of public office: for instance, in 1885 in New York County, a Tammany nomination for sheriff cost the candidate $10,000. The amount supposedly was easy to recoup from a post with annual fees of $50,000. To be nominated in 1905 for a seat on the state Supreme Court, where the term was fourteen years, the fee was a year's salary, $17,500. Commercial companies doing business with the city were expected to pay in stock or cash for their contracts, and illegal enterprises regularly paid bribes for protection. In addition, Tammany had what it called "honest graft," such as a tip that a subway extension was planned, say, to Hunts Point in the Bronx, allowing insiders to buy plots along the line at low prices that doubled or tripled when the project was announced.[15]

Other Tammany schemes, such as the Ice Trust, exposed in 1900, stole directly from the poor. In this case, Tammany members colluded with the American Ice Company to give it sole right to land ice at the municipal docks, in effect creating a monopoly in ice. In return, the company gave stock to Tammany officials, including the mayor, Robert C. Van Wyck, whose holding rose in value to almost $700,000 before exposure burst the bubble.[16] In those days before air-conditioning and refrigerators, ice was an important commodity, especially in the hot, cholera-threatened summers. Though the rich could escape to the mountains or shore, the poor had to stay in their tenements. Ice then not only could chill a refreshment or soothe a fever but was a necessity to preserve food. The realization that Tammany's politicians had enriched themselves by gouging the poor shattered the loyalty of many who had always voted the Tammany line.

But if exposure of the Ice Trust did more than most such investigations to change votes at the poll, equally sensational, and better remembered in future years, was Tammany's role in the era's vice scandals. Tammany, and most notoriously "Big Tim" Sullivan, operated protection schemes for saloons, gambling dens, and houses of prostitution, taking money to ensure that police or firemen did not inspect the premises for violations. Or, if an arrest was made, protection ensured the judge's favorable decision. The leader of the ring that organized the city's gamblers, said to number 10,000, was "Big Tim," and he had a hand in the gangs of petty thieves and gunmen, and in the supply of young girls, mostly recruited from the tenements, for the city's red-light districts.[17]

On 14 February 1892, the Reverend Charles H. Parkhurst, pastor of the Madison Square Presbyterian Church, mounted his pulpit and with a sermon opened a campaign to root out "the polluted harpies that under the pretense of governing this city, are feeding day and night on its quivering vitals." He had studied the corruption in person by going in disguise to the saloons and brothels, together with a detective to whom he paid six dollars a day and expenses. On successive Sundays, Parkhurst shocked his congregation with descriptions of what he had learned and seen. He gave the addresses of the saloons, brothels, and gambling dens, and named the politicians profiting from them. His account of one brothel reached a high point of sorts with a description of a "dance of nature" in which, to a piano played by "the Professor," five naked girls danced a can-can. This was followed by a game of "leapfrog," in which the five girls, still naked, jumped over a frog. (Dr. Parkhurst had been reluctant to play the frog, and that role was taken by the detective.) And after each Sunday's sermon, Monday's newspapers repeated it in detail.[18]

Before winter passed, everyone knew of Dr. Parkhurst, and his revelations led directly to the appointment by the state legislature of a commission that held public hearings, called witnesses, and confirmed Parkhurst's tales.[19] In the next election for mayor, in November 1894, the city's voters rejected the Tammany candidate and elected a reformer, William L. Strong. More exposés followed. But for popular excitement none matched Dr. Parkhurst's tours of the underworld.

Reformers were grateful to Parkhurst, of course, but Lowell, for one, thought his role misconceived. "You know, Charlie," she said to CCB, "I don't think that's the function of a clergyman. I think his function is to hold up an impossible ideal." She spoke what he often had heard Phillips Brooks preach, and fifty-one years later, in recalling Lowell, he repeated her remark with approval.[20] Nevertheless, what Parkhurst and others had achieved in the 1894 election had a direct effect on CCB, for as part of Mayor Strong's reform administration in 1895, he took his first public office, as "trustee of common schools" in the Twenty-first Ward.

In the coming battle to reform the city's public school system, CCB's part in two previous reform movements served as preparation. These campaigns were more purely political, and the first started in 1892 with the founding of a network of Good Government Clubs in twenty-three of the city's twenty-four assembly districts. Their aim was to break Tammany's hold on the city by electing reform candidates in the November election of 1894. For two years the club members rang doorbells, issued pamphlets, provided speakers, and on Election Day had poll-watchers at each booth. CCB's friend Richard Welling, a lawyer and a founder of the clubs, though in spirit a man of peace, in size and strength was a giant, and in his autobiography he recalled no violence, saying only, "Shrewd Tammany politicians have more than once admitted that our Clubs manned the polls and watched the count so closely that this gave Strong the victory."[21] Poll-watching as then practiced was not among CCB's talents; nor was public speaking on street corners. He was physically slight, and his voice, though well tuned for a small hall or courtroom, could roar only briefly. His gifts lay elsewhere, and Welling remembered how one day when depressed by a setback, he was rallied by CCB's good humor and ability to keep the distant goal in sight.[22]

Another campaign in which CCB participated was for the adoption of civil service reform and the principle of appointment to office by merit, not patronage. Tammany politicians mocked the idea, calling it "Snivel Service." One, George Washington Plunkitt, described it as "the biggest fraud of the age. It is the curse of the nation. There can't be no real patriotism while it lasts. How are you goin' to interest our young men in their country if you have no offices to give them when they work for their party?"[23] For CCB, however, the Civil Service Reform League and its long campaign to limit the spoils system in government jobs was a familiar cause. Lowell's brother-in-law, George William Curtis, had been its national leader for twenty-five years, until his death in 1892, and the study in the Curtis house on Staten Island, where CCB spent many weeks recuperating from his breakdown, was a library of the movement's history, much of which CCB had absorbed or heard from Curtis himself.[24]

In this long crusade, CCB had a small but continuous role, not without influence. In May 1900, for example, Governor Theodore Roosevelt wrote to him concerning the civil service classifications of city and state jobs: "As soon as I received your letter of the 8th inst. I started in on the stiffening business with the Civil Service Commission." And on the same day, on the same matter, Roosevelt wrote to Silas W. Burt, the civil service commissioner representing New York City, "The inclosed explain themselves. I think Burlingham a pretty good fellow." Both campaigns, for good government and for civil service reform, suggest what CCB was becoming: a man of resilient humor who could rally the dispirited, and who by a letter could stir a powerful official to action.[25]

Undoubtedly CCB's work for the Good Government Clubs, backed by a recommendation from Welling, brought him to Mayor Strong's attention, and the appointment as a trustee of common schools pleased him. His interest in education was strong and not surprising, given its role in his father's life and his own, and the work concerned his home ward, the Twenty-first, stretching from Sixth Avenue to the East River and from Twenty-sixth to Fortieth Street. Encompassing Murray Hill and, to the east, a large area of tenements, it had three primary and three grammar schools. (At that time, the city had no high schools.)[26]

Each of the city's twenty-four wards had a committee of five trustees who were the lay authorities in charge of their schools. To a large extent these trustee committees were autonomous, able to hire and fire teachers, decide which textbooks would be used, initiate plans for new school buildings, and control for the most part their construction. The trustees' plans, however, needed approval by the city Board of Education (twenty-one commissioners appointed by the mayor) and by the city superintendent (appointed by the Board of Education), to whom the city's Board of Estimate, which appropriated funds for school needs, looked for advice on budgets.

Whatever the system's original virtues, by the 1890s it had grown overly complex, inefficient, and open to corruption. Aside from lacking the will, trustees lacked the power (which resided in the state legislature) to redraw ward lines so as to bring the number of pupils in each ward into better balance. (Shifts in population as the city expanded northward had created startling differences: the small downtown Third Ward, for instance, by 1893 had no schools, whereas the large uptown Twelfth Ward had twenty, some with as many as forty teachers—one ward's organization being "larger than the school system of Buffalo.")[27] The system's ambiguities in responsibility frustrated parents and reformers alike. Nominally, education was a function of the state, which set the basic laws governing the formation of school districts, construction of buildings, and administration of the system. But the city or its agencies wrote the minor laws and regulations required to implement the greater, and much of the money to support education was raised through municipal taxes. In theory the citywide Board of Education was more powerful than any committee of trustees, but in fact the trustees of the larger wards were lords in their own fiefs, often declining appointment to the board. Everything about the school system, wrote one reformer, "appears to be involved in a most intricate muddle."[28]

Throughout the 1890s the chief sage and advocate of reform in all matters educational was Nicholas Murray Butler, later president of Columbia University but in this decade dean of its philosophy faculty. In addition, he was the founder and first president (1886–91) of what became Columbia Teachers College. He and his wife lived on East Thirtieth Street, close to Josephine Shaw Lowell. Sometimes CCB, alone or with Louie, on the way home after dining with Mrs. Shaw or Lowell, would stop by the Butlers' for a chat. CCB evidently found Butler's ideas convincing, for in the various posts he held in the years to come, he worked steadily to implement them. Intellectually, he admired Butler greatly; socially, he had reservations that hindered intimacy, for he found Butler without humor and "very stuffy."[29] And he was not alone in this view. (A sentence from Butler's autobiography suggests the defect: on hearing word that President McKinley had been shot, "because of my cordial political and personal relations with the President and my intimate friendship with Theodore

Roosevelt, then Vice-President, I was even more agitated and concerned than most others.")[30]

Nevertheless, Butler's ideas for reform in the school system seemed right in essence: (1) centralize power in a city superintendent and a Board of Education, abolishing the trustees; (2) professionalize the teachers and the city superintendent by promoting teachers on civil service principles instead of "pull" with a trustee; (3) procure a leading educator for city superintendent who could revise the curriculum, reduce the amount of learning by rote, and offer a greater variety of courses; and (4) modernize the system's financial administration so that projects of every kind, from school construction to teachers' pensions, could be accomplished more quickly.

Many people advocated this program in whole or in part. One Good Government Club that devoted itself to public school problems, analyzing issues, distributing pamphlets, and presenting lectures, had an offshoot, the Public Education Association, of which CCB was an active member and which was led by Mrs. William S. Rainsford, wife of the rector of St. George's Church. But no one was so politically astute, tireless, and articulate as Butler in promoting the reform program. In 1891, with William H. Maxwell, superintendent of the schools in Brooklyn, Butler founded the *Educational Review*, which quickly gained national importance. Diane Ravitch, a historian of the New York public schools, has named Butler the "field marshal" of the school reform movement: "He was involved to some degree in virtually every organization that joined the fight . . . Every important reform document about the public schools was either written or edited by Butler."[31]

The need for action was plain, for New York's school system was visibly failing its purpose for thousands of children. In 1895, for instance, quite aside from the number of truants or the quality of the education offered, the schools had to refuse admission to 24,000 children for lack of space, and in 1896 the figure rose to 28,825. The following year Mayor Strong appointed CCB to the Board of Education,[32] and each year that CCB was a school official, 1895–1903, the city built new schools. In 1898–99 it opened nineteen, with 388 classrooms and seats for 18,077 pupils; the next year it opened fifteen, which, with enlargements of old buildings, added 456 classrooms and 20,220 sittings; and in 1900–1901 it opened nineteen new buildings and eight additions, providing 596 classrooms with seats for 27,491. Still, the increase did not meet the need. In the most crowded neighborhoods in Manhattan, Brooklyn, and to a lesser extent Queens, some schools went to part-time classes, a program affecting 52,231 pupils. As the Board of Education's secretary lamented in his report, "In spite of all endeavors, it was impossible to provide room for the children clamoring for instruction in the public schools." The number of immigrants, annually increasing, was overwhelming.[33]

In November 1897, primarily for reasons other than the schools, the reformers lost the election, and Tammany again controlled City Hall. The defeat checked school reform, leaving many problems unsolved and festering. Adding to the confusion and delay of the next few years was a major shift in the city's structure brought about by the Consolidation Act of 1898. On New Year's Day of that year, Greater New York came into being, an imperial port city where the Hudson and East Rivers join to meet the ocean, encompassing a far greater area than before and divided into five boroughs, Manhattan, Bronx, Queens, Brooklyn, and Richmond (Staten Island). CCB's term on the Board of Education ended in 1900, just as the city's new charter was revised to correct some weaknesses, and among the lesser new provisions were several that strengthened the powers of the Board of Education and city superintendent. But at least the trustees had been abolished—a drastic shift in power no doubt made possible in part because, as CCB noted, the posts of board member and trustee were unsalaried.[34]

Tammany's mayor, Robert Van Wyck, reappointed CCB to the Board of Education in January 1901, but in the early autumn CCB quietly resigned, apparently because he felt the board had ceased to be an instrument of reform. It was dominated, as often in the past, by the city superintendent of Manhattan and the Bronx, John Jasper, who had assumed his post in 1879 and who was an obstacle to reform not because of any venality but for lack of vision. He could see that more schools were needed, and cooperated in building them, but he saw no need for any change in curriculum or in how teachers were appointed or promoted. Born in 1837, he had been educated in the public schools of his day and was content with their learning by rote and with the teachers that Tammany's district leaders recommended, often the least prepared or adventurous of the candidates, but politically the most loyal.

Then, in November shortly after CCB's resignation, another reform candidate for mayor, Seth Low, won the election. A Republican businessman, educator, and politician, he had served two terms as mayor of Brooklyn (1881–85), been a trustee of Columbia College since 1881, and was president of the university (1890–1901) and chiefly responsible for its move from mid-Manhattan to Morningside Heights. Concurrent with Low's election, a revision of the city's charter expanded the Board of Education from twenty-one to forty-six members, giving Low a chance to appoint a majority. (On the enlarged board Manhattan had twenty-two commissioners; Brooklyn, fourteen; Bronx and Queens, four each; and Richmond, two.) At Low's request CCB rejoined the board on 20 January 1902, and was promptly elected its president.[35] He clearly set forth the intent of the city's revised charter concerning the public school system:

> The fundamental principle of this system is the separation of business functions from those purely scholastic. Although the initiative in all matters scholastic rests with the Board of Superintendents [dominated by Jasper] the final responsibility falls upon us [the new Board of Education]. On the business side, it is for us to determine the policy, devise the means for carrying it out and through our executive officers bring it to a successful completion.[36]

In effect, CCB was giving notice that even though Jasper might initiate scholastic changes, "final responsibility" for them lay with the board. Jasper cannot have been surprised by this challenge, for CCB's position was well known, no doubt the reason for his appointment.

When in 1896 the reform mayor Strong had asked Donald C. Gilman, president of the Johns Hopkins University, to be city superintendent, Burlingham had regretted Gilman's last-minute withdrawal, and in an open letter to the Board of Education's *Journal* had written:

> Valuable as I think Mr. Jasper is to the school system, his most devoted friends must consider that he is not to be compared with a man like Dr. Gilman. The one is a great educator and administrator, the other an able clerk. Mr. Jasper should be placed where he can be of real service to the schools, as a chief clerk, and the Board of Education should take time to find a Superintendent of the same type as Dr. Gilman.[37]

It would seem that Mayor Low, whose chief political adviser on educational matters was Butler, who had succeeded him as president of Columbia University, put CCB on the board primarily to ease Jasper out. Only this would free from opposition the man the commissioners of 1898 had elected first city superintendent of Greater New York, William H. Maxwell, then superintendent of the Brooklyn schools. Maxwell, a friend of Butler, had progressive ideas about teaching, and his election had reduced Jasper to second in rank in the school system, but Jasper still had considerable power and the discord between the two soon flared into open hostility.[38]

CCB, of course, had other goals besides easing out Jasper. One, requiring a further revision of the charter, was to permit the use of school buildings "for recreation and other public uses." Plainly tenement communities would be better served if people could use the buildings after school hours for meetings, sports, adult classes, and other extracurricular activities. He wanted, as did everyone, a desk for every pupil so that no child would be turned away. He wanted the curriculum revised to be more flexible and imaginative. He wanted teachers advanced on merit, not "pull." And he hoped, working with the Board of Health, to put nurses into the schools so that children with ailments were not mistakenly sent home or kept in school. Perhaps because of his own experience of ill health, he knew how enfeebling it could be, and was eager to combat it. In 1903 he recommended this program to Mayor Low as especially worthy of support, and in the next decade, at St. George's Church, he helped to organize dental and health clinics that by the 1920s would be serving 9,000 patients a year.[39]

The most immediate job, however, was to remove Jasper, who would be sixty-five, retirement age, in August. CCB worked out an agreement with him: at the board meeting in May Jasper would not oppose a resolution that accepted his retirement effective 1 September and assured him of an annuity of $2,000 in recognition of his forty-five years' work in the school system. But at the meeting a group of Jasper supporters among the commissioners sought to reelect him to another six-year term as superintendent of Manhattan and the Bronx, and they insisted that no application would be made for retirement until after 1 September—with no date specified. Jasper's part in this revolt is not clear. The dissension at once split the board, but reform commissioners were in the majority, and they adopted the resolution incorporating the agreement between CCB and Jasper—but not without a row that spilled into the newspapers. Still, Maxwell was freed of a second in command who actively opposed him. Reform in other areas could proceed faster.[40]

In trying to promote better, more imaginative teachers, CCB was helped by his work as a trustee and an inspector, which had brought him into contact with teachers, good and bad, and in William McAndrew he saw one who was good, though too independent to please Jasper or Tammany. Against considerable opposition he managed to advance McAndrew to principal of the Girls' Technical High School (later Washington Irving High School), where McAndrew served until 1924, when he left to become superintendent of the school system in Chicago. By then he was one of the country's outstanding educators. Of his career in New York, he wrote to CCB, "I have had a superb time here. Burlingham, he started me."[41]

But not all went easily. A scandal erupted in the special school for truants, whose principal, Alfred T. V. Brennan, and assistant, Marcus L. Brown, were accused of beating two boys, or, as the *Herald* called the boys, "scholars." Brennan allegedly used a rubber hose on an eight-year-old, and Brown a ruler studded with nails on the head of a boy of nine. For the latter a doctor was needed to stitch the cuts. For several weeks the Special Schools Committee of the board conducted a quiet investigation, finding the hose but not the ruler, and then suspended the two men, pending a final decision by the full board. The story meantime broke in the newspapers, causing an uproar. Brennan had friends in Tammany, and many persons believed that for truants physical beating was the only effective discipline.[42] Questioned by a reporter, CCB stated: "I was very much surprised when I learned the character of the charges against Mr. Brennan. I knew that there had been complaints from the school for some time, and my idea was that there, as has been the case in other schools, the employees had used some mild form of chastisement. It never occurred to me that brutality such as is described in the charges had been practiced."[43]

The temporary suspension was discussed at a December meeting of the full board where a Tammany commissioner and Brennan supporter, Thomas B. Connery, angrily attacked CCB and Maxwell, charging them with "a disgraceful conspiracy" to oust Brennan, "who was an obstacle to President Burlingham's pet scheme for reorganization." Connery's voice rose in passion. "You—I am speaking to you, Mr. President—you, whom the canons of honor should have held back, you, who hold the lofty office of president of this board, you, President Burlingham, who should by the rights of your office be every teacher's friend, came into that room on the last day of the hearing and forced the scale of the balance against Brennan."

At that moment Commissioner Jacob W. Mack interrupted and ironically urged President Burlingham not to cut off Connery's oratory "on account of the excited condition he is in and on account of his age and gray hair." "Never mind my age or gray hair," roared Connery. "I can take care of myself."

CCB asked him to continue. "The entire proceedings," shouted Connery, "were shameful, shameful, shameful!" The *Tribune* headlined its story as the "Wildest Scene in Board of Education's History." But despite Connery's effort on Brennan's behalf, the board in its final vote sustained the suspension 24 to 8, with two abstentions.[44]

In a lecture at Columbia two years later, CCB commented on the recent agitation to restore corporal punishment to the schools. "It is an extraordinarily fatuous movement," he said. "Does any one in his right mind suppose that whipping, having been put out of the schools, can ever be put back? I have no doubt that there are many boys who would be the better for a sound licking, but the fatal and unanswerable objection to corporal punishment is that no principal or teacher is fit to administer it."[45]

Having served a full year as he promised the mayor, CCB resigned as president of the board on 2 February 1903, giving no reason other than that "things are running so smoothly now." But everyone seemed to accept as fact his need to return to full-time legal practice and earn some money. A school principal wrote to him, "I hope you may grow rich very fast, providing of course, you can become rich without being spoiled."[46] Mayor Low praised CCB's skill in leading the board through the first year of the revised charter "with so little friction and so large a measure of efficiency." CCB's ability to avoid or lessen friction, whatever the job in hand, was a quality that many people in his long life noted, and it surely lay, at least in part, in his instinctive avoidance of sarcasm. He might grow angry but was seldom sarcastic and never malicious. Butler, in the heat of an editorial, could write of a "school ring" whose members should be described "anthropologically, not figuratively," as the "savages and barbarians" of Tammany Hall, but CCB's most personal attack on anyone was his open letter about Gilman and Jasper, and though he spoke disparagingly of Jasper's qualifications, he did not make fun of the man's face, accent, or background. As a result, those he opposed seldom took personal offense.[47]

Though departing leaders traditionally are showered with meaningless praise, in CCB's case some who wrote to him touched on qualities that shone throughout his life. A district superintendent, for instance, after echoing Low's point on efficiency, "You have produced order from the chaotic conditions of last winter," added: "Though you do not claim to be a democrat, you came nearer the rank and file of teachers than any of your recent predecessors. The lowest teachers in the rank had your ear as well as the highest official. This may be termed good democracy."[48]

To achieve a sense of democracy in a school system as large as New York's is not easy. In the school year 1903–4, that system had 501 schools, 13,131 teachers, total expenditures of $27,848,853.16, total registration of 622,201, and—a sign of partial failure—average attendance of only 466,571. By 1914–15, with immigration still increasing, school registration would soar to 776,000, a figure greater than the combined total of the country's next five largest cities, Chicago, Philadelphia, St. Louis, Boston, and Cleveland. New York's problems, at least in numbers, were unique.[49]

Commissioner Mack, over CCB's objections, organized a farewell dinner of CCB's colleagues on the board. "It is none of your business what this dinner will cost," he wrote to his reluctant guest of honor, "because the dinner itself is but a vehicle to gather your friends." When CCB sought to escape by pleading a previous engagement, Mack replied, "No matter what peremptory engagement you have for the evening of February 14th, you will have to abandon it." Mack already had in hand "nearly forty" acceptances and the dining room in the Hotel Savoy was hired. So, the *Tribune* reported, there was a "sort of family gathering," and after the dinner, several speeches, and a reply by CCB, "many informal remarks were made and many good stories told." And among those who came to dine that night with CCB was Thomas Connery.[50]

9

Improving the Bench

THE FIGHT OVER the future of the city's schools in which Burlingham had a part exposed for many in New York and other states a significant difference between the leaders of Tammany and those of reform. As one scholar-politician later wrote of the Tammany bosses: "They never thought of politics as an instrument of social change—their kind of politics involved the processes of a society that was not changing."[1] The reformers saw more clearly society's ills and needs, but vision alone did not produce victory at the polls; public support was needed, and on few issues did the public respond as readily as on housing, schools, and prostitution. Tammany's grip on the judicial systems of the city and state, for example, was openly corrupting but usually more difficult for reformers to dramatize. The public knew little about the courts and, barring a huge scandal, cared little, perhaps in part because so many people liked a bit of judicial corruption—fixing a traffic ticket—and so few had any direct experience of it in larger matters. But then in the summer of 1898 occurred an event that reform-minded lawyers seized upon to focus attention on the courts.

For the elections in November Boss Croker refused to renominate for the state Supreme Court in Manhattan (the trial court of general jurisdiction) a respected judge, Joseph F. Daly. Judge Daly had angered Croker by failing to appoint as his clerk the man Croker had recommended, and by denying an order in a suit affecting Croker's real estate interests—despite word from the boss that the matter was "personal."[2] To Croker, the affair was merely a case of Tammany's internal discipline. "Legitimate patronage is legitimate politics," he told a reporter. "If a victorious party can present for office men better than or as good as those whom it has conquered, why should it not be entitled to some favors at the hands of the men it has made? Judge Daly took everything and turned his back on the men who gave him his position." But to reformers, Croker's refusal to renominate a sitting judge who during two terms had proved exceptionally able was a break in custom and a threat to the judiciary's independence.[3]

In place of Daly, Croker put forward David Leventritt, whom the City Bar Association, led by the chairman of its committee on judicial nominations, Elihu Root, promptly declared "unfit." Root, a fervent Republican and for the past decade one of New York's leading lawyers, within the year would become secretary of war for President William McKinley and already had close ties to Theodore Roosevelt, who in the election was running for governor of New York. His manner, as he himself acknowledged, was cold, and his self-image, which was also as others saw him, was as a Roman in the days of the republic, proud, reserved, incorruptible, and stoic; he even cut his hair in the Roman style, with a short bang across the brow.[4] In Root, the more open and emotional Croker had a stern and unforgiving opponent.

The bar association promptly announced a "Committee of Fifty" to support Daly and to nominate a nonpartisan "Independent" slate for all three openings on the court. Manhattan Republicans, relishing Croker's discomfort, also put Daly on their ticket for one of the three contested seats, along with the respected judge William S. Cohen and a lawyer, Henry W. Taft, proposed to them by Root's committee. (Taft, a friend of CCB, was the younger brother of the country's future president, William Howard Taft.)[5]

On 21 October reformers, led by the bar association, held a public meeting in Carnegie Hall to stress the identity of its Independents' slate with that of the Republicans, though without fusing the two: the candidates would appear on the ballots as both Independents and Republicans. CCB, though nominally a Democrat, worked as a lawyer and Independent for Taft, whom he considered "one of the best men at the Bar to put on the Bench."[6]

In the last weeks before the election, the Republican and bar association tickets received strong support from Roosevelt, campaigning for governor. Having returned from Cuba as a hero of the Spanish-American War, he was running against Croker's candidate, August Van Wyck, brother of the city's mayor, and in his speeches Roosevelt made judicial independence his main issue. He hardly mentioned his opponent but campaigned against Tammany, speaking again and again on Croker's refusal to renominate Daly.

Nevertheless, in the votes for the Manhattan Supreme Court Tammany's three candidates won easily, defeating Daly by 33,000, Cohen by 48,000, and Taft by 51,000. The *Herald* judged the size of Tammany's victories "one of the many surprises of the day." Root ascribed the defeat in part to the difficulties of the election process: many voters, he felt, had refused to split their votes among the parties for fear of disqualifying their ballots by a mistake in marking them.[7]

In the race for governor, however, the issue of judicial independence served Roosevelt well. As a Republican he carried the upstate counties with such strength that the *Herald* trumpeted, "Rural New York Met Van Wyck's 80,000 at the City Line and Buried It Completely." But at the final count the margin was close, only 17,794 of 1.3 million votes cast. Still, at age forty, vigorous and eager to push reform, Roosevelt became governor of New York. For Croker, it was a major defeat, and stirred revolt among his district leaders.[8]

Roosevelt's move to Albany, and then later as vice president and president to Washington, and Root's to Washington as secretary of war for McKinley and then secretary of state for Roosevelt, were symptoms of the importance of New York City to the country. The city was the country's largest as well as its financial and commercial center, and the state was then the country's most populous and industrial. Hence, the investigation of the city's tenements and the two-volume report that followed were of national importance, and fights with Tammany, even those the reformers lost, had national repercussions, illuminating the problems in other cities and suggesting solutions. As for CCB, as reform leaders like Roosevelt, Root, and others less famous rose from the city to the state to the federal government, they took with them their New York experiences and friendships, and provided him with a cadre of increasingly powerful politicians and bureaucrats ready to listen and perhaps be persuaded.

In the spring following the election of 1898 Tammany suffered an even worse defeat. With Governor Roosevelt's support, a special committee of the state legislature, the Mazet Committee, began to investigate the city's government, with special attention to the appointment of judges and their behavior on the bench. Both Croker and judges were called as witnesses, and their testimony was conclusive: with few exceptions, judges nominated by Tammany, with election all but assured, bought their positions for prices ranging from $10,000 to $25,000 (or set at six months' salary). In addition, court appointments, particularly those of clerks and referees, had to be made as Croker ordered, and the counsel for the Mazet Committee described the city's government as "an absolute monarchy." Croker, holding no elective office, was king, and "blind obedience is the rule."[9]

In this instance, the exposure of corruption did not lead to important reform, yet the effort was not without result. Within Tammany, the revolt against Croker gathered strength, causing him, after Seth Low's election as mayor in November 1901, to retire to his estates in England and Ireland, where he bred bulldogs and racehorses. (In 1907 his horse "Orby," at odds of 100 to 9, won the Derby at Epsom Downs.) Meanwhile in New York, after a struggle among the district leaders, Charles F. Murphy emerged in 1902 as Croker's successor and set out to improve Tammany's reputation. Where he could, he nominated better candidates for office, and he ruled less crudely than Croker.

In the years CCB served on the Board of Education, he had only a small role in efforts to improve the judiciary. Six or seven months before the November election of 1906, however, he realized there would be ten Supreme Court judges to elect in the First Judicial District (Manhattan)—eight of them to new seats added by a recent amendment to the governing law. In addition, the patronage-rich post of New York county surrogate would be on the ballot as well as several lesser judicial posts. The Good Government leader Richard Welling later recalled: "No one except Charles C. Burlingham seemed alert to the exceptional opportunity. He went around from office to office, a most unwelcome caller after his message was known, and asked the influential lawyers of the city what they proposed to do about it."[10]

By mid-May, CCB's question had produced a group of thirty-five lawyers calling itself "Judiciary Nominators." Joseph Hodges Choate, recently returned from six years as ambassador to Britain, was chairman but served chiefly as a figurehead until the final weeks when he became the Nominators' most effective speaker. CCB as the group's secretary did the daily work, most of it from his office on William Street. Welling, as he had in earlier campaigns for reform, served as chairman of the Committee for Meetings and Speakers.[11]

From the start the Nominators included several important political figures, adding others as it expanded. Among its Republicans were Root, now secretary of state, and Charles Evans Hughes, who as counsel for a legislative commission investigating insurance fraud had earned a statewide reputation and was running for governor of New York against Tammany-supported William Randolph Hearst, whose newspapers had a circulation of more than a million and who was in his second term as a congressman from Manhattan. Hearst, whose papers frequently descended to "yellow journalism," with sensational and sometimes falsified reporting, was not a Nominator, but chief among the group's reform Democrats was Edward M. Shepard, who had often battled Tammany and was greatly respected.

A subcommittee for Announcement and Program, of which CCB was secretary, was supposed to announce the Nominators' candidates as soon as qualified men were selected, but trouble arose. The *Herald*, on 26 June, reported that they were unable to agree with either the Democrats or the Republicans on any candidates. It quoted CCB denying a deal with either party: "We shall nominate a ticket by petition. That is in our constitution, and we have never had any other idea. We can not tell when the ticket will be ready." The paper, calling the situation "a jangle" of factionalism, headlined its story: "Chaos Is Now Predicted."[12]

In the end, the slate was weak, largely because no Republican lawyers of stature would run. Most men believed they had no chance of election in Manhattan against a Tammany candidate, especially if the race was a three-way contest (such as the Committee of Fifty had lost eight years earlier in trying to reelect Daly). And probably equally disheartening was the rumor that Hearst, with his abusive *Journal* in New York, was said to be spending half a million dollars to ensure the election of Tammany's ticket and himself as governor.[13]

The possibility of a Democratic landslide in the state led to a difference of opinion between New York's two most prominent Republicans, President Roosevelt and Hughes, and offered another example of how New York experience and politics reverberated right up to the White House. Roosevelt, who had become president on McKinley's assassination and then in 1904 had been elected in his own right, wanted more New York Republican clubhouse politicians on the Nominators' ticket: "We are going to have with us anyway the people whom the great lawyers could influence. We don't want to drive away the others." Hughes disagreed: to select men more active as politicians than as lawyers, or worse, to make a deal to split the posts with Hearst and Tammany, would "turn a current of criticism against us at a critical time. It would seriously reflect upon the sincerity of the position we have taken." The *Times*, the paper most strongly supporting the Nominators' campaign, in mid-October nervously editorialized that the city's Republican organization should adopt more of the Nominators' candidates, "especially as it would reduce the number of parties running and number of names on the ballot."[14]

In the election, Hughes defeated Hearst by 57,897 votes, but his victory failed to pull even one of the Nominators' judicial candidates into office. The *Times* lamented, "The movement of the Judiciary Nominators, backed by the cordial support of the Republican organization, has proved a total failure ... A very considerable portion of the lawyers of the city, and many of good standing and influence, failed to show any interest in the matter. The bar as a body clearly was not enlisted. We think the fact discreditable to the profession."[15] Welling in his memoirs remarked less harshly: "It is hard to excite the town over the qualifications of judges ...

It was an uphill campaign from the start, and though it cost a lot of work, the record stands as a threat to Tammany to beware of low-grade judges." But it seems doubtful that Tammany, having elected all its judicial candidates, felt threatened. More likely it noted that in a tough gubernatorial campaign, with interest focused on the high office, it could nominate for the bench, and elect, anyone it chose.[16]

As for the would-be reformers, the lesson learned was the one Roosevelt had urged on Hughes: in New York City to win even a single judgeship against Tammany, reform Democrats and Independents must early and fully merge their efforts with those of the Republican organization. Partial fusion was not enough.

On another occasion in this first decade of the 1900s, CCB sought to improve the judiciary, but in a fashion quite different. Whereas the Judiciary Nominators had been a sudden six-month affair, full of committees and the play of important political personalities, this second project came about slowly and privately. It began when Burlingham befriended an unhappy, confused young lawyer named Learned Hand, whose company he enjoyed and whose talents, he saw, held promise if better harnessed. Ultimately, by his interest he helped to launch an important judicial career.

By mid-century Hand (1872–1961), though he never sat on the Supreme Court, was the most admired judge in the country. Indeed, by then for many lawyers he was "the greatest contemporary judge in the English-speaking world."[17] Not just for his legal opinions, delivered during fifty years on the federal bench, but also for the kind of person he was. Perhaps in part because he never was advanced to the country's highest court, the source of his authority was all the clearer. It lay in his capacity to listen, to think, to understand, and then to decide with justice and compassion. "His major legacy," according to his biographer, "lies in his demonstration that wise and detached judging is in fact humanly possible."[18]

In 1904 this paragon was merely an associate in a small New York City firm where he felt he was neither earning enough money to support his growing family nor doing work interesting enough to exercise his talents. Born and raised near Albany in a family of lawyers, Hand had received a classical education that carried him easily to Harvard College. There, unathletic, not very popular, and failing to be elected to the Porcellian Club, which he greatly desired, he felt himself an "outsider." Socially he moped; intellectually he blossomed, studying chiefly political economy under CCB's classmate Frank Taussig and philosophy and history of art with William James and Charles Eliot Norton. Upon graduation with highest honors, he took a master's degree in philosophy, and Taussig offered him a place on the economics faculty, but Hand declined. Still unsure of himself, he followed family advice and entered Harvard Law School, where he again distinguished himself, thriving on Langdell's method of teaching by analyzing cases, which admirably forced the students, in Hand's view, to "dig out the truth for themselves."[19] On returning to Albany in 1897, he found practice in a small firm unbearably dull: "Nothing but foreclosures, mortgages, settlement of estates. Everything was petty and formal. Nobody wanted to get behind a problem." Life brightened in 1902 with marriage to Frances Fincke, a Bryn Mawr graduate with friends among Josephine Shaw Lowell's many nieces, and shortly thereafter he and his wife left Albany for New York.[20] Two years later, when he met CCB, he was an associate in the firm of Gould & Wilkie and repeating the disappointments of Albany.

Hand was good at analysis, examining a problem from all sides and then writing a memorandum; poor at the continual interaction of personalities in a law firm's daily practice; and downright bad at attracting business. In five years at Gould & Wilkie, he brought the firm only two clients and one case of any importance. Though he could sparkle in conversation and write an excellent brief or article, as a practicing lawyer he was a failure, and the gap between his obvious intellectual abilities and his lack of worldly success distressed him. It also bothered his wife, his father-in-law, and his friends—all of whom offered advice.[21]

How CCB, fourteen years older, first met Hand is not recorded, but evidently a quick sympathy soon developed into a friendship. Their correspondence, a vast collection of letters, notes, and cards exchanged over fifty-five years, begins in July 1904, when Hand was thirty-two and CCB forty-six. By then CCB and Louie were dining with Hand and his wife, Frances, and CCB was taking an interest in the younger man's career. He had begun to send him papers in upcoming cases, asking him to analyze the law and the facts and even to write an occasional brief, in one case pointing out that though "the text books are in our favor," the outcome was uncertain, and adding, "If you get busy, or if this doesn't interest you, send it back." And in the same letter he offered "a harder question and perhaps a more interesting one," arising out of a collision at sea of two British ships, in which both were at fault, but only the one represented by CCB had sunk with her whole cargo. At issue was a question of insurance: whether British or American law should apply. And he closed his letter, "This is perhaps too hard a nut for summer cracking. We had a fine time last night. I hope we shall see you both again soon."[22]

Hand's analysis of the case does not survive, but presumably it pleased CCB, for the friendship thrived and apparently there was more back-and-forth about admiralty cases. In the next three years CCB advanced to "My dear Learned," signing "yours affectionately," and then to "My dear B." The latter was used by friends and family, and recalled Hand's first name, "Billings," which by age thirty he had dropped as "vastly formidable" and "pompous"—though some questioned the improvement in substituting "Learned."[23]

Hand himself, along with his friends and admirers, thought he would be well suited to be a judge—because of his diffidence not a state judge, who must win periodic elections, but a federal judge, appointed for life. Also, because he was a Republican in a Democratic town, an appointment to a federal court seemed a more likely possibility. In 1907 an opportunity appeared to open when Congress seemed about to add a fourth judge to the three in the District Court for the Southern District of New York. This was Addison Brown's court, to which, mainly because of the large increase in business and admiralty cases, Congress had added a judge in 1903 and another in 1906. But Congress failed to act, and the effort on behalf of Hand aborted. It led him, however, to join his local Republican Club, and in the 1908 election he even attempted several street-corner speeches. More important, he published in the *Harvard Law Review* an admired analysis of the Supreme Court's decision in *Lochner v. New York*.[24]

This case, decided 5 to 4 by the Court in 1905, ruled that the New York legislature's Bakeshop Act of 1895 that limited the hours of bakery workers to ten a day or sixty a week was unconstitutional because it violated the Fourteenth Amendment's due process clause. At the time, particularly in the smaller bakeries often located in the damp cellars of tenement houses, many bakers worked a hundred hours a week, and the state legislature had passed its law (unanimously in both houses) to improve the sanitary conditions at the bakeries and the working conditions of the bakers. The Supreme Court, however, refused to consider whether the Bakeshop Act was reasonable, or whether the sanitary and economic reasons for it had some basis; for the Court's majority it was invalid because it attempted to regulate the right of men, worker and boss, to contract for labor, a right guaranteed by the amendment. Four justices disagreed, and Oliver Wendell Holmes and John Marshall Harlan wrote strong dissents to the effect that the New York legislature had the right to grapple with the issues of sanitation and working conditions; indeed, under the separation of powers, that was peculiarly the duty and right of the legislative branches of government. Hand's article warned bluntly against the danger of judges trumping legislatures

on debatable issues such as sanitation and economic welfare. As summarized by his biographer, it was "a fervent plea for judicial restraint, a strong
endorsement of legislative power to engage in experimentation, [and] a
sharp attack on exercises of judicial authority in the *Lochner* mode," and it
spread the growing belief that Hand should be a judge.[25]

When, in February 1909, Congress finally authorized a fourth judge
for the Southern District Court, Hand's friends, led by CCB, at once revived their campaign. William Howard Taft was the country's new president and eager to improve the federal judiciary, and his attorney general
was George W. Wickersham, a New York lawyer whom CCB saw frequently at St. George's Church. Another Hand supporter and friend of
CCB was Henry W. Taft, the president's brother and Wickersham's law
partner. Unquestionably the attorney general was "the critical element,"
as Hand's biographer writes, but CCB "deserved, claimed, and received
much of the credit for Hand's nomination." The Senate soon confirmed
the appointment, and on 30 April Hand became a judge in New York's
Southern District. He was thirty-seven, one of the youngest men ever appointed to the federal bench.[26]

Decades later, in March 1947, Hand recalled to CCB "a walk we took
out by Corlear's Hook, soon after I was appointed. It was a bright Sunday
morning, I think; that hardly seems possible, and yet so it remains in my
mind. Anyway, it was a bright spring morning; and with your frankness,
then as now, you let me see that I was a shot in the air—that I might hit
and that I might miss—that it was fifty-fifty, so to say." And he was relieved to have "hit."[27]

Nevertheless, after taking his seat in June 1909, Hand had worried,
writing to CCB: "I wonder how I am doing. I am certain of one thing, and
that is, that I have an irrepressible tendency to talk too much." More con-
fidently he added, "I am going to try some admiralty cases."[28] And ultimately he became in his generation probably the country's greatest judge
in admiralty.

On the first day of March 1905 CCB's father died. Though for any generation collectively the shifts in thought, belief, and mode of living may
seem gradual and continuous, for individuals the changes often come in
spurts, set off by a death, a new home or job, or the adoption of some tech-
nological invention that powerfully alters behavior. For all these reasons,
CCB and Louie's way of life changed more swiftly than usual in the years
1905 through 1912.

For a decade Aaron Burlingham had been housebound, too weak to work, and in his last years semiparalyzed, until at age eighty-three he was freed from pain and frustration by pneumonia, then called "the old man's friend." In the fifth year of his trial he had written: "I try to be submissive; sometimes it is difficult. But for grace I could not rest content. Jesus holds me. Let us keep to him. It won't be long." Then, nineteen months after his death, his wife and companion in faith also died.[29]

They had lived in Mount Vernon for twenty-three years, and their home and needs had kept CCB and his brother,, Albert, in touch as the sons cared for, visited, and worried over their parents. Albert, a bachelor, had been an attentive uncle to CCB's children, generous with his time and affection. He continued now to live in Mount Vernon for another quarter century, becoming a well-known figure in the town. He married a widow, acquired a stepson, founded a printing company closely associated with his old employer R. Hoe & Company, and after a brief illness died in 1934. But without their parents to bring them together, the tie between the brothers loosened. Albert, with new concerns of his own, soon ceased to be a presence in CCB's family.[30]

Eight months after Dr. Burlingham, Josephine Shaw Lowell died. Her mother, Sarah Shaw, had died before her, on New Year's Eve, 1902, and three years later it became clear that Lowell, though only sixty-one, had cancer. She spent part of her final summer in Ashfield, Massachusetts, where CCB and Louie in past years often had rented a cottage to be near her and her family. One friend who stopped by there for a last visit was Jacob Riis, who sat beside her before the fire, holding her hand. She had seen his distress and to ease it had spoken directly of her husband, killed in the Civil War, and of her own near death, which would end "my waiting for my husband for forty-one years." Softly she repeated the thought, and at her memorial service Riis quoted it, remarking on her joy "in the re-union."[31]

For CCB and Louie, there would be no more dinners with Lowell, no more discussions with her of political or social issues, no more sharing, however vicariously, in her campaigns for reform. One of her last had been against the foreign policies of Presidents McKinley and Roosevelt, which, she along with others—notably William James, Charles Eliot Norton, President Eliot of Harvard, and Senator George Frisbie Hoar of Massachusetts—had opposed as imperialistic. To them the conquest of the Philippines, far more deadly and devastating than the war in Cuba, was especially terrible: the American army of 70,000 had lost 4,234 men, and the Filipinos some 20,000, while an estimated 200,000 Filipino civilians died from war-related disease or injury.[32]

In Lowell's eyes, the United States in this war violated the principle of its own Declaration of Independence: government by "consent of the governed," and did what it had condemned Spain for doing in Cuba. Moreover, there were dismaying documented reports of American atrocities, use of torture, internment camps, and mass killings, which Roosevelt and Secretary of War Root tried to excuse as aberrations of war. Roosevelt, in a private letter, dismissed Lowell and her views: "Mrs. Josephine Shaw Lowell is an utterly unimportant annoyance." She, also in a private letter, proclaimed: "[There must be some] who will keep on the watch, and be ready to point the moral and to lead the way." Trying to be practical, early in 1905 she founded with others a Filipino Progress Association, with CCB on its executive committee. But against Roosevelt's popularity and raucous patriotism the anti-imperialists accomplished little.[33] Still, Lowell's undiscouraged efforts to follow her parents' example and her husband's prescript for a life "useful" to society, a life of thought and deed based on moral principles, became an ideal for many. As for CCB, though in his generation morality seemed to lose strength as a measure of worth for political or social action, he never wavered from his commitment to a moral basis for life.[34]

For the two summers following Lowell's death, the Burlinghams spent their vacations with her daughter Carlotta, visiting the latter in 1906 in Ashfield and the next year in England. Meanwhile, with most of the older generation now dead, they began to look for a suitably modest place of their own for the summers, and found it at Black Point, Connecticut, a long flat thumb of land poking a mile into Long Island Sound east of Saybrook.[35]

The Point, narrowly bordered by rock and scrub, stood only ten or twelve feet above the water, and its soil, though sandy in spots, was fertile. In the mid-nineteenth century it had been a two-hundred-acre farm, with cornfields and orchards growing close to the low bluffs and reeds along the water's edge. About 1880, on the death of the owner, "old Mr. Bond," his eight children, instead of splitting the property, held it together, sharing its revenues. Gradually the family ceased to cultivate the farm's outer rim and sold or rented small parcels along the shore while retaining for themselves and their new neighbors rights-of-way to "pass and repass" along the waterfront and among the cottages. Meanwhile, they maintained income by selling fruits and vegetables to the summer residents, many of whom came from Hartford or New York and built cottages for weekend or vacation fishing. Black Point thus became a haven of like-minded folk, and they soon by informal handshake began to share transportation from the railroad station, maintenance of the interior roads, and access to the only bathing beach (where the "thumb" joined the mainland). Who told CCB or Louie of the Point is not known, but in any case it pleased Louie, for it was on the water, and it pleased CCB, since it was easy to reach (roughly three hours on the New York-Boston railroad to stations at either Saybrook, New London, or Niantic). In 1909 they bought a small plot, barely two acres, on the Point's western shore, not at the squared tip of the thumb but modestly back toward the first knuckle. Their land was an open field, dropping in a tangle of rock and weeds to the water, and reached by a dead-end spur of the farm's perimeter road. This brief lane, shared with a neighbor, stopped short of both cottages, so that anyone arriving, whether by carriage or car, in fair weather or foul, had to walk, or run, the final yards to the house.

The Burlinghams put up a simple wooden cottage, two floors with peaked roof and porch, shingled, and the trim painted white. It had a central chimney and fireplaces but no cellar or insulation, and its interior was painted uniformly white. The furniture was cheap wicker, and the few pictures initially were prints of birds, ships, and an attack by Japanese soldiers on a Chinese castle. Upstairs in his study, CCB tacked to the walls beside his desk his map of Paris in the 1880s, showing every boulevard and monument, and a sepia reproduction of Augustus Saint-Gaudens's memorial to Robert Gould Shaw and the Massachusetts Fifty-fourth Regiment. Throughout the house bookshelves swiftly filled with books whose spines promptly spotted with mildew. (By way of comparison that same year, 1909, J. P. Morgan's partner Henry P. Davison built himself a summer home at Peacock Point, 4,000 acres jutting into the Sound near Port Washington, Long Island. The brick house had a two-story portico supported by four Greek pillars topped with urns and more than forty rooms, including an organ loft and billiard room, and required twelve indoor servants—among them a full-time laundress, a seamstress, and a cook for the staff.)[36]

At Black Point Louie often had a cook and a maid, and later a chauffeur to assist her, but she and Nancy did much of the shopping and household work. What the cottage had in abundance was light, air, and a view. From the porch, the prospect westward was unbroken—to the left, open water; to the right, a distant curving shore; and straightaway a mile or so, two small barren islands. Beyond these was the Saybrook Light, and onward, somewhere below the horizon, New York City. CCB did not swim, sit on the beach, sail, fish, or garden; his pleasure was either to play croquet, on an uneven court that curved around the house, or to sit on his porch conversing with friends about the problems of New York or the nation. At Ashfield there had been an academy, organized by Charles Eliot Norton and George

William Curtis, which each summer had offered a series of speakers for the summer and town people, and at Black Point, for neighbors and guests, there was CCB on the porch, conducting a continuous Platonic dialogue.[37]

Over the years, as more people came and built houses on the Point, the handshake agreements about its communal life evolved into a more formal association, with bylaws, rules, and covenants. This Black Point Association held for shared use the beach, the tennis courts, and a well-kept croquet lawn; its contractor kept the roads in repair and mowed the public lands; and when necessary, it enforced its rules and regulations. Over the years, on the former farm's well-cultivated fields the residents' landscaping grew into magnificent trees and hedges, so that in midsummer the Point's interior became marvelously green and shadowed even as its shoreline continued silvery blue and transparent. In the early 1930s the Burlinghams bought cottages on the inner side of the perimeter road for Charles and Nancy. These houses, which were adjacent, had no view of the Sound, but their occupants shared in all the Point's activities. Charles, married and with children, steadily occupied his, but Nancy, still unmarried, continued to stay with her parents, allowing CCB to rent her house cheap to friends or relatives.[38]

In their earliest years at the Point, CCB and Louie had perhaps rented a horse and carriage for the summer from the Bonds, or more likely made some arrangement with the family to be met at the railroad station and taken on shopping trips into nearby Niantic. But soon after World War I they bought a very small cottage in the center of the Point, a half mile from their own, where they installed a chauffeur and kept a car. By then, though neither of them ever learned to drive, like most of their neighbors, they had decided that a car was a necessity.

They were slower than most to enter the age of the horseless carriage, for even before the war many middle-class families were investing in cars, which were swiftly forcing changes in everyone's way of life. Already in 1896 William Jennings Bryan had been the first presidential candidate to campaign by car, and by 1912 it seemed every politician was doing it. In 1905 Roosevelt had driven down Pennsylvania Avenue to his inauguration in a horse-drawn carriage, and so did Taft in 1909, but also that year Taft converted the White House stables into a garage.[39]

By then automobiles were popular in cities where streets were paved, and tickets for speeding were becoming common. Reputedly the country's first was issued in New York, in July 1899, to a cabdriver, Arthur Driscoll, trying to earn a fifty-dollar tip for making a train connection and weaving down Fifth Avenue at the incredible speed of thirty-five miles per hour, terrifying horses and pedestrians.[40] Two months later the city, and perhaps the country, had its first automobile fatality, as a Mr. H. H. Bliss, descending in the middle of the street from a trolley at Central Park West and Seventy-fourth Street, turned to lend a hand to a lady following him. At that moment he was struck from behind and his head and chest crushed by an electric car (a cab) passing unexpectedly on the trolley's right.[41]

Before the car, children often had played in the streets. But in 1901 a chauffeur driving two businessmen to Wall Street, while passing through the Lower East Side, hit and killed two-year-old Louis Camille, a child of Italian immigrants. Residents of the street mobbed the driver, who was rescued by police. In 1910, 195 of the city's 376 traffic accidents involved children, and by World War I motorists in New York had killed more than 1,000.[42]

Inevitably, the car increased class antagonisms. Louis Camille's parents had no car; but in 1905, according to *Harper's Weekly*, two hundred New Yorkers owned five or more, and John Jacob Astor had thirty-two. And soon those who lived in the city but owned no car began to find themselves restricted by the disciplining of those who did. In an effort to accommodate the car, the city in 1904 had its police begin to "direct traffic," and the next year it created its first "rotary" (at Columbus Circle and Broadway). In 1910 it began to widen streets, usually by cutting down trees and narrowing sidewalks, first on Twenty-third Street, then Fifth Avenue, then Madison. Eventually it introduced one-way streets, traffic lights, and painted center lines. (The first center line in the country appeared in 1911 on the curves and bridges of Wayne County, Michigan, put down by a county commissioner who had seen a horse-drawn carriage and a car dispute the center of a bridge. Not long after, an eighteen-mile stretch was painted on a road going north from New Haven, Connecticut, possibly the first continuous white line on a highway.)[43]

Moreover, the car increased class separation. The middle class—of which the Burlinghams with their place at Black Point were typical—now found it easier to maintain a place of their own in the country. Thus, the car not only changed a way of life in the city, turning streets that had been social, recreational, and commercial centers for neighborhoods into traffic arteries dangerous to pedestrians, but also created a new form of suburban life. At Ashfield or Cornish, or any of the small New England towns where the Burlinghams had once spent their summers, city and country folk had mixed together. The summer visitors typically came for several months, often renting house, horse, and carriage from a local farmer, relying on him for food, and on his wife and family for many services, such as laundry, cleaning house, or painting. Summer life was in the village, organized around the town hall, church, and library. And it included everyone, summer and winter folk. But Black Point developed differently, as a one-class community in which the summer visitors came often for shorter periods, typically owned their houses, and, by the miracle of the car, increasingly shopped on the mainland for life's necessities. The cottages soon were not tied to the Bonds' farm or even to a village. To CCB's parents or even to Lowell's generation, the life there would have seemed strange.

In September 1909 CCB went to Europe as one of four delegates appointed by President Taft to represent the United States at what later were known as the Brussels Conferences on Maritime Law. The Belgian government had called the meetings to consider proposals of the Comité Maritime International to codify, amend, and make uniform the differing laws of maritime nations, especially the laws of salvage, collision, and limitation of ship owners' liability. The Comité was (and is) a nongovernmental international organization, founded in Antwerp in 1897, for the purpose of aiding the development of maritime law, and in particular to keep it uniform and abreast of changes caused in the shipping industry by politics, economics, and, most important at the time, by invention (the steam engine, steel hulls, radio). Seagoing peoples and nations have long had a seemingly instinctive desire to make the law of the sea uniform, both on the high seas and, if possible, in port, and hence the Comité was a modern outgrowth of an ancient and continuous urge. Since the advent of the steam engine in maritime commerce, the world had been shrinking. As the obstacles of wind and tide lessened, speeds and tonnage increased, schedules tightened, and the amount of commerce entering and leaving the world's harbors steadily rose. International cooperation then seemed ever more necessary, and those concerned with the sea, especially those working with its law—businessmen, diplomats, and lawyers—generally viewed the Comité and its purpose with approval.

The members of the Comité (by 1996 fifty-five countries were represented) are not individuals but national organizations, and in 1899 American admiralty lawyers had to create such a group so that the United States might be represented. And to that end, on 21 June 1899, some 106 admiralty judges and lawyers from every section of the country met at the Association of the Bar of the City of New York to found the Maritime Law Association of the United States, the MLA, a private, nongovernmental group like the Comité, and with a conforming purpose: "to advance the Maritime Law of this country, and to act with foreign associations in their efforts to bring about greater harmony in the Shipping Laws of different nations."[44]

CCB apparently had attended this first meeting of the MLA, at which Robert Dewey Benedict, of New York, was elected president. An elderly, handsome man with strong features, noble brow, and splendid white hair, mustache, and beard, Benedict bestowed dignity and respectability on the infant organization. Two months earlier, in a short article on the city's admiralty bar, the *Times* had led off with Benedict's image before going on to say that "notable among the younger men" were Harrington Putnam, Wilhelmus Mynderse, J. Parker Kirlin, and Henry G. Ward. All were CCB's friends, and two of them, Ward and CCB's partner Putnam, were put on an executive committee. In later years Putnam and then two more of CCB's partners would serve as president, but CCB himself, except for the summers of 1909 and 1910 when a delegate to the Brussels Conferences and a brief term ten years later on the executive committee, had little part in MLA activities. He evidently was content to let his partners represent the firm while he pursued other ventures.[45]

Now, however, with the three others of the U.S. delegation to the 1909 Brussels Conference, he sailed in mid-September on the Cunard Line's newest ship, the S.S. *Mauretania* (30,696 tons). He knew none of his colleagues well, but in sharing a stateroom with Walter C. Noyes, a judge on the Second Circuit Court of Appeals and an expert in railroad law, he soon made a friend of the younger man. Noyes was a distant cousin of Learned Hand, who had sent a basket of fruit to the stateroom, and CCB, in thanking Hand for it, wrote of "Coz. Walt" lying "in his berth with Hughes on Admiralty on his lower bosom and the stem and apex of a pear in his hand. The grapes hang from the electric light bracket and they are going, too."[46]

The liner, CCB added, "is *the* ship—a marvel of comfort, elegance, and speed—588, 588, 596! How's that for 3 days runs! Leaving New York Wednesday at 10 a.m., we expect to dine in London on Monday evening . . . We are paying the minimum $125 [delegates had $1,200 for expenses], and live like princes on the A deck—brass beds, windows (not portholes), bureaus, washroom, silken hangings on walls, a fine table, abundance of room, and splendid deck spaces." Noyes, whose home was modest and whose courtroom was in the ugly Post Office Building, reveled in the beauty and luxury of A deck, and for the return voyage insisted on the *Mauretania*.[47]

Stopping for a few days in London, CCB wrote to Louie that the city "is as familiar to me as New York." The previous year, he, Louie, and their three children, all now grown, had spent a summer in England, sightseeing and visiting Carlotta Russell Lowell, who had taken a house in Surrey. Now, having seen the sights and temporarily unhitched from Noyes and the others, he whirled about the city for his firm, calling on solicitors and insurance companies, lunching with Lotta Lowell and the Sedgwicks—Louie's friend May Minturn had married CCB's friend Harry Sedgwick—and several times dining with Francis and Helena Hirst, an English couple. Francis Hirst, editor of *The Economist*, knew everyone, and took him to meet John Morley, the biographer of Gladstone and the government's secretary for India. Unfortunately, CCB wrote to Louie, Morley "was going to the Cabinet meeting; so *O* happened." On the other hand, "My call on Winston Churchill," president of the Board of Trade, "was most interesting; but too long for a letter"—hence lost to posterity.[48]

Another event of that September was in the London newspapers and promptly reported to Louie. Robert Hoe III, the colonel's nephew and Louie's first cousin once removed, had died and the world learned what the family had long suspected: the world-famous bibliophile and leader of R. Hoe & Company, father of nine, with a wife in New York, had kept a mistress in London. As the facts emerged and a court fight over the estate developed, newspapers in New York picked up the story, and Hoe relatives there followed it closely. But of the warmth that the colonel and Brightside had injected into the family, little remained save the legacies to his grandchildren, and among the many cousins descended from him and his brothers and sisters there was no longer much communication.[49]

Once in Brussels, CCB to his delight discovered that his ability to understand French, the language of the conference, was adequate. Twenty-three nations were represented in the meetings, and among the delegates there were many—Hungarians, Greeks, Italians—who spoke no English and were charmed by CCB's willingness to make of himself in French (his words) an "Old Fool." As he wrote proudly to Louie, "In spite of the family warning I converse fluently in French with Mr. Lyen-Caen, Doyen de la Faculté du Droit of the University of Paris, a grand old man who has promised me a certificate that I comprende tous et parle tres bien. This in answer to my statement that I have been *défendu* by my *famille* to *parler Français*." And to his youngest son, Robert, now a junior at Harvard: "If you don't learn to speak French you are a G O A T. My poor feeble knowledge of that language has been a means of grace and a reason for gratitude to God . . . My conversational powers as you know are of a limited nature, but I have talked and jabbered away on all occasions without regard to syntax or genders!"[50]

He seems to have been the only one of his delegation who had any fluency in the language or was willing to try it, and his efforts added greatly to his enjoyment of the receptions and dinners surrounding the conference and often made him a leader in his committee assignments, one of which concerned "liens on collision." (Liens on salvage were taken up in the full conference.) By the second week in October the delegates had drafted and signed international conventions on both collisions and salvage, and had postponed to the next year any action on limiting ship owners' liability. These conventions had no force in any country until adopted by that country's governing body, of course, and the first of the treaties approved by the U.S. Senate was the convention on salvage, in 1913.[51]

Twenty-one years after the conferences, CCB prepared a speech for a meeting of the Maritime Law Association which, for some reason, he did not deliver, but which was fully prepared and recorded his feelings about what was and was not accomplished at Brussels in 1909 and 1910:

> We went and discussed and signed conventions. We came home and reported, and our reports are still reposing in the pigeon holes of the Department of State. The treaty on salvage which we signed was of little importance and brought the law of the other nations into complete conformity with our own. So the treaty was ratified . . . But the far more important convention on collisions, which would have changed our law of damages from the *judicium rusticum*, by which in case two vessels are at fault the damages are divided equally, to the more civilized Continental rule of apportioning liability according to the degree of fault, was never even sent to the Senate. Great Britain changed her rule to conform to the convention, and for twenty years the new system has worked there as well as it has worked on the Continent for generations.[52]

The failure of Taft and succeeding presidents to send the convention to the Senate rankled CCB for many years. In 1938, for a time, after Franklin Roosevelt had sent it to the Senate, it seemed likely to be adopted, and CCB wrote to Felix Frankfurter, "The only opposition is from cargo underwriters, who are foolish fellows. I hope it will go through now."[53] But it did not, then or later in CCB's life. What bothered him was not only that the United States did not adopt as law the best thinking of the day on an important subject but that it failed to stand by an international agreement it had helped to initiate. The performance seemed not only foolish but ir-responsible. In his undelivered speech, he stated his feelings more mildly:

> It is a humiliating experience for a delegate of the United States to attend a conference and agree on the terms of a convention and perhaps take a more or less important part in shaping the convention, only to find him-self repudiated by his own country. Well, that is an experience which I have no doubt many of you have had, and others will have in future.[54]

Though his disappointment in his country's response to the work of the conference lay in the future, there was meanwhile the present to make the most of. In 1909 CCB was one year past fifty, which then, when life's expectancy was shorter, was considered a turning point; he nevertheless filled every free moment with sightseeing and new experience. When the conference ended, he did not go to Paris with his three American col-leagues but started alone on a trip to Cologne, up the Rhine to Basel to see works by Holbein, and then on to Lucerne, Bern, and Geneva. "It seems odd for me to be travelling about alone," he wrote from Cologne to his daughter, Nancy, "very odd and even absurd. But here I am with my little bag, my hot water bag too, which I carry in the catch-all with my thick overcoat, and a great comfort it is. Before I lay down for a nap I fill it, and I have used it very often in Brussels." And he described for her in detail the cathedral at Aix-la-Chapelle.[55]

Away from his family for the first time of any length, he wrote to them all profusely. His letters to Louie have their usual declarations of love and also continual reports about his health, for evidently they both feared that the conference with its new faces and ideas might prove too stimulating, leading to overwork and a recurrence of his nervous illness. To "Young Charles," his eldest son, who had graduated in the spring from Harvard Law School and was working in New York for the firm of Cravath, Hen-derson & de Gersdorff, he wrote about the coming election in the city for mayor and about his fellow delegates in Brussels: "I could give the U.S. Govt. some points on Delegations—Who's who and who ain't." In closing he was suddenly very open in his affection: "I love you, my darling boy. What a comfort you are to me. To know you are *there, right there*, is a sup-port and source of the greatest satisfaction." A joy of parenthood that often comes late and with a surge of relief is the realization that an adult child is close by, loving, and competent.[56]

To his younger son, Robert, twenty-one and planning to become a sur-geon, he wrote almost as freely, offering thoughts about college courses

though without pressing advice on him or closing with such an open declaration of affection. Robert's health worried his parents, though neither
put a name on the trouble. After graduating from Middlesex, a boys'
boarding school in Concord, Massachusetts, Robert grew into a tall, remarkably handsome young man, but troubled at times by excessive emotions, usually outbursts followed by remorse. While he was in college,
Louie once reported to CCB: "I hope you will be happy about R. now, for
he has been too tired by the strain of hours and rush etc. that he had nothing left for us to go on. But now we can do a great deal for him if his letters are not too crushing. *However*, your company has been a great boon
and made everything much easier for everybody." As Robert grew older,
his swings in mood increased, and parents of a later generation might have
suspected some chemical-hormonal imbalance, or—given the medical
history of Louie's father and the suicide of her Uncle Darius—a genetic
tendency to manic depression. To Louie, however, Robert was simply
"over-tired."[57]

For his daughter, Nancy, CCB had a lightly phrased complaint: "Good-
night, darling Nanna. I have had one letter from you beside a steamer letter. You ain't much of a writer, be you? But you are a very comfortable and
darling lady, and I hope I can bring you a nice present."[58] Her future was
not clear, and he worried. She was twenty-three, unmarried, and living at
home, and though named after Annie Hoe, she lacked her great-aunt's
assurance and personality. She was shy, inexperienced, and not very
attractive. She had attended the Brearley School for girls until sometime
in her teens when her mother, thinking her too high-strung for the
school's regime, had taken her out and continued her education at home.
She had become an accomplished pianist and knew much about art, at
least of the Joe Evans and Abbott Thayer school, but the pattern of her
life, as lady-in-waiting in her mother's home, was already old-fashioned,
and her mother's oversight perhaps excessively severe. Louie one summer
at this time wrote to CCB: "I fancy now N. will be buying gay garments
for the winter. Yes, indeed (I will ever remember your last remarks). She
does enjoy the luxurious income—never forgetting how her precious father has heaped every blessing on her, as I do never forget, but it is the
spiritual things that I know to be most precious of all." Apparently Louie
thought her daughter lacked spirituality, and Nanna's views, if she had any,
were not heard.[59]

After Switzerland, CCB went to Paris, where he spent an afternoon in
the Bois de Boulogne with the Sedgwicks and their baby. CCB still loved
Paris, as planned by Napoleon III and Baron Haussmann, especially its

boulevards, parks, and thousands of trees. (In New York in 1904, the Municipal Art Society, criticizing New York's lack of greenery, had conducted a campaign to plant more trees: Paris, in that year, had 80,000 shade trees, including 7,000 on the grounds of its public schools, all grown in municipal nurseries and tended by municipal park departments; New York, on the sidewalks of its five boroughs, had only 4,000 trees, and even these, by the Parks Department's admission, had been "sadly neglected in recent years.") For CCB as for many New Yorkers, Paris was still the model of what New York ought to be.[60] Then, after two farewell days in London, CCB sailed for home on 23 October 1909, departing with Noyes from Southampton on the *Mauretania*. In his last letter home he promised Louie, "This is positively my last tour alone . . . Yesterday, I was *désolé*; I am always *désolé* except when I am with somebody who knows me and *mine* . . . I can never write or tell you what you are to me. Think of it, we have been together far more than half of your life and more than half of mine."[61]

No doubt he believed every word he wrote to Louie, but his six weeks on his own, more briefly repeated the next summer for the conference's second year, may have conveyed a different message to the old friends he met abroad and to the many new he made. These more likely saw a man over fifty displaying a remarkable ability to continue to grow. At an age when many men turn stodgy, he was full of the world's affairs, hurrying about Europe alone, with his hot-water bottle, eager to see the sights, to pursue new projects, and to share his thoughts.[62]

In the years to come his love for Louie did not lessen, nor did hers for him. Yet with these trips to Brussels a change starts in their relations. She stands still; he moves forward. She remains a wholly private person, not even involved in the work of her church; he begins to develop a public character quite separate from wife or family. However partial the view of those outside his family who saw him as an individual, alone and complete in himself, that was increasingly how he appeared to the world.

IO

Building a Law Firm

IN NOVEMBER 1909, shortly after CCB's return from the first Brussels Conference, his law firm had a sudden crisis. Early that month William J. Gaynor, a judge for sixteen years of the New York Supreme Court (the court of original jurisdiction, not the highest appeals court), won election as mayor of New York City and resigned from the court. Governor Hughes had to find a replacement, and he sent Edward M. Shepard, a leading reform Democrat, to ask if CCB had any objection to the appointment of his partner Harrington Putnam.[1]

Putnam likely knew of the call and its purpose, for it was a tactful way of handling what was often a difficult problem for a law firm: the sudden loss of an active senior partner. All the city's admiralty lawyers at the time were aware that Robinson, Biddle & Ward, having lost two partners to the bench in 1906 and 1907, was now floundering as Robinson, Biddle & Benedict. At Wing, Putnam & Burlingham, Henry Wing, almost seventy, had recently retired, and now the firm was losing Putnam, leaving CCB with only two junior partners, Everett Masten and James Forrester, and a young associate just out of Yale Law School, Chauncey I. Clark. Yet as Hughes no doubt expected, CCB rejoiced in Putnam's appointment, perhaps in part because at fifty-one and in good health he would inherit the firm, but also surely because he thought Putnam would be an excellent judge. But the problem for the firm was acute: it needed to quickly recruit some experienced lawyers, for the workload for those remaining was, as CCB later wrote, "too heavy a load to carry."[2]

The fifty-eight-year-old Putnam soon proved his ability as a judge, despite some complaints that he was slow in deliberation. To that charge, Putnam's friends replied that he had never been in a hurry, waiting until fifty-two to marry; and after he was on the bench he startled many by walking from his home in Brooklyn to hold court in Riverhead, Long Island, covering the seventy miles in two days and thinking nothing of it. In November 1910, having completed the remnant of Gaynor's term, he stood for election on the Democratic ticket for a full term and won.[3]

Meanwhile, CCB, searching for some established lawyers to stabilize his rump firm, fished where he knew there were six, in the roiled waters of Robinson, Biddle & Benedict, and caught four. (The other two joined A. Leo Everett to create the firm of Everett, Clarke & Benedict.) One of the four was CCB's friend William S. Montgomery, who perhaps influenced the others to come along. In any case, on 1 July 1910, a new firm was formed, Burlingham, Montgomery & Beecher. CCB later said simply, "I formed a new firm," but he may have exaggerated, for Montgomery and Beecher were two-thirds of it and presumably had a good deal to say about its organization.[4]

Montgomery, a Kentuckian, was a graduate of the Naval Academy and had been on the flagship with Admiral Dewey at Manila Bay. He evidently had great charm, for as CCB noted, "clients adored him." As for Beecher, a fine litigator, he "had a highly nervous temperament and was wearisomely argumentative." (The trait soon "wore him out," and in 1917 he left the firm.)[5] Below the three senior partners, the firm's stationery listed Masten and Forrester followed by the newcomers George H. Emerson and Morton L. Fearey. (The single associate, Chauncey Clark, was not listed.)

Possibly the four junior partners, despite their place on the letterhead, were not full partners, and instead of a share of the firm's profits, they may have received a guaranteed annual salary. Such an arrangement was not uncommon, its reason often having less to do with the man's ability or social position than with his financial resources. A lawyer whose only asset was his share of the profits was no use to a firm that had none and was calling on partners to pay the firm's debts out of personal assets. Or sometimes to appease an important client a firm would list a lawyer as a partner when in the privacy of the partnership agreement he was something less. In a partnership the variations in profit-sharing, voting, or liability were boundless. Relationships could be fashioned to fit any need and refashioned in less than an hour, which is why small businesses often preferred partnerships to a corporate structure.[6]

Whatever the relationships in the new firm, they changed again when in January 1912 Montgomery died suddenly after an operation, and the firm's partners looked to CCB for leadership. The firm was now his. And soon after, CCB again altered the firm's structure in a way that not only displayed his dominance but had consequences that lasted for the rest of his life, the life of his son Charles, and the lives of several of his partners.

A year before Montgomery's death Montgomery and CCB had hired a second young lawyer as an associate, Roscoe H. Hupper, son of a Maine sea captain. Hupper had grown up on a farm, from which he had worked his way to Bowdoin College, graduating in 1907, and then to George Washington Law School, 1910. Both Clark and Hupper would be with the firm for fifty years, and ultimately would outrank all but CCB. Each in his way was brilliant. Clark, who had a quiet manner and a somewhat solitary personality, tended to practice law from the firm's library and was outstanding at analysis, particularly in towage, the complicated law of tugs and their tows. Hupper, more outspoken and harsher in manner, was splendid in a courtroom. Justice Felix Frankfurter once named him the best "oral advocate" he had heard. Hupper was also important to the Maritime Law Association, serving frequently on its executive committee in the years 1924–40 and as president 1940–42. By the mid-1930s Clark and Hupper would be the firm's leaders, and, though friends, there was always a spark of tension between them. One day after CCB retired, Hupper was late for a partners' meeting. When he appeared, Clark said testily, "You're late." "No," snapped Hupper. "The meeting does not begin until I arrive."[7]

A few months after Hupper joined the firm, CCB and Montgomery hired still another young lawyer as an associate: CCB's son Charles, who had graduated from Harvard Law School in 1908 and since then had been working in New York at the firm of Cravath & Henderson (later Cravath, Swaine and Moore). Young Charles—often so called and formally distinguished from his father by the absence of any middle initial—had matured into a handsome man and competent lawyer. Before college he had attended the Cutler School for boys in Manhattan, whose graduates included Teddy Roosevelt, J. P. Morgan Jr., Waldorf Astor, several Vanderbilts and Havemeyers, but despite the social cachet, the school offered a spartan environment, an emphasis on outdoor sports, and a rigorous curriculum aimed at college.[8] Young Charles had thrived at Cutler, done well at Harvard, and at the Cravath firm had a job with one of the best in the country; he had won the respect of his colleagues and could have practiced law in any city he chose. Though details are lacking, apparently it was CCB's idea to bring his son to the firm, and Young Charles acquiesced.[9]

From the moment he appeared, in September 1911, Clark and Hupper viewed him with suspicion. And then, one day in 1912, about six months after Montgomery's death, Clark and Hupper went out to lunch together and, returning to the office, now at 27 William Street, saw a painter adding a name to the list of partners on the glass door: Charles Burlingham.[10] Both Clark and Hupper felt superior as lawyers to Charles and also had seniority in the firm; yet Clark would have to wait four years before CCB advanced him to partner, and Hupper, five. Eventually the two forgave the father, but never the son. Thereafter, though civil to Charles in the hall, in the library, and in the courthouse, they often were contemptuous in private, infecting some others in the firm with their attitude.[11]

In the decades ahead, people frequently spoke of CCB with amazement. He seemed tireless, able to do the work of three; and besides managing a successful law firm and practicing law, he carried on a huge correspondence and took a lead in his church, in the bar association, and in city, state, and national affairs. One explanation, apparent to those who saw him at home or in the office, was the almost daily assistance he received from his highly competent son. After CCB's death, Charles murmured to one of his much younger law partners, "I feel as though my life's work has ended."[12] Over the years, many who knew the situation in the Burlingham firm and family discussed the unique subordination: Who was responsible for the dependency? Father, or son? And to what extent was the father injuring the son? Most persons assumed the relationship benefited CCB, not Charles. But those raising the questions soon moved on to other matters. The Burlinghams, after all, seemed content.

Meanwhile, CCB presided serenely over the conflict of personalities beneath him, managing the firm as he saw fit and always encouraging his junior partners to participate, in whatever way they found congenial, in the affairs of their city—not only in their professional groups, such as the City Bar and Maritime Law Associations, but in support of their churches, schools, hospitals, and other charitable organizations. In this he was not unique—many lawyers in New York shared his sense of municipal citizenship—but in this respect his firm's record was outstanding, and in the municipal elections of 1909 and 1913 he added to its reputation.

In the summer of 1909, many New Yorkers initially wondered why Charles F. Murphy, boss of Tammany, should have so feared losing the municipal election to reformers that he gave the nomination for mayor to William J. Gaynor, an outstandingly honest and able judge. Gaynor, from Brooklyn, was such an "independent Democrat" that he had first been elected to the State Supreme Court, in 1893, as a Republican. He was blunt in speech, irascible, passionate for civil service reform, and outraged by police corruption and brutality. In the three-way race for mayor against the Republican-Fusion candidate Otto T. Bannard, an admirable, public-spirited citizen, and the Independent William Randolph Hearst, whom Hughes had defeated three years earlier in a race for governor, Gaynor's choleric remarks and upright character caught the public's favor. And in November he won decisively (proof of Murphy's judgment, for only Gaynor was elected on Tammany's slate). Yet as Richard Welling, one of Gaynor's civil service commissioners, remarked, Tammany "never could have expected 'recognition' from him, and he never gave them a crumb." When asked, after election, what he would do for Boss Murphy, Gaynor mused, "Suppose we give him a few kind words."[13]

Reformers thought the opening months of Gaynor's four-year term wholly admirable. Without regard to Tammany's wishes, he appointed many reformers to municipal office, eliminated sinecures and useless positions, started a revision of the city's fiscal procedures, and set about curbing police corruption, which then was much involved with gambling and prostitution.[14] With his work well begun, he planned a four-week holiday in Europe for the summer of 1910, and on 9 August crossed the Hudson to Hoboken to board the *Kaiser Wilhelm der Grosse*, famous for its speed.[15] Members of his staff came to see him off. While they were all on deck saying their farewells, a crazed former municipal employee, who felt Gaynor had deprived him of work, suddenly came up and shot him in the back of the neck. The bullet lodged in the roof of Gaynor's pharynx, at the top of his throat, and could not be removed.[16]

He recovered enough to return to work in October, but the experience seemed to have exhausted him and to have shattered the last brake on his temper. He now quarreled with friends as well as enemies, increasingly berating deputies, the press, and supporters. When a scandal erupted in the Police Department, he opposed the investigation of it and accused the chairman of the investigating committee of extortion. Sued for libel, he was unable to back up his charge and forced to write a public letter of apology.[17] People soon realized they were watching a tragedy, the deterioration of a potentially great public servant. For despite his worsening troubles, he still was accomplishing much for New York in housing, education, sanitation, and food inspection. But as the 1913 municipal elections approached, the Democratic Party refused to renominate him. A proud man, he entered the race as an Independent, ultimately the nominee of only one small reform group, the Citizens Committee. Fate spared him defeat; two months before the election he died.

Almost a year earlier, alarmed by Gaynor's declining health, ten reform-minded citizens who held no public office had met informally to discuss what might be done. The meeting was called by Joseph M. Price, president of the Improved Mailing Case Company, and on 10 December 1912 the ten met at the Murray Hill Hotel, nine men and one woman—Lillian D.

Wald, founder and leader of the Henry Street Settlement. Among the men, besides Price and CCB, were George W. Alger, a lawyer with an interest in government and social problems, and Henry Moskowitz, a Romanian immigrant who had grown up on the Lower East Side, worked in settlement programs, and founded a Downtown Ethical Society—all three, friends of CCB.[18] These ten soon enlarged their group to somewhat more than thirty, who then invited to a conference not only many well-known Independents but also party men provided they were not in office. The purpose of the conference was "to preserve and advance the best standards of City Government divorced from partisan politics."[19]

Curiously, the thirty who sent out this invitation did not include five of the original ten members. Among those missing were Wald and Alger. Wald seems to have dropped out of the movement altogether, perhaps because women did not yet have the vote, but why Alger and three other men were not listed, though continuing to work for the cause, is not clear. They may simply have stepped aside to make room for others and ensure a balance among the thirty hosts of the city's boroughs and parties.[20]

Some three hundred people attended the conference, held on 19 March 1913 at the Fifth Avenue Hotel, and adopted a series of resolutions: chiefly, to organize a large representative Citizens Municipal Committee, with members apportioned as expediently as possible to represent the five boroughs and all shades of anti-Tammany opinion. To carry out this job, the meeting created a Committee of Twenty, with Moskowitz as temporary chairman and CCB and Price among the members.[21] (Wishing to be appropriately representative and appraising power and politics in the city as they appeared in the winter of 1913, the committee recruited itself as follows: from Manhattan, ten members; Brooklyn, five; Bronx, two; Queens, two; and Richmond [Staten Island], one; and from the four anti-Tammany parties the allotment was: Democrats, nine; Republicans, four; Progressives, five; and Independents, two.[22] It held four meetings, at the last of which, on 23 April, it announced to the public the names of the 107 members of the Citizens Municipal Committee that in July would choose a slate to present to voters in November. CCB later dated the birth of Fusion politics in New York City, whether defined as a committee or a party, to this announcement.[23]

Unfortunately, newspapers have used the term "Fusion" loosely, and historians and reference works often give it different meanings. Some historians, for instance, describe an anti-Tammany Democrat or Republican nominee who gains support from an independent party or civic group as a Fusion candidate, running on a Fusion ticket. For example, contemporary newspapers as well as *The Encyclopedia of New York City* (1995) list Seth Low as a Fusion candidate for mayor in 1901 because as the nominee of the Republican Party he won the backing of many civic and Democratic reform groups.[24] But CCB felt that Low and his campaign did not qualify as Fusion. Low had been the nominee of the Republican Party, and its leaders, though accepting support from other groups, controlled his campaign. For CCB, Fusion presumed that a citizens' group, not a political party, selected the candidate regardless of party, and then won for him the nomination of one or several of the city's political parties, after which the citizens' group ran the campaign, or at the very least had a forceful role in it, though not providing a line on the ballot. The candidate's name appeared on the lines of established parties, such as Republican, American Labor, or Socialist.

In a speech in 1949, CCB defined his view:

> I have been asked to give my hearers the history of Fusion in New York City—it is a brief story. Fusion here is only 36 years old. In 1913 we formed a Committee of about 100 to see if it was possible to unite all Anti-Tammany bodies in an effort to drive out of office the five Democratic County organizations. The Republicans had discovered that theirs was a minority party. Their candidates had been defeated year after year, the only exceptions being William L. Strong in 1895 and Seth Low in 1902. Now and then a strong man by force of character fought the bosses on the inside and was nominated, e.g., William P. Grace in 1885 and William J. Gaynor in 1910 . . . Fusion Committees are not political parties. They have no column on the ballot. Their function is to bring together all political parties and bodies which are opposed to Tammany, to represent independent citizens who have no party affiliations, to recommend and bring about nominations and a well-balanced ticket, and to take an active part in the campaign.[25]

In 1913 the extent of the minority position of the Republican Party in New York City is clear in the apportionment of members of the Committee of Twenty. That year, the Progressives, the Teddy Roosevelt or "Bull Moose" wing of the party, which had bolted from the regulars for the national election of 1912 and advocated far-reaching regulatory and social reforms, were rated more powerful than the more conservative regulars led by William Howard Taft. Taft and Roosevelt, both former presidents, had split the Republican vote and lost the presidential race of 1912 to the Democrat Woodrow Wilson. Yet even if the two wings in New York combined, they still would equal only the anti-Tammany Democrats, who numbered far less than the Democratic regulars. This weakness was seemingly hard for Republican leaders to acknowledge. The party could win the country's presidency or the state's governorship, why not the mayor's office? Why not, at least, one or two of the city's five posts of borough president? With each municipal election, hope sprang anew, often blinding Republican leaders, as well as rank and file, to the need for compromise and allies.

The large Citizens Municipal Committee appointed an executive committee of thirty that was charged with securing the fusion of all the anti-Tammany parties.[26] According to CCB (who was not on this committee), a portion of it, usually numbering eleven and with Price presiding, "met almost daily and heard the suggestions of delegations and individual citizens."[27] But by the middle of the summer the executive committee was unable to agree on a candidate for mayor. It divided in equal thirds for George McAneny, Independent; John Purroy Mitchel, anti-Tammany Democrat; and Charles S. Whitman, Republican; so on 31 July, at the Fifth Avenue Hotel, the full Citizens Municipal Committee met, with 89 of 107 members present, to resolve the tie.[28]

The choice was not easy; all three men were qualified for the office. McAneny, the Independent, was then Manhattan's borough president. In the past he had been president of the City Club, secretary of the Civil Service Reform Association, and a member of the commission in 1908 to revise the city charter. Mitchel, the anti-Tammany Democrat, had made a reputation in 1907 as special counsel for the city investigating corruption among the borough presidents (removing from office those of Manhattan and the Bronx while spurring the man in Queens to seek a European vacation); in 1909, on the same ticket as Gaynor, he had been elected president of the Board of Aldermen and during Gaynor's illness had served as acting mayor. Whitman, the Republican, who had been a city magistrate and a judge of the Court of General Sessions, was presently district attorney for New York County, in which office he was winning a statewide reputation for his prosecution of the sensational "Becker case."*

---

*At two in the morning on 16 July 1912 four thugs, "Lefty Louie," "Gyp the Blood," "Whitey Louis," and "Dago Frank," had shot and killed—five bullets in the body—the gambler Herman Rosenthal as he came out of the Café Metropole, at Forty-third Street between Broadway and Sixth Avenue. The killers were seen speeding away in a gray Packard touring car. Whitman soon charged that the murder had been ordered by a police lieutenant, Charles Becker, to prevent Rosenthal from testifying that morning to Becker's "partnership" in a gambling house. Convicted, Becker went to the electric chair in 1916, the first member of the city's police force executed for criminal conduct.

The full Citizens Municipal Committee, however, had as much diffi-culty as its executive committee in selecting a nominee. On the first ballot, the vote was McAneny, 28; Mitchel, 32; and Whitman, 29. On the third (with one of the 89 no longer voting), McAneny 25; Mitchel, 34; and Whitman, 29. On the eighth, McAneny, 21; Mitchel, 35; and Whitman, 32. Support for McAneny, the Independent, was slowly fading, but neither leader was close to the required majority of 45.[29] Though the hour was close to midnight, the Republican members of the committee, led by Otto T. Bannard and Henry L. Stimson, a lawyer and friend of CCB, asked for a recess and retreated to an upstairs room to debate how they might gain votes for Whitman. To pass the time while they were gone, CCB went to the hotel bar with Willard Straight, a journalist soon to found *The New Republic*, with Herbert C. Croly and Walter Lippmann as its editors. Inas-much as CCB never drank, except "a little white wine" at weddings, he presumably enjoyed Straight's conversation, for the two lingered there for an hour until Bannard and Stimson came downstairs.[30]

The Republican leaders had talked to McAneny by phone, pointing out that votes for him were dwindling and urging him to release his support-ers to vote for either Whitman or Mitchel. McAneny then phoned Price, his floor leader, asking that the votes be cast for Mitchel—whereupon McAneny's supporters, in caucus, as CCB later reported, "voted 18 to 5 to throw their votes to Whitman. But when they got in the room again and saw the Republicans still voting stolidly *en bloc* for Whitman, some of them, being wholly irresponsible as Reformers always are, threw their votes to Mitchel."[31] During the roll-call vote for the ninth ballot, accord-ing to the *Herald*, "amid wild excitement, Mr. McAneny's following went to pieces," 11 of the group's 21 votes went to Whitman, whose total rose to 43, and 10 went to Mitchel, giving him 45, a majority of the 88. Con-sequently, the Citizens Municipal Committee at 2:30 a.m. declared Mitchel its nominee for mayor.

Bannard, Stimson, and several other Republicans walked out in anger, and as CCB observed, "there was some difficulty in holding the body together to complete the ticket."[32] This was managed, however, and ulti-mately among other nominees were Whitman to continue as district at-torney and McAneny to be president of the Board of Aldermen. In early August, after seven months of intense work, the Citizens Municipal Com-mittee had a fusion slate to offer New York's parties and civic groups, a job it left to its executive committee, which succeeded in effecting a true fusion—persuading the Republican and most Independent groups with lines on the ballot to adopt the Fusion nominees—in all the boroughs but

Queens, where the Republicans supported Tammany's candidate for borough president.[33]

With Price still chairman the executive committee promptly started the Fusion campaign, which in November met with success. Mitchel defeated Tammany's candidate, Edward E. McCall, a justice of the state Supreme Court, by 121,000 votes. And in all the more important posts the Fusion candidates took office (except in Queens, where the Tammany man became borough president).[34]

With reform triumphant, the Citizens Municipal Committee considered its job all but done. Meeting on 18 November, it approved its treasurer's report of expenditures of $143,581.23 and receipts of $154,666.18, and then voted to disband.[35] On the first of the new year Mitchel, only thirty-four, became the youngest mayor in the city's history. He was also one of its best, not only in the people he appointed to lead his administration but in his own energy, competence, and integrity. (He appointed the first woman to head a city department: Katharine Bement Davis, former head of the State Reformatory for Women, who became commissioner of corrections.)

The effect of eight years of good government—Gaynor followed by Mitchel—was strong. With momentum gained, a new level of competence was reached, and became expected. In the judgment of one New York City historian, Mitchel's administration, building on the work of his reform predecessors, "was, from its beginning, a legend of well-nigh perfect government."[36]

CCB's chief task in the Fusion campaign had been to organize a subcommittee on judicial nominations[37] and select candidates for five positions: a judge for the City Court, two for the General Sessions Court, and two for the state Supreme Court, First District (Manhattan and the Bronx). Having picked a slate, the subcommittee would propose it to the executive committee, and if the latter approved the nominations (carrying with its approval the backing of its parent committee of 107), it would try to persuade the political parties and civic associations that formed the Fusion group to adopt them.

CCB's subcommittee began its work, as had the executive committee, by holding open meetings to hear suggestions from individuals, civic groups, and political leaders. Everyone agreed that Justice Eugene A. Philbin, an independent Democrat whose term on the Supreme Court was ending, should be nominated to succeed himself, and all agreed that one of the two men for General Sessions, which dealt with criminal law, should be Charles C. Nott, a distinguished district attorney and a Republican. But over the other three posts the politicians snapped and snarled so viciously that CCB compared them to "a pack of hounds."[38]

The most prestigious of the three contested positions, justice of the Supreme Court, caused the greatest trouble. Republicans wanted William H. Wadhams, who though a member of a Republican family in Albany practiced law in New York City. But CCB thought Wadhams "second-rate" and sought someone better, planning to propose Wadhams, if necessary for political reasons, for the City Court.[39] He and his four-man subcommittee reviewed the possible nominees for the three posts, those most worthy and those most likely to accept. "We thought we had some political wisdom, and we thought we'd like to nominate a Jew for the Supreme Court. So we lighted upon one named Frank"—Julius J. Frank.[40]

Broadly speaking, among reformers there are two types: those who think that tinkering with the system—revising the charter, passing a law—will improve government; and those who think that improvement lies in recruiting better men and women into public service. Those inclined to the latter view argue that a bad politician can wreck a good system, regardless of safeguards, whereas a good one can make even a bad system function. CCB, by temperament and experience, was in the latter group. In a long life as a reformer, he spent little time lamenting the ethnic politics of the city but played the game as it was dealt, confident that in every group there were good men and bad. The trick was to recruit the good.[41]

Before CCB talked to Frank, he had Henry Moskowitz to Black Point for a night, and after a dinner with Louie and Nancy and while enjoying the August evening on the porch, the men discussed the subcommittee's choices. When CCB mentioned the Supreme Court and the possibility of Julius Frank, Moskowitz exclaimed: "You haven't got the right kind of a Jew. Frank is a Felix Adler Jew, a Modernist. You want to get a man who is a real Jew. I'll tell you the man, Cardozo. He is in the Portuguese Synagogue."[42] Moskowitz, a member of an Ethical Society, was himself a "Felix Adler Jew," meaning a relatively secular German Jewish one, whereas the Portuguese Synagogue, founded in 1654 by twenty-three Sephardic refugees from Brazil, was the city's first and oldest. The Cardozo ancestors of Benjamin Nathan Cardozo, whom Moskowitz was recommending, were members of the dispersed Sephardic community and had arrived in the New World in 1752, coming from Portugal via Holland and England. They had gone first to Connecticut, on to Charleston, South Carolina, and then to Philadelphia. By 1830 they had settled in New York, joining the Portuguese Synagogue and working in trade, banking, and the law. Like other Sephardic Jews, they married within their community and remained always a little apart. In their own eyes, and certainly in those of many other Jews, the Portuguese Synagogue and its members, Shearith Israel, had a special status.

In Boss Tweed's time, however, the Cardozo family name had tarnished. Its leading member in 1872, Albert Cardozo, a justice of the Supreme Court, First District, and the father of six children, including the then two-year-old "Ben," had resigned his seat to avoid impeachment on charges that he had done favors for the Tweed Ring. With his resignation, after public hearings, the charges were dropped, allowing him to avoid disbarment, but in the eyes of many his resignation won him only further dishonor, for he had agreed with two other judges facing removal or impeachment that, to avoid any appearance of guilt, none would resign; and he had betrayed his fellows. Though for the thirteen years of remaining life he was able to practice law and support his family, of all of Tweed's judicial henchmen Albert Cardozo was the most reviled.[43]

His youngest son, Benjamin, had grown up eager to erase this stain on the family name. At Columbia College he had majored in philosophy, graduating in 1889 with honors and earning a master's degree. Entering Columbia Law School, he attended only two years, leaving, as then was not uncommon, without a degree; and upon admission to the bar in 1891 he had joined his elder brother, Albert, and a first cousin, Michael H. Cardozo, in the family law firm. Of the three, Ben soon proved the most talented, developing a courtroom reputation for intelligence and hard work, for being bookish and polite. He was also modest, somewhat reclusive, and, on the death of his brother in 1909, the sole support of two sisters, the elder of whom kept house for him in the city.[44]

CCB had a slight acquaintance with the Cardozo family. In 1906 the Judiciary Nominators had proposed Michael Cardozo, then fifty-five and with a reputable career, as one of thirteen judges for the expanding Supreme Court, First District, and CCB remembered that the nominee had been "overwhelmed with joy." Though bearing a dishonored name, "he was a man of high character and perfect integrity; so grateful for this recognition at the bar, he didn't care whether he was elected or not." Four months before the election, however, he died.[45]

CCB's next contact with the family occurred in 1909, soon after Taft had become president of the United States, and early that year Taft's attorney general, George Wickersham, asked CCB to talk with Benjamin Cardozo about a possible appointment to the Southern District Court of New York. Cardozo's reputation as a trial lawyer was growing, but he was even more esteemed for his arguments before the state's Court of Appeals, concerning whose jurisdiction he had published in 1903 a much admired treatise. "I went to see him," CCB recalled. "If I knew him before that, I'm not sure, but I very likely didn't. I put it before him, and he said, 'No,' he couldn't possibly do it because he had two sisters to support and the pay was very small [$6,000 annually]. That ended the episode."[46]

When in 1913 Moskowitz spoke of him, CCB seized the idea and, once back in New York, called promptly on Cardozo, and this time Cardozo agreed to be a candidate, though CCB felt "quite sure from talks with him later that he didn't expect to be elected."[47] Events followed fast. A few days later Stanley Isaacs, a district leader for the Progressive Party who was later to become an important figure in New York City politics, called on CCB in the latter's office.

> I went down to see him to enter the nomination of a Progressive for judge—W. Holden Weeks, who was a good lawyer and a very decent person.
>
> Burlingham was very cordial to me. He said, "What do you think of Ben Cardozo for a judicial nomination?"
>
> I happened to know Ben Cardozo very well. He was then just a practicing lawyer and looked upon as one of the ablest members of the Bar—the younger members of the Bar—and most experienced in the Appellate Division. Naturally I had to say, "I think he'd be magnificent if you could get him to run."
>
> I found that Burlingham used him as a touchstone to test every other candidate that was mentioned. Nobody else thought of him except Burlingham, but Burlingham forced his nomination for the Supreme Court.[48]

The Republicans still wanted Wadhams or some other Republican, however, and Cardozo, though unpolitical, was a Democrat. They thought that if CCB's subcommittee was to carry out the agreement for distribution of office among the parties, then the Republican Party was owed the position. As CCB was proposing to assign the nominations, both seats on the Supreme Court would go to reform Democrats (Philbin and Cardozo), while the Republicans (with Nott and Wadhams) would gain only the two on the less prestigious Court of General Sessions. The Progressives, though less vocal about their grievance, also felt slighted, for they received only the post on the City Court.

Throughout mid-August in Republican district clubhouses the party's alleged mistreatment was recited, condemned, and action demanded. Two leaders, Bannard and Samuel Koenig, called on CCB to urge him to withdraw Cardozo's name, "but I told them they were too late." Some Republicans even talked of nominating a third ticket, with a Republican at its head. But Whitman and Wadhams, by refusing to lead the movement, blocked it.[49]

CCB submitted his slate to Price's executive committee. For four hours in a meeting he defended his subcommittee's nominees, using Cardozo as the test by which other suggestions failed. Ultimately, he prevailed,[50] and when the Citizens Municipal Committee forwarded its recommendations to the Progressive Party, urging adoption, Isaacs in the latter's convention gave the nominating speech for Cardozo. The party adopted the Fusion slate,[51] and in the end the Republicans, too, accepted it, so that on the ballot Cardozo appeared as candidate of the Progressive, Republican, and Independent Parties. Further, he was supported by most of the important newspapers except Hearst's *Journal*, which endorsed Bartow S. Weeks, the Tammany candidate.

Cardozo, out of shyness, refused to campaign, and the chief workers on his behalf were three young lawyers, Walter H. Pollak, Walter Meyer, and Louis Marshall. Pollak, then an associate in Cardozo's firm and later a famous civil libertarian lawyer who argued often in the U.S. Supreme Court (notably in the *Gitlow*, *Whitney*, and "Scottsboro" cases), served in effect as his campaign manager. In the final week before the election he even was able to persuade the *Sun*, which had a reputation as the thinking man's paper, to endorse Cardozo.

CCB surely had a hand in a statement by 130 members of the bar extolling the candidate's virtues: "Mr. Cardozo's great learning, ability, and devotion to the highest ideals of his profession have won for him in remarkable degree the confidence of the courts and the respect of the bar. His nomination came to him unsought and as a spontaneous recognition of his qualifications." The praise was fulsome, but its power lay in its list of sponsors, led by Joseph H. Choate, with whom CCB had often worked in the past.[52] Cardozo, who was finding the campaign and publicity hard to bear, refused to allow the statement to be published in the newspapers, and the most he could bring himself to approve was its circulation among members of the bar. His reluctance perhaps excited his advocates to work even harder on his behalf. Plainly, he was no ordinary candidate.

For most of Election Day Tammany's candidate, Weeks, ran some 1,900 votes ahead of Cardozo, but then, as returns from the Bronx came in, his lead dwindled. At the final count Cardozo had won, 152,594 to 149,798. Fusion had done unexpectedly well in the Bronx, yet a switch of only

1,400 votes would have elected Weeks. Cardozo, in his modest fashion, ever after would say he had won only by a misunderstanding: immigrant Italian voters in the Bronx, seeing a name ending in *o*, had thought he was Italian.[53] Whatever the cause of victory, on 5 January 1914 he took his seat on the state's Supreme Court, First District, the same court from which his father had resigned in disgrace. He would repair the family name.[54]

Then fortune with a spin upended plot and scheme. The Court of Appeals, which had seven judges elected for terms of fourteen years, occasionally made use of a Supreme Court judge to assist in reducing the backlog of cases. One of these "temporary" appointees had recently won election to the Court of Appeals, leaving a vacancy that Governor Martin Glynn, a Tammany Democrat, could fill by appointment. The appeals judges asked him to appoint Cardozo, but Glynn hesitated, reminding them of Cardozo's lack of judicial experience—he had as yet to write his first opinion. The judges repeated their request, noting Cardozo's unusual abilities, and no doubt adding that despite his Fusion origin, he was a Democrat. Support from the New York bar was strong and organized, and the appointment, in any case, was temporary, ending in three years. On 2 February 1914 Glynn signed the order, and Cardozo, who had neither political skill nor even a full month's service on any court, advanced to the state's highest court.[55]

So solid was Cardozo's work as a temporary judge that he won election as a regular member of the court in November 1917. Becoming chief judge in 1926, he led the court until March 1932, when, by appointment of President Herbert Hoover, he advanced to the U.S. Supreme Court. Governor Glynn later said of his appointment of Cardozo that he "was prouder of that designation than of any other act of his career."[56] And a historian of the New York Court of Appeals concluded: "The arrival of Cardozo at the Court was an event so significant that it opened a judicial era . . . He won for himself a place of worldwide esteem in the common law."[57]

With the great rise in industry that was reshaping American culture, commerce, and law, the New York Court of Appeals found itself at the center of a conflict between old law, which was proving inadequate to new conditions of life, work, and trade—railroads, automobiles, regulatory statutes—and new law, which needed developing. As the highest court in the country's greatest commercial state, it had been wrestling with this conflict before Cardozo arrived, and continued after he departed, but in his eighteen years on the court he led it to an extraordinary competence. Under Cardozo, the court became, quite appropriately, the premier court of commercial law in the country. Courts in other states looked to its decisions with confidence, often following its reasoning in difficult cases, as Cardozo and his colleagues successfully refashioned the ancient forms of common law to respond better to modern lay ideas of what might constitute fair play in the new world of commerce and industry.[58]

Many who appreciated Cardozo's importance also appreciated the person chiefly responsible for opening the door to it. Years later Stanley Isaacs stated, "I think C. C. Burlingham was responsible for that, almost single-handed."[59] And on Cardozo's appointment to the U.S. Supreme Court, Felix Frankfurter wrote to CCB, "For you it is, more than any one single person, who gave him to the state and thereby to the nation."[60] Perhaps these statements claim too much, but without CCB to propose him and to stand firm against all efforts to remove him from the ballot, the shy, reclusive lawyer might never have reached the New York Supreme Court, the threshold to his rise. It has been said that in the twentieth century the four greatest American judges were Oliver Wendell Holmes Jr., Louis Brandeis, Benjamin Cardozo, and Learned Hand—two from Boston; two from New York. In starting the judicial careers of both New Yorkers, CCB was crucial.[61]

Though the public would need time to recognize the qualities of Hand, Cardozo, and others less famous whom CCB worked to put on the bench, within a widening circle of lawyers, journalists, and politicians, his work in improving the city, state, and federal judiciaries was increasingly recognized and admired. And to those aware of it, one of its most surprising aspects—what seemed most extraordinary—was his lack of any party or public office, or desire for one. He acted simply as a private person, a citizen.

Part Two

A LEADER OF THE BAR

Defending the White Star Line

ALL LEGAL REPUTATION has in it an element of luck. Lawyers who have won some fame and fortune and yet are modest know that without the exceptional case or client, or some rare political opportunity, hard work and competence may lead not to failure but to a limbo where financial ease and public esteem are ever just beyond reach. During World War II, CCB's friend Thomas D. Thacher, who was in succession an outstanding federal district judge, solicitor general of the United States, civic reformer, and judge on New York's Court of Appeals, recommended a New York lawyer for a job in Washington, describing him as "able and brilliant," but a man "who for some reason or another has not been financially successful in practice" yet "is well regarded in the profession and in my judgment thoroughly competent to render excellent service . . . Whether he could afford to give up the small practice he has, I do not know."[1] Among lawyers in any big city there are many such. And in his own success, Thacher could see no pattern or guiding principle. He replied to a young lawyer seeking advice on a career in public service, "As I look back, it is quite impossible for me to understand how, or why, my professional activities turned out to be what they were. I had no particular aspirations except to practice law . . . [and] so far as public office is concerned, that, I believe, was a mere matter of chance and luck."[2]

For CCB, the case that gave him a national, even international reputation began with the sinking of the *Titanic*. The ship's owner, and CCB's client, was the White Star Line, established in 1871 and by 1912 dispatching fleets of freighters and some of the biggest liners crossing between New York and Southampton. White Star was owned by a British company, Oceanic Steam Navigation, which in turn was owned by a trust or conglomerate known as IMM, short for International Mercantile Marine Company. This holding company, IMM, was the ultimate owner of seven steamship companies, five British, two American, with White Star and its liners accounting for half the tonnage of the seven. The White Star ships (typically named after regions or peoples ending in *ic*, Nordic, Baltic, etc.) were built in Britain, registered there, and sent to sea with British captains and crew, yet IMM was American, owned chiefly by the seventy-five-year-old J. Pierpont Morgan and his partners.

In New York, the White Star office was at 9 Broadway, and its most important piers, which it rented from the city, were among the nine new "Chelsea piers" on Manhattan's West Side, in the North or Hudson River.[3] Located between Eleventh and Twenty-second Streets and built by the city (1902–5) at a cost of $15 million, these Chelsea piers were designed to dock the world's largest liners and to ensure New York's preeminence among American ports. From the start, in one respect, they were unique. They achieved their exceptional length of 825 feet in part by excavating, for the first time in Manhattan's history, *into* the island. Even so, they soon proved too short to accommodate White Star's largest liners, 882.5 feet, and two of the nine piers were extended a further 100 feet into the river. The pier sheds offered structural innovations: steel trusses supporting the roofs gave to freight handlers an unobstructed covered floor more than a sixth of a mile in length; and sliding panels in the walls gave them access to the ships' holds at any height or position. In their location and construction, the piers marked the changes taking place in shipbuilding and in New York's formerly close and visible connection to ships. Coming to an end was three hundred years of wooden sailing ships docking in the East River in open, visible berths, with cargo piled on the street, and bowsprits stretching overhead; emerging on the West Side was the era of larger steel-hulled ships needing the Hudson's greater width for turning and, when docked and loading, screened from the public by a continuous four-storied wall of masonry between street and water.

White Star had two berths at the foot of West Nineteenth Street and others at West Eleventh. With freighters continually arriving and departing and liners sailing twice a week, its daily business in tugs, cargo, passengers, food, and coal was immense. Its five-pointed white star on a red field, and its liners' salmon-colored stacks, topped by a wide band of black, crowded the waterfront and harbor.

For a law firm, White Star was a most desirable client. William Montgomery and Norman Beecher had brought it with them when they had merged with CCB in 1910 to form Burlingham, Montgomery & Beecher. And CCB had contributed such clients as the Anchor Line (sailing chiefly to Glasgow or Scandinavian ports), the Holland America Line, Nippon

Yusen Kaisha, and several other European and South American companies as well as some Atlantic Coast lines. Yet despite the new firm's six partners, three associates, and substantial roster of clients, it was not the city's largest or the most distinguished firm in admiralty practice.[4]

Then, three months after Montgomery's death in January 1912, while the firm was still shorthanded, overnight a huge and incredible White Star case exploded. Shortly before midnight on 14 April the line's newest ship, the *Titanic*, on its first transatlantic crossing, from Southampton to New York, scraped an iceberg. Within three hours it sank, with the greatest loss of life at sea till then suffered in peacetime. Of the 2,208 persons aboard, only 711 were saved.[5]

The liner, at gross tonnage 46,329, was the world's largest. Its owners and builders had claimed it was "unsinkable," and until the iceberg showed otherwise, most people believed it was. It had an almost flat, cellular double bottom, designed so that if the lower, outer bottom was pierced but not the inner (located five feet apart), the entering sea water would fill only the small cellular compartment between the two. The ship also had fifteen transverse bulkheads rising from the keel; when the doors between these were closed, which could be done from the bridge by an electrical switch, they created sixteen so-called watertight compartments—watertight, however, only to the height or deck the bulkhead reached. Of the fifteen, the shortest rose only to F deck, two and a half feet above the ship's waterline; of the others, eight rose to E deck, and six to D. The compartments thus were like pails, watertight on the bottom and sides, but not at the top. As long as the ship had buoyancy, with the surrounding sea lapping at or below the ship's waterline, seawater entering any compartment would rise no higher than the sea level outside, and hence would remain contained in its compartment. But if the ship began to lose buoyancy, so that its waterline sank below the sea's surface, then the entering water would, depending on the height of the transverse bulkheads, begin to spill into the next compartment, gradually filling it, and then over into the next, and so on. But the spillage would take time, and meanwhile the ship's pumps would be ejecting water and the crew perhaps able to block or slow its entry.

If the *Titanic* had been rammed amidship, its builders claimed, it could have floated with two compartments flooded, and in a calm sea probably even with three. If it had hit the iceberg straight on, by all estimates it could have floated with the front two or perhaps three compartments flooded. But it hit the iceberg a glancing blow, five feet above the inner bottom, and the ice ripped holes in the first five forward compartments, two more than the most generous estimate of the number which could be flooded and the ship remain afloat. With so much water entering, the ship's bow began to lower into the sea, so that sea level rose above the ship's waterline, speeding the spillover from one compartment to the next. Within twenty minutes of the collision the ship's captain and the builders' agent knew their ship was doomed. It would sink, they estimated, in less than two hours. In fact, it survived two hours and forty minutes.

News of the disaster, received via radio, filled the morning papers, with the front page of *The New York Times* displaying a three-column headline ending: "Last Wireless at 12:27 a.m. Blurred." The unaccustomed speed with which Marconi "wireless" reported news from the vague and distant scene drew large crowds in cities across the country and in Britain to hear and read the latest bulletins, which the papers posted. At first, the uncertainty of the ship's fate fed the excitement; then, after its sinking was confirmed, reports of ships speeding to the rescue; and always the uncertainty of how many and who had been saved. Not until three and a half days had passed, when the Cunard liner *Carpathia* docked in New York with survivors, was there any certainty, and even then the search for bodies of the drowned continued for an additional month, with 328 found, of which some were shipped home for burial, some were buried at sea, and some in the cemeteries of Halifax, Nova Scotia.[6]

In the rush of events that followed the sinking, CCB's primary work was twofold. On Thursday evening, 18 April, with the arrival of the *Carpathia*, his immediate task was to guide *Titanic* crew members and White Star officials through seventeen days of hearings in New York and Washington before a U.S. Senate committee, and his second and ultimately more important task was to defend White Star against claims for loss of life and property because of the line's alleged negligence.

The two tasks were allied. Though the captain of the *Titanic* had gone down with his ship, the Senate committee's report eventually blamed him for continuing at full speed despite three warnings from other ships of ice ahead. It blamed the second officer, who survived, for much of the confusion in the lowering and loading of the lifeboats, which had allowed some 500 places in them to go unfilled. It blamed the British Board of Trade for a regulation requiring a ship to carry lifeboats sufficient only to save 27 percent of the crew and passengers. And it blamed White Star's president, J. Bruce Ismay, who survived, for urging the captain to excessive speed in a dangerous situation, saying that, if not by spoken word, then merely by his presence, Ismay declared the line's hope for a fast crossing. Thus, the Senate's report laid ground for claims against the company for loss of life and property due to negligence.[7]

The Senate hearings undoubtedly were hard for CCB and his clients, particularly for Ismay. Harsh newspaper headlines and stories repeated what everyone asked: with the accepted rule for loading lifeboats "Women and Children First," how could the company's president have taken a place in one when some 1,500 of his passengers and crew, including women and children, went down with the ship? Even as the hearings opened in New York, Senator Isidor Raynor (of Maryland) denounced Ismay on the Senate floor as "a coward" and stated that the White Star Line was "criminally responsible" for the disaster.[8]

The Senate committee's chairman was William Alden Smith (Republican, of Michigan), a member of Congress since 1895 and a senator since 1906. A somewhat eccentric lawyer, he liked to crusade for what he believed was right, and often did so with skill and courage; at the same time he could be remarkably deaf to the opinions of others, however reasonable their views; and though considered sincere, honest, and competent, he was also thought to be quite unpredictable and at times bluff, even brutal, in his treatment of others. He tended to be against the rich or famous and enjoyed stabbing them oratorically and creating headlines, and he no doubt saw in the *Titanic* a chance to attack J. P. Morgan and reap national, even international fame.[9] Within three days of the sinking he had arranged for his committee to be appointed, armed with powers of subpoena, and himself named chairman; even as the *Carpathia* steamed into New York Harbor on the evening of 18 April, he arrived in the city by train and went immediately to the ship to subpoena witnesses.

The next morning at 10:30 a.m. he opened the hearings in the ornate East Room of the old Astoria Hotel, at Fifth Avenue and Thirty-third Street, calling Ismay as his first witness. Though there were six other senators on the committee, Smith asked the questions, made the rulings, dominated, and was generally admired for his work.[10] In one aspect of the sinking, his seventeen days of interrogation probed deeper than the British Court of Inquiry, which followed in May. By taking testimony from all three classes of passengers aboard, of whom he questioned almost as many as he did of the crew, he was able to picture more clearly the confusion aboard ship as passengers and crew slowly grasped that it would sink. That confusion was not to the credit of the White Star Line, its captain, or its crew, but it did make plausible many of the contradictory statements about the loading of the lifeboats and offer an explanation of why so few were properly manned or filled. Yet in his eagerness to name heroes and villains, Smith also somewhat distorted the picture of what happened and why. The British inquiry, by contrast, was less concerned with praise and blame, and, taking testimony mainly from the crew and naval architects, stuck close to technical questions of the ship's construction and the captain and crew's performance. Its report, issued on 30 July, promptly was dubbed a white-wash of the captain and of the British Board of Trade, chiefly because it concluded that the captain, while he had made "a very grievous mistake" in speeding into a known ice field, was not legally negligent—because it was an established practice in clear weather not to slow down because of ice warnings.[11] In future, however, it noted that such action *would* consti-tute legal negligence. The court also exonerated Ismay for boarding a lifeboat: "Had he not jumped in he would merely have added one more life, namely his own, to the number of those lost."[12]

To Senator Smith and to most of an excited American public and press, Ismay was a villain. In addition to the ambiguity of his position aboard ship—was he a mere passenger or responsible official?—there was the fact of his survival when so many had died. Further, in his statements to the committee and to the press he often sounded arrogant and snobbish, em-bodying for many Americans the most hated aspects of British upper-class arrogance. *The American*, an anti-British paper owned by Hearst, on the first day of the hearings published a photograph of Ismay, with a caption that accused him of ordering the ship's excessive speed in icy waters and of being "a coward" who "escaped in the lifeboats with the women and chil-dren." It spelled his name "J. Brute Ismay."[13] Other newspapers were only slightly less unkind, but CCB could do little to defend his client in the press. He coached him for the hearings, however, and some of Ismay's statements about his role in the disaster sound as if drafted by counsel. But CCB later told Walter Lord, historian of the *Titanic*, "Ismay was the most arrogant client I ever had," and ultimately that arrogance, Ismay's air of being a British gentleman hounded by American dogs, kept him from winning any part of public opinion.[14]

Meanwhile, the Senate hearings, in which many judicial rules of fair-ness and procedure do not apply, began badly for Ismay. He apparently had hoped to make a statement and then be dismissed, but it soon became clear that Smith was not about to release the president of the White Star Line, and after questioning him for several hours Smith required him to remain in the city subject to the committee's wishes. By the close of the first day's hearing, which did not adjourn until 10:30 p.m., it was also clear that Smith intended to hold in the city all 215 survivors of the crew until he saw fit either to call them to testify or to release them. The prospect of this brought on the longest exchange in the hearings between him and CCB, who pointed out that most of the crew were destitute, having lost everything—clothing, property, job—and had been temporarily lodged by IMM aboard a Red Star ship, the *Lapland*, scheduled to sail the next morning. The men were understandably eager to go home, and CCB asked that the great majority of them, all but the four officers and twelve men under subpoena, be permitted to depart.

Smith refused: "I am not going to release the others."

CCB: "But they are not under subpoena."

Smith: "They are not."

CCB: "Thank you. We understand, Sir."

Smith: "I don't want to release anybody."

The drift of this confused, softly stated exchange apparently alarmed the senator, for it hinted at the bad press he might receive if he appeared to trample on the men's misery. CCB pushed the point harder: "If the committee wants to herd them up, that is one thing," he said, but "it is perfectly impossible for a steamship company to take care of 200 people without any steamship to put them on." And when the *Lapland* sailed the next day, though Smith had subpoenaed an additional 20 crew members, the remaining 170 started for home.[15]

CCB could not do so well for Ismay. In addition to the trauma of the sinking, which Ismay shared with other survivors, he was also the president of a company hit by a catastrophe, and there were decisions to be made, conferences to be held, schedules to rearrange. But on the third day of the hearings, Monday, 23 April, Smith moved them to Washington, requiring all those under subpoena to follow him there, and except for what Ismay could do by phone and telegraph, he was kept from his responsibilities. When Smith did not recall him as a witness, Ismay asked for permission to depart and was refused. The fourth day, still not recalled, he asked again and was refused. On the fifth, Wednesday, he and CCB paid a call on the senator, to no avail. Sometime on the sixth, Ismay delivered to Smith a letter, apparently drafted by CCB, in which he asked politely that, if he were to be recalled, he be summoned at the earliest time possible, so that he might then return to England. Smith's reply was abusive. He wrote of how hard he was working and how Ismay should be helping, not hindering, the investigation. And he did not recall Ismay until the tenth day of the hearings, 30 April.

This second interrogation went on for several hours as Smith took Ismay through the financial structure of IMM and its relation to White Star. Before starting, however, Smith read into the record Ismay's letter to him and his own reply. Then he inquired at length if Ismay was satisfied with the committee's procedures, with his treatment by the committee's chairman. Ismay assured the senator he was satisfied. When the torturer's hand is on the screw, the victim on the rack, if well advised, will not complain of ill treatment. Further, Smith asked, would Ismay return from England if requested and provide experts to answer technical questions? Ismay promised. Neither a witness nor his counsel can rein in a senator who is chairman of a hearing, with the power of subpoena, the power to deny counsel the right of cross-examination, and the power to order who is heard, when, and for how long. Despite Smith's tone, Ismay throughout was polite and CCB silent.[16]

Smith also asked why Ismay had sailed on the *Titanic*, and Ismay replied that he wanted to see how passenger facilities might be improved. Why had Ismay entered a lifeboat? "Because there was room in the boat. She was being lowered away. I felt the ship was going down, and I got into the boat."[17] And when the long interrogation on the corporate structure of IMM and White Star finally ended, Ismay was released and left for England.

The second part of CCB's defense of the White Star Line began when survivors and relatives of those who had drowned filed claims in federal and state courts for loss of property and lives. In accordance with the social mores of the time, relatives of the grandest persons lost did not sue. Mrs. Astor declined to put a value on her husband's life, the Wideners on their son's, or the Guggenheim, Thayer, or Straus families on the lives of their relatives. These they memorialized in other ways. To recall Isidor and Ida Straus, their family and friends gave New York, at Broadway and 106th Street, a small park with a water basin and dripping fountain beneath a reclining pensive figure of the goddess Memory, mother of the Muses. The inscription recalled Ida Straus's decision not to leave her husband: "Lovely and pleasant were they in their lives, / And in their death they were not separated." The Wideners, to commemorate their son Harry, a book collector, built at Harvard the magnificent Widener Library.[18]

Other folk did differently. Mrs. Henry B. Harris, widow of a Broadway theater owner, valued her husband's life at $1 million, which the historian Walter Lord cites as the largest claim. And he lists among the smallest Edith Rosenbaum's of $2 for a lost hot-water bottle and Mary McGovern's of $20 for time lost in court listening to lawyers.[19] Altogether the claims filed in the Unites States courts totaled $16,804,112. Both Britain and the United States, however, had statutes limiting the amounts a shipping company could be required to pay in a shipwreck, even one caused by negligence of the captain or crew. These "limited liability" statutes were intended to encourage commerce. (Ships, the two governments recognized, were extremely expensive to build—the *Titanic* cost about $7.5 million; in 2004 dollars, roughly $140 million. And once a ship was launched on the high seas, its owners, usually on land, had little or no direct control of it. In legal terms, in a shipwreck the owner typically had no "privity or knowledge" of the accident's cause.)

Yet these limitations on liability were computed quite differently in the two countries. In the United States the total allowed was the value of what was salvaged from the wreck and the money paid by passengers and shippers for a safe delivery that was not accomplished. Moreover, any insurance the owners collected for the ship's loss was not included. Of the *Titanic*, all that was salvaged was fourteen lifeboats, having an estimated secondhand value of $4,520. This amount, when added to the charges paid by passengers and shippers, made a total of $97,772.17.[20]

In Britain a different method of computation, based on the ship's tonnage, produced a figure of $3,450,000. But many passengers, British as well as American, feared that the British Board of Inquiry's opinion of "grievous mistake," not negligence, as the cause of the disaster would bar any recovery in Britain. So they sued in American courts, though claiming that the British statute, with its more generous allowance, should control. Their lawyers argued that the *Titanic* was after all a British ship with a British captain and crew, and, the iceberg being stateless, no other nationality was involved.

To limit these claims, and to meet the argument underlying them, CCB started a suit on 4 October, six months after the sinking, in the Admiralty Division of Federal District Court for the Southern District in New York. He sought a ruling that the White Star Line, though a British company, could apply to American courts for a limitation on its liability for the shipwreck and that the United States statute, not the British, should control. He did not seek to preclude claims from starting in British courts, or applying to those the British Statute. Nevertheless, a passenger who was a British subject, William J. Mellor, opposed him, arguing that the laws of Britain should apply, both as to jurisdiction (the proper court) and to the limitation of liability (which statute should control). Mellor's attorneys argued that the *Titanic* had not sunk in American territorial waters, which it never reached; the wreck was of a British ship on the high seas, with no other nationality involved. The district court agreed, deciding against CCB on both counts.[21]

CCB then took the case to the Second Circuit Court of Appeals, where he won the right to carry the case still higher. The circuit court, in place of writing a decision, certified three legal questions, the heart of CCB's case, "upon which this court desires the instructions of the Supreme Court": (a) "Whether in the case of a disaster upon the high seas" that matched in facts the ownership of the *Titanic*, the owner could sue in American courts under certain federal statutes; (b) "Whether, if in such a case" the law of the foreign country of registry provided limitations of liability different from those of the United States, the owner could sue in American courts under certain federal statutes; and (c), if the answer to (b) is "yes," "Will the courts of the United States . . . enforce the law of the United States or of the foreign country in respect to the amount of such owner's liability?"

On 13 and 14 January 1914, CCB argued the three questions before the Supreme Court, and on 25 May the Court published its opinion, written by Justice Holmes. The decision on questions a and b was 9 to 0 in favor of White Star's right to seek protection in the United States court, and on question c, 8 to 1 that the limit on liability should be calculated according to U.S. law. (Nothing in the decision stopped anyone from suing in a British court.)[22] Years later one of CCB's young partners recalled that in the Holmes opinion "a serious legal issue was handled by a very correct court in a fairly informal manner."[23] The description fits. Holmes summarized the facts and law in five pages of plain prose, without footnotes. That also was CCB's courtroom style. He did not pretend to be a legal scholar or a forensic actor, but in court he was confident, clear in presenting the facts and law, and succinct in summing up. For these reasons he usually stood well with judges, and if the case had a jury, equally well with it (though in admiralty suits for historical reasons juries were extremely rare).[24] In addition, his manner was spry, his clothing always neat and clean, and his expression open and friendly. People inclined to like him.

After this victory on the technical questions, CCB attempted to negotiate a settlement with the claimants, now joined as a group. But they still hoped to prove that White Star—through Ismay, an owner and the company president being aboard—had sufficient "privity or knowledge" of the captain's negligence in speeding into the ice field (as the Senate committee had found) to disallow the limitation on liability, and thus to remove any cap on awards for losses suffered. So the attempt at settlement failed.[25]

CCB then returned to his original suit in the New York Southern District Court, now claiming (1) there was no negligence on the part of the captain or crew (citing the conclusions of the British Court of Inquiry) and therefore no possibility of a claim against the owners; and (2) if the court should find that the captain or crew had been negligent, there still was not enough privity or knowledge on the owner's part to hold it liable. The statute, therefore, would limit the amount of the awards. The question now was: who, if anyone, was negligent?[26]

The judge—there was no jury—was Julius M. Mayer, whom CCB later described as "not a man of learning, but a good, practical, business-like judge."[27] The trial began on 22 June 1915 in Mayer's courtroom in the District Court Annex, on the twelfth floor of the Woolworth Building, and it continued for two weeks, with much of the testimony of the Senate hearings and British Court of Inquiry repeated. The claimants argued that the captain was negligent, chiefly because of Ismay's presence and urgings, while CCB countered that the ship's officers had taken full precautions and, on hearing of ice ahead, had doubled the lookout. (The validity of the logic, four eyes better than two, seemed unassailable, and therefore was useful. But privately CCB remarked to one of his partners that one lookout in the crow's nest was better than two: one will look, two will talk.)[28]

In the trial's second week the claimants called an expert witness, Rear Admiral Richard M. Watt, described as "chief constructor in the U.S. Navy." He stated that if the *Titanic* had been built with a watertight deck extending across the top of its sixteen "watertight" compartments, the ship would have stayed afloat. This perhaps was true. But the admiral over-reached; he also made a number of statements about the construction of the ships *Lusitania* and *Kronprinzess in Cecilie*, and upon cross-examination by CCB had to admit he was not an expert on the construction of either ship. CCB then put on the stand Ernest R. Rigg, chief naval architect of the New York Shipbuilding Company, who testified that the *Titanic* had been built according to the established practices of the day.[29]

At the close of argument, one claimant's counsel stated the issue, as he saw it, to Judge Mayer: "The question your Honor will consider is whether the company was guilty of negligence in rushing into the danger zone at high speed and whether Mr. Ismay was the person who directed this speed." The judge thereupon adjourned court until 27 July, when he heard both sides sum up and promised soon to begin deliberation.[30]

CCB felt he had won the case, but sometime in the next month or so, because White Star was losing money and was eager to be free of the *Titanic*, he again opened negotiations for a settlement. This time the line offered to add $500,000 to the $97,772.17 allowed by the limitation of liability statute, bringing the total available to claimants (including accrued interest on the initial amount) to $664,000. And on the evening of 17 December, CCB announced that the proposal had been accepted.[31]

On 28 July 1916, a full year after Judge Mayer had opened the case, he signed the final decree, in which he stated that the sinking with its losses was "incurred without the privity or knowledge of the petitioner" [technically, the Oceanic Steam Navigation Company], the petitioner "is not liable to any extent for any loss," any future claims "hereby are forever barred," and all those who had filed claims "are perpetually restrained and enjoined from bringing or instituting and from prosecuting any action . . . whatsoever in any county or jurisdiction . . . for any loss."[32]

The decree, signed by all the claimants' attorneys, followed the ship's sinking by four years, three months, fourteen days. In that time, claims against White Star in American courts, with interest added, had risen to roughly $18 million. CCB had won for his client a settlement of $664,000, less than 4 percent of that potential liability.

The saga of the *Titanic* was the twentieth century's longest-running news story, beginning with a single event that had lasted only a few hours. Even in the 1990s any survivor dying was assured an obituary recalling the incident, and even today any exhibit or event concerning it will draw an audience. In the days immediately after the sinking, the continually renewed and often confusing radio reports pushed all other news aside, and then throughout the months of the Senate hearings and the British Court of Inquiry, the story's facts, surmises, and survivors' tales and photographs daily took up four, five, or six pages of the newspapers.[33]

Everywhere, people saw in it elements of myth: impassive nature humbling man's pride in his technology, and, though perhaps more slowly grasped, the doom of a social era. Three years more, and a world war began to narrow the vast difference between traveling through life first class or in steerage. On the *Titanic*, those in first class embarked with maids, valets, dogs, automobiles, and some with more than fifty pieces of personal luggage; in steerage, many had only their hopes of a better life in the New World.

In addition, there were the small, sharp pictures of human behavior under stress: the ship's eight-man band playing its cheery numbers to the end; the richest man aboard, John Jacob Astor, after putting his young, pregnant wife in a lifeboat, going to the dog pens to release his Airedale terrier "Kitty"; the elderly Ida Straus, whose family owned Macy's department store, declining to leave her husband; and, in contrast, the socialite William Carter, of Philadelphia and Palm Beach, who, having abandoned his wife and children to save himself, later greeting them aboard the

Carpathia, "I never thought you'd make it." Mountaineers in Appalachia who had never seen an ocean or a liner soon had composed a hundred-verse ballad with the refrain: "It was sad when that great ship went down."

Eighty-five years later, at the end of the century, the saga still had enormous appeal. In 1994 a Japanese company announced it would build a replica of the *Titanic* to use as a hotel and conference center; the next year a monument to commemorate the disaster was unveiled in Greenwich, England; and in 1997 it was the subject of Broadway and Hollywood spectaculars. Meanwhile, in 1985 a Franco-American expedition located the liner on the ocean floor and was able to examine parts of it, resolving some old questions while raising new. Among those answered was the liner's position at the time of sinking, fixing it at eighteen miles, not ten, from the *Californian,* a fact moderating criticism of the latter's captain for not speeding to the rescue. Among the new questions raised: what caused the hole near the ship's bow, which must have hastened its sinking? Was there some internal explosion? None was reported.[34]

For CCB's small firm, the ship's disaster was the foundation on which he and his five partners were able to build and expand, giving them greater leeway than had most such firms to choose clients, partners, and young associates. To the thirty-six firms or attorneys who signed Judge Mayer's final decree, CCB and his firm were now well known, as they were also to many farther afield who had followed the case. Across the country, the *Titanic* litigation made CCB's firm a leader in admiralty law, a position strengthened as commerce in New York's harbor steadily increased. By 1922 an attorney in Minneapolis, writing to a friend in New York, would refer to CCB as "the dean of your admiralty bar."[35] And when CCB died in 1959, the London *Times* wrote, "As one of the outstanding mercantile lawyers of his day he handled litigation in the American courts arising out of the *Titanic* disaster. It was this connexion with maritime cases that won him high esteem in the British legal fraternity."[36]

More personally for CCB, the case and its aftermath brought him financial ease. The firm's fee for his defense of the White Star Line is not known, but it must have been substantial. As the senior partner, he would have had the largest share, possibly as much as 50 percent, and most of it received before federal and state governments began to tax income. After 1916, at the age of fifty-eight, because his tastes were moderate, he now had enough money to do as he wanted.

A book of the Old Testament that he liked to quote was Ecclesiastes, which in 9:11 warns: "The race is not to the swift, nor the battle to the

strong . . . but time and chance happeneth to them all." He did not pretend to himself or others that his good fortune was based solely on skill or
hard work; he knew that much of it lodged in a unique maritime disaster.

In early February 1916, after CCB had settled all claims in U.S. courts
for the sinking of the *Titanic*, his health collapsed and Louie took him to
the Princess Hotel, in Bermuda, to recuperate. There they remained
throughout the spring, returning directly to Black Point, where he stayed
through June. In all, he was out of his office five months.[37]

The symptoms of his illness seem to have been the same, though less
severe, as those he suffered in 1892, which he later characterized as "nervous prostration," with fatigue, giddiness, inability to concentrate, and a
loss of confidence in his physical and mental abilities. This time, he seems
to have suffered chiefly from fatigue.[38] In April, from Bermuda, he wrote
to Learned Hand: "Peace and quietude reign here, the excitement roused
by the arrival of the steamer soon passeth away. The boat brings only the
newspaper of its sailing day and the previous Sunday, and the Bermuda
daily is an emptiness—all of which spells Rest, and makes letters trebly
dear."[39] In June, back in Black Point and again writing to Hand, he discussed the war news from Europe and national politics. (With the presidential election still five months ahead, he offered Hand "a prophecy,
which you can seal up and open November 7, 1916." His prediction—that
the candidates were to be Woodrow Wilson and Charles Evans Hughes,
and that Wilson would win—proved correct.) Then he suddenly inter-
jected: "How are your intestines? My blood pressure has risen to 115. But
I *still* soar a bit." So perhaps there were blood pressure or other circulatory
difficulties.[40]

Plainly, this second breakdown was less serious than the first. He was
physically less ill, out of the office only half as long, not financially
pressed, and as the triumphant head of his firm was assured of his place
whenever he wished to resume it. Moreover, he and Louie, having weath-
ered the more serious illness of 1892, knew that a full recovery was possible and believed they knew how to achieve it: through rest. His recovery
seemed to prove it, for by July 1916 he was back at work full-time.[41]

From the two illnesses he claimed to have learned that prolonged,
hard-pressed work threatened his equilibrium, yet he soon again was in a
situation where his health threatened to fail, and in April 1918, having
taken on extra patriotic duties because of the country's entry into the war,
he anxiously wrote to Hand:

I am at present hoping to get relieved of my job as chairman of Local Board Div. 8 as it has proved rather more than I can stand—Eight to ten hours a day for two months and a half has rather done me up—in fact my doctor told me if I did not quit there was serious danger of a complete break up again—So as soon as I can get a successor appointed I must get away for a good rest. All of which means that there can be no question of my going to Washington—I've had my try at really hard work and find I can't stand it—It's humiliating, but there can be no doubt that it's better to quit now and be able to do a certain amount of work in the future than to hang on for a month or two longer and then be permanently laid up again.[42]

In view of CCB's good health in all but two periods of his life, and especially considering his vitality in his last forty years, his two "prostrations" (with a third threatened) are mysterious. He thought the breakdowns of 1892 and 1916 were both the result of overwork. Though he himself never said as much, the first might be seen as the nervous collapse of an anxious young lawyer whose pay barely supported his family, and the second perhaps has a surer explanation: the temporary collapse of a fifty-eight-year-old lawyer who, having defended an unpopular and highly publicized client for four years, finds himself, after suddenly winning the case, exhausted and momentarily bereft of purpose. To CCB the cause as well as the cure in both instances was entirely physical. Today, with advances in psychiatry and the use of drugs to control depressions, others might be inclined to think the illnesses were, in some part, mental. But what part? He seems happy in all respects: wife, children, friends, church, outlook, work.

Moreover, nervous breakdowns of his type were then not uncommon among the educated urban middle class, and were generally ascribed to overwork. New York lawyers typically worked long hours, and until the late 1930s most went to their offices on Saturdays, staying at least until early afternoon. Their profession being adversarial, they competed daily with rivals in the courtroom, in negotiations, and even within the firm, and there were frequent opportunities to be agitated, to feel exhausted, defeated, or failing. Hence lawyers and their families often judged a breakdown to be merely a physical revolt of overtaxed nerves, with the attendant symptoms, often loss of interest in any activity and extreme fatigue without cause, being surely temporary.

Before World War I many American men regained their health, or perhaps resolved unacknowledged emotional problems, by going out West, where the outdoor life supposedly was more basic and simple, and therefore more healthy. Two lawyers who went to the West for a cure, both college mates of CCB, were Theodore Roosevelt and Owen Wister, and the latter created out of his Western experience that seminal novel of cowboy myth *The Virginian* (1902), with its famous drawl, "When you call me that, *smile!*" After the war, New York lawyers suffering breakdowns typically stayed closer to home and office, many retreating for a cure either to Four Winds, a country estate in Katonah, New York, or to Silvermine, a sanitarium in the woods behind Norwalk, Connecticut. Though some stayed many months and received psychiatric treatment, others went only for ten or twelve weeks, during which they slept well, ate a controlled diet, and perhaps worked in the carpentry shop. In the 1920s many referred to their experience as "unwinding," "taking time out," or "recharging the battery." By the 1930s, when psychiatry had become fashionable at least among the educated young and the rich, talk of its use in a breakdown was more open, yet many who stayed for long periods at these sanitariums were little inclined to say so, and their families often assured friends that both the illness and the cure were purely physical.

CCB was not ashamed of his breakdowns and made no secret of them; indeed, after 1918 he offered them constantly as the reason for rejecting any suggestion of public office. Though to the world he seemed remarkably healthy, especially in his last forty years, he thought of himself, as did his wife, as physically weak and without the normal reserves of strength.[43] Yet curiously, this second illness, though imposing a sense of physical limitation, seems to have been spiritually liberating.

In August 1916, when he turned fifty-eight, CCB had a life expectancy of twelve or fifteen years, and soon was writing to Hand that for physical reasons he would never be "going to Washington" or into any official position. Yet in this decade the gaiety and humor, so much admired in him in later years, steadily increased. His entries for his periodic Harvard Class Reports, which hitherto had been perfunctory—"Nothing extraordinary has happened to me . . . My firm name continues the same, Wing, Putnam & Burlingham" (1905)—began to tell more of his life and thoughts, lightened by such self-deprecating twists as "I cannot see how any of this is of the slightest interest" (1929). His classmates, however, found his bits of news and humor attractive, and also discovered, as he attended more college functions, that he himself, in his forthright way, was charming. Thus, some forty years after leaving Harvard, where he had made few friends as an undergraduate, he slowly became a fondly admired figure in the Class of '79.[44]

Whatever effect CCB's illness in 1916 (and threat of its recurrence in 1918) may have had on his disposition, it did not lessen his interest in trying to improve the judiciary. On returning to his office in the summer of 1916, he picked up where he had left off in scheming to bring better men to the federal district courts and to advance the best of them to the Second Circuit Court of Appeals. Generally speaking, in lobbying to advance men within the federal system there was no need for large impromptu committees, rallies in Carnegie Hall, and private meetings with the district leaders. Federal appointments, made by the country's president on the advice of his attorney general, chiefly required access to a few highly placed politicians.

The record of CCB's influence in appointments to the federal judiciary in New York is often spotty and inconclusive, for much of his work necessarily was done behind the scenes, in personal meetings, letters, and phone conversations. But every now and then a surviving letter, a public statement, or an anecdote in someone's oral history illuminates his actions and principles. Writing in 1924, for instance, to William Howard Taft, then chief justice of the U.S. Supreme Court, CCB lamented that some recent appointments to the federal bench had been "pretty good; but no name was considered unless the man had been active in the party. Often a man who has been a stiff party man, like Judge Wallace, makes a very fine judge, but the best lawyers are usually not politicians; is not that true? In this district we need just now another learned man or two." Besides good character and judicial temperament, he wanted more legal learning.[45]

One man whom CCB had believed was outstandingly qualified for appointment to a district court, and then later for advancement to the Second Circuit Court of Appeals, was Charles Merrill Hough (1858–1927), who early in 1906 had been a partner in Robinson, Biddle and Ward (predecessor to the firm from which, four years later, CCB recruited Montgomery and Beecher). Though the firm did much admiralty work, the client most often employing Hough was the Pennsylvania Railroad. In one respect Hough was an unlikely candidate for the bench. Though happily married, he had a prickly, isolated personality. The son of an army veteran who in the Civil War had risen from private to brigadier general, he adored his father, and had turned to law instead of the army only because of poor eyesight. He had adopted, however, a gruff military bearing, and because he had an ugly face as well as an inclination to bark at those whose minds moved slowly, many lawyers found him intimidating.[46]

CCB, however, once again drawn to the odd or crippled individual, became friendly with Hough, and insisted to others that beneath the man's harsh exterior was a streak of sensitivity, even sentimentality. Though some may have questioned Hough's temperament for the bench, none doubted the caliber of his mind, and in the city an influential group of lawyers urged his appointment to the Southern District Court.[47] Their efforts soon made the appointment seem assured, another example of loyalties embedded in New York City politics reaching high into the federal government. Hough was a Republican, and in 1906 Theodore Roosevelt was president, with Root as secretary of state, W. H. Taft secretary of war, and William H. Moody attorney general. All three cabinet members were enthusiastic for Hough, and in addition he had the support of two important New York Republican leaders, the head of the party organization in Manhattan, Congressman Herbert B. Parsons, and the state's leading senator, Chauncey M. Depew. Yet suddenly, in the early spring of 1906, the movement for Hough stalled. Roosevelt, in full cry against big corporations and trusts, wanted a man less identified with the Pennsylvania Railroad.

CCB at the time happened to be in Vermont, not far from Hanover, New Hampshire, and Dartmouth College, of which Hough was a graduate. Telegraphed by a friend in Washington that the appointment was in trouble, CCB hurried to Dartmouth's president, William Jewett Tucker, and, explaining the situation, drafted a telegram for Tucker to send to the president, the gist being that Hough's work for the railroad was an added reason to appoint him because he knew the ways of big corporations. But surely more persuasive than the telegram was the urging of the cabinet officers and of the party leader, Parsons. Roosevelt, bowing to pressure, on 21 June 1906 appointed Hough to the Southern District Court.[48]

Seven years later, when Noyes resigned from the three-judge Second Circuit Court of Appeals, a door opened to advance Hough, and this time CCB's actions were more directly influential. In 1913 the Democrat Woodrow Wilson was president, with James Clark McReynolds his attorney general and Colonel Edward M. House, who held no public office, his chief friend and political adviser. CCB began his campaign for Hough in his usual manner, talking to other lawyers, exciting them to recommend Hough, while he started a correspondence with Colonel House that soon became friendly. Attorney General McReynolds objected to Hough for a number of reasons, but mainly because he was a Republican, and the appointment ultimately went to Henry Wade Rogers, then dean of Yale

Law School (the first of several deans from that school to serve on the Second Circuit bench).[49] Though disappointed, CCB waited, watched, and early in 1916, with the resignation of another judge from the appeals court, had a second chance to propose Hough. By then President Wilson had moved McReynolds to the Supreme Court and Thomas Gregory was attorney general, a far more genial and less rigid personality than McReynolds. And Colonel House, already favorable to Hough, thanks to CCB, was still advising the president.

Burlingham and others who favored Hough promptly revived their campaign, and in the course of it CCB and James Byrne, two of New York's leading Democratic attorneys, went to Washington to see Gregory. They had to wait till evening to meet with him, but the attorney general, a Texan and a bit deaf, was full of Southern courtesy. He greeted them to his office, and against the winter's chill had the fire lit and chairs placed before it. After pleasantries, he stated the problem: Hough was a Republican. "Can we get a Democrat?" he asked. "Isn't there a Democrat that would fill this place?" His Democratic visitors replied: "There's no Democrat that's equal to Hough." Back and forth went the discussion, but CCB and Byrne held firm. Later, after the campaign had succeeded and Hough was on the court, CCB said, "We'd never have got it but for Colonel House. *Never.*" Yet he and Byrne surely impressed Gregory to some extent.[50]

On both the trial and appeals court Hough proved an exceptional judge, in competence, industry, and learning. In his ten years on the district court, despite bouts of ill health, he conducted more than 1,200 trials and filed 1,809 written opinions. A fellow judge noted of him that in a trial, "the high initial velocity of his mind was conspicuously effective in mastering facts, analyzing evidence, and applying general principles to concrete cases." But that swiftness could unnerve lawyers unable to keep abreast, and many found his failures of patience quite terrifying.[51] In his ten years as an appeals judge, Hough was equally industrious, participating in the hearing of 2,047 cases and writing opinions in 675. He was strong on bankruptcy, patent, and admiralty law, and considered to be one of the best judges in the English-speaking world for commercial cases. In addition, he found time to lecture, to serve as president of the Maritime Law Association (1919–27), and to make use of his scholarly bent by writing a history of the Southern District Court and its judges and by editing, with a "Historical Introduction and Appendix," *Reports of Cases in the Vice Admiralty of the Province of New York and in the Court of Admiralty of the State of New York, 1715–1788.* His only flaw was his occasional lapse in judicial temperament. CCB, speaking of him after his death in 1927, recalled him as "impatient of irrelevance, incompetence and prolixity" and at times presenting "a formidable and even alarming exterior," adding that even such a confident young lawyer as Felix Frankfurter confessed to walking round the courthouse twice before going in to face Hough.[52]

Not all lawyers aided by CCB to the bench reached Hough's level of excellence, and a difficulty in any judicial nomination is that no one, not even the candidate, can be sure how well or poorly the lawyer will transform into a judge, whether for trials or appeals. One who, in CCB's opinion, proved merely adequate as an appeals judge and might have done better in a trial court was his friend (and Hough's former law partner) Henry Galbraith Ward, whom President Roosevelt in 1907 appointed to the Second Circuit Court of Appeals, where he served for fourteen years. Despite CCB's friendship with Ward, who had helped him financially in his first illness, CCB, ever honest, wrote of him in a memorial: "Judges and lawyers are soon forgotten—only the greatest survive. Judge Ward was not one of these." He might have been, wrote CCB, if appointed to a district court where in conducting trials "his experience at the bar, his firmness, courtesy, good sense and knowledge of the world" would have counted for more. Though Ward, as CCB took care to note, was an exceptionally good man and a fine lawyer, his best qualities did not flourish on the appeals court, where he tended to be impatient of discussion.[53]

One lawyer who proved an outstanding success as both a trial and an appeals judge was Learned Hand's first cousin Augustus Noble Hand. Two years older than "B," cousin "Gus," despite a similar background of family, Harvard College and Law School, had a very different personality. Learned, who was rather mercurial, inclined to worry, and easily depressed, always saw multiple sides to every question, was skeptical of any belief, but had a mind capable of original thought and the ability to express that thought in memorable language. Augustus, though less brilliant in style and thought, wobbled less in doubt and was perhaps even surer in judgment. To CCB, Gus was "so stable," he seemed "like a part of nature itself," like a "mountain" or "a great oak." In later years, when the cousins were together on the Court of Appeals, a quip among lawyers and judges was that in writing briefs or decisions, one should "quote B, but follow Gus."[54]

CCB's part in Augustus Hand's appointment in 1914 to the Southern District Court (which had gained a fourth judge in 1909) is obscure, in part because Gus, unlike Learned, was quite unself-conscious and did not preserve his papers. Yet his first law clerk, Charles E. Wyzanski Jr., who became an intimate friend and later himself a district court judge, declared in a memorial address: "President Wilson, following the suggestion of this Association's beloved member, Charles C. Burlingham, appointed Augustus N. Hand." And later Felix Frankfurter, either echoing Wyzanski or writing from his own knowledge, said the same.[55]

In trials, what happens in the courtroom is often more important than the judge's written opinion. In this respect, A. N. Hand fulfilled the judge's chief duty almost to perfection. He conducted trials in such a manner that the jury, the counsel, the spectators, and even the defendants left his courtroom persuaded that the issues of fact and law had been raised and considered and the court in its rulings and procedures had been fair. And the same was true in hearing arguments on appeal; Hand's attentive presence exuded the quiet certainty of his intellectual processes and his religious faith, faith being defined not as adherence to a particular creed or sect (though he was an active vestryman and warden of Grace Episcopal Church, in New York) but, in Wyzanski's words, as "that search for meaning, which though it never reaches its goal, gives life a structural unity."[56] In that respect, CCB and Gus Hand were alike, whereas Learned, the religious skeptic, was different.

In the American legal world, as acquaintance with the Hands and their works began to spread, each of the two judges whom CCB had befriended, though so different in character, persuaded those who worked with them and watched them that an honest search for truth, conducted with learning, rectitude, and generosity, can be achieved and that it is one of humanity's noblest triumphs.

One judicial attribute that CCB ranked high and sought in the candidates he recommended for the federal bench was an ability to write—at very least with clarity and, still better, with some style. This attribute he put to the fore in the selection in 1910 of a judge for the Eastern District Court. In 1907 President Roosevelt had appointed Thomas Chatfield to the position once held by Charles Benedict, and then, in the spring of 1910, Congress, responding to the increase in the court's business, authorized a second judge for it. This was the position to be filled by President Taft, who had Wickersham as his attorney general. To Wickersham in August 1910, CCB wrote an analysis of the five leading candidates for the new judgeship, preferring Van Vechten Veeder, whom he knew mainly through the man's writings.[57]

Veeder had practiced for ten years in Chicago before coming to New York in 1900, where he had formed a two-man firm that took some admiralty cases but whose chief clients were several Long Island street railway companies. But what stirred CCB's enthusiasm were the scholarly articles

Veeder wrote about English cases and legal figures, which had won praise even in England. CCB, sending several of the articles to Learned Hand, commented on Veeder's combination of workaday practice, the trolley lines, and legal-historical scholarship: "We know that good writing doesn't mean good judging or vice versa but seriously, I find Veeder very strong on the practical side."[58]

To Wickersham, who knew Veeder well, CCB wrote: "As to politics— Who cares now in New York. In three days I would get all the political support for any candidate you should name, however inconspicuous or unknown. You know well how many politicians there are who are only too happy to learn the name of the man who is to be named to declare that he was always their candidate." And then, with a jibe at the judge whom Veeder would join on the Eastern District Court, CCB closed: "Remember that with Chatfield on the Bench for life, there is especial need of a lawyer near him. He might learn something at lunch."[59] The following winter, 1911, President Taft appointed Veeder to the post, where he served with distinction for six years—until lured back to private practice by CCB, when he once again sought a lawyer of a particular sort for yet another reorganization of the Burlingham firm.[60]

Just as CCB had worked to advance Hough from the Southern District Court to the Second Circuit Court of Appeals, he hoped to advance Learned Hand, who, though an excellent trial judge, seemed likely to be an even finer appeals judge. On appeal, the subject matter typically is less concerned with fact and more with legal analysis and application of principles, areas in which Hand was particularly strong. For these reasons as well as for the increase in pay and prestige, he, too, was eager to make the move, and in the spring of 1917, following a judge's resignation from the court, Hand actively sought the post, backed by an impressive group of lawyers and journalists, including CCB, George Rublee, a leading Washington lawyer, Felix Frankfurter, currently in President Wilson's administration as a labor mediator, and Walter Lippmann and Herbert Croly of *The New Republic*. While CCB worked to widen and organize support among the New York bar, Hand went to Washington and met with Attorney General Gregory, but without success. No appointment was announced, and as the summer passed, Hand's chance seemed to fade.[61]

In November, CCB wrote a second time to Gregory, stressing that by then Hand had been sitting for two months on a temporary assignment to the appeals court, where he "has not only given satisfaction to the Bar, but, as I am sure you would learn from any of the Circuit Judges, has been a most helpful colleague. His logical power and his wide and deep legal learning are greatly needed in the Court. No other District Judge can compare with him in these respects." But in March 1918, Martin T. Manton, a judge on the Southern District Court, with fewer and less distinguished years of service than Hand, was promoted over him.[62]

The chief reasons were two: Manton was a faithful party Democrat whereas Hand was a Republican, and, perhaps more damning, Hand in a recent decision had shown his independence of mind by ruling against the government and popular feeling. In *Masses Publishing Co. v. Patten* (1917), a case of First Amendment rights exercised to criticize the government in wartime, Hand had supported the idea that dissent, even in wartime, was a constitutionally protected right, but he had promptly been reversed by a unanimous Second Circuit Court of Appeals, smudging in the eyes of some his reputation as a judge.[63] Before the reversal, in October 1917, confident that he had judged rightly, Hand wrote to CCB:

> I think all this building [the federal courthouse in Manhattan], plus Veeder, is against me, although Ward does not commit himself. Gus thinks of it as nothing more than another instance of my natural perversity. The perversity is there all right and God knows how much my subconscious self, which is no doubt a cross-grained critter, may have been fooling with my cerebral centres, but I never was better satisfied with any piece of work I did in my life. I do not mean that I was pleased with it as a judicial performance, but with the result. There is a bit of it that is arguable, no doubt; in the main outline I have been very happy to do what I believe was some service to temperateness and sanity.[64]

World War I had to end before others could see the wisdom and patriotism in Hand's analysis defending the right to publish articles and cartoons decrying government policies. But time justified him. His analysis of the question "When, if at all, may the state penalize political dissenters?" first won the attention and then the gradual adherence of Justice Holmes, who echoed several of the decision's ideas in one of his famous dissents, and ultimately in 1969 the Supreme Court adopted Hand's analysis, which then became "the law of the land." As his biographer points out, Hand's decision in the *Masses* case was "the most important, pathbreaking opinion of his trial court tenure."[65]

In 1921 Hand had another chance to rise following the resignation of CCB's friend Ward from the Second Circuit, but all signs prophesied against him. In the White House was President Warren Harding, an "Old Guard" or "Taft" Republican, who would remember that in the 1912 battle between the Taft and Roosevelt wings of the Republican Party Hand had supported Roosevelt. Worse, he had run in 1913 as a Roosevelt Progressive against the conservative candidate for chief judge of the New York State Court of Appeals.[66] And though he had lost in the subsequent three-way race, winning only 195,000 of the 1.5 million votes cast, his tally had allowed the Democratic candidate to beat the Taft Republican by a mere 3,000 votes, a defeat that stung the Republican loyalists.

In that election Hand had refused to campaign, thinking electioneering inappropriate for a judge, and it is a close question whether in these years he was more politically active than a federal judge should be. His biographer, while pointing out that custom then was more flexible than now, states that even then Hand was "treading a thin and occasionally imperceptible line." Hand himself soon came to believe he had crossed it, and though continuing to follow politics closely, never again played a part in them.[67]

Thus, the promotion of Hand to the appeals court in 1921 seemed so unlikely that he and his admirers instead backed a campaign for the appointment of Julius M. Mayer. And Harding, in 1921, did indeed promote Mayer—like Manton, Hand's junior on the district court—to the Second Circuit, where he served until 1924, when he resigned to return to private practice.

By then the political situation in Washington was quite different. Harding had died in disgrace, shamed by the corruption in his administration (of which the "Teapot Dome" oil scandal was the worst). Vice President Calvin Coolidge had succeeded to the presidency in 1923 and had replaced the unsavory Attorney General Harry M. Daugherty with Harlan Fiske Stone, a New York lawyer, former dean of Columbia Law School and a friend of CCB. And Chief Justice Taft, who had advised Harding against any consideration of Hand for the U.S. Supreme Court because Hand had "turned out to be a wild Roosevelt man" who had "made an ass of himself by running for the New York Court of Appeals," relented—somewhat. He urged Coolidge to appoint Hand to the Second Circuit Court "as the best man" available.[68]

This 1924 campaign on Hand's behalf went easily, as the joking tone in CCB's letter to Stone suggests:

> I need not tell you that the resignation of Mayer is a very severe blow to our Circuit Court of Appeals. It was feeble enough anyway and now it is tottering. With all proper deference and respect, I am sure I am right in my conviction that the best man on the bench to fill Mayer's place is Learned Hand. Politically he is unstable enough, but by learning, expe-

rience and character, he is perfectly fitted for the Appellate Bench. Now, may I make a brash suggestion to Your Excellency? If your honorable chief [Coolidge] is elected, he can do anything. If he is defeated, ditto.[69]

When Coolidge won the presidency in November 1924, defeating Democrat John W. Davis, in the first week of December he sent Hand's nomination to the Senate, which confirmed it unanimously. And on 29 December Hand took a seat on the Second Circuit Court of Appeals, sworn in by the senior judge, Charles M. Hough.

CCB's work to improve the quality of the federal bench in New York was inevitably episodic. He had to wait for the opportunities to open, and they weren't always favorable; but when they were, then there he was, as Learned Hand once wrote, "busy as a bee intriguing."[70] But in another area of his life, his work for St. George's Church, his focus could be constant, and there he brought to his work all the same skills and contacts that he deployed in trying to improve the federal bench. In both areas he displayed the same social and civic consciousness without distinguishing in any way between church and law. He saw life whole; and increasingly people commented of him that he was always the same person whether momentarily engaged in politics, economics, or legal or social matters. It was a source of strength.

Religion, Social Justice, and Brotherhood

ON 1 DECEMBER 1914, CCB was elected to the vestry of St. George's Church, which he had joined in 1891.[1] As he had been drawn into its activities, his attachment to it had deepened, and he had an increasing part in shaping its response to New York City's social, political, and religious problems. For roughly half a century, 1885 to 1935, St. George's was a leader in what became known as the Social Gospel movement, and though that pleased CCB, it did not please everyone, not even all Episcopalians.

In essence, the Social Gospel movement sought to give equal weight to both parts of what Jesus preached as the great double precept: love thy God and love thy neighbor. As reported by St. Mark, Jesus gave neither command a preference, saying, "For the second is like . . . There is none other commandment greater than these."[2] Yet traditionally American Protestants, with their Calvinistic heritage, had emphasized the first, seeing salvation principally in obedience to God, a personal, even private act and relationship. Those now drawn to the Social Gospel interpretation tended to redress the balance in the precept, or even to give preference to the second command, seeing the best, if not only, method of achieving salvation in the acts of loving thy neighbor.

When CCB joined St. George's, the church had been engaged for eight years in a major reorganization. Founded in 1752 on Beekman Street as a "chapel" of Trinity Church, it had moved in 1848 to Stuyvesant Square at Second Avenue and Sixteenth Street, where for twenty years it had enjoyed great success as an Episcopal evangelical "low" church, noted for great preaching and an exceptional Sunday school. By the spring of 1881, however, many of the neighborhood's richer families, whose pew rents had provided half or more of the church's income, had moved farther uptown, leaving the church with a roster of less than two dozen families, a growing annual deficit, and a discouraged rector about to depart in defeat for a church in Baltimore.[3]

St. George's problems were not unique. In Manhattan during the last quarter of the nineteenth century perhaps as many as forty Protestant churches left the area below Twentieth Street to follow their congregations uptown, even as hundreds of thousands of immigrants poured into the old neighborhoods, turning single-family houses into tenements. In the Episcopal churches, the governing vestries—typically a rector, two wardens, and eight vestrymen—usually concluded that the only sensible course was to relocate their church farther uptown.[4]

At St. George's, the vestry—ten lawyers, bankers, and businessmen, of whom J. Pierpont Morgan soon became the most famous—began a search for a new site, judging the most likely to be the southeast corner of Madison Avenue and Seventieth Street. Yet ultimately the men voted to remain on Stuyvesant Square, though the block-sized park was now a soiled desert, its fountain dry, its grass scuffed, its bushes crushed brambles. For those who had grown up in the church, the decision to stay may have been primarily sentimental; for others, financial; for one or two, perhaps, convenience. But however mixed their reasons, they also believed strongly in St. George's evangelical style of service, with its emphasis on preaching and on Sunday school, and some may have felt a duty to the neighborhood. In any event, in May 1882 they invited a dynamic young preacher from Toronto to become their rector, offering to support him in a complete reformation of the church.[5]

This man, William Stephen Rainsford (1850–1933), the eldest son of an Anglican minister, had grown up in Ireland and England but in the mid-1870s had come to preach in the United States and Canada. Invited in 1878 to Toronto to conduct a mission at St. James Cathedral, he had attracted large crowds, stirring many to rejoin the church, and by May 1882 was the cathedral's assistant rector. And because he expected soon, on the present rector's retirement, to be elected to the post, he declined St. George's invitation.

The vestry hesitated, for it had not seen any man it liked so much. Rainsford was thirty-one, tall, fair-haired, athletic, full of energy and enthusiasm. He seemed just the man to revive St. George's, making it a house of God's Word for the thousands living nearby who never entered it. In October the vestry reissued its invitation, proposing to send two members to Toronto to speak with Rainsford. Instead he came to New York. A new bishop of Toronto, insisting he should have been consulted before

Rainsford's election to the cathedral post, had refused to confirm it. So in November, at a vestry meeting in Morgan's house, Rainsford listened to a gloomy report of St. George's depressed condition, and then, with plans he had prepared for Toronto, outlined his idea of what St. George's might be—a great urban parish, serving rich and poor alike. If they would back him, he would lead. Responding for the vestry, Morgan said, "Done."[6]

First, pew rentals were abolished, and with weekly announcements in the *Herald* and *Times*, St. George's became the first large Episcopal church in the city to proclaim its seats "free." No longer could a family reserve a pew for its exclusive use. The brass nameplates were removed, and in the case of several pews, the vestry had to buy out unexpired contracts. But from Rainsford's first day as rector, the church was open to all, invited to sit anywhere.[7] Then, to replace the pew rents, so vital to the budget, a system of weekly contributions by envelope was started, any amount welcome and its size, large or small, concealed. (Not for many years, however, did income from this source match what pew rents had furnished.)[8]

To reach the church's new tenement neighbors as well as former parishioners still living nearby, Rainsford and two assistants in his first fifteen months made 10,872 house calls, one of which took him to Staten Island. He had found on a list of names a "Mrs. Croker," and learned she was the mother of Boss Croker, the Tammany leader. Rainsford, whose idealism did not preclude calculation, promptly called on the old lady, who was pleased and asked him to return to give her communion, which he did. Soon after, he received a letter of thanks from Boss Croker, and lo! the city cleaned up Stuyvesant Square, kept it tidy thereafter, and assigned a genial Irish policeman to patrol it on Sundays and holidays.[9]

To reach those in tenements, Rainsford opened a mission several blocks east of St. George's, on Avenue A between Fifteenth and Sixteenth Streets, where he hired a room behind a saloon, hoping to lure men, women, and children into simple services. For the first meeting, with a roomful of women and children and a man's head occasionally poking in from the saloon, he intended perhaps only a hymn, a prayer, and an invitation to the church. But before he was well started, a gang of boys charged him in a scrum formation, knocking him flat to the floor. With some assistance— Rainsford had brought with him two laymen who believed in "the church militant"—he managed to eject the ringleaders. Later, as he walked back to the church, the neighborhood boys marched behind, banging cans, chanting, and mocking.[10] Soon this sort of trouble ceased, brought to an end perhaps on the day Rainsford knocked out cold a surly drunk who was plaguing a female volunteer by whispering smut at her. The watching boys were impressed, and within the year the Sunday school in the saloon, conducted mostly by volunteers, had 150 students.

Next, the church opened a kindergarten on Avenue A, only the second of its kind in the city. For Rainsford, there was not only Christ's command, "Suffer little children to come unto me," but he also believed strongly that though the elder generation of immigrants might be lost to the church, their children might be won. And in twenty years he brought St. George's from an active enrollment of about 100, mostly members of some twenty families, to 8,290, of which fully a third were the children of German immigrants. Attendance at Sunday school, meantime, rose from 300 to 2,300.[11]

By 1906, when Rainsford resigned, exhausted physically and spiritually, St. George's, with its 4,000 communicants, daily services, large plant, and numerous organizations, was the largest and most active Episcopal parish in the United States. It had a Boys' Club, for which a trade school, New York's first, had been developed; a Girls' Club; a Girls' Friendly Society, the country's largest, working to improve conditions for girls in poor homes; several seaside cottages to which parishioners and their families were taken for a day, or a week; a Men's Club, whose track team in 1911 would win a national marathon; and a parish house, the first in America designed for group activities, with club rooms, an auditorium, and a gymnasium where, to the horror of conservative Episcopalians, Rainsford allowed dancing.

In addition, the church had an outstanding choir, with a black baritone soloist, Harry T. Burleigh, who in 1894 had won the post over fifty-nine white contestants, making St. George's the city's first large church to have an interracial choir. Initially, his presence had stirred some opposition among parishioners, but that soon dissolved, for Burleigh was an exceptional person, and not only as a musician, but as a singer, composer, arranger, and preserver of Negro spirituals. Soon, through concert tours, he became a national figure, yet he continued to sing at St. George's until 1946, fifty-two years in all, during the last thirty of which he was one of the most admired members of the church.[12]

But if, as CCB once declared, "Rainsford drew us to St. George's," there were many Protestants, including some Episcopalians of "high" church persuasion, who questioned the development of such an "institutional" church, asking what a social program like a track team or a seaside cottage had to do with sin and salvation.[13] In this they somewhat resembled the conservative evangelical Protestants, especially in Baptist and Methodist churches, for whom religion continued to be a quest for individual regeneration, with signs of progress a public confession of sin followed by a conversion. For such persons, social programs, and even more dubiously the political positions into which attempted resolutions of urban social problems seemed to lead, such as supporting the formation of labor unions, were quite outside the province of religion.[14]

Roughly speaking, according to a historian of the Social Gospel movement, it "took root and grew most vigorously among Unitarians, Congregationalists, and Episcopalians—three American religious bodies inheriting the state-church tradition of responsibility for public morals."[15] This was especially true of those who, like Josephine Shaw Lowell, Theodore Roosevelt, or Rainsford, lived and worked in large cities where the hardships and evils of the new industrial age were most apparent. For these Protestants, many of whom became Progressives in their politics, the movement was an attempt to revitalize traditional American Protestantism so that it might have more influence on the country's social problems.

For CCB, a disciple of Brooks, Rainsford probably seemed to carry forward what Brooks often had implied and might have preached more directly had he not died in 1893. Brooks had emphasized the centrality of Christ in the Trinity, not God as a distant Father but God come down to earth as man to struggle directly with the ills of society. And Rainsford, in his preaching and activities, stressed not so much "love thy God," sin and conversion, as "love thy neighbor," brotherhood and justice.[16] Certainly CCB, by choosing to join St. George's and to work for it for sixty-eight years, proclaimed his belief in its efforts to meet the social ills of the industrial age as he saw them appear in New York.

One of St. George's programs on which he worked hard, one not fully achieved until 1919, was the establishment of free health and dental clinics, the first in New York to be set up by a church. The health of children in the public schools had long concerned CCB, and in 1908 he became chairman of a Committee on Physical Welfare of School Children, under the aegis of an association that later became known as the Community Service Society. But all these programs faced opposition, sometimes even among those who might have been expected to embrace them. Among parents in the tenements, for instance, particularly among the Italian and Russian Jewish immigrants, who by then were replacing the Germans and Irish in the area south of St. George's, there was much superstition, ignorance, and fear.[17]

These primal emotions occasionally sparked attacks on the schools, as happened during the "Adenoid Riots" of June 1906. In this instance, doctors and nurses assigned by the city to the public schools had begun to remove adenoids, free of charge, from the mouths of students who had trouble breathing through their noses. The operation was simple, and often performed at home, the doctor merely snipping overgrown beefy lymphoid tissue from the top of the pharynx behind the nose. Typically, no dressing or treatment was added other than a dab of antiseptic. Yet, as the *Times* reported on 28 June:

> Yesterday morning [the operations] were the cause of riots which threw the lower east side into a panic. The Jews in that section, most of whom cannot speak or understand English, heard that their children's throats were being cut in wholesale fashion by the City Government. Tearing their hair and talking wildly in Yiddish, the parents stormed a dozen public schools ... "You cannot imagine their excitement," said Miss Lizzie E. Rector, principal [of the school on Rivington Street].[18]

The attacks on the schools were simultaneous, and at Public School 4 Miss Rector opened all doors, letting the parents rush through the classrooms, screaming their children's names. The next day "frantic Italians," some with stilettos, mobbed three buildings, and it was discovered that many had sent their children to school with salt, knives, and instructions to throw the salt in the eyes of any doctor approaching and to stab him. To quell the uproar the schools were dismissed; and later, though with less turbulence, the riots spread to schools in the Brownsville section of Brooklyn.[19]

An inquiry traced the cause of the panic to "doctors" with perhaps little or no medical training who practiced in the tenements. At least twenty-five Jewish parents reported that a strange man had come to their flats urging them to run to the rescue of their children. According to the *Times*, the "doctors" disliked the Board of Health's program for schools because it deprived them of "the 13 and 28 cent fees which form the bulk of their income."[20]

In light of such ignorance and fear, St. George's began its medical program slowly, with house calls by one of Rainsford's assistants who was a doctor and could write prescriptions. Then, in 1902, Morgan, guided by his personal physician, Dr. James Wright Markoe, a vestryman of the church (1899–1920), opened on Stuyvesant Square the New York Lying-In Hospital, which in its early years handled 60 percent of all hospital births in Manhattan. Though the hospital technically was not a church program, because entirely paid for by Morgan and separately funded, many who knew of Morgan's and Markoe's connection to St. George's thought of it as a church project. And doubtless the relationship between the two in such matters as recruiting volunteers was close.[21]

In 1909, under Rainsford's successor, St. George's started a tuberculosis class and clinic fitted to the schedules of working men and women. Ten years later it opened a Nutrition Clinic, the work of its Institutional Committee, which had as cochairmen CCB and Dr. Markoe. The clinic was free and available to all on Tuesday, Thursday, Saturday afternoons, and Friday evenings for those who worked during the day. The pediatrician, recruited by Markoe, was backed by the parish nurse, who through the church's *Bulletin* called for volunteers "for this work which, it is hoped, will be far-reaching in the Preventive Work for which the Parish stands." Markoe concerned himself primarily with the project's medical side, and CCB with all else. And though the vestry put the "matter of a plan for obtaining funds" on "a committee composed of Messrs. Burlingham and Markoe," that burden fell chiefly to CCB.[22]

A dental clinic followed, and on 3 January 1920, in a letter revealing CCB's distinctive style in his church work, he wrote to his dentist, Dr. George E. Rice:

> Here is a check for you to help meet the H.C.L. [high cost of living].
> And how about my dental chair that you were to get me for St. George's, cheap as dirt, or cheaper? And the fine set of second-hand tools from a dead dentist—if they ever die? We need them right away. We have a nutrition clinic, with 250 children on our list, and they need to have their teeth looked after. My hope is that if I get a fine, handsome chair and a set of tools, some kind lady or gent will come in and see them and say, "Where is the dentist?" and we will say, "He is not yet caught or bought," and she or he will say, " I will pay for him for a year or less." See?
>
> Happy New Year,
> C.C.B.[23]

Within four months the parish *Bulletin* announced: "A dental chair and complete equipment have been secured and are now on view in the Clinic." And it all but promised a dentist to begin work in the near future.[24]

Then, on Sunday, 18 April, at the church's midmorning service, a small, shabbily dressed man, intending to shoot J. P. Morgan Jr., fired a pistol point-blank at the vestryman offering him the collection plate, and Markoe fell in the aisle, a bullet in his left forehead. The man, firing wildly and without effect, fled the church, pursued by two vestrymen in cutaways, who tackled him in Stuyvesant Square. Markoe, carried to the Lying-In Hospital, was declared dead. The assassin had escaped from a mental institution.[25]

Despite the loss of Markoe, St. George's two clinics thrived, so that the doctor in charge could state in her 1926 report: "The children who came to us as babies seven years ago have now passed through the first years of childhood and arrived at school age and comparative safety as far as health is concerned." CCB, as the clinics' administrative head, gave the figures: visits to the nutrition clinic of babies, schoolchildren, boys over twelve, and adults totaled more than 8,000, not including examinations of 589 for various summer programs. Visits to the dental clinic totaled nearly 2,000. The cost to the church for the previous year, with no value assigned to volunteers, was $8,361.13, incurring a deficit of $377.20. All the figures went into CCB's annual appeal for contributions.[26]

Meanwhile, early in 1925 CCB ran into a personal embarrassment at St. George's. The rector, Karl Reiland (1912–36), had suggested that CCB be elected to the vacant post of junior warden, but the senior warden, Robert Fulton Cutting, while enthusiastic, had raised a question to which CCB replied by letter:

> You are quite right. I have never been confirmed. I have put it off, waiting for a more convenient season, and I have become a little shy about it, I think. I ought to have been confirmed with my children. If I should be confirmed now, I should feel like a German Jew being baptized in order to hold office under the Kaiser.[27]

In place of himself, CCB recommended the election of vestryman George Wickersham, who after four years in Washington as attorney general for President Taft (1909–12) had returned to New York and was devoting much time to St. George's. As CCB pointed out to Cutting, their parish had "not always been in step with the diocese, and I think that Wickersham would help us in that regard." He was hinting—what he knew Cutting would grasp—that Bishop William T. Manning and his assistants liked to associate with the rich and powerful, and Wickersham, though personally modest, came clothed in the aura of great office. Moreover, as Cutting no doubt recalled, it was CCB himself who most recently had put St. George's out of step with the diocese.

At the 139th annual Diocesan Convention, held in 1922 on the grounds of the slowly rising Cathedral of St. John the Divine, CCB as a lay delegate from St. George's had publicly questioned Bishop Manning's wisdom. Manning had opened the convention with a speech calling on all his clergy and communicants to support the Volstead Act, "to see prohibition fairly tried, and to stand in this matter with their whole strength for that respect for law which is vital to the life of our country and which is the first obligation of loyal citizens." The statement, delivered in sonorous tones by a bishop in full regalia, seemed one to which no delegate could take exception.[28] But CCB immediately had stood and introduced for the delegates' consideration a resolution that began: "We recognize the right of citizens to protest against the Volstead Act and to seek by all proper and legal methods to secure its modification or repeal." Agreeing that of course everyone must obey the law, he pointed out that its burden fell very unevenly on rich and poor. The rich easily could evade it at their "clubs, in restaurants, and social parties," a fact that led the poor to "class antagonism" and "class hatred." His resolution was referred to a Committee on Miscellaneous Business, but the next day the delegates passed in its place a resolution that "This convention records its emphatic approval of the sentiments expressed in the Bishop's address regarding obedience to the law." To the bishop's supporters, CCB's resolution was just the sort of impertinence that St. George's too often produced.[29] And if someone in the bishop's party had known that CCB was not confirmed, he could have been challenged, ruled improperly present, and ejected.

So in 1925 Wickersham became junior warden and, on Cutting's death in 1934, senior warden, at which time CCB became junior warden. Two years later, when Wickersham died, CCB became senior warden, which he remained until his death in 1959. The question of his confirmation never again was raised, and he never spoke of it. Everyone seems simply to have assumed that such an active vestryman was a communicant. Meanwhile, he took communion regularly. Presumably, at some point lost in time, he had begun the practice, or possibly had waited until after confirmation in a private ceremony or in some other church. Perhaps in 1925 Cutting and Reiland decided to count him a communicant in fact if not in canon law.[30]

On 14 September 1914, at St. John's Episcopal Church in Cold Spring Harbor, Long Island, CCB's younger son, Robert, married Dorothy Tiffany, youngest child of Louis Comfort Tiffany, vice president and artistic director of Tiffany and Company and head of Tiffany Studios, glass manufacturers. Despite her father's eminence, at Dorothy's request the wedding was simple, with only fifty or so members of the two families present. Robert was twenty-six, a doctor about to become a surgeon, and Dorothy almost twenty-three, a shy heiress living at home where she shared, often unhappily, in her widowed father's frequent social and sometimes exotic activities. Because of her father's objections to the marriage, which he never fully stated—he similarly had objected to the marriages of her three older sisters—the couple's courtship had been difficult, and so, too, would be their married life, with much injury done to them and their children by themselves, their families, and their psychoanalysts.[31]

Dorothy's life had not been easy. When she was a child, her nurse often compared her unfavorably to her nearest elder sister, who had died, and when she was twelve her mother slowly died, groaning and crying in pain. Her father took first to drink and then to a mistress, a nurse he took into his home to live beside his daughters. A family friend persuaded him to send Dorothy to a girls' boarding school, St. Timothy's, near Baltimore, but as she neared graduation, much to her distress, her father, apparently out of loneliness, called her home to live with him. He formally introduced her to society with a "coming out" party in 1911, and sometime around then, at other parties, she met Robert Burlingham, who had graduated from Harvard College in 1910 and was studying medicine at Columbia's College of Physicians and Surgeons, expecting to graduate in the spring of 1914. Sometime in 1912 or early 1913 Dorothy's father and Robert had an argument, and he ordered the young man out of the house, forbidding Dorothy to see him for a year. When the year passed, with the couple still in love, he tried again to delay the wedding, permitting it only after his eldest daughter and her husband had agreed to live with him in the Tiffany five-story fortress on the northwest corner of Madison Avenue and Seventy-second Street. For Dorothy, though she loved Robert, marriage was also an escape from her father.[32]

In June before the wedding in September, Robert, while visiting his parents at Black Point, had an illness that Dorothy later described as a nervous breakdown.[33] His health always had been variable, inclined to periods of nervous disorder that both his mother and father ascribed to fatigue from overwork; but with age these were becoming more protracted and frequent. According to Robert and Dorothy's biographer (a grandson), Robert suffered from "a manic-depressive psychosis" which in 1914 was "uncontrollable," and which today is considered "to be the product of a chemical-hormonal imbalance which can be transmitted genetically."[34] And his mother's family, in successive generations, perhaps offered an example of it.

Louie Burlingham's father, DeWitt Lawrence, had suffered a long depression, aggravated by drink, and periods of insanity. Her alcoholic uncle, Darius Lawrence, had hallucinated and killed himself. Her elder sister Mellie, with Bright's disease, had turned reclusive and died of causes undiscussed in the family. And, still in the future, Louie's youngest sister, Edith, in the 1920s would have a breakdown, enter an institution, and die when only fifty-five. Meanwhile, in tending Robert, Louie persistently minimized the severity of his illness. Possibly, knowing that rest had led to full recovery for CCB, she hoped the same prescription would cure Robert, and at least initially it must have seemed to do so, for with each return to health, he no doubt seemed wholly cured. But if for a time the father's and son's problems appeared similar, Robert's soon proved far more troublesome.

Eleven months after the wedding, the couple's first child was born, Robert Burlingham Jr., known as Bob. As a baby, he was plagued with eczema, asthma, allergies to breast and cow's milk, and given to stunning fits of screaming when Dorothy left the room. He needed a mother with the very strongest instincts of nurture, what Dorothy's generation called a "natural mother," but Dorothy, in this regard, seems to have been only average. She hired nurses, consulted doctors, and followed their advice faithfully, but an early picture of her with her baby on her lap shows Bob lying awkwardly on his stomach, with neither mother nor son smiling. And unhappily, none of his nurses seemed able to provide the spontaneous understanding that his mother apparently lacked.[35]

Sometime in late 1916, when Dorothy was again pregnant, Louie suggested that the couple move from their apartment on West Fifty-seventh Street, close to Roosevelt Hospital, to a house at 129 East Thirty-eighth Street, across the street from herself and CCB. Robert's elder brother and sister, both unmarried, were still living with their parents, and Louie's suggestion was made, no doubt, with the best of motives. Yet according to Dorothy's grandson and biographer, the move to Thirty-eighth Steet was "the mistake of her marriage."[36]

Bob's asthmatic attacks continued. Every time his mother left the house without him, he would cry, cough, gasp, and cling to his nurse, screaming, and Dorothy, on calling home, would be assured by the nurse that he was now calm. One time CCB, returning from work, from across the street heard the screams, and upon investigating discovered the nurse had locked Bob in the closet. Without waiting to consult Dorothy, he (or perhaps he and Louie) fired the woman. CCB later claimed that Dorothy had angered him further by writing the nurse a good reference. But even without that aggravation, relations between the two houses by now were strained, with Robert too docile a son to pick up his family and move.[37]

Dorothy's displeasure with the elder Burlinghams increased when Louie, inviting her for tea one afternoon, laid out some pictures by Abbott

Thayer, Joe Evans, and a few others of their contemporaries and asked Dorothy to discourse on them. Whatever Louie may have intended by her questions and proddings, Dorothy felt she had been given and failed a test, and just as Robert, despite his medical skills, was not prepared to face down his parents, neither was the younger Dorothy. As Tiffany's daughter she probably knew more than Louie about art, and if she had been less diffident, she might have turned the discussion to the new artistic styles exhibited in the 1913 Armory Show, styles of which Louie knew little. But Louie, like CCB, would dominate, if allowed.[38]

By 1920 Dorothy had borne two more children, daughters, and Robert had suffered several more breakdowns. These, by his grandson's account,

> were ferocious, starting with a leap from childlike exuberance to full-blown mania in which it was difficult to predict his behavior. When manic he tended to verbal abuse, rashly charging into situations, confronting people unnecessarily. Then he plunged into an abysmal depression steeped in self-recrimination, blaming himself for his lack of control, and especially for dishonoring his family. Tragically, he seemed to believe that these episodes should have been controllable by the force of his will.[39]

Sometimes, when depressed, Robert would radiate a powerful sexuality. He was a handsome man, physically strong, and though usually sweet and gentle, when ill could be domineering. At such moments even his handshake could be bone-crushing, and some women, doubting his self-control, felt threatened. In later years a male nurse-companion whom CCB hired for him, at the first sign of a gaze or grip held too firmly or too long, would say quietly, "Enough of that," and Robert would ease up.[40]

Soon Dorothy was pregnant again, and desperate. Before giving birth to a son in March 1921 she left Robert in New York for a house in Connecticut, taking the children with her. She had enough money to support herself, the children, and a staff, and in effect she abandoned Robert and the care of him to his parents, particularly to CCB, who thereafter selected the doctors, rest homes, and relatives with whom Robert might live while recuperating. To CCB and Louie, Dorothy's abandonment of Robert was an appalling abdication of her wifely responsibilities, and they never could understand how she could leave her husband at this juncture, especially when Robert—and Dorothy never denied it—so clearly loved her and the children. As soon as he recovered, he would try to rejoin her, sometimes seeing her and the children together, sometimes apart. He lived in the hope of reuniting the family. But probably to Dorothy, her leaving Robert was the price she had to pay to be free of his parents' continual interference.[41]

For four years Dorothy and the children lived apart from Robert. To help Bob's asthma, for several winters she took them all, including a sister's asthmatic child, to live in Tucson, Arizona, and they spent two summers in Wyoming and another in Switzerland. Meanwhile, she periodically sent Robert reports of the children's health, and he, during vacations from work or illness, occasionally managed to see them. Despite a succession of tutors, however, their education was a casualty of their disturbed life: by the summer of 1924, when Bob was nine, Mabbie (Mary) seven, Katrina five, and Michael three, not one had set foot in a school.[42]

By 1924 Dorothy began to hear accounts of psychoanalysis, including the possibility of using it to cure an organic disease like asthma. She also learned that Sigmund Freud's daughter Anna had begun to treat children in Vienna; and through friends she discovered an English-speaking school in Geneva which would take "the Four," as CCB called his grandchildren. She sailed with them on 1 May 1925, intending to stay six months or a year in Geneva, with a visit to Anna Freud to discuss the possibility of analysis for Bob.[43] And she left without informing Robert or his parents.

In the next six years Robert contrived to visit the children in Europe several times, and CCB saw them there in 1929. But not until the summer of 1931 did Dorothy allow any of the children to visit their father or grandparents in the United States. By then the two oldest, Bob and Mabbie, had long been in analysis with Anna Freud, and Dorothy, who was preparing to become a psychoanalyst, with Freud himself. Meanwhile, in New York, CCB hired one of the city's leading psychiatrists, Dr. George Amsden, to take charge of Robert's medical treatment, while he himself organized and provided whatever at any moment seemed necessary—an institution, a home (with his parents, with Louie's sister Grace, or some other friend or relative), a male nurse or companion, or, when Robert was in good health, openings to medical jobs he could perform. What more could be done? No one knew.[44]

Psychoanalysis, with its strange vocabulary, id, ego, libido, and its challenging new ways of interpreting human behavior was but one of the ways in which life in the United States after the world war seemed very different from life before it. There was also, as of 1919, Prohibition, radio as entertainment, an enormous increase in advertising, and as of 1920 women voting and, perhaps even more astonishing, drinking and smoking in public. In 1925, with the development of new paints, cars, hitherto always black, suddenly blossomed in all colors, and started to be built as closed cars rather than open carriages.[45]

Meanwhile, New York architects, forsaking efforts to make New York beautiful in the beaux arts style of Napoleon III's Paris, in a ten-year building boom had created the city's own new style of urban design. By the 1920s the midtown area around Grand Central Station (opened in 1913) soared skyward in a cluster of tall buildings, the most beautiful and imaginative of which was the seventy-seven story Chrysler Building, completed in 1929 by the automobile magnate Walter P. Chrysler. It was the first to use exposed metal in its design, and its decoration, which included stainless steel eagle heads and large metal disks resembling Chrysler radiator caps, and a helmetlike top ending in a gleaming steel spire, was the most distinctive on the city's skyline. Though it soon was surpassed as the world's tallest building by the Empire State Building, the Chrysler Building even more than its rival proclaimed to the world a new American civilization that was proudly and unmistakably "modern."[46]

Equally dramatic changes occurred in women's clothing. In 1919, before the Constitution's Nineteenth Amendment extended voting rights to women, skirts hung to the ankle, as they had for centuries, but by 1927 their hems hovered at the knee. As the ideal woman's figure changed from the "Gibson girl" to the boyish "flapper," layers of clothing were peeled away: the corset, the petticoat, and sometimes even the brassiere. Cotton underclothes gave way to rayon and silk; cotton stockings, to flesh-colored silk or lisle. The *Journal of Commerce* estimated that the amount of material needed for a woman's complete costume (exclusive of stockings) had dropped from 19¼ yards in 1913 to 7 in 1928. And along with lighter, fewer clothes came bobbed hair. In 1918, a "bob" had been a symbol of radicalism, but by 1929 it was universal among the young, and not uncommon even in women of sixty or older.[47]

One who did not embrace the new fashions was Louie Burlingham, who by 1929 was fifty-six. By then she suffered with Milroy's disease, an edema that swelled her legs and thighs, causing her to walk with a cane and in shuffling short steps, yet with an erect posture. Perhaps to hide her affliction she continued to dress in the old style, always a long, full black skirt, a white blouse, and over it a black overcoat. By then, too, her hair was gray, soon to be white, and in some earlier year she had caught an eye infection that had blinded her left eye. She always wore spectacles, covering the lost eye with a blackened glass. The effect of clothes, stance, and patch was startling, and severe. At Black Point, where she liked the croquet, the children called her "the Pirate."[48]

Louie's younger sister Grace, who in 1906 had married Robert Longley Taylor, a professor of romance languages at Williams College, possibly also had Milroy's disease, for after her husband's death in 1923 Grace's figure began to resemble Louie's, whom she soon surpassed in weight. In contrast, the figure of their youngest sister, Edith, was thin, even wiry. The tendency to Milroy's disease is hereditary, and in time Louie's grandchild Bob, and then his daughter, would suffer from it.[49]

Just as CCB and Louie had acted as guardians to Grace and Edith in the 1890s, so they did again in the 1920s, when Grace was widowed and Edith fell ill. Grace's husband had left her an annual income of about $6,000 and three children to educate—Lawrence, age thirteen, Philip, eleven, and Rosamond, eight. The money, in addition to what Grace had inherited from Colonel Hoe, might have been enough, except that she liked to entertain and had little sense of economy. If she needed money, she borrowed, and then found the sum hard to repay. At some time, probably in the early 1930s, to prevent liens from attaching to her house in Williamstown, CCB bought it, or at least transferred title to his name. Years earlier, in 1893, he had bought for Grace and Edith, or more likely merely acted as their agent, seven acres of farmland in Plainfield, near Cornish, New Hampshire, where the sisters built a house, designed by Charles Platt, and spent their summers. In 1935 Grace, with her assets much reduced by losses in the Depression, sold the Williamstown house and moved to Plainfield. But on her death in 1940 her estate, after paying her debts (many owed to a housekeeper for daily expenses), had little left for the children.[50]

Of these, the eldest, Lawrence, as a boy had shown a talent for botany, but in his schools and college, possibly because often ill, seemed unable to develop it. Later, after graduating from Williams and farming for several years the family home in Plainfield, he took a degree in education at Dartmouth and became a schoolteacher in the academies and public schools of Vermont and New Hampshire. He had an inquisitive mind, a gift for teaching, and a personality that perhaps was more at ease with students than with adults. CCB, despite a lifelong affection for "Lawrie," seemed to find his nephew, this farmer-teacher isolated in northern New England, a bit of a puzzle, an anomaly in the modern urban world.[51]

Rosamond, Grace's youngest child, had the easiest time with her "Uncle Charley," moving steadily through school, graduating in 1936 from

Bennington College, and soon thereafter marrying a young lawyer, John L. Burling, who had graduated from Harvard Law School, a pattern of life that CCB could understand. In contrast, Phil, the middle child, bounced from school to school, and his relations with his uncle were often troubled. "When young," said Phil, in his eighties, "I was interested in girls, cars, and aeroplanes. Uncle Charley understood the first, but not the second, or third. He never drove a car himself, and although in the 1920s and 1930s he kept a Cadillac and a chauffeur named Edward, he couldn't tell a Cadillac from a Buick." And airplanes "were quite out of his ken." Yet for Phil, his boyhood's most memorable experience was driving to Springfield, Vermont, on 26 July 1927, to greet Charles A. Lindbergh. The flier was then on tour, stopping in every state to show off himself and his plane, *The Spirit of St. Louis*, in which, alone and nonstop, he had flown the Atlantic, from New York to Paris.[52]

Though Phil showed a talent for making of iron or wood anything mechanical, his formal education was spotty. From an early age he attended a succession of boarding schools, and by the ninth grade he was in the Hoosac School, in Hoosick, New York, in beautiful country between Troy and the Vermont border. Founded in 1889 by a "high" church Episcopal minister, the school had a strong academic and religious tradition, and though Phil was no more unhappy or unsuccessful there than in other schools, CCB grew impatient with it. He disliked its Anglo-Catholic ways and complained to Phil that it celebrated too many saints' days and spent too long preparing its Christmas pageant. At the close of the spring term in 1927, CCB came up in the Cadillac (driven by Edward) to tell the headmaster that Phil would not return in the fall. Fifteen-year-old Phil, hanging listlessly on the edge of the conversation, heard CCB, possibly to avoid the true reasons for the withdrawal, announce, "The boys here are too fat!" Later he heard the headmaster protest, "You have treated the school like an old shoe!" Then his uncle whisked him away in the Cadillac.[53]

CCB then put Phil in a school near Williamstown, where he stayed two years, doing poorly, until CCB in desperation moved him to Phillips Academy, at Exeter, New Hampshire. There, perhaps merely because of greater age—Phil was now seventeen and entering Exeter's tenth grade with many fourteen-year-olds—he did better. Yet he left before graduating (though listed as a member of the Class of 1932) to enter Williams College.[54]

He had wanted to go to the Daniel Guggenheim School for aeronautical engineering, at New York University, but CCB insisted on Williams, where the tuition for a deceased professor's son was less, explaining to Phil that he was paying bills for a number of young relatives and must keep costs down. So Phil drifted through two and a half years at Williams, taking what engineering courses he could, and then left, in good standing, for California and a job with Lockheed. But lack of imagination more than of money may have led CCB to insist on Williams for Phil. CCB liked to repeat patterns of living and apparently, despite Phil's poor academic record, he hoped the boy would turn to law. It took CCB many years to accept Phil as God had made him and to stop trying to remake him into someone else. Yet despite the continual turmoil and disappointments, Phil as an adult liked his Uncle Charley, kept in touch, and when in New York stayed with him, though he always felt that, in not becoming a lawyer, he had disappointed the old man.[55]

Perhaps if the family had been differently structured, if CCB's brother, Albert, had still been a presence, or Grace's husband still alive, or if Young Charles had been more independent of his father, one of them might have helped Phil to the Guggenheim school for aeronautical engineering.[56] But in the family's planetary system there was only one sun, a single source of energy, light, and opportunity—CCB. No relative, young or old, wanted to be left in darkness, so all turned toward him. They might have profited if their heaven had displayed a second sun, a brother, uncle, aunt, or grandparent, equally rich and well educated, who was ready to laugh at CCB, pointing out his mistakes and biases and offering an alternative to him. But for the Burlingham children and their three Taylor cousins there was only CCB.[57] Yet despite his failure with Phil, what is most remarkable about CCB as he advanced in age, reaching seventy in 1928, is not the rigidity of his views but his ability to adapt. In part, no doubt because he worked outside the home, more than Louie he felt the temper of the times and, unconsciously perhaps, somewhat adjusted. Yet with his daughter, Nancy, in part because events played out within the home, where he deferred to Louie, he and Louie together stumbled badly.

By the mid-1920s Nancy Burlingham was approaching forty. Still unmarried, still living at home, she helped her mother with the family's domestic affairs, and every October in the 1920s she would accompany her mother (Edward would drive them in the Cadillac) to Williamstown to spend a month with Grace. Mother and daughter would have a suite in the Williams Inn, bedrooms flanking a sitting room, and almost every afternoon Louie would take Grace and Nancy for a drive. Grace, who, more than Louie, liked people and company, was a pianist of professional skill, and often in the mornings she and Nancy would play duets. Whatever

Grace's failing in managing her money, she ran her house and children with a looser rein than did Louie, and to Grace's daughter Rosamond, thirty years younger than Nancy, her older cousin, whether in New York or Williamstown, had the life of "a handmaiden" or "slave."[58]

In the New York apartment Louie always wore the same black skirt, white blouse, and black overcoat, she always sat in the same Victorian chair in her living room, with a huge jigsaw puzzle on a card table before her, employing, for her one good eye, a large magnifying glass. At meals, when she became restless, she would rise and leave the room. "Her personality was rigid, stern. By her lights she probably was never less than fair, but she allowed no individuality, variation in others." Rosamond came to feel that Nancy, unlike Charles and Robert, who had escaped to college and graduate school, was "squashed" at home, for Louie, as much as CCB, was a strong parent.[59] Rosamond and others who knew the family sometimes wondered whether if in Nancy's youth her father had been more attentive to her education and future, she might have escaped some of her later problems. But even close attention, prelude to any action, would have required CCB to interfere with Louie in an area in which he ceded sovereignty to her. With Nancy, he perhaps showed some of the same lack of imagination that he had in his dealings with Phil.

In one sense Nancy had seen much of the world. She had been several times to England and France, though always with her mother, and when CCB fell ill in 1916 she accompanied her parents to Bermuda. And then, in July 1922, on a trip arranged by his son Charles, CCB took Charles and Nancy with him to the American Bar Association meeting in San Francisco. "It is a quick sort of rubber-neck trip," he wrote to his friend Judge Ward:

> A special train starts from Chicago on the 28th, stopping a day at Colorado Springs, another day at Salt Lake City, three days in Yellowstone, four or five days in San Francisco, and then we go up to Vancouver and back by the Canadian Pacific. Charles has figured it out 8300 miles to be done inside of 30 days. I hope we shall survive. I have never been west of Colorado, and I am keen to see something of the West.[60]

Nancy's comments on this excursion do not survive, but for her it was at best only another trip with a parent and elder brother. Quite possibly, as several relatives surmised, Nancy reached forty without ever having held a man's hand.

One bit of scrappy undated evidence suggests that at some point, possibly during or soon after this trip to the West, on which CCB saw Nancy daily for almost a month without Louie present, he began to fret about his daughter's life. Buried among his personal papers in a family trunk is a memorandum, unmistakably in his hand, the outburst of a frustrated, worried man. He writes of Nancy:

> You are wasting your life in doing trifles which are not of the least value to yourself or any one else. And you are in danger of becoming *queer*, like a miserly, old woman.
>
> Your poverty is your own fault. You could support yourself amply as a teacher or otherwise.
>
> You are very social, charming in conversation, but you have given up almost all your friends—because of your poverty and lack of clothes I suppose.
>
> Now, what does this tirade come to?[61]

Most likely he laid the note aside, undelivered. But even the thought was unfair, as he must have known: he and Louie had not educated Nancy to be self-supporting. If, subservient to her mother's guidance and example, she dressed drably, how could he complain? If she protested her "poverty," and according to others she occasionally did, it was because she saw women of her age married, independent, with homes of their own, and money seemed part of their freedom. To Phil Taylor, his Uncle Charley had in Nancy "a problem he couldn't resolve, or fully understand." In later years, when she telephoned her father from Williamstown or Black Point, CCB, frustrated with her complaints, would thrust the phone on Phil, saying, "Here, you talk with her."[62]

To everyone's surprise, CCB's eldest son, Charles, in the summer of 1928 when he was forty-four, engaged to marry. Until then Charles had seemed entirely happy and fulfilled in serving his father and the family. He lived with his parents in New York and at Black Point, worked in his father's firm, was good-looking, wore clothes well, and had considerable wit; in addition, he was by nature quiet, well mannered, and little inclined to assert himself. When looked to for leadership or support in a family crisis, he usually stepped aside, saying, "A hundred years from now it won't make any difference." Then he met the youngest daughter of J. Alden Weir, a distinguished American painter who had died in 1919. Eight years younger than Charles, she was Cora Weir Carlin, a widow with a one-year-old son.[63]

Unlike Dorothy Tiffany, Cora entered the Burlingham family as a mature woman. "A lovely person and exactly the right sort for Charles and for all of us," CCB wrote to a friend. A graduate of the Brearley School, during the world war she had served with the Red Cross in a hospital in Brest, writing letters home for American soldiers who had been blinded by gas or were dying. In France she had met and married William Carlin, an older man, and they had come back to the United States to a life of remarkable activity. They worked and traveled, fishing in Canada, hunting ducks in North Carolina, and riding camels to the pyramids in Egypt.[64]

Her first child, William Carlin, was born in 1927, but then early the following winter her husband died, leaving her financially independent. She was handsome, played the piano as well as Nancy, and, as Alden Weir's daughter, knew more about art and artists than Louie. She was also a good executive (for thirty-five of her later years she would be in charge of all exhibits at the New York Botanical Garden). She knew what she wanted in life, and was self-assured and skillful enough to outmaneuver CCB and Louie without confrontation. Her marriage to Charles would last fifty happy years, and all the while, gently but firmly, she increased his independence of his parents. In 1930 she bore him a son, Charles Burlingham Jr., who years later at a service for his father would say of his parents' marriage what many had long thought, "She saved his life."[65]

Right from the start CCB's urge to dominate the couple was denied full expression. The wedding, on 2 April 1929, was to be in the Weir family's church, the Episcopal Church of the Ascension, the first church built on Fifth Avenue (in 1841), on the northwest corner of Tenth Street. But as CCB complained to a friend only six days before the date: "I find it almost impossible to get Charles to invite anyone to the wedding. To almost every suggestion I make, he replies, 'Oh, who wants to go to a wedding, especially at noon?' Mrs. Weir [Cora's aunt and stepmother] has had a lot of trouble with her heart lately, and the consequence is that the wedding breakfast or luncheon is to be an almost exclusively family affair."[66]

Came the day and the ceremony, and CCB wrote to another friend:

The wedding was simple and cosey tho' in a church—about 200 of us. The sole usher was George Montgomery who arrived rather late in a thrush brown suit looking cunning but flustered. I deposited my topper in the front pew with Nancy, Mattie [Albert's wife], and my brother, and bestirred myself to get our side (the right), properly filled up so as to balance the host of Weir relatives (Mr. Weir being one of sixteen children) on the left. I moved a lot up front and stopped and talked to everybody and introduced a few, so the church solemnity was a bit dissipated.

Then the lady organist struck up the W.M. and in from the right entered Charles and Robert in blue double-breasted jackets, looking very serious, and, I may say, handsome, followed by Cora and Page Ely, her bro.-in-law. They took their places in the Chancel and, as you know, it was only a jiff and they were M. & W.—no just reason being stated why they shouldn't be. Then they came down the aisle at double quick, and Jerry whisked them away and we came tumbling after. Charles was all smiles, and Cora as red as a rose was she, and later she told us she saw nobody hardly.[67]

All in all, though perhaps not planned as he would have liked, not so bad either.

13

CCB as Public Sage

THE YEARS IMMEDIATELY following the war were perilous for admiralty firms, for as CCB later wrote: "World War I worked a great change. The value of ships rose by geometrical progression, the cost of repairs likewise. The Government built and chartered thousands of ships, and the Admiralty flourished. Young men clamored to enter the offices of established admiralty firms, and new firms were formed."[1] Two or three mistakes in hiring lawyers or making partners could end in discord or even a split, leaving the firm crippled and in decay.

Among the new firms was an old one reorganized. Burlingham, Montgomery & Beecher had come into being in 1910, but in 1912 Montgomery had died and in 1917 Beecher resigned, leaving CCB, aged fifty-nine, the sole senior in a firm with six junior partners, of whom the two eldest, Everett Masten and George H. Emerson, though fine lawyers, were not leaders of the bar or within the firm.[2] As CCB saw the situation, what the firm needed was another senior partner, a lawyer of such distinction that CCB could bring him into the firm, giving him the second largest share of the profits without stirring revolt among the junior partners. He resolved on Van Vechten Veeder, fifty years old and generally thought to be the better of the two judges on the Eastern District Court— the same man whose appointment to the bench in 1911 he had worked to achieve.[3] So, reversing his usual role, he set out to lure an able judge off the bench and into his firm.

He opened his campaign in the summer of 1917, inviting the judge to Black Point, and four of Veeder's letters give a rough picture of the firm, its division of earnings, and its reins of power. CCB negotiated with the judge, for instance, without consulting any of his partners (though sometimes using Young Charles as a courier),[4] and an undisputed premise of their talks was that Veeder's position in the firm would be second: in the firm's name and in sharing its profits. Money was CCB's chief enticement. Veeder, married and with two children, had an annual salary of $7,500, and CCB offered a guarantee of $25,000 or 16 percent of the firm's profits, whichever was higher. Veeder reported himself "content" with that amount "so long as" all partners understood it was "for the first year only." He did not want to enter the firm "upon an equality (approximately) with Masten and [Morton L.] Fearey," the partners closest to CCB in percentage points.[5]

Seemingly, CCB estimated the firm's after-expense profits for 1918 at $155,000, suggesting that in the new firm the four leading partners, CCB, Veeder, Masten, and Fearey, would share, at a minimum, $100,000— perhaps $30,000, $26,000, and $22,000—leaving $55,000 for the other four. Though compared to the salary of a district judge the partners' shares may sound grand, compared to the earnings of many other lawyers they were not, and CCB with reason could write a corporate lawyer in 1920 that there was "no money" in admiralty, "except for a few."[6] Nevertheless, with the changes in shipping brought on by the war, both CCB and Veeder were optimistic about the future, and on 1 January 1918 they opened Burlingham, Veeder, Masten & Fearey, a firm with five junior partners (the fifth advanced from associate), as well as several associates.

Veeder, a tall, gaunt descendant of early Dutch settlers, brought much to the firm besides a knowledge of admiralty law. He read widely (outside the law his favorite author was Thomas Hardy), published scholarly articles on legal history, and was an authority on libel and slander as well as international law. He frequently was named to arbitration panels and further burnished the firm's reputation when he served for six years, 1930–36, as president of the Maritime Law Association.[7]

In choosing partners and associates CCB countered the usual practice in these years of a small New York firm. Typically, one started with two or three competent, colorful, dynamic lawyers banding together and, having established themselves, hiring competent but colorless young lawyers as assistants, lawyers who would not offer competition or argument, but quiet, efficient backup service. Then when the founding partners began to die or retire, the aging colorless men would lack the dynamism to keep the firm vibrant, and it would lose health, often picked to death by livelier firms who wanted its clients or perhaps a lawyer or two for the back room. This was never CCB's way. He usually was drawn to hire as an associate or take in as a partner a vigorous personality, someone like himself, with interests, opinions, and a flair in pursuing them, and consequently the firm always had younger members who were restless and eager for promotion. Yet by reputation the Burlingham firm was a good place to work. Though its salaries and shares were small compared to those offered by the big corporate firms, young lawyers flocked to it for jobs.[8] They had heard, or knew, or suspected that there was more to this small firm than the money to be earned, or even the specialty of admiralty law; there was the quality of its men.

Among the firm's younger partners, the three leaders were CCB's son Charles, Chauncey Clark, and Roscoe Hupper, the latter two still resenting Charles's promotion to partner ahead of them.[9] In August 1918 CCB wrote to his friend Tom Thacher, then with the American Red Cross in Russia, about a possible adviser for Admiral W. S. Sims, commander of U.S. naval forces in European waters, and after discussing the qualifications of a former naval officer who was "about 45, a man of experience, but not of the *best* legal training, and perhaps a trifle slow, tho' very sound," he went on to say:

> If it is general admiralty law that is called for either R. H. Hupper or my son Charles would fill the bill. They have both had a great deal of experience as advisors and had big responsibilities put on them. Hupper is a Bowdoin man, 35 or 36 years old. Charles is of Harvard College and Law School, aet. 34. Hupper has more learning and is very judicial. Charles is more a man of the world, in the good sense of the *word*. He is on his pins intellectually all the time. He has a slight physical disability, which makes him ineligible for military service. He is now one of the Deputies of the N.Y. Director of Draft.
>
> As to Hupper—he is the best lawyer of his age at the Admiralty bar. He has had many offers of public positions and for partnerships. I have advised him not to enter War Service until he got a chance to use his brains. May be this is it.[10]

Nothing came of CCB's recommendations, but they suggest the quality of his leadership. Though Hupper had received many offers to leave the firm, he had chosen to remain, and despite his anger at CCB for putting Charles ahead of him as partner, he continued to consult CCB about choices for the future. Beneath the roiled surface of their relations lay a bed of trust, which CCB's letter justified. He neither hid Hupper's light under a bushel nor tried to hold him in the firm to his disadvantage. Plainly, in this firm, the partners judged each other's worth not solely by the percentage of profits.

Though CCB had been elected to the City Bar Association (as the Association of the Bar of the City of New York was commonly called) in 1882, he took little part in its activities until after World War I. Meanwhile, he dutifully attended its meetings, so that in 1946, at the Association's seventy-fifth anniversary, when he was the only lawyer living who had been a member for more than sixty years, he could say of its 231 founders, "I knew 36, and by sight a good many more."[11]

The Association's chief project in the 1880s and 1890s had been a long, bitter fight in the New York legislature to defeat a replacement of the state's "unwritten" common law by a series of "written" codes. Across the state the proposal had agitated many lawyers, especially those practicing in the state courts where common law dominated statutory law, to lobby the legislature or, at very least, to contribute their opinions to the campaigns for and against the proposed codes. The Association's leaders in the annual battles, which to contemporaries loomed very large, were James C. Carter, the Association's president in the mid-1880s and at the time a much admired philosopher of historical jurisprudence, and Theodore W. Dwight, head of Columbia Law School. Their chief opponent was David Dudley Field, the author of the codes and an unpopular though respected member of the Association.[12]

To some extent, those who favored codification of the law looked back to an earlier period, when Napoleon I had systematized French law into five greatly admired and much copied codes (civil law, civil procedure, commercial, criminal, and penal law). But after Napoleon III's defeat in the Franco-Prussian War of 1870, German thought and techniques supplanted French, and just as in education American universities imitated German models—Harvard and Johns Hopkins—in the history and philosophy of law there was a similar movement. Carter, for one, dismissed the Napoleonic Codes as merely a despot's self-serving tools, while exalting England's common law as "the natural growth and development of free institutions through the centuries of time." Others, searching still further back in time, saw the origins of these free institutions in the customs of those Germanic tribes who had fought Rome and escaped its legal tradition.[13]

Later the pendulum of thought started a backward swing, but this continuing historical and philosophical debate, which stirred so many lawyers to ecstasy and battle, did not excite CCB—perhaps in part because, after joining Wing, Shoudy & Putnam in 1883, most of his work involved admiralty law and the federal courts. But his lack of interest also reflected his personality. In his correspondence, theoretical ideas about the law's history and philosophy do not arise; his focus always is on the immediate and practical: law, today, in a courtroom; how to improve its substance and procedures; how to improve the quality of bench and bar. Yet within the Association, its defeat of Field and the proposed codes reverberated for years, and on its fiftieth anniversary, in 1920, its historian happily recorded, "This chapter in the history of law demonstrates the learning and devotion of the Association's representatives."[14]

Besides dominating the Association's thinking in these decades, James C. Carter also set its style. For evening meetings, dress was formal (black tie); discourse was civil and cool; in politics, most members were Republican, though many, including CCB, were not; and for membership, an Anglo-Saxon New England heritage was preferred, though not required. Annual dues were kept high, and by 1908 had reached fifty dollars with an entrance fee of one hundred dollars. By then, however, the number of members was shrinking. Despite seeking members from all five of the city's counties, despite a splendid new building at 36 West Forty-fourth Street, and despite some 16,000 lawyers in New York County (Manhattan) alone, the Association had only 1,750 members, one in nine of New York County lawyers, whereas in 1875 it had achieved a ratio of about one in five. By 1908 the Association was "Old Guard."

That year a New York County Lawyers' Association was founded with dues at ten dollars a year, no entrance fee, and within the year, 3,401 members. Of the latter, seventeen were women (lawyers excluded by the older association, despite efforts by CCB and others, until 1937). Yet the new organization, its founders insisted, was not intended to rival the old. Seventeen of its thirty officers and directors were members of the older Association, and they viewed the new "County Lawyers" as merely an association of a different sort, an ally to the elder in the pursuit of better justice in the courts. Among the many who joined the new without leaving the old was CCB, though not a leader in its affairs.[15] His chief interest in these years was the Maritime Law Association, attending the Brussels Conferences in 1909 and 1910, serving on an MLA committee to revise the Pilot Rules for Inland Waters, and in 1918–20 on its executive committee. Still, he regularly attended meetings in both the county and city bar associations, and when the latter overnight in January 1920 suddenly flamed into action, he had a small part in fanning the spark.

The occasion arose on the suspension, on 7 January, of five Socialist Party members—duly elected, sworn in, and seated—from the New York State Assembly. The Republican Assembly leaders, who commanded a majority of 110 to 35 Democrats and 5 Socialists, passed a resolution, 140 to 6, referring judgment on the Socialists' right to sit on a Judiciary Committee, still to be named, and meanwhile ordered the five Socialist assemblymen to vacate their seats. They refused and, one by one, were ushered from the chamber by the sergeant at arms.[16]

In that winter of 1920, the United States, already agitated by prosecutions for treason under the 1917 Espionage Act, was in the midst of a "Red" scare aggravated by recent news from Russia. In Moscow, the Third Communist International had issued a manifesto declaring war on the trade union movement and on all the democratic parties of the world (including the Socialist Party of the United States), because they pursued reform through the ballot box. The manifesto's ringing phrases of class warfare had led Attorney General A. Mitchell Palmer, only the week before the suspension of the Socialist assemblymen, to order a series of "roundup" raids of Communists and suspected Communists. Some six thousand or more people were jailed, many without warrants or evidence against them, and held for days or weeks without charge.

The Republicans in Albany, led by Speaker Thaddeus C. Sweet of Oswego (said to have ambitions to be governor), assumed that Americans and especially New Yorkers would approve their act. The Socialists, Sweet told the Assembly, "had been elected on a platform that is absolutely inimical to the best interest of the State of New York and of the United States." He equated the party with the Bolsheviks in Russia: "It is not truly a political party, but is a membership organization admitting within its ranks aliens, enemy aliens" who had sworn allegiance to Communist class warfare. Quoting from both the Socialist and Communist International manifestos, he tried to show that the five men were committed to the violent overthrow of the state and nation.[17]

New York's five Socialists were all familiar politicians in the city, however, two of them having served in the previous Assembly. Their party, recognized in every state, had recently elected representatives to city, state, and national legislatures without any problems. The party's views on reform by peaceful means were well known, and the New York *World*, formerly Joseph Pulitzer's paper, promptly responded to the Assembly majority with an editorial condemning its act as legislative tyranny.[18] A few other newspapers followed its lead, but more important than editorials was a public letter from Charles Evans Hughes to Assembly Speaker Sweet.

Hughes, who in 1906–10 had been an outstanding governor of New York and thereafter an associate justice on the Supreme Court until 1916, was currently the Republican Party's national leader, having only narrowly lost the 1916 presidential election to Wilson. His rebuke was front-page news:

If there was anything against these men as individuals, if they were deemed to be guilty of criminal offenses, they should have been charged accordingly. But I understand that the action is not directed against these five elected members as individuals, but that the proceeding is virtually an attempt to indict a political party and to deny it representation in the Legislature. That is not, in my judgement, American government.[19]

Like CCB, Hughes was the son of a Baptist preacher, and his letter blazed with moral indignation. Even so, a sizable majority of the legislature and public did not support him, and he prepared for a fight with fervor and energy. Though he was at the time president of the County Lawyers' Association, he chose the older city association as his instrument, doubtless because, as one of the five Socialists, Louis Waldman, later noted, it "was the most powerful organization of lawyers in the country."[20] Hughes called for others to join him, and thirty-four members of the Association, including CCB, responded. Through the newspapers they announced their plan to present to the Association, at its annual meeting on 13 January, a resolution denouncing the suspension as contrary to the spirit of representative government and calling for the appointment of a special committee of the Association to help defend the Socialists before the Assembly's Judiciary Committee. No doubt chiefly because of Hughes's political eminence, several New York newspapers had front-page stories announcing the time and date of that annual meeting, with the text of the proposed resolution and a list of its sponsors. And on the scheduled evening more than four hundred lawyers, an unprecedented number, turned up for the Association's proverbially dull annual meeting.[21]

The debate on the resolution was conducted in "Old Guard" style. Hughes, in black tie, offered the resolution and his reasons for it, and William D. Guthrie, a fellow Republican, also in black tie, answered in a prepared speech, arguing that the Association should not judge the Assembly's action until its Judiciary Committee had its hearing on the men's loyalty to American forms of government. Amendments were offered, with speakers for and against. CCB did not speak, but he was present and active. Hughes wanted a well-known Republican lawyer from Buffalo, John Lord O'Brian, to speak, knowing O'Brian would be sympathetic to the cause and persuasive to western New Yorkers, and he sent CCB to find him. CCB discovered him standing at the back of the hall—it was the start of their friendship—and O'Brian spoke briefly, passionately on the issue as one not of "constitutional interpretation" but of "fair play."[22]

At 12:45 a.m., after much parliamentary maneuvering, the members still present resolved, 174 to 117, that "this Association is unalterably opposed" to the exclusion by the Assembly of duly elected representatives who do not advocate change of government by violence, and requested that a committee (which plainly Hughes would lead) be appointed to argue the point before the Assembly's Judiciary Committee. Political passion and partisanship were high, yet bitterness was avoided, chiefly because of the "Old Guard" ideal of civility in discourse. (In 1946, at the Association's seventy-fifth anniversary, Chief Justice Harlan Fiske Stone said of that meeting: "Rarely have I heard any public discussion conducted with more power and skill and resourcefulness"—"rarely" in part because even by 1946 the ideal of professional courtesy had begun to fray.)[23]

Hughes led a five-man committee (not including CCB) to Albany, and though the Assembly's Judiciary Committee chairman tried to silence him by interruption, he stood his ground, delivered an oral statement, and distributed copies of the committee's brief. As word of their action passed across the country, Hughes and the Association increasingly won support. But the Judiciary Committee voted 7 to 6 to expel the Socialists, and in the Assembly debate that followed, one member proposed a lynching: "These five men ought to be made an example to the other traitors and violators of the law. They ought to be strung up to the nearest lamp post, with their feet dangling in the air."[24] On the final Assembly votes, taken individually on the five men, in each case a majority in both parties, Democrat as well as Republican, voted for expulsion. Many people rejoiced in the outcome, and in an editorial the next day *The New York Times* purred: "It was an American vote altogether, a patriotic and conservative vote. An immense majority of the American people will approve and sanction the Assembly's action."[25] In fact, a majority began to think the Assembly's action was ridiculous, and state politicians soon sought to distance themselves from it. The episode, however, revitalized the bar association. In the period 1919–25 the number of out-of-town members rose from 347 to 716, and city residents from 1,810 to 2,685. With more members, the number of the Association's projects multiplied, increasing its presence and significance, both of which gained further with the election of Hughes to its presidency in 1927, followed by CCB in 1929.

For CCB and his generation, the suspension of the Socialists served, much as had the fight over codification for the previous generation, to show how a bar association, under strong leadership, could be used to affect government. Before Hughes and the Socialists CCB had taken little interest in the Association; after the episode he became one of its most active members. And the event warmed his friendship with Hughes, a man who perhaps wanted intimacy with friends but found it hard to achieve. Theodore Roosevelt had dismissed him as a "bearded iceberg," but CCB, though addressing him always as "My dear Hughes," nurtured a mutual confidence that allowed the two to discuss freely anything pertaining to the law. Hence, when Hughes in 1930 succeeded Taft as chief justice, CCB continued to be able to confer directly on any legal matter with the country's highest judicial officer; and with Harlan Fiske Stone, who succeeded Hughes in 1941, he was similarly congenial. Thus, for a quarter of a century, 1921–46, CCB had the ear of America's chief justice, which gave him no power, but considerable opportunity for influence.[26]

Among lawyers in New York in 1921, Hughes was generally thought to be the leader in appellate work, CCB in admiralty, and Max D. Steuer in jury trials, civil or criminal.[27] Steuer, everyone agreed, was unmatched in cross-examination, having an infallible ability to recall testimony and yet keep in mind the whole case, so that he always asked the crucial question, but never the one too many. His jury trials always drew an audience of lawyers, and in this respect he was the only successor to the great advocates of the past, Choate or Evarts, a fact reflecting the extent to which legal practice had changed. Many of the best minds now concentrated on corporate or appeals work, most of it done in an office or library, not in a courtroom.[28]

In April 1921, however, another outstanding trial and appeals lawyer joined the city bar when John W. Davis, after resigning as ambassador in London, chose to settle in New York. Despite having been Woodrow Wilson's solicitor general, 1913–18, and before that a West Virginia lawyer and congressman, he still had to wait six months for admission to the New York bar though meantime able to practice in Virginia, West Virginia, and the federal courts. (Ultimately, by the year of his death, 1955, he had argued more cases in the U.S. Supreme Court, 140, than any contemporary.) A gracious man of learning, wit, and charm, Davis joined the firm of Stetson Jennings & Russell, which in 1925 (after Davis, as Democratic candidate for president in 1924, had lost to Coolidge) became Davis Polk Wardwell Gardiner & Reed. The firm had a roster of extraordinary corporate clients, including J. P. Morgan, Guaranty Trust, Standard Oil of New Jersey, Erie Railroad, International Paper, and the Associated Press. In addition it handled estates for the very rich and did considerable trial work. The only fields of law beyond its usual scope were admiralty and patent.

The partnership agreement initially guaranteed Davis $60,000 a year and 18 percent of the firm's net profits, which for seven months of 1920 had totaled $469,000. Thus, depending on the amount of new business he and the firm could develop, he would earn annually upwards of $150,000, far more than most lawyers (though far less than Steuer, who reportedly earned $1 million).[29] His purported earnings, his clients, and their retainer fees to the firm, however, were continually raised to question his fitness for public office and even his personal integrity, and the charge of having "sold out to Wall Street" first appeared during a movement, enlisting CCB, to have Davis appointed to the U.S. Supreme Court.

The chance for an appointment arose under Republican Warren G. Harding, who, though president for only two years before dying in 1923, had the opportunity to name four men to the Supreme Court. He first appointed, to the post of chief justice, William Howard Taft; and then as associate justices, George Sutherland, Pierce Butler, and Edward T. Sandford. It was for the seat eventually taken by Pierce Butler that Davis, strongly supported by the new chief justice, was considered. Taft wanted Davis because as a Democrat he would bring some political balance to a court now heavily Republican, and yet personally he was socially and politically conservative.[30]

Despite widespread support, Davis stopped the nomination. He wished to be a lawyer, not a judge; Mrs. Davis did not wish to live in Washington; he only recently had completed ten years of public service, with the last three as ambassador, a post that had consumed all his savings; the annual salary of an associate justice, though free of income tax, was only $15,000, with no pension on retirement; and he wanted economic independence. As he explained to CCB, "I have taken the vows of chastity and obedience, but not of poverty."[31] Taft was disappointed and angrily wrote to CCB, "It is not so easy to select a judge as you reformers think . . . If you people in New York were not so eager for money and would be content to live on a reasonable salary . . . you might have some representatives on our bench, but you are all after the almighty dollar. Now put that in your pipe and smoke it."[32]

The issue of Wall Street money, lawyers, and clients rose again in 1924 as Democrats around the country debated the choice of a candidate to oppose Calvin Coolidge, who had succeeded Harding as president. In late June the party delegates gathered in Madison Square Garden, as a heat wave blistered New York. Finally, on the fifteenth day of the longest convention in presidential politics, after more than 103 ballots, the two leading candidates, Al Smith and William G. McAdoo, withdrew in favor of Davis, who won on the next ballot.

Long before then, CCB and Felix Frankfurter, then in his eleventh year as a professor at Harvard Law School, had started an epistolary argument over Davis's qualifications—their first sustained discussion in a correspondence and friendship that would continue until CCB's death in 1959. In February 1924, Frankfurter opened the exchange, "Dear Mr. Burlingham," with a compliment on CCB's remarks, published in the American Bar Association's *Annual Report*, favoring a bill to hold the United States liable for damage done by its ships. Then, referring to the corruption in Washington, the Teapot Dome scandal, and "the disgrace of a Daugherty as an Attorney General," he regretted that leaders of the bar—he named none, but Davis was then the American Bar Association's president—were failing to speak out against it. "I don't know why I say all this to you except that you are one of the few leaders that I know who share these feelings. Besides, you are a sort of father confessor of mine though you may not know it. But the fact is that I was sent out of the public schools of New York over the imprimatur of C. C. Burlingham" (who as "acting president of the Board of Education" had signed the diploma).[33]

In August 1894 Frankfurter, then eleven, and his family had come to New York from a Viennese ghetto and settled in a cold-water tenement in a German Jewish district on East Fourth Street. And often, in his first American years, he had gone for warmth and German newspapers to the reading room of Cooper Union. He was short (when grown only five-foot-six), walked with a bounce, and when talking, which he did in torrents, became "mostly head, eyes, and glasses." At fifteen or so he ceased to be a practicing Jew, becoming in his term a "reverent agnostic," yet one who asked for a Hebrew prayer at his death. Leaving Public School 25 in 1897, he entered City College's five-year course that combined high school and college. Tuition then was free, the students numbered 774, and the college's only building was a small Gothic structure at Twenty-third Street and Lexington Avenue. Graduating in 1902, he worked for a year in the city's Tenement House Department, and then entered Harvard Law School, where every year he led his class. After various legal jobs, including three years as an assistant U.S. attorney for the Southern District of New York under Henry L. Stimson, he returned in 1914 to teach at the law school, though during the war he also served as a federal labor mediator, a job that put him several times at the center of controversy. By the fall of 1919 he was back at the law school, where he remained until appointed in 1939 to the Supreme Court. By 1924, when he started his exchange of letters with CCB, he was already one of the country's best-known legal scholars and writers, and CCB hastened to reply.[34]

"My dear Felix," he began. "Yes, we are a poor lot. But what would you have us do? A statement signed by men of light and leading like yourself" might carry "a certain amount of weight, but most of us merely express our sympathies or antipathies, praising the men we like or reviling those we hate—and that gets nowhere."[35] In further letters, CCB asked to hear some "practical" plan of action. Frankfurter replied vigorously: "Let's stop being 'practical' for a season! . . . Don't you think it would be like a breath of fresh air in our dank national atmosphere if a few lawyers who did matter would say we don't like all this degradation and enveloping commercialism and general corrupting atmosphere?" And for the moment, the exchange stopped.[36]

In October, with Davis now the Democratic presidential candidate, it resumed when CCB discovered that editorials in *The New Republic*, which were strongly anti-Davis, had been written by Frankfurter,[37] who charged Davis with lack of courage and other qualities of leadership, and preferred Robert La Follette, who had united in a third party the remains of the Progressive and Socialist Parties and a coalition of farmers in the West. "I am for Davis," wrote CCB. "If I were young, I should probably be for La Follette, but now that I am old and have seen the righteous so often forsaken and begging bread, I could not vote for the grizzled old plush-head, with his stale and worn out programme." As for Frankfurter's complaint that Davis had failed to provide the bar with leadership, CCB commented: "I took no stock in the criticism that he ought to have made loud barking sounds after he took up the practice of the law; nor that he went into the Stetson firm instead of hanging out his shingle."[38]

Instantly Frankfurter replied: "Let me say a very blunt word. You old men know not what you do. Partly because you are too modest—you don't realize that you shape the ideals, or lack of them, of the next generation because they all want to be like you. And that's why I feel so deeply the unspiritual quality of Davis' career." To save time in writing he enclosed a copy of a letter on the same subject that he recently had sent to Learned Hand.

> For what is Davis' career? We are told he was anybody's and everybody's lawyer—in West Virginia, when he was an unknown fellow. But from the time that public office gave him a prestige to be capitalized, he capitalized it in terms of big money-making for himself and of service to the powerful. You know very well that I don't think of politics as a battle between the angels and the devils, in which all the rich are devils and all the poor are angels. But surely you will agree as heartily as I do in believing that it bodes ill for the state if talent and power and prestige are predominantly in the service of power.
>
> Look at Davis' life! When he came back in 1921, he could have commanded the most successful possible career as a free advocate. He could

have been what Hughes became after he left the bench. Instead of that consider his career, and its spiritual implications . . .

You will tell me Davis had to make a living . . . He could have made a handsome income if he had established himself as a free lawyer, instead of becoming a necessary part of the financial-legal complex which gave him an income (I have every reason for knowing) of not less than two hundred thousand dollars. He had to make a big living. But he went in for a Long Island living because that's the kind of a fellow he is. And it is good neither for these lads that I see passing through this School from year to year, nor for this country . . .[39]

CCB replied by return mail, saying of the letter to Hand that it was "quite like the editorials in *The New Republic* to which I took violent though unexpressed exception." He plunged on:

The contrast between Davis and Hughes is too ludicrously unjust and that $200,000 stuff strikes me as equally foolish.

Davis came back from England dead broke. He would have opened an office of his own but he had not the price. He did not have a snug firm berth to go back to like Hughes and so he weighed and considered the offers that came to him . . . Wisely he went with the Stetson firm. They needed him as much as he needed them . . . Davis gave them what they most needed, a head who was a lawyer.

Should he have hung out his own shingle? Should he have returned to Charleston, W. Va., or should he have become a member of the Washington bar? Why? He was not a candidate for office . . . He is just a law lawyer. He likes it and he likes to earn money, but his money-earning is only incidental. To me it is extraordinary that you reproach him for living on Long Island. It is a mighty good thing for the Long Islanders and will never spoil him or his wife. They are absolutely democratic. You should see them with their W. Va friends and neighbors.

Now as to Hughes. Did you ever consult him professionally after he returned to our bar? Were his clients the poor and oppressed of this world? And what about his charges? I know from experience something of his scale. No man at our bar made so much by counsel work as Hughes did in that brief period between the Court and his secretaryship [of state, for Harding].

I do not consider Davis a very enlightened person, socially or industrially, but he is so intelligent that if elected he would learn and he has no predilections for the "interests" or "big business." His chief defect is

a lack of enthusiasm—a fatal defect as a campaigner. He has nothing of
the crusader in him. He is too calm, too humorous, possibly too cynical.
I wish his heart had beaten hard and loud for the political prisoners
[convicted under the espionage acts]. I wish his great talents had been
joined to a burning hatred for wrong, but they are not. I am sure that
if you had gone to him and asked him to fight for the liberties of the
downtrodden, he would have done it and then would have cooled down,
or perhaps never have warmed up. That is not the best sort of president
for the American or any other bar association, but he would make a very
good president of the United States—a good administrator, a good
judge of men, a good appointer of judges.[40]

Frankfurter raised a serious issue about law and lawyers, which a biographer of Davis has summarized: "To accept a regular retainer was to
change the character of one's practice and to restrict one's political and
professional independence."[41] Or, as laymen would say, a lawyer on retainer is "a dog on a leash." William E. Hocking, in *The Yale Review*,
phrased the issue more concisely than Frankfurter: "When Mr. Davis
scorned the suggestion that he should change his occupation to make
himself a fitter possibility for the presidential nomination, he was right;
when he asserted that occupation and activities have no psychological influence upon perceptions of public policy, he was wrong. Associations
alter interpretations."[42] CCB in his view was closer to Hocking than to
Frankfurter, for he did not believe that a lawyer's corporate or criminal
clients of necessity rendered him unfit for office. Though CCB's analysis
of Davis was remarkably acute, he was unable to shift Frankfurter's views
of the man by even a hair. Yet both CCB and Frankfurter found their exchange stimulating, and for the next thirty-five years they argued back and
forth, never more enjoyably than over small disagreements when each felt
he could speak bluntly.

In the years to come, Frankfurter's call for more vigorous action by
leaders of the bar returned to haunt him. By 1937, when President Roosevelt threatened to "pack" the Supreme Court to end its rejection of his
legislative programs, Frankfurter was not only America's leading law
scholar but its leading journalist about the court's history and procedures.
Yet to the distress of many, though he was believed to disapprove of Roosevelt's plan, he would neither speak nor write on it publicly. Many then
thought his silence sprang from a reluctance to risk losing a possible
appointment by Roosevelt to the Supreme Court. His grand pronounce-
ments about a lawyer's duty and honor then began to sound hollow, and

his criticisms of Davis, when recalled, seemed tainted by the envy of an academic who begrudged a practicing lawyer the rewards of a different choice of career.[43]

But despite some serious disagreements with Frankfurter, requiring some subjects to be temporarily banned from discussion, CCB's correspondence with him never faltered. Though CCB publicly opposed Roosevelt's "court-packing" plan and privately called on Frankfurter to speak out, he evidently decided after a time to ignore Frankfurter's silence. Other aspects of their friendship were more important. As a practicing lawyer, CCB knew that nothing in the courtroom is as pure and perfect as presented in the classroom. Life is more complex than any lecture can convey, and in life no one achieves full consistency. An occasional lapse should be overlooked; first-class minds don't always agree, and first-class friendships temper sympathy with detachment.

As their correspondence continued, CCB began to realize how different had become the law professor, as a type, from the practicing lawyer.[44] A hundred years earlier the two had been one and the same, and even in CCB's youth they frequently had coincided. But by the 1920s Frankfurter had become in many respects the prototype of a new profession: the legal scholar who, despite arguing an occasional case, is primarily a teacher in a law school and yet who, in public journals, pursues a cause. This scholar or professor, feeling he knows more in certain areas of the law than the less specialized practitioner, seeks through editorials, articles, and political influence to have a dominating hand in legal and public affairs.[45] As CCB aged, despite his affection and admiration for "Dear Felix," he began to wonder whether such men could or should be leaders of the bar and came increasingly to doubt their fitness for the bench.

Having plucked Veeder off the federal bench, CCB continued trying to push good men onto it and also, when he saw an opportunity, to improve the administration and procedures of New York's federal courts. Though he was not crucial to the promotion in 1924 of Learned Hand to the Second Circuit Court of Appeals, he was greatly pleased by it and wrote: "My dear B. This is no ordinary event. The world may be unshaken, but we who understand know that your appointment saves the Court."[46] His few words, though seemingly dashed off, were meaningful. With Hand's accession the court now had four judges; of the other three CCB thought chief judge Henry Wade Rogers, a former dean of Yale Law School, was lazy; he respected Manton's abilities but was suspicious of his political ties and activities; and though greatly admiring Hough, he feared the judge's

ill health would end soon in death. In that likelihood he could declare that
Hand's appointment "saves the court" because it ensured for it at least one
first-class mind and worker. As happened, however, Rogers died before
Hough, in 1926. Because the court's jurisdiction included Vermont and
Connecticut as well as New York, tradition called for one of its four judges
to come from a New England state, and to succeed Rogers, President
Coolidge appointed Thomas W. Swan, of Connecticut. Born in the state,
in Norwich, Swan had graduated from Yale College and Harvard Law
School and practiced corporate law in Chicago until called in 1916 to succeed Rogers at the Yale Law School. In his ten years there Swan had greatly
improved its quality and reputation, and his chief supporters for the court
were Chief Justice Taft and Learned Hand. CCB, unenthusiastic about
another law school dean, stood aside. In this he perhaps was in the majority, for in 1926 many lawyers still believed that law grew best by accretion,
each step, after argument in a court, leading to the next. Legal theorists
and professors expounding doctrines of wide generality were suspect.

In Swan's case, however, Taft and Hand gauged better than CCB the
man's potential as a judge. Twenty years later, in describing Swan's qualities, Hand sketched a standard of judicial behavior at its best:

> His manners on the bench were, and are, a model and—be it said in all
> humility—often an admonishment to others whose composure is not
> equally proof against irritation. He speaks but little, and is no "ill-tuned
> cymbal"; he never seeks to bring out in advance what will appear in
> season; nor does he lead the argument far afield into pastures whence
> the return is tortuous and uncertain. When he does speak, it is to put a
> narrow question, directed to inconsistencies already apparent, or to the
> untoward consequences of that which has been said. He is never in
> the teacher's chair, nor does drive counsel to confusion by successive
> advances, designed to end in rout.[47]

With Swan on the Second Circuit the court was not only saved but
improved. But in 1927 when Hough died, the agitation and search for a
better-than-average successor began again. Manton by seniority became
the court's chief judge, and CCB's choice for Hough's successor was Augustus Noble Hand. Even before Hough's death, he had written to Frankfurter, "The one thing we need most is to get A. N. Hand promoted to the
C.C.A. and that, I think, can be accomplished."[48]

Though President Coolidge was a Republican, he allowed himself to be
persuaded to the merits of a Democrat, and in 1927 Learned's first cousin

"Gus" joined him and Swan on the Second Circuit. Reportedly the chief agents in achieving the promotion were Taft, Attorney General Harlan Fiske Stone, and Hughes, just starting his term as president of the City Bar Association.[49] CCB, as usual, was meddling in the background, and in a letter to Hughes in May 1927, the week before Hand joined the court, he explained why the Manhattan Republican organization had acquiesced in the appointment of a Democrat:

> A. N. Hand's promotion was made much easier by the hope of the [Republican] Organization that they might put in one of their own men as District judge, and the man [Ogden L.] Mills and S. Koenig [Republican leader in Manhattan] want is F. J. Coleman. He has, of course, a great sheaf of letters, but neither by training nor experience is up to the standard.
>
> Hand is to be sworn in next Tuesday, and unless the bar speaks, Coleman will be nominated by default. I have suggested to the Judiciary Committee [of the bar association] that they tender their good offices to the Attorney General immediately. They did an exceptional thing in the case of Hand by definitely recommending him. Their usual practice is to pass on names submitted to them [ruling "qualified" or not]. It is quite likely that if a few Republican lawyers would recommend some good lawyers, like Alfred A. Wheat, who has been in with the Department of Justice for the last three years or so and has argued many cases in the Supreme Court, or Alfred C. Coxe or [Bernard] Hershkopf, who (the last two) were on the Organization list when [T. D.] Thacher was appointed [to the district court in 1925], the Attorney General might recommend a lawyer rather than a politician.[50]

Thomas Thacher had taken Learned Hand's place on the district court and was proving to be an excellent trial judge. CCB now hoped to be as lucky in the successor to A. N. Hand, and he continued to barrage Hughes with suggestions and information. Ultimately the appointment went to Francis G. Caffey, a former U.S. attorney for the Southern District whom CCB had recommended in 1917 and who, he now assured Hughes, was A. N. Hand's choice for the post "if a Democrat is possible."[51]

The appointment of judges, however, was not CCB's only concern with the federal courts. The Second Circuit had the heaviest load of the country's nine circuit appeals courts, and Manton, in the spring of 1925, had devised a plan for redividing the country into six circuits so that the work would be more evenly distributed. He wrote a summary of his ideas to

Chief Justice Taft, and also discussed the plan with CCB, who thought well of it. CCB thereupon proposed to Taft that the issue be raised in some fashion at the next meeting of the American Bar Association, in Detroit in September 1925: "But I don't want to mess into it without your approval."[52] Evidently Taft approved, for a few weeks later CCB asked Hughes, at the time the American Bar Association's president: "What would you think of a Resolution to be offered at Detroit asking the Committee on the Amendment of the Law to consider whether it is desirable to re-circuit the United States?" In summarizing Manton's plan, he pointed out that in 1924 the First Circuit (Massachusetts, Maine, and New Hampshire) had heard 77 appeals, and the Second, 441.[53]

Despite the attention given to the recircuiting plan, it died aborning, though not before a number of judges and lawyers had been reminded of a problem that needed solving. Yet, as reformers then used to say, to harvest one viable idea, you must seed and hoe ten. And in 1929 Congress eased the pressure on the Second Circuit in another way by authorizing the addition to its bench of a fifth regular judge. CCB and Learned Hand hoped to advance Thacher from the district court, but Coolidge, from Vermont, named Judge Harrie Brigham Chase of the Vermont Supreme Court.[54] Chase spent most of his time in Brattleboro, deciding those cases that arose in his home state. On occasion he came down to New York to help out, but by choice and pattern of work he remained somewhat apart from his colleagues. L. Hand's biographer describes Chase as a "modest" judge of "integrity and competence" who "never claimed to be an intellectual or a penetrating student of the law." He "preferred his outings on the golf course to his struggles with arguments and judicial opinions," but "unlike Manton, he was not a political judge preoccupied with cronyism."[55] He was never at the court's center.

Even before the addition of Chase, during the 1920s Chief Justice Taft often assigned Judge Julian W. Mack to the Second Circuit on a temporary basis. Mack's position in the federal system was odd. A good lawyer and judge, he had been named to the U.S. Commerce Court in 1911, a new court created to review railroad regulation cases, and with its three judges given the rank of circuit judges. But the court soon had been abolished, with one judge impeached for accepting bribes and the other two, holding lifetime appointments, left "floating" and available for temporary assignments. Until Mack's retirement in 1940, he sat frequently with the Second Circuit, so much so that to many laymen and even lawyers he seemed more permanent than temporary. The court in New York frequently sat in panels of three judges, with Mack one of the three, and although he seldom wrote an opinion, suffering, it was said, from "pen paralysis," he participated in many decisions. He was congenial with Swan and the two Hands, less so with Manton, and saw little of Chase.[56]

After Chase's appointment in 1929, the court had no further change until 1938, and in that period it settled into a pattern of highly productive work. At its core were Swan and the two Hands, all of whom would serve on it for more than twenty-five years, giving it a quarter century of stability. And during that time, they made of it, in both the number and quality of its decisions, the leading federal appeals court in the United States.

In the more numerous state courts, it was harder for a private citizen like CCB to have an impact, but even here his continual efforts to advance Judge Cardozo in some small measure helped the New York Court of Appeals to one of the brightest periods in its history. Cardozo's judicial career initially had moved at an astonishing pace. Within a month of taking his seat in January 1914 on New York's Supreme Court, First District, he had advanced, by temporary assignment, to the Court of Appeals, and less than four years later, having served continuously as a judge on assignment, he was elected in November 1917 to a regular seat, with a term of fourteen years.[57] And by 1926 he was an obvious contender for the post of chief judge, which was soon to open when Frank Hiscock, as required by law, retired at age seventy.

By then Cardozo was known across the state and popular with its lawyers, who appreciated his patience with their problems. These he once summarized in a speech before the New York County Lawyers' Association in a characteristic long sentence: "When I meditate on these things, the enthusiasms of forensic efforts, the fire that goes into them, the meaning of defeat or victory, not merely to the pocket of the advocate, but still more to his pride, his repute and his sense of duty done, I think with mounting wonder of the spirit of professional fellowship which animates the profession even now—the good temper, the humor, the acceptance of fortune fair or foul as all in the day's work."[58]

In this decade Cardozo, though still bookish, shy, and reclusive, increasingly was celebrated not only as a judge but as a person, and not surprisingly CCB, in his enthusiastic way, wanted to draw him out, to introduce him to others, so that they, too, might enjoy the man. Hence, one day in 1923, CCB and Harlan Fiske Stone, then dean of Columbia Law School, suggested to Cardozo that he allow them to propose him for membership in New York City's Century Club. He was, they urged, just the sort of member the club desired, and he could leave the work of nomination to them.

The judge, CCB recalled, was "modestly reluctant, and said that he thought it might be embarrassing to him and to us." At the time, the Century had a number of Jewish members, mostly of German heritage. But because of the influx after 1900 of Russian Jewish immigrants to the country—in New York by 1925 among residents one in four was a Jew and among lawyers almost one in two[59]—anti-Semitism was on the rise. And Cardozo delicately reminded his friends that his being a Jew might be a hindrance. They insisted it would not, and after further discussion, according to CCB, Cardozo agreed to leave the decision "entirely in my hands."[60]

CCB loved the Century. Among American clubs it was relatively old, dating back to 1825, and by its constitution its purpose was to gather in a congenial setting "authors, artists, and amateurs of letters and the fine arts." Put more bluntly: amateurs of the arts—rich lawyers, doctors, publishers—were to subsidize in a club impecunious artists, primarily by charging the artists considerably lower dues and admission fees. But the club had trouble maintaining a balance between rich and poor. Artists, it was discovered, were apt to hold grudges against each other, and painters, for example, who were in the club were quite prepared to keep out whole schools of colleagues whose styles they disliked. Lawyers, if not more forgiving, were at least more forgetful, and usually willing to allow in any colleague not yet convicted of a crime. So lawyers were easier than artists to elect and in their number threatened constantly to be too many. Also, artists tended to be hermitlike creatures who had trouble mustering the necessary number of letters in support to win election, whereas lawyers, who by trade had an acquaintance with most of the town, overwhelmed the Admissions Committee with testimonials. One of the most pithy of these purportedly read: "I have been asked by Mr. McPush to write to the Committee in regard to his candidacy. This is the letter."[61] And of course, from time to time among the members, besides personal hatred, other passions, moral, racial, or political, rose high and toppled judgment.

Periodically, grave mistakes in admission were made. The disappointments among the artists typically were those who, in their reclusiveness, seldom appeared and contributed little to the club's purpose, whereas in the "talking" profession, the mistakes were all too present. Tocqueville had written eloquently on the difficulty of stopping an American bore, and at the Century these were usually lawyers, clerics, or professors. The lawyers, at least, were accustomed to interruptions by the judge or opponents and did not take them personally, but clergymen and professors, unused to having their monologues halted, often grew huffy.[62]

After 1891 the club's home, at 7 West Forty-third Street, was a handsome five-story Palladian house designed by McKim, Mead & White, with a skylit gallery for displaying the works of member artists. The rest of the building primarily offered the club's 1,200 members spaces for conversation. A wide staircase, dividing at a landing and turning back on itself, led to the piano nobile, where to one side was a very large room, with many groupings of chairs, and across a spacious hall, another half as large. In summer, members could enjoy a shaded wooden deck in the back, dominated by a bronze reproduction of the Roman she-wolf suckling Romulus and Remus. On the floor above, facing the winter's warming sun, was a small loggia, a handsome, well-stocked library, and a dining room set up to stimulate talk, with a center "long table" at which members took any seat vacant with the certainty of being drawn into conversation by neighbors.[63] A fourth and fifth floor had private dining rooms and several offices, but the club had no bedrooms, no sports facilities (beyond billiards), and did not allow gambling. Talk was what was wanted, talk and the exchange of ideas.

CCB first spoke privately to the twenty-one members of the Admissions Committee and determined that it would favor Cardozo's election. But that by itself was not conclusive, for the committee could only recommend: if one-fifth of the club members present at a monthly meeting objected to a candidate, his name would be returned to the committee for further consideration. (By this method, the committee hoped, "the evils of oligarchy and the excesses of democracy both are avoided.")[64] Next CCB asked Elihu Root, the club's president, to propose Cardozo, but Root refused, thinking it inappropriate for the president to propose a candidate; he agreed, however, to second the nomination. So CCB wrote a note to John G. Milburn, like Root a former president of the City Bar Association: "We have elected you to propose him [Cardozo], and I feel sure that you will be glad to do so . . . This is rather highhanded business on my part is it not?"[65] But he no doubt thought: with Root signed on before, could Milburn lag behind? And in addition he gathered a sheaf of supporting letters from all his usual friends: Stone, the two Hands, Hughes, Stimson, Veeder, Wickersham, Frederic Coudert, Henry W. Taft, John Finley, and more.[66] Leaving nothing to chance, he wrote to Learned Hand, "Dear B, May I suggest that in your letter you dwell particularly on Cardozo's social side—manners, charm, etc. Everybody knows his ability and will write about that, but you have had him at your house and can write a good strong letter for him."[67]

As the monthly meeting neared at which Cardozo's name would come up, CCB reminded him of their conversation now two years past, and when election was achieved he had a note from the judge: "Your friendship and your energy are alike without limits. Of course, I remembered the talk, but I fancied that you had found it prudent to let the matter drop. I ought to have known that you never give up—at least when by keeping on you can be helpful to a friend."[68]

A friend of both men who disapproved of the outcome was Felix Frankfurter. He thought Cardozo should not have joined a club that had some reputedly anti-Semitic members, and in an interview in 1960 he told Cardozo's biographer, "From my point of view a little stiffer austerity would have been in order." He added that "when he himself was on the Supreme Court, he had turned Burlingham down when Burlingham wanted him to join the Century because the problem of anti-Semitism had persisted."[69] But Cardozo enjoyed the Century. When in New York City he often lunched at the club's "long table" and soon became a well-known figure there.

In this same period CCB worked to advance Cardozo from associate to chief judge on the Court of Appeals, a more complicated affair. The court had seven judges elected in statewide campaigns for fourteen-year terms—except that by custom a judge who completed a full term without discredit was entitled to renomination by both the Republican and Democratic Parties and was thus sure of reelection; the new term therefore was effectively until death or age seventy, when by statute judges were required to retire. A similar sort of exception lay in the governor's power to fill a temporary vacancy, due to death or resignation, by an appointment whose term ran until the next Election Day; this often (though not always) led to an endorsement at the next election by both political parties.[70] Consequently, vacancies without an heir apparent were rare, and lawyers and politicians knew that if they wanted to influence the selection of candidates, they must act together and long before Election Day. What they liked least was a contest between two good candidates, with one sure to be wasted in defeat, or, worse, between two picked for political ties without regard to legal ability. Given the predominance of Republicans in the state, except in a few large cities, the political ratio on the court in these years remained constant, roughly 60 to 40 percent Republican to Democrat.[71]

CCB began his push for Cardozo in August 1925, when the Democrat Al Smith was in the midst of his third term as governor. Writing to Hughes, at the moment in private practice but with influence in the state's Republican Party, and noting that the court's chief judge, Frank H.

Hiscock, would turn seventy the following April and be forced to retire, he observed: "It is not too early for the bar to be thinking about his successor. [Associate judge] F. Crane is already busy. [Ex-]Governor Miller would probably be for [associate judge Cuthbert] Pound. Cardozo is the best I think, but in any case an effort should be made to have both Parties unite on some one man. How to do it is the question." Ex-governor Nathan L. Miller, the only man in five elections to defeat Smith for the office (the terms then were two years) was a Republican, and so, too, were Judges Crane and Pound. Cardozo, a Democrat, owed his place less to party politics than either of them, but on the Democratic side, as CCB added, there was a complication.

> There is one factor which must not be lost sight of. The Cardinal [Joseph Patrick Hayes] was deeply pained that [associate judge John W.] Hogan was succeeded not by one of his faith but by [Irving] Lehmann, leaving the Court without a single member of the true Church. So we may be sure that when the time comes, the Cathedral will not sit idly by. I have written to Wickersham, [William D.] Guthrie, and Stimson and have heard from the first two. Guthrie writes that he believes Cardozo "is justly regarded, both in and out of the State, as the most scholarly and able of the judges of our Court of Appeals." As President of the Association of the Bar he must be "circumspect" he says. But he thinks there should be an exchange of views, and he suggests I write to you and to Mr. Root and Governor Miller.
>
> I have asked Stimson and Wickersham to speak to Mr. Root. Gov. Miller I know only slightly. I should suppose he would favor Pound [both being upstate Republicans]. Wickersham strongly favors Cardozo, Milburn would too, I'm sure. What do you suggest?[72]

CCB closed with a list of dates of appointment to the court, showing that although Cardozo was the youngest of the three likely candidates, he had "the longest service in the Court."

In the succeeding months the political intrigues became ever more contorted, and two months after Hiscock retired, CCB wrote in frustration to Frankfurter: "It really doesn't make an awful lot of difference whether Pound or Cardozo is chosen. The main thing is that there should not be two tickets." And by midsummer of 1926 the leaders of both parties had agreed on Pound. Or thought they had.

In September, at a meeting with Republican leaders, Governor Smith suddenly announced he wanted Cardozo, declaring that he had only just learned that Cardozo had seniority. The Republicans were outraged, or so they pretended, but within two days they had agreed to a plan to which Pound graciously acceded: both parties would endorse Cardozo for chief judge and a Republican, Henry T. Kellogg, to replace associate judge Chester B. McLaughlin (retiring because of age). Then, after the election, Smith would appoint to Cardozo's former seat the Democrat John F. O'Brien, whose religion pleased the cardinal.[73]

Writing to Frankfurter soon after this September shuffle, CCB acknowledged that he did not "know all the inside work," and gave primary credit to Smith's adviser Joseph M. Proskauer, though editorials in the *Times* and in *The World* "may have done something." As for himself, "I burnt the wires with telegrams . . . but my influence is slight."[74] And after winning the November election, on 1 January 1927 Cardozo became the court's chief judge.

As such he became responsible for the court as an institution. In January 1917 it had moved from the Capitol Building in Albany to a building of its own, the Court of Appeals Hall. Built in 1842 and close to the Capitol, but enlarged and refurbished for the court, the building's Ionic design featured a domed rotunda encircled by columns and with hallways leading off it. The courtroom on the main floor was wood-paneled, with brass rail, portraits of former judges, and a magnificent onyx fireplace. On the floors above were a library, a conference room, judges' chambers, and offices for the clerks.

One court tradition, which Cardozo continued, was to assign cases by rotation: this differed from the custom in the federal courts, where cases were often assigned to judges specializing in a given area of law: admiralty, patents, or torts. Under the Court of Appeals system, sometimes the judge with the greatest expertise in the subject matter would not write the opinion in the case, and many lawyers wondered if rotation was the best way to assign cases. One virtue of it, however, was that it increased the court's collegiality. There was no bickering about the number of cases assigned or the quality of them—for judges as much as lawyers want the famous cases—and Cardozo regularly took his share of the unexceptional.[75]

During his six years as chief judge, Cardozo's learning, manner, and civility had a chance to exert their charm, and the court was a remarkably happy institution. Its seven judges, coming from all sections of the state, when in Albany put up at the Hotel Ten Eyck, at the foot of State Street, ate most of their meals together, and, or so it was said, all took to reading books because Cardozo, at mealtime, liked to talk of them.[76] Indeed, ever since 1914 he increasingly had set the court's intellectual tone. New York being the country's most populous state as well as its commercial and financial center, its Court of Appeals was preeminent, and its decisions set precedent across the country; among the most frequently cited cases many were written by Cardozo.[77] He was personally conservative but in his social and economic thinking slightly ahead of most lawyers. And he was ready, when occasion offered, to reinterpret and expand the common law case by case, in its traditional, incremental manner.

His most frequently cited opinion was *MacPherson v. Buick Motor Co.*, decided in 1916, when cars were beginning to dominate the road.[78] The law in New York then stated that if a consumer wanted to sue a manufacturer for a defective product, he must have bought it directly from the manufacturer (in legal terms, have privity of contract with the manufacturer), with an exception for an object whose normal use was to injure or destroy, such as poisons, explosives, or deadly weapons. In *MacPherson v. Buick*, Mr. MacPherson had bought a new Buick from a dealer. One day soon after, while he was driving on a road at 8 mph, one of its wooden-spoked wheels collapsed; the car lurched, and he was thrown out, injured, and sued not the dealer but the Buick Company, which, he claimed, should have inspected for and corrected the defective wheel.

The company offered several defenses, among them that it had no privity of contract with MacPherson, who had bought from a dealer, and that the car was not an inherently dangerous instrument and therefore not within the exception to the general rule. Having lost in the lower court, the company appealed, and Cardozo wrote the decision.

> Beyond all question, the nature of an automobile gives warning of probable danger if its construction is defective. This automobile was designed to go fifty miles an hour. Unless its wheels were sound and strong, injury was almost certain. It was as much a thing of danger as a defective engine for a railroad. The defendant knew the danger. It knew also that the car would be used by persons other than the buyer. This was apparent from its size; there were seats for three persons. It was apparent also from the fact that the buyer was a dealer in cars who bought to resell . . . Precedents drawn from the days of travel by stagecoach do not fit the conditions of travel today. The principle that the danger must be imminent does not change, but the things subject to the principle do change. They are whatever the needs of life in a developing civilization require them to be.[79]

By ruling that the car was an inherently dangerous instrument, Cardozo extended the law of liability for a defective product to an important new industry. His language was quiet, and he presented the decision as merely a commonsense restatement of existing law; yet the extension of product liability past the dealer to the manufacturer was quite revolutionary and, in another judge's view, "managed to change profoundly the climate of opinion regarding privity of contract." In achieving this end, Cardozo's soft-spoken style was important, and it served to bring his fellow judges to a 6 to 1 decision, whose near unanimity helped to damp opposition to the new concept. Seeking in this gentle manner primarily to resolve a conflict, not to debate a grand issue, Cardozo advanced the law to meet the emerging problems of the industrial age.[80]

CCB greatly admired this style. When, in 1944, justices of the U.S. Supreme Court seemed unable to render any decision without the clanging discord of multiple concurring and dissenting opinions, CCB wrote an anonymous letter to the *Herald Tribune* protesting the turmoil and extolling Cardozo's judicial administration as a model. "It is one of the essential functions of a Chief Justice," wrote CCB, "to persuade his associates not to insist on differences which can be adjusted."[81] When four justices offer four concurring opinions, each with a different set of reasons for reaching one decision, who can say which set controls? What is the law?

Besides an ability to win support for rulings by writing in an unaggressive style, Cardozo also could make a point memorable by a literary flourish, though the more plainspoken CCB complained that sometimes the writing was "a bit too fluorescent."[82] A typical Cardozo flourish occurred in a case concerning the city of Utica and its desire to build an airport. The state legislature in 1928 had authorized cities to establish airports, and Utica had bought land and was planning a bond issue when a citizen sued to stop the project, contending that an airport, though built for a public purpose, was not a proper municipal purpose. The question stirred interest, for air travel was new and exciting, and a number of cities were planning airports. The case did not turn on Cardozo's specialties, torts and contracts, but came to him by rotation, and yet by a sentence or two he made it solely his.

> We think the purpose to be served is both public and municipal. A city acts for city purposes when it builds a dock or a bridge or a street or a subway . . . Its purpose is not different when it builds an airport . . . Aviation is today an established method of transportation. The future, even the near future, will make it still more general. The city that is without foresight to build the ports of the new traffic may soon be left behind in the race of competition. Chalcedon was called the city of the blind

because its founders rejected the nobler site of Byzantium lying at their feet. The need for vision of the future in the governance of cities has not lessened with the years. The dweller within the gates, even more than the stranger from afar, will pay the price for blindness.[83]

When the opinion came down, lawyers throughout the state began to talk of Chalcedon and Byzantium, and if one asked, What have they to do with Utica and airports? The answer was, Everything!

But of course it was not the literary flourishes that made Cardozo nationally known, nor were they the reason why the court, under his leadership, attracted such admiration; it was the steady quality of its decisions, not all of which were his. Yet much of the credit accrued to him personally, and by 1932 he was undoubtedly the preeminent judge in the country who was not sitting on the Supreme Court. It was no surprise that in January 1932, when Oliver Wendell Holmes Jr. resigned, President Hoover acted promptly and offered Cardozo the Supreme Court appointment on 15 February, and Cardozo accepted.[84] Within the week his mailbox overflowed with congratulatory letters (among them, he told Learned Hand, were two offers of marriage). As always, he disliked the publicity and evidently had moments when he regretted exchanging New York for Washington. But Hand thought him "not as unhappy at the prospect of pulling up his stakes as he thought he would be." New Yorkers, on the other hand, were sorry to see him go.[85] At the Century Club, to celebrate his appointment, some of the artists and writers, counting him a fellow "author," gave him a dinner—though probably few if any had read to the end of his *Nature of the Judicial Process*. Nevertheless, they had read the man, and considered him an artist (CCB, as a mere "amateur of the arts," was not invited), "and the whole occasion, by turns frivolous and serious, revolved around books."[86]

On 14 March, he was sworn in at the Supreme Court building in Washington, and wrote that same day to CCB: "Beloved Burlingham, What a joy it was to see your dear face in the Court room! Many, many thanks. Affectionately, B.N.C."[87]

In April 1920, the same month the New York Assembly confirmed the expulsion of five Socialist members, in South Braintree, Massachusetts, two men with pistols stole a shoe factory's payroll, killing the paymaster and his guard. The murders took place on the main street, at about 3 p.m., and the gunmen sped off in a car driven by another. The payroll was $15,776.51, and the murdered men, F. A. Parmenter and Alessandro Berardelli, had families.[88] Several weeks later police arrested two Italian immigrants, Niccolo Sacco and Bartolomeo Vanzetti, charging them with murder. Both were philosophical anarchists, perhaps Communists, and certainly, by the day's standards, radicals. Though both had come to the United States in 1908, neither had become a citizen or fluent in English, and both, to evade the 1917 armed services draft, had fled to Mexico and now risked deportation. Sacco worked in the shoe factory, and Vanzetti was a fish peddler. Their trial by jury, held fourteen months later in the Superior Court in Dedham, Massachusetts, ended in conviction, with death the likely sentence.

The trial at first was little noticed in local newspapers or elsewhere in the United States. In Europe, and in Central and South America, however, the leftist, anticapitalist papers made much of it, their reports leading to boycotts, riots, and attacks on U.S. embassies. In Paris, at a demonstration for the two men, a bomb was exploded, killing twenty people.

Gradually, as motions and appeals on Sacco and Vanzetti's behalf were made and lost in the Massachusetts courts, lawyers, laymen, and political activists in other states began to follow the proceedings. They were impressed by the bearing of the two men, saw real or imagined flaws in the case, and divided in opinion on the fairness of the trial and subsequent court rulings. Soon the guilt or innocence, execution or reprieve of Sacco and Vanzetti was as dominant an issue in the United States as the Dreyfus case had been in France twenty-five years earlier.

CCB's part in the debate was marginal, and he came to it only in April 1927, by which time the Massachusetts Supreme Judicial Court had overruled the last appeal, returning the case to the trial court and Judge Webster Thayer for sentencing. By then Frankfurter had become the principal and most effective spokesman for all those who thought the original trial, conducted by Thayer in 1921, had been tainted by his prejudice against "radicals" or who thought sufficient new evidence had been produced to warrant a new trial. For both reasons Frankfurter believed a new trial was justified, and, if granted, the men would be found innocent. In an article for the March 1927 *Atlantic Monthly*, he reviewed the case in detail, and in the same month, with footnotes and appendixes added, published the article as a small book, *The Case of Sacco and Vanzetti: A Critical Analysis for Lawyers and Laymen*.[89] His statement was probably the most cogent published on either side; but besides jolting many to rethink their opinions, it projected him personally into the controversy. Some thought he should not publish such an article while the state's Supreme Court had an appeal in the case under consideration, others that a law professor should keep himself and his school out of the fray; still others argued that because Frankfurter himself was a "radical," or at least "liberal," he was biased in the men's favor, or alternatively, a defense by one so patently biased only aggravated the prejudice against the men. For years thereafter he was praised or reviled for his actions, while meantime, on all sides, passion outpaced reason.

On 9 April Judge Thayer sentenced the men to death by the electric chair, with execution in the second week of July. Three days after the sentencing, five citizens of Massachusetts, among them the Episcopal bishop William Lawrence, the Harvard professor Frank Taussig, and a leading Boston lawyer, Charles P. Curtis Jr., wrote a letter to Governor Alvan T. Fuller which he promptly made public. The writers petitioned softly: "Knowing well your sense of justice . . . we ask with great earnestness that you call to your aid several citizens of well known character, experience, ability, and sense of justice to make a study of the trial and advise you." They urged him to appoint a panel of distinguished citizens to advise him on his power to pardon or to order a new trial.[90]

CCB received a copy of the letter, probably from Taussig. But by then he had sent one of his own to the *Times* and to the *Tribune*, published by both on 20 April. Its opening paragraph set a calm, unaggressive tone: "In the midst of the turmoil and shouting of the Reds and Whites it may be enlightening to some to know in what respect the Massachusetts law of appeals in capital cases differs from that of New York and Great Britain and the resulting difference in the relation of the Governor to the pardoning power." He briefly stated the law in England and, at greater length, as it was in New York, showing how the governor's power in Massachusetts was greater than in New York. The final paragraph read:

> In Massachusetts the Governor has the right, and in certain cases is in duty bound, to look into the facts, review the action of the trial Judge, consider newly discovered evidence—in other words, perform the functions which in England and in New York are performed by Appellate Judges. Whether he takes the sole responsibility for this or calls to his aid a commission of inquiry is a matter for him to determine. In this State [New York] in two notable murder cases—the Carlyle Harris case and the Charles F. Stielow case—the Governor appointed a commissioner to aid him. In the Harris case the Governor refused clemency. In the Stielow case he not only pardoned the defendant but restored to him his civil rights.[91]

On the morning the letter appeared in the *Times* and *Tribune*, CCB, apparently as an afterthought, sent a copy of it by messenger to Walter Lippmann, editor of the afternoon *World*. Lippmann replied, also by hand, scolding "Dear Burlingham" for coming late to *The World* but planning to use the letter. Newspaper editors do not like to limp after competitors, however, and Lippmann, instead of publishing the letter, based an editorial on it, stating that the chief issue in discussion "has been clearly defined by Mr. Charles C. Burlingham, a distinguished lawyer of this city." After publication in city newspapers of several more letters by CCB, he became for many New Yorkers, and even for some farther afield, a welcome guide to the Sacco and Vanzetti case.[92]

Meanwhile, CCB wrote to Taussig, eager to support the suggestion to Governor Fuller but fearing that even "a moderate statement" by a group of New York lawyers might strike the governor as an "impertinence," a butting-in by "outsiders." And he wrote a similar, more detailed letter to the president of the Boston Bar Association. Taussig replied by return mail: "If New York lawyers made a statement, there would probably be a howl about interference . . . My present feeling is that you better let things alone . . . Chances seem to me that Fuller will commute the sentence . . . I have no idea whether he will act on the suggestion of appointing an investigating body, but rather think he will . . ."[93]

On 22 April, CCB, still searching for a way to act, wrote to Bishop Lawrence, who was about to retire as Episcopal bishop of Massachusetts:

> You need no praise from me . . . that you have intervened with so admirable a suggestion to Governor Fuller . . . Here in New York many of us lawyers are interested but do not see exactly what we can do . . . Counsel for Sacco and Vanzetti in the trial court were palpably incompetent, failing to take exceptions as they should. Judge Thayer has reviewed his own decision and considered the new evidence and declared it wanting, and your Supreme Court has felt itself compelled to regard the findings of Judge Thayer and the jury as final. Whatever Governor Fuller may do in this case, I hope that your system of appeals in capital cases will be changed.[94]

That same day he wrote to Frankfurter, whom he had seen in New York the previous evening. (Most likely they had dined with friends at the Century Club, close to Grand Central Station where Frankfurter could board the night train to Boston.) "I hope you were not worn out by the discussion last night. Perhaps I did wrong to precipitate it. But I thought it most illuminating, and it must have shown you—if you did not know it already—that there are men of intelligence and not completely closed minds who take a different view from you and me. Of one thing I became convinced, that if we wish to get conservative support, we must not *knock* the judges—even W.T. [Webster Thayer]."[95]

Then, on 14 May, *The World*, in an editorial, mistakenly included CCB's name among a group of thirty who had petitioned Fuller to review the case. CCB seized the opportunity to write another letter to *The World*, published on the eighteenth, correcting the error and ending with what he described to a friend as "the sting in the tail":[96] "Without reading the record one cannot express an opinion on the guilt or innocence of Sacco or Vanzetti, but the opinions of Justices Braley and Wait of the [Massachusetts] Supreme Judicial Court leave one, as Mr. [Emory] Buckner said after reading Prof. Frankfurter's book, with an 'uncomfortable' feeling that Sacco and Vanzetti may be judicially and officially done to death not for murder but for being draft-dodgers and Communists."[97]

On 1 June, Governor Fuller appointed a committee of three—President A. Lawrence Lowell of Harvard, President Samuel W. Stratton of the Massachusetts Institute of Technology, and Judge Robert Grant, a retired probate judge—to advise him on the exercise of clemency. On 27 July the committee reported to Fuller that the two men had been properly convicted, and on 3 August he denied clemency. There followed a flurry of appeals and petitions to various judges (including four on the Supreme Court: Taft, Stone, Brandeis, and Holmes), all of whom refused to intervene.

While Frankfurter used all his legal talent and remarkable physical and emotional energy to pursue every possibility of preserving the men's lives, CCB continued trying to persuade others to that end through public and private letters. Frankfurter came to New York for an evening meeting with CCB and Lippmann, and the next afternoon, 19 August, *The World* devoted its entire editorial page to an analysis of the "Lowell Report," focusing attention more on its weakness than on its strength. The analysis was unsigned, but journalists soon had an inkling of CCB and Frankfurter's part in it, for that evening the *Times* asked CCB to write a briefer summary of it—which the paper published over his name the following morning. Later CCB wrote to Taussig: "I have no doubt that the Governor and the Committee are convinced of the guilt of the men and of the fairness of the trial. The report I consider a very unconvincing document. It was as much a plea for the prosecution as Frankfurter's was for the defense." But he sensed, as he later told Frankfurter, "the time to convince had then passed." Like all his correspondents, in his letters he never mentions the murdered men or their families.[98]

In the last days before the scheduled execution, he signed, along with sixteen others, including such notables as Jane Addams of Hull House and Mary Wooley, president of Mount Holyoke College, a public appeal to Governor Fuller for a stay of execution.[99] Privately, he wrote to Bishop Lawrence's successor, Charles L. Slattery:

> Why are our clergy silent on a question which is agitating the whole world? We are not under the Mosaic dispensation. Massachusetts will stand even if her Governor should temper justice with mercy and common sense by a commutation which deprive these poor deluded Communists of their martyr crown and prevent the possibility of remedying a possible wrong at some future time. Human justice is not so perfect that death must follow judgment inexorably, even after seven years of delay.
>
> I have no request to make of you. I wish I could hear the voice of one of our own clergy ring out full and clear asking mercy, not sacrifice.[100]

Slattery replied that to ask the governor to commute the sentence was to ask him to surrender to clamor and to set an unhappy precedent; he would remain silent. No eleventh-hour appeal, no last-minute petition was effective, and early on the morning of 23 August the men were executed.[101]

Six days later CCB wrote of his feeling to an English solicitor, Frank Douglas MacKinnon (later a lord justice of appeal), a friend remote from the inflated emotions swirling about the case.

> We have had a terrible time over here with the Sacco-Vanzetti case. Poor old Massachusetts, with its worn out system of criminal appeal, limiting the appellate judges to a review of the law, quite different from our New York system, which is like yours under the Act of 1907, has been made a byword and mockery. It has wrapped its filthy rags of righteousness about it and told the rest of the world to go to hell. To you it must seem incredible that more than seven years should pass between indictment and execution. I have felt that a decent respect for the opinions of mankind demanded a commutation of sentence, and have said so as strongly as I could. I don't think the men had a really fair trial, and my personal opinion is that they are innocent and that the crime was committed by professionals; but whether guilty or innocent, they should not have been executed.[102]

In the coming months, CCB saw one last thing he could do. With ten other men, among them John W. Davis, Elihu Root, and the noted lawyer, philanthropist, and Zionist Bernard Flexner, he sponsored the publication of *The Transcript of the Record* of the case, in six volumes, making available for study virtually the entire proceedings from the start in 1920 to the end in 1927.[103] The cost was roughly $30,000, the bulk paid by John D. Rockefeller Jr. and Julius Rosenwald, the president of Sears, Roebuck; the balance by CCB, Flexner, Root, and Charles P. Howland.[104] Free copies were distributed to major libraries across the country. CCB and Flexner were in charge of publication, and probably responsible for what CCB described as the "cold, unemotional preface which we have prepared,"[105] which stated: "The Sacco-Vanzetti case is without doubt an historical trial. As such it promises to be the subject of controversy and discussion for many years to come . . . Without the record, comment and criticism must be partial, if not partisan; with it, there can be no excuse for misrepresentation through ignorance or design."[106]

The sponsors' expectations of interest were met, for a flow of books about the trial still continues, with occasional bits of new evidence added.[107] Perhaps most informed readers today believe that Sacco was guilty and Vanzetti innocent. But that judgment does not resolve the question of the fairness of the trial, which for many was the greater issue. In 1948, writing of this to a man who had coauthored a book on the trial's "legacy,"[108] CCB recalled a conversation twenty years earlier with Francis John McConnell, a Methodist bishop serving in Pittsburgh and later in New York. The Bishop had read the trial record, and CCB asked him, "Why?" "I wanted to know for myself whether they had a fair trial." "Well, what did you think?" "I think the judge ruled properly on the evidence, but I don't think they had a chance, for they were being tried when the atmosphere of the courtroom was worse than unfavorable and the men were being tried as 'radicals.'" To which CCB added in 1948, "Not everyone agrees with the Bishop, but he was right."[109]

The case cast a long shadow across Frankfurter's subsequent career. In any discussion of Sacco and Vanzetti, some voice was sure to rise in anger over what many saw as his unseemly interference and bias. And he himself was never free of the fever. One day in 1930, he had a discussion with another "liberal" lawyer, Edward S. Greenbaum, whose client, *The Nation* magazine, had been sued for libel. The plaintiff's claim rested in part on some Sacco and Vanzetti testimony, and if brought to trial, might offer a chance to validate it. When Greenbaum mentioned the advantage to *The Nation* of a settlement before trial, leaving the evidence untested,

Frankfurter exploded: If Greenbaum put his client ahead of Sacco and Vanzetti, then he was "a fake liberal." And thirty years later Frankfurter, then on the Supreme Court, still talked of Governor Fuller (whom Taussig had described to CCB as an "honest man" and "courageous") as a "crude, illiterate, self-confident, purse-proud creature."[110]

With the Sacco and Vanzetti case, Frankfurter posed in starkest terms the difficulties that arise for a law professor, supposedly a dispassionate scholar, when he undertakes to be active in public affairs. A decade later Learned Hand, speaking at Harvard on the role of university scholars in troubled times, phrased the scholar's dilemma in a way that for many brought Frankfurter to mind: "You may take Martin Luther or Erasmus for your model, but you cannot play both roles at once; you may not carry a sword beneath a scholar's gown, or lead flaming causes from a cloister." The price for doing so is high, and for the rest of his life Frankfurter paid it.[111] But in contrast to Frankfurter and others, throughout the tumult of Sacco and Vanzetti, CCB kept his balance better than most, while managing on occasion to shed light on some of its issues. And his reputation as a writer of public letters grew. Besides his work in August for *The World* on the Lowell Report, he had received a request from the *Times* for a letter on it. In October he answered an inquiry from a lawyer in Ohio about views he had expressed at the time of the execution, and in December the dean of Harvard Law School asked for a letter to newspapers on a recent report of the Massachusetts Judicial Council on the Sacco-Vanzetti case. The latter CCB declined to write on the ground that after the men's execution, with the exception of publishing the *Transcript*, he thought the controversy should be allowed to die. Thus, without intention, from the nettles of the notorious case CCB plucked a reputation as a sage and writer on public affairs, opening for himself an avenue of influence of which he made much use in the years to come.[112]

14

CCB as Bar Association President

In May 1929 CCB was elected president of the City Bar Association, succeeding Charles Evans Hughes,[1] but his new duties scarcely changed his daily routine, for he was already spending many hours a week on Association affairs. The disadvantage of the post was its daily concern with the Association's domestic affairs—the upkeep of the building, its library, staff, debt, and personnel. The advantage was the president's power to set priorities, to assign projects to the special committees, and to appoint committee members and chairmen. It also offered, for those with the will to use it, a pulpit for preaching to New York and its lawyers. The term of office was one year, but by tradition a president, upon completing his first year, was reelected to a second.

The job, if well done, was both expensive and exhausting. Critics of the Association in these years complained that it drew its presidents too often from the larger Wall Street firms, but only these firms could support a partner on what amounted to a two-year leave of absence without cutting his partner's share. Single practitioners or lawyers in small firms seldom could afford the job. CCB, throughout his two years, drew his full partner's share from Burlingham, Veeder, Masten & Fearey. Moreover, the job was exhausting, because to be effective a president had to always keep pushing. The Association, despite its large building and 3,500 members, was never more than a voluntary group, hard to move from talk to deed; most members came to the meetings only after a day's work elsewhere, and some of the Association's failures, particularly failures to act, must be measured against its members' limited time and energy.

Charles Evans Hughes, a man of extraordinary energy, had managed to stir the Association to action, so that besides its regular winter's work of analyzing new laws presented to Congress and the New York state legislature, and its continual fussing over the qualifications of federal, state, and municipal judicial candidates, it also had undertaken to review the evils of "ambulance chasing" and the administration of the bankruptcy laws. In each case Hughes had responded promptly to proof of professional wrongdoing trumpeted in the newspapers, and in both, the Association contributed to significant reform.[2] For the bankruptcy investigation, for example, in February 1929 Hughes appointed a special committee with CCB as chairman, who accomplished much before resigning to succeed Hughes as president; thereafter, he steadily pressed forward the committee's review and report (even as its expenses mounted to $43,000, requiring extra contributions from members).[3]

One project to which CCB continually returned, regardless of office, was to increase openings for women in the legal profession and elsewhere. In 1912, in one of his earliest letters to Franklin D. Roosevelt, then a New York state senator, he had written, "I want to say that I am strongly in favor of any proper bill which helps along the cause of women's suffrage. I have believed in this for twenty-five years, or more, and am glad to see that it seems to be coming along." Even after the Nineteenth Amendment (ratified in 1920) secured for women the right to vote, he continually campaigned for their right to be admitted to law schools, as lawyers to be elected to bar associations, and in the Episcopal church to serve on vestries or as delegates to diocesan conventions.[4] He had seen what Josephine Shaw Lowell could do, had served as a director of Lillian Wald's Henry Street Settlement, was acquainted with leaders in the National Consumers' League such as Josephine Goldmark and Florence Kelley, and he knew and admired Frances Perkins, appointed in 1929 by Governor Roosevelt as industrial commissioner, the first woman to hold a cabinet post in New York's state government. Four years later, as President Roosevelt's secretary of labor, she would be the first woman to hold a cabinet post in the federal government. CCB did not doubt women's abilities.[5]

Perhaps the first institution he sought to change in its stand against women was his law school, Columbia. In 1921, he wrote to district court judge Julius M. Mayer:

My dear Judge:
I am your Vice Chairman, or one of them in the Columbia Law School Alumni Association. I have never attended a meeting or done a thing, and perhaps I never shall, but this thought has come to me: Why should we not at least inquire into the subject of opening the School to women? It seems absurd that the two best Law Schools in the country—Columbia and Harvard—should close their doors to women, when the

Bar is open to them and all the other schools let them in, the P. & S. [Physicians and Surgeons] too.

Some years ago I inquired into it and discovered a curious thing: The Faculty objected here; at Cambridge, the Trustees. At that time Columbia seemed fearful that, if it let women in, all their best men would go to Cambridge. Whether a similar feeling existed in Cambridge, I don't know. The situation has now changed and I believe both Schools are over-crowded. At the Harvard Law School they are plucking the men unmercifully, in order to reduce numbers. It may be that the Schools will say now: We haven't enough room for the men; so why let in the women? But, it would seem better to me that they should raise their standard still higher and weed out the weaker brethren and make room for the stronger sistren. What think you, wouldn't this be a good subject for the President to bring up somehow, somewhere? The best way would be to have Harvard and Columbia act at the same time.[6]

No doubt CCB was one of many urging a change in admissions policy, and probably not the most influential. Still, he was pleased when in the winter of 1928–29 Columbia Law School began to admit women—and displeased with Harvard, which failed to act.[7] In the coming decade, whenever he had occasion to write to James M. Landis, dean of the Harvard school in 1937–46, he raised the subject. In 1939 he complained, "I don't like to see women shut out from the best school in the U.S.A." In 1942, dissatisfied with the lack of progress, he published a letter in the *Harvard Alumni Bulletin*: "The Harvard Law School is the only law school in the United States that excludes women. Yet women are people—they vote; they are admitted to the Bar, practise law and become judges; they are members of State legislatures, and of the House of Representatives . . . A woman [Frances Perkins] has sat in the Cabinet for nine years. Why should they be denied the privilege of preparing . . . at the Harvard Law School . . . ?"[8] He exaggerated. In the mid-1940s, Harvard was not "the only" law school to exclude women, but it was one of the very last important schools to do so, and to many persons its position began to seem witless. In 1943, again to Dean Landis, he wrote, "I wish my LL.B. was from Harvard so that I might rightfully assume the role of St. George and try to slay the Dragon of indifference which keeps women out of the H.L.S." And two years later, "Why don't you open the doors of the Law School to 'vimen'? Most other doors are open. Why keep this one shut?"[9]

Landis, trying to defend the school, told CCB that "shortly after Pearl Harbor a majority of the faculty actually voted to admit them but we were afraid to take action at that time" for fear it "might be interpreted by our detractors as being action guided not by those pure intellectual consider- ations that ought to govern us but perhaps by our necessity for increasing the income from tuition. So we have decided to mark time."[10] CCB replied that "your reason" was not "good."

When the war ended and still the law school did not act, CCB com- plained in 1949 to Grenville Clark, a member of the Corporation, Har- vard's governing body, who replied, "Yes, Law School opening to women long overdue, of course. But, as I'm sure you know, the delay was caused by vacillation in the Law School. It wasn't ever held up in the Corpora- tion."[11] Eventually, in the autumn of 1950, Harvard Law School accepted women, and its historian, writing in 1967, reported that "when it hap- pened there was no difficulty at all."[12]

At the City Bar Association, the campaign to admit women, at least after Hughes became president in May 1927, took a different turn. The Association's leaders for the most part—Hughes, CCB, Wickersham, James Byrne, and Henry W. Taft—were in favor, but found they could not rally enough members to cut through the alleged legal tangle. In 1886 the state constitution had been amended to include women among those per- sons eligible to be admitted to the bar,[13] but the Association continued to refuse them on the ground that under *its* constitution, adopted in 1870, the word "person" describing those eligible for membership could not have included anyone then ineligible to be a lawyer. In January 1926 the executive committee restated this tradition in a formal resolution as an ap- proved policy, but then, with Hughes as president, the same committee in March 1928 took an informal poll and found itself 9 to 3 in favor of re- scinding the resolution. An Association member, Wilson Powell, urged delay, however, in order not to endanger a large gift or bequest allegedly on its way, and again the issue stalled.[14]

The fate of the supposed gift or bequest is not known, but CCB, on be- coming president, moved quickly to reopen the question. He immediately faced an obstacle: How to get around, through, or over the standing reso- lution without stirring its supporters to wrath, especially those—always some on hand—who in any debate seem to care most that each proposal meet the exact requirements of law, custom, and *Robert's Rules of Order?* CCB consulted the Association's secretary, who charted only three safe paths: amend the Association's constitution, let the executive committee by itself reverse its predecessor's resolution, or let the Association by vote of its members reverse the resolution. CCB chose the first, presumably as the most open and conclusive way to settle a contentious issue,[15] and he carefully prepared for a debate at a members' meeting on 10 February 1931. To speak in its favor he scheduled three of the Association's most popular former presidents—Wickersham, Byrne, and Taft—and on the appointed night, with four times the usual number of members present, twelve members spoke in favor of the proposed amendment and ten against, arguments of common sense, fair play, and the Association's purpose as a professional group, not a men's club, versus arguments about the cost of remodeling the building to accommodate women, the disruption of its atmosphere, and the likely reluctance of women to pay the entrance fee and dues. After two and a half hours of debate, CCB ordered a vote. Two-thirds of the 249 present, or 166, were needed to carry the amendment; it failed by 30.[16] What most discouraged CCB and his allies was that, in reverse of the situation at Harvard Law School, at the Association its "Old Guard" mostly favored the admission of women, and it was the young men who had kept them out.[17] (At the time, according to the newspapers, the city had some 500 practicing women lawyers, of which 189 were members of the County Lawyers' Association.[18] In addition, women were enrolled in both the New York State and American Bar Associations.)

Six years later, in 1937, the older men, again led by Byrne, CCB, and Taft, and again with careful and proper advance notice, presented a resolution that under the Association's constitution "as correctly interpreted," women were eligible for membership. This time the debate lasted only forty-five minutes, and no one spoke directly against the resolution, though Taft later wrote that many members felt it was "a forced interpretation." Needing only a majority vote, the resolution passed, and "thus," concluded Taft, "the fight for the admission of women to one of the oldest and most conservative associations in the country was won." The decision by then was hardly adventurous or praiseworthy—though still thirteen years ahead of the dithering Harvard Law School.[19]

Predictably, at some point while president of the bar association, CCB would confront Tammany on its nominations for state and city courts. As events unfolded, a scandal in 1929 in the city's Magistrates' Court raised the issue, and then led to an unexpected, greater confrontation with Tammany in which its corruption of all parts of the city's government were investigated and exposed.

The earlier improvement in New York City's administration that had been achieved under Mayors Gaynor and Mitchel had stopped in 1917 when Tammany defeated Mitchel's bid for a second term and elected in his place a county judge from Brooklyn, John F. Hylan. The architect of that

Tammany victory, which ousted reformers from many municipal posts, was Boss Charles F. Murphy, possibly the most skillful, intelligent leader the organization ever had. A short, stocky man, always called *Mr.* Murphy, he spoke little and kept his expression inscrutable. When a reporter at a Fourth of July function asked a Tammany stalwart why *Mr.* Murphy didn't join in singing "The Star-Spangled Banner," the man surmised: "Perhaps he doesn't want to commit himself."[20] Yet Murphy was farsighted enough to back some progressive social and economic laws as well as Good Government reforms, not only to win votes but seemingly because he approved of them. For several years in the state legislature his lieutenants, Assemblyman Al Smith and Senator Robert Wagner, leading Tammany's disciplined troops, introduced and passed such laws as the Workmen's Compensation Act (1911) and some much-needed reform in the organization of the state's government. Meantime, Murphy took care to keep his lieutenants free of scandal.[21]

His choice of "Red Mike" Hylan for mayor, however, was far less satisfactory. Though personally honest, Hylan was barely competent and at times seemed dim-witted. (At a hearing on whether a tunnel under the Hudson River was more feasible than a bridge, Hylan listened to several hours of testimony, then turned to those proposing the tunnel and asked how they would build it: "By the open cut, or by the bore method?" Al Smith, chasing after two reporters, persuaded them to drop the story.)[22] Moreover, in choosing his commissioners and aides, Hylan so dutifully relied on Murphy's advice that even the boss one day was heard to say, "No Tammany mayor has ever been more liberal to Tammany in the matter of patronage."[23] Yet here, too, Murphy was cautious, recommending only men who would not be too greedy or outrageous, and for eight years under Hylan city government drifted: not much happened, bad or good, while Tammany politicians quietly enriched themselves. When Murphy died in April 1924, his estate was valued at more than $2 million.[24] That same year, George Washington Plunkitt, leader of the Fifteenth Assembly District, died, leaving more than $1 million—most of it acquired, as he liked to say, by "honest graft." For his tombstone, Plunkitt, "the Sage of Tammany," suggested: "He Seen His Opportunities and He Took 'Em."[25]

After Murphy's death, Tammany's support for reform of any kind waned, even as conflicts he had controlled grew greater. One problem for the Manhattan leaders was the city's growth and shift in population. In 1923 Brooklyn had become the most populous borough, and by 1930 it outnumbered Manhattan in residents 2,560,401 to 1,867,312. By then both the Bronx and Queens, profiting from subway extensions, had each grown to more than a million. In the politics of Greater New York, Manhattan was losing electoral clout, and in the outer boroughs it was not popular, its parochialism caught in Plunkitt's assertion: "A Brooklynite is a natural-born hayseed, and can never become a real New Yorker."[26]

To succeed Murphy as boss, the district leaders elected his able son-in-law, James A. Foley, a former Democratic leader of the state senate and since 1920 one of the two judges in New York (Manhattan) County's Surrogate Court. But Foley, more scholar than politician, refused the call, preferring the court and becoming, by his death in 1946, possibly the best judge in its history.[27] The leaders then, after much maneuvering, in July 1924 elected a judge of the Court of General Sessions, George W. Olvany, the first Tammany boss to hold a college degree. But he came to the post as a compromise candidate, without the full backing of either Mayor Hylan or Governor Smith, and was never wholly at ease in the job. To the eye of Edward J. Flynn, county leader in the Bronx, "The crown that was placed on Judge Olvany's head weighed heavily"[28]—though not so heavily that he and the law firm to which he had nominally returned on leaving the bench lacked for benefits. In his five years as boss he pocketed some $2 million, and the firm more than $5 million, most of it from real estate interests seeking variances from the Board of Standards and Appeals.[29]

Though perhaps lacking the temperament for boss, Olvany sought to rule, and in choosing Tammany's candidate for mayor in the 1925 election he, Governor Smith, and the Bronx and Manhattan clubs—again failing to lure Foley from the bench—opposed Brooklyn-based Hylan's bid for a third term and instead nominated Jimmy Walker, a state senator from Greenwich Village. As the Democratic primary approached, many persons thought Hylan, now claiming to be more honest than Tammany, was the sure winner, for he had the backing of the Brooklyn, Queens, and Staten Island organizations, as well as the support of Hearst's morning *American* and evening *Journal*. Yet in September, after a bitter campaign, for Hylan felt Tammany had betrayed him, Walker won easily, even taking Brooklyn by 5,000 votes, and in November he swept past his Republican opponent, Frank D. Waterman (of the fountain pen company), by a plurality of 402,123, carrying into office all his running mates. For the first time since 1897, when Croker's candidate defeated Seth Low, Tammany had a total victory.[30]

Taking office on New Year's Day, 1926, Walker became the city's one hundredth mayor.[31] Standing only five-feet-eight-and-a-half, he was dapper, elegant, with pipe-stem legs and arms, and he favored suits specially cut to flatter his slight figure, usually adding for outdoors a hat, spats, and cane. He liked Broadway, composed songs—one of which, "Will You Love Me in December as You Do in May," became popular—and though married, had several chorus-girl mistresses with whom his relations were well known. Mentally quick and always charming, he was a good speaker, and no mayor ever led a parade up Fifth Avenue with greater style. To his admirers he was "Beau James," who could do no wrong. An early, steady supporter, Flynn, wrote of him later:

> No one in New York politics was more personable or more generally liked than Jimmy Walker. No one could ever become really angry with him. When, as frequently happened in my relations with him, he would do something that annoyed me, I found that his manner was so boyishly disarming that my resentment usually evaporated. This was a beguiling characteristic, but one which was destined ultimately to give him much trouble. Many of the people who surrounded him were superficial and rapacious. He found it hard to believe that any of his friends were bad— or even wrong. In the end, he became the victim of some of these so-called "friends."[32]

Walker's first term, 1926–29, went easily, for the country was prosperous, the city happy in its Jazz Age, with its flappers, nightclubs, and bootleg booze. And of all the fizz, and glamour, along with a whiff of corruption, Walker was the personification. Still, from time to time, signs of trouble surfaced, and one of the most extraordinary occurred in a speech given by Max D. Steuer, the trial lawyer, at a banquet at the Brooklyn Law School in May 1925, the spring before Walker's election. Steuer was Tammany's preferred attorney, hired by its leaders when they needed defending in court and constantly asked to be the toastmaster and orator at its functions and testimonial dinners. No one more regularly, more fulsomely extolled the leaders, their wives, their service to the city. Yet this night, according to the *Brooklyn Daily Eagle*, he told the law students: "To aspire to the [New York] Supreme Court bench you must be subservient to your district leaders and at the same time sell your manhood. That is the only way I know to attain the bench. There was a time when judges were considered dishonest. That is a thing of the past. The trouble with judges today is that they do not know anything. They are stupid."[33]

The next day reporters hurried to the courts to ask the judges if they were stupid. Some judges retreated into pomposity, and a few, smiling, said "Yes."[34] Steuer promptly claimed to have been misquoted, and the

Eagle, perhaps because of Steuer's position in Tammany circles, published what amounted to a retraction.[35] Steuer was not known as a drinking man, and people speculated on why he had made such a statement, but few doubted its implication: Tammany was selling judicial nominations.

Steuer formally apologized in November in a speech before the Lawyers' Club in Brooklyn: "At no time in the history of the American nation has the standing and integrity of our judges, nor their learning and ability been greater than it is today." And further, "I would like to say a few words about self-styled leaders of the legal profession who in the last few years have led an onslaught on the character and ability of the lawyers of today and have attacked, by invidious comparison with judges of the past, those now occupying the bench." He named none of the "self-styled leaders," but presumably one he had in mind was CCB.[36]

After Walker's reelection in November 1929, the Democratic district leaders ousted Olvany and installed as boss John F. Curry, whose close friend and adviser was Steuer.[37] In all ways, Curry was a more conventional leader. Born in Ireland, he had come to New York as a child and grown up in the "Hudson River badlands," the streets in Manhattan's Sixties, west of Eighth Avenue. Leaving high school, he caught his district leader's eye by playing shortstop for the Palisades Ball Club and running the hundred-yard dash for the West Side Athletic Club. He became in time a West Side district leader, and then, with Walker's backing, won control of the party throughout the city. Personally, he was a good family man and churchgoer; politically, he was a throwback to Croker, and he opposed the efforts of Smith, Wagner, and Foley to create a more honest, forward-looking "New Tammany." After Al Smith in 1928 had lost the presidential race to Hoover, and Franklin Roosevelt, despite the Republican tide, was elected governor of New York, Curry was able to sideline Smith and his followers in the city Democratic clubs. He shared with Walker undisputed control of municipal appointments, but with Walker's attention mostly on nightclubs, Broadway shows, and the chorus girl Betty Compton, Curry dominated the alliance, and appointments were often for the worse. Scandals of police and judicial corruption in the city increased.[38]

In November 1928 Arnold Rothstein, a well-known gambler, bootlegger, drug dealer, labor racketeer, and friend to many of Tammany's district leaders, had been shot dead at a card game in the Park Central Hotel; the murderer was never identified. Many New Yorkers suspected that the police failure was deliberate, ordered by Tammany to keep its ties to Rothstein concealed. In the 1929 mayoral election, the Republican candidate,

Fiorello La Guardia, made much of the unsolved case, pointing out that city magistrate Albert H. Vitale, who was drumming up the Italian vote for Walker in the Bronx, had been a friend of Rothstein and had borrowed $19,600 from him. But Walker was able to ride out the scandal, carry every borough, and win by a margin of almost half a million votes.

A month later Vitale was back in the news in a story which, because it made readers laugh, gathered more attention than he wanted. At a dinner in his honor, given by the Tepecano Democratic Club at the Roman Gardens in the Bronx, scattered among the guests were some criminals (of which the best known was Ciro Terranova, the "Artichoke King"). Just as Vitale rose to respond to applause, more bandits arrived: six masked men, guns in hand, burst into the private dining room and ordered the guests against the wall. Vitale managed to hide his diamond ring in his trousers, and a former magistrate, Michael Delagi, got his ring into his shoe. Others were not so lucky, and the thieves took thousands of dollars and jewelry from guests as well as a revolver from one who was a city detective. On their departure, Vitale, feeling his honor smirched, erupted in rage. Preferring a display of power to discretion, he hurried to the Tepecano clubhouse and within two hours returned every penny, ring, and revolver to its owner. Whereupon the public took a big interest in Magistrate Vitale's underworld connections.[39]

Newspapers, civic groups, the Bronx County Bar Association, and CCB at the City Bar Association called for an investigation. CCB suggested to the presiding justice of the Appellate Division, State Supreme Court, First Judicial District, which supervised the inferior courts of Bronx and Manhattan, that the bar association conduct it. Replied the justice, "I cheerfully accept."[40] Vitale, meantime, continued in volcanic rage. Asked by the chief magistrate to account for what had happened, he protested: magistrates are not "schoolboys" whose master can "call upon them to give an account of their daily doings."[41]

CCB assigned the investigation to the association's committee on criminal courts, law, and procedure, led by Kenneth Spence, and it held hearings at which witnesses were examined while Vitale was present with his counsel, Steuer. Failing to find enough evidence for charges on the Roman Gardens incident, the Association's committee prosecuted Vitale on two others: borrowing without interest or date of repayment $20,000 from a notorious criminal, Rothstein, thereby undermining the integrity of justice by bringing the Magistrates' Court into disrepute; and freeing a thief, a henchman of Rothstein, after receiving the loan. The Appellate Division, all five judges sitting, heard the case, and at noon on 13 March announced its decision. At the prosecutor's table were CCB and the two counsel for the Association, Spence and George Z. Medalie; at the defense's table, Vitale and Steuer. The court began by dismissing the second charge, though it called Vitale's action in freeing the thief "gross negligence and incompetency." But on the first charge—which Steuer had tried to reduce to a simple question: Can a judge borrow money?—a unanimous court found the loan corrupt. "The whole tendency of the transaction was to put the judge in the power of the lawyer or the gambler, or both. It had a tendency to bring the court of which he was a member into public disrepute and suspicion and undermine the integrity of justice." Citing La Guardia's campaign charges against Vitale as an example of dwindling public respect, the court concluded, "This actually happened." It then removed Vitale from office.[42]

Yet little was gained. For in Vitale's place Mayor Walker, over the Association's protests, appointed yet another organization Democrat, George B. De Luca, while Tammany maintained Vitale's income by having other municipal judges assign him refereeships.[43] CCB, meanwhile, tried to persuade the public that the issue was larger than the evil deeds of one or two magistrates. Only a week before Vitale's removal he had spoken to the monthly meeting of the New York Chamber of Commerce, on Liberty Street. This organization, chartered by George III in 1770 and reportedly the oldest of its kind in the world, had 2,000 resident members, among them the city's most prominent bankers and industrialists. He explained: "The magistrates are appointed by the responsible head of the City Government without check or balance . . . They have fixed terms of ten years. They have an adequate salary of $12,000 a year. They have fixity of tenure, and they can be removed only by a very high court, the Appellate Division, for cause after notice with an opportunity to be heard. All these magistrates who are now under suspicion and who have brought their courts to such low esteem were appointed by Mayor Hylan or Mayor Walker."[44] Since suggestions for improvement "made sporadically by lawyers in casual talks or even by committees of bar associations or commercial bodies do not carry us very far," he recommended as perhaps the only solution to the problem the creation of a "continuous and permanent body with the duty of watching the administration of justice and the working of the courts." This idea, he noted, had already been partially tested in Massachusetts and California.

In 1930 the idea of such a council or commission was rather radical, and many good judges and lawyers opposed even a limited version of such oversight. But, as CCB stressed, history showed that tinkering with the nominating system was not likely to help. Until reform under Mayor

Strong (1895–97), he reminded his audience, magistrates had been elected. Then, "in a period of moral upheaval the law was changed" and the mayor given the power of appointment. Yet still the quality of justice delivered—in the Magistrates' Court mostly to the poor—was rotten. If a "continuous and permanent body" could be constituted, then it should be, he thought, "an unpaid commission with an adequately paid full-time staff." But he failed to persuade the business leaders of the need.[45]

At the Association's annual meeting in May 1930, CCB again spoke bluntly on the intrusion of politics into the nomination of state and city judges.

> We thought it a sign of promise when a few years ago the political organizations for the first time sent our committee the names of persons whom they were considering as candidates; but we cannot flatter ourselves that any serious attention has been paid to our opinions or recommendations . . . No one can be certain that even a good lawyer will prove to be a good judge; but it must be conceded that learning, experience and character afford a better assurance than political activity and party fealty. I cannot believe that the lists submitted by the political organizations to our Judiciary Committee represent the best lawyers available for judicial office.[46]

The next morning the *Herald Tribune* and the *Times* carried full reports of this speech beneath headlines alleging the declining quality of judges in the lower courts. In his President's Report to the Association, CCB further analyzed the problem: "The efforts of our Committee on Criminal Courts to aid the Mayor [Walker] . . . in the choice of magistrates have not been successful. Our offer to assist him has not even been acknowledged . . . It is not a theory but a condition that confronts us. With a majority of 500,000 behind them, the politicians are free to select judges at their own pleasure."[47]

Then, within only a few weeks, another scandal blossomed in the Magistrates' Court, this one initially discovered by the federal district attorney's office investigating income tax frauds. The wife of a lawyer named George F. Ewald had given a check for $10,000 to a municipal clerk who had endorsed it to a Tammany district leader who was also the city's deputy commissioner of plant and structures. The "loan," reportedly given to help the commissioner to buy a house, was unsecured, without interest, and the house never bought. But two days after the check had passed, Ewald was appointed a city magistrate.[48]

Civic groups clamored for further investigation, and CCB, after meeting with Association committee chairmen and members, wrote to Governor Roosevelt asking that an independent counsel conduct a thorough investigation of New York's Magistrates' Court. Or so the newspapers were left to guess. CCB was too astute a reader of Roosevelt's personality to force the issue in the press. For some years he had been writing bulletins to the governor about judicial and city affairs—short letters with news and observations relayed in a bright, gossipy style[49]—and now he was careful not to put too much public pressure on him. Refusing reporters' requests to reveal the substance of the letter, he insisted that was the governor's "privilege."[50]

Roosevelt's political position at the time was awkward. In November, he faced an election for a second two-year term, and he wanted, perhaps needed, Tammany's support. He would act, therefore, only if forced by public pressure, and then usually in limited measure. His response now was to call a special term of the Supreme Court, First Judicial District (Bronx and Manhattan), to investigate its Magistrates' Court. This narrowed the probe to only two of the city's five boroughs, but within that limit he enlarged the investigation's scope to the entire court and anyone—police, lawyers, politicians—doing business with it. And he took this larger investigation, though not the Ewald case, away from New York County's district attorney, Thomas C. T. Crain, a Tammany leader whose work had struck many as perfunctory, and gave it to a yet unappointed independent counsel.[51]

To explain to the public what was at stake, CCB wrote a half-page article for the *Times*, published on 24 August, stating what had happened, why, and suggesting how the further investigation might be handled. The question was not Mrs. Ewald's check,

> but whether appointments can be purchased in New York City by political or other contributions or payments. No one is so simple as to believe that money is, or ever has been, paid to the Mayor of New York . . . That is not the way things are done. Analogies are never perfect, but if appointments are purchased the method is not unlike the English sales of peerages . . . England has her scandals. But things there are not standardized as they are in the land of Henry Ford.

He went on to show how the corruption worked in a standardized way—"There is no law in New York against contributions to party funds by relatives or friends of an aspirant to judicial office"—and he displayed how it seemed likely that the cost of nomination for magistrate was close to one year's salary, $12,000, and for a position on the Supreme Court, $25,000. A schedule of payments amounting to these sums would be worked out;

> assuming that "the system" exists—and no legal evidence of its existence has yet been adduced—it would not involve [necessarily a single payment] . . . All the candidate need do would be to adhere to this schedule and make his payments in a mutually convenient way, and ultimately the money would find its way into an appropriate bank or trust company. Busybodies and wiseacres are able to give the names of the financial institutions commonly supposed to be available.[52]

With remarkable clarity, CCB went on to discuss the statutory basis of the governor's action and the sort of legal proof required to convict anyone of "unlawful acts . . . committed in connection with or arising out of or in any way relating to the appointment [of Ewald], and for such other proper matters as may come before the court." Who could be the appointed investigator? He dismissed Crain as a "Sachem of the Tammany Society," a man both incompetent and biased, and showed why, in order to lessen the intrusion of politics into such a potentially wide investigation, the state's attorney general, Hamilton Ward, also was unsuited: Ward once had sought the Republican nomination for governor and perhaps was doing so again. Careful as before not to impinge on Roosevelt's freedom of action, CCB closed his article without suggesting a candidate.[53]

Two days later Roosevelt recommended to the Supreme Court that it employ Samuel S. Seabury as its referee or investigating counsel. Seabury, a reform Democrat, had been a judge on the Court of Appeals until resigning in 1916 to run a losing campaign for governor. Since then he had been in private practice in New York, making a specialty of appeals in civil cases. Many New Yorkers thought Roosevelt's action too little and too late, and the following month, in a letter to Frankfurter, CCB reported: "I told Roosevelt this morning that if he didn't look sharp the public would think he was protecting Tammany, which I don't believe for a moment he is." Seabury, CCB was sure, would conduct a good investigation.[54] He knew him well from their work together at the Association, and he publicly applauded Roosevelt's recommendation, telling reporters that the Supreme Court "could not have selected a better man."[55]

Seabury soon proved a brilliant leader of a team of sleuths who could trace money through the pockets of banks and politicians to its source in vice. In addition, he was scrupulously honest, and in his marriage happy, so that no slander, however much Tammany whispered, could stain him. In battling corruption he was tireless, viewing the investigation as a campaign of good against evil, angels of righteousness harrowing the fallen. He was the son of an Episcopal clergyman and the great-great-grandson of Samuel Seabury, the first Episcopal bishop in the United States, and though addressed as "Judge," he often was referred to privately as "the Bishop," since his flaws of character, if such they were, struck many as ecclesiastic. These were a tendency to sermonize, to take himself too seriously, and to see issues and people too much in black-and-white.[56] Yet for a crusader against corruption, these defects perhaps only increased perfection, and the Seabury investigations, which ultimately numbered three, were among the most thorough Tammany ever sustained, and possibly the most damning.

Once public hearings began in late September 1930 they continued through the winter—Seabury and his staff, many of them bar association members, uncovered a racket in which a network of police, bondsmen, lawyers, court clerks, and magistrates framed women as prostitutes. One woman, Vivian Gordon, was found strangled in Van Cortlandt Park just before she was to testify. From the testimony of others, it became clear that politicians behind the magistrates controlled appointments in the lower courts. Once on the bench, a magistrate was expected to pay off his district leader again and again. One magistrate acknowledged at least forty intercessions in cases before him. "That," testified a leader in the Bronx, "is the way we make Democrats."[57]

The public was shocked by the treatment of the women, and the Appellate Division removed two magistrates (one, Jean H. Norris, was the city's first woman judge)[58] while three others resigned and one fled the state. Six police officers were convicted of extortion, the vice squad was reorganized, and the City Bar Association, jointly with the New York County Lawyers' Association, started disbarment proceedings against sixteen lawyers. Seabury's recommendations for improving the court's structures and procedures were eventually adopted, at least in part. But nothing was done about the basic problem of political selection and interference with judges.

Seabury's second investigation started before the first closed, and focused on the New York County district attorney's office. As the scandals of the Magistrates' Court unfolded, the public had begun to ask why District Attorney Crain had not done more to prosecute corruption. Everyone knew of his failure to secure an indictment of Magistrate Ewald. In January 1931 CCB wrote privately to Roosevelt that he hoped "before long you will be compelled to remove T.C.T.C, the most incompetent person who has ever attempted to fill the office of District Attorney of any county." Finally responding to public pressure, Roosevelt called a special grand jury and superseded Crain with a special prosecutor. Yet despite strong circumstantial evidence of a bribe, three juries refused to convict Ewald or his district leader, and in January 1931 the case was dismissed. By then, however, Ewald had resigned from the court.[59] Two months later, again in response to public outcry and to a petition from the City Club which CCB had helped to draft, Roosevelt appointed Seabury as his commissioner to investigate Crain's inaction and to make recommendations. Crain promptly retained Steuer as counsel.[60]

Beginning in March 1931, this second investigation exposed a vast scheme of business blackmail. Throughout New York City, almost every business, large or small, was the prey of criminals, many of them city officials seeking bribes, payoffs, or shakedowns. Crain, a former judge, was now old, incompetent, and easily manipulated by Tammany, yet because he seemingly was more befuddled than dishonest, Seabury did not recommend, and Roosevelt did not order, his removal. A more political reason for mercy may have been that Curry reportedly planned to reelect Crain to office in November, and as everyone knew, Tammany had a 500,000-vote margin by which to do it. After the election Curry could then claim the voters had repudiated the governor's action and the evidence of the investigation.

Meanwhile, as fresh proof of Democratic corruption continually emerged, the state legislature, controlled by Republicans, appointed a joint legislative committee to investigate, with Republican state senator Samuel H. Hofstadter as chairman and Seabury as committee counsel in charge of the investigation, which he drove hard, despite efforts of Democrats to harass him.[61] Soon the investigations recalled those of Boss Tweed's administration sixty years earlier. Seabury and his staff uncovered bank accounts of salaried city officials running into millions of dollars. For example, the sheriff of New York County, Thomas M. Farley, with an annual salary of $8,500, in six years accumulated nearly $400,000. Unwilling to explain the source of the money, he was removed from office by Governor Roosevelt.[62]

Tracing the web of corruption into all five boroughs, Seabury showed that the Manhattan Tammany leaders received a cut from almost every conceivable governmental function: from issuing marriage licenses to granting approval to remodel a house. Despite the economic depression, despite Tammany's claim to be the friend of the poor, it was rewarding its Democratic faithful—many with cars in the garage and maids to clean the house—by looting a $10 million fund appropriated by the city to help the unemployed.[63]

Once again, as in CCB's youth, Lord Bryce's charge that American democracy had failed in municipal government was heard around the country. In an editorial *The Nation* articulated what many were thinking: "As long as Tammany remains in charge of New York the entire system of city government in America is disgraced." There was talk once again of city charter reform, last accomplished in the formation of Greater New York in 1898. But the American people do not recast the structure of their federal government, or even of their state government, every thirty years. Where was the flaw? In the charter? In the democratic procedures? In the people?[64]

In late May 1932 Seabury's investigation reached its climax, a confrontation with Mayor Walker, who was to testify, under subpoena, having signed a waiver of immunity. Though technically only a hearing, the event had many aspects of a trial. The legislative committee convened in the New York County Courthouse, it sat in a courtroom at the judges' bench, and witnesses testified from a chair on a dais. The room normally seated 300, but now 700 people, including some 340 spectators, crushed into it, while 6,000 more milled through the corridors and waited outside.

Walker arrived in a blue limousine, flashing a ring with a blue stone and dressed entirely in shades of blue—single-button double-breasted suit, tie, shirt, and pocket handkerchief. He testified glibly, sometimes brilliantly, and his admirers applauded his every joke and sally. When he appeared on the courthouse steps, the crowd cheered. When Judge Seabury came out, many booed. Yet by the end of the second day Seabury had established that Walker had taken bribes from businessmen to further their interests with the city. One such, who had sought to sell tiles to the city for its subway stations, had paid Walker a two-year total of $246,693. At a stock brokerage firm, Walker had accounts running close to a million dollars but refused to explain the money's source. Meanwhile, his financial agent, who might have done so, had fled to Mexico.[65]

Seabury sent a report of the testimony to Roosevelt,[66] who managed to avoid taking any action until after the Democratic convention in Chicago in July 1932. Then, as governor *and* Democratic candidate for president, he summoned Walker to Albany to answer charges that he was unfit for office and should be removed. Again, the hearing resembled a trial, held in the Executive Chamber of the Capitol's Hall of Governors, with counsel present, reporters, and members of the public. Roosevelt as judge, though reluctant to punish Tammany further, conducted the hearing fairly and forcefully. A lawyer himself, he refused to be lectured by counsel, and from the start made plain that this was his show, not Seabury's, not Walker's.[67] During three weeks of testimony, Walker increasingly convicted himself, and rather than be removed from office, a growing certainty, he abruptly resigned. Roosevelt, released from a hazardous decision in the midst of a presidential campaign, promptly declared the hearing and investigation at an end—a morally ambiguous act distressing to many, for it allowed public servants accused of corruption to avoid any hearing or trial. Walker, complaining he had been mistreated, like Croker retreated to Europe with his fortune intact. And for several months, until after an election in November 1932, the president of the city's Board of Aldermen, Joseph V. McKee, was acting mayor.[68]

The City Bar Association supported Seabury throughout all three investigations, but its role after the first, on the Magistrates' Court, declined. On the second, concerning the competence of District Attorney Crain, it left leadership to the City Club, though CCB had a hand there.[69] But on the third, the probe into Walker's administration, the Association did little beyond passing a resolution, in May 1932, condemning the tactics of lawyers acting to obstruct the investigation. Yet the resolution was forceful and praised by the *World-Telegram* as a "stinging rebuke to Tammany," delivered by "the organized Bar at its best," and CCB, as he retired from office, talked bluntly of the profession's failure to do its full duty to improve the integrity of justice, particularly in appointing and nominating judges. Still, compared to the Association's work in 1870, when it put Boss Tweed in jail, or in 1930 in ousting Magistrate Vitale, its actions in 1931–32 were more like cheers from the sideline.[70] The reasons for the Association's decreasing impact on municipal affairs are not altogether clear, though two are plain: Seabury was doing the job well, and John W. Davis, who in 1932 succeeded CCB as Association president, brought less energy to the job. Also, CCB may have felt that he had been warned by Roosevelt not to push too hard. In their exchange of letters in January 1931, he received one marked "Personal": "I expect shortly to see the P.J. [presiding justice of the Appellate Division] about the personnel of the inferior courts. I think it would be a mistake for the Bar Association to make the first move if it can come from the Appellate Division itself." That is, Roosevelt wanted pressure on himself as governor to act on the magistrates or Crain to come, if possible, not from a private, civic group but from the state's judiciary. This was the sort of plea to which CCB, trained by Josephine Shaw Lowell, was sensitive: Don't bludgeon a public servant into action if he or she can be motivated to it.[71]

In this, CCB differed from Seabury who became expert in putting pressure on Roosevelt by creating newspaper headlines, as a result of which Roosevelt came quickly to dislike him. And the dislike hardened when Seabury, his headlines streaming across the country, began to cast himself as a dark-horse Democratic candidate for president. Pinch Roosevelt's political nerve, and he would react. As CCB once wrote of him: "He is all political, the most political man I know." In this respect, CCB, famously not wanting any office or perquisite for himself, had an advantage over Seabury: Roosevelt never saw CCB as a threat.[72]

Moreover, for better or worse, CCB was capable of a sort of compromise that came easily to Roosevelt but was impossible for Seabury. In a handwritten letter to "My Dear Governor," 21 July 1930, CCB reported: "I had a very satisfactory talk with John F. Curry the other day. You observed, did you not, that Jimmy [Walker] sent us 4 names [for possible judicial appointment]. We kept them *confidential*, approved 2, and he appointed them, rejecting the 2 we disapproved." Seabury, whose hatred of Tammany had been called "a mania," would not have talked to Curry, not even to ensure the pick of a judicial litter.[73]

For some blend of these reasons, when the second Seabury investigation started, CCB as Association president held back. Yet four weeks after Walker had resigned and the investigations were ended, when CCB was no longer president, he suddenly took fire. On 30 September 1932, with the Association in full cry behind him, he ignited an extraordinary anti-Tammany crusade.

The episode started abruptly, following an announcement by the Democratic and Republican Parties of two candidates for election to seats on the state Supreme Court, First District. To the public's amazement, both parties had named the same two men: Aron Steuer, son of Tammany's lawyer, and Samuel H. Hofstadter, a Republican state senator and chairman of the legislature's committee investigating Walker. Plainly, Boss Curry and his Republican counterpart, Koenig, had made a deal. Its crux, most people assumed, was that the Republican Hofstadter, who without Tammany's endorsement had no chance of being elected in the First Judicial District (Bronx and Manhattan), had agreed to suppress Seabury's final report on Walker. And worse, many people feared the Republicans had agreed to drop from the election campaign any call to reform the city charter. Less serious, some lawyers were distressed that the Democratic nominee was not

Judge Samuel I. Rosenman, already on the court's bench by Roosevelt's interim appointment; by hitherto unbroken tradition any judge nominated by a Democratic governor to fill a vacancy would receive the party's endorsement at the next election, but dumping Roosevelt's friend and appointee was Tammany's revenge for all its faithful forced from office. But Rosenman's fate—within a year he was reappointed to another vacancy on the court—was the smallest part of public indignation: what stirred wrath was the supposed threat to Seabury's final report and the arrogance of the political parties.[74]

On 3 October twenty-one members of the bar association, led by CCB, petitioned for a special meeting to be held three days later. More than 600 members attended and, by a vote of about 580 to 20, they adopted a resolution that condemned the "parceling out of these judicial nominations for bi-partisan political purposes in defiant and contemptuous disregard of public and professional sentiment and of civic decency"; declared Hofstadter and Steuer unfit to hold judicial office for having accepted the nominations under such circumstances; declared that independent nominations of qualified candidates ought to be made and supported; and invited the New York County Lawyers' Association, the Bronx Bar Association, and other civic and commercial organizations in the city to join the campaign.[75]

At once CCB and his swelling band of supporters met a problem: the Association by its charter could not support a political ticket. So they founded an Independent Judges Party, with headquarters in the Association's building, and a campaign committee with Nicholas Murray Butler, John W. Davis, Elihu Root, and Seabury as honorary chairmen. The next day candidates were announced, both well-known lawyers: George W. Alger, a Republican, had been appointed by Governor Smith to investigate the state's prisons, by Governor Roosevelt to the commission on paroles, and was presently chairman of the Commission on the Cloak and Suit Industry; and Bernard S. Deutsch, a Democrat, president for three years of the Bronx Bar Association, secretary of the Appellate Division's Special Calendar Commission, and a leader of the American Jewish Congress.

For Deutsch's and Alger's names to appear on the ballot, nominating petitions signed by at least 3,000 voters had to be filed, and there was some doubt whether these could be collected in time. Within three days, however (though one was a half holiday, one a Sunday and one Yom Kippur), lawyers, members of the Citizens Union (a nonpartisan group monitoring city affairs), and law students at Columbia and New York Universities secured 8,300. The professional politicians sneered and predicted the Independent candidates would poll a mere 50,000 votes.

The newspapers supported the campaign, however, and the *Herald Tribune* pointed out: "The last time a race of this sort was made where the leaders of the bar nominated candidates in opposition to those of the major parties was in 1906 when the Judiciary Nominators put a ticket in the field."[76] In late October, CCB spoke to the public on radio, explaining why a political deal had so outraged reformers that they had created a Judges Party to elect two judicial candidates.

> Apparently neither Mr. Koenig nor Hofstadter himself had the faintest idea that this deal would arouse the indignation of the Public . . . They saw only the chance to get one more Republican on the Supreme Court Bench. Of the thirty-six Justices of that Court in Manhattan and the Bronx only four are Republicans [with one about to retire] . . . Hofstadter would bring a little patronage to Sammy [Koenig], who is pleased with any crumbs that fall from the richly laden table of Tammany . . . [A reason for the deal] was to seal the mouths of the Republicans on the investigation and the disclosed corruptions of Tammany Hall. Rumor has it that it was Jimmy [Walker] himself who was most eager to have Hofstadter nominated. And this part of the deal was completely successful. No Republican candidate . . . has said one word about the Hofstadter-Seabury inquiry. The Republican candidate for Mayor [Lewis H. Pounds] talks a little about the budget and expense of Government, and gives the history of his life and makes a few promises, but that is all. The best issue of the local campaign was thrown away in order that Koenig could get a Republican judge on the bench.[77]

Like all candidates on the Democratic and Republican tickets, throughout the campaign Hofstadter and Steuer never mentioned or explained the deal by which they had been nominated. Summoned as members of the Association to appear before its Grievance Committee, both men resigned. Their behavior and silence, and even more the silence of the Republican Party on "the best issue of the local campaign," convinced many voters that the deal, whatever its terms, was rotten.[78]

On the night before election, the Independent Judges Party, its supporters, and its candidates, Alger and Deutsch, met in Town Hall, with CCB presiding. Seabury was the main speaker and broadcast over radio station WOR, but CCB opened with a speech on the reason for the campaign, its history, and his belief that the question at hand was larger than one political deal.

> This is not a political meeting. Its purpose is ethical—what I may call practical ethics—moral principles put into practice . . . Since 1846 we are supposed to have had an elective judiciary, chosen by the sovereign people, and everybody knows, here in this City judges are appointed—not, however, by the Governor or any responsible person, but by an irresponsible boss. Nomination is equivalent to election. I don't, for a moment, think that our citizens are satisfied with this system. They are rather cynical about judges, and no wonder. But if they knew how to get them they would like to have learned, able, industrious, honorable and independent judges, but they simply don't know how to go about getting them. Businessmen and the press have for several years lately laid the fault at the door of the bar. They charge, and with reason, that we are indifferent, apathetic and lethargic.
>
> Well, whatever our failures of the past have been, we are leading now.[79]

The next day at the polls, as foreseen, Alger and Deutsch lost. Yet to everyone's astonishment, they secured nearly 300,000 of the 850,000 votes cast, running far ahead of the Republican candidates for any office, even of Hoover for President, and in four assembly districts they defeated Steuer and Hofstadter. The vote, CCB told reporters, would serve as "a warning to the bosses to keep hands off."[80]

In a report (seemingly written by CCB) of the Independent Judges Party to the three bar associations that had supported it, the lesson of the campaign was summarized as follows:

> The loss of the election in itself was of minor importance. Volunteer efforts with scant time and funds and little organization could hardly be expected to defeat the combined strength of the two major parties.
>
> The important results are the public interest aroused, the assumption of leadership by the Bar, and the opportunity afforded for the future. For the first time in the present generation large numbers of the public have individually become conscious of the evils of political domination of the bench, and of the insolence with which political leaders barter and control judicial office . . .
>
> We feel confident that the Bar is finally aroused, and ready to assert its right to lead, and that the public, now keenly alive to the vital im-

portance of this problem, is looking to the Bar and is ready to follow its leadership.[81]

But nothing happened as expected. Hofstadter did not pocket Seabury's report in committee—though perhaps the adverse publicity of the election made that impossible—and both he and Steuer soon proved better than average judges. Nevertheless, to many of the public there still seemed much amiss in the system of nominations. As Al Smith had observed in testifying before Hofstadter's committee, "No man sitting on the bench should feel that he owes anything to anybody."[82]

As to the bar's assumption of leadership in attacking the problem, CCB was too sanguine. Along with others who had helped in the campaign of the Judges Party he called a meeting at the Association after the election to consider forming a permanent organization to prevent future trading of judicial nominations among political bosses.[83] But the meeting failed; nothing came of it. Undoubtedly that collapse, when the time seemed ripe, the bar aroused, the Association ready, and he and others eager to lead, was one of the great disappointments of CCB's life. He had hoped that just as Hughes in 1920 had been able to revitalize the Association in the crusade to defend the Socialists' right to sit in the Assembly, so too he could revitalize the Association in 1932 and through it achieve some permanent improvement in methods of judicial selection. But to no avail.

The next day, for one of the few times in his life, he allowed his disappointment to show. In a letter to his friend Tom Thacher, the solicitor general in Washington, he wrote:

> Our vote for Alger and Deutsch amazed the politicians. They gave us not more than 50,000 to 75,000 votes, and we got 293,000 more than Hoover, or Donovan, or Pounds got in N.Y. and Bronx Counties. We raised only $16,000 and have no deficit. We got very little help from the bar. They voted at the meetings of the Association and gave a little money, but only a handful did any work. Our organization was pathetically amateurish, the best workers being four or five women. But we had the whole press . . . We do not fool ourselves that we could do it again. So crude a deal won't be tried again for quite a while.[84]

In that last prophecy, he who had tried it twice was correct: It has not been tried again. Indeed, the question of what procedure is best for selecting judges for state and city courts, by appointment, election, or some mixture of the two, continues to perplex American politics and law. Many variations have been tried, abandoned, rethought, and tried again; but no system can inoculate itself against abuse or against interference by politicians.

Possibly one reason no permanent improvement was achieved in the era of the Seabury investigations was that the public and most lawyers did not understand the extent to which the city Magistrates' Court, and their counterparts throughout the state, were necessities of machine politics as then practiced. Only a few saw, as did CCB, that no amount of transient indignation or tinkering with procedure could take politics out of an institution so important to the economy of politicians. The public did not grasp that the state and city judiciary, numbering upwards of 3,000, was the politicians' most valuable asset. In the lowest courts judges could be used for small favors, freeing a thief or fixing a traffic ticket. And in the Supreme and Surrogate's Courts they had an enormous amount of patronage to dispense in appointments as receiver, referee, guardian, or administrator; in settling a decedent's estate, for instance, the fee, depending on the estate's size, can run into millions of dollars. Such fees, in politically hard times, can keep a political party or faction alive, and there are always many mouths to feed.[85]

For a meeting in October 1932 of Greater New York's five Democratic county committees to nominate a candidate to succeed Mayor Walker, notices went out to 32,075, of which 20,000 gathered in Madison Square Garden. As Warren Moscow, a *Times* reporter, wrote: "The local party organizations in any county are more intimately concerned with the election of a state Supreme Court justice than they are with the Presidency of the United States . . . They make more noise campaigning for the latter, but there is more intra-organization rivalry over selecting the former."[86] Though much has been written on how to insulate judges from political pressure, no system yet has proved sure.

On this question, while the Seabury investigations were under way, a high school student in Virginia wrote to Charles C. Burlingham, president of the Association, asking his opinion. CCB replied:

16 March 1931

Dear Miss Hollis,

I have your letter of the 5th instant in which you inform me that the high schools of Virginia are debating this year the question whether judges should be appointed by the Governor, subject to confirmation of the General Assembly. The subject is an interesting one. Most lawyers in this State, I believe, would prefer an appointive to an elective system if it were practicable, but as we have elected our judges now for more than eighty years, it seems entirely improbable that we could revert to the former method of appointment by the Governor. The elective system works well in some states, especially where no party has an overwhelming majority. In New York City, where the Tammany candidate for Mayor at the last election received a majority of more than 500,000, the politicians are able to dictate the nomination of judges. Where in a city like Cleveland, Ohio, the parties are more evenly divided, the politicians have to be on their good behavior, and the Bar is able to make its influence felt in the selection of candidates for the bench. My own opinion is that better judges would be secured if they were nominated by the Governor and confirmed by the Senate or a council. Federal judges have been appointed since the adoption of our Constitution, and I think there are few who would wish to change this method of selecting judges. On the whole it has worked very satisfactorily.

Sincerely yours,

Charles C. Burlingham[87]

15

Contesting the Freuds

FOR CCB AND LOUIE the pain of their son Robert's illness never eased. By 1918, or possibly even earlier, CCB at least understood that Robert's breakdowns, unlike his own, could neither be prevented nor even much relieved. Though CCB seldom discussed Robert's symptoms and seems to have avoided the term "manic-depressive illness," by 1920 at the latest he had grasped that Robert's health was cyclical. Though Robert might seem to recover fully from his most recent "nervous breakdown," there always would be another. And no one, wife, doctor, or loving parent, could stop the fearful repetition. Louie spoke of Robert as merely "overtired," but CCB, paying the bills and conferring with the doctors, knew better.

In ill health, Robert needed close medical and custodial care, and though in his depressions he never struck anyone, his verbal rages, to those not expecting or understanding their nature, were terrifying; while in good health he was charming, loving, competent in his medical skills, and able to hold a job. Yet each blessed healthy period, though it might last for months, bore the seed of the next breakdown.

Two events in Robert's marriage stand as turning points in his life, both precipitated by his wife, Dorothy. The first occurred in March 1921, when she, pregnant with their fourth child, left him in New York City to start a separate household for herself and the children in Connecticut. Not trained for any job, she did not attempt to work, but as a Tiffany, with the Burlinghams now assuming all the expenses of Robert's illness, she had income enough to support herself and the children. Her move was an act of desperation—she did not want a fifth child, she could not handle Robert when he was ill, and his behavior in his depressions frequently upset the children. The second event came with Dorothy's secret departure for Europe in May 1925, putting herself and the four children beyond Robert's reach. Though by this move she no doubt increased her chance for peace and stability, she lessened his. For Robert, as a college classmate observed, "yearned for love from his family and friends."[1]

By her sudden departure she also wounded CCB and Louie, who awoke one morning to discover that their only grandchildren had been swept away out of sight and hearing. Going first to Switzerland, Dorothy soon went on to Vienna, where she settled, and as the months passed without any talk of return in her letters, the separation of wife from husband, of children from father and grandparents, began to seem permanent. In addition, it slowly became clear that Dorothy was attaching herself and her family ever closer to Sigmund Freud and his daughter Anna; by 1927 Dorothy was in analysis with "the Professor," and the two eldest children, Bob and Mabbie [Mary], with Anna Freud. The third child, eight-year-old Katrina, also started analysis with Anna in that year, and then in 1932 the youngest, Michael, at age eleven.[2]

Today, when the lay public is more familiar with the theories of psychoanalysis, it is hard to recall the distrust and skepticism that the new science, as it declared itself, aroused in many who learned of it only slowly and often inaccurately. It appeared to be, as Freud himself once described it, the third great blow to man's pride: first, Copernicus and Galileo had shown he was not at the center of the universe; then Darwin, championed by Huxley, had displaced him from a unique position in the animal world; and now Freud and his disciples suggested that he was not even master of his own mind.[3] As the public dimly understood Freud's teaching, a person's mind was filled with ill-repressed fantasies of an often violent, sexual nature which could be brought to the surface, or so Freud claimed, by a process called "free association." But if true, would not his liberated patients run riot, indulging their fantasies to the injury of others? Freud in five lectures delivered in 1909 at Clark University in Worcester, Massachusetts, had tried to allay this fear, but few came to believe that unconscious impulses would lose strength if brought to the conscious surface and faced with understanding. Instead, many feared that the theories of psychoanalysis would allow people to evade responsibility for their actions. Or, as Freud's biographer Ernest Jones summarized that fear, "The admission of unconscious processes might lower our cultural standards." Anxious laymen put it more simply: if, as Freud taught, a person's character is essentially formed by the age of three and thereafter can only be modified, not altered, who can be held responsible or blamed for anything?[4]

Throughout the 1920s and much of the 1930s, to most of the public the practitioners of psychoanalysis seemed a cult of Central European Jewish doctors who preached disturbing, even dangerous, new doctrines. And inevitably Freud became a lightning rod that attracted the storm of public controversy. To most educated people of the day in universities, churches, and professions, he initially seemed merely a doctor with some odd ideas about sex that he preached to patients who plainly were extremely sick. At the same time, to those who believed in him, an increasing number, he was close to a god.[5]

In Vienna Dorothy and her children became intimate members of Freud's circle, so much so that in January 1929 he wrote to a friend and fellow psychiatrist: "Our symbiosis with an American family (husband-less), whose children my daughter is bringing up analytically with a firm hand, is growing continually stronger, so that we share with them our needs for the summer."[6] As reports reached the United States of how Dorothy was paying expenses for the Freuds, transporting them hither and yon in her car, renting houses and taking vacations with them, build-ing a school for twenty or so children who could be educated according to Anna's ideas, and presumably paying fees for the many hours of analysis she and the children absorbed, friends of the Burlinghams began to assume—as CCB and Robert never did—that the Freuds had found in Dorothy a rich American who could be milked for benefits. Among these friends of the family she sometimes was referred to as "the mad Dorothy," or as one who, in joining the Freudian cult, had passed "beyond the reach of reason"; and there was much agreement that she unfairly kept the chil-dren from their father.[7]

She had defenders, among them her sisters and their families, who pointed to the complications of her marriage. Despite Louie and CCB's ef-forts to contain and minimize Robert's depressions, they were not a secret, and aside from their injury to his role as husband and father, they clearly were spoiling his chance to have a career. By 1928, instead of surgery at Roosevelt Hospital in New York, he had shifted to research in the pathol-ogy laboratory of the Albany City Hospital, where it was easier to arrange long periods of absence.[8] In the summer of 1927 he visited Dorothy and the children in Vienna and even had several consultations with Freud. The following year he returned for another visit, going on to Budapest to see the distinguished American psychoanalyst Dr. George S. Amsden, whom he had been consulting for more than a year in New York. While Robert was in Budapest, the Freuds, perhaps without Dorothy's knowl-edge, tried through their contacts to persuade Amsden to keep Robert there in order to lessen his upsetting influence on his family.[9] His visits disturbed the children and depressed Dorothy, causing her to have severe diarrhea, brought on presumably by fear of his questions about the future of the marriage and education of the children.[10] And he, upon returning home without satisfying answers to his questions, would have a depression.

In these troubles Louie concerned herself with Robert, making a home for him in New York and writing consoling letters to him in Albany.[11] She left relations with Dorothy and the grandchildren to CCB, whose infrequent reference to Louie in writing to Dorothy suggests that he thought the breach between the two women was unbridgeable. He saw that Dorothy and the children wrote regularly to Robert, and in his own letters to Dorothy he tried to preserve a friendship. In September 1927 he wrote a friend who recently had seen her in Austria: "You confirm what everybody else has told me about Anna Freud. I am sure she has a very fine influence. I have no doubt that analysis has helped Dorothy." He did not pretend to understand Freud's theories, and concluded, "In the great hand of God we stand!"[12]

Yearning for his absent grandchildren, he tried to establish some direct contact with them by sending the occasional present or letter. On Christmas Day, 1928, recalling the performing lions he had seen as a boy in Paris, he wrote to the youngest, seven-year-old Michael:

> I don't know whether you like lions or not, I certainly don't like to see them in small cages, but when they are in a big place where they can move and have some exercise and enough to eat, I think they are better off than when they are being hunted in Africa with spears and guns. I am sending some pictures of lions on a lion farm out in California which maybe you will like.[13]

Then, in the summer of 1929, he accompanied Robert to Vienna. The prospect of their arrival agitated Dorothy, who became haggard, and also Freud, whom a friend reported as pacing his garden: "He's so afraid, so terrified for Dorothy with Robert coming."[14]

Nevertheless, CCB's appointment book records that Dorothy did a fine job of arranging for him to see the sights of Vienna and Salzburg, including a performance of *Hamlet* in Salzburg's Cathedral Square and also one of von Hofmannsthal's *Jedermann*. But most exciting for CCB was his pleasure in his grandchildren. "Mabbie lunches with me," he jotted in his appointment book. "Oh, joy, oh rapture!" And in the last week of August he shared a traditional Austrian birthday party with Bob, CCB's seventy-first and the boy's fourteenth.[15]

The next day, 26 August, he and Robert had an interview with Freud, the second that summer for Robert, the first for CCB. Robert, who was keeping a record, made the following notes immediately after the interview.

> CCB: What is your diagnosis of Dorothy's condition?
> SF: Hysterical or obsessive neurosis, with fear.
> RB: Just what did you mean yesterday, when you told me you were teaching Dorothy to control her sex[ual] feelings. Am I to understand that you are attempting to come between Dorothy and me?
> SF: I never come between husband and wife.
> CCB: What about the children returning home?
> SF: That is a legal matter.
> CCB: Dorothy has at times thought that we might kidnap the children. You consider us gentlemen, do you not?
> SF: Dr. Burlingham is a gentleman, but you are a lawyer.[16]

According to Robert, the interview ended on that note, and two days later he and CCB left for New York, without even the eldest child, Bob, whom they had hoped to start in an American school to prepare for an American college.

Freud seemingly, either with conscious deceit or in self-deception, misled Robert in saying "I never come between husband and wife," for he was attempting to do just that. In the previous day's interview he had told Robert that his visit to Vienna offered a "temptation" to Dorothy, for she had "a conflict between her physical desires to return to you and her judgment."[17] In the opinion of Dorothy Burlingham's grandson, Michael John Burlingham, who has written the most detailed study of this domestic tangle: "The cornerstone of Freud's self-mastery program for Dorothy, then, was an intellectual preoccupation [psychoanalysis of children] so engrossing as to reroute her sexual drive. Desexualization is not an attractive concept, but that was nonetheless Freud's intent. His denials to Robert aside, he was raising an absolute barrier between husband and wife."[18]

The situation dragged on unresolved. In Vienna, the children continued in analysis with Anna Freud, and Dorothy published her first long paper, "Child Analysis and the Mother" (1932), which earned her, though she was not a doctor, associate membership in the Vienna Psychoanalytic Society. In New York, Robert on his father's advice declined to challenge Dorothy's exclusive control of the children by a legal action.[19] He had no wish to shatter the family in a law court; he lived to reunite it, a hope in which his parents, with their strongly religious view of marriage and family, sustained him. Nor was this view limited to the "older" generation.

Among Robert's contemporaries were many men and women who still thought of marriage as primarily a religious commitment undertaken, in the words spoken by Dorothy, "for better for worse, for richer for poorer, in sickness and in health, to love and to cherish." To such people, a professional career might be suitable for Anna Freud, unmarried and without children, but it was no longer an option for Dorothy, who had married as an adult and with full knowledge of Robert's breakdowns. Her place was at his side, alleviating his problems, not, by her absence, aggravating them. For those who knew of the selfishness of Louis Comfort Tiffany, an analysis of Dorothy, however un-Freudian, was easy: like father, like daughter.

The marital deadlock continued, but as the four children matured, their positions in the family began to change. Beginning in the summer of 1931, when Bob first returned to the United States, Dorothy sent them over (though never all at once) to visit their Tiffany cousins and aunts on Long Island, the Parker and Gilder families, and their father and relatives at Black Point. At first, with neither branch of the family did the children find their visits easy. All four spoke German-accented English, had a mostly Austrian cultural background, and knew little of American customs and history. Katrina later recalled that before her first visit to Black Point, she had never heard of the American Civil War.[20] From Long Island in 1932, while at the Gilders, fifteen-year-old Mabbie wrote to her mother, "Uncle Rodman made jokes about dreams and Professor," and in such situations "I always laugh and say nothing." And one time at Black Point CCB, when told of Freud's book *Jokes and Their Relation to the Unconscious*, guffawed, "What does Freud know of humor? He *has* no sense of humor!"[21] Everyone laughed and said nothing, though all might have profited if some adult present had asked CCB if he had read the book or knew enough of Freud to judge. But in this family no one splashed cold water on the patriarch.

Yet in another respect the visits at Black Point went more easily than expected. Freud, though raised in an observant Jewish family, as an adult was indifferent to religion, having discarded any belief in God or immortality, and feeling no need for them. Dorothy had warned her children that their Burlingham grandparents took religion seriously, but she heard from Katrina during the first visit in 1932: "It is really not so bad as I thought it would be. We don't have to pray at table and don't have to go to church. But perhaps that will come soon."[22] It did not. At Black Point, CCB omitted church; and in New York, while he, often without Louie, attended St. George's, and Charles and his wife, Cora, went regularly to Ascension,

Robert and Nancy seldom entered a church. As for prayer, CCB knelt in private and did not thrust his religious beliefs and habits on his family.

The children soon responded to the obvious love of their father and grandparents, and took to calling CCB "Bompa," perhaps a contraction of "bon Papa." They had been warned of their father's illness and were on the watch for symptoms. But as Mabbie wrote to Dorothy, "He really is lovely when he is not sick . . . In reality he loves you because all the things he likes in us are because they are like you." Then she added about CCB: "Bompa is so queer. He encouraged us to be wild at meals and then all at once yesterday he told Daddy that we had to be more formal." Amused, she closed, "Now we are so proper!"[23]

Finally, in August 1932, Dorothy made an effort to resolve the stalemate in her relations with Robert. That month she made a round-trip visit to New York on the new North German Lloyd liner *Bremen*, traveling with twelve-year-old Katrina, who had just returned from Black Point. Dorothy planned to stay in the country only one day, and her purpose was twofold: at lunch on Long Island to see her father, eighty-four and in failing health, and after dinner in New York to ask Robert for a divorce.

Leaving Katrina for the day at 860 Park Avenue, and with more confidence than ever before, she went alone to face the scourge of her childhood, her father. Stooped, weak, and often confused, Louis Comfort Tiffany was no longer a threat; and in five months death removed him from her life.[24]

Returning to Park Avenue, she was greeted by CCB, Katrina, and Robert. As it was summer, Louie and Nancy were at Black Point, and Charles, now married, in his own home. At some point in the evening, before leaving with Katrina for the *Bremen*, she took Robert to his room to speak to him privately of her wish for a divorce. But she had miscalculated: if over the past seven years she had gained in confidence, he had lost, and when she suggested a divorce, it meant to him a final destruction of the family. He locked the bedroom door, trapping her inside. Their voices rose, and Katrina later recalled "a lot of screaming" and a situation "very frightening." In the hallway, CCB knocked and knocked at the door, and when Robert finally unlocked it, Dorothy and Katrina fled to the ship. According to Dorothy's biographer, she now "realized that there could be no divorce; they would never even become legally separated."[25]

Within five months, on 1 January 1933, Hitler came to power in Germany, causing CCB to fear that a German invasion of Austria or a local coup by Austrian National Socialists would follow by midsummer. At his request, the Department of State sent its consul general in Vienna to offer Dorothy aid, if needed, in leaving the city. She, however, saw little reason for fear and none for help. In New York, CCB wrote to a friend, "Louie has been very anxious about the children in Vienna and thinks I am not vigorous enough in trying to get them away."[26] So, in April, he wrote to Tom Thacher, ending his term as solicitor general for President Hoover:

> I wish our four grandchildren were not under the same roof with Professor Freud in Vienna. Dorothy is devoted to the Professor and would not forsake him, and for that matter the influence of the Freuds, particularly Anna F., on D. is valuable . . . Now here's the request: Can you quietly, in your own way, find out what they really think in the State Department about conditions in Austria? Is Hitlerism to prevail there too?[27]

Thacher's reply perhaps was less soothing than CCB had hoped. The situation in Austria was reported to be "very tense," yet unlikely "for the present" to worsen. For the moment, there seemed to be "no immediate cause for apprehension"; and there was a chance that Mussolini might prevent Hitler "from gaining too much headway in Austria."[28]

CCB and Dorothy's letters in May and June 1933 chiefly concerned the children's summer visit to Black Point, and he received one that he told a friend was "rather rough": Dorothy accused him of not trusting her to want what was best for the children. She evidently feared that he planned to keep the children in America. He replied softly, saying that he thought the Freuds' influence on the children was beneficial and that he always wrote frankly, in the belief that frankness helped understanding.[29] His answer cannot have satisfied her, for he next had a letter from her lawyer in New York, Paul D. Cravath, an acquaintance of CCB and, at the time, one of Wall Street's distinguished corporate lawyers.

At his first meeting with Cravath, who plainly found his role in the family drama uncomfortable, CCB trumped all complaints by demanding, one grandfather to another, how Cravath "would like to see his grandchildren for [only] three or four weeks in nine years." Cravath had replied that "he wouldn't." Yet at their second meeting Cravath asked CCB to cable Dorothy with a letter immediately following to state "that the children would go back at the end of their visit." CCB refused: "Under no circumstances would I write any such thing," for the political situation was too uncertain. He had already written Dorothy about steamers each way and beyond that would "make no promises whatever."[30] Of all this, Robert apparently was told nothing, for fear of upsetting him needlessly, and at the end of the summer, Hitler having not yet invaded Austria, the children returned from Black Point to Vienna.

The next summer, there was much the same preparatory fuss, though without Cravath's intercession, and in the midst of the children's visit, when Dorothy herself came briefly to the United States, CCB wrote her a long letter in which, after a preamble, he stated his thoughts in numbered paragraphs.

I am getting very old, and while I never stand on rights, which I consider vastly inferior to duties, I have a right to talk plainly to you, and we have always talked to each other plainly and frankly, have we not?

1. You have done wonders with the children; the Freudian influence has been all to their benefit; they are four remarkable personages.

2. . . . I do not think the atmosphere of Vienna is salubrious or proper for the bringing up of children in their teens . . . What I think is serious is the psychological effect of the sad condition of Vienna—poverty, oppression, suppression of liberty of speech, writing and action, cruelties worthy of the Nazis themselves—these are the things that subconsciously affect us, even joyous children in their teens.

3. I am far more interested in the children than I am in either you or Robert. I think the younger ones are now being deprived of opportunities which they are entitled to. They have got all the German or Austrian Kultur they need. I think they should be in American schools . . . [where] there is the companionship of young and happy children doing things together . . . They would get on famously with other children.

4. If you are adamant against their entering American schools, then they should be in Switzerland or France and acquire the *Latin* culture.

Well, I have written you perhaps too much and in too great haste. I recognize that you are acting according to your best judgment and your conscience, but some of the bitterest suffering in this world, from the Middle Ages down, has been caused by people who were following their conscience. It would not be fair for me to close this letter without my telling you plainly that while Mother and I have always and inevitably told Robert that he must do nothing which would break up the unity of the family, even at the greatest cost to himself, we have never spoken of you to him or to anyone else except in kindness and love. But not withstanding this, I feel it my duty to put down in black and white my opinion, which is that you have failed to treat him fairly and justly in the matter of the children. You observe that I leave the rest of us out.[31]

Dorothy was not persuaded. The children continued in Viennese schools, with the two eldest, Bob and Mabbie, still in analysis with Anna

Freud. In April 1934, without Dorothy's knowledge, CCB asked an American consul in Vienna, George S. Messersmith, to look out for the family,[32] and after Dorothy, in the summer of 1935, called on Messersmith to ask about the political situation, he wrote CCB a detailed account of the conversation.

> I took the liberty of telling her that I thought it was a very fine thing for the children to have this opportunity to be at home for after all they were Americans and it would be a good thing for them to spend a continuous period there, but I felt that this had very little effect on Mrs. Burlingham. I think she has the feeling that the Austrian surroundings are really more beneficial for the children than what they would have at home . . . [She] seems to have some rather strange ideas about our own country, and I feel that she does not know it quite as well as some of the rest of us.[33]

Yet it seemed that Robert and his father had won a partial victory in the struggle over cultures and schools for the children. In September 1933, Bob, the eldest, having failed to pass the examinations to enter Harvard, started college at Antioch (Ohio), from which he was able to transfer to Harvard in the fall of 1936 by entering the Class of 1939 and repeating a year. His father and grandparents were delighted, and those who recalled CCB's transfer to Harvard from a Western college by repeating a year were amused by the seeming pattern.

In CCB and Louie's generation, when the life expectancy for men was fifty years and for women only slightly more, few couples reached a fiftieth, golden, wedding anniversary. Louie's grandfather Colonel Hoe, though married fifty-one years, lost his first wife, Louie's grandmother, after only eight, and in his second marriage died seven short of the golden fifty. Louie's parents were even more unfortunate. Her mother died at age forty-six, and her father, though remarrying, died within ten years. CCB's parents celebrated their fifty-*first* as their golden anniversary, because the previous year his mother had been seriously ill, and so a year late, on 11 November 1902, they held a small evening reception at their home in Mount Vernon.[34]

For couples who reached their anniversary in health and prosperity, the occasion was one for great rejoicing, not only within the family but for friends, neighbors, and, if the town was small, the whole community. The model of such for CCB was the three-day party at Windsor, Vermont, in

August 1893, given by and for William M. Evarts and his wife, Helen.[35] Evarts was then possibly America's most distinguished lawyer and states-man. He had successfully defended President Andrew Johnson in his im-peachment trial (1868), represented the country in the Geneva arbitration with Great Britain (1870), served as U.S. attorney general and secretary of state in the cabinets of Presidents Johnson and Hayes, and had recently been elected senator from New York. He had led in founding the New York City Bar Association and had been its president for its first ten years. Several of his famous cases, such as his defense in 1875 of the Reverend Henry Ward Beecher against a charge of adultery, had held the country's attention for months. In addition, he was a frequent public orator, noted for his wit and ability to match words to the occasion. Newspapers rou-tinely reported his opinions and doings, and also the events of his golden wedding anniversary.

Though Evarts practiced law in New York City, he and his wife had de-veloped a large farm, Runnemede, at Helen's home in Windsor. The Con-necticut River valley was then more cultivated, less wooded than now, and noted for its quiet beauty, order, and civilization—often compared, and not only for its agriculture, to the Chianti hills of Tuscany. On the outskirts of its many small towns along the river, such as Windsor and Brattleboro in Vermont, and Cornish, Lebanon, and Hanover in New Hampshire, gath-ered many outstanding artists, lawyers, doctors, and educators. In the 1890s, among the artists was the sculptor Augustus Saint-Gaudens, while among the lesser folk, for four summers, were the Burlinghams. They rented a house in Cornish from Evarts's law partner and son-in-law, Charles Beaman, who liked to fill houses he controlled with poor but interesting people whom he charged barely more than the legal "peppercorn." Louie and the children were in Cornish for part of the summer of 1893, but CCB was not with them, for that was the year of his nervous breakdown and the family's summer was cut short, precluding a share in the Evarts festivities.[36]

These began with a small dinner party at Runnemede, entertaining sons, daughters, and guests, such as Massachusetts senator Hoar, Mrs. Hoar, and the New York lawyer Joseph Hodges Choate. The next morning the household gathered for readings from the Psalms, followed by the pre-sentation of gifts to the couple from their four sons and four daughters. Shortly before noon, the people of Windsor came to present their con-gratulations and were greeted in the gardens. In the afternoon, the seven-teen grandchildren offered their thanks and presents, which was followed by another, larger dinner party, at which healths were drunk, speeches made, and a golden loving cup passed round the table.

The next day many reunited and were joined by many more at Blow-Me-Down, Beaman's farm in Cornish, New Hampshire, just two miles across the river. There, the farmers, in the fields bordering Beaman's lane, had raked the mown hay into the initials W.M.E. and H.W.E, and over the noon hour Evarts and his wife greeted guests in the parlor. Later, on the lawn and to music by a band from nearby Claremont, there was dancing.

As CCB and Louie approached their golden anniversary, on 29 September 1933, they had no such plans. Times had changed, and such grand parties were now rare, though a fiftieth wedding anniversary was still a cause for celebration. But the Burlingham family in 1933, compared to the Evarts family forty years earlier, quite aside from its lesser wealth, was far smaller and somewhat in disarray. CCB's brother, Albert, was alive, but CCB had met few of his Burlingham and Starr first cousins and knew none of them well. Louie's family was closer, but of her five siblings only the widowed Grace Taylor survived, and only with her family were the Burlinghams intimate. Of their own children, Charles, Nancy, and Robert, only Charles was married happily. Nancy was still single, Robert was often ill, and his wife, Dorothy, with their four children, was in Vienna with the Freuds. Thus to CCB and Louie, an anniversary party may have seemed more likely to stress the family's troubles than its unity. So they planned nothing.

Then their neighbors at Black Point surprised them. As CCB wrote to his friend the economist Francis Hirst in London:

> Saturday night at Black Point all our neighbors, fifty or more, gave us a surprise party for our golden wedding. It is really the 29th, but they were afraid we might have gone home [to New York City] by that time, so they anticipated the date. It was a great affair. The whole Point came marching in on us, two by two, singing, and brought gifts of one sort or another that glittered, although not gold, and a magnificent wedding cake, with a bride and groom in Louis Seize costumes on top, with orange blossoms.[37]

And of course, though he does not say so, toasts were offered, healths drunk, and speeches made. A happy evening at the Point.

By 1933, aside from their apartment in the city, Black Point was almost the only place where Louie and CCB appeared together. In the later years of their marriage, by her choice, she restricted herself and her activities to home and family. She never accompanied him in any of his legal or political activities or associated herself with him publicly. Even at St. George's Church she seldom appeared, and after the war, if he went to the theater,

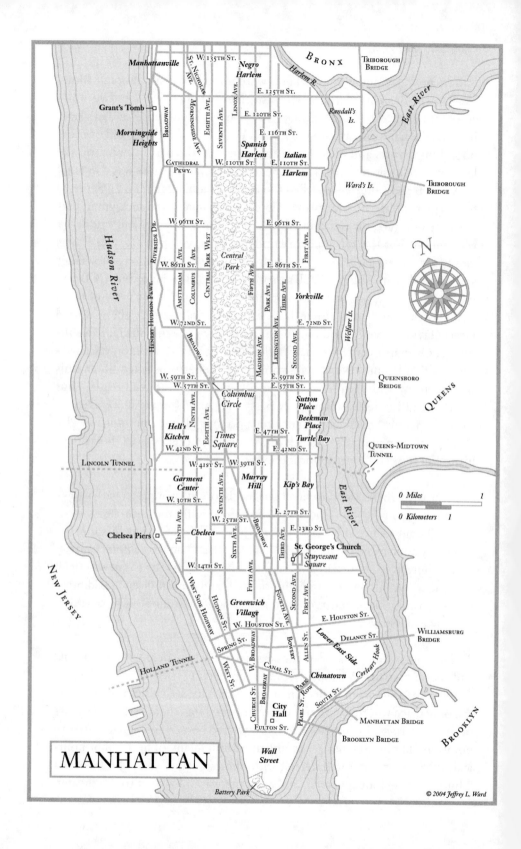

MANHATTAN

BRONX

TRIBOROUGH BRIDGE

Manhattanville

W. 135TH ST.

Negro Harlem

Harlem R.

Grant's Tomb

E. 125TH ST.

Randall's Is.

E. 120TH ST.

Morningside Heights

E. 116TH ST.

Spanish Harlem

Italian

TRIBOROUGH BRIDGE

CATHEDRAL PKWY.

W. 110TH ST.

E. 110TH ST.

Harlem

Ward's Is.

W. 96TH ST.

E. 96TH ST.

Central Park

W. 86TH ST.

E. 86TH ST.

Yorkville

Welfare Is.

W. 72ND ST.

E. 72ND ST.

Hudson River

W. 59TH ST.

E. 59TH ST.

QUEENSBORO BRIDGE

W. 57TH ST.

E. 57TH ST.

Columbus Circle

Sutton Place

QUEENS

Hell's Kitchen

Beekman Place

Times Square

E. 47TH ST.

Turtle Bay

QUEENS-MIDTOWN TUNNEL

W. 42ND ST.

E. 42ND ST.

LINCOLN TUNNEL

W. 41ST ST.

W. 39TH ST.

Garment Center

Murray Hill

Kip's Bay

W. 30TH ST.

E. 27TH ST.

W. 25TH ST.

E. 23RD ST.

Chelsea Piers

Chelsea

St. George's Church

W. 14TH ST.

Stuyvesant Square

NEW JERSEY

Greenwich Village

E. HOUSTON ST.

W. HOUSTON ST.

WILLIAMSBURG BRIDGE

SPRING ST.

Lower East Side

Corlears Hook

HOLLAND TUNNEL

CANAL ST.

Chinatown

City Hall

FULTON ST.

MANHATTAN BRIDGE

BROOKLYN BRIDGE

Wall Street

BROOKLYN

Battery Park

© 2004 Jeffrey L. Ward

East River

East River

0 Miles 1
0 Kilometers 1

his children or friends more often accompanied him than Louie. In the activities at Black Point, however, the croquet, the frequent houseguests, and their neighbors' summer parties, they were a couple. At the Point everyone knew Mrs. Burlingham, "the Pirate," with the black patch on her left eye. In New York City many of the men and women who worked closely with CCB had never met her.

Yet their city apartment might have been a gathering place for more than a few friends and family if she had wished to make it so. They had left their brownstone house on Murray Hill in 1925, after more than thirty years there, because the newer, taller buildings rising around 140 East Thirty-eighth Street had put the house in shadow, and the consequent lack of light made it hard for Louie, with only one good eye, to read or sew by daylight, or to do her jigsaw puzzles. By then Park Avenue was fast becoming a residential boulevard, its railroad tracks covered and the use of steel stilts between them making possible huge buildings above that did not vibrate with the passing trains. As a result, the avenue, twice as wide as most, gradually was lined from Forty-sixth to Ninety-sixth Streets with grand apartment houses that enjoyed exceptional light, and in one of the more ordinary of these, at 860 Park, on the northwest corner of the avenue and Seventy-seventh Street, the Burlinghams took the top floor, the thirteenth (which the management, to soothe the superstitious, numbered "fourteenth").

The apartment, the only one on its floor, had four large bedrooms for CCB and Louie, Charles, Nancy, and Robert. Later, after Charles married in 1929 and moved out, a room was always ready for guests. At the back were a large kitchen and pantry and two small rooms for a cook and maid. Almost a third of the floor was given to three rooms. A living room at the corner contained a grand piano, a card table for Louie's picture puzzles, Abbott Thayer's portrait of Annie Hoe, and the big armchair she had given CCB and Louie for their first home. Facing Seventy-seventh Street was a dining room, with the portrait of CCB's father, and facing east onto the avenue, a study for CCB. Though lacking architectural distinction, the apartment was spacious and comfortable, and their pictures and books gave it character. But aside from putting up family and a few friends, Louie seldom entertained. If CCB wanted to meet someone, he generally did so at his office or at one of his clubs.

Over the years Louie seems to have developed a somewhat difficult personality. Certainly her daughter-in-law Dorothy thought so, and even CCB, though always loving his Louie, recognized that at times she could be a touch critical. In 1932 he wrote to Francis Hirst's wife, Helena, in England, about Molly Hamilton, a friend and Labourite member of

Parliament: "I will keep all that you have said as confidential, not even telling Louie, for while she admires Molly greatly, she has always felt that there is in her a defect of taste. This L. excuses because M. has had to fend for herself. I might discover it even with the naked eye, but why should I? She is a grand person, and who am I to look for motes?"[38] Others saw in CCB and Louie the difference he remarked.

Louie doubtless intimidated some people merely by her appearance: tall, heavyset, and always in a floor-length black skirt to cover the swelling of her legs caused by Milroy's disease. She was slow to smile, and her face could seem severe, with its patched eye or painted spectacle. And her manner could be harsh. When in 1936 her widowed sister Grace Taylor had a wedding in her family (the eldest son Lawrence marrying Edith Howard, in the Howard house in Norfolk, Massachusetts), neither CCB nor Louie was present. Yet both were fond of Grace and the children, for whom CCB had acted as guardian as well as uncle. They may have had other reasons for their absence, but the bride put it down to snobbery: Mrs. Burlingham thought the Howard family socially inferior to the Lawrences.[39] What Louie thought is unknown, but clearly she did not cover her absence by any satisfactory explanation or effort to repair the breach. The alleged slight rankled, but CCB, though equally absent, was not equally blamed, a split in judgment that seems frequently to have occurred.

To CCB, however, Louie was always the perfect companion; and he would seize almost any occasion to write her a bit of verse, doggerel no doubt but nice to receive. On St. Valentine's Eve, 1936, when he was seventy-seven and she was seventy-two, he fancied himself arriving in Heaven before her:

> My Louie's still my Valentine,
> And will be till I die
> And if I meet the Saint in Heaven,
> I'll ask him, with a sigh,
> To take this message to my love:
> Tell her that all's not well above
> While she is down below
> And I should like to know
> The day, the hour, the minute, too,
> When I shall see my darling Lou.[40]

Out of habit or perhaps feigning fear that, despite the uniquely bad handwriting, she might fail to identify the poet, he added, "C.C.B."

. . .

As CCB grew older—he was seventy in 1928—and continually increased his engagement in public affairs, the pressure for some readjustment of his position in his law firm inevitably increased. The partners had never set a limit on the amount of charitable work one could undertake, and presumably, if the issue had come up, something might have been said of business brought to the firm by CCB's prestige. But the subject did not come up. CCB's outside work, as one of his later partners observed, "was just a fact of life."[41]

Nevertheless, aside from the money—in 1928 CCB reportedly still took the largest share of the firm's profits[42]—there was pride to be considered, and that year Clark and Hupper, both of them middle-aged, active, and increasingly distinguished, forced a minor but noticeable change. On New Year's Day, 1929, the firm's name became Burlingham, Veeder, Fearey, Clark & Hupper.[43] The change included not only the addition of two names, Clark and Hupper, but the dropping of one, Masten.

Everett Masten, however, continued as a partner until 1934, when he withdrew from the firm though maintaining an association with it until 1942. An authority on marine insurance, charter parties, bills of lading, and an expert in drafting the necessary documents, he apparently had made himself a niche, was content with it, and was not bothered by the demotion, if such it was. In CCB's words, Masten "found great joy in his gardens which he cultivated with rare taste. And withal he was a man of wide culture, home-keeping but most hospitable."[44] Sometimes on Sundays, his partners went to Staten Island to lunch with the Mastens and to see his gardens; and if they had children, they took them along. Masten was always genial and the outing pleasant.[45]

It is not clear to what extent the firm's new name signified a change in the partners' shares. Presumably the four older men, Burlingham, Veeder, Masten, and Fearey, gave up some percentage points to Clark and Hupper, but the listing and ordering of partners' names on the firm's stationery remained as before: after Burlingham and Veeder came Masten, Emerson, and Fearey; then (in order of becoming a partner) Burlingham fils (1912), Clark (1916), and Hupper (1917), and to end the list, three junior partners.

Then there was the annual dinner party that in the 1920s the firm gave its associates. Held at the Yale Club (where Morton Fearey was active and celebrated as "Yale's greatest baseball pitcher"), the dinner was a dignified affair with everyone in black tie and with a speaker, usually a judge recruited by CCB: in 1924, Frederick E. Crane of the state Court of Appeals; in 1925, Augustus Hand of the federal Southern District Court; in 1926, Charles

Merrill Hough, of the Second Circuit Court of Appeals; and in 1927, Francis A. Winslow, of the federal Southern District Court. But by then, with Prohibition and bootleg whiskey in their eighth year, among some of the younger associates, at least, the evening's dignity was fraying. That year, according to an associate, Fearey, in order "to show he was a good sport," he smuggled in a bottle of Scotch. Whereupon, later in the evening, a young associate "slid under the table during Judge Winslow's speech. This shocked CCB, and the annual dinners were called off." It was still CCB's firm.[46]

Most important, the firm's profits were up, and there was more to share, and so, even without readjustment, shares were bigger. Because of the war, New York's port facilities had greatly expanded, and the growth thereafter continued, so that by 1930, according to a Port Authority bulletin, New York was "the largest, most frequently used, and best-known port in the world." The *Maritime History of New York* reports that in 1930 "a ship arrived or departed every ten minutes of daylight hours . . . There were fifty ship-repair yards in the Port . . . Five hundred steamship piers and deep-water berthage totaling seventy miles of side wharfage were available. During the 1920s more deep-water steamship berthage had been added to New York's already developed waterfront than existed in the entire Port of New Orleans."[47]

With the size of ocean liners constantly increasing, plans were already drawn for a new Transatlantic Steamship Terminal (Piers 88, 90, and 92) on the Hudson River between Forty-eighth and Fifty-second Streets. France, Britain, Germany, and Italy were building liners larger than the *Titanic*, and the companies wanted better facilities to turn around such huge ships as the *Normandie, Queen Mary, Bremen,* and *Rex.*[48] Though the new piers opened only in 1936, even before then the port had made a startling record in "turnaround time." Cunard's *Berengaria*, docking at 9 a.m., had unloaded 1,000 passengers and nine hundred sacks of mail and freight, reloaded, and sailed at midnight. The even larger *Île de France* accomplished a "turnaround" in an hour less. To pass the debarking passengers and freight swiftly through customs and off the pier, the port kept available a force of 3,700 inspectors.[49]

The Burlingham firm shared in the port's growth and prosperity. Whereas in 1910 it had seven partners, by 1928 it had eleven. Then, in late 1933, with business declining because of the Depression, Clark and Hupper pushed through a bigger change. By then CCB was seventy-five, Veeder sixty-six, and Hupper and Clark both fifty. Tradition among later members of the firm holds that this was "a shoot-out." The two older men were told either to move over and become "of counsel," or the two younger would depart, taking with them clients, presumably some associates, and perhaps a partner or two.[50]

In those years, becoming "of counsel" usually meant the elderly lawyer was allowed an office and the occasional use of a stenographer, and was consulted about legal matters only infrequently and about office affairs almost never. He was expected to come to the office seldom (his room often being used for conferences), to stay for a decreasing number of hours, and after a few years to drift away or die. And with the reduced status came a large cut in the partner's share or a transfer to some sort of pension, usually guaranteed for only a year or two.

Early in 1934 the firm's name became Burlingham, Veeder, Clark & Hupper, with the two oldest partners now listed on the right-hand side as "of counsel." But in the reshuffle more happened: Fearey withdrew, taking with him a junior partner, William Paul Allen, and an associate; and with them and another lawyer, Samuel C. Coleman, he formed the firm of Fearey, Allen & Coleman. Fearey had done much of the Burlingham firm's trial work defending suits against the Pennsylvania Railroad, White Star Line, United Fruit Company, and smaller steamship companies, and his new firm's immediate success suggests that he took much of this business with him.[51] Masten (perhaps shifting to a salary) elected to stay with the firm, as did CCB's son, though both were demoted in the rank of active partners, which now read: Hupper, Clark, Burlingham (the son), Masten, Emerson, Ray Rood Allen, and John L. Galey; the firm once again had only seven active partners. And though Clark's name still preceded Hupper's in the firm's name, reflecting his historical precedence, Hupper's name now preceded Clark's in the list of active partners: experts in the meaning of such placements might have concluded that Hupper by a small margin had become the firm's leader.

Tradition, backed by sparse circumstantial evidence, holds that in this reorganization CCB gave up his entire financial share in the firm.[52] He was seventy-five, thirteen years beyond his life expectancy; he lived moderately; and evidently he felt he had money enough to give up making more. (Veeder's arrangements were more complicated: apparently he retained some financial interest in the firm until at least 1937 and perhaps later; meanwhile, he accepted appointments from the courts—as referee in a railroad reorganization and arbitrator in a motion-picture tribunal—gradually moving himself from the firm's payroll to the courts'. In 1940 he gave up his position with the firm as "of counsel," and two years later died.)[53] Tradition also states, though with less supporting evidence, that

Charles Burlingham the son agreed to a smaller share of the firm's profits. Allegedly he did not care, because he had "a rich wife." If so, she made no great display of wealth. But in any case the mid-1930s seem to have been his most difficult years in the firm: pushed down and scorned by Clark and Hupper he had, most observers agreed, a "hard lot."[54]

The reorganization occurred on the eve of what became probably Hupper's most famous case. On 8 September 1934, the Ward liner *Morro Castle* caught fire off the New Jersey coast, in sight of Asbury Park. Airplanes bearing photographers soon swarmed above her, and for a week or more in the movie houses of the nation the public avidly watched newsreels of the billowing smoke, the listing ship, and the circle of rescue boats that dared not come too close. Everyone knew that the fire had been discovered in a locker off the port-side writing room, that the ship's captain had died from indigestion only hours before; and that the fire had spread too far to be stopped. Ultimately, 125 passengers and crew died, the cargo was a total loss, and the ship itself, a red-hot hulk, was beached beside the Asbury Park convention hall, where it briefly became a tourist sight. As often occurred in admiralty cases, insurance soon became the main issue. Hupper, arguing for the Ward Line, ultimately won a decision in 1940 that the line should be repaid by Continental Insurance for money paid in damages to the disaster's victims. And that same year Hupper was elected president of the Maritime Law Association.[55]

Throughout the winter and spring of 1934, as CCB spent more and more time on civic affairs, he tried to wind up his cases for the firm. On 24 April, writing to his English friend Helena Hirst, he described what was probably his final appearance in a trial.

> I have been in Court for several days in a very sensational case. Ridley, a miserly old fellow, was murdered in his cellar office last May, with his secretary. The secretary had drawn up and had him sign—he was nearly blind—a fraudulent will. The witnesses confessed and are now in Sing Sing Prison. We thought everything was settled until recently when an old Norwegian, Jens Nelson, appeared, first claiming to have a note of Ridley's for $150,000 to purchase some fly-trap invention, and later claiming to be a son, born in a lumber camp in Michigan in 1866. He produced a certificate of his mother's marriage and of his own birth and baptism signed by a Norwegian Lutheran Pastor. We knew the documents were forged—modern pulp papers, modern ink, illiterate writing, a forged signature with the wrong initials, all of which we proved. But the lawyers for the claimant persisted until we exploded a terrific bomb

yesterday in Court, calling a jeweler from Poughkeepsie who testified that he had engraved the seal for Jens three months ago. Then the lawyers were thoroughly scared and, professing that this was their first assurance that their client was an imposter, they asked leave to withdraw from the case, which they did, and the Surrogate threw the claimant out of Court and sent him to the Police Court to be prosecuted.

This is about my last case. I think I have one more appeal, but I have enough—perhaps too much—to do, with one sort of thing and another.[56]

Part Three

BLOOMING IN OLD AGE

16

La Guardia's Fusion Campaign

THE DOOR TO REFORM in New York City politics, which "regular" Democrats had slammed shut with their total victory in 1917, had jarred open in 1930–32 with Seabury's investigations of Tammany's corruption. Many New Yorkers determined, at their first opportunity, to show their anger at the polls. The occasion came in November 1932 in the special election that followed Mayor Walker's resignation in September and the succession of Joseph McKee as acting mayor. At issue was who, starting New Year's Day, 1933, would serve the remaining year of Walker's term.

McKee himself did not stand for election, yet because in his few weeks in office he had been straightforward, honest, and competent, he received almost 250,000 valid write-in votes. Yet Tammany's candidate, John Patrick O'Brien, on 1 January took office, having defeated his nearest opponent, the Republican Lewis H. Pounds, by 600,000 votes. In O'Brien's margin of victory, as all would-be reformers knew, lay the chief obstacle to reform. In a city of 2,250,000 voters, where registered Democrats outnumbered registered Republicans almost four to one, Tammany, even when proved corrupt, had a cushion of half a million votes. The lesson was plain: for any reform party to win, whether Democratic, Republican, Socialist, or Independent, it must have allies; it must fuse.

To that end, preparing for the regular election for mayor in November 1933, groups of Republicans, Independent Democrats, Socialists, businessmen, and enthusiasts of all kinds for better government had early joined in a large Fusion Coordination Committee. Their sense of crisis, of the absolute need for reform, was strengthened by the severity of the country's economic depression. By the end of 1932 New York State had some two million men unemployed, and in Buffalo the percentage of the workforce unemployed was 32.6 with only 44 percent of male workers having full-time employment. The Welfare Council of New York City, for example,

estimated that during the winter of 1931–32 the city's government would
have to provide not less than $20 million for emergency work and wages,
and cities all around the state had discovered that their needs for such programs were four times greater than in 1929, and funds were giving out.
The Depression made even the sunniest day gray as men stood idle in the
streets, defeated and increasingly derelict, or, as happened in Washington,
D.C., in 1930, 5,000 women stood in line to apply for two hundred openings as charwomen in government buildings.[1]

Though most New York reform groups by the spring of 1933 had
joined the Fusion Coordination Committee, by mid-July, with the primaries looming, they still had no candidate for mayor. By then the committee, though without full agreement or enthusiasm, had offered Fusion
backing to at least ten men, and all had refused it. Until the committee's
groups could unite on a candidate, most politicians, however reform-
minded, could not be lured to run for mayor and certain defeat. As July
ended and August's heat settled on the city, the movement for reform,
despite its initial strength, seemed likely to splinter.[2]

In a search for unity, three reform leaders met for lunch on 2 August:
Seabury, George Z. Medalie, and Roy Howard. Medalie, a Republican
and an outstanding lawyer, was a former U.S. attorney and future judge on
the New York Court of Appeals; Howard was the editor and publisher of
the liberal-leaning afternoon daily the *World-Telegram*. Medalie proposed
a small, inner "Harmony" Committee to lead the discordant groups of the
larger committee to a candidate, a plan to which the others agreed, and
they discussed who should be the committee's members and chairman.
After lunch, as spokesman, Medalie went to Burlingham's office to ask
him to organize and lead it.[3]

At the time, most people thought Seabury should be the Fusion candidate. He was sixty, at the peak of his ability, with a national reputation
from his investigations of Tammany, and he had some political experience.
He usually was addressed as "Judge," for he had been elected to the City
Court in 1901, to the state's Supreme Court in 1906, and to the Court of
Appeals in 1914. In 1916 he had resigned from the Court of Appeals to
run as a reform Democrat for governor. Looking for allies, he had been
promised by Theodore Roosevelt the backing of the Progressive Party—
Roosevelt had told him, "I will never give my support to [Charles S.]
Whitman," the conservative Republican running for reelection. Then,
mainly for reasons of national politics, Roosevelt had endorsed Whitman,
and the betrayed Seabury had lost. (Before the election, in an episode displaying Seabury's characteristic moral passion, and what to some seemed

his pomposity, he sought out Roosevelt, lashed him verbally, and left him speechless by concluding, "Mr. President, you are a blatherskite!")[4]

Now, in the Fusion Coordination Committee, Seabury again faced Whitman, whom he similarly despised. If he sought revenge, he could have it by taking the nomination for mayor, for Whitman, though twice governor, could not deny Republican endorsement to the man who embodied reform and who had driven Mayor Walker in disgrace from office. But for reasons not entirely clear (concealed perhaps in Seabury's personality), he continually refused the nomination; and to impede a draft for it he shifted his legal residence from the city to East Hampton, Long Island. Yet he remained a force within the Coordination Committee, in effect having a veto on its choice. For CCB and the Harmony Committee, Seabury's hatred of Democratic Tammany leaders and of Whitman were two prickly complications.

A third thistle, though with a seed of hope, was a split developing among Republican leaders. The more conservative, led by Whitman, favored Major General John F. O'Ryan, a World War I hero, a former member of the city's Transit Commission, and a leading member of a new reform group, the City Fusion Party. (Though he called himself an Independent Democrat, O'Ryan's conservatism made him agreeable to Whitman.) Younger Republican leaders, however, were beginning to favor Fiorello H. La Guardia, who in 1916 without help from his party had become the first Republican ever to win the Fourteenth Congressional District (Manhattan south of Fourteenth Street), and had represented it for two terms. He then had served five terms, 1922–32, for the Twentieth District, in East Harlem, where, as before, he campaigned in both Italian and Yiddish. And in the city's government, in 1919–21, he had been president of the city's Board of Aldermen and in 1929 had run for mayor against Walker, and lost. He had the political experience that O'Ryan lacked, and from his work in Congress had a national reputation as a Progressive Republican—opposing child labor, a national sales tax, and the electric power trusts. In addition, he and Nebraska's Senator George W. Norris (another Republican who took party ties lightly) had led and won the fight for a labor anti-injunction bill (1932), strengthening the workers' ability to strike by giving them greater substantive and procedural rights in federal courts. To conservative Republicans, Norris and La Guardia were as bad as Democrats.

La Guardia, having lost his congressional seat in the Democratic landslide of 1932 and unsure of whether he'd get Republican backing for mayor, sought to become Fusion's candidate, but many on the Fusion Coordination

Committee thought him a demagogue. Stout and short—only five-foot-two—La Guardia in public speaking was prone to fierce, dramatic gestures and a theatrical rhetoric delivered in a voice that in excitement (a frequent state) could rise to a piercing whine. In 1932, while still in Congress, he had loudly called for the impeachment of Hoover's secretary of the Treasury, the banker Andrew W. Mellon. But except to gain La Guardia headlines, his charges had come to naught. Since then, as the Depression worsened, he had widened his targets: In a May 1933 article for *Liberty* magazine, he wrote that American bankers were "more to blame" than any others "for the present depression." And the "banketeers," as he liked to call them, had colleagues—stockbrokers, bond salesmen, lawyers, and judges—who were just as greedy and dishonest, and he explained how frauds on bank depositors were rigged. He painted in stark colors, and his picture of the banking industry was ugly. Many on the Fusion Coordination Committee thought themselves or their colleagues libeled, and they loathed La Guardia.[5]

CCB apparently met him first in May, introduced by Adolph A. Berle Jr., a professor of corporation law at Columbia and one of President Franklin D. Roosevelt's circle of advisers known as the "brain trust."[*] Berle had worked closely with La Guardia in the lame-duck session of Congress following the November 1932 election and preceding Roosevelt's inauguration in March 1933, and had come to admire him as an effective politician with ideas for meeting the economic crisis not unlike those Roosevelt was considering for his New Deal. In Berle's opinion, if La Guardia was a demagogue, he was at least "demagoguing in the right direction,"[6] and sometime in May 1933 Berle invited CCB (also possibly Seabury) to dinner to hear La Guardia's ideas on municipal politics and the Depression.[7]

The latter, as it affected the city, was a subject on which CCB knew more than most. He was then president of New York City's Welfare Council, which coordinated the work and policies of some seven hundred voluntary and one hundred governmental social and health agencies throughout the five boroughs. The council, as the *Herald Tribune* once explained, was "the city's engineering plant in the field of social fact finding and planning." And as a vestryman of St. George's Church and active in its

---

[*]According to William E. Leuchtenburg, *Franklin D. Roosevelt and the New Deal, 1932–1940* (New York: Harper & Row, 1963), 32: "Roosevelt referred privately to this quintet [Raymond Moley, Samuel Rosenman, Rexford Tugwell, Basil O'Connor, and Berle] as his 'privy council,' but in September, James Kieran of *The New York Times* called them the 'brains trust' and it was this name, later shortened to 'brain trust,' which caught on."

social programs, CCB had seen "with my own eyes" how private charity and even public emergency relief, after 1931, had been overwhelmed by the immensity of the Depression. In October 1933 (two years before the Social Security Act was passed), he declared in a feature article for the *Times*, "We must devise some reasonable and fair system of unemployment insurance." By then, one in three workers in the city was unemployed, one in five public school students suffered from malnutrition, and one in six (roughly 400,000) families was on some form of relief. CCB could see advantage to the city in a mayor familiar with the federal government and able to work with Roosevelt's administration. Perhaps as early as July, in the search for a Fusion candidate he favored La Guardia.[8]

For Seabury, less concerned with welfare than with municipal corruption, it was enough that La Guardia was honest, was vigorously anti-Tammany, and, because of the city's large Italian immigrant population, had a chance to win. In late July his support of La Guardia was hardened further by rage when the Coordination Committee, without consulting him and eager to end the stalemate between O'Ryan and La Guardia, chose for its nominee Robert Moses, chairman of the State Emergency Public Works Commission. The committee had polled its members and found that Moses outscored La Guardia 18 to 5—a seemingly decisive margin. Moses, an Independent Republican as well as a protégé of Democratic ex-governor Al Smith, was popular with reformers, but in Seabury's eyes, because he had opposed some reforms the latter favored and because of his tie to Smith, he was suspect.

Seabury, taken to lunch and told of the choice before it was to be released to the newspapers, banged the table, yelling, "You have sold out to Tammany!"[9] Trailed by his host, he strode from the room, summoned reporters, and proclaimed that Moses would be merely a front for Smith, who would defer to Tammany. Unable to placate Seabury, the committee shelved its proposal; and La Guardia, asked by reporters to comment, purred, "I will stand shoulder to shoulder with Judge Samuel Seabury."[10]

Meanwhile, Moses had checked with Smith, who, while certainly not pro-Tammany, refused to endorse a candidate who would run against the Democratic Party. Lacking Smith's support as well as Seabury's, Moses phoned Joseph Price, the committee chairman, and asked to be withdrawn from consideration. The committee next compromised on Whitman's candidate, General O'Ryan, further enraging Seabury. Again calling in reporters, he suggested that Whitman's conservative Republicans and Tammany's leaders probably had made a deal, and anyway, O'Ryan couldn't win. Once more, as CCB remarked to a colleague, Seabury "blew his trumpet blast," and the next day, 1 August, the *Herald Tribune*, an important Republican paper, had a lead story proclaiming, "Seabury Tells General O'Ryan He Can't Win."

Tammany leaders no doubt laughed at the sight of Seabury shooting down one reform candidate after another, but reformers were appalled. And it was the next day at lunch that Medalie proposed to Seabury and Howard his idea of a "Harmony" Committee and afterward invited CCB to lead it.[11]

The city sweltered in the summer's worst heat wave. Nonetheless, that afternoon, 2 August, CCB called a meeting in his office at 5 p.m. of eight reform leaders, not including Whitman or any of the three who had suggested the new committee. (It seems likely, however, that he first talked with both Seabury and O'Ryan either personally or by phone before 5 p.m.) Evidently his organizational meeting went well, for he immediately sent a letter by hand to Whitman explaining what had happened, naming those who had met in his office, and asking Whitman to appoint some delegates to meet with the new group before Whitman's Republican Mayoralty Committee met the following afternoon. Whitman did not reply.[12]

Next CCB sent a letter by messenger to Geoffrey Parsons, an editor of the *Herald Tribune*. "The H.T. has said nothing editorially on the fusionist mess," he began. "Before you speak, may I make a suggestion or two?" And after describing the situation as he saw it, he went on:

> Seabury's intransigent position as to the General . . . seems to make it impossible to obtain a unification of anti-Tammany forces in support of O'Ryan. The matter seems to rest with the Republican Mayoralty Committee. If, at their meeting tomorrow, they would pass a resolution reciting that in view of the apparent dissension in Fusion ranks, and the position of Seabury, they will not approve Whitman's recommendation without a further attempt to bring about complete harmony, some unification might be had. To that end, they should appoint a small committee to confer with all other persons and bodies interested, and perhaps form a new committee . . . I think the H.T. is in a position to affect that committee by its statement. It is not necessary now to declare for or against O'Ryan, or for or against La Guardia. A broader central conference committee should be created immediately.[13]

The next morning, 3 August, the *Herald Tribune* had a lead editorial, "Let's Fuse," urging the Whitman committee to appoint "a subcommittee wholly divorced in personnel from the blunders to date, to confer with a similar committee representing the various other bodies interested (such a committee as that already formed under the informal chairmanship of Mr. Charles C. Burlingham) and with Judge Seabury."[14] An unenthusiastic editorial in the *Times* that morning suggested General O'Ryan might be the best Fusion candidate; and Roy Howard's afternoon *World-Telegram* editorially inquired, "Who is Mr. Whitman that he should be permitted to wreck fusion?" But that day the *Herald Tribune*, because it spoke to and for many Republicans, was the most important.[15]

At 6 p.m. that evening, as the tarred streets softened in the heat, CCB held a meeting on the second floor of the bar association's building on West Forty-fourth Street. Present were the eight persons of the previous day plus six more, including Seabury but not Whitman, O'Ryan, or La Guardia; this expanded Harmony Committee, however, did include a group of mostly younger members from Whitman's Republican Mayoralty Committee, which had met that afternoon and, in response to the *Herald Tribune* editorial, had forced the withdrawal of ex-Governor Whitman's proposed endorsement of O'Ryan and won authorization to act in conjunction with CCB's committee.[16]

In the first two hours of CCB's evening meeting, until the break for dinner, the committee's members discussed a number of possible candidates, interspersing their proposals with pleas to Seabury to reconsider and run. But he refused. After they reconvened at 9 p.m., discussion focused on La Guardia and O'Ryan, and turned fierce. The businessman Joseph Price, representing a group calling itself the Independent Fusion Committee, at one moment cried, "If it's a question of La Guardia or bust, I say bust!" And Seabury, continually rising to speak for La Guardia, became ever more vehement until CCB shouted, "Sit down, Sam, sit down!"[17]

There was silence. Few in the room had ever heard the Judge addressed by his first name, and none had heard him commanded to sit. But he did sit, and the incident, though not inducing harmony, may have brought it closer. Near midnight a majority, 9 to 2, voting by groups, was prepared to agree on La Guardia. CCB then telephoned O'Ryan, explained what had happened, and asked him to withdraw his name, which O'Ryan did. Thereupon the vote was made unanimous: La Guardia would be the Fusion candidate to run against Tammany's nominee, Mayor John O'Brien. Yet there was no harmony.[18]

When the meeting broke, at 12:40 a.m., and its members came down the stairs to the building's lobby, where reporters were waiting, CCB, as the conference had agreed, announced its decision: La Guardia. But as he finished, Price began to speak. "You can't do that, Joe," said CCB. "You are not authorized to speak."

"I'm speaking for myself," countered Price. He was as old as CCB, and over the years the two often had worked together for reform.

"Go ahead," said CCB, standing to one side as Price passionately declared, "I consider the manner in which the vote was taken as very unfair." His emotion obscured his reasons, but clearly he resented Seabury's pressure. "The conference was absolutely dominated by Judge Seabury who repeatedly said that he would consider any other qualified name as well as Mr. La Guardia—Such a name was offered in the conference but not accepted by Judge Seabury, even for consideration."[19]

In the next few days several newspapers and much of the public rallied to La Guardia as the reform candidate. On the ballot his name would appear on two lines: the Republican Party and the City Fusion Party. And his campaign was managed not by the regular Republican organization but by a Fusion Campaign Committee with William M. Chadbourne, an elderly Republican, as chairman and Seabury, CCB, and La Guardia as core members. Promptly this committee began meeting every weekday morning for breakfast at Chadbourne's Park Avenue apartment, and according to CCB, besides the four "steadies," three others frequently were present: Berle, Howard, and Maurice Davidson of the City Fusion Party. Chadbourne, who had a staff to cook and serve, presided while the others, including La Guardia, gave reports and debated the campaign's progress. In these discussions the candidate's voice frequently rose in agitation, and then Chadbourne would murmur soothingly, "Now, Fiorello . . ."[20]

In mid-September, the committee added an eighth regular: Paul Windels, a Republican who had managed La Guardia's campaigns for alderman in 1919 (an upset victory) and for mayor in 1929 (when defeated by Walker). Besides other Republican activities and a private law practice with his brother, Windels had worked as counsel to the State Bridge and Tunnel Commission and associate counsel to the Port of New York Authority. He knew La Guardia both as a political candidate and as a friend and neighbor, for La Guardia recently had rented a summer cottage behind Windel's in Westport, Connecticut. Windels had followed the 1933 reform movement from his law firm, taking no part in Fusion activities until September, when, mostly over the back fence in Westport, he warned La Guardia that the reform campaign was stalling. At La Guardia's request, and to the delight of the others, Windels joined the committee full-time. Far more expert than Chadbourne in the briars of municipal politics, he brought to the Fusion campaign not only skill and judgment but also his standing with Republican district leaders throughout the city.[21]

Of others who came occasionally to breakfast, two of the more important were Walter Lippmann, a syndicated columnist for the Republican *Herald Tribune*, and Herbert Brownell, age twenty-nine, state assemblyman from Manhattan's Tenth Assembly District. Brownell, who later would be President Eisenhower's attorney general, had come to New York from Nebraska via Yale Law School and won his first public office only in 1932. He brought to the Fusion Committee's support the Republican organization of his district, which included most of Greenwich Village, the garment center, and mid-Manhattan from Union Square to Grand Central. Equally important, as a newcomer to city politics he was relatively free of political ties and debts and thus well placed to become—if La Guardia won—the mayor's frequent spokesman in Albany, presenting to the state legislature the bills the new city administration wanted passed. With the city teetering on bankruptcy and the problems of unemployment and relief so vast, La Guardia and his reform team already were drafting many of these. They wanted programs ready to go from the day La Guardia might take office, 1 January 1934.[22]

Besides this "brain trust" operating from Chadbourne's apartment, the Fusion Campaign Committee rented a floor of the huge Paramount Building overlooking Times Square. The cost, because of the Depression, was sixty dollars a month.[23] The City Fusion Party, a constituent of the Campaign Committee and with a line on the ballot for La Guardia as well as political clubs in all five boroughs, took the floor below. The Republican Party, also with a line on the ballot for La Guardia and with representatives on the Fusion Campaign Committee, operated out of its own headquarters and district clubs—supposedly in coordination. But keeping all the constituents happy was a daily chore for CCB, as frequently one group saw the efforts of another as poaching on posted preserves. There was constant conflict over candidates to fill out the ballot, and others equally severe over possible post-election appointments. La Guardia campaigned on a theme of turning Tammany out of office and replacing the crooks with honest, competent officials drawn from all groups. But local political clubs, before ringing doorbells and setting up meetings, wanted to know: What's in this for our boys?

Major campaign speaking was left almost entirely to La Guardia and Seabury, who often appeared together, and in striking contrast. La Guardia, short, stout, and swarthy, was fiery and theatrical; Seabury, tall, lean, and white-haired, in his wrath at Tammany's corruption seemed an Old Testament prophet. La Guardia's energy was extraordinary. He sometimes gave as many as sixteen speeches in a day, ending usually with one before an Italian audience whose enthusiasm for their own "Fiorello" would recharge the hopes of the exhausted managers and candidate.

Though La Guardia had not graduated from high school, he had developed his natural talents to a remarkable extent, not only in the law, in which he held a degree from New York University (1910), but in areas as diverse as music, airplanes, and financial accounting. He spoke six languages: English, Yiddish, Italian, German, Hungarian, and Croatian. With the first four he could, as Mayor O'Brien could not, speak to the great majority of the city's voters in their own tongue. Further, he had a gift for the happy phrase and the ability to tie it to the moment. CCB recalled an occasion when, attending a meeting with La Guardia, they arrived backstage and waited while a choir sang a spiritual, "I heard of a City called Heaven, and I started to make it my Home." After the final chord, La Guardia went on, made his speech, and ended by saying, "I heard of a City called New York, and I started to make it Heaven."[24]

He had been born on Sullivan Street, in lower Manhattan, and though raised in Arizona, where his father was a bandmaster in the U.S. Army, he loved New York. And so clearly could he project his feeling for it that his emotion seemed to embrace every part and person of the city. All, that is, except the Tammany crowd, who, he would shout, must be driven from office, for they plundered the relief funds, corrupted judges, clerks, police, and firemen, stealing money and justice from the people. That was the core of his message, constantly repeated, to which he added rather more vaguely that if he was elected, he and his team of honest experts, appointed only on merit, would build schools and hospitals, create work for the unemployed, and raise money to relieve the distress of the homeless and hungry. The money for the programs, he implied, would come in part from the federal and state governments. Some who heard him thought he was a demagogue peddling dreams to the poor in exchange for power. Others, dreading the intrusion of Washington and Albany into city affairs, considered him a "half-baked socialist."[25]

In addition to questions of strategy and policy discussed at the breakfast meetings, CCB worked mainly in three areas, raising money for the campaign, preparing a balanced slate of candidates to offer voters, and preparing another of executives to be appointed if the election was won. The money-raising was hard. Many of the city's rich Republicans distrusted La Guardia, and many of their Democratic counterparts chose to follow the lead of ex-Governor Smith, to be loyal to Tammany while hoping to reform it from within. Fusion, rich in volunteers, was always cash-poor.

On the other hand, CCB enjoyed the work of balancing the ticket and the administrative appointments, for it took him into the heart of the political parties to bargain with the district leaders and bosses, men whom he found interesting, whether or not honest. As early as 16 August, for instance, the Fusion Committee endorsed for reelection two Tammany judges for the New York County Surrogate's Court, James A. Foley and James A. Delehanty. The decision was easy, for the men were outstanding. But Fusion's endorsement, when added to Tammany's, ensured their election without campaign costs—a point for CCB in talking to Tammany boss John Curry about other judicial candidates.[26]

Similar give-and-take applied in selecting men for future appointment. La Guardia, for example, asked CCB to find out if Tammany's current commissioner of docks, John Mackenzie, was honest and worthy of reappointment, an act that would please Curry. CCB, using his contacts as an admiralty lawyer, reported: "I . . . discovered, without exciting the slightest suspicion, that the North German Lloyd people also had the highest opinion of him. They have carried on long negotiations about new piers at the foot of Canal Street, which neither the City nor the company has money enough to finish. They seem to have no doubt of Mackenzie's honesty." Mackenzie, therefore, was marked for reappointment. There were many such behind-the-scenes investigations and reports, for depending on the number of posts won in the election, there were hundreds of jobs to be filled.[27]

Fusion's slate for the election—chiefly mayor, comptroller, president of the Board of Aldermen, district attorney, and the five borough presidents—was balanced carefully between candidates of Italian, Irish, Jewish, and Anglo-Saxon background. It likewise included representatives of all the major reform parties: Reform Democrat, City Fusion, Republican, and even, for some of the judicial posts, Tammany Democrats. Its diversity contrasted sharply with Tammany's ticket, which, as had become usual in the last thirty years, was strongly Irish and Catholic—an increasingly risky lack of balance, for Italians and Jews combined were now close to 45 percent of the city's population.

In mid-September, the primary elections gave Fusion a promise of victory in November. In the Republican primary, the party's elderly Manhattan boss lost to a younger man, who promptly pledged the party to La Guardia. In the Democratic primary, though Mayor O'Brien won the right to run for reelection, the party showed itself badly split when three of Tammany's eight incumbent district leaders lost. Fusion's ticket, in contrast, was uncontested and ran strongly. A *Literary Digest* poll, taken shortly after, showed La Guardia leading O'Brien 4 to 1. Then, in the last week of September, a "spoiler" entered the race.

In Washington, D.C., the day after the primaries, President Franklin D. Roosevelt, who, though a Democrat, owed nothing to Tammany, conferred with two New York Democratic "bosses," both to some extent anti-Tammany. These were Jim Farley and Edward J. Flynn, heads of the party in New York State and in the Bronx. Roosevelt wanted neither O'Brien nor La Guardia to win. In Roosevelt's eyes O'Brien, though personally honest, would continue Tammany's wasteful and corrupt control of the city, while owing no allegiance to the Democratic Party nationally. Equally bad, La Guardia, the Fusion-Republican, would increase Republican power. To avoid the dilemma, he proposed that Flynn persuade a retired Democratic politician from the Bronx, Joseph McKee, to run against them both, promising Flynn to give McKee a public presidential blessing as the election approached.[28]

McKee was a viable candidate because in his four months as acting mayor (following Walker's abrupt resignation in September 1932) he had been an effective executive, independent of Tammany, and had proved popular with the voters. He was personable, a devout Catholic, a Wall Street lawyer, currently the head of a bank, and in his integrity and conservatism appealed to the rich in both parties. (Possibly, if Tammany had nominated McKee instead of O'Brien in either the special or regular election, Fusion would not have been born and La Guardia would never have become mayor.) In less than a week, Flynn, helped by the publicized approval of Roosevelt and Farley, created a "Recovery Party," which on 29 September offered itself to voters, with McKee as its candidate for mayor. It presented itself as the best alternative to Tammany—"best" because it was a Democratic party in a Democratic city and thus had a chance to win. Along with the public endorsements of many prominent New Yorkers, money poured into his campaign treasury.

On the stump, La Guardia and Seabury cast McKee as a front for Tammany. If McKee won, they warned, the old corrupt Democratic organization would still control; but even if he lost, the Fusionists feared, so, too, might La Guardia, for McKee would divide the anti-Tammany vote. Increasingly in October, as newspaper endorsements showed, the race for mayor had ceased to be La Guardia against O'Brien and become La Guardia against McKee. Backing La Guardia were the *Times*, *Herald Tribune*, *World-Telegram*, and *Evening Post*, with a combined circulation of 1,375,000. Supporting McKee were Hearst's *American* and *Evening Journal*, the *Daily News*, *Daily Mirror*, and the conservative Republican

Sun, with a combined circulation of 4,150,000. Supporting O'Brien was only Tammany's house journal, the *Democrat.*[29]

On both sides, the campaign between Fusion and the Recovery Party grew harsh, and on one issue, anti-Semitism, splashed through mud. Seabury, always inclined to take politics personally, began in his speeches to attack the Democratic governor, Herbert H. Lehman, who was a Jew but who was not up for election and irrelevant to the campaign. But Seabury, disliking some of Lehman's policies, therefore disliked the man, and, despite pleas by La Guardia and others, continued to attack him. CCB, doubting he could influence Seabury, wrote directly to Lehman, regretting the attacks and suggesting they were the result of "fatigue and strain," or "more likely" sprang from Seabury's "sense of wrong which has long o'er-crowed his spirit—the feeling that so far as the mighty are concerned there has been little recognition by them of his work in exposing Tammany misrule." His analysis was shrewd and fair. Roosevelt, Lehman, and Senator Robert Wagner all kept Seabury at arm's length, and honors that might have been paid to a great reformer, such as a judgeship or ambassador's post, were withheld.[30]

McKee and his backers soon suggested, however, that Seabury and, by association, La Guardia were anti-Semites. In reply Windels dug out an article written in 1915 by McKee in which he had regretted that Catholic children, by preferring parochial to public schools, were leaving the latter to be dominated by atheistic Jews, many of whom were secular socialists rather than God-fearing. The issue was fake; none of the three, La Guardia, Seabury, or McKee, was anti-Semitic, but in a city 27 percent Jewish, in a year when Hitler was in the headlines, the charge resonated. And in the battle of nastiness La Guardia, who once claimed to have invented the "low blow," won. In the last ten days of the campaign McKee's chief financial backer, Samuel Untermeyer, a Jew, publicly withdrew his support.[31]

Flynn asked Roosevelt for the promised presidential blessing of McKee, a public statement, perhaps, or an invitation to the White House. Roosevelt was evasive. Flynn appealed again. Finally, he concluded from the president's inaction that Roosevelt had decided for political expediency to do nothing. "At any rate," Flynn later wrote, "nothing is what he did."[32]

Meanwhile, in mid-October Fusion ran out of money. Raising any at all had been difficult—McKee in a shorter time had done twice as well—and as CCB explained to a friend, "The few Wall Street men who gave money hid their names." Some of the rich he had approached had been willing to give only indirectly, not to La Guardia or Fusion but to some allied and less controversial group. The Rockefeller family, for example, contributed $7,500 to the Honest Ballot Association, which during registration week and on Election Day deployed 20,000 poll-watchers to prevent fraud and intimidation at the booths. The head of the Morgan bank, Thomas W. Lamont, who privately favored La Guardia, offered CCB personally, not the Campaign Committee, $4,000 "to do with as pleased me." But CCB, out of scruples he himself later questioned, declined the gift and declined it twice again when it was reoffered. Ultimately, the Fusion Committee ran its campaign at a figure variously reported as between $115,000 and $180,000 (not including separately managed Republican funds), but even at the largest estimate the Fusion budget was small for a citywide campaign.[33] At a special meeting of Fusion leaders, on the evening of 18 October, David M. Heyman, the campaign treasurer, reported on the financial crunch: large printers' bills and no money with which to pay them. As Windels recalled the situation, it was "so desperate, we didn't know what we were going to do . . . [but] shortly after that things happened that brightened the skies considerably."[34]

What caused the skies to brighten? The morning after the special meeting CCB lent the Campaign Committee $4,000 on the understanding that if it ended solvent, he would be repaid. The amount was large for him, a retired lawyer aged seventy-five, and with dependents. In his law practice he had done well but never matched the fees of the great corporate or criminal lawyers. He was "comfortably off," with his Park Avenue apartment and a summer cottage on the Connecticut shore. In these Depression years, however, his cash contributions to worthy causes seldom rose above $100, and probably his initial gift to the campaign had been in a range of $250. In addition to the $4,000 loan, he contributed $400 to a syndicate formed to pay off the Campaign Committee's post-election debts, as well as lending $500 on his usual terms to the City Fusion Party. Meanwhile, he continued his appeals, writing to one man, "We are in the vocative for money. We have hardly enough for postage and nothing for posters nor for the radio. Can you not help us get something now?"[35]

CCB's appeals, whether spoken or written, on behalf of church, college, or some other cause, usually stirred a response. Donors admired his lack of self-promotion or seeking, and they had confidence in his statements of purpose and need. Trusting him, they gave. In this case they had twofold reassurance: Seabury's close association with La Guardia undoubtedly confirmed for many that La Guardia, despite some overheated rhetoric, was personally honest and truly intended reform. In any event, the appeals brought in enough cash for the committee to go ahead with plans for a final gathering in Madison Square Garden on the night of Thursday, 2 November.

The rally began at dusk with torchlight parades from various parts of the city—the *Herald Tribune* estimated 50,000 marched—to the Garden, at Eighth Avenue and Fiftieth Street. On its outside, the building was a dull blank of windowless walls decorated only by the tracery of black-painted fire escapes, but inside, entered through an arcade of shops and filled with a crowd of 25,000, it throbbed with color and excitement. CCB, as chairman of the meeting, spoke briefly of the indifference that Fusion had faced at the start:

> The revelations of the legislative investigation anticipated by La Guardia four years ago and proved by Seabury did not seem to stir the citizens at the time. The leaders of business and the professions showed no great interest. Few of the *first* citizens, if there are any such, even rendered lip service. But now it is plain that the people were aroused. What we have seen in the last six weeks is a rising of the waters to flood. You may be sure that on November 7th the bosses and their creatures will be over-whelmed.[36]

At 10:25 p.m., La Guardia entered, the band struck up his campaign song (sung to "The Halls of Montezuma"), and the crowd shrieked, yelled, stomped, and sang. Ten minutes into the uproar, CCB raised a sign over his head announcing that La Guardia was about to speak on the radio, and the crowd quieted. Once again La Guardia returned to his campaign's theme: the destruction of Tammany and its crony style of government and the making of a more responsive, more beautiful, more humane city.

On the following Tuesday, the vote was La Guardia, 868,122; McKee, 609,053; and O'Brien, 586,672. Though La Guardia had less than a majority, only 40 percent of the total vote, and although Fusion, because of McKee, had lost to Tammany many posts it had hoped to win, on New Year's Day La Guardia would become the city's mayor.

After the election La Guardia went to Puerto Rico for a quick vacation, and CCB returned to raising money to pay off the campaign's debts. In late December, for example, he wrote to Arthur Woods, the agent for the Rockefeller family: "The tumult and the shouting being over, we find that the Fusion Committee has a deficit of a few thousand dollars. I am sure you won't take it amiss if I modestly suggest that your great and good friends, having given $7,500 to the Honest Ballot Association, might supplement that gift by $2,500 to help wipe out the deficit."[37]

By then the deficit was not large, in part because the previous month he had received a large unsolicited contribution made to himself personally. After the election Thomas Lamont had written: "Dear Charles, I understand that you sacrificed yourself rather recklessly to keep things going in the recent Fusion campaign. I think you did a grand piece of work, and if you will let me fill in your personal deficit to the extent of $6,000, as per attached cheque, I shall be glad." This time, on Lamont's fourth effort, CCB accepted the personal gift and the next day forgave repayment of his loans to the Campaign Committee and the City Fusion Party, adding to the latter an additional contribution of $250.[38] The campaign, CCB assured Woods in December, "was the cheapest ever run. It cost only about $115,000. The treasurer, Heyman, was adamant against spending unless the money was either in the bank or on its way there." By New Year's Day, when CCB for his work in La Guardia's nomination and campaign was to be called New York's "First Citizen," a title he thought "the bunk," he and his colleagues were able to start New York's greatest mayor in office with a financially clean slate: all campaign debts paid.[39]

CCB, 1936, drawing by Alexander Iacovleff

Aaron Hale
Burlingham, CCB's
father, circa 1860,
as a young man

Aaron Burlingham
in middle age

Albert, CCB's elder brother,
and CCB, circa 1863

CCB, circa 1879, at Harvard College

Colonel Richard March Hoe

Annie Corbin Hoe, circa 1882

Phillips Brooks

Adeline Hoe
Lawrence and her
five daughters,
including CCB's
future wife, Louisa
(sitting), in 1877

Louisa L. Burlingham
and her son Robert,
in 1888

Miss ELLEN TERRY as PORTIA

Joe Evans he drew it from a fotograf by Winter & Brou
53 a Baker Street Portman Square London W

AND AFTER
MANY CURIOUS JOURNEYINGS
GIVEN TO
CHARLES BURLINGHAM THE YOUNGER
ON THE
FIRST ANNIVERSARY OF HIS BIRTHDAY

EIGHTH JUNE MDCCCLXXXV

Ellen Terry as Portia; drawing by Joe Evans

Joe Evans, "Uncle Joe"
to CCB's children

Theron G. Strong

George William Curtis

Richard G. Welling

Learned Hand, in 1909

THE ILLUSTRATED LONDON NEWS,

REGISTERED AS A NEWSPAPER FOR TRANSMISSION IN THE UNITED KINGDOM, AND TO CANADA AND NEWFOUNDLAND BY MAGAZINE POST.

No. 3811.— VOL. CXL   SATURDAY, MAY 4, 1912.   SIXPENCE.

The Copyright of all the Editorial Matter, both Engravings and Letterpress, is Strictly Reserved in Great Britain, the Colonies, Europe, and the United States of America.

Ismay (hand to moustache) testifying at the first Senate hearing at the Waldorf-Astoria hotel in New York. Senator William Smith, the chairman, is reading with his right elbow on the table.

CCB at a *Titanic* hearing, *Illustrated London News*, 1912

Nicholas Murray Butler and CCB, walking up Fifth Avenue after
a morning service at St. George's Church, Easter Day, 1930

Thomas D. Thacher

Paul Windels

CCB and his wife on the porch at Black Point, circa 1930

CCB in his eighties

The silver oar, made in 1725,
symbol of the Admiralty Court

CCB alone on the porch at Black Point,
circa 1950

St. George's Church

CCB (in the white suit) at City Hall in 1945,
with La Guardia and Eisenhower

17

CCB as Mentor to La Guardia

FIVE MINUTES AFTER midnight tolled the New Year, 1934, La Guardia took his constitutional oath as New York's 103rd mayor.[1] Symbolic of the fresh start that he and his Fusion-Republican reformers offered New York after sixteen years of Tammany corruption, the ceremony was simple, private, and without cost to the almost bankrupt city. At La Guardia's request, it was held in the oak-paneled library of Samuel Seabury's house on East Sixty-third Street, with only a few press and others present. Among the latter were La Guardia's wife, Marie, his barber, Cheech Giordano, and the reform leaders who had helped him to power, Berle, Windels, Seabury, and Burlingham.[2]

The reformers wore evening clothes, black or white tie; La Guardia, with an actor's appreciation of appearance, a business suit—a man of the people, ready for work. And so the morning papers pictured him. Yet he surprised reporters by ending a brief promise to provide honest, nonpartisan government with a paraphrase of an oath from classical Athens. In the afternoon, to close a national radio address, he repeated the oath, and the next morning the *Times* published it in a box on page one: "Oath of the Young Men of Athens" (sworn when, on turning eighteen, they entered the city's program to train Athenian male citizens).

> We will never bring disgrace to this, our city, by any act of dishonesty or cowardice nor ever desert our suffering comrades in the ranks. We will fight for our ideals and sacred things of the city, both alone and with many. We will revere and obey the city's laws and do our best to incite a like respect in those above us who are prone to annul them and set them at naught. We will strive unceasingly to quicken the public sense of civic duty. Thus in all these ways we will transmit this city not only not less but far greater and more beautiful than it was transmitted to us.[3]

Asked why he had chosen this fragment of antiquity, La Guardia replied that he could find nothing "more expressive of our duty, our determination and our steadfastness."[4] Perhaps some in the city, as it struggled with the problems of municipal corruption and economic depression, found the ancient idealism stirring. La Guardia, however, was a complex man and may have had additional reasons for resurrecting the oath. He may have wished to remind his college-educated reform backers that though he lacked a college degree, he was as well educated as they. He may have wished, because most of them (Seabury, Berle, Windels, and Burlingham) had Anglo-Saxon or German backgrounds, to remind them that the Mediterranean people were civilized when the English and German most certainly were not. He was ready to acknowledge their help in his election, yet—lest any mistake—he was his own man.

La Guardia came to power at an extraordinary time in New York's history. Not since the days of Boss Tweed and Boss Croker had the city suffered as much from corruption as it had for the previous eight years under Bosses Olvany and Curry and Mayor Walker. Moreover, by 1934 every third jobholder was out of work, funds for relief were all but exhausted, and as tax receipts declined, the city was fast losing its credit. Its budget was wholly out of balance, and it continually was borrowing from the banks at high interest to stave off bankruptcy, while operating under a bankers' agreement that guaranteed the banks first call on any revenues collected. Chicago had already defaulted on its bonds, and New York was close to doing so. Yet in his campaign La Guardia had promised to cut jobs, save money, and regain the city's credit.[5]

Fulfilling that promise was now more difficult than it might have been because in the three-way election La Guardia had won only 40 percent of the vote, his Fusion-Republican ticket had captured only twenty-five of the ninety-four elective offices at stake, and Tammany still controlled the citywide Board of Aldermen (later the City Council), the Bronx and Manhattan borough presidencies, the New York County district attorney's office, and all other county offices, as well as the appointments of many court clerks and secretaries. Tammany, after previous defeats by reform movements, had always recovered, and now—because of Roosevelt's third-party "spoiler"—was well placed to do so again.

The city's most pressing problem, meanwhile, was its budget and credit. The sums involved were huge. Tammany's proposed budget for 1934 showed expenses totaling $551 million, with revenue short by at least $30 million. In addition, there was always the unexpected: on New Year's Eve it had snowed, costing the city $1 million to clear the streets; and the winter, unhappily, would be unusually severe, with fifty-two inches of snow and an average temperature in February of 11.5 degrees Fahrenheit that hindered melting. Meanwhile, the city faced $500 million in short-term debt, of which some $200 million were revenue bills issued against prospective tax collections.[6]

Only with credit restored would New York be eligible again for grants from the state and federal governments. But reducing expenses, though an economic necessity, was also a political battle, for it meant putting people out of work when there was no unemployment insurance and little money for relief. Further, the mayor's power to terminate a job, or to order a worker onto unpaid, involuntary leave, or even to reduce a salary, was severely restricted by the city's limited grant of power from the state.[7] Similarly cramped was the city's power to raise money through taxes, other than on real estate, and there the limit, as the rising delinquencies signaled, had been reached.

To meet the emergency, La Guardia wanted the state to grant him emergency powers, and on 2 January he presented to the legislature in Albany an "Economy Bill" that for a period of two years would greatly empower the city and its mayor, changing the city's relation to the state.[8] He and Berle had drafted the bill, basing many of its provisions on those of similar emergency powers that President Roosevelt the previous year had sought and received from Congress. But Tammany Democrats combined with Republicans to defeat it in the state legislature, and Governor Lehman, though consulted in advance, had not grasped the extent of the proposed shift in power. In a twelve-page letter he publicly scolded the mayor for seeking "dictatorial powers" and described the bill as "essentially unAmerican."[9]

Reform leaders and much of the public were startled. They had expected the Economy Bill to pass easily. La Guardia and Berle hurried to Albany and, after more consultation with Lehman, redrafted the bill, compromising on many issues. Thrice more the bill, with further compromises, was presented and, despite the governor's support, was defeated. Clearly, the problem lay with the many Democrats in the legislature who continually voted against the bill, and to lessen their opposition La Guardia went to Washington to see Roosevelt, who was sympathetic. Presumably the president thereafter talked bluntly to Farley and Flynn, who handled federal patronage in New York, while he himself lectured several of the Democratic legislative leaders whom Lehman brought down to see him.[10] Early in April, on its fifth presentation and shorn of much of what La Guardia had sought, the bill passed, and was signed. At once the mayor began cutting salaries (including his own) and putting municipal workers who earned more than $1,200 annually on unpaid leaves ranging from a week to a month.[11] Throughout the bill's difficult passage La Guardia had never lost his temper, had shown himself willing to compromise, had cemented his relationship with the governor and the president, and yet had fought on until winning some of what he wanted. His performance rallied newspapers and the public to him.[12]

Yet all these qualities as an executive leader were still only part of what the depressed times required. During the struggle over the Economy Bill, CCB wrote to Felix Frankfurter in England, "The talk about dictatorship is all bunk." The bill included sufficient political and judicial checks. More important, "It remains to be seen whether LaG. has administrative ability. His appointments have been good, but he interferes with his heads [of departments]." Emergency powers alone were not enough. Good administration was also needed, and in that respect La Guardia was sometimes not so strong.[13]

For his corporation counsel (the city's lawyer), he wanted his friend and campaign manager, Paul Windels. The two men were in many ways opposites, for Windels was tall, lean, Germanic, controlled, and somewhat reserved. Each appreciated the other's qualities, and as Windels once noted, "For some curious reason I seemed to have a quieting influence on him, and we got along very well together. He kept his temperamental outbursts pretty much for other people." Yet when offered the post, Windels hesitated and, before accepting, set a condition: "There was to be only one corporation counsel, and that would not be the mayor of the city—that I would have absolute control over my appointments without any interference either from the mayor or political leaders or anybody else." La Guardia thereupon asked "in a rather wistful way" if he could offer an occasional suggestion. Windels agreed to hear a few, but insisted, "I'll have the final word."[14]

Thus, he who knew La Guardia best established his administrative independence before taking his post; others who tried to establish it afterward had trouble. As CCB had told Frankfurter, La Guardia interfered with the heads of departments: "I have braced up one or two of them to stand up to him. That is the only way to deal with him, and he really likes it. He told me that he was going to appoint so-and-so, but a minor official 'must go.' I told him if I were a Commissioner and he told me that, I would go immediately myself. And that particular head stood up and won."[15]

In the corporation counsel's department, Windels created a legal firm as good as any in the country, public or private. At the end of four years, it had recovered for the city from cheaters of all kinds some $50 million, and had prevented new graft and swindles of incalculable amounts.[16] Windels had an easier time than most department heads in part because his staff was relatively small: "I believe I had more appointments to exempt positions [free of civil service rules] than all the rest of the administration put together." (He underestimated the number of such positions, but not his department's high share. "We had over a hundred exempt places . . . superimposed over a Civil Service staff of about one hundred lawyers and a corresponding number of clerks and other types of assistants." In the police, fire, and sanitation departments, "where there were only a *few* exempt persons superimposed over a great mass of Civil Service employees," the commissioner and his few appointed deputies had a harder job changing habits and attitudes.)[17]

Seeking young, competent lawyers to fill his exempt positions, Windels consulted reform leaders as well as friends in private firms. On Seabury's advice, he hired some who had worked on the investigations into municipal corruption; through CCB, who talked with the dean of Columbia Law School, he drew some top recent graduates; and from private firms he lured several who wanted public service experience. His recruiting was made easier by the growing enthusiasm for La Guardia and the nationwide dearth of jobs. Finding work, any work, was hard, and what Windels had to offer was exciting.[18]

On going through the files, Windels and his staff found "an enormous number of cases buried." Actions of all kinds, from questions of franchise to suits by the city against others, had been allowed to lapse, and it was clear that during Walker's mayoralty the exempt employees had spent much of their time in private practice, violating the city charter. Windels reorganized the department so that every important position, including his own, was covered by a second person; if the first was absent, the second could take over, and the case could proceed without interruption.[19]

In addition, his deputies reported that many of the corporation counsel's offices were filthy, and Windels organized a thorough scrubbing. After the mop-up, he noted, morale of the "nonexempt" civil service employees rose, and he found most of them "hard-working, sincere, honest people who resented the neglect of prior years." By midsummer the department was operating efficiently, and Windels took a short vacation. While he was gone, La Guardia had "some personal dealings with members of the staff, and developed his usual irritations and impatience. When I came back, he had a long list of assistants he wanted dismissed. I laughed and told him to forget it. For a while there was a little strain between us, but that was soon forgotten."[20]

With Windels so strong, CCB uncharacteristically all but ignored the corporation counsel's department and focused his attentions elsewhere, for example, the Municipal Civil Service Commission, which Tammany had corrupted. As a young lawyer he had known George William Curtis, a national leader for civil service reform, had joined the Civil Service Reform Association, and could remember the day in 1883 when New York and Brooklyn became the first cities in the country to adopt any regulations. Now, fifty years later, he was a vice president of the association (led by his friend Richard Welling)[21] and, like most reformers, was eager to revitalize the city's civil service.

When La Guardia took office, under the commission's regulations city posts were divided into four groups: (1) exempt (the mayor could appoint free of the rules); (2) competitive (applicants had to take a competitive examination); (3) noncompetitive (applicants had only to pass a qualifying test); and (4) labor (selection by order of application). Tammany continually had bent these rules to reward its Democratic faithful, creating exempt posts, failing to publicize the place and date of competitive examinations, giving insiders advance information about them, and often testing by requiring an essay which a marker could grade as he wished. In the Sanitation Department some 12,000 workers were hired without any examination; the city-operated IND subway similarly employed some 6,000 outside the rules; and the city's relief programs had 10,000 exempted from the rules on the grounds that they were only temporary help. In sum, 45.5 percent of the city's workforce held jobs without competitive examination. Moreover, salaries for similar jobs often differed depending on the holders' ties to political clubs.[22]

La Guardia appointed as his commissioner of civil service James E. Finegan, a Brooklyn lawyer and a founder of the City Fusion Party. CCB, in a letter to La Guardia in which he numbered the subjects discussed, turned in "4" to civil service: "Now that the Honorable Jim is president, I hope you will be able to get him a couple of side partners [deputy commissioners] to tell him what's what, for it is essential that the Municipal Service Commission should be first chop and watch the departments like a lynx." Three days later CCB was back at it: "I think this is a good time for you to instruct your Commissioners as to the enforcement of the Civil Service Law, and particularly direct them to select the man at the top of the list in every case except where good reason to the contrary is shown. The best Civil Service reform Mayor we have ever had was not Low or Mitchel, but Gaynor, who insisted on this principle, as did Woodrow Wilson and Theodore Roosevelt."[23]

La Guardia was as eager as CCB for this particular reform, for without it the city's workforce would continue to be Tammany-controlled. And though La Guardia little resembled a wiry, watchful lynx, he prowled often through Finegan's department, frequently berating him for being slow to act. Yet Finegan and his deputies were effective. In 1933, Tammany's last year of control, only 6,327 people had bothered to apply for civil service positions; in 1939 the number was 252,084. In the same period, exempt positions almost halved, dropping from 853 to 443, and the percentage of city employees holding jobs by competitive examination rose from 54.5 to 74.3, while the percentage of the noncompetitive group dropped from 17 to 14. In addition, the tests were made more searching, and their marking fairer. As the quality of the employees rose, the city was better served. And as the hold of Irish-dominated Tammany on city jobs weakened, the workforce became more representative, reflecting the shift in population toward Jews, Italians, and Negroes.[24]

In 1905 state senator George Washington Plunkitt, Tammany's sage and a Manhattan district leader, had warned the Democratic Party against what he called "this college professor's nightmare . . . civil service reform!" Mocking the reformers of the day, who had just suffered a defeat, Plunkitt asked, "Could a search party find R.W.G. Welling? . . . The fact is that a reformer can't last in politics . . . I see a vision. I see the civil service monster lyin' flat on the ground. I see the Democratic party standin' over it with a foot on its neck and wearin' the crown of victory." But in 1934 Plunkitt was dead, Welling was leading the Civil Service Reform Association, and La Guardia's Civil Service Commission had a foot on Tammany's neck.[25]

All in all, the improvement in civil service was more of a revolution than a reform. La Guardia and his administration had gone far to erase what Lord Bryce had called the great failure in America, the "spoils system" that more than any other factor had corrupted its municipal governments.[26]

Ironically, in an area of city government always close to his heart, the courts and their judges, CCB soon discovered that if he had a suggestion for La Guardia he must introduce it with care. La Guardia, though himself a lawyer and with friends in the profession, usually spoke ill of it and especially of judges. In 1931, while a congressman, and interviewing a young man who wanted to join his legal staff, La Guardia asked, "Why do you want to become a lawyer?" The fellow replied, "Because I believe in justice." Whereupon La Guardia shouted: "To live off the people? To take their earnings? When a decent world comes, there won't *be* any lawyers."

Sometime later, in his mercurial way, he was laughing, and hired the man. But he seldom gave bar associations any credit for their efforts to clean house, and he frequently said the caliber of judges in New York was poor, not only in legal learning but in character: the "scholarly, upright, hard-working, fair; they are the exceptions."[27]

CCB's usual manner for discussing judicial candidates was blunt and purposeful. In December 1933, just before La Guardia took office, he was shocked by a *Times* report that Governor Lehman might appoint John P. O'Brien, the Tammany candidate who had lost the election, to a position on one of the state or city courts. Instantly writing to the governor, CCB cited one of O'Brien's decisions as proof of why "it would be far better for him to enjoy his pension of $14,000 than resume judicial duties." He urged, instead, a search for a "real lawyer." Whether or not Lehman considered the advice, he did not return O'Brien to the bench.[28] With La Guardia, CCB at times was equally direct. "I heard a rumor . . . of your appointing Gus Hartman to the Domestic Relations Court. I denied it . . . Yours, with a passion against Gus' service." But often, it seems likely, such a comment followed or perhaps initiated a discussion in the mayor's limousine. La Guardia, who after taking office continued to live in his apartment on the edge of Harlem, began a custom of stopping in the mornings at 860 Park Avenue to pick up CCB, and then on the way downtown the two would discuss the issues of the moment. Or sometimes in the late afternoon CCB would stop at City Hall and urge the mayor to quit for the day, and they would drive uptown. No record of their talks survive, beyond an occasional reference surfacing in a letter, but in Hartman's case CCB most likely gave reasons for his "passion against Gus" in the limousine, and was persuasive, for the man was not appointed.[29]

One day early on with the mayor, CCB was sharply rebuffed. The men were sitting in La Guardia's backyard in Westport with Windels and his son, a La Guardia favorite, and CCB was urging the mayor to heed the recommendations of the bar association's Judiciary Committee. La Guardia listened attentively and then broke a long silence, sighing dramatically: "Charles, Charles, Charles. I know all about your committee. I've done some investigation. One member is over eighty and the others all want to be judges." His tone signaled finality, and even young Windels caught the sudden tension.[30]

CCB, that afternoon, chose not to argue with La Guardia. Instead, he changed tactics. If La Guardia objected to the use of the bar association as a tool to improve the bench, then CCB would not use it. And in future CCB almost never mentioned the Association or its committees to

La Guardia, typically launching suggestions as personal observations, couched in a playful style to which La Guardia happily responded.

January 21, 1936

Dear C.C.

Thanks for paragraph 1 of your letter of January 20th. I did invite you [to a public ceremony] and asked if you would go with us, but as usual you scorned and pooh-poohed and I didn't say anything more. I am always so frightened to even make a suggestion and everything you say goes with us, therefore

2. I am sorry I cannot appoint the gentleman you suggest.

3. I am sorry I have practically made up my mind on appointments to the bench.

I am, sir,

Your obedient servant,
Fiorello[31]

Despite or because of the playfulness, much was accomplished. When La Guardia had to appoint a presiding justice for the municipal courts, he got a long note from CCB (again perhaps following a discussion in the limousine), warning against promoting "a Tammany-bred Municipal Court Justice . . . or any protégé of any of the county leaders." A presiding justice should have administrative ability to deal with court calendars, firmness and tact in dealing with other judges, and a determination to place the judges' clerks and their assistants under competitive civil service. Advising against one candidate who seemed too close to his political leader, CCB suggested: "Your best bet is [Pelham St. George] Bissell. You must know him. Why not ask K. [Kenneth] Dayton to report on his fitness." Dayton, a lawyer working for the city, was not a bar association figure, and La Guardia, in this instance, followed CCB's advice and appointed Bissell.[32]

CCB was not against politics in a judicial candidate's background. As he once wrote to Roy Howard of the *World-Telegram*, "Politics is a good school. Many of our best judges were politicians before they went on the bench. The important thing is that they should discard politics [on the bench]." Yet even at the Court of Appeals, CCB thought the Tammany-schooled judges "inclined to favor the Organization on a close question of civil service positions." He noted that "when La G. cut the salaries of clerks of the Municipal Court from $3,200 to $1,200 at one fell swoop, four of the judges [a majority] held, wrongly as I think, that the budget could not be altered." Besides competence, CCB wanted character.[33] And here La Guardia agreed, believing that "the personality of the judge has the greatest effect on the course of justice." As a congressman, he had brought impeachment proceedings against several federal judges who, he felt, "were neither upright nor scholarly" and "bore no resemblance to Caesar's wife," and as mayor he frequently voiced his prejudice against judges. But as CCB observed to Howard, "La G.'s ferocious attacks on the Courts are an obstacle, not a help, to his ends. I have suggested to him that for a change he might praise *one* judge *once*—treat them as he does the police—some crooks and rascals but on the whole a fine body of men etc. etc." But he could not soften La Guardia's antijudicial bias.[34]

Similarly, he could not persuade the mayor to stop condoning inappropriate public comments by the police commissioner, Lewis Valentine. An "honest cop" from within the department who did much to improve it, Valentine was prone to tough talk to his men or to reporters—such as saying that the gangster "Dutch" Schulz should be brought into the police station "in a box," or suggesting that "roughing up" suspects was in order: "There will be promotions for the men who kick those gorillas around and bring them in." His views made headlines, and probably most New Yorkers agreed with them, for in the previous three months the department had six men killed on duty. Valentine's most famous statement echoed across the country in November 1934. An unidentified gangster had shot a cop fatally, and the commissioner, after a visit to the dying man in the hospital, returned to the station to a lineup of suspects. Among them was a young thug who had been arrested for the murder of a garageman. He wore a Chesterfield coat, a pearl gray fedora, and a smirk on his face. His record showed eighteen arrests but no convictions. Valentine, turning to the police beside him, barked: "When you meet such men draw quickly and shoot accurately. Don't be afraid to muss them up . . . Blood should be smeared all over that velvet collar." Interviewed later in the day by excited reporters, he announced: "It will be the crooks who are carried out in boxes, not the cops . . . With the criminals, racketeers and gangsters, the sky is the limit."[35]

Many cheered such talk, but others, editorial writers and even some police commissioners, publicly protested. CCB promptly wrote the mayor a two-sentence note: "I really think Valentine's brutal and foolish remarks call for some statement by you in the nature of reproof. I did not think he was capable of such an offensive outburst."[36] La Guardia replied that same day with a three-page letter, insisting, "The Commissioner's remarks were entirely directed to the officers defending themselves." As he recounted the history of police deaths in the last three months, his emotion colored every sentence: He was entirely with the police, and CCB should calm down.[37]

CCB responded softly: "I don't suggest that you should let down V. or publicly reprove him, but with your fine *Nordic* hand at an appropriate time you could divorce yourself from the mussing up doctrine, dwelling on the provocation that led V. to his extreme statement . . . I greatly hope that you will have a little fatherly talk with V."[38] But no such talk took place, nor did any such statement appear. CCB tried once again, still more softly, and then quit. On police behavior, just as with the bar association's recommendations on judicial appointments, La Guardia had his view and was not to be moved. CCB turned to other subjects where he might have more influence.[39]

One matter on which CCB and the mayor easily agreed was the importance of giving all ethnic groups some representation in the city's government. "I was amused," CCB wrote to the mayor in February 1934, "at the religious character of the Housing Authority." La Guardia had appointed to it a Jewish Socialist, a Catholic priest, a woman social reformer, a housing reform evangelist, and as chairman, a Protestant of English-American background.[40] In the same vein, in April 1935, he wrote La Guardia about a judicial appointment, "If you want a Jew, why not Irving Ben Cooper? . . . If you want a R.C. . . . I know one who has been recommended [to me] by Monsignor Keegan and others."[41] Two months later La Guardia privately consulted Francis Martin, the presiding justice of the state Supreme Court in Manhattan, about the possibility of appointing a Negro, the first, to the Magistrates' Court. Evidently Judge Martin advised against it, but CCB reported:

> I tried the question on several Federal Judges today, including Judge Francis G. Caffey, a real Southerner from Alabama, and not one of them thought there was the slightest reason why a Negro should not be appointed. Delany was Assistant U.S. Attorney and appeared before these judges often. Rivers they also know and think very highly of. Paige none of them knew. Delany and Rivers are members of the Bar Association.
>
> Some time you may learn that Martin, P.J. [presiding justice], is usually wrong about everything.[42]

Perhaps because advice was conflicting, La Guardia did nothing. Then, the following April, the subject revived, and CCB wrote again:

> If you really think that Frank Martin has more sense than I have, O.K. by me, but I really think a Negro magistrate would be another sprig of

laurel in your administrative wreath, and I don't care many damns
whether it is Rivers or Paige. Rivers is the better lawyer, and your objection that his brother is a district leader and a mere cloak for him does
not move me, for it is an article of my creed that a judge is a great deal
better for having had political experience, provided he will cast away
politics when he climbs or is kicked onto the bench.

I have a new Aryan for you—James M. Gifford, a grand young fellow,
assistant to the Dean of Columbia Law School, and if you would like to
see him I'll bring him down and you'll probably appoint him on the spot.

Also I have a fine bunch of Semites for you.

But I forgot—you want a Lutheran, don't you?[43]

This time La Guardia made the appointment, and on 2 September 1936
he swore in Myles A. Paige as one of the city's forty-nine magistrates, the
first Negro to sit on that court, which more than any other deals directly
with the public. At the ceremony Paige, six-foot-two and a former football
star, though positioned by the photographers one step below the mayor,
still towered over him. A Roman Catholic, Paige had gone to Harvard and
put himself through Columbia Law School while working as a Pullman
porter, and since had done a great deal of church and community work. In
1940 the mayor promoted him to the city's three-man court of "super
magistrates," the Court of Special Sessions.

Three years later La Guardia appointed Francis E. Rivers to the City
Court, the first Negro to sit there; and later still Rivers was advanced to
the New York Supreme Court, at the time the highest judicial position
attained by a Negro jurist. Long before then, in 1929, he had become the
first Negro member of the bar association, where in 1963, after retiring
from the bench, he served as chairman of the Association's Special Committee for Civil Rights Under Law.[44]

La Guardia was not the first New York mayor to appoint Negroes to
the bench. Walker in 1930 had appointed Charles E. Toney to the Municipal Court, where he served for twenty years, and the next year James S.
Watson to the same court, but La Guardia's choices were perhaps based
more on merit and less on clubhouse politics than Walker's, and for them
historians have awarded him a "sprig of laurel."[45]

In appointing women La Guardia did as well, though he almost lost one
of the best in a two-sided spat of temper. She was Justine Wise Polier, the
daughter of the city's well-known Rabbi Stephen A. Wise, and La Guardia
started her with a three-month temporary appointment to the Domestic Relations Court (today the Family Court). She was knowledgeable and

particularly wise about relief, juveniles, and the courts, but from La Guardia's point of view she one day spoke out of turn. She had been outraged by harsh statements about the unemployed made by Hugh Johnson, who in the summer of 1935 was in charge of the city's relief programs. Johnson, La Guardia's personal choice, was a rough-hewn, hard-drinking retired general and former director of the federal National Recovery Administration program. He was eager in his new job to bring order out of what he saw as chaos, and in his style began with flamboyant overstatement.

Judge Polier wrote directly to him, saying he didn't have his facts right, didn't know what he was talking about, and shouldn't talk in such a way when he was new to the job. She sent a copy of her letter to La Guardia, who immediately phoned her. He wished to treat Johnson gently, he said, in order not to antagonize the great man's connections in Washington, whence came funds for the city's relief programs. He told her that he had called Johnson to ask him to return the letter unopened, and now he wanted Judge Polier to call Johnson to confirm that such was her wish. She refused. He threatened not to reappoint her to the court. She said that was up to him. He said he would have her fired. She said that was up to the presiding judge. After more threats and obstinacy, he hung up. Their quarrel did not make the papers, but at the end of her three-month term he did not reappoint her.

Polier, now unemployed, went to visit her daughter in the Adirondacks. As soon as she was back in New York, her phone rang. It was CCB: "What's this trouble between you and La Guardia?"

Surprised, she asked, "What do you know about it?"

"Well, he came up to visit me [at Black Point] this past weekend and Felix Frankfurter was there with me. La Guardia asked our advice for a member of the court, and I said, 'What do you mean, you're not going to reappoint Justine?' And La Guardia said, 'I've got to have discipline in the judiciary.'"

The remark had ignited both CCB and Frankfurter, and they had scorched the mayor. "Now," said CCB, "I think he's sorry that he got out on a limb, and he doesn't know how to get back in, or he wouldn't have come up. Will you call him, speak to him?"

"No. I made my decision, he's got to make his."

Another mediator might have stopped there, but CCB kept on. He asked if she had liked the work, and she replied, "I find it fascinating, but I find this intolerable." Ultimately he got her to say: "There's only one thing I think I can do honorably. I'm willing to write him, if you ask me to, saying that you called me and asked me to, and if he wants to speak to me I'd be glad to see him." And on CCB's urging, she sent a longhand note to the mayor.

The next morning Polier's phone rang. La Guardia: "Justine, how are you?" He was at home, having his hair cut, and he invited her over for a chat. He did not dispute the truth of what she had written to Johnson, but when she said she had done only what he should have done and perhaps for political reasons could not, he said: "That's just like you Wises. You do whatever you think is right and you don't give a damn about the consequences." Yet they parted in agreement. She was sworn in the next morning in his apartment, without publicity (about which she cared not at all), and they breakfasted together on "scrambled eggs."[46]

CCB did other good deeds for the Domestic Relations Court. In 1937 he became chairman of a public relations committee for it and advised the mayor on "the very real need of additional probation officers and professional and clerical assistants in the Court." But possibly nothing was more important than saving for the court, and for the city's people, Judge Polier, who became in thirty-eight years on the bench a national authority on juvenile justice and children's rights.[47]

One serious problem that plagued La Guardia during his first term, serious because it brought him into conflict with President Roosevelt, was the construction of a multiple bridge across the Harlem and East Rivers that would connect Queens, the Bronx, and Manhattan. For twenty-five years only four vehicular bridges spanned the East River, joining Manhattan and Long Island, with the two newest, the Williamsburg and Queensboro, both opened in 1909. And while plans for a fifth, triborough bridge across the river's northward Hell Gate channel* were drawn up in 1910, World War I had intervened; when construction finally began in 1929, the Depression soon stopped it. Thus for a generation of New Yorkers only three bridges had tied Manhattan to Brooklyn (the Williamsburg, Manhattan, and Brooklyn) and only one to Queens. These four, all de-

---

*According to *A Maritime History of New York* compiled by the WPA writers' program, 204–5: "The channel was the nightmare of Long Island Sound navigators until the middle 1870s. The name Hell Gate is a corruption of the Dutch *Hellegat*, meaning 'entrance to hell.' It was a fitting name to give a channel in which so many vessels were wrecked or seriously damaged . . . Losses continued chiefly because of Hallett's Point, a jagged rock seven hundred feet wide extending three hundred feet into the channel, which created a strong current tending to throw ships off their course. In 1869 Congress appropriated funds to begin the work of blasting . . . and Hallett's Point disappeared at a total cost of less than two million dollars."

signed for horse-drawn carriages, could not meet the needs of an automobile age, let alone the city's expanding population, particularly in Queens.

Among La Guardia and his close advisers, only CCB had known the East River (strictly speaking, not a river but a sixteen-mile tidal strait connecting New York Harbor and Long Island Sound) before the Brooklyn Bridge became, in 1883, the first to span it. La Guardia, Windels, and Berle knew their city's history, and they liked to draw examples from its events and personalities, but CCB—seventy-six in 1934—had an advantage: he could recall, with personal anecdotes, a New York that most others had never seen: with wood-hulled whalers docked along South Street, Herman Melville as a customs inspector, and the Black Ball Line sailing to Liverpool.[48]

One day in 1937, in his capacity as president of the Welfare Council, CCB spoke at the laying of the cornerstone for a new hospital for the chronically ill on Welfare Island (today Roosevelt Island). Long and narrow, Welfare Island (until 1921 named Blackwell's and after 1971, Roosevelt Island), lies in the midst of the East River, stretching roughly a mile and three-quarters, from Manhattan's Fiftieth to Eighty-sixth Streets. Bought from the Indians in 1637 by Washington Irving's neckless, potbellied, pipe-smoking Governor Wouter Van Twiller,[49] who used it to grow tobacco and graze cattle, it had passed into other hands, become a pasture for hogs, and then, for more than a century, was farmed by members of the Blackwell family until a descendant sold it to the city in 1828 for $32,500. By 1860 the city had built on it a prison, an almshouse for the poor, a workhouse for petty offenders, a lunatic asylum, a charity hospital, and a smallpox hospital. CCB could remember those days:

> My recollection of Blackwell's Island goes back to the early 1870s when a cousin of mine was the chief medical officer of Charity Hospital on the Island. As small boys my brother and I visited our cousin there. We went to the foot of 50th Street, I think it was, and waved a handkerchief and a rowboat put out from the Island manned by prisoners of the penitentiary in stripes, the officer in charge at the stern with a gun. The hospital employees were prisoners from the Work House. I can smell that hospital now.[50]

Between 1870 and 1909 the city added more buildings for hospitals, prisons, and staff, and by 1909, when the island became the mid-river crutch for the Queensboro Bridge, it was becoming urban.* By 1935, when the last prisoners were shifted upriver to Riker's Island and the hospitals and apartment houses expanded further, little bucolic beauty remained.

When La Guardia took office, the four East River bridges were nagging symbols of how badly Tammany had served the city. From 1910 to 1930 the city population had grown from 4.7 million to 6.9 million, with most of the increase in the Bronx, Queens, and Brooklyn; and by 1931 more than 800,000 cars clogged the city daily, trying to move on streets not greatly changed since plotted by the Commissioners' or Grid Plan of 1811.[51] By 1933, on an average weekday, some 240,000 cars and trucks used the four bridges. On the Queensboro, which then carried more cars than any bridge in the country, the pavement was slippery, with narrow lanes unmarked by painted lines. Bumping and scraping accidents were common, and a police study in 1931 reported that during rush hours the average time for crossing the bridge's longest span, 1,182 feet, was forty-three minutes. One reason cars moved across the Queensboro at less than a half-a-mile an hour was the lack of ramps or adequate approaches: traffic was spewed at either end onto a city street, where traffic lights regularly stopped all movement. In an effort to speed the crossing, Mayor Walker's administration in 1931 had built two new lanes on the bridge's upper level, but the design was faulty. Heavy curbstones made the lanes too narrow for cars, and the lanes were closed while the curbs were chipped away—a project that took three years.[52]

On 25 October 1929, Mayor Walker had broken ground for the Triborough Bridge first proposed in 1910, but the ceremony took place the day after the stock market began its crash, and the bridge's future was soon in doubt. The city's initial allocation of $5.4 million was largely consumed by condemnation awards and counsel fees, many swollen by Tammany's graft. And before work stopped the next year, only seventeen concrete piers, intended to carry the bridge's central span across Ward's Island in

---

*The Queensboro Bridge is the only one not built in the suspension style. Instead, it is a cantilever of steel a mile and a half long, carrying two levels for traffic (including rails for a subway), of which the lower level is 135 feet above the river. As the bridge crosses Roosevelt (Welfare) Island, it rests on a ten-story concrete building that has elevators to take cars and people down to the island. This multipurpose bridge looks awkward and angular, and it looms over the island and buildings, casting down noise, dirt, and shadow. A nonvehicular, four-track railroad bridge crosses the East River at Hell Gate, joining Queens to the Bronx. When the Pennsylvania Railroad completed it in 1917, it was the longest of its kind (steel arch) in the world and beautiful.

the East River, had been completed—each forty feet thick, eighty feet long, and more than a hundred feet high. But even these highly visible monuments failed to suggest how bad was the design and planning of the Tammany-dominated Triborough Bridge Authority (created by the legislature a few years before): as on the Quensboro Bridge, the traffic lanes were too narrow for cars, and no provision was made in any of the three boroughs for ramps or approaches.[53]

La Guardia was eager to have Robert Moses, president of the New York State Parks Commission, do for the city what he had done for the state with the public beaches and highways on Long Island and in Westchester County. Moses was difficult, brilliant, devious, and arrogant, and as he accreted power would become more so, but La Guardia wanted his energy and imagination for the city. By state law, however, state officials could not be appointed to city posts, and Moses would not give up his state position; he argued that the development of the car and its highways had blurred the boundaries between city and state. La Guardia, therefore, submitted a bill (drafted by Moses) to the legislature in Albany that would permit dual officeholding in certain circumstances, and would replace the city's five borough Parks Departments (each with a commissioner responsible to the borough president) with a single citywide department run by a commissioner appointed by the mayor. The Tammany-controlled legislature, fearing Moses would dismiss all the political appointees, voted this down, but on resubmission the bill passed, and Governor Lehman signed it on 19 January 1934. That afternoon La Guardia appointed Moses New York City's first commissioner of city parks.

Immediately after taking his oath, Moses fired all the employees in the new consolidated department who held exempt positions—chiefly the five borough parks commissioners, their superintendents, personal secretaries, and stenographers. Almost as fast, his deputies (many of whom he brought with him from his state staff) began to assign lazy workers, who thought they were protected by civil service, to difficult jobs, at inconvenient hours, miles from their homes. Many resigned. Additionally, many more in unprotected "labor" positions—those late for work, slow to work, or unable to work—were fired on the spot. Like Windels, Moses had a department to clean out, and he did it swiftly. His biographer, Robert Caro, states that by spring "seventeen hundred renovation projects had been completed; everything in the parks had been repainted, every lawn reseeded, and every tennis court resurfaced. Miles of walks, bridle paths, and playing surfaces had been refinished. Hundreds of comfort stations, drinking fountains,

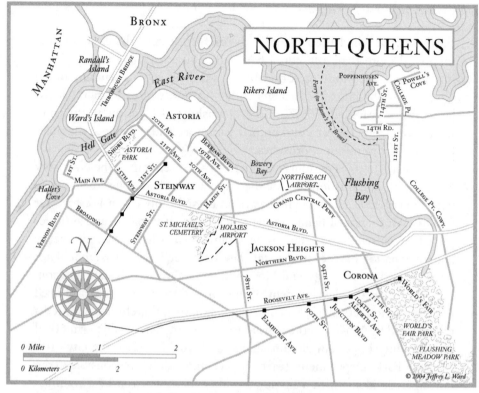

NORTH QUEENS

BRONX

MANHATTAN

Randall's Island

East River

TRIBOROUGH BRIDGE

Rikers Island

Ferry (to Clason's Pt.–Bronx)

POPPENHUSEN AVE.

POWELL'S COVE

COLLEGE PL.

117TH ST.

Ward's Island

Hell Gate

ASTORIA

14TH RD.

121ST ST.

SHORE BLVD.

20TH AVE.

ASTORIA PARK

21ST AVE.

BERRIAN BLVD.

19TH AVE.

Bowery Bay

NORTH BEACH AIRPORT

Flushing Bay

COLLEGE PT. CSWY.

1ST ST.

Hallet's Cove

MAIN AVE.

15TH AVE.

31ST ST.

20TH AVE.

STEINWAY

HAZEN ST.

GRAND CENTRAL PKWY.

VERNON BLVD.

BROADWAY

STEINWAY ST.

ASTORIA BLVD.

ST. MICHAEL'S CEMETERY

HOLMES AIRPORT

ASTORIA BLVD.

N

JACKSON HEIGHTS

NORTHERN BLVD.

78TH ST.

94TH ST.

CORONA

WORLD'S FAIR

ROOSEVELT AVE.

90TH ST.

JUNCTION BLVD.

104TH ST.

ALBERTIS AVE.

111TH ST.

WORLD'S FAIR PARK

ELMHURST AVE.

FLUSHING MEADOW PARK

0 Miles   1   2

0 Kilometers   1   2

© 2004 Jeffrey L. Ward

wading pools and park benches were repaired, thousands of dead trees uprooted, sandboxes refilled and nineteen miles of fences put up." New Yorkers were delighted.[54]

The biggest job Moses tackled was the Triborough Bridge. The plan was to link Manhattan, the Bronx, and Queens at the juncture of the Harlem and East Rivers, making use of relatively cheap land on Randall's and Ward's Islands as stepping-stones for a complex of causeways and four bridges that would make up the whole. When built to redrawn plans, the bridge over the Harlem River linking Manhattan to Randall's Island was the largest vertical lift in the world; the bridge over the Bronx Kill linking the Bronx to Randall's Island was a six-lane triple truss; only slightly less extraordinary was a wide viaduct and bridge on trestles crossing Little Hell Gate, an arm of the East River, and linking Randall's to Ward's Island; finally, most spectacular, across the East River at Hell Gate, was a half-mile suspension bridge using enough cable wire to circle the globe twice and linking Ward's Island to Queens. All in all, the system of sorting roads, ramps, and bridges was a colossal engineering feat worthy of the city that La Guardia, Moses, CCB, and others thought New York ought to be. To bring it into being Moses had assumed yet another position, chairman of the Triborough Bridge Authority, which, like the Parks Department, he wholly reorganized and greatly expanded in purpose and powers.[55]

Finding money for the project was left mostly to Mayor La Guardia, and despite the Depression, largely by straight talk he persuaded his citizens to accept three new taxes, on sales, cigarettes, and public utilities. The Triborough Authority also sold bonds, promising to pay interest and principal out of tolls collected on the bridge after it opened. But the chief source of money for municipal projects like the Triborough complex was Washington, funds allocated by the various federal public works and relief programs.

La Guardia worked hard on his relations with President Roosevelt and secretary of the interior Harold Ickes, chief dispenser of federal funds for public works. As soon as he was sworn in, according to Windels, "he rushed down to Washington and wiggled his way in to FDR. He got chummy with Roosevelt, who was a politician and was always playing along with the good vote-getters. He undoubtedly thought, 'Well, if La Guardia is willing to go along with me, I'll go along with La Guardia.'" And soon the city was receiving big sums from Washington. As Windels noted, "The money would have come just the same if O'Brien or McKee had been elected . . . The point is that we got it and Robert Moses and men of his type spent it, and the city got something permanent for it."[56]

CCB could do little to help La Guardia in raising money, but he did what he could. Writing to the mayor in February 1934, he concluded: "I have just come back from Washington where I had a grand time—tea with Mrs. Roosevelt, a half hour with the President, dinner with Cardozo, another with Brandeis, and a call on Holmes, J., aet. 93 in March." Unstated but understood was that he had spoken well of La Guardia to the president. Roosevelt was after all a former governor of New York, who had practiced law in the city, kept a house there, and was a member of CCB's Century Club; he cared for the city and surely asked about its new mayor, for he was always eager to hear CCB's opinions.[57]

Then, in late February 1934, disaster threatened. Ickes summoned La Guardia to Washington. Though construction on the bridge was progressing well, he demanded that Moses be removed from the Triborough Bridge Authority or the bridge would have no more money from the Public Works Administration. The order, Ickes explained, came from the president. Stunned, La Guardia asked for a few days to see what could be worked out.

Returning to New York, La Guardia in his limousine picked up Windels, and while the two were driven around the city, La Guardia gasped out his predicament: "Jesus Christ, of all the people in the City of New York I had to pick the one man whom Roosevelt won't stand for, and he won't give me any more money unless I get rid of him." According to Windels, La Guardia kept "shaking his fists in the air and shouting, 'Jesus Christ! Seven million people in the city, and I had to pick the one Roosevelt can't stand!'" Windels kept repeating, "You've been elected mayor on the theory that you are going to run an absolutely independent administration . . . You can't start off by knuckling under to outside dictation."[58]

Worse yet, Moses, when consulted, refused to resign. If forced to leave the Triborough Authority, he threatened, he would also resign as commissioner of city parks, and he would go complaining loudly. As La Guardia soon learned, the hostility between Roosevelt and Moses was extraordinarily deep and mutual, rooted in slights and slurs, real or imagined, suffered in their activities in the state government in the early 1920s.[59] La Guardia stalled, assuring Ickes that he was trying to resolve the situation in a mutually agreeable fashion. CCB counseled, "There is only one course to pursue, and that is to stand like a rock against Ickes and all the rest. It is none of their d— business. Apart from that, as a matter of policy, nothing would do your administration more harm than to have one of the very best men in it crowded out. F.D.R. is too smart not to know that R.M. is a dangerous nettle to fool with." The historically minded Berle wired the President, THINK THIS IS ONE OF THE THINGS YOU CANNOT DO UNLESS THERE ARE REASONS OTHER THAN PERSONAL GIVING GROUND FOR PUBLIC DEFENSE. Berle warned Roosevelt that his demands might soon become public, adding: "I hardly know Moses but suggest there might be more real devils to fight. Remember the execution of the Duke [sic] D'Enghien broke Napoleon." Roosevelt wired back a charming evasion, beginning, "I love your suggestion that Bob Moses' real name is the Duc d'Enghien . . ."[60]*

The stalemate continued throughout the spring and early summer, with La Guardia continually promising Ickes that Moses's resignation would soon be in hand. As Windels recalled, "It was, 'Give me this payment and I'll get rid of him next week'—that kind of thing." Then Ickes

---

*The Duc was a Bourbon prince living in Germany, and in 1804 Napoleon, while first consul, had him kidnapped, brought to Vincennes, tried by court-martial on false charges of treason, convicted, shot, and buried in a grave already dug. The incident seemed a gangster's act and haunted Napoleon's regime, turning many against him and causing Talleyrand famously to remark: "It is worse than a crime, it is a blunder."

increased the pressure, threatening to hold up funds not only for the bridge but also for other projects—schools, hospitals, and subways.[61]

Meanwhile, Moses made a mistake. He accepted from a conservative wing of the Republican Party (led by Trubee Davison, a son of the former chief executive of the Morgan bank) the nomination to run for state governor. To many people his act seemed a betrayal, for he had been the protégé of Al Smith and in the 1920s had fought leading conservative Republicans, most famously in creating the public beaches and highways of Long Island. Now, to run against the admired and popular Democratic Governor Lehman, he was allying himself with the most plutocratic and conservative wing of the state's Republican Party.[62]

Almost at once, because of Moses's strange ideas of how to run for elected office, the chief issue became his personality. In a meeting with the Young Republicans, some of whom questioned his new sponsors, Moses ended by calling the young men names. Then he irritated the old conservatives, the press, his former Democratic friends, and even the nominally Republican La Guardia: without consulting the mayor, he announced to the press that he had his endorsement, after which a furious La Guardia would say only that Moses would make a good governor without ever suggesting that he'd make a better one than Lehman. Ignoring his managers' advice that he was not well known outside of New York City and Albany, Moses refused to campaign upstate and ultimately gave only twelve formal speeches. Yet he managed to offend almost everyone. He appalled many Jews by denying his heritage. To any question about it, he would reply, "It's nobody's business what my religion is." And that, according to Windels, "got a lot of people very angry."[63]

Moses also attacked Lehman personally. The governor was "stupid," "weak," a "puppet of Tammany," and even a "liar." That got more people angry. Finally, swept away by his own rhetoric, he accused Lehman of corrupting the state's Court of Claims, though the governor had no part in the court's proceedings or administration. When challenged to cite the court's failings, Moses named a drunken judge who, it turned out, had been dead a year. Lehman was not the only man he attacked: Seabury was a demagogue with "a messianic complex," and Roosevelt's former law partner, Basil O'Connor, a "fixer and a chiseler."[64]

For the most part, Governor Lehman ignored Moses, leaving many of the wildest charges unanswered. Then, as the election neared, Lehman's secretary of state, Edward J. Flynn, Democratic boss of the Bronx, suggested in a speech that Moses was "emotionally unstable" and a "political blatherskite." By then many voters were prepared to believe that Moses, the man who could "get things done," was a monster of ambition and arrogance.[65]

On Election Day the vote was Lehman, 2,201,729, and Moses, 1,393,638. According to Caro, the 35 percent for Moses was "the smallest percentage polled by a gubernatorial candidate of any major party in the 157-year history of New York State." Worse yet for the Republicans, they lost control of both houses in the state legislature for the first time in twenty-one years, as upstate towns and villages that had never done so before now went Democratic. The *Herald Tribune* called the election "the greatest defeat the Republican Party has ever encountered in this state."[66] In Washington, Roosevelt and Ickes smiled, and began again to press La Guardia to force Moses from the Triborough Authority. Surely now he could be ousted.

Throughout November and December, while Ickes refused to advance any money for New York City projects, La Guardia consulted almost daily with Windels and CCB—and continued to stall. Moses, meanwhile, strengthened his refusal to resign by pointing out to La Guardia that under the statute creating the Triborough Authority, he could not be removed except on charges of wrongdoing.

Growing impatient, Roosevelt had Ickes, on the day after Christmas, issue on behalf of the Public Works Administration "Administrative Order Number 129," aimed directly at Moses, both as city parks commissioner and as a commissioner and chief executive of the Triborough Authority: "Hereafter no funds shall be advanced to any authority, board or commission constituting an independent corporation or entity created for a specific project wholly within the confines of a municipality, any of the members of the governing body of which authority, board, or commission holds any public office under said municipality."[67]

The order was not issued publicly, but Ickes sent a copy of it to La Guardia, who discussed it with Moses. On 3 January 1935, La Guardia went to Washington, where he talked to both Ickes and Roosevelt and apparently promised to implement the order promptly. But before he had time to return to New York and fulfill the promise, Moses leaked the order to the press, accompanied by his explanation of it: "There are certain facts which should be known to the public." The order was an attempt to force him from his job. "When the Mayor explained this situation to me I told him that I should be glad to retire from his administration entirely if he wanted me to, but that I would not take a back door out of the Triborough Authority merely because there was pressure to get me out for personal or political reasons."[68] The public, unaware of the enmity between Roosevelt and Moses, assumed the president wanted Moses "out" because in his campaign against Lehman he had criticized Roosevelt's New Deal. Suddenly, from being the town's most unpopular man, Moses was again its hero, and many, even some who disliked him intensely, rallied to his defense.

CCB put some thoughts on the situation into a note to La Guardia:

I spoke to Price, and he has talked with R.M.

1. I don't believe that Ickes or anybody else in Washington can hold up or stop payments on the Triborough Bridge legally. Ask Windels. It has to be finished within a certain time and the contracts are made.

2. This morning it is rumored that the President's message will recommend a reorganization of the P.W.A., which may take it out of Ickes' hands.

For these two reasons, why not stand pat?[69]

A few days later CCB wrote to Frankfurter: "Last night I wired Louis Howe [FDR's friend and adviser] thus: 'Kindly tell Skipper universal sentiment here pro-Moses. Hope he will devise face-saving formula for secretarial retreat from order 129.'" CCB added, "This has been going on for many months and LaG. should have set his back up long ago. I told him last night that if he did not look out the guns now directed against Washington would be turned on him. It is intolerable that personal spite and spleen should affect loans."[70]

Meanwhile, in mid-January 1935, twenty-three civic, social, and commercial groups united in a "pro-Moses" rally, and later asked the nationally known lawyer William D. Guthrie to write a brief on the order's constitutionality. At the same time, in Albany, Herbert Brownell submitted a resolution to the Assembly petitioning the president to withdraw it. Weeks passed, and more and more groups and individuals raised their voices and passed resolutions.[71]

The president and Ickes, aware of public feeling against them, suggested a compromise to La Guardia: that he promise in writing to Ickes not to reappoint Moses to his Triborough post when his term expired on 30 June 1935. This would deprive Moses of any official role in the ceremonies at the bridge's opening, projected for July 1936.

While La Guardia was considering this ploy—and even as the Triborough Authority began to run out of funds—CCB sent him a memorandum "Re Moses":

You know my views on this subject; but I think I will put them in writing as my considered opinion, for my own clarification, if not for yours.

You have told me that you do not think one man should be permitted to obstruct or imperil the relief of hundreds of thousands.

That one man, however, has become a symbol. Washington has taken the position the English Kings took toward the American Colonies. The question, therefore, is whether you, as representative not of New York City alone, but of every municipality and State in the Union, will submit to an unreasonable and tyrannical order from Washington.

If you have already committed yourself expressly or by implication, I think you should make it plain to the Secretary [Ickes] and the President that the sentiment of New York is so strong that as our representative you must respect it, and that unless good reason is shown to the contrary you intend to reappoint Moses as Triborough Bridge Commissioner on the expiration of his term.

I have tested public sentiment at all points possible for me, and it is unanimous. Even those who dislike Moses for his bad manners and rough stuff agree that it would be far better to let the work on the Triborough Bridge cease than to yield to Order 129.[72]

Moses's biographer has called this statement "definitive," and perhaps in a limited sense it is. The ideas were not CCB's alone, however, for several weeks earlier Walter Lippmann had touched on several in his column for the *Herald Tribune.* But Lippmann had not written so succinctly or so directly to La Guardia. If, as one La Guardia biographer has said, one of CCB's important functions for the mayor "was to keep reminding Fiorello of first principles," this is an example.[73]

Public sentiment was, indeed, unanimous, and Roosevelt was barraged with mail and visitors telling him to back down. Joseph Price, in telling friends of his interview with the president, reported that Roosevelt had asked plaintively, "Isn't the President of the United States entitled to one personal grudge?" "No," said Price. Yet the president had seemed to want to be conciliatory. On 22 February CCB wired Roosevelt: "Never have seen such unanimity of feeling. Issue far transcends Moses or New York . . . Way out can and must be found."[74]

Two days later La Guardia met with Roosevelt on a train taking the president from Washington to Boston. To avoid reporters, La Guardia boarded in Philadelphia, carrying with him the draft of a letter to Ickes in which he promised to abide by Order 129 in future but suggested a modification: that he not be asked to apply it retroactively, for there were two appointees affected, Moses and Langdon Post, who was commissioner of housing and head of a recently created New York City Housing Authority. In the draft letter, much was made of Post's predicament, and Moses was relegated to a postscript, where La Guardia added, "I assume the ruling on one [Post] will be applicable to the other [Moses]."[75]

After a few days of delay, the president dictated such a modification of the order for Ickes to sign. Again, much was made of Langdon Post, and Moses was mentioned only in passing: "Since a like situation exists with reference to Mr. Moses, of the Triborough Bridge Authority, this interpretation shall also apply to him." But the newspapers proclaimed a victory for Moses—"Feud Ended, Ickes Pays, Moses Stays," chimed the *Daily News*—and the headline of the *Herald Tribune*, "a resounding" defeat for the president.[76]

In March, CCB wrote a personal letter to the vanquished president, addressing FDR with what he knew would be considered an endearment, and he sent it, with a covering letter, via Marguerite LeHand, one of the president's personal secretaries: "Will you be good enough to hand this to the President at an appropriate time. Don't bother to send me any acknowledgment. I am glad to learn that Colonel Howe is better. Please give him my regards."

March 18, 1935

Dear Governor:

Thank you for your *magna pars* in settling the Ickes-Moses row. R.M.'s tongue is an unruly member. Indeed, he is quite a blackguard, sparing neither friend nor foe. His treatment of Lehman was particularly offensive.

However, he is one of the most efficient persons extant, and in my opinion Order 129 was what B. Franklin would call an *erratum*.

Yours,
C. C. Burlingham[77]

Thus, in some small part, because CCB had reminded Roosevelt as well as La Guardia of "first principles," construction on the bridge could move ahead, and it opened for traffic on 11 July 1936. The average citizen might not see the improvement in the corporation counsel's office, but the Triborough Bridge was a visible triumph of La Guardia's promise to make New York a better city.

18

Harvard and FDR

BECAUSE CCB'S ROLE in fighting Tammany was much noted in New York and New England newspapers, colleges and universities in the Northeast began to give him honorary degrees, their citations stressing his work as a private citizen for the public good. The first to celebrate him in this fashion was Williams College, in 1931.[1] Although CCB had no formal connection to it, he had acquaintances in Williamstown through his sister-in-law Grace Taylor, a professor's widow living there with her children, and a good friend in Dr. Albert H. Licklider, a professor of English literature he sometimes joined at the theater in New York and to whom he wrote chatty letters about plays seen. At commencement that June, he felt among friends.[2]

Invited to speak, he touched briefly on New York's "lurid" corruptions and Judge Seabury's investigations, stressing that even these would achieve little if the public did not maintain its interest in civic affairs. On that point he quoted the contemporary Greek scholar Alfred Zimmern: "The state is in fact as the Greeks call it τὸ κοινόν, the common interest, or as the Romans said, 'Res-publica,' everybody's business." And noting that Williams had many students from New York, he asked, "Can we count on them to be interested in their city and make its affairs their business? If we can, they may leaven the lump, destroy the lions, yes, the tigers in their path, remove mountains—do all these things, however mixed the metaphors may be."

Still, the job would be difficult.

We cannot hope to stir the mass of the citizens even to a desire for good government; they are too much occupied with their own affairs. We should seek to reach the intelligent minority and secure a majority of that minority. Even a democracy is ruled by minorities. I have been speaking of municipal government, where America seems weakest, but what I have said applies in greater or less degree to State and National government.

He quoted Edmund Burke on the importance of participation in politics: "Public life is a situation of power and energy; he trespasses against his duty who sleeps upon his watch, as well as he that goes over to the enemy." And he followed with a remark of Dr. Samuel Johnson on youth: "Sir, young men have more virtue than old men; they have more generous sentiments in every respect. I love the young dogs of this age; they have more wit and humor and knowledge of life than we had." Finally, after flattering his audience, he warned them with an adaptation of St. Paul's letter to the Ephesians, 6:13, that to meet the corruption of the cities, "youth must put on the whole armor of God that it may be able to withstand in the evil day, and having done all, to stand."

The occasion was not one of great moment, but the speech was well fashioned to it—some personal thoughts on an important subject embroidered with a little Latin, a little Greek, Burke, Johnson, and indirectly a little Phillips Brooks, all delivered in five minutes.[3]

Two years later he was similarly honored by Columbia but he did not speak at the commencement, probably to his relief. In the previous four years, while leading a reorganization of the Law School Alumni Association, of which he was now president, he had spoken often—only eight months earlier, at a ceremony commemorating Theodore W. Dwight, the law school's founder.[4] And at Harvard in 1934 he was one of nine honored, and his citation, composed in Latin by President James B. Conant, referred to him as "a distinguished champion of good government, who for more than 50 years has used his talent for the benefit of his fellow citizens."[5] Writing gratefully to Conant the following week, CCB congratulated him on the concision of his Latin and closed with a characteristic postscript:

As you are a man of science and not a lawyer, may I be so bold as to say that there is a word which we lawyers use very often and not all of us know how to pronounce, but I believe there is only one correct pronunciation of the word and that is to put the accent on the penultimate—inquiry. I said to C.F.A. [Charles Francis Adams], "Tell the President at an opportune occasion the way that word should be pronounced." His characteristic reply was, "Do it yourself," and I am doing it.[6]

Conant, perhaps pleased that his Latin had drawn praise, promptly replied, noting about the pronunciation of "inquiry" that "I shall try to become a lawyer in this respect if in no other!" With many people Conant had a reputation for coldness, but from this time forward, despite their difference in age, his relations with CCB were sufficiently warm to help them both in a few years through a far more difficult commencement.[7]

CCB's allegiance to Harvard had been tepid as an undergraduate and cool as a young lawyer, when he had skipped all class reunions. But it had warmed as his sons, Charles and Robert, had entered the college, and in 1904, when Charles was at the college, CCB had gone to Cambridge for his twenty-fifth reunion. He was not a class officer, was not asked to speak until his thirtieth reunion, and not until the class report for 1914 did he bother to write an account of himself in any detail. That same year, he appears for the first time in the history of the Harvard Club of New York City, which he had joined as early as 1885 but little frequented, suddenly at the center of an artistic imbroglio that some members felt was of his own making.[8]

The club had on its walls portraits of many of its presidents by distinguished artists, including a magnificent full-length pair by John Singer Sargent of the lawyers Joseph Hodges Choate and James C. Carter. To these, CCB had suggested another be added, smaller and seated, of ex-judge Peter B. Olney, club president in 1911–13. Though not so great as Choate or Carter, Olney had an admirable career, particularly in bankruptcy actions, and in addition he looked and behaved judgmental, with craggy brows, hard blue eyes, a harsh voice, and a temperament accustomed to wielding the gavel. CCB persuaded him to the idea and recommended as the artist George Bellows, whose paintings and drawings, particularly of prizefighters, recently had won praise. The club's Art Committee agreed to the plan, and the artist and the judge met for sittings.

Bellows's first attempt pleased neither the artist nor the judge, nor the few others who saw it, and was withdrawn. A second effort, displayed in the club's main hall, also displeased most people. Where Sargent had painted luminous faces against somber black and brown clothing and background, Bellows's colors throughout were brighter, and as the only portrait of its kind in the vast, dimly lit hall, it seemed to most members not the beacon of a brilliant new style in portraiture but merely a badly painted picture. CCB was told by the club's secretary to tell Bellows it was rejected.

"There's an awful how-de-do," CCB wrote to Bellows. Olney "has now come out in the open and said he cannot bear to have it hung. Of course those chaps up at the Club don't know the difference between a portrait and a Uneeda Biscuit advertisement." Later he wrote, "As was said by a famous lady to a strong man of old, 'The Philistines be upon thee' . . .

Meanwhile, I think the portrait had better go back to your studio." He proposed to pay the artist's fee himself. Bellows refused the offer but wrote to the club secretary proposing to settle for $750, half the fee, if "allowed to retain the painting." In the end, the club paid him nothing, but he had the portrait, which he showed many times.

Meanwhile, the club, committed to Olney, hired Ellen Emmet Rand, whose portrait is not very different from Bellows's except in its more conventional dark coloring. She presents a strong-featured mustached Olney peering from under bushy brows as if into some legal tangle. With Bellows, he is more the personification of Old Testament justice. The pose is stiffer, and the well-modeled face has a slightly withdrawn quality, suggesting perhaps a touch of fanaticism. Olney and his generation preferred the Rand; club members today might think the Bellows more interesting.

The Harvard Club's building, at 27 West Forty-fourth Street, was almost directly across from the bar association building at No. 36, and so lawyers have often used its private dining rooms for meetings, and in the 1920s, as CCB's activities at the bar association increased, he was also in and out of the Harvard Club far more often and began to attend class and university functions there. In his fiftieth class report (1929), he wrote about his activities in detail, mocking their importance with a quip: "At last I've gone to Bachrach's [photographer]. Now, my next duty is to write the supplement to my autobiography. How much better to write the biography of my auto!"[9] Five years later the university gave him an honorary degree, and in October he was elected president of the Harvard Alumni Association.[10]

The association, a corporate entity, had a permanent office at the university, a full-time paid general secretary to do its president's bidding, and a *Bulletin*, published weekly during the academic year that went to all 65,000 university graduates. Its president's most visible function, however, was to preside at the annual general alumni meeting on commencement afternoon.

In those years, Commencement Day was divided in two. In the morning were academic exercises, by ancient tradition opened by the sheriff of Middlesex County, in full regalia, advancing to the front of the platform, thumping three times with his sword in its scabbard, and commanding, "The meeting will be in order."[11] In the afternoon, after gala luncheons, the alumni, arranged by class in order of seniority and led by a chief marshal selected from the twenty-fifth reunion class, marched from Harvard Yard to the adjacent Sever Quadrangle, where, in an area capable of seating 15,000, the assembly was addressed by the governor of the Commonwealth, the president of the university, and three or four of the honorary degree recipients. "As the presiding officer," the alumni association's general secretary informed CCB, "you introduce the speakers and lead off with a comparatively short address."[12]

The alumni president also was expected to attend dinners throughout the winter at Harvard Clubs in New York, Chicago, and other cities, all formal occasions at which he had to speak, and to write explanatory letters for alumni election to various posts such as the overseers, marshals, alumni offices, and the Harvard Fund Council. He could make much or little of the job, but in case he took it lightly, the association provided an efficient secretary.

In the spring of 1935, CCB's preparations for Harvard's commencement on 20 June went easily until the last eight weeks. That spring the university planned to award college degrees to 679 (CCB's class had numbered only 199) and honorary degrees to twelve, who included such notables as Albert Einstein, Thomas Mann, William Allan Neilson (president of Smith College), and Henry A. Wallace (secretary of agriculture). The question for CCB was which of the twelve to ask to speak. The decision was eased by Harvard's practice in these years of not revealing the recipients' names to the public until Commencement Day morning—indeed, even the recipients weren't told of their selection until mid-May. Hence CCB could reflect and choose in private.

Nevertheless, there were problems. Of the twelve, the two best known, Einstein and Mann, both spoke English with strong German accents. Einstein, at the Institute for Advanced Study in Princeton, perhaps was familiar with Harvard's procedure, but Mann was not; he wrote from Zurich directly to Conant asking if he was to speak. If so, he said, he would talk on Goethe, preferring to speak in German, though if necessary he could manage English. Conant's secretary, consulting CCB, was told: "I don't think we want any speeches in German or broken English at the alumni meeting, and to invite Mann might break Einstein's nose." Therefore, neither.[13]

To the secretary of the Harvard Corporation, the university's governing body, CCB explained: "I was keen to have a man of science, but I cannot bear to think of a broken English speech by Einstein—let them look at his head of hair." Several other scientists he dismissed because "I don't see them making good speeches."[14] In the end, to his introductory remarks and the two preordained speeches of Conant and Massachusetts governor Curley, he added only Neilson and Wallace, at least one speaker less than usual from the degree recipients. But an hour and a quarter of speeches, he told Conant, was "enough."[15]

Whereupon he found himself in the midst of a political storm. The rumor that Secretary of Agriculture Wallace might receive a degree brought protests to university officials from a number of graduates, chiefly from two Republican congressmen.[16] At the time Republican feeling against Roosevelt was fierce. The Supreme Court recently had collapsed much of the New Deal, holding the National Recovery Act unconstitutional, and Roosevelt had begun to hint that he might change the structure of the Court. Many persons, not only Republicans, feared he was aiming at dictatorship. The two congressmen predicted alumni outrage at an honorary degree for any New Deal official as well as angry editorials across the country. And along with rumors of the nomination of Wallace, stories arose of petitions circulating among the alumni demanding that the Wallace selection be withdrawn.[17] The situation worsened in early June when Wallace, in an impromptu interview on his way to speak at Bowdoin College, in Maine, and later in his speech there, offended many New Englanders by suggesting they were poor sports to protest so loudly on behalf of their textile industries against a new processing tax.[18]

CCB had no vote on whether the selection should or could be reversed—that lay with the university's Board of Overseers—but because he had asked Wallace to speak, he was kept informed. Ultimately, the overseers let the nomination stand and, with it, the invitation to speak, but Conant noted in his autobiography that this commencement was the most troubled of his tenure (1933–53) and the only one in which even the possibility of such a reversal was discussed.[19]

CCB, without discounting New England's hostility to Wallace, steadily defended his place as a speaker. After all, he wrote, Wallace was

> a Cabinet Minister, the only one to attend, and it would seem to me something of an affront not to have him one of the speakers. Besides I thought that it would give him an opportunity to recant or modify his Bowdoin speech . . . A member of the Board of Overseers called me the other day, said he knew W. well enough to tip him off, and would do so. I guess it will go all right. We [Harvard] have stood a lot and can stand a lot more, and this will be a fine exhibition of our tolerance, for in spite of his shooting off his mouth, I fancy that W. is an able chap.[20]

To Wallace he wrote, "I don't know whether you see the Boston papers which are raising a little Hell about you, but I feel confident that an old hand like you will not be disturbed . . ." After discussing the order of speakers and putting Wallace last, he added, "I have a sort of sardonic and ghoulish glee at the thought that while I am praising Harvard for its enviable record of academic and other freedom, Harvard Alumni are grousing because of a speech made by the Secretary of Agriculture in a free parliament at Bowdoin!"[21]

The possibility of an ugly protest against Wallace was only part of Harvard's commencement's troubles. In the past year Hearst newspapers around the country had campaigned against Communism in colleges, and a number of states, including New York and Massachusetts, were debating the need of "loyalty oaths" for school and college teachers. On this issue, too, passions among alumni, politicians, and educators ran high. Governor Curley was known to strongly favor such a bill in the Massachusetts legislature, which Smith College president Neilson was known to oppose strongly. A confrontation between the two, even if only in words, could turn the ceremony sour. Besides, CCB wanted to talk on the subject himself; and perhaps, too, he hoped to defuse it. On Commencement Day, in his brief introductory speech, he said genially that he personally had "no contribution to make on higher, or any other education."[22] Instead, "I will venture to tell you what Gertrude Stein said when she recently revisited" New England:

> Education is thought about and as it is thought about it is being done in the way it is thought about, which is not true of almost anything. Almost anything is not done in the way it is thought about but education is done in the way it is thought about and that is the reason so much of it is done in New England and Switzerland. There is an extraordinary amount of it done in New England and in Switzerland.
>
> In New England they have done it, they do do it, they will do it and they do it in every way in which education can be thought about.
>
> I find education everywhere and in New England it is everywhere, it is thought about everywhere in America everywhere but only in New England is it done as much as it is thought about. And that is saying a very great deal. They do it so much in New England that they even do it more than it is thought about.

The predominantly New England audience, feeling somehow flattered by this modernist talk, smiled, though later one alumnus, in congratulating CCB on his ability to quote Stein "so comprehensibly," confessed: "I do not feel quite sure what all of it meant, but I expect that is my own stupidity. At any rate, it gave me much pleasure at the time."[23]

CCB touched lightly on one of the day's sore topics, remarking on how Harvard differed from Columbia, or from the state universities in California or Illinois, and finding its "distinctive" quality in its "long record of freedom and tolerance." He admitted that the founders of the college in 1636 "were not tolerant or open-minded men"; and the Patriots, during the Revolution, gave the Loyalists "a pretty hard time." Further, in the nineteenth century, despite "the liberalizing effect of the Unitarian movement," the abolitionists "did not fare well at the hands of the Cotton Whigs" who dominated the university's committees and boards before the Civil War. "But for the last seventy years our record has been without spot or blemish." And he cited the university's recently retired president A. Lawrence Lowell's defense of teachers' rights during World War I: "In spite of the risk of injury to the institution," Lowell had said, "the objections to restraint upon what professors may say as citizens seems to me far greater than the harm done by leaving them free."

In this respect, CCB noted, how unfree were many faculties in Continental Europe and "in some of our State Universities or denominational colleges." Praising Lowell for defending academic freedom even when he was personally out of sympathy with the teachers' views, he challenged his audience to match Lowell's integrity and tolerance:

> How often we have heard our own alumni say they will never contribute a cent to such and such a department so long as so and so is in it! I will not say with St. Peter, "Thy money perish with thee." No, we need all there is to be had. But I will quote from the Acts of the Apostles [8:21] what St. Peter added: "Thou has neither part nor lot in this matter; for thy heart is not right in the sight of God."
>
> I am well aware that many of the martyrs in the cause of Academic Freedom are very foolish gentlemen, poor stuff for heroes. But as Professor Einstein has said, "If we want to resist the powers which threaten to suppress intellectual and individual freedom, we must keep clearly before us what is at stake. Without such freedom there would have been no Shakespeare, no Goethe, no Newton, no Faraday, no Pasteur, no Lister . . . Only men who are free can create the works which make life worth living."

Before closing with a general statement about freedom and truth, CCB offered his own opinion:

> I see no reason why a good teacher or student should be dropped from the rolls of any college because he is a pacifist, a communist, an atheist, or any other form of "ist," provided he sticks to his last in the classroom

and is a propagandist only *extra mures* . . . I have no fear of Fascism in this country, but I confess that I look with some apprehension on the successes of self-styled patriotic societies in putting on the statute book laws . . . requiring teachers in private as well as public schools to take a loyalty oath.

Reminding the alumni that the university's seal bore the word *Veritas*, he rejoiced that Harvard had such leaders as Lowell and Conant: "For eternal vigilance is the price of liberty." And swiftly he called Curley to the lectern, announcing, "The Governor of the Commonwealth of Massachusetts."

Curley, dropping his usual campaign Irish brogue, spoke eloquently on the state and country's economic problems and the obligation of colleges and universities to help in their solution. Later he told CCB that he wished he'd thrown the speech aside to answer CCB on oaths for teachers, but realized that it would have been inappropriate.[24] Curley, an excellent impromptu speaker, might not have been so restrained had he followed rather than preceded Neilson, who, with the danger of rebuttal past, gave much of his ten minutes to a vigorous plea for academic freedom, extolling what he called the English practice: "the open safety valve, a method which has the great advantage to begin with, of greatly lessening the risk of explosion, and, in the second place, of leaving the road open for the discovery of new truth."[25]

CCB allowed himself a comment on Neilson's speech as he introduced Conant, perhaps with the idea of lowering tensions: "I think in his reference to the English method, Dr. Neilson must have had in mind that recent picture in *Punch*, of a [police] bobby in Hyde Park, in the communistic crowd. And the bobby says: 'Those as wants to burn Buckingham Palace to the left; all others to the right." The alumni laughed, CCB announced, "The President of the University," and Conant spoke on Harvard's internal affairs.

Then came Wallace, wittily introduced, who discussed the country's confusion in the Depression and the difficulty in maintaining a balanced economic life among divergent regions, groups, and interests; he stressed the need for unified action. He mentioned some of Secretary of State Cordell Hull's trade treaties and some of his own agricultural policies, pointing out—without mentioning Roosevelt by name—that many Harvard graduates were contributing to choices being made and efforts to unify the country. Whereupon CCB swiftly closed the meeting.

The next month the *Alumni Bulletin* reported, "Throughout the addresses . . . on the afternoon of Commencement Day ran an undertow of tension."[26] But CCB's handling of the day won praise on all sides, not least because he had spoken forthrightly yet not given offense. Within the university he was now considered a graduate worth consulting, and Harvard officials began to seek his thoughts on troublesome issues. He enjoyed this, responding promptly and with the gift, as always, of sounding in his letters just as he talked. After six years of back-and-forth with CCB, Joseph R. Hamlen, publisher of the *Bulletin*, remarked: "I hope you are not entirely bored with my letters. You are responsive and stimulating, and I get more pleasure from your correspondence than anyone else's."[27] One problem Hamlen took privately to CCB concerned preparations for the university's tercentenary celebration in September 1936. Former Harvard president Lowell was refusing to introduce or even sit on the dais with either Governor Curley or President Roosevelt. His reasons had more to do with ego and misunderstanding than politics, and CCB had a part in restoring peace.[28] A disagreement between Conant and the faculty over salaries and retirements threatened to be more divisive, but it, too, was resolved successfully.[29] And in June 1940 the alumni association inaugurated an "Alumni Medal" for service to the university by awarding it to CCB. His continuing success at Harvard, both public and private, added to the weight of his opinion elsewhere, not least in Washington, where many Harvard graduates, including the president, followed the university's affairs.

On 5 February 1937, President Roosevelt sent a bill to Congress that until then he had kept secret, consulting almost no one during its preparation except Attorney General Homer Cummings.[30] The bill's arrival in the Senate and the House caused astonishment, confusion, anger, joy, and in New York the next morning the front page of the *Herald Tribune* gave it and its reception seven of the eight columns. Around the country other papers did much the same, with their editorials mostly disapproving.[31] The bill proposed that Congress authorize the president to appoint one new justice, to a maximum of six, for every justice of the U.S. Supreme Court who, having passed the age of seventy and having served for ten years, did not retire.

Under the Constitution, Congress had the power to fix the number of judges on the Supreme Court and had done so six times in the past.[32] In 1891 Lord Bryce, in commenting on that power, had summarized: "The Fathers of the Constitution studied nothing more than to secure the complete independence of the judiciary. The President was not permitted to remove the judges, nor Congress to diminish their salaries. One thing only was either forgotten or deemed undesirable, because highly inconvenient, to determine—the number of judges in the Supreme court. Here was a weak point, a joint in the court's armour through which a weapon might some day penetrate."[33]

Roosevelt's bill struck at that "weak point." It did not compel retirement at age seventy but merely allowed the president, if the justice had served more than ten years, to appoint another judge to the bench. Six of the nine sitting justices were over seventy, had served more than ten years, and had announced no date to retire. If Congress, where the Democratic Party controlled both the House and the Senate, passed the bill that winter, the president by spring could appoint to the court, with approval of the Senate, six more judges.

Behind the bill lay a year of momentous events. In 1935 and 1936 the Court, on various grounds, had declared most of Roosevelt's New Deal legislation unconstitutional, invalidating the National Recovery Act, the Agricultural Adjustment Act, the Railroad Retirement Act, the Guffey-Vinson Soft Coal Act, the Municipal Bankruptcy Act, and the Frazier-Lemke Farm Mortgage Act; and it had denied the president the power to remove a hostile member of the Federal Trade Commission. There was virtually no area of American life in which Roosevelt's efforts to combat the Depression and his administration's right to act had been affirmed. Many of the decisions had been 5 to 4, with the majority usually Butler (age seventy-one), McReynolds (seventy-five), Sutherland (seventy-five), Van Devanter (seventy-eight), and Roberts (sixty-one). The minority usually had included Brandeis (eighty-one), Cardozo (sixty-six), Stone (sixty-four), and Chief Justice Hughes (seventy-five). To Roosevelt and those who agreed with him, the Court's "nine old men" were blocking the expressed will of Congress and the president. And when FDR was elected to his second term, in November 1936, by a huge popular and electoral majority, he believed he had a mandate to bring "into the judicial system a steady and continuing stream of new and younger blood."[34]

The proposed bill authorized additional judges for the lower federal courts as well as the Supreme Court, with a limit of new judges set at fifty. The country's attention, however, focused on the Supreme Court. To support his argument for the need of reform FDR released a report from his attorney general that showed the Court was behind in its work and needed additional judges to catch up.[35] Initial public response may have been more cautious, even hostile, than Roosevelt had expected. Outside Washington, plainly, reverence for the Court as an institution was still great. But Roosevelt was not daunted: his party controlled both houses of Congress, and he believed that the majority of the people were with him. In addition, he would have the fifty judicial appointments to hang as carrots before legislators who were hesitant or opposed. His position seemed strong.

CCB's immediate reaction to the bill, as solicited by the *Times*, was typical of many lawyers, notable only in that he was a Democrat who had openly criticized some of the Court's recent decisions. A judge's age by itself was a poor test of competence, he noted, for aging was biological, not chronological, then added: "I think some of the President's recommendations are excellent. But I am strongly opposed to an increase in the size of the court."[36] The next day, his thoughts more collected, he wrote to Frankfurter, at Harvard:

> The most despicable figure in this wretched business is the A.G. [Homer Cummings]. He should have resigned rather than lend himself to such a contemptible scheme. Frank's specious plea should have been punctuated by real lawyers.
>
> That the S.C. has brought this on itself is no excuse.
>
> You who know the business of the Court—that it needs no relief, that a Court of 15 is absurd, that a high court of parts is worse, that constitutional questions can be taken up by the S.C. speedily, that the *certioraris* are a nuisance but are manageable, that every member of the Court is in full *mental* vigor, that it is an insult and a humiliation that the old Justices should have their successors seated by their side—*you* are the one who should speak out loud and clear against the proposal.[37]

The next day, with more detail in hand, he wrote to New York's senator Robert F. Wagner, enlarging on several ideas and responding to FDR's claim that the court was behind in its work:

> . . . 5. The heavy toll of applications for *certiorari* is handled without undue difficulty by the Court—a large part during the summer vacation, each Justice considering each application. The large proportion denied is reasonable and proper, for, in the main, only questions of real importance should be brought before the Supreme Court.
>
> 6. If an age limit is thought desirable, it can be provided by amendments for the future, in which case doubtless those Justices who have reached the limit set would retire. I know of only two cases of superannuation in the history of the Court—Mr. Justice Grier in 1869 and

Mr. Justice Field in 1897. By amending the Judiciary Act so as to permit a Justice to retire at 70 or 75 with full pay, even if he has not served ten years as is now the law, any case of superannuation can be taken care of and special acts as in the case of Mr. Justice Moody [served only four years] will be unnecessary.[38]

He closed on a more personal note: "I have strongly criticized several of the recent decisions of the Court, notably the Minimum Wage decision and the grounds of the R.R. pension decision; but these decisions should not be met by packing the Court. And no matter how the Court is changed, an amendment to the Constitution will still be needed to clarify and broaden the scope of the Commerce Clause and to limit the Due Process Clauses of the Fifth and Fourteenth Amendments."

Wagner did not reply, and five months later, in July 1937, CCB wrote to his sister-in-law Grace Taylor, "I am thoroughly ashamed of our Senator Wagner, who has not even yet stated his position." Royal S. Copeland, New York's other senator and also a Democrat, had come out against the bill in February.[39]

Trying to do more than write letters, CCB and Samuel Seabury on 24 February 1937 presented a resolution on Roosevelt's bill to a special meeting of the City Bar Association; the more than 600 members present voted 517 to 88 to oppose the bill: "It is the considered judgment of the Association of the Bar of the City of New York that, however its members may differ in their view of recent decisions of the Supreme Court on constitutional questions involving the scope of the federal and state power in social and economic legislation," Roosevelt's proposal "would, if enacted, make the Court suspect of subservience and the executive of domination; it is unsound in principle and dangerous as a precedent, and violates the historic American principle of the independence of the judiciary."[40] The Association thereafter published briefs, booklets, and letters and sponsored radio addresses opposing the bill, and also sent some younger members to Washington to work with a similar group from the American Bar Association to research legal and historical issues that arose and to brief anyone who asked, chiefly congressmen and reporters. Very soon Roosevelt's claim that the court was behind in its work was proved false, and he dropped it, admitting later that its use had been a mistake. It had stamped his proposal with an air of deceit he could never fully erase.[41]

CCB was one of the Association's radio speakers, over WEVD on 28 March, and before then much had happened to influence his views. He had written to Roosevelt in late February suggesting that a constitutional amendment would be a better way to proceed than the proposed bill, and FDR's reply anticipated much of what he was about to say in a coming Fireside Chat to the nation:

> To get a two-thirds vote [in Congress], this year or next year, on any type of amendment is next to impossible . . . Finally, if an amendment were to be passed by a two-thirds vote of both houses, this year or next, you and I know perfectly well that the same forces which are now calling for an amendment process would turn around and fight ratification on the simple ground that they do not like the particular amendment adopted by the Congress . . . Therefore, my good old friend, by the process of reductio ad absurdum, or any other better-sounding name, you must join me in confining ourselves to the legislative method of saving the United States from what promises to be a situation of instability and serious unrest if we do not handle our social and economic problems by constructive action during the next four years. I am not willing to take that gamble, and I do not think the Nation is either.[42]

CCB was not convinced, and he increasingly disliked Roosevelt's public statements. At the Democratic Party Victory Dinner on 4 March, Roosevelt charged the nine justices with usurping power in striking down his New Deal legislation. Five days later, in the Fireside Chat, he asserted that the Court "has improperly set itself up as a third House of the Congress—a super-legislature . . . We must take action to save the Constitution from the Court and the Court from itself."[43] To many people, his pose of saving the Constitution put the picture wrong way round. And CCB in his radio speech tried to set it straight.

> The real purpose of the legislation proposed is to secure through additional judges a reversal of some of the recent decisions of the court. This is not the American, the Democratic way. It was precisely what the Stuart Kings did in England in the 17th century, it is what the royal governors of the colonies tried to do here in America in the 18th century. It is not our way, and it is not the right way.
>
> The right way is to proceed by Constitutional Amendment and let the whole body of the people decide what they want and not leave it to a Congress elected on other issues and dominated as this one is by the Executive through patronage and refusal of patronage.[44]

He also warned that the six additional justices when appointed, however independent they tried to be, would be objects of contempt: "They would be King's men."[45]

Before this late March speech, CCB had written twice again to Frankfurter, at Harvard, urging him to speak out: "In my opinion . . . every professor in every law school should express his opinion of the President's proposal," Frankfurter most of all, for he was the country's authority on federal courts. CCB could understand neither Frankfurter's silence nor his explanation of it, which, rather than clarifying his position, evaded discussion. In a letter to CCB on 16 March, Frankfurter wrote: "You . . . think it my duty to 'speak out.' Evidently my 'duty' in this instance is two-faced. For according to the unsolicited advice tendered me by other valued friends (some of them passionate opponents of the President) it is my duty not to speak out now."[46]

Another friend of CCB, Grenville Clark, a partner of Root, Clark, Buckner & Ballantine and also a member of Harvard's Corporation (its governing body), had similarly urged Frankfurter to "speak out." "The thing that is really not understandable to the average man is why, at a time like this when everyone is seeking light, you of all others should remain silent."[47] And Frankfurter had replied:

> Why have I not spoken out? Fundamentally, because through circumstances, in the making of which I have had no share, I have become a myth, a symbol and promoter not of reason but of passion. I am the symbol of the Jew, the "red," the "alien" . . . I would be heard and interpreted . . . not as the man who by virtue of his long years of service in the government and his special attention to problems of constitutional law and the work of the Court spoke with the authority of scholarship, but as the Jew, the "red," and the "alien."[48]

The tone and ideas here, as CCB and Clark undoubtedly discussed, were uncharacteristic of Frankfurter. His friends had not asked him to agree with them, although some of his published writings suggested he would, but only that he discuss the issues and state an opinion, lending his expertise and authority to the national discussion.[49] After a while, they ceased their urgings. "I will just add this," Clark wrote, "that there is one reason that should be important, viz., your personal relations to F.D.R. If that is it, everything would look different, and I wonder if that isn't really it, although you have not mentioned it."[50] In the coming weeks, as eighteen of Frankfurter's colleagues at Harvard Law School, acting as individuals, signed a public protest (reported in the *Times*) against Roosevelt's plan, his silence rang ever louder.[51]

CCB, at this time, was arranging for Frankfurter to speak to a small group of Harvard Club members in New York, mostly lawyers, and wrote him: "As to subject anything will serve. It's you they want to hear, and we wish to reveal you to them as hornless. Of course, the Court is the most interesting subject in New York now, but I assume you don't wish to talk about that." At the meeting, on 7 April, Frankfurter talked of the Court as an institution, the background to the crisis, but said very little about the president's bill.[52] This puzzled his listeners, as well as the far greater number who hoped, week after week, to read in some journal his analysis of the issues. Gossip surmised that as a reward for it Roosevelt had promised him a position on the Court. That suspicion of a bribe for silence stuck to Frankfurter for life, and for many people was confirmed when eighteen months later, in January 1939, Roosevelt appointed him to the Court.

The truth came out in 1968, with the publication of Roosevelt and Frankfurter's correspondence, long after Roosevelt, Frankfurter, CCB, and Clark were dead. According to the editor of the correspondence, Roosevelt had phoned Frankfurter right after the announcement of the bill, told him that he intended one day to appoint him to the Court and did not want him (in the editor's words) "entangled in this particular controversy. Would Frankfurter help him to get out of this mess? . . . What Frankfurter never told anyone was that, while remaining officially neutral, he had been a central and constant adviser of the President";[53] from 6 February onward he had been a major player in the President's campaign, writing Roosevelt letters of advice, secretly visiting the White House to confer, and urging the president not to compromise. Unknown to CCB and Clark, Frankfurter was their active opponent.[54]

At the same time that CCB was arranging a speech for Frankfurter in New York, Clark was forming a National Committee for Independent Courts to oppose the Court-packing bill. Clark, an expert in railroad rates and reorganization, was a good organizer. Outside his legal practice, he was best known in the 1930s for having started the 1916 Plattsburg movement to train army officers, who would be needed if the United States entered the war.[55] Now, in early March 1937, he sent a young lawyer from his firm, Cloyd Laporte, to Washington to sound out the senators who were known to oppose the Court-packing bill, and Senator Arthur Vandenberg, Republican from Michigan, made the suggestion, which Clark adopted, that the committee be restricted to Democrats who had voted for Roosevelt in the last election.[56] Later, a bracketed phrase on the committee's stationery, directly below the title, would state: "A Committee of Citizens, All of Whom Favored the President's Election in 1936, and All of Whom Are Opposed to the President's Supreme Court Proposal." Cochairman with Clark was Charles C. Burlingham.

When CCB made his radio speech in New York on 28 March, urging the President to proceed by constitutional amendment, he spoke as a former president of the bar association, but when he testified nine days later before the Committee on the Judiciary of the U.S. Senate, he spoke as a leader of Clark's committee, which was beginning to form (Frederic R. Coudert, four days later, spoke for the bar association). The gist of CCB's two speeches (the radio address was the better, being more succinct) was the same: in the lessons of the country's colonial history, CCB found reason to oppose the bill, and he noted a full congressional debate on a constitutional amendment, as well as those following in the forty-eight state legislatures, would be useful. "I cannot help thinking that such debates and discussions would serve as a new Federalist for the education of all the people of the United States." He concluded, "I devoutly hope that the light of reason will dawn on the misguided advocates of this plan, unnecessary, unwise and most dangerous as a precedent."[57]

The *Herald Tribune* stressed that CCB had described the president as stumbling into "a great blunder" from which he should withdraw and then proceed by proposing an amendment. The president, CCB had said, would be "the last man in the world to claim that he is a great lawyer," and the attorney general had led him into "a shabby enterprise." (He had also said, however, which the Republican paper ignored, "I am not one of those who imagine that the President is reaching for more power to make himself a dictator. That is absurd and unthinkable. But President Roosevelt is not the last President of the United States; there will be others.")[58]

CCB was only one of several witnesses testifying on 6 April, but he made his appearance memorable, charming the senators with quotations from Emerson and Shakespeare and disarming the hostile William H. Dieterich of Illinois, by a courteous gesture: "Mr. Dieterich inadvertently let a piece of paper drop on the floor," reported the *Herald Tribune*. "Spry Mr. Burlingham hopped out of his chair, like a mere youngster of seventy, picked up the paper and handed it to the Senator with a courtly bow. By the time he had finished his testimony even Mr. Dieterich was smiling."[59]

The issues of the debate gradually shifted. At the hearing on 21 March, Senator Burton K. Wheeler of Idaho, a Democrat opposing the bill, read a letter from Chief Justice Hughes that showed the Court was up to date on its work. Equally important, on 7 April, the Court handed down four decisions that to a great extent reversed its anti–New Deal rulings. In one case, on the minimum wage law, it reversed itself, 5 to 4, with Justice Owen Roberts now joining the former liberal minority. (Actually, this decision had been reached the previous December, and publication had been delayed for other reasons.) In the three other cases, though there was no direct reversal, the shift in stance was still dramatic. A new Frazier-Lemke Act, for example, redrafted to meet the Court's previous objections, was sustained. Finally, on 12 April, the Court, 5 to 4, upheld the National Labor Relations Act, with Hughes writing the decision: "We have no doubt that Congress had constitutional authority to safeguard the right of respondent's employees [steelworkers] to self-organization and freedom in the choice of representatives for collective bargaining."[60]

By mid-April, therefore, many people thought the debate on the president's bill soon would die. Roosevelt had his favorable rulings, and in a sense had won; similarly, the Court, having shown it was abreast of business and could correct itself when seemingly wrong, also in a sense had won. So, as wits remarked, "why shoot the bridegroom after the shotgun wedding?" Yet Roosevelt, advised by Frankfurter, continued to fight for his bill, and the battle's focus shifted from the Court to the Senate, becoming less a matter of constitutional issues than of counting votes, first in the Senate Judiciary Committee and then in the Senate.

On 18 May, as the debate over the plan was about to enter its fourth month and the country was growing weary of the turmoil, Justice Van Devanter submitted his resignation from the Court, effective at term's end, ensuring Roosevelt, in June or July, his first appointment to it. (And six days later the Court, in opinions written by Cardozo, upheld, 5 to 4, the unemployment provisions of the Social Security Act and, 7 to 2, the old-age insurance provisions.)[61] Again an opportunity for compromise opened, but Roosevelt had a difficulty. He was widely believed to have promised the first opening on the Court to the Senate majority leader, Joseph Robinson, of Arkansas, whose fellow senators on word of Van Devanter's resignation had thronged about him with congratulations. Robinson was far from a New Deal Democrat, however, and how he would rule on important cases was doubtful. FDR, therefore, made no announcement and continued to press for his bill, hoping perhaps to force either its passage or further resignations from the Court. Either way, he then could appoint one or two judges of more liberal persuasion along with Robinson.

As the controversy simmered, Clark went to Washington to launch the National Committee for Independent Courts at a meeting in the Mayflower Hotel on Friday evening, 21 May. In the previous six weeks the committee had enrolled 110 influential community leaders from thirty-three states with invitations out to more.[62] CCB had helped to recruit members from around the country, and had written and spoken to senators and representatives in Washington, but most of the work had been done by Clark and his assistant, Cloyd Laporte. The object of the dinner, Clark explained in his invitation to friendly congressmen and senators, will be "to confer with a few Senators and Representatives as to how best the proposed organization can function." The next morning, smaller meetings to deal with details would follow.[63] Several Democratic senators attended, among them Tom Connally of Texas and Burton K. Wheeler of Montana, both members of the Judiciary Committee who had put hard questions to witnesses favoring the bill. According to Laporte, Wheeler "was at that time in a blue funk and indicated that he thought it was impossible to win. He was bucked up at the meeting, particularly by the more optimistic statements of G.C. [Clark], reinforced by G.C.'s obvious determination to carry on the fight to the end."[64] By August the committee had 230 members from forty-two states and perhaps unexpectedly was strong and effective throughout the Democratic South.[65]

Polls taken in the Senate, meantime, were slowly shifting against the president. And then, on 14 June, after two months of debate, the Judiciary Committee issued its report on the bill. By a vote of 10 to 8 (one member absent), it recommended "the rejection of this bill as a needless, futile and utterly dangerous abandonment of constitutional principle." The language was harsh: the President's proposal was "without precedent or justification . . . Under the form of the Constitution it seeks to do that which is unconstitutional . . . It is a measure which should be so emphatically rejected that its parallel will never again be presented to the free representatives of the free people of America." No minority report was filed, and seven of the committee's fourteen Democrats voted with the majority.[66]

Roosevelt's response was wondrously resilient. Two days later he invited all 407 Democratic congressmen to a three-day picnic at a Democratic fish and game club on Jefferson Island in Chesapeake Bay. There, in an old fishing jacket, he played the genial host, swapping stories, treating the disloyal kindly, and belying the image of a would-be dictator. His charm soothed and penetrated, rekindling among some doubters the flames of faith. By all reports he revived support for his plan, already redrafted as a "compromise" or "amended" bill.[67]

This new bill, introduced to the full Senate on 2 July by Senator Marvel Logan, Democrat from Kentucky, would authorize the president to appoint an additional judge for each member of the Court who remained on the bench after reaching seventy-five, but he could appoint only one such additional judge each year, and a limit was set at five. This meant that by the end of January 1938 Roosevelt would be enabled to appoint three new justices—one to replace Van Devanter, one in 1937, and another in 1938—and would have the certainty, regardless of resignations, of at least one more on 1 January 1939. As opponents noted, he had given up little. Nevertheless, Senate majority leader Robinson was able to orchestrate a groundswell in favor of the "compromise" bill, and a Gannett poll on 7 July estimated that the Senate likely would pass it 52 to 44.[68]

Opponents of the "compromise" bill now struggled to delay a vote, and CCB on 6 July had a letter in the *Times* insisting: "The Logan bill is a mere face-saving device. No such operation is needed. The President does not need it. Nor do the Senators, nor does the Democratic Party, nor does the New Deal. The best way to remedy a blunder is to admit it." Five days later he had a more detailed letter in the *Times*, which the *Boston Herald* picked up the next day in its lead editorial, quoting long parts (in italics) with approval, among them:[69]

> Mr. Burlingham finds these two significant circumstances in the senatorial debate:
>
> *1.—The eight members of the Senate judiciary committee who voted for the original bill in committee failed to submit a minority report.*
>
> *2.—In the debate on the floor of the Senate, so far as it has gone, not one word has been uttered by any of the supporters of the substitute bill on the merits of the proposal or on the principle involved. The leaders have filled the air with appeals to party loyalty and attempts to make it appear that the opposition is seeking to split the party for ulterior purposes.*
>
> *Nothing could demonstrate more convincingly that the proposal is indefensible and that the arguments against it are unanswerable.*[70]

The City Bar Association's Committee on Federal Legislation, meanwhile, with its chairman now Laporte (appointed on CCB's suggestion), was preparing its detailed report on the new bill, as were similar groups around the country.

For more than a month, however, Roosevelt privately had been preparing an attack on his opponents, and he hinted at his pleasure at what was to come in a letter to CCB on 27 May: "Under your hat—within a few weeks quite a storm is going to break over the heads of individuals who have been cheating their own government. Watch and see how many lawyers condemn them and how many lawyers condone them."[71]

In late May, FDR had submitted a bill to Congress to close well-known loopholes in the tax code, and though in June little happened, on 1 July, at a joint congressional committee hearing, seven so-called tax evaders were named, and the first was Grenville Clark. In the *Times* report of the hearing, Clark was said to have created sixteen family trusts with an annual saving in taxes of $90,000. Supposedly, the Treasury Department had a rule of confidentiality with taxpayers that forbade the release of names and figures where no crime was charged. But the president, encouraged by secretary of the Treasury Henry Morgenthau Jr., had overridden the rule (two of the Treasury's leading lawyers resigned in protest).[72] So, at the hearing, seven rich men were held up to scorn and details of their tax returns made public, though they were not charged with illegal acts and some of their so-called tax dodges, such as Clark's use of family trusts, were conceded to be legal. Roosevelt, however, in his message to Congress accompanying the tax bill, had stigmatized the as-yet-unnamed men as eager "to dodge the payment of taxes which Congress based on an ability to pay" and thereby to shift the tax load to "others less able to pay ... mulcting the Treasury of the Government's just due."[73] The threat to Clark was plain: that he could be called to testify before a congressional investigating committee, an arena in which slander is common and privileged.[74]

The tactic backfired. Newspapers, instead of howling about rich men and their trusts, were asking why the executive branch of government had waited so long to close such well-known loopholes. On 16 July *The New York Times* announced, with revealing quotation marks in its headline: "'Evaders' of Taxes Not to Be Called." Roosevelt's sneak attack had collapsed.[75]

Events followed fast. In Washington, in the summer's suffocating heat, the senators, perspiring and angry, debated the "compromise" Court-packing bill. No one worked harder than majority leader Robinson, struggling to hold his margin of one or two, and on the night of 13–14 July, alone in his apartment, he had a heart attack, and died. On 17 July, the *Times* published the bar association's detailed, adverse report on the bill.[76] And on 20 July, on the front page of the *Times*, Governor Lehman addressed Senator Wagner, asking, "as a citizen of the State of New York, which you represent in the United States Senate, to voice my opposition to the Court Bill and to express the hope that you will vote against it."[77] The paper quoted CCB praising Lehman for his stand and criticizing Senator Wagner for his long silence: "It has been a great disappointment to many of us who have supported Senator Wagner that ... [he] should have permitted five months to pass without expressing his opinion on a question of vital importance to the people of the state he represents."[78]

Frankfurter, on the other hand, wrote to Roosevelt, "I was—and am—hot all over regarding Herbert Lehman's letter. Some things just aren't done—they violate the decencies of human relations and offend the good taste and the decorum of friendship." How he judged his deception of CCB and Clark, he never stated.[79]

After a recess for Robinson's funeral in Arkansas, eight Democratic senators who had been supporting him in his fight for the "compromise" bill announced they would vote against it, and finally, on 22 July, after several weeks of bitter debate, the Senate voted 70 to 20 to return the bill to committee, a congressional form of burial.[80] Senator Wagner was among the seventy, still avoiding any statement on its merits, though in a letter to the *Times* he assured Governor Lehman that when the need arose, he would vote his "conscience."[81]

Even now Roosevelt sought to keep the issue alive, and on 26 August, in signing a bill that authorized him to make some generally approved procedural reforms in the lower federal courts, he announced he would continue to fight for "a thorough-going reformation of our judicial processes."[82] CCB, writing to Clark, concluded, "F.D.'s statement was deliberately misleading. I do not think any bill to increase the Supreme Court will pass; but unless deaths or resignations occur the first decision that runs counter to F.D.'s plans will lead to some of these evil proposals . . . So our Committee should continue."[83] And he agreed with Clark's suggestion that the committee be moved from Washington to Clark's office in New York and be put on hold, ready for quick reactivation.[84]

No need for revival arose, for within the next twenty-one months "deaths" and "resignations" allowed Roosevelt to appoint four justices to the Court. The third, in January 1939, was Frankfurter. Less than four years after the defeat of Roosevelt's original proposal he had named eight judges to the Court, more than any president except George Washington.[85]

All historians agree that Roosevelt's defeat on the Court-packing plan was significant, though often differing in their reasons. He himself liked to say that though he lost the battle he had won the war; within eighteen months, after all, he had a safe majority on the Court, ready to approve the legislation he wanted. Historians in Roosevelt's thrall tend to adopt this view without question, yet at best, it is only partly true. And many Americans saw his victory as a stunning defeat, a defeat all the more remarkable for being delivered by his own party and only months after an overwhelming reelection.[86]

William E. Leuchtenburg, in his essay on "FDR's 'Court-packing' Plan," suggests six ways "in which FDR lost the war." In briefest summary:

The Court struggle . . . helped blunt the most important drive for social reform in American history . . . [It] deeply divided the Democratic party. In state after state, it precipitated factional wars . . . [Because of it] the middle-class backing Roosevelt had mobilized in the 1936 campaign ebbed away . . . [It] produced divisions among reformers of many types . . . [It] undermined the bipartisan support for the New Deal. Many of the Republican progressives had become growingly disquieted about the men around Roosevelt . . . [And it] affected Roosevelt's conduct of foreign affairs. At a minimum, it proved distracting . . . More important, the controversy gave hostages to opponents of his foreign policy . . . [and to several important senators, such as Hiram Johnson and Wheeler] it seemed to reveal what they deplored about his foreign policy—that it was devious, and that it sought too much power for the executive.[87]

It is difficult to set a value on the work of Clark, CCB, and the National Committee for Independent Courts. Many historians do not mention the committee or either man, except perhaps to subsume them in such phrases as "congressional mail ran heavily against the bill."[88] Yet Roosevelt's effort to disparage and disgrace Clark by falsely portraying him as a "tax evader" suggests that to FDR he was more than a bothersome gnat. And the gathering at the Mayflower Hotel, the constant stream of adverse bar association reports, letters to editors, and speeches against the proposal (often seeded by Clark's committee) surely stirred many of the protests that flowed to representatives in Washington. Moreover, the committee provided a structure to which Democrats in forty-two states who wanted to oppose the bill could turn—and many did turn to it for guidance.

From the perspective of CCB's life story, what is interesting is how congenial he found Clark's quick turn to a voluntary association for taking action, and equally or even more important the way in which both he and Clark played their parts. Their temperate and measured rhetoric did not flag. Neither, though provoked, spoke in anger, and CCB always deflected blame for the blunder on to Cummings, not FDR. Their temperance and decency in debate surely inclined some, perhaps many, to their views, and in setting their example both found that when the fight was won, they still could work happily on other matters with FDR and with Frankfurter. Civility in discourse had its reward.

19

Family Deaths and Sorrows

IN THE SPRING OF 1934, Louie had an attack of bronchitis complicated by a mild pneumonia, and though she recovered, she thereafter seemed more prone to illness. In midsummer 1937, at Black Point, she developed a number of infections and began to lose strength, enough so that reports of her condition began to circulate, and in mid-August, Cardozo wrote to CCB, "Nothing touching you or your life can be foreign to me. I hope that by this time the dear lady is well."[1]

Apparently she did improve, or seemed to, for that month CCB accepted appointment to a Committee for the Reelection of La Guardia and came down from Black Point for the meeting. He had no doubt the mayor, running again as a City Fusion–Progressive–American Labor–Republican candidate, would defeat Tammany's Jeremiah T. Mahoney. La Guardia's record was good, and "the plain people," as CCB designated the politically inactive, knew it was good, and "*they* will elect LaG."[2]

In September, Louie was well enough to return to town, but CCB warned Grenville Clark that because of her illness he would be "very irregular at the office"; and instead of going to the Episcopal Church Convention in Cincinnati, he sent an alternate, after placing a long letter in the *Times* about church affairs. By mid-October he wrote to Frankfurter that his hopes for Louie had risen slightly: "She is taking more nourishment, but she is very weak." Meanwhile, he undertook to lead a Citizens Committee to elect Thomas E. Dewey to the post of New York County District Attorney.[3]

But as fast as Louie rid herself of one ailment, she succumbed to another, and by late October she was in New York Hospital, which CCB described to Cardozo as "a wonderful institution."[4] Yet despite his efforts at cheer, he soon realized that Louie was leaving him. As he remarked to one friend, her decline was a "long acquiescence—not a struggle,"[5] and told another, "She got weaker and weaker and finally faded away." She died on the evening of 7 December. "We had a very simple little service by her bedside as she had wished. For myself, with 54 years of perfect companionship, I cannot and do not repine." That was the reply he gave to all his friends who, as then was the custom, wrote him notes of sympathy, even busy men like Roosevelt, Stimson, Cardozo, Frankfurter, and the two Hands. As Stimson put it: "This note is just the grasp of the hand which is about all that a friend can do at such a time."[6]

For the most part, the notes that survive and CCB's replies conceal more than they reveal. To make a display of grief was not in CCB's nature, nor was it the style among his friends for responding to a wife's death. One or two of his replies, however, add a line to Louie's portrait. To a college classmate, CCB confided:

> Two kinds of letters have been very interesting. One, the first from men who were [his son] Charles's contemporaries and came to our house thirty years ago and they have seen little of us since, having married and been absorbed in their own lives. They write now of what a welcome they had in those days from Louie and what a deep impression she made on them. The other class is of those who saw her only once or twice and yet felt her aura and knew that they were in the presence of a being serene and beautiful who had attained. I wish you had seen her oftener and I feel sad to think that she and your Alice never met.[7]

Though CCB's letters confirmed the extent of Louie's withdrawal from most social relations beyond family or neighbors at Black Point, he seemed quite unaware of her increasing reclusion. In no letter did he question, complain, or ponder the reason for it. He decreed, as she had requested, that her funeral service should be private, not even in a church, only for immediate family—which was unusual for the wife of one of the city's distinguished citizens, one with an exceptionally wide acquaintance. Further, as the brief obituaries in the *Times* and *Herald Tribune* noted, she was born a Lawrence, a family well known in the city, and was a granddaughter of Richard March Hoe, "the inventor of the rotary printing press." But, strange for the time, neither paper reported any church affiliation.[8] Apparently CCB did not see Louie's withdrawal from the world as either odd or a failure.

Similarly, in a letter to Frankfurter he seemed unaware of how his description might cause her to appear to one who knew her less well.

> Think of it, fifty-four years of perfect companionship, with joys and sorrows shared. Would it not be unworthy if I now repined!

Lonely—yes, very; but really not overwhelmed with grief or submerged in sorrow.

You perceived how choice I think L. was. She had *attained.* For Nancy it is hard work, for we three were closest . . .

Louie tested people—have I not said this to you—if at first sight one perceived that he was in the presence of something rare and precious, then he thereby proved himself worthy. That perception, I feel sure, Marian and you had.[9]

What he meant by "attained" is unclear, though he used the term more than once, and perhaps some of those who failed to prove themselves "worthy" of Louie thought her snobbish, unduly dismissive. But his loneliness without her was with him for the rest of his life; and though he sought to keep it concealed, on one occasion he described it as "inconsolable."[10]

Shortly after her death, in writing to an English friend, Frank MacKinnon, he confessed, "My faith in personal immortality is far from strong," and a decade later he wrote to Helena Hirst: "I had hoped to be eternally with L. But in these last ten years my hopes of personal relations after death have become fainter and feebler." Perhaps, after the body's death, the soul in some fashion persisted, but not in a way to allow personal relations. The withering of that hope and belief apparently continued. But he never ceased to say of Louie that with her he had enjoyed "fifty-four years of perfect companionship." In her, he "had been blessed far beyond my desserts."[11]

In the summer of Louie's worsening health, CCB was at first pleased and then disappointed in the actions of his eldest grandchild, Bob Burlingham, who in the fall of 1936 had transferred as a junior from Antioch to Harvard. Bob apparently had such a jolly time in Cambridge that he did no work and was dropped from the class in the spring. Stung by the defeat, he went to summer school, earned reinstatement, and in late August left on a quick visit of triumph to his mother in Vienna. While there, he started a relationship with a Norwegian girl, Rigmor "Mossik" Sorensen, whom he would soon marry, and shortly learned—a shock to everyone—that his mother had tuberculosis. Instead of returning to Harvard, despite anguished telegrams from his father and CCB, Bob, after consulting Anna Freud, remained in Vienna, and to resolve his emotional turmoil resumed full-time analysis with her.[12]

By now Anna Freud's role in Dorothy's family had become thoroughly ambiguous, especially for Bob and Mabbie, each of whom already had ten years or more than two thousand hours of analysis. Worse than ambiguous, it was perhaps even hypocritical, for she had allowed herself, even sought for herself, to become a surrogate parent.[13] Like her father, she had worked to separate Dorothy from Robert and in time had supplanted him in Dorothy's life in both intellectual and emotional terms, though her relationship with Dorothy seems to have remained platonic.[14] When the children had problems of anger, guilt, or confusion over their displaced father and heritage, she undertook to advise them, but by now, relying on Dorothy's daily presence and assistance as well as enjoying the children's attention and dependency, she was no longer a disinterested party.

The situation and relationships grew ever more burdened, causing Mabbie one day to write her mother: "Oh it's awfully *blod* [stupid] because everything has its unknown reasons. I with my many troubles and unknown reasons. Everything has an unknown reason. Oh reason after reason, everything with its reasons. It nearly makes me mad." As Dorothy's biographer noted of Anna Freud's work with Mabbie, "This was hardly the desired result."[15]

Ultimately, the only child to escape the family's entanglement with the Freuds was the youngest, Michael, who broke with his mother at age seventeen, leaving Vienna for the United States in early March 1938 and traveling with his father, who, on hearing of Dorothy's tuberculosis, had come to visit her. Michael already was sure that he wanted to be an engineer, to go to the Massachusetts Institute of Technology, and to lead an American life. In later years he stressed that his break was not with his family but with his mother.[16] He had grown impatient with the psychiatrists, he later explained, always so "secretive." His mother would tell him not to be alone with his father, and he would ask, "Why?" Would his father abuse him? No. Still, better not to be alone with him. Michael never did hear a reason; just whisper, whisper. Did he love his father? He asked the question rhetorically and replied: "Yes and No. How can a child love an adult with whom he has seldom been, has been prevented from being for any length of time?"[17]

At seventeen, Michael came to the United States to stand on his own feet, and he succeeded. His siblings would do less well, all of them as adults returning periodically to adolescent dependency on Anna Freud and more analysis by her. Katrina perhaps did the best, attending Bennington College and becoming a talented amateur photographer, Bob in time became an architect, would divorce, remarry, become less and less effective as a person, and in 1970, at age fifty-four, die of an asthma-induced heart attack—his later life seeming an unprotested retreat into death.

Four years later, at age fifty-seven, Mabbie—after many years as a teacher of arts and crafts to children and in apparent good health though with frequent visits to Anna Freud—had a breakdown, left her husband to return to Anna Freud for more analysis, and soon, by an overdose of sleeping pills, killed herself. Happily for CCB, these events culminated after he had died, but as early as 1947 he saw their shadows approaching.[18]

Soon after Michael left Vienna in March 1938, Hitler and his army marched in, and from Switzerland Dorothy, though ill, helped members of the Freud family to reach England, where she eventually joined them. There, she and Anna continued their work with children, and London replaced Vienna as the center of her life.

Meanwhile, at 860 Park Avenue the winter of 1937–38 was also momentous, starting with Louie's slow decline and death in early December. As the New Year began, CCB stoically faced his loneliness alone, keeping his grief private; Nancy, from whose life the dominating personality was now removed, at least had the chance to lessen her grief by taking a greater role in family affairs; but for Robert there was only the staggering loss of his mother's supporting love and then the news from Vienna that his wife had tuberculosis. Abruptly he left to visit her, returning with his son Michael in March.

The following month, as the Germans occupied Austria, Robert's hopes rose that Dorothy might return to the United States, and her plan to follow the Freuds to London was a blow: she intended to create another home in Europe for their children. Apparently until that decision he had believed that in some fashion the family could be reunited, though his parents as early as the summer of 1936 had realized that whatever position he might achieve as father, his role as husband, was ended.[19]

In late April 1938, when Robert visited Katrina, a sophomore at Bennington, he lamented to her that, with the children growing up, he was losing his family. Two weeks later he may have felt it slip away further when he learned that Mabbie, in England, in a quickly planned wedding had married her fiancé, a young Viennese architect named Simon Schmiderer. There had been no time for Robert to go over, and even Dorothy in Switzerland had been unable to attend. Robert grew agitated, restless, and unable to sleep. As he and CCB bid good night, after a game of cards on the evening of 27 May, his father reminded him to take a sleeping pill.[20]

Early the next morning, the building's superintendent called CCB down to the avenue sidewalk to identify a body in blue pajamas. Robert. According to the *Times* the next day,

Dr. Burlingham's father issued the following statement:

Dr. Robert Burlingham, son of Charles C. Burlingham, killed himself
at 5:30 o'clock this morning by leaping from a window of the family
apartment at 860 Park Avenue. He had not been sleeping well for about
ten days and acted from a sudden impulse.

Dr. Burlingham was 50 years of age. He was graduated from Harvard
in 1910 and from the College of Physicians and Surgeons in 1914 . . .
The funeral services will be private.[21]

For its day, when suicide was considered shameful and seldom acknowledged, the statement's honesty was startling—admired by some, deplored
by others. Even two years later, Robert's college classmate who wrote a
memorial of him for the class report did not follow CCB's lead and merely
referred without explanation to a "tragic death."[22] The *Times*, treating
the story as news, not obituary, reported that no note had been found in
the apartment. "The victim had been under the care of a nerve specialist
recently, it was learned. The body was removed to a downtown undertak-
ing establishment following a visit to the scene by a member of the Medical Examiner's Office." The reporter named the doorman who found the
body, the superintendent who summoned the father, the doctor who
pronounced "the victim" dead, and the two detectives who investigated
"the case."[23]

Through it all, the seventy-nine-year-old CCB did whatever was asked
of him, even responding, on 1 June, to a call from a social worker for the
American Council of Jewish Women. She was at a pier, meeting a ship
carrying refugees, and had discovered a man from Vienna who had only
five dollars and a letter of recommendation from Dorothy Burlingham.
She had recognized the last name and called CCB. Would he put up the
fifty dollars needed to forestall the man's transfer to Ellis Island? He sent
the money down by messenger. Regardless of circumstance or feeling,
Dorothy's word must be made good.[24] By the end of the summer, however, he was exhausted, and had a heart attack, from which, with several
months' rest, he seemed to recover fully.

Dorothy, meanwhile, had a letter from her sister urging her not to feel
responsible for Robert's death, and Freud, too, absolved her of guilt, recalling "how overpowering was the influence of his illness, which made it
impossible to have a satisfactory relationship, and which has to be accepted as yet another of those acts of fate that fall upon us human beings
and cannot be changed by any brooding or self-analysis."[25]

No letter from CCB to Dorothy has been found, but he surely wrote to her, for they continued to correspond regularly. Some members of the family felt that in him coals of anger against Dorothy, though well banked, never ceased to burn. Her grandson and biographer reported: "On at least one occasion, he flatly stated that he held Dorothy responsible for Robert's death. But his indomitable faith made it possible for him to survive without rancor."[26] His feeling about Robert CCB put in a letter to his sister-in-law Grace Taylor in April 1940: "Not once since he died have I wished Robert back. He could not have borne the sorrows of D. and the children being so near and yet so far. A week ago today D. sailed by the Italian Line for London via Genoa. She obtained her leave thro' [William C.] Bullitt, who has been touched by the magic Freud. D. was wild to go. The children do without her; they are very independent."[27]

The following year, having heard from a friend in London of the work Anna Freud and Dorothy were doing with children, he wrote back:

What you write of Dorothy's work is most interesting . . . D. is very efficient—would make a fine business man. Her lack of education and of natural brain power exposes her to emotional appeals. But the Freuds have helped her greatly and this work suits her perfectly. Through the lines of the Reports, I see the trail of psycho-analysis. S.F. was a great man no doubt, but his disciples have done great harm and D. has not had enough mental training to practice the perilous art.[28]

A decade later he was still writing to Dorothy, long, chatty letters of family and political news, which he signed "Father." And though he continued to speak his mind, often disagreeing with her about what the children should or should not be doing, she would reply, addressing him "Dear Father." In a letter sent shortly before his ninety-second birthday, she wrote, "One of my greatest sources of pleasure is that you never turned from me. I do appreciate how wonderful you have been to me. It would be another world if everybody was as loving as you."[29]

After Louie's death in 1937, CCB received many letters of condolence from friends, and in replying to several of these, after commenting on his happiness in marriage to her, he remarked on the greater loss suffered by their daughter, Nancy. As he wrote to Frankfurter: "For Nancy it is hardest, for we three were the closest, and L's death presages mine, and that means even greater loneliness for N. She is so quiet and unvocal that only a few know the strength, tempered and tried, and the nobility of her nature. She is grand now, and she will endure nobly all that Fate brings her."[30]

Fate, however, had been swift and cruel following Louie's death in December with Robert's suicide in May and CCB's heart attack in August. The full burden of running a complicated, upset household (including a chauffeur, cook, and usually at least one maid) had fallen on Nancy. She was aided, both in Black Point and New York, by her elder brother and his wife, though Charles and Cora had their own home, two boys to care for, and their own activities. As the months passed, it became clear that Nancy could not manage the budget, the meals, the visitors and guests, and the constantly changing schedule. She was not as decisive as Louie in dealing with the staff, and her health was not always the best. Sometime during this period CCB hired a nurse companion to help her, a woman who recently had cared for Louie.

By 1938 Nancy was fifty-three, a shy, wan spinster. CCB could call her "quiet and unvocal," but to others in the family—she knew no one well outside it—she had troubles deeper than these surface traits. She sometimes brought to a situation more emotion than it warranted. Good-byes, particularly with small children, could become difficult, leaving the child confused and upset. Even before Robert's death, she enjoyed taking his children shopping and to buy handsome presents for Mabbie and Katrina. But as Katrina later remarked, this was not something the girls' Tiffany aunts did, though they were far richer; but then, the Tiffany aunts had families of their own to love. To Katrina, at Bennington, Nancy clearly was brooding her failure to marry and have children.[31]

Decades earlier she supposedly had attracted a suitor. Her brother Charles, at a party on Crane's Beach (north of Gloucester, Massachusetts), had introduced her to a friend, a lawyer working for a Boston firm, who had been drawn to her. But she had been too unsophisticated to handle the man's attention and had retreated to her parents in New York.[32] Her nieces and nephews, debating in later years who or what was chiefly responsible for her troubles, divided in their opinions, ascribing her unhappy situation in different proportions to heredity, to CCB, and to Louie. Yet most agreed that if heredity was the initial cause—perhaps another instance of Lawrence bad blood—its effects had been aggravated by both parents.

Unquestionably, CCB's extraordinary energy and intensity were hard on his children and grandchildren. On occasion, some found the force of his personality greater than their small experience and emotional strength could sustain. Even unrelated adults at times found him disconcerting. On subjects that interested him he knew a great deal and liked to keep the conversation on them. And because the range and quality of his acquaintance was so remarkable, he was apt to be abreast or even ahead of new opinion. Few houseguests or friends questioned his views but were eager to hear more, for that was the purpose of their visit, and he delighted in not disappointing them. Those who saw CCB at the root of Nancy's real or imagined troubles noted that the Burlingham household, its schedule, family, and staff, was organized to serve him. Marriage for Nancy would have inconvenienced CCB, and therefore, according to this view, he encouraged her to stay home and unmarried. Despite his support for women's causes and independence, he had not urged her to college, or to prepare for a job or any sort of life outside the family.

Others were inclined to hold Louie more responsible. In the opinion of her niece Rosamond Taylor, who knew her well, "Aunt Louie was a great moulder of persons." Louie had talked of Nancy's frail health and the need to protect her against the buffetings of the world. Louie was the one who had taken her out of school, breaking her friendships with other children, and had arranged for tutoring at home—an education, chiefly in piano, tea, and the domestic arts, that prepared Nancy for a world that was already passing.[33]

At home, CCB bullied her as he did anyone who allowed him to do so. For example, he had an obsession about mail. Any letter he wrote had to be posted at once, and if at Black Point, then taken to a railroad station for quick pickup. But at Black Point even the nearest station was a considerable drive. If the chauffeur or Nancy was not available, CCB would ask Charles to take the letter. One night he phoned Charles late, and Cora told him firmly that Charles would mail the letter in the morning. Such defeats for CCB were rare. He hated the phone and could be brutal on it. At Black Point he would call Charles or Cora and demand his grandson Charlie for lunch. "One p.m.," he would shout, and crash the phone on its cradle. At meals, he forever was sending one child for the dictionary, and another for the atlas. His eldest grandson's wife, the Norwegian Mossik Burlingham, recalled his behavior at table as "bossy, and disruptive." The meal frequently was spoiled because too often it was a time of tension. She was glad not to be "a close, blood relative." Yet because Bob Burlingham was not earning much, CCB would send Mossik a monthly check for fifty dollars "because he wanted women to have money of their own." In time, he raised the stipend to a hundred dollars. "He was *very* generous."[34]

Sometime in late 1939 or early 1940, Nancy suffered a "nervous breakdown." She became sick without apparent cause. Physically, she felt exhausted, and frequently took to her bed; emotionally, she was depressed, unable to complete the simplest chore, much less manage a household. In these years, before psychiatry and pharmacology became common, the cause of such a collapse usually was ascribed if not to menopause then to heredity, alcoholism, trauma, or grief, any of which except for alcoholism seemed possible in Nancy's case. And the usual initial treatment for such a breakdown was a long rest. (The first antidepressant drug, Iproniazid, was not available until 1957.) To that end CCB arranged for her to enter Brooklea Farm, in Port Chester, which he described to Thacher as "a beautiful sort of sanitarium mansion." He went on to explain, "I could not bring Nancy back to the cares of housekeeping. She is awfully tired and worn and has been put to bed now." He visited her regularly, often spending the night at the sanitarium, and from time to time she would come to the apartment in New York to try a night or two at home.[35]

Months passed, but she did not improve. To his friend Helena Hirst in England, CCB wrote that the worst of it was Nancy's belief that she would not recover. "I have called in a well-known physician to consult and if possible inspire N. with hope and give her the assurance the M.D.s feel that she will recover completely."[36] But his scheme had only slight success, and one night in the New York apartment, seemingly in 1940, she had a setback.

On this occasion, Rosamond Taylor and her husband John Burling had come for dinner. Burling was then an assistant U.S. attorney in the Southern District—before that he had worked for Tom Dewey in the New York County attorney's office—and CCB was eager to hear the younger man's views on city affairs. The dinner went well enough, though Nancy, before coming down from the sanitarium, in some sort of protest, had taken scissors and butchered her hair. She had always been plain; now she looked odd and sick.

After dinner, CCB, wanting Burling to himself, told the two women to play the piano, as Rosamond recalled, "in a tone in which one might tell a dog or cat to get off the chair." As the women went to the piano, CCB took Burling to a sofa at the side of the room. A few bars into the piece Nancy broke into convulsive sobs, saying she would never get married, never have a child, and that Rosamond was the child she should have had. Rosamond looked to CCB for help, but he ignored her and kept Burling on the sofa beside him, talking. As soon as the young couple felt they decently could, they left, both deeply upset.[37]

Nancy's symptoms grew worse, and increasingly she turned her rage for her illness on her father. She had no rein on her tongue. Anything could be said and was. He was responsible for her illness. He had kept her from having a family. He had ruined her life. Her niece Katrina recalled the tirades as "quite terrifying" and so "extreme" they could only have been "the result of illness." Mossik later concluded that Nancy was "manic-depressive."[38]

In cases of breakdown where rest brought no improvement—and by July 1942 Nancy had been at Brooklea Farm for two years—the last hope lay in electric shock treatments. If administered with a general anesthesia, these were not painful. The theory behind them was that the electric shock would induce a muscular seizure, which in turn might jar and re-arrange the neurons in the brain. These neurons released chemicals into the brain, and thus, possibly, a series of shocks might change the chemical balance in the brain.

In Nancy's case, the decision to try electric shock treatment was made after a disastrous visit with CCB at Black Point. Just what happened is not known, but word of it brought from Gus Hand a letter to "Dear Burleigh." After expressing hope that the shock treatment might prove helpful, Hand added: "I am sure you ought not to live with a person in her condition. I shall never believe that it is good for either of you, and heaven knows that there are enough troubles and alarms in this world so that some real di-version from them is necessary to get along. You need it and cannot get it if you are always on the job. This frank 'realistic' statement, as the chil-dren of light would say, doesn't lessen my thoughts and sympathy."[39]

A fortnight later CCB wrote to Thacher:

At last I have good news. N. is decidedly better after 8 treatments by electric shock therapy at Bloomingdale, where she went July 21 after 3 weeks here. She said she was too ill to be here and was willing to go anywhere for help. I had read a little of this modern method and after consulting my old friend Dr. Adolf Meyer of Johns Hopkins gave my consent. I have had two letters from N. just now and she writes that she feels like a different person. She must now wait a month before further treatments. I have had my 3 great-grandchildren here and 2 mothers and (for weekends) 2 fathers, and they have been a boon.[40]

By the end of the year, he wrote the Hirsts: "The news from Nancy is very good. I was in the lower depths and wrote letters and adjured the doctors when suddenly the third series began to take effect and our family physi-cian and Miss Irwin [N.'s nurse companion] found a very marked change and improvement."[41]

Yet full recovery remained elusive. The following spring Nancy was worse, then better, and CCB prayed for the improvement to last. To the

Hirsts he wrote: "All the doctors assure me that she will get well and that I must be patient. I thought I had been, but I must remember Job!" That day he had the Bible much in mind, for he had bought one to take to Nancy, but was told by a nurse that Bibles weren't allowed in the hospital. "So I wrote to the chief medical officer and asked him whether he thought a psalm of David was deleterious—no reply yet!"[42]

By June 1945 Nancy still was not well enough for even a short visit to Black Point, and CCB relayed his disappointment to the Hirsts. The doctor had told him, "When she is as well in the morning as she is in the afternoon and evening then she may come." To which CCB added a comment: "I have less and less respect for psychiatrists. I have known a great many and only one stands out, or possibly two." But he did not name them.[43]

Two years later, in July 1947, her health had stabilized enough for her to think of leaving the sanitarium, and CCB bought her a house in Greenwich, Connecticut, close to the sanitarium and not far from New York, adding to her nurse companion a cook and a housekeeper. Nancy was apprehensive about the change, however, and did not leave the sanitarium until the end of the year. But once settled in her house, at 60 Glenville Road, she seemed to enjoy it, and by the summer of 1948 was making short visits to Black Point and the Park Avenue apartment.

The worst of her illness lasted ten years, 1938–48, a decade in which CCB aged from eighty to ninety, and during which, as he confessed to the Hirsts, his mind had turned frequently to the event he called "Brother Death." "I think of him often in the night watches. Death seems to be the most natural thing in the world. To me birth seems far more wonderful and mysterious." Though at an age when most men are tired and ready to lie down, CCB by nature was an optimist, and he never quit trying to win health and a life for his daughter. Returning to New York from Black Point in 1950, he wrote happily to the Hirsts: "Nancy drove me down Saturday afternoon and stayed for tea and supper, which was a great comfort to me."[44]

Yet some aspects of their relations he could not change. Apologizing to Helena Hirst the next spring for Nancy's failure to answer a letter, he wrote: "I have given her an addressed envelope with a 15-cent stamp, but I don't know whether she will write. She loves to have word from you, and I hope you will keep on writing."[45] He probably thought with the stamped addressed envelope he was helping his daughter; she probably thought he was bullying her.

Her recovery was never complete. One of her great-nephews remembers that on leave-taking, "she would burst into tears, get too emotional, and her keeper would come up and try to soothe her." And her nephew Charles, in answer to her complaint that his father had nicer furniture than she did, explained that much of it had been brought to his father by his mother.[46] But a reasonable answer could not ease an unreasonable grievance, and in this and other respects she continued to feel unfairly treated within the family. From time to time she would call her father and assert a complaint, though seldom with any workable plan for redress. CCB, deaf, hating the phone, unable to focus her words on anything specific, would lose his temper, and thrusting the phone at the nearest person would bark: "You talk to her."[47] When he died, he left two-thirds of his estate in trust for Nancy, who would have the income for life, allowing her to live in comfort. But as a relative observed, "The last forty years of her life"—she lived until 1974, aged eighty-eight—"were very little."[48]

Nancy's absence from CCB's household set his life's pattern for his last twenty years. He continued to live at 860 Park Avenue, with a housekeeper in charge, ultimately Nora Brennan, an Irish immigrant, who became in time his ears, eyes, secretary, and friend. If someone wanted to come for the night, a meal, or tea—and CCB welcomed visitors—he or she would call and speak to Nora, who kept CCB's schedule and would make all the arrangements. People dropped by constantly to discuss Fusion politics, church affairs, civil service reform, or any of the other projects in which he was involved. While La Guardia was mayor, he continued to frequently pick up CCB in his limousine, and the two would ride downtown together. Almost every morning young Charles, by then in his sixties, would stop by on his way to the office and check on his father's wants and plans. St. George's Church began to hold its vestry meetings in the apartment, and lawyers from the bar association were continually in and out.

By 1946, at eighty-eight, CCB had started a cataract in each eye, but hardly anyone outside the family was aware of this new problem. His grandson Charles, spending a week with him at Black Point, came home late one night and discovered CCB reading in bed. He had pillows at his back, a goose-necked lamp, magnifying glass, and flashlight, and he was reading *Paradise Lost*, he said, "for the last time."[49] But those who saw him up and about in his apartment in New York or in his law firm (where he had excellent assistants) hardly noticed the dimming of vision. He was active, vital, and still astonishingly well informed. He met life with élan. Reproved one day by Nancy for backseat driving, he replied with a poem:

The Back Seat Driver

I know an old gaffer—he's called C.C.B.
Who's the worst backseat driver one ever did see.
    He's as deaf as an adder and blind as a bat;
    What difference does that make, he says thro' his hat.

He doesn't know whether the light's green or red,
If eether or eyether, he yells "Go Ahead."
    He bawls out dear Wallie [N.'s companion] when she's at the wheel,
    And cries "Left" or "Right" with impenitent zeal.

What to do is the problem, a hard one to solve,
And all we can think of is to firmly resolve,
    To bind up his eyes with a kerchief of linen
    And shut his mouth, too, to keep him from sinnin'.[50]

But remorse was brief; he continued to drive from the backseat.

Whatever Hupper, Clark, and others in the law firm may have expected, CCB did not behave as do most lawyers who become "of counsel." Spurred perhaps by loneliness, he came to the office as regularly as before; worked almost as many hours, and called just as often on his son or other lawyers in the firm to help him with legal or historical research. He used the stenographers constantly, and if for any reason he found himself at home in the middle of the day, he'd telephone for one to be sent to his apartment in the early afternoon. After she arrived, he would dictate for an hour or two, and then have the maid bring in tea and cookies. The stenographers considered it a good assignment, for tea usually appeared by four o'clock, and after a cup she was free to go home. One time after tea, Emma O'Connor went to Bloomingdale's department store, where she left her notepad with the dictation on a counter. The next day CCB did not come to the office until after lunch, and through the morning Emma suffered. When he arrived, expecting to sign his letters, she went to tell him her story. Afterward she told her colleagues: "He listened to me, thought a bit, then threw back his head, laughed, and told me not to worry, that doubtless what he had dictated was a lot of nonsense anyway."[51]

Five, ten, fifteen years passed, and CCB, with astonishing vitality, did not die or fade away. One day in the office, while Grace Stanley was taking his dictation, he leapt from his chair like a boy, saying, "Look, look," and waving her to the window, pointed to an airplane flying close by. Another time, when Grace was with him, the phone rang. As she later recounted: "The firm's operator said to CCB, 'The president wants to speak with you'—'The president of what?'—'Of the United States.'—And indeed," said Grace, "it was President Franklin Delano Roosevelt."[52]

Despite the friends in high places, CCB's manner was democratic, friendly yet formal, and for Emma O'Connor's young son he regularly cut from his letters the signature of anyone famous and saved any stamps from other countries. Later Emma's son, grown and at Dartmouth, shifted his interest to cars, and in 1944 bought what he considered a great treasure, a dark blue 1929 Studebaker "President." Eager to show it off, he called his mother, drove the car to William Street and parked it under the eye of an amused policeman who gave him ten minutes to race up to the office and point it out to his mother. Upstairs he was hurried into CCB's office, where Emma, a few others, and CCB were hanging out the window, gazing at a blue dot on the street. Exclaiming as loudly as any was CCB, who couldn't tell a Buick from a Cadillac but was always on the side of youth.[53]

Being "of counsel," CCB was supposed not to meddle in office affairs, but he liked meddling, and by sly questions to the staff and the firm's young lawyers, as well as almost daily conversations with his son, he kept abreast of what was going on. Typically, having gathered his information, he then would confront Clark or Hupper with direct questions that were hard to evade for he knew the answers. Hupper would protest to the other partners, and no doubt to CCB, that being "of counsel" he had "no right to ask such questions. No right!" Nevertheless, a shared affection bound the two men, and it deepened with the years.[54]

In this, CCB was fortunate, for another leader of the firm, say, the lawyer who succeeded Hupper, might not have been so patient. This man was the highly competent but somewhat harsh and aggressive Eugene Underwood, who rose to dominance in the 1950s and whose most celebrated case was the defense of the Italian Line in the sinking of the *Andrea Doria* in 1956. Twenty years earlier he had "shot" his way into the partnership by delivering an ultimatum to Clark and Hupper, who capitulated and thereafter were never fully at ease with him. Though CCB had hired Underwood in 1922, the latter seems to have been less sentimental about the old man than Clark and Hupper.[55]

Yet even between CCB and Hupper friendship could not always smooth the conflict of egos. When in 1958 Hupper's partners wanted to give him a seventy-fifth birthday party, he agreed to it only if CCB, who was a hundred that year, was *not* invited, for if CCB were present or heard of the party in advance, he would want to run it, to tell everyone how it was to be. Hupper's partners understood, and so the party was held without CCB.

And when he learned of it, his feelings were hurt. One partner, attempting to soothe the old gentleman, wrote him a letter about office affairs, suggesting in a tortured paragraph that the party was an impromptu affair because legal matters kept interfering: "Therefore, you understand that birthday parties were not very important in the picture."[56]

CCB soon forgot or forgave, for he was little inclined to hold a grudge. More important, and not to be forgot, was that his partners, for almost a quarter of a century, 1934–58, had given him a base from which to sally forth and do what pleased him. That was worth remembering.

All courts have their traditions, their heroes, and their villains, and surely nothing corrodes public faith in a judicial system so swiftly as corruption on the bench. Rightly, most citizens believe that the judge, however brusque, prejudiced, or incompetent, is honest, that the court's decision is not for sale. And the higher the court's rank, the greater the strength of the public's trust. At the lowest level, say in traffic court, many people believe in the possibility of a "fix," but in the higher trial courts the number dwindles, and in appellate courts trails off. Moreover, trust is strongest in the federal system where the appointed judges have life tenure and do not have to win reelection.[57] Yet even in the federal system the courts have an occasional villain, and one appeared in 1941 on the Second Circuit Court of Appeals, ending in a fall from the bench that has been called "the most momentous judicial disgrace in the Anglo-American judicial system since Francis Bacon was impeached in 1621."[58]

A lesser fall had occurred in 1929 with the resignation of Judge Francis A. Winslow from the Southern District Court. He had been charged with "serious indiscretions," especially in the appointment and oversight of receivers in bankruptcy cases—allegedly he had appointed favorites and approved excessive fees—and a congressional subcommittee was appointed to investigate. Even earlier, at the request of the U.S. attorney, the City Bar Association had appointed a special committee, with CCB as chairman, to investigate the court's bankruptcy procedures. Not daring to face the congressional charges, Wilson resigned his seat, an act that by custom stopped the investigation, the theory being that with the judge removed, there was no need to proceed further.[59]

The bar association committee, however, continued to examine the court's procedures, and ultimately, in May 1930 (by which time CCB was the Association's president), it produced a long report which it offered to the district court with recommendations for improvement. In time, Congress and the federal courts adopted many of its suggestions, and thus, out of the Winslow scandal some good was achieved.

But there was no such gain in the disgrace that led to Martin T. Manton's resignation in 1939 as senior judge of the Second Circuit Court of Appeals. He had been appointed to the Southern District Court in 1916 and only eighteen months later had been promoted, over the head of his senior colleague Learned Hand,[60] to the Second Circuit Court, where in 1927 he became the senior, or chief, judge. Since then, by hard work, by force of personality, and because of the court's importance, he had become the country's best-known federal judge after the nine on the Supreme Court.[61]

Faced with evidence that he had accepted bribes, asked litigants for loans, and sold his decision in patent cases, he at first protested his innocence and then resigned. Unlike the Winslow case, however, this time the U.S. attorney did not stop on the judge's resignation but proceeded to prosecute Manton on criminal charges of obstructing justice and intent to defraud the United States. Though U.S. Attorney John T. Cahill probably needed no urging, he was prodded to it by a challenge from the New York county attorney, Thomas E. Dewey, who had gathered considerable evidence against Manton[62] and who announced publicly that if the federal government did not prosecute the judge, then the state would. Whereupon, with Dewey cooperating, Cahill charged Manton with eight instances in which he had accepted some $186,000 in bribes and loans from parties before his court—this was, of course, only the easily proved residue of allegedly much larger sums.[63]

Because all the federal judges in the local district and circuit courts were acquainted with Manton, Chief Justice Hughes appointed a district judge from Maryland, W. Calvin Chesnut, to conduct the trial, which started on 22 May 1939 and ended on 3 June; in his charge to the jury Judge Chesnut observed, "The charge of conspiracy to sell justice, made against an appellant Federal judge, is hitherto unprecedented in the 150 years of the Federal judiciary."[64] The jury, after deliberating four hours, returned a verdict of "guilty," and Chesnut sentenced Manton to prison for two years with a fine of $10,000. Finally, in February 1940, after losing his appeal to the Supreme Court, Manton paid the fine and on 7 March was taken to prison. The newspapers, for more than a year, had followed his resignation, trial, and appeal, and the public knew to the day when he went to jail. After serving his term, he went to live in Fayetteville, New York, a suburb of Syracuse, where he died in 1946, "unwept, unsung, and dishonored."[65]

CCB had worked with Manton from time to time on court affairs, notably in 1925 on a plan, never adopted, to redistrict the country's nine federal circuit courts, and though he did not like the man's style, he had not thought him corrupt. In manner, Manton was flashy, eager for honors and publicity; in temperament, harsh and aggressive; in politics, a Tammany Democrat, strongly supported by the city's Catholic church and laity. CCB thought him a good lawyer and a hardworking judge; in ten years, 1929–39, he had presided over some 2,000 cases and written some 650 opinions.[66]

Nevertheless, he distrusted Manton. In November 1932, writing to Thacher, who had left the district court to be solicitor general for Hoover and would soon be returning to private practice, he said: "I wish I could get M.T.M. out and make way for you."[67] But there was as yet no ground on which to ease out Manton. By then, however, due to the failure of the Bank of the United States, the size of Manton's borrowings and real estate dealings was beginning to be known, and he was reputed to be one of the richest of federal judges. Addison Brown, while a judge on the Southern District Court (1881–1901), had carried on a flourishing private business in real estate, but not on such a scale, not in an economic depression, and never involving parties before him in court. But as the Depression continued, Manton's widespread interests were increasingly threatened by tenants who could not pay rent, by collateral called, and by mortgages foreclosed, and from the evidence at his trial, not until the Depression did he begin his unscrupulous scramble for money.[68] He acquired it often by composing self-serving court orders. One sequence in 1932 led a dismayed legal historian to summarize: "The Chief [Manton] appointed *himself* a district judge and in his capacity as the senior circuit court judge, entered an order directing the district judge (himself) to take jurisdiction over the Fox bankruptcy. Then, in his capacity as district judge, he appointed two personal cronies as receivers . . . Manton was tireless in milking the Fox receivership." Of this Manton maneuver, CCB exclaimed to Thacher, "There is nothing like it outside *The Mikado*."[69]

By mid-1933, he was warning Chief Justice Hughes against Manton.[70] Yet there still was no complaint of corruption, only of behavior that brought the Second Circuit Court into disrepute. By 1938, however, Manton's conduct was arousing graver suspicions, and CCB about this time wrote to President Roosevelt urging him "never to give him [Manton] any honors." More bluntly, he told Frankfurter, "I wouldn't believe Manton under oath."[71]

Then, on 27 January 1939, the *World-Telegram* began a series of articles on Manton's abuse of the court. Two days later Dewey, in a letter to the chairman of the House Judiciary Committee, listed six cases of Manton's corrupt behavior with more under investigation. All the leading New York papers put the story on the first page, and the next day Manton sent President Roosevelt his resignation. At that point no one, except perhaps Dewey, was thinking of a trial on criminal charges. Most presumed that, as had happened with Winslow, the judge's resignation would end the investigation.[72]

CCB, startled by Dewey's revelations and perhaps not even now fully convinced of the judge's guilt, promptly wrote to Manton about his resignation:

1 February 1939

Dear M.T.M.

I have a feeling that you must be very sad, and I am so truly sorry that you are that I cannot refrain from sending you these poor lines.

I have a notion that you have failed to appreciate the sentiment of the bar and the public which has been growing stronger and stronger in recent years against judges taking part in business transactions. I imagine that, feeling assured that your decisions were not influenced by your business relations, you have not perceived how strong the public sentiment is.

We have been friends for a good many years, and I hope you will not object to my expressing myself thus frankly, for I am truly and sympathetically yours,[73]

The letterhead of the existing, unsigned copy of CCB's letter to Manton—860 Park Avenue—suggests that it was typed in CCB's apartment. A retired judge, Samuel C. Coleman, who read this copy after CCB's death, penned on it a note of disbelief: "Manton? Was this sent?"[74] But whether or not the original was sent, the copy surely represents CCB's feelings both then and later. For in 1952 he wrote to a colleague, "It can be said of Manton that he really did not think he was doing anything wrong in being nice to his friends."[75]

In view of what was revealed during Manton's criminal trial, the lack of condemnation in CCB's later statement may seem strange, but it accurately reports Manton's thinking about his own behavior. A lawyer who talked to Manton soon after conviction recorded, "It was fascinating to observe . . . he had no realization whatever of having done anything wrong in taking money from litigants. Hadn't he decided all the cases before him correctly?" CCB's comment, however, also suggests the defect of his own virtue: he hardly could bring himself to believe that a high-ranking federal judge could sell his decisions, but that is what Manton had done.[76]

By 1940, though CCB had ceased to practice law, because of his activity in civic affairs he was still well known to the press and public and still considered the leader of the admiralty bar. In that capacity, in early December 1940, he received a letter from Julius Goebel, historian of Columbia Law School, about the twenty-two inch silver oar that for fifty years during the eighteenth century had served as the mace of the British vice admiralty court of the province of New York.[77]

Before 1776 some twenty-five or more British vice admiralty courts on the American East Coast and in Bermuda, the Bahamas, and the Caribbean islands each had a silver oar. Their size and design were similar, each had engraved on one side of its blade the Royal Arms of Great Britain, and on the other, the Crowned Anchor, the seal of the Admiralty Court of Great Britain. The oar for New York's court, made circa 1725 by the city's best silversmith, Charles Le Roux, also bore on its handle the words "Court of Vice Admiralty New York." Mounted on a pole and carried into the courtroom before the judge, the oar opened the court's session. Throughout the sitting it lay in a small cradle on the judge's desk, directly before the judge and in full view of the court; and to close the session it was carried out before the judge.[78]

In 1775, amid the turmoil of the Revolution, New York's oar disappeared, leaving the vice admiralty court's successors—the Admiralty Court of the State of New York, which in 1789 became a U.S. district court, and in 1814 the Southern District Court of New York—without their emblem of admiralty jurisdiction. Other colonial admiralty courts also lost their oars, and for over a hundred years the only one known to survive was that of the Bermuda court. Then one day in the early 1890s, the whereabouts of the New York oar had been disclosed, though its holder refused to give it up. Appeals were made, in which CCB had a part, but to no avail.[79]

Then, almost fifty years later, CCB received Goebel's letter.

November 30, 1940

Dear Mr. Burlingham,

    The famous and beautiful oar of the New York provincial Vice-Admiralty Court has passed into the hands of Robert Ensko [silversmith] of 682 Lexington Avenue. Mr. Ensko who has a thorough appreciation of the historical significance of the oar prefers to have it go to an institution rather than some private collector. I understand that Yale is endeavoring to work on the sympathies and pocket book of Judge Woolsey [one of the Southern District Court's eleven judges]. I should feel very bad if an object, so intimately connected with the history of our state should pass into a jurisdiction where the authority of admiralty courts was consistently contemned. I am accordingly writing to inquire whether you can suggest some way of interesting the admiralty bar in purchasing the oar and perhaps presenting it to Columbia. I think it can be obtained for as little as Twenty-five Hundred Dollars.

Unfortunately with the exception of yourself my acquaintances among the affluent are all of the Common Law variety and their mental outlook is still colored by the prejudices of Sir Edward Coke. Please pardon me for bothering you.[80]

Goebel's appeal, sure to excite CCB, failed in only one respect. From the start CCB wanted the oar for the court, not Columbia, and to that end he enlisted as a colleague his friend Tom Thacher. The ex-judge, though a Yale graduate and ardent "Eli," was presently a fellow of the Yale Corporation, the university's governing body. Regarding the oar, however, CCB correctly gauged that Thacher's loyalty to the city and the court would be greater than to any university, and in Thacher CCB would have an ally powerfully placed to frustrate a bid from Yale. And lo!—Yale promptly sent a visitor to Thacher. But the discussion did not go as Yale's emissary had hoped. Thacher reported to CCB: "John Phillips is very anxious to get the Oar for the Yale Art Collections of old silver. He is the Curator of the Garvin Collection. I told him it was out of the question—that the Oar belonged in New York. He was insistent that it would be lost in the court. I was equally insistent that Yale should not have it. In the course of our talk he said that he thought it was overpriced by Ensko."[81]

That same day, CCB went to Ensko's shop and afterward wrote to Thacher:

I saw the oar this morning. It is a beautiful creation, made by Charles Le Roux who was assistant Alderman of the East Ward from 1735 to 1738 . . . Ensko, Inc., bought it from the Manufacturers Trust Company, Trustee of one of the Ludlow, for $2,500—so they told me this morning, and can show the bill of sale. I got a refusal on it until January 15th, so you and I ought to be able to raise the money, and I will rough out an appeal which you must smooth and polish.[82]

One Thomas Ludlow, as CCB explained to those who asked how the oar had passed out of public into private hands, had been the last provost marshal of the English vice admiralty court. Sometime in 1775 he apparently had taken "the oar into his own possession." Though CCB was prepared to believe that his motive had been custodial, "safekeeping," still, Ludlow's "descendants came to regard the oar as their private property; but about two years ago one of the latest Ludlows put up the oar as collateral for a loan from a National Bank of this District." And the bank, on Ludlow's failure to meet payment, had sold the oar to Ensko.[83]

The Burlingham-Thacher letter of appeal went out on 30 December to some fifty admiralty firms and individual lawyers "in the hope that by gifts of from $50 to $100 we may collect the fund necessary to make the purchase within the next few days." Checks were to be sent to CCB.[84] Response was quick. Within a day the three firms of Crawford & Sprague; Haight, Griffen, Deming & Gardner; Kirlin, Campbell, Hickox, Keating & McGrann; and Samuel Seabury had altogether contributed $350. The two canvassers also had a refusal, from Loomis, Williams & Donohue:

> We cannot but feel that it would be of questionable propriety for a United States Admiralty Court to display, during its sessions, as symbolic of its authority and jurisdiction, an emblem of British Royalty bearing the British Royal coat of arms and the seal of its ancestral British Court. We are satisfied that our Revolutionary forebears would have sternly frowned on such a practice and put a peremptory end thereto . . . While we are thus barred from the acceptance of your invitation, nevertheless, we should be most happy to join in the purchase of the Silver Oar and contribute thereto an amount substantially as great as that which you mentioned in your letter, if the device of the British coat of arms should be effaced and supplanted with the National coat of arms of the United States; and if, too, the seal of the old British Admiralty Court should be hammered out and replaced with the seal of our United States Admiralty Court.[85]

Ignoring this refusal, CCB and Thacher urged the president of the Maritime Law Association to have its executive committee consider if the association might donate to the cause $500. And this was easily accomplished, for the MLA's president was CCB's partner Roscoe Hupper, and the committee met in the office of Burlingham, Veeder, Clark & Hupper. The association's secretary soon reported to CCB that the contribution had been "enthusiastically" approved. In addition, since the two campaign managers had forgotten to send a copy of their appeal to Burlingham's firm, Hupper volunteered its check for $100.[86]

Even so, on 14 January, the day before the option to buy was to expire, they were short $600, and CCB asked and received from Ensko an extension to the twentieth. But he worried still about Yale, warning one contributor, "Yale College is after the Oar."[87] That threat may have moved at least one lawyer to his checkbook. Harrison Tweed, of Milbank, Tweed & Hope and a grandson of William M. Evarts, sent in $100 with the comment: "Anyway, I am glad that if Yale wanted it they are not going to get it. I have always regretted the fact that I gave them the best of the Hunt portraits of Senator Evarts."[88]

As the option's expiration drew near, CCB and Thacher still lacked $290 but dared wait no longer. Making up the balance themselves, they sent a check for $2,500 to Ensko on the seventeenth, only to discover that they had forgotten the sales tax of $50. Meanwhile, they continued to dun firms that had declined to contribute. "I must say," CCB wrote to Thacher, "the refusal of Cadwalader, W[ickersham] & T[aft], of [Emory] Buckner, and of Root, Clark, B[uckner] & B[allantine], has peeved me quite a bit. If we could get $100 from each of them and from Davis, Polk, we'd be all right." Thacher thereupon extracted $100 from Davis, Polk, and a second $100 from the anti-Yale Tweed.[89]

A few days later CCB wrote to Goebel: "We have bought the Oar and paid for it, and in due course it will be presented formally to the Court *en banc*, and I will see to it that you are duly notified, for you are the true begetter of this delight. Ensko acted very handsomely. He extended our option four or five days, although he could have sold the Oar to Yale for $3,500."[90]

By the first week of February, CCB was able to tell Thacher, "We are now $185 ahead, so I enclose a check to your order for $100, your extra contribution . . . Now, why not go ahead and arrange with Knox, J. [chief judge] for a session of the Court *en banc*, and you are hereby designated as the Orator of the Day."

Thacher promptly replied with a handwritten note:

Don't talk of an orator of the day. We're in Admiralty and want an *Oar-ator*—You're the only one because you have had the sea in your veins longer than all the rest. The bar loves you for many things and when we venerate the Admiralty your presence and your presentation of this venerable relic will do more honor to the Admiralty and the Court than anyone else. It is quite preposterous to suggest one who, when you were already a leader, did not know that a bottomry bond was not an ancient plumbing fixture . . . You should perform this simple task because it is yours and no one else should be permitted to do it. You can do it so beautifully, so simply, and so briefly . . . This has been my thought all along, and I should not have cared about the plan if I had thought you would not do this in a way which I am sure will be no burden at all to you and will be tremendously appreciated by those who love you and the Court in which you have practised so long.[91]

So, at ten-thirty on the morning of 14 February, before a crowd of lawyers in room 506 of the federal courthouse, on Foley Square, and before all eleven judges of the Southern District of New York, CCB presented to the court its ancient symbol of admiralty jurisdiction. He spoke briefly to the point: an emblem of historical interest, lost to the court for 166 years, had been found, purchased for the court by the admiralty bar, and returned to its rightful owner. Following Louie's advice given him many years earlier, he had written out his remarks in order not to omit the name of anyone who deserved thanks, yet also, as usual, he peppered his text with impromptu remarks, so that it sounded vivid and spontaneous.

The *Times*, in a story anticipating the event, explained to its readers that "the Southern District Court is said to have had a larger share in developing the law of the sea than any other United States Court." CCB, at eighty-two, had practiced before it longer than anyone living, and now, after fifty-eight years, on a unique occasion and with a characteristic flourish, he made his exit.[92]

20

Moses, Roosevelt, and CCB

WHEN ROOSEVELT'S FIRST term as president began its final year, in January 1936, Americans had reason to hope that the worst of the Depression had passed. By the end of that year the national income had risen from $39.6 billion in 1933 to $64.7 billion, and the number of unemployed had dropped from somewhere between twelve and thirteen million to between six and eight. Though millions still suffered, a full economic recovery seemed possible. Writing the next month to his English friend Helena Hirst, CCB quoted a letter from Frank Taussig, professor of economics at Harvard, to express his own feelings about Roosevelt: "With all his political ambition, love of political gain and willingness to do dubious things in order to win, I have faith that he is sincere in his general attitude, genuinely despises the Wall Street crowd, whom he knows and knows about, and has an unfailing sympathy for the under-dog."[1] As if in confirmation, Roosevelt on the night of 27 June, in accepting the Democratic nomination, spoke of how "Governments can err, Presidents do make mistakes, but the immortal Dante tells us that divine justice weighs the sins of the cold-blooded and the sins of the warm-hearted in different scales. Better the occasional faults of a Government that lives in a spirit of charity than the consistent omissions of a Government frozen in the ices of its own indifference." That, too, reflected CCB's feelings; and in general he favored the New Deal's efforts to foster relief and recovery.

In the November election Roosevelt won forty-six of the forty-eight states, all but Vermont and Maine, and in January in his second inaugural address he stressed the need to continue those efforts—"I see one-third of a nation ill-housed, ill-clad, ill-nourished"—after which people waited expectantly to hear his plans to assist that third of the nation. But to their surprise, instead of a program for new social or economic legislation, he introduced his bill to enlarge the Supreme Court, an issue on which he misgauged the public's feelings and on which, by the end of July, he had been roundly defeated. Then, in August, the economy faltered. In three months the production of steel fell from 80 percent of capacity to 19; by late October Dow Jones stock averages had dropped more than a third; and by year's end an additional two million people were out of work. The "Roosevelt recession" of 1937–38 severely challenged the worth of his previous efforts, and some began to doubt that full employment ever again was possible. One such was Mayor La Guardia, who in April 1939 wrote to Senator James J. Byrnes, of South Carolina, "Instead of considering the situation as an emergency, we accept the inevitable, that we are now in a new normal"—with nine million unemployed.[2] Ultimately, only World War II gave work to all.

In her husband's first year as president, Eleanor Roosevelt became a major figure in American life. She traveled constantly—reportedly 40,000 miles in her first year—speaking at schools, colleges, and formal or informal meetings of all sizes and kinds. She seemed to be and go everywhere, and *The New Yorker* pictured her ubiquity in a cartoon of a grimy coal miner exclaiming, "For gosh sakes, here comes Mrs. Roosevelt!" She did indeed go down a mine, and wherever she went she carried words of encouragement to the frightened or suffering and promised to carry their words of misery back to the president. Her sympathy for the oppressed included Negroes, and she offended many white traditionalists by her support for Negro rights, and by inviting Negroes to the White House. To reach a wider audience with her thoughts and experiences she started a syndicated daily newspaper column, "My Day," which in its plain speaking and common sense was easily mocked, yet appealed to millions of readers. No previous first lady had been so active, so constantly in the news, and there were many who disapproved. CCB was not one. Having sent a severely anti-Eleanor article to Helena Hirst, he assured her in his next letter, "I don't think that E.R. was disturbed in the least by that piece or would be by any other of the same sort. As you know, I have the greatest admiration for her."[3] They were after all siblings under their skins: they both liked to meddle in public affairs.

For CCB, by the summer of 1937 one pressing engagement was the campaign of La Guardia for a second term as mayor. He never doubted La Guardia would win: the city's "plain people" had grown fond of the mayor, approved of his record, and would reelect him.[4] And on 2 November, with Seabury again stumping the boroughs beside him, La Guardia defeated Tammany's Jeremiah T. Mahoney, 1,344,630 to 890,756, becoming the first reform mayor in the city's history to win a second term. Worse still for Tammany, unlike four years earlier, Fusion candidates this time also won the presidencies of the City Council and the boroughs of Brooklyn and Manhattan, as well as the post of district attorney of New York County (Manhattan). As before, La Guardia took his oath of office in Seabury's library on East Sixty-third Street.[5]

Though CCB, as a member of the Citizens Non-Partisan Committee to Re-elect La Guardia, wrote letters, consulted, and raised money,[6] he was less active in the 1937 campaign than he had been in 1933. The committee's chairman was Seabury, aided by Windels, who on the evening of 29 July, in possibly the campaign's most important event, quelled a revolt of Brooklyn Republicans and held the county organization for La Guardia.[7] Windels's success in preventing defection and a primary contest most likely influenced the Manhattan Republican leader, Kenneth Simpson, with whom La Guardia and CCB had dealings, to conclude before the primaries that he and his district leaders likewise should support La Guardia.[8] Consequently, the 1937 mayoralty campaign and election was straightforward, a Fusion-Republican candidate against a Tammany Democrat, and no "spoiler" like McKee to split the reform vote.

Doing less for the mayor, CCB shifted time and energy into electing Thomas E. Dewey as New York County district attorney. In 1935 Governor Lehman had appointed the Republican Dewey a special prosecutor to investigate organized crime in the city, particularly a mob known as Murder Incorporated, and Dewey had been so effective that in August 1937 the Manhattan Republican leader easily recruited Fusion backing for him, starting with CCB, who agreed to be chairman of a Thomas E. Dewey Citizens Committee.[9] As CCB stressed in a speech for Dewey, "The office of District Attorney is the stronghold which Tammany must have to maintain its power. Four years ago we almost carried that fortress, but we failed, and the big shots enjoyed peace and security until Dewey was appointed Special Prosecutor to do the work the District Attorney should have done."[10]

In the election Dewey won even more votes in New York County than La Guardia, and his years as district attorney carried him a long way toward becoming governor in 1942, an office he held for three terms (twelve years). For CCB, the 1937 campaign ensured him Dewey's attention, which was useful in the years ahead.

But from neither the La Guardia nor the Dewey campaign did CCB draw his usual pleasure, for spoiling both was the distraction and distress of his wife's illness. In mid-October, when Louie entered New York Hospital, CCB daily sat at her bedside until, on the evening of 7 December, she died.

Throughout those weeks, perhaps as a relief to anguish, he continued to pepper La Guardia with comments, and soon after the election he wrote:

> You see the notes are beginning again.
>
> 1. I am awfully sorry Windels [corporation counsel] is getting out— a very wise guy. You have done absolutely the right thing in putting [William C.] Chanler in. You will never have any trouble with him. He is a fine lawyer, with good judgment and all the courage in the world.
>
> 2. I am deeply interested in the City Planning Commission [a powerful group created by the new city charter approved in 1936] and have a lot of very good ideas on the subject, which I won't bother you with here now.
>
> I wish some time you would sit down with two or three people— Windels, perhaps [I. N. Phelps] Stokes and me—and talk a little about the type of people you want. Everybody seems to think Moses is the man, but that means no Board at all, and while he is a wonderful creature and has done wonderful things, I have my doubts as to his power to look ahead 50 years, as Andrew H. Green, who was the begetter of not only Central Park, but of all the Bronx parks, did.[11]

Whether or not La Guardia was influenced by CCB, he ignored Moses, who was already the city's parks commissioner and head of the Triborough Bridge Authority, and named as the Planning Commission's chairman Adolf A. Berle Jr.; when, after a year, Berle resigned, he appointed Rexford Tugwell, also a member of FDR's "brain trust," a former professor at Columbia, and an authority on agricultural economics. Tugwell soon found himself constantly opposed by Moses and not always well supported by La Guardia. Disgusted and increasingly isolated in the political infighting, at the end of La Guardia's second term Tugwell withdrew to become governor of Puerto Rico, and La Guardia designated Moses as chairman of the City Planning Commission. CCB's prophecy then became reality: Moses, adding yet another post and its powers to his already swollen portfolio, dominated the commission and ignored long-term planning in favor of immediate projects, the more striking and visible the better.

As before, La Guardia sometimes resisted CCB's suggestions, though usually offering him a reason. In June 1938 CCB wrote him, "I greatly hope that you will not re-appoint [Ferdinand Q.] Morton a Civil Service Commissioner. You know who I think is the best man for the post—[H. Eliot] Kaplan—and I think his knowledge and wisdom are needed."[12] Morton, a protégé of Tammany leader Charles Murphy and the first Negro civil service commissioner, had held his post since 1922, but apparently what alarmed CCB were reports of Morton's activity in Democratic politics in the city's Nineteenth Assembly District.[13] Kaplan was the executive secretary of the Civil Service Reform Association, constantly in touch with city officials, and CCB, as a vice president, knew his ability. For several weeks La Guardia was silent, so CCB reopened the subject, with a barrage of Latin and French: "*Morton delendus est.* He has played ball [cooperated] with P. Kern [the commission chairman] and he would continue to do so while *you* are in, *mais ce n'est pas assez. Prenez garde.*"[14]

This time La Guardia replied: "You speak of Morton. Well—after all the intent of the law, I suppose, is to give the opposition a voice on the Commission . . . Guess I will re-appoint Morton. Besides everyone in Harlem good, very good and excellent as well as bad, poor and indifferent is a candidate." In refusing earlier to act on CCB's advice concerning Lewis Valentine, he had defended his commissioner of police swiftly, hotly, out of emotion; with regard to Morton, where his reason was more political than emotional, he was jocular.[15]

Throughout the summer of 1938, following Robert's suicide and his own subsequent slight heart attack, CCB spent more time than usual at Black Point, and consequently he and La Guardia were less often together. La Guardia that summer had taken a cottage for his family at Northport, Long Island, and in place of his frequent talks with CCB, he often wrote him from there, chatty letters, full of news, affection, and typing slips (here left uncorrected).

Am here today after a terrible week. So happy to have found your letter. This is the first time for many years that I have ussed a typewriter. Had to search to whole house for paper and these scraps were given me by Eric [his adopted son]. He said he had them hidden where the other Kids could not find his supply . . .

I have not seen you since my talk with F.D.R. when he came to the City. Will save it untill I see you. May run out some day soon to visit, if I may. Will tell you all about it . . .

I have two vacancies in Special Sessions in Bklyn and Queens. Expect to promote Magistrates Wiboldt and Finnegan. What say you?

What is this you say about your hearing? Are you spoofing, is it temporary ? I am sure we will be able to carry on our talks—x I will invoke all the habits of my Italian father and jewish mother—surely we wil get enough action out of that. But what will you do with your soft voiced Union League Club friends? . . .

Do take care of yourself. Let me come up some afternoon (weekday) to visit.

Marie and the children (we have five in the Summer)* send love—and so does

[Then, pressing the key to change the color of the typewriter ribbon to red, he tapped out]

"fiorello the red"[16]

CCB's deafness that summer came as a surprise to him and to his friends. One, "Gus" Hand, suggested hopefully that it was merely a nervous response to Robert's suicide, and so would be temporary.[17] But it persisted, and on 20 July CCB wrote to La Guardia: "I should like to have gone with you to Cardozo's funeral—we have been to quite a few funerals together, have we not? My reasons for not going were (1) I am as deaf as a post and have been for several weeks; (2) B.N.C. was very dear to me and needed no such tribute from me. And ninth and lastly, the service was, as I expected, worse than awful—Sephardic—even Irving Lehman, who stopped in the other afternoon, said so."[18]

La Guardia wrote once a week, CCB less often. In an August letter, La Guardia began: "No letter from you this week—so I guess there is nothing wrong in the city . . . Simpson [Manhattan Republican leader] has a bad case of grandiose mania and would make an ass of himself if nature had not already attended to that little matter. I am happy to be out of politics and for ever! . . . Hope you are well and that your hearing is improving. There is so much choice and spicy gossip going around that it just will be necessary that you get in good shape."[19]

But by mid-September, when CCB returned to New York, his hearing had not improved. The next month he advised his friend Thacher that he was still "too deaf to be of any use. I should have to snuggle up to the speaker and could not hear the discussion." He already had tried and discarded one hearing aid, had an appointment to test another, and eventually settled on one without much satisfaction. He tried to be philosophical—he was after all eighty—but he found the frustration of deafness hard to

---

*The family that summer included himself, Marie (his second wife), their two adopted children, Jean and Eric, a nephew, a neighbor's daughter, and the son of their Negro housekeeper. According to Kessner (1989), 441: "This mélange caused a small ruckus when the La Guardias went calling on the Roosevelts at Hyde Park and brought along the black housekeeper's son to visit the president. Local gentry were outraged . . ."

bear. He would say later that he hated deafness more than blindness, because the lack of hearing had cut him off from the theater. Meanwhile, his own speaking voice grew louder, and his characteristic gesture, especially with those speaking softly, became the quick thrust of a microphone into the speaker's face.[20]

CCB had a rule for growing old, which one day he urged on Frankfurter: "Take care to remember that the forties are not the thirties; that the fifties are not the forties; that the sixties are not the fifties, and so on and so on. Do you see? One thing more: form the habit of lying down for an hour before dinner every evening." Turning eighty in August 1938, by his rule CCB should have been letting up, but others saw little slackening.[21]

The Civil Service Reform Association hailed his eightieth birthday with a resolution passed without his knowledge, and published as a news story by the *Times*. Citing "the charm of his youthful understanding," the resolution allowed him to celebrate only fifty years:

> Whereas, the mere lapse of recorded time does not measure the amount of effective time given [to reform and good works] . . . Whereas in the good-humored activity and vigor in all these works . . . Whereas the age of Charles C. Burlingham may not therefore be estimated on any dimensional basis . . . Now, Therefore . . . [our] natal congratulations to Charles C. Burlingham on what the committee has with careful deliberation appraised as his fiftieth birthday.[22]

Nevertheless, he tried to remember a man's eighties are not his seventies, and in February 1939 he resigned the presidency of the Welfare Council of New York, a post he had held since 1931. His successor, Alfred H. Schoellkopf, graciously described him as "New York's First Citizen," and the city's newspapers in their editorials repeated the title. The *Herald Tribune* particularly praised him for his "attempt to bring about harmonious co-operation between public and voluntary efforts to prevent and to alleviate" human suffering.[23] CCB thought this task of mediation was important, and in a private letter to Schoellkopf he stressed it: "You know without my telling you that not all our friends downtown know, as you and I do, the ability and wisdom of the leading social workers of New York. I think you will be more successful than I have been in *selling* them to each other."[24]

By "downtown" CCB meant not only the politicians, bankers, and stockbrokers of City Hall and Wall Street, but all those who served them, the city's lawyers, doctors, accountants, and others who made up New York's professional middle class—the people who traditionally volunteered to serve on church vestries, hospital committees, school boards, libraries, and a host of other charitable jobs. In noting the need to "sell" these good people and the social workers "to each other," CCB touched on a troublesome aspect of social change that he had noted in his work for St. George's and for the Association for Improving the Condition of the Poor (after 1939 part of the Community Service Society), on whose board of managers he had served since 1906.

The older professional middle class and the newer professional "social workers" were often at odds, and each developing a strong bias against the other. One unhappy aspect of the gradual professionalization of social and charity work (in part initiated by Josephine Shaw Lowell and her colleagues and greatly accelerated by the programs and rhetoric of Roosevelt's New Deal) was the professional social workers' disdain for volunteers, church workers, or even individuals with money to give. The social workers seemed to delight in telling the others that they had never helped the poor, only patronized them, and now must step aside for the new professionals, who, better trained, more compassionate, and with money from the state, would do better. It was not an attitude that led to liking or cooperation.[25]

An editorial in the *Sun* on CCB's retirement from the Welfare Council touched on the problem in contrasting the views of Schoellkopf and a leading social worker, Harry Hopkins, on the future of the nation's welfare programs. Schoellkopf hoped to keep the various work programs temporary, because he thought they demoralized the recipients. Hopkins, who was head of the federal government's Works Progress Administration, the WPA, and soon to become Roosevelt's confidant and secretary of commerce, hoped to institutionalize them, taking relief workers into civil service, because he thought they could find useful work for the next twenty or thirty years.[26]

Learned Hand, in a November 1940 letter to CCB, let his irritation with the social workers in the federal bureaucracy steam forth: "I am voting for F.D.R. and while it would be too much to say that I do so *con amore*, I am getting relatively more comfortable about it. If only I could wean myself of my dislike for the complacent, self-righteous, self-seeking crew of social-workers who surround him, always caterwauling about their love for humanity, I should feel happier." He wrote privately, but spoke for many. The friction, as CCB warned his successor on the Welfare Council, was a real problem.[27]

·   ·   ·

On 22 January 1939, with an unexpected announcement, New York's city parks commissioner Robert Moses precipitated a struggle between himself and many of the city's reform groups that embroiled the mayor and eventually the president of the United States. Ultimately, it changed the way many persons in New York felt about Moses and his projects, and though it greatly increased his power, it also bore the seeds of his decline—some would say disgrace.

Moses proposed that in place of the planned Brooklyn-Battery Tunnel, designed to link the southern tip of Manhattan at Battery Park to the partially built motor parkway that skirted Brooklyn's shore, there should be a bridge. Or rather, because the distance to cross was great, there should be two linked suspension bridges. Each would arch from its shore, in Brooklyn and Manhattan, and come down on a huge concrete anchorage pier to be planted in the East River where it joins the Upper Bay just north of Governor's Island. Because the concrete pier would be placed close to Governor's Island, it allegedly would not hinder shipping using the harbor's Buttermilk Channel, which passes between the island and the Brooklyn waterfront and connects the Upper Bay to the East River. According to a brochure Moses issued, the cost of the double bridge, including all the necessary ramps and approaches in Manhattan and Brooklyn, would be $41.2 million, whereas the tunnel would cost $84 million.[28]

Behind his figures, which were promptly challenged, lay a struggle over money and power. Moses, who did not control the city's Tunnel Authority but had long wished to do so, wanted the bridge as the most notable jewel in his emerging system of parkways ringing and joining the city's two most populous boroughs. To persuade La Guardia to the idea, he had taken the mayor on a boat ride in the harbor, extolling a bridge's beauties and explaining where and how it could be built—and in describing an architectural vision, Moses could be inspiring. La Guardia was not averse to another visible monument to his administration, but he wanted the Brooklyn-Battery crossing, whether tunnel or bridge, primarily as a source of employment for the city's workers. His difficulty with the tunnel idea, first proposed in 1925 and now fully designed, was money. It would be the longest continuous underwater tunnel for motor vehicles in North America, and its designers estimated it would cost $65 million, not including the cost of some planned connections to parkways. La Guardia, who in most circumstances controlled a majority of votes on the Board of Estimate, was ready, as he had done before, to allocate a large portion of the city's annual budget to parks, parkways, tunnels, and bridges instead of to schools, hospitals, libraries, and subways (not controlled by Moses). Yet however he juggled the figures for the tunnel, he lacked roughly $30 million.[29]

Meanwhile, the city's Tunnel Authority had no record yet of earning money—its first project, the Queens-Midtown (Manhattan) Tunnel, was not scheduled to open for another two years—and therefore no gauge of use from tolls collected. Hence it had small basis on which to offer bonds to finance a second tunnel. Again and again La Guardia had gone to Washington hoping to close the $30 million gap by persuading federal agencies to increase their grants to the city, but always without success. Then, to his surprise, he discovered that the Moses-controlled Triborough Bridge Authority was earning large annual surpluses, banking millions of dollars each year from the bridge tolls. In 1937, for example, the authority reported that 11,171,956 vehicles of all kinds had used the bridge, an average of 30,608 a day, and receipts from tolls totaled $2,845,109. With such a record of use, the authority could easily raise $30 million from bonds issued against future earnings.[30]

And the price Moses asked of the mayor for providing the money? A written promise of eventual control of the Tunnel Authority, a power grab that La Guardia had blocked in 1936.[31] Now, in September 1938, he surrendered. He wanted the tunnel for the city's workforce and as a step toward completion of Moses's "Circumferential Parkway." This "Belt Parkway," as it soon was called, would carry tunnel traffic from southern Manhattan through and around southern Brooklyn and through the borough of Queens to the new Bronx-Whitestone Bridge, scheduled to open on 30 April 1939.[32] This suspension bridge, at the time of construction the fourth longest in the world, was the sixth for motor vehicles across the East River and the farthest yet to the north and east, crossing from the Whitestone section of Queens to the Bronx east of Hunt's Point; from there, connecting roads led to the Hutchinson River Parkway, allowing motorists to drive from Long Island to upstate New York and New England while avoiding Manhattan altogether and bypassing most of Queens and the Bronx. The concept of a perimeter parkway was truly grand, but unless largely self-financed by tolls, as people were beginning to realize, its construction was likely to bankrupt the city, if not in the initial building, then in the future costs of maintenance.

That realization caused an angry confrontation in mid-October at hearings by the city's Board of Estimate. At issue was money to build a stretch of Moses's Circumferential Parkway in the Gowanus section of

Brooklyn. City comptroller Joseph D. McGoldrick, Manhattan borough president Stanley M. Isaacs, and president of the City Council Newbold Morris together controlled eight of the Board of Estimate's sixteen votes, enough to block the parkway appropriation in favor of more money for hospitals and schools, which they favored. Moses, expecting trouble, packed the hearing with his Parks and Triborough employees, who hissed and booed anyone who spoke against his parkway. He also asked the mayor, who had the right to preside over the board's meetings, to attend. The three dissenting officials, though their financial and social arguments were strong, were not aware of how much stronger was Moses's grip on the mayor: The Triborough Authority's ability to raise the needed $30 million for the tunnel was crucial to that larger project. Moreover, if the tunnel were not built, the city would lose some $55 million in federal money allocated to it and the connecting parkways.

So the mayor called the board into executive session and—though the dissenting officials were Fusion candidates elected to their positions, not appointed by him—put the issue to them on a personal basis: "You've got to go along with me on this." After four hours of closeted argument, the three dissenters gave in, making the final vote in favor of the allocation for a section of parkway unanimous. As McGoldrick later explained to Moses's biographer, Robert Caro, refusing such an appeal would have meant a complete split with the mayor, after the second-term Fusion administration had been in office only ten months. "[We] knew that we couldn't at that early stage have a break with the Mayor—it would have thrown the whole administration into chaos."[33]

With Moses assured of the city's contribution to the Gowanus section of his Circumferential Parkway, paperwork on the tunnel could proceed. La Guardia could arrange details of the financing, for which Moses, in return for his contribution, had obtained, by a secret memorandum with him,[34] the promise of eventual control of the Tunnel Authority. Members of the latter, knowing nothing of this secret agreement, went ahead with their next step, winning the approval of the U.S. Department of War: because navigable waterways are under federal, not state or municipal, jurisdiction, the War Department had the right to veto any crossing of a harbor that might interfere with shipping. A tunnel, however, offered no obstruction, and approval came through promptly.

Then, on 22 January 1939, Moses called his news conference. Instead of a tunnel built by the Tunnel Authority, he proposed a bridge built by the Triborough Authority. A bridge, he said, would cost less, be easier and quicker to build, and able to carry more traffic. He distributed a brochure with some comparative figures on cost and drawings of the proposed bridge. The Tunnel Authority's architects and engineers were outraged.[35]

New York's newspapers at first were puzzled, and inclined in their reports to assume that anything Moses said must be true and, at the very least, worthy of study. The public's reaction took several days to coalesce into an opinion, but soon a majority seemed against the bridge. The proposed ramps and elevated approach roads on the Manhattan end would all but destroy Battery Park, a small but much appreciated open space at the tip of the island, with grand views of the harbor—past Governor's Island to Brooklyn, past the Statue of Liberty and Ellis Island to New Jersey, and, on a clear day, past Staten Island, out the Narrows, to the Atlantic Ocean. In addition the small park had a historic fort, Castle Clinton, built about 1808 to protect the harbor from the British; it later had been converted into a theater (Castle Garden) where in 1850 Jenny Lind had sung her recitals, then it became, in 1855–90, the chief entry port for the country's immigrants, and in 1896 was converted again, this time into the city's aquarium, one of the best in the world and attracting annually some 2.5 million visitors. On reviewing Moses's proposal, many people concluded that it threatened both the Aquarium and Battery Park.[36]

People with the time and ability to analyze his estimates of comparative costs soon came to believe that his figures were deliberately false. No estimate of the tunnel's cost had ever set it at $84 million. Moses claimed in his brochure to have received the figure from the tunnel's designer, Ole Singstad, an assertion that Singstad denied. The figure he had given to Moses was $65 million. Moreover, the estimate of $41.2 million for a Brooklyn-Battery bridge was plainly too low, for the cost of the Bronx-Whitestone, half as long, two lanes narrower, and almost completed, was $39 million.[37]

Good Government groups that had joined to defend Moses in the building of the Triborough Bridge against the interference of federal Order 129, now organized to oppose him and to save Battery Park. Though there would be much skirmishing over comparative costs, the crucial issue was aesthetics. The bridge would all but destroy the park. Stanley Isaacs, the Manhattan Borough President, uncovered what Moses in his brochure seems to have tried to conceal: that the bridge's anchorage in the park would be a block of solid masonry equal in size to a ten-story building; that the ramp linking the bridge to the West Side Highway would be wider than Fifth Avenue, supported on concrete piers, and would cut through the park at close to a hundred feet in the air; that many of the nearby office buildings on State Street and Battery Place would have their views of the harbor replaced by a view of the underside of an elevated highway; and that the degrading of the area would cost the city in twenty years some $30 million in real estate taxes—a cost not appearing anywhere in Moses's estimates.[38]

In late July the Good Government groups formed a Central Committee of Organizations Opposing the Battery Toll Bridge.[39] Its claimed purpose was to win time to study the plan for the bridge, but its real purpose, as everyone understood, was to defeat the proposal. Its plan, the same as had proved successful in the battle over Order 129 in the building of the Triborough Bridge, was to educate the public on the issues and create such a surge of public opinion that Moses and his supporters would have to give way. The committee's chairman, the lawyer Albert S. Bard, sent out speakers with corrected figures and drawings to talk to any group that would listen, and assigned CCB to talk to the mayor before the next and crucial meeting of the City Council.

Roughly speaking, cities in New York State have no power except what the state grants them. To exercise those granted powers, "home rule," the cities often must seek approval of the state government, which grants approval usually in the form of a legislative act signed by the governor. Conversely, the state in many circumstances cannot make changes in the granted powers without a city's approval, usually stated in the form of a home rule message from the City Council and mayor to the state legislature. For the Triborough Authority, a state-created entity, to build another bridge, it needed the state's approval for a change in purpose. To that end, Moses had submitted a bill to the state legislature. But he also needed the city's approval in a home rule message. That placed the struggle between him and his opponents in the City Council, where it seemed likely but not certain that Moses would prevail. If he did, then the reformers had one last chance—the mayor. In anticipation of the City Council hearings, CCB, acting for the Opposition Committee, went to City Hall, where the mayor, as always, dropped what he was doing and took the old man into his office.

Just what was said and promised in that meeting is not known. Robert Caro, however, was able to interview two men to whom CCB reported the meeting, Windels and Ole Singstad, and gives this summary of their memories:

> La Guardia [had said] that while he would support a home-rule message
> for the bill authorizing Triborough to build a Crossing, he would not

support—or sign—one for the bill stripping the Tunnel Authority of *its* authorization. The Mayor told Burlingham that he would wait until the War Department, which . . . had scheduled a hearing on the bridge in April, had formally given approval to build it.[40]

Even that restricted promise did not endure, however, for Moses, who was in Florida, telegraphed the mayor that unless the possibility of a tunnel was killed at once, the Triborough Authority would not advance any money. In short, if any crossing was built, it must be a bridge. Whereupon the mayor told the leaders of the City Council that to preserve a crossing and its federal funding they must support the bridge—on Moses's terms.[41]

The City Council meeting on 27 and 28 March was long remembered for the way in which Moses's arguments in favor of the bridge were shown to be based on false premises, and for the arrogance with which Moses attacked personally those who opposed him. He began by saying of borough president Isaacs, "It's getting to be so that nothing will please them but a Communist state, which we know is so pleasing to Mr. Isaacs." The remark drew loud boos, which the Triborough Authority claque tried to drown in cheers.

Then Moses turned to the Regional Plan Association's spokesman, George McAneny, a former borough president of Manhattan, a planner of the New York World's Fair (soon to open), and since 1892 one of the city's outstanding citizens. Though McAneny was eleven years younger than CCB, he looked ten years older, shrunken, wrinkled, and stooped. Yet he had spoken eloquently against the bridge, suggesting that a more worthwhile project might be to improve the Brooklyn approaches to the Brooklyn Bridge and put a toll on it. "No man in his right mind would do that," said Moses, noting that the idea was fit only for a man who is "not going to run for public office again." Then, turning to look directly at McAneny, who was seated behind him, he added, "He's an extinct volcano. He's an exhumed mummy."[42] There was silence. Moses went on to other matters, ending: "This is a showdown project. Either you want it, or you don't want it. And either you want it now or you don't get it at all."[43]

The next day the full council voted 19 to 6 to give him the home rule message he wanted, in effect killing the tunnel. In Albany, where Moses was much courted by legislators because of his double position as president of the State Parks Council and the Long Island State Park Commission, the Assembly passed his bill 106 to 6, and the Senate 41 to 1. Then Governor Lehman signed it, saying defensively that New York's elected officials clearly wanted it.[44]

To opponents of the Battery Toll Bridge, their campaign seemed doomed. Despite success in rousing the public to oppose the bridge, at least among civic groups and newspaper editorials and letter columns, they had failed to win over the politicians. As a last effort, some committee members asked Windels to consult CCB, who had attended the council meetings, on what now might be done.

Windels went to CCB's office, put the question, and CCB, after thinking for several long minutes, suddenly smiled and said: "Call Eleanor."[45]

Shortly thereafter, on 5 April 1939, in her newspaper column "My Day," Eleanor Roosevelt had a paragraph beginning,

> I have a plea from a man who is deeply interested in Manhattan Island, particularly in the beauty of the approach from the ocean at Battery Park. He tells me that a New York official, who is without doubt always efficient, is proposing a bridge . . . This, he says, will mean a screen of elevated roadways . . . I haven't a question that this will be done in the name of progress, and something undoubtedly needs to be done. But isn't there room for some consideration of the preservation of the few beautiful spots that still remain to us on an overcrowded island?[46]

Her question probably reached, and perhaps stirred, hundreds of thousands of New Yorkers who lacked the time or interest to follow events in the City Council, Planning Commission, or state legislature. Windels had done his part; CCB, meanwhile, had been doing his. He wrote a long letter to the *Herald Tribune*, published on 6 April under the headline "The Case Against a Battery Bridge; Charles C. Burlingham Opposes It as Dangerous, Extravagant and Disfiguring."

> To the New York Herald Tribune:
>
> The position you have taken on the Battery bridge seems reasonable—"go slow," but I should have preferred "stop it." No one can admire Mr. Moses more than I do. His work for the city and state is incomparable. But he is not infallible in judgment, nor even in taste.
>
> At the risk of being called an extinct firecracker, I venture to say . . . Mr. Moses is the only public official fit to consider the questions involved who has given the proposal unqualified support . . .
>
> 1. I am not qualified to express an opinion on the financial questions involved . . .
>
> 2. As to the effect of such a structure on navigation I can speak with some confidence, for my whole professional life has been given to the

practice of admiralty . . . I know the dangers of abutments and structures in mid-river. I know of my own knowledge the value of Buttermilk
Channel to navigation. A clear, unobstructed way through that channel
is of the greatest importance . . . Let no one think that it is a simple
thing for tugs to tow or assist a steamship in the East River; the North
River is child's play comparatively. No difficulty should be added to the
grave perils of navigation which already exist . . .

3. . . . I need not repeat the incontrovertible statement at the hearings
that a bridge depreciates while a tunnel increases real estate values . . .

4. An unanswered and unanswerable objection to the proposal is that
it will injure irreparably the aspect of New York. I am amazed that any
true friend of the city can have the effrontery to suggest an anchorage of
solid masonry, equal to a building ten stories high, 175 feet long by 125
wide, and a new elevated road curving round the northerly and westerly
portions of the park, in a space which in its all too small compass epito-
mizes so much of the history of our beloved city.

Charles C. Burlingham.[47]

A few days later CCB wrote to President Roosevelt, scrawling across
the top of the typed page, "In graveyard confidence."

Dear Franklin:

Nobody fit to have an opinion wants the Battery Bridge except Bob
Moses. It should have been stopped by the City Planning Commission.
It might be stopped even now by the Art Commission. It can easily be
stopped by the War Department.

Now please *stop* and read my letter to the Herald-Tribune.

The War Department can stop it, and if I weren't so deaf and old I'd
try to convince them of the danger to navigation. Rumor has it that the
New York & New Haven, Long Island and Pennsylvania Railroad
Companies, who know these dangers, as their car-floats have to round
the Battery all day and every day, have been told to keep their mouths
shut and not oppose the bridge.

The Board of Engineers of the War Department is to hold a hearing
in New York on the 25th instant. It is not their custom to subpoena witnesses; so the railroad companies will probably not attend. It will not
be difficult for advocates of the bridge to pick up masters and pilots of
tugboats and steamers who will minimize the dangers of navigation.
But the fact is that the channel of the East River should be widened, not

narrowed or obstructed. It is 1600 feet from shore to shore, and I am told it could be widened in places to 2000 feet.

One other Federal Point. Jesse Jones [head of the Reconstruction Finance Corporation], as well as the bankers, should satisfy themselves that the financial plan is sound. The cost estimated by Moses is $41,500,000. According to the New York Tunnel Corporation, it will be much more. Again, the effect of a new bridge on the Queens tunnel bonds must be considered by the R.F.C. and the P.W.A.

Verb. suf. sap. [A word to the wise is sufficient], especially when the sapient being is a lover of New York, as well as President of the United States and Commander in Chief of the Army.

Yours,

C. C. B.[48]

A word to the wise might be sufficient. But such a word whispered to one who hated Moses, who had been humiliated by him in the fight over the Triborough Bridge, was even surer. Roosevelt replied: "Thanks for the note. I know little about the bridge except a bee-oo-tiful picture of it in the Sunday supplement—but I will look into it and keep your name out of it."[49]

CCB, perhaps recalling how Moses had been able to reposition himself as the aggrieved party in the Triborough fight, hastily replied with a scrawl on scratch paper: "It was *your* name, not *mine*, I wished kept out. I merely thought that if you agreed that the *PONS* was *Asinorum* you might kill it. Hence my extreme *secrecy!*"[50]

In addition, CCB wrote to La Guardia, who was about to go to Washington for the War Department's hearings on the bridge: "All I ask is that you do not exert yourself [on its behalf] in Washington or elsewhere." La Guardia, ignoring the request, lobbied hard for the bridge.[51]

Meanwhile, Roosevelt sent CCB's letter to Secretary of War Harry Woodring, asking him to look into the bridge, and several days later he had an aide send a note to the chief of the War Department's engineers asking the latter to "speak to The President before you make any report on the subject." Plainly the president and commander in chief was taking a personal interest in the outcome. There would be no precipitous approval.[52]

Of all of this Moses and La Guardia were unaware, and they waited impatiently for the War Department's review board to issue its opinion. Meanwhile, in early June CCB had another letter in the *Herald Tribune* which the paper headlined "Battery Bridge Called a Costly Delusion," to which Moses replied: "I see Mr. Burlingham is back in the papers again . . . There is nothing new in his last letter excepting the reference to the depressing effect of bridges on surrounding real property . . . What he says on this subject is wholly inaccurate."[53]

Finally, on 17 July 1939, Secretary Woodring issued the War Department's ruling: the bridge crossing was not approved because the bridge would be "seaward of a vital Navy establishment . . . the U.S. Navy Yard at Brooklyn." There might be a danger, if it were damaged in a war, of blocking the approach to the Yard. There could be no appeal.[54]

Moses was furious. The existing Brooklyn and Manhattan bridges, though further up the East River, were both seaward of the Navy Yard. He suspected the president's hand in the decision, but had no proof. He tried to insinuate that idea to reporters, hoping they would trace some link to Roosevelt, but they either missed his point or failed to uncover any evidence.

In a gleeful note scrawled to Windels, CCB asked: "Who killed Cock *Robert*? 'I' said Sec. Harry, 'with my *poisoned* arrow.' I thought Woodring's reasons asinine, and I don't wonder Bob M is mad—and he certainly is. I wonder whether he will *name* F.D.R. He has almost by reference to Ickes and the Triborough. Some time I'll tell you a little inside dope. Hiz Honor [the mayor] took it nicely."[55]

La Guardia's pain was further eased when the federal Reconstruction Finance Corporation suddenly decided it would lend the Tunnel Authority not the previous maximum of $39 million but $59 million, and in addition would reduce the interest on the loan. This reconsideration brought the total estimated cost of the tunnel down to $59 million. As for the reasons behind such an abrupt shift, no one seems to have asked.[56]

Moses considered the defeat the greatest of his career, even though he won from it control of the Tunnel Authority. At least he was now in charge of the tunnel's construction, which began in 1940 but was stopped by World War II. In 1950 the tunnel opened to traffic, and by then the Tunnel and Triborough Bridge Authorities had merged, with Moses as chairman.

He never ceased to resent the loss of his bridge. According to August Heckscher, a biographer of La Guardia and editorial writer for the *Herald Tribune*, at any mention of it Moses's eyes would burn with anger. At one such moment, after building a bridge across the Narrows between Brooklyn and Staten Island, he muttered, "Nevertheless we did it. We built the Verazzano bridge *seaward of the navy yard*."[57] Today, when the Upper Bay is clear of fog, that distant bridge, opened in 1964, can be seen from Battery Park, which still offers an unrivaled view of one of the world's greatest harbors.

Though the facts of this dispute are established, thanks in part to Caro's interviews with many of the main actors, their interpretation and implication for municipal government are still divisive and troubling. Caro sees the episode as the moment when Moses ceased to think of himself as an official of New York's city government but its equal. The combination of his state and municipal positions, as well as the financial independence of the Triborough Authority, allowed him to create a government within a government over which the mayor and the citizenry began to lose control. Conversely, Roger Starr, an editorial writer for the *Times*, in his book *The Rise and Fall of New York City* (1985), insists that Moses was pursuing "goals that he knew the people wanted," and rejects most criticism of him as coming "from people who had no knowledge of the times of which they were writing . . . and [had] a phobia on the subject of political and governmental power."[58]

Yet reformers like CCB, trying to arouse public opinion to the realities of the proposed bridge, believed they were acting appropriately and were not phobic about political power. What could be more democratic than to educate the electorate through public action and hearings? Moses, in reply, could say that in every city and state agency or governmental division that held hearings he won a majority of votes. What could be more democratic? Yet in the end, all these democratic procedures counted for little.

To students of city government, especially those who like to think their subject is a branch of political science, the episode is alarming. Some focus their distress on the ability of Moses, a mere parks commissioner, to deliver ultimatums to the mayor and City Council, and to control, free of any city direction, millions of dollars that might better have been dedicated, at least in part, to the city's general needs and purposes. Surely, in permitting such a result, something in the structure of city government has gone askew. Others shake their heads over how the question ultimately was decided: not by New York's mayor, City Council, or citizens, but in secret, on specious reasons by a vengeful president of the United States. And still others, if they knew of it, might protest the role played by a deaf old man who, because he held no public office, was accountable to no one at all. City government in the United States, most scholars seem to want to believe, should be more rational in its theories and procedures, more of a predictable science, less of a human art.

21

War and Presidential Politics

CCB's INTEREST IN world affairs, born of a boyhood trip to England and a winter in Napoleon III's Paris, never staled. Before World War I he continually refreshed it by further trips to Europe, by his experience as a delegate to the Brussels Conferences on Maritime Law in 1909 and 1910, and more generally by his maritime practice, which brought him into contact with lawyers and businessmen from other countries. In the years between the two world wars he went only once to Europe, in 1929 to visit his daughter-in-law Dorothy and his four grandchildren who were living in Vienna, but their fate, after Hitler's rise to power in 1933, kept him focused on European politics to detect signs of war. And even without the family in Vienna, he would have followed the news closely, for always more important to him than the sites and history of Europe were the friends he made abroad, especially among lawyers and diplomats in England, who wrote anxiously to him, and he to them, at each new ominous event. Their mutual alarms gave meaning and even perhaps urgency to his international work.

One scholarly project that held his interest, though it progressed only slowly, was the further development of international law. Doubtless what drew him to this work was his experience at the Brussels Conferences, where, with representatives of twenty-five nations and French the common language, he had participated in the drafting and signing of international conventions on collision at sea and on salvage. In 1912 the U.S. Senate had ratified the salvage treaty, but twenty-five years later it was still unwilling—to CCB's undiminished distress—to consider the one on collision.[1]

Nevertheless, he continued to work for international accord when the opportunity offered, notably as a member of the advisory committee of a group awkwardly titled Research in International Law under the auspices of the Faculty of Harvard Law School. The project's director and moving spirit was Manley O. Hudson, a Harvard professor of international law, who starting in 1936 was also a judge on the World Court at The Hague.[2]

The research project's aim was to compile accurate information on the practices of states and international courts and to produce a series of model conventions on such subjects as nationality, state responsibility, aggression, and the law of treaties. In the years 1927–40 it produced thirteen such conventions, which had considerable influence on the development of international law after World War II. There were also intermediate projects, one of which caused CCB in 1929 to report to his Harvard classmates: "This is really hard work. Last month we spent three whole days from 9:30 a.m. to 6 p.m. working out the text of a chapter on Territorial Waters. The codification is being made for our State Department, which will send delegates to the Conference of Experts to be held next year in Geneva."[3] In the spring of 1936, with the group still working on its proposed conventions, he was elected chairman of its executive and advisory committees, succeeding George W. Wickersham in both posts, but by midwinter 1939 his increasing deafness prevented him from presiding at meetings, though he remained active where he could work one-on-one.[4]

In the winter of 1939–40 he tried to persuade Congressman Sol Bloom of New York City to introduce a resolution in Congress to provide the World Court* with $80,000 toward its budget for 1940. With the war, he wrote to Bloom, the League of Nations was collapsing, and because of "the destruction of so many of its members by Hitler and Stalin, the funds of the Court are running very low and there is great danger that it may die, which would be a great loss to civilization." But Bloom would not introduce the resolution without White House approval, and Hudson reported to CCB that FDR thought it "too dangerous politically—said he would not oppose it—said U.S.A. ought to pay something, to cover salary of the American judge at any rate, and suggest it be paid out of 'contingent

---

*The World Court, properly titled the Permanent Court of International Justice and sitting at The Hague, was established in 1920 and dissolved in 1945 when its functions were transferred to the new International Court of Justice. It all but ceased to function, however, after the Germans seized Holland in 1940. The United States never joined the Court, which had fifty-nine member states, though one of the fifteen judges was always an American: John Bassett Moore, Charles Evans Hughes, Frank S. Kellogg, and Manley O. Hudson. In its twenty-five years the court rendered thirty-two judgments and twenty-seven advisory opinions. One judgment, for example, in 1933 awarded sovereignty over the northern coast of Greenland to Denmark, rejecting Norway's claim.

fund' of Dept. of State." A few hours later Secretary of State Cordell Hull told Hudson the fund was exhausted "and suggested private funds be appealed to. Thus it goes!" Over the ages maritime lawyers generally have worked to develop international courts and codes of law and their governments have been slow to bind themselves to agreement. Meanwhile, at least, CCB enjoyed the stimulation of interesting colleagues.[5]

He also followed world affairs through the Council on Foreign Relations, a New York group with membership by invitation that aimed to bring together lawyers, journalists, businessmen, and scholars to study issues of foreign policy. Founded in 1921, it held frequent meetings with knowledgeable speakers, published the quarterly magazine *Foreign Affairs*, and eventually developed affiliated groups in other cities. In October 1932 CCB wrote to Francis and Helena Hirst, his English friends in London, describing several private receptions in New York for Lord Reading, who had served briefly as foreign secretary in Prime Minister Ramsay MacDonald's cabinet. "We gave a party at the Bar Association, and I took the chair, as you say. He made several speeches here, none of them of any moment. We had a dinner without reporters at the Foreign Relations Council, where he talked for an hour about India and parried questions, like the excellent lawyer that he is."[6] And in March 1933, also to the Hirsts, he relayed a dinner speech by Governor Philip La Follette of Wisconsin: "A charming type of American, is he not? He told us his impressions of Eurup as an Amurican, and it was truly a story of an innocent abroad; e.g., he said that 750,000 Berliners lived in little cabins outside the city" (actually, he had seen the sheds where city folk kept tools to farm small gardens), and "he reported that there was no talk of depression in Europe, but much of war, and advised us either to build a wall around ourselves or go in and do our part in Europe." And a few days later, "we had a reception for [Yosuke] Matsuoka, a Japanese statesman and diplomat, at the Foreign Relations Council." Matsuoka defended Japan's invasion of China, seizing the province of Manchuria, and bombing Shanghai to break a boycott and force acceptance of Japanese goods. To CCB, Matsuoka appeared "an almost German type of Japanese, very able, very resolute, almost brutal and ruthless. I feel that they would be more persuasive if they acknowledged that they had made a mistake in the case of Shanghai and then insisted that they had certain treaty rights in Manchuria which they must protect."[7] (Some historians in hindsight believe that world war in the Far East "really began on 18 September 1931" with the Japanese invasion of Manchuria.)[8] In any case, Matsuoka, after leading Japan out of the League of Nations in 1933, became Japan's foreign minister in 1940, allied

Japan with Italy and Germany in the Pact of Berlin (1940) and signed a five-year peace treaty with Russia (1941).

With the Depression worldwide and the turmoil abroad, each week seemed to bring news of a new cause for agitation, and in his letters CCB frequently referred to the prospect of war. In April 1933 he wrote, "No matter what is said, I don't envisage war just yet. Hitler's hands are full, Mussolini's, too, and M. is comparatively stable, though very hard up, I am sure."[9] And then there were Dorothy and the children in Vienna. That same month he told the Hirsts, "We are unable to make any dent on Dorothy, whose will is her most powerful faculty. I have tried to make clear to her that while those who are under a duty should stay, American children who have no obligation should come away." But a month later he reported, "Nothing budges Dorothy. Yesterday one of our friends saw a movie showing the barbed wire entanglement and the machine guns in Vienna May 1, while Dorothy was cabling, 'Peaceful May Day, all well and happy.'"[10] Meanwhile, events grew more frightening. In 1935 Italy invaded Abyssinia (Ethiopia), the emperor Haile Selassie sought help from the League of Nations, which could not agree on any action, and Italy took over the country. The next year Germany, in violation of treaties that had ended the world war, reoccupied the Rhineland and, without opposition from France or Britain, began to build fortifications. And in July 1936 a rebel Spanish army led by General Francisco Franco crossed the Straits of Gibraltar from Africa and attacked Spain's republican government. In the United States general opinion was overwhelmingly pacifist: the country should stay out of the Spanish Civil War, especially because it seemed likely to start another general European war, as the Fascist governments of Germany and Italy began to aid the rebels.

CCB wrote in September to Hirst, "As to Spain, my first thought, or rather my second, was that [Léon] Blum [prime minister of France] was wise in insisting on neutrality, but under the true doctrine of neutrality the Government in power is entitled to arms and apparently this [Spanish] government is receiving none while the rebels are getting aeroplanes and all sorts of munitions of war through Portugal and other ways."[11] Therein lay a troublesome question, and as CCB pondered it, he was distressed and soon joined a small minority of Americans who sought repeal of the United States Neutrality Act of 1937. This act, which Roosevelt in deference to isolationists in Congress had signed, imposed an embargo on the exportation of arms to Spain, prohibiting the sale of weapons to either the legitimate government or the rebels. CCB thought the act was not only perverse in its result but a "humiliating" policy for the United States to adopt. What was the effect of such neutrality when Germany and Italy by 1938 were openly arming the rebels and sending troops to fight? Undermining Spain's legitimate government![12]

On 31 January 1939, CCB and Philip C. Jessup, a professor of international law at Columbia, published a letter in the *Times* arguing that the United States with its act was following not its traditional policy of neutrality, but a perversion of that policy. Their long legal argument possibly caused many readers to turn the page; but it was also clear and well founded in American history. According to them, "traditional neutrality" called for the United States, when a civil war broke out in Europe, "to do nothing in the way of restricting the commerce in arms."[13] Congressional leaders, however, ignored the letter.

In publishing it, the *Times* had put CCB's name first, identifying both men as "authorities on international law." But privately CCB wrote to a member of the research project: "I need not tell you that the Embargo letter was all Phil's—a few words and phrases changed or the prominence of its position in the Times mine!"[14] The paper, either because the letter was too long for the editorial page or perhaps to give it prominence, had made a major article of it, a full half page with its own six-column headline.

Then, on 1 September 1939, Hitler sent his army into Poland; France and Britain came to Poland's defense, and World War II began. Within sixteen days the Germans had overrun western Poland, and on 17 September Russia, which had signed a nonaggression pact with Germany but was eager to keep German soldiers off its borders, attacked Poland from the east. By the end of September all Polish resistance had ceased. Before then Roosevelt had asked Congress to repeal the Neutrality Act and return to our "traditional neutrality." But isolationist feeling still dominated the country and Congress balked. Finally, after six weeks of debate, it repealed the arms embargo, but hedged the repeal by including in the new act a proviso that forbad American ships to enter belligerent ports. Meanwhile, as Germany on its eastern front divided Poland with Russia, on its western it faced the French army and a smaller British expeditionary force. Throughout the winter there was no movement, and then suddenly on 10 May 1940 Germany invaded neutral Holland and neutral Belgium, all but destroying Rotterdam by aerial bombardment, and in ten days smashed through both countries and drove deep into France, trapping the British expeditionary force with its back against the English Channel. Then came "the miracle of Dunkirk." To save its army the British sent every available boat of whatever kind and size, warships, ferries, freighters, private yachts, and fishing skiffs, and while the Royal Air Force kept German planes from the skies and a division of men held off the German army, the motley flotilla carried some 338,000 men to safety, but of necessity left on the beaches their heavy arms and equipment.

On 10 June Mussolini declared war on France, invading along the Mediterranean Riviera and through the Maritime Alps, and on 22 June the French government sued for peace. The German army took over Paris, which had fallen undefended, and the northern half of the country; the French government, relocating itself in Vichy, had the southern half, "Unoccupied France." After the winter's "phony war," when nothing happened, suddenly in six weeks the war seemed over, for only Britain was left to oppose Germany, and it was badly crippled.

On 11 August 1940 CCB and three other lawyers—Tom Thacher, George Rublee, and Dean Acheson—with his name again put first, published a letter in the *Times* arguing that there was no legal bar to President Roosevelt's transferring to the British government fifty overage destroyers deemed no longer essential to United States national defense. Again, the thesis, though technical, was clear and well founded, and CCB, writing to a friend in England, stated: "Acheson wrote the letter, the rest of us were merely signers." Explaining the argument, he said: "The method of disposal was worked out by reference to several acts of Congress. The Navy could not make the transfer [of the destroyers] directly, but Navy and Army could sell or give any properly to each other. So the sale could be effected by giving the destroyers to the Army, which under another statute could sell them to private persons who could sell them to England."[15]

In September, when England received the fifty destroyers (with ten Coast Guard cutters added), the rationale for the transfer was different: American security would be enhanced by trading the overage destroyers for ninety-nine-year leases on six British air and naval bases in the British West Indies. Yet the earlier letter had not been without effect. Four days after it was published, Senator Josh Lee, Democrat from Oklahoma, reportedly "fresh from an interview with President Roosevelt," floated the idea of transferring the destroyers as "a trial balloon" in the Senate, and he cited the letter in support. Though CCB might have said he had no part in the letter's composition, others assessed his contribution more highly. Henry L. Stimson, who in July 1940 had become secretary of war, scratched out a personal note: "My dear Burley, Sometime I hope I shall have a chance to tell you what a part your opinion (jointly with Tom Thacher, Acheson and Rublee) played in world politics. The job is not yet finished, for it is a tough one, but I think it will come out all right."[16]

By autumn 1940, as shocked Americans began to grasp the implications of Hitler's success—what it would mean to the United States to have all of Europe, from the Russian border to the Atlantic Ocean, controlled by Fascist powers, the markets perhaps closed to American goods, the German navy operating out of French Atlantic ports, the shift in power and alliances in Africa and also, with Japan increasingly hostile, in Asia—many began to doubt the wisdom of self-imposed isolation as a policy and to want aid for Britain, and at home preparations for self-defense, perhaps even war. Around the country a grand and sometimes furious debate began on what should be done: CCB, Stimson, and those like them believed the United States could best protect its national interest by opposing Hitler's expansionist policies at once rather than later, and in whatever way was most effective. Roosevelt made clear to them that he privately felt the same, but for political purposes he often spoke publicly in ambiguous or duplicitous terms. But besides national interest in a purely military or political sense, Roosevelt, CCB, and many others also opposed Hitler on moral grounds, and here CCB was one of the first to speak out.

On 29 May 1933, only three months after Hitler came to power, CCB and fifty other prominent New York City lawyers had published in the *Times* a petition from the City Bar Association to Secretary of State Cordell Hull asking him to protest "the action of the German Government toward the bench and bar of Germany." The German government was "depriving judges duly appointed for life or during good behavior of their seats on the bench, and prohibiting lawyers from practicing their profession, because of their race or religion." Though the lawyers pitched their protest primarily on legal grounds—a violation of German pledges made at the Paris Peace Conference in 1919—they also expressed a moral revulsion at "a violation of the elementary principles of justice." To deprive a man of his profession, of his ability to earn a living, on grounds of race or religion, was to degrade him as a human. "We had hoped that these reports were exaggerated and that later information would show that reason and justice had not been overthrown. The first reports have, however, been confirmed authentically." They asked the secretary of state formally, publicly, to protest the actions to the German government.[17]

John W. Davis, then president of the bar association, came first on the list of lawyers, but CCB (who was second) had had the idea for the petition, wrote it, and gathered the signatures. He explained to the Hirsts:

> I have got up a petition to the Secretary of State protesting against the treatment of the Jewish judges and lawyers by Hitler. At first Mr. Root would not sign because he was unwilling, he said, to ask the Secretary to

do something which he would not do himself, but I revised the document and threw in the fact that in 1919 the German Government made a pledge to the Allies and to us to protect the rights of minorities, and in 1923 they successfully invoked the jurisdiction of the World Court to enforce the rights of German minorities in Poland. On seeing this, Mr. Root signed and as Davis and others had already signed, the other lawyers followed the bellwethers. When we have all the signatures we wish, about fifty, and it has gone to the State Department, I will send you a copy. Who knows it may ring round the world.

When I was in Washington I saw the chief of the Brain Trust, Moley, and he approved sending the paper to the Secretary. I made it easy by putting in the words, "if it is consistent with diplomatic precedents and usage"; so it may find itself into the official waste basket. But I could not sit silent and let these outrages be perpetrated on our *brethren* without a word of protest.[18]

Two weeks later, again to the Hirsts, he reported: "Our petition has not been acknowledged by the State Department; but it may be of some influence." But it apparently was never acknowledged, had no influence, and CCB did not mention it again.[19]

He had the gift and the curse of seeing the looming war not only in abstractions, fascism versus democracy, but also in terms of people, of individuals in danger and suffering, not only Dorothy and his grandchildren in Vienna (though all ultimately got out in time), but even more immediately Jews in Germany. When war came and France fell, he worried most about England, the mother of parliaments, the source of the Magna Carta and its rights and of the common law. Alone, ill armed, with German submarines sinking British shipping around the world, could it survive a defeat like Dunkirk? And as Hitler in the summer of 1940 rushed the building of landing crafts to carry his army across the Channel, and meanwhile started the nightly bombing of English cities, the Blitz, CCB worried about his friends in England. Most of them lived in London, and were old. Under the pressures of war, under German air attack, how would they fare, how survive?

At the center of one group of his English friends were Francis and Helena Hirst. Francis, born in 1873, the son of a prosperous Yorkshire wool merchant, had the reputation of being a Victorian liberal with "a completely closed mind," especially in his chosen field of economics. As a disciple of Richard Cobden and Adam Smith, he believed in free trade and in all circumstances laissez-faire. As his friends joked, in his wife, Helena, he most appropriately had married Richard Cobden's great-niece. As a young man, tall, fair-haired, Hirst had enjoyed a starry career at Wadham College, Oxford, where two close friends were F. E. Smith (from 1922 Lord Birkenhead) and John Simon (from 1940 Viscount Simon), both of whom served in several positions in British cabinets. All three were brilliant students of the classics and, in succession, presidents of the Union, Oxford's debating society; all three also studied law and, though their politics differed, continued close friends. Through Hirst, CCB knew Birkenhead and Simon.[20]

Also through Hirst, CCB met Molly (Mrs. Mary Agnes) Hamilton, a Socialist, Labour politician, journalist, and writer who in the early years of the twentieth century cut a figure as a liberated woman. She was opinionated, cigarette-smoking, and separated from her husband, just the sort of woman Hirst usually deplored.[21] Yet she and Hirst were close friends because, as she once wrote, "he is not only an individual of delightful distinctness but endowed with a very high degree of personal charm, as well as a 'pawky' humour there is no resisting. It is one of his most attractive traits that, rigid as he is in doctrine and capable of bearing gladly the most shocking bores if they have the right opinions, he sticks to his friends through thick and thin."[22] Like the Hirsts, when Molly Hamilton passed through New York, she was apt to stay at 860 Park Avenue, whose spare rooms, after Louie's and Robert's deaths and in Nancy's absence, CCB offered to friends as the "Hotel Burlingham."[23]

Hirst's career after Oxford rose steadily, though not in the law, which he soon gave up. Turning to journalism, he became a potent pamphleteer, and in 1907–16 was the editor of *The Economist*. While there, though famously opposed to women's suffrage, in 1912 he surprised everyone by hiring as a writer for the magazine the unorthodox Mrs. Hamilton. With his exceptional knowledge of classics, politics, and economics, Hirst had a well-stocked mind which he deployed in an attractive, personal style, and under his leadership the weekly *Economist*, possibly the world's most consistent and enduring proponent of free markets and trade, steadily increased in circulation, advertising, and liveliness of content.[24] CCB had first met him in 1905, and four years later, when he returned to London, Hirst, who by then knew everyone, had introduced him all around.[25]

By midsummer 1916, however, Hirst's rigidity of mind cost him his job. Before August 1914 he had crusaded for peace, retrenchment, and reform, not believing that Europe possibly could be so foolish as to go to war. Even after the fighting began, he continued to campaign for his ideals, denouncing the war, waste, and the suppression of civil liberties. The magazine's historian suggests, "The 1914–16 period was probably only the third occasion in the paper's life when no one would have been surprised if the windows had been smashed." Hirst's moral courage in continuing to advocate Cobden's well-known triad of "Peace, Free Trade, and Goodwill" no doubt was great, but in time of war to many people, even to friends, his views began to seem irrelevant, even on occasion offensive.[26]

Thereafter his career drifted downward, for he could not adjust his opinions to the times; and though he continued to write and lecture, people grew less inclined to read or listen. After Hirst's death in 1953, CCB wrote of him, "He was a man really concerned about the public weal . . . and really not concerned with personal prizes or what is called 'having a career.' This was as well, for it was his lot to live for fifty years with strong currents sweeping the country in the opposite direction to that he believed it should steer." For the last half of those years, even more than his talent as a writer and lecturer, his gift for friendship sustained him, and also the presence at his side of his uncommonly articulate, perceptive wife.[27]

Even after Germany in March 1938 invaded Austria, Hirst predictably called for diplomacy, peace, and better trade relations with Germany. In September he supported France's and England's concessions to Hitler at the Munich Conference, approving the dismemberment of Czechoslovakia and the transfer of its Sudetenland to Germany. Presumably he believed Hitler's statement that there would be "no further territorial problem in Europe . . . We want no Czechs."[28] But when Hitler's troops, in March 1939, marched into what remained of Czechoslovakia, Hirst fell ill, partly at least, in his wife's opinion, in response to the shattering of his hope for peace.[29] Six months later, after Hitler attacked Poland, which triggered Britain's declaration of war against Germany, he was struggling in his letters to be philosophic, but by then, as CCB told a friend, his discussions with Hirst had gotten "so bad," he had written to him that "while nothing could break our friendship," he would express his political views one last time and then "not write further on the subject."[30]

CCB picked up from a passing remark, however, that Hirst was beginning to have financial troubles. Freelance journalists, at best, were paid little, and with paper rationed in wartime England, magazines and newspapers could print fewer articles.[31] Furthermore, to pay for the war, England had begun to tax unearned incomes ever more steeply, and then Helena wrote that Hirst had needed an appendectomy. With his usual stubbornness he had forbad her to call a physician or even to take his temperature until she had rebelled and called an ambulance—just in time. But the delay caused complications, and recovery was slow. John Simon lent them his house on

Walton Heath for convalescence, but Hirst, hating to be away from his books and desk, would stay only a few days.[32]

CCB, perhaps recalling how in illness he once had been rescued by friends, proposed to three of Hirst's American friends, all acting or retired presidents of universities, that the four of them send Hirst a gift of $1,000 to cover the costs of the operation.[33] And it was done:

> Dear Francis:
>
> The enclosed draft is a Christmas gift from four of your old friends. We cannot wish you a *Merry* Christmas, but we do wish you and Helena and Britain and the World a happier year than this has been.
>
> The mails are so uncertain that I cannot wait to have this properly signed or better written, but I know I speak *du coeur* for your friends and mine, Bryan, Butler and Lowell as for myself.
>
> Yours,
> Charles C. Burlingham[34]

Helena's letter of thanks came first: "My dear C.C.B. This is *your* doing!" She described Hirst's initial inability to utter his feelings: "All evening he was like a man dazed that such a load has so suddenly fallen off him. When I settled him into bed, he said: 'I can't get over their amazing generosity—such a gift—it is such a relief! I think it must be what they wanted it to be—so I think I may accept it?' And he couldn't say any more."[35] He let slip in his own letter, however, the magnitude of his relief: "I suppose you must have guessed our plight—war taxes, loss of work, and then this stroke of bad luck. Helena was very brave about it, as she thought more of my recovery than of our losses—if we left our home it would be unsaleable—nearly all our neighbors have evacuated their homes in the idiotic panic flight." Not only was income down, but in the collapse of the real estate market, a sizable part of capital was illiquid and increasingly valueless. But the "splendid gift" would enable the Hirsts "to remain here for some time to come and for me to continue my work for a reasonable and negotiated peace."[36] Within two months he sent CCB an article he had written on "War Aims and Peace Terms." To which CCB, breaking his ban on political discussion with Hirst, wrote a long reply, ending: "Your hope of good trade relations with Germany and a reduction in armaments are pious, and I hope they will be fulfilled, but I have my doubts."[37]

Instead, the war intensified. In May 1940 Holland, Belgium, and France collapsed, Britain was mauled at Dunkirk, the air "Battle of Britain" began in July, and the Blitz on 7 September. When, as Helena wrote, "it got to things falling through our roofs," the Hirsts found the sleepless nights, the terrors, the tensions unbearable, and they moved to Richard Cobden's old home, Dunford House, in Sussex, where a doormat greeted the world, "Peace, Free Trade and Goodwill."[38]

CCB had another English freelance journalist about whom he worried, but Samuel Kerkham Ratcliffe was a very different sort of person. He knew Hirst not from Oxford, youth, or shared ideals, but because the journalistic world in England was small. Though five years older than Hirst and less of a scholar, Ratcliffe was far more contemporary in his ideas. Physically a small man, he could be huge in the flood of his views on England, the United States, and world affairs. His letters to friends and colleagues were interminable, raising more issues than any correspondent could answer; but fortunately he would accept replies that were occasional and partial. Beginning in the late 1920s, he had created a career for himself explaining British politics to Americans and vice versa, touring first one country and then the other, speaking in educational institutions, over the radio, through newspapers and journals. In a comment to Learned Hand about Ratcliffe, CCB named him "the Apostle to Main Street."[39]

Like Hirst, Ratcliffe knew everyone, and when Molly Hamilton's book of reminiscence came out in 1944, he at first was pleased, for she described him as "the prince and doyen of lecturers." Then she spoiled it by calling a speaking tour in the United States "that lowest of missions, the great resource of the intellectual unemployed." In a letter to CCB, Ratcliffe cataloged her mistakes in the book, remarking: "There is, of course, a glowing eulogy of yourself. Her special tributes would be more satisfying if all her birds were not swans. I am calling attention to the alleged fact that most of them have blue eyes! As we all know, the blue eye has become rare. Here in Glasgow, for example, as in Australia, 99 out of every 100 have grey." Ratcliffe was a Master of the Miscellaneous Fact.[40]

CCB, on reading Hamilton's description of himself, also complained. He wrote to the Hirsts, though with less heat than Ratcliffe: "I fail to recognize myself . . . I seem to be a sprightly little chip sparrow, hopping about pretty well *pour un ancien*." On the other hand, "Considering how far apart politically and economically F. [Francis] and M. [Molly] are, she has been quite nice, don't you think?" Neither Hirst took up the question. Nevertheless, among these friends, though they spoke to and of each other bluntly, none bore grudges. Even the gossipy Molly Hamilton they forgave, perhaps because they recognized that in hard times she, like others, had to earn a living.[41]

Ratcliffe's answer to wartime taxes and shrinking income was to take a job he didn't want as an editorial writer for the *Glasgow Herald*. Though seventy-five and with a wife who was ailing, the two leased their cottage, safely outside of London and with a prized vegetable patch, and moved to Scotland's greatest industrial city, where they stayed for almost two years. "There can't be anything better in horrible days such as these than a useful routine job," he wrote. CCB at once began to send him clippings from American newspapers and magazines. These were important to Ratcliffe, for with paper rationed, the English newspapers and journals had little space for American news. Further, he appreciated CCB's comments on the news, for they "give me fresh points on the U.S. political situation." In this way, perhaps some of CCB's views entered Glasgow homes.[42]

Not every old friend, however, could match Ratcliffe's resilience. Geoffrey W. Russell, though nine years younger, was often exhausted by his wartime jobs and the constant bombing of London. A solicitor of uncertain health, he had looked forward to retirement in September 1939, but when the war started that month, he went to work for the Custodian of Enemy Property, advising on matters of insurance: questions of enemy premiums, claims, and reinsurance balances. He reported to CCB that the work was "exceedingly difficult and laborious."[43] Worse still, the government could not allow him a typist or telephone receptionist. He might have enjoyed the difficulties, he wrote, "when I was forty or fifty, but now I find it hard to concentrate on cases." And when the Blitz began, his health broke and often kept him at home.[44]

His relief lay in books. For many months the most exciting to him was the correspondence of Justice Oliver Wendell Holmes Jr. with the great English legal scholar Sir Frederick Pollock. Though this two-volume work was published in the United States in 1941, despite Pollock's stature in England it did not appear there until after the war because of the paper shortage. But as word of it crossed the Atlantic, English lawyers begged American friends to send over copies, and CCB sent one to Russell, who hoped to review it.

Meanwhile, CCB had the lead review in the Sunday book section of the *Herald-Tribune*, 23 March 1941, but his effort was strangely dull. After giving the background of both Holmes and Pollock, he quoted an apt appreciation by Cardozo of Holmes's literary talents and offered examples of his and Pollock's epistolary style, but neither man came alive, nor did the issues they discussed. Holmes had died in 1935, with his reputation at its height, his glory puffed by the adoration of Frankfurter, who for twenty years in talks, articles, and pilgrimages to his home had celebrated him as a heroic man and jurist. CCB, imbued with this attitude, missed what others were beginning to see in Holmes as defects of character. A friend in Chicago, a lawyer who had always admired Holmes's legal opinions, confessed to CCB that on reading the judge's letters he had been repelled by the man's "intellectual arrogance," and CCB, perhaps sensing failure—Frankfurter sent him only the faintest praise—chose not to mention the review to most friends, dismissing it quickly to one as "superficial."[45] His delightful breezy style, it seemed, could flourish only in public and private letters; in a formal piece, before what he conceived to be Holmes's greatness, it froze.

Russell received the book with delight, and managed to write the first review of it to appear in England, in *The Spectator.* Thereafter he wrote to CCB: "Holmes-Pollock. It will be long, I think, before there is a letter between us two without something about this . . . You must remember that there is a more recent and more fresh excitement here about that book and among our lawyers than there is with you." And he went on to minor points about the famous correspondence that he and friends in England had been discussing. For both men "Holmes-Pollock" was a diversion from the bombing, at a time when each morning's newspaper must have caused CCB to wonder if he ever again would hear from Russell.[46]

Another of CCB's old English friends was Frank Douglas MacKinnon, who, after nine years on the King's Bench (a trial court), in 1937 was named a lord justice of appeal. An outstanding lawyer and judge, it was said that while a trial judge he never needed to reserve judgment, always being ready to deliver his decision orally at the trial's end. CCB had first met MacKinnon in 1905 at a lunch in London that included Simon and F. E. Smith (not yet Lord Birkenhead), and thirty years later MacKinnon could write, "I suppose since then I have met Simon a hundred times as often as you . . . And I *know* him only about a hundredth part of the degree in which I know you!"[47] Some persons found MacKinnon, a Scot, hard and closefisted. Others, like CCB and Russell, saw that harshness as self-protective and brushed it aside. Russell remarked after MacKinnon's death, "He was in many ways one of the kindest and most generous men I have known, but he always thought that to other people his head would be more attractive than his heart."[48]

MacKinnon, a man of letters and an antiquary, cared deeply about England's monuments and rituals, and closest to his heart were the Inns of Court in London—Lincoln's Inn, Gray's Inn, the Inner Temple, and the Middle Temple—the four legal societies which controlled admission to the bar. Though today mainly eating clubs and professional societies, in olden days they had been the schools of the common law, for in England, unlike the Continent, the universities at Oxford and Cambridge had taught only the academic branches of law—Roman, canon, and civil law. The buildings of the Inns, interspersed with offices for solicitors and barristers, dated back to the thirteenth century and earlier (the two Temples, with halls, libraries, and a Norman church, were the seat of the Knights Templar). By the 1940s the Inns of Court, with barristers in gowns and wigs hurrying through the tangled alleys, made a medieval warren in the heart of modern London. MacKinnon, like most young lawyers in the late nineteenth century, had read law in a barrister's office, and then had been called to the bar from the Inner Temple, to which he was intensely loyal.

German night-bombing, which as MacKinnon wrote to CCB had to be indiscriminate because "what with balloons and guns they can't get down to aim," first destroyed three nearby chancery courts. About the loss of these, MacKinnon could joke: "If Hitler were not illiterate and monoglot one might impute to him a special hatred derived from *Jarndyce* v. *Jarndyce*."[49] But a few weeks later he grieved "for my beloved Inner Temple," which on the night of 18 September was hit in its library and tower, which housed the main staircase. Six nights later a bomb struck the northwest corner of the great hall.

> The walls are standing. But every one of the stained glass windows was destroyed. And the chaos of debris inside, when I went to see it next day, was indescribable. Oddly enough most of the pictures (we had long ago removed the more valuable) left on the walls were hanging unharmed, though one or two (old but not valuable) were destroyed. I never saw such a horrible sight.
>
> The Middle Temple is an institution for which I have no affection. But their hall as you know, is one of the finest things in London. From the aesthetic point of view I rejoice that it has had no bomb. Nor has the hall of Gray's Inn, which is almost as good though smaller.[50]

Though MacKinnon as a lawyer cared little for the Middle Temple hall, as a lover of Shakespeare he revered it. For, in a curiosity of English theater history, *Twelfth Night* had its premiere there in 1601, and he had attended a commemorative performance there in June 1934. But in October 1940 a bomb shattered the building, and MacKinnon sent CCB pictures of the destruction. By the following May most of the Inns of Court, the seat and source of the common law in the United States as well as England, lay in ruins.[51]

Then CCB received a handwritten note:

17 Feb. 1941

My dear Charles

You are one of my best & oldest friends. So I must tell you of the disaster that has come upon us.

My dear girl Julia, her child of 18 months, & her husband were on a ship. It was torpedoed & every human being on board was lost. I suppose I may tell you this much, but the details are treated as very secret.

My wife is wonderful. Indeed I am at times alarmed at her calm. She does not talk to me about it, & I dare not talk to her.

As for me.—I was 70 last week. I have had a happy life, and now I wake of a morning from uneasy sleep, and wish I had never waked.

As for those fiends in Germany—!!

Ever yours
F D MacKinnon.[52]

Throughout the years leading up to and through World War II, a principle by which CCB judged many leading men and issues of world affairs, such as whether to support Roosevelt for a third and fourth term as president, was his desire to save England—not the British Empire. He distinguished sharply between the two, including in his definition of England those other British states (chiefly Canada and Australia) that shared a common heritage in law, language, theater, and political development.[53] Many American lawyers at that time felt as he did. They knew that their institutions and common law had their origins in English history, and they admired that law, not only for the rights it conferred, such as trial by jury, but also as a system of thought and education, as well as a means of social reform by incremental change. By midsummer 1941 CCB was plotting a scheme for Americans to rebuild the damaged parts of the Inns of Court. "I have in mind a plan which I know will interest all American lawyers— to restore both the Middle and Inner Halls, the Master's House and the

Church, no matter how many millions it may cost," he wrote to Geoffrey Russell. "If America restored the Louvain library,* why should we not do the same for the Temple?" He persuaded a friend in the American Bar Association to introduce a resolution to that effect, and it was adopted in the fall of 1941. Later, as the war drew to a close, an ABA committee collected contributions and after deducting expenses was able to present a total of more than $40,000 toward rebuilding the Inns—a gift that today might be the equivalent of $250,000. Something, but to CCB's disappointment it was nothing like the million raised for the Louvain library.[54]

Between the Munich pact in September 1938, sacrificing Czechoslovakia to German expansion, and the Japanese attack on Pearl Harbor on 7 December 1941, many in the United States continued strongly isolationist in their views. For CCB, however, the Fascist threat to England and America and to their institutions, law, and culture was clear, and magnified daily by the battle reports and distress of friends near the front. For him, the war was never a distant abstraction, pins on a map, but a fight at the front door for survival. On 24 May 1940, in the week of Dunkirk, as France collapsed and the Germans reached the English Channel, CCB, in his eighty-second year, wrote to Samuel Seabury, "This is Queen Victoria's birthday. Who could have imagined 40 years ago such a world as this? . . . These are the worst days I have ever had."[55]

Contributing to CCB's distress over the war was the uncertain future of Fusion's movement for reform in New York, a fate by then tangled in La Guardia's political ambitions. The question, for instance, of what office La Guardia might seek at the end of his second four-year term arose before the term was half over. On 17 June 1938 New York's junior senator, the anti–New Deal Democrat Royal S. Copeland, suddenly died, and there was talk that La Guardia might run for the post. Publicly, he scotched the idea, declaring that the opportunity came too soon after reelection as mayor; privately, perhaps, it was a post he did not want.[56] He had served fourteen years in the House of Representatives, winning a national repu-

---

*Louvain, a Belgian city, was famous for its medieval buildings, of which one, the Clothworkers' Hall, housed the library, founded in 1426 and containing a unique collection of 750 medieval manuscripts and over 1,000 incunabula. For six days in August 1914 the Germans burned and sacked the city, and the library was completely destroyed. Most of the Western world, its governments and people, vigorously protested, and the fate of the library became a major disaster for the Germans, since it confirmed a widespread belief that they truly were barbarians. The library was rebuilt with American funds but destroyed again by the Germans in World War II.

tation as a liberal legislator, and in his first six years in City Hall he had won another as a fiery, combative mayor—imaginative, compassionate, incorruptible. After the experience of leading America's greatest city, even a place as senator may have had little appeal, junior to Robert Wagner and merely one of ninety-six. Since 1935 he had been traveling around the country as president of the U.S. Conference of Mayors,[57] fostering a new relationship between the country's larger cities and the federal government and meanwhile developing his own national constituency. He now thought of himself as a national figure, representing more than a city or state, and so did many others. When he first thought seriously of running for president in the 1940 elections is not clear, but surely before Copeland died. But by then—what La Guardia did not know—Roosevelt for more than a year had been thinking of seeking a third term.[58]

As those who worked with La Guardia soon became aware, he longed for greater power and glory. Stanley Isaacs observed that though La Guardia had "made up his mind to be the best Mayor the city ever had— and he was," the purpose was conceived in part "to achieve his other ambitions." Paul Windels said, "He never lost his interest in his political future. He was at it all the time." And by his sixth year in office those other ambitions began to affect his work for the city. CCB said, "He got damaged really by power."[59]

An episode that signaled the troubles ahead began quietly in October 1939 when the city's Board of Higher Education invited the English philosopher and mathematician Bertrand Russell to teach some advanced courses at City College. The appointment was to run for seventeen months, the three semesters February 1941–June 1942. Russell, a renowned mathematician (and an English earl)—he was to win the Nobel Prize in Literature in 1950 for his *History of Western Philosophy*—accepted the post, and the appointment was announced on 26 February 1940.

Despite an editorial in the *Sun* deploring Russell's views on capitalism and conventional morality, the appointment seemed likely to win general approval. Most people saw it as a coup for the municipal college, which hardly ranked with Harvard or the great state universities. But then the Episcopal bishop of New York City, William T. Manning, in letters, sermons, and speeches began to preach a crusade against Russell, not for his mathematics or philosophy, but for his morals.[60]

In the 1920s Russell had published a series of books on education and social mores of which the chief, *Marriage and Morals*, had appeared in 1929. The books were well written, scholarly, and aimed at an educated audience. Their tone, however, was often offensive. There are less provocative ways to describe Christian baptism than writing: "The Pelew Islanders believe that the perforation of the nose is necessary for winning eternal bliss. Europeans think that this end is better attained by wetting the head while pronouncing certain words." Or, to state that the author's aim is "to cleanse sex from the filth with which it has been covered by Christian moralists."[61]

For married couples without children, Russell advocated what then was called "a companionate marriage," distinguished from usual marriage by three characteristics. "First, that there should be for the time being no intention of having children, and that accordingly the best available birth control information should be given to the young couple. Second, that so long as there are no children and the wife is not pregnant, divorce should be possible by mutual consent. And third, that in the event of divorce, the wife should not be entitled to alimony." In an earlier book, *Education and the Modern World*, he had proposed for university students what, in the phrase of the day, was called "free love": "University life would be better, both intellectually and morally, if most university students had temporary childless marriages that would afford a solution to the sexual urge neither restless nor surreptitious, neither mercenary nor casual, and of such nature that it need not take up time that should be given to work." In sum, "all sex relations which do not involve children should be regarded as a purely private affair," with adultery permissible and even desirable. As for Christianity, "Through its whole history it has been a force tending toward mental disorders and unwholesome views of life."[62]

Russell's views initially had caused a stir, but then most people, when the sun continued to rise daily, forgot them. At the time of his City College appointment *Marriage and Morals* was out of print. Nevertheless, Bishop Manning, who had kept a file on Russell, began at once from his pulpit and by his pen to warn parents against the pollution of their children's minds. Russell was a "recognized propagandist against both religion and morality," he declared, and a man who "specifically defends adultery."[63]

CCB wrote to La Guardia, a fellow Episcopalian, "I hope you will keep out of the Bertrand Russell mess . . . If Bishop Manning had kept his fourteenth-century trap shut, the noble earl would have come and gone without notice." The bishop's alarums, however, stirred the city's Catholic hierarchy, its church journals, and laity, arousing a far larger audience than merely conservative Episcopalians. Probably unknown to CCB, La Guardia meantime promised Manning he'd do what he could to stop the appointment, acting "within the limits of such powers as I have."[64]

On 15 March 1940, the *Herald Tribune* published a letter signed "Church-man and Taxpayer" noting that "the three subjects" on which Russell had been hired to teach were "advanced logic, the philosophy of mathematics, and the relation of philosophy to the sciences." The writer, in whom many doubtless recognized CCB, pointed out that few students would take the courses (limited to juniors and seniors), and the true issue in the bishop's "stirring of the educational broth" was not academic freedom within the university but toleration within the community for different views. Privately, CCB told Windels he had tried by the letter "to eliminate" the question of academic freedom. And though he did not say so, he may have written anonymously in order to avoid the appearance of an attack by "low" liberal St. George's Church on its high-church conservative bishop.[65]

Meanwhile, Manning continued to thunder against Russell. He ignored the subjects Russell was to teach, and stressed, often by lifting out of context, his views about sexual relations, masturbation, and homosexuality. In a sermon in the Cathedral of St. John the Divine, with La Guardia in the congregation, Manning warned that Russell threatened "those foundations of religion and of moral life upon which alone our nation can endure." Earlier, in a letter to the *Times*, he had asked, "Can any of us wish our young people to accept these teachings as decent, true, or worthy of respect? . . . The heads of colleges are *in loco parentis* and they are responsible for the influences brought to bear on their students."[66]

Then, on 14 March, the day before CCB's "Churchman and Taxpayer" letter was published, the City Council, by resolution, ordered the Board of Higher Education to rescind the appointment. The board, however, voted 11 to 7 against reconsideration, and La Guardia, who seemed ready to stand firm, had a note of praise from CCB: "I'm sure you won't let our anachronistic cinquecento Bishop or the Tammany Enquirer press you to press the Board of Higher Education to press the Adulterous Peer out of his post . . . It is largely a fake issue . . . You were wise to leave it to the Board."[67]

Yet the turmoil continued. A city taxpayer, Mrs. Jean Kay, a dentist's wife in Brooklyn, petitioned the state Supreme Court to revoke the appointment because Russell's teaching of logic would be "lecherous, salacious, libidinous, lustful," as well as "unscholarly." It would subvert not only her children's morals but their intellects. Neither of her two children, however, was enrolled in City College; the eldest, still in high school, even if she entered after graduation, would not become eligible to take any of Russell's courses before his brief tenure had ended.[68]

Nevertheless, on 31 March Justice John E. McGeehan—a Catholic and best known for seeking to expunge from a courthouse mural a portrait of

Martin Luther—at a hearing on Mrs. Kay's petition, found in her favor. He first denied the corporation counsel's motion to dismiss the suit because the petition failed to state facts sufficient to constitute a cause of action. He then concluded that Russell's appointment was revoked because he (1) was neither a citizen of the United States nor declared his intention to become one, (2) had not taken a competitive examination for the post, and (3) was advocating behavior against the public policy of the state and nation. Had Judge McGeehan limited himself to the first two grounds, based on the state's laws for "teachers" in public schools, many people might have thought him wrong but within reason. Unhappily, he declared the third ground "the most compelling," and gave to it most of the decision, repeating Manning's quotations and condemnations of Russell's views, to which, offering little as legal basis, he added strictures of his own: "The appointment of Dr. Russell is an insult to the people of the city of New York . . . [and] the board of higher education [in making the appointment] "to be paid by public funds, is in effect establishing a chair of indecency."[69]

His decision probably pleased the majority of those following the case in the newspaper headlines. But many felt he had overstepped his judicial function at a hearing on a petition. After ruling on the motion to dismiss the case, which was the only matter before him, he had improperly gone ahead to hold a trial and render judgment. "Lost was the immemorial right to answer charges filed; ignored were objections to irregularities of process," stated one critic, while others lamented a judicial rhetoric that puffed the hurricane of bigotry blowing through New York. Meanwhile, in Los Angeles, a startled, stunned Russell, unrepresented at the hearing, kept silent.[70]

Years later one critic characterized the decision as owing "less than nothing to the law and a great deal more than it ought to the Catholic interests in the Bronx Democratic Party who had secured McGeehan's appointment." At the time, CCB described it to the mayor as "one of the worst I have ever read," and like many others he assumed that the Board of Higher Education, acting through the city's corporation counsel's office, would appeal it.[71]

La Guardia and CCB's personal views of Russell's ideas probably were much alike and not untypical of a decade when the Episcopal church refused to officiate at a marriage of a divorced person whose former spouse was still living. Many people then, like the austere Presbyterian Henry Stimson, would not entertain in their homes anyone divorced, much less a known adulterer. La Guardia's views on relations between men and women were courtly, even old-fashioned for the time, and he had as a rule of his administration that adultery was a cause for discipline and even dismissal because "prejudicial to the good name and interest" of the city. CCB had once warned a Harvard official that a candidate for dean of the college, whose job in part would be to counsel undergraduates, was said to be in the midst of an extramarital affair with "a secretarial or typist lady," and therefore should be considered carefully. Plainly, however, CCB distinguished between a college dean, with a permanent appointment to counsel students of all ages, and a visiting professor who, though twice divorced, thrice married, and an adulterer, would lecture on logic and philosophy only to older students.[72]

Before the initial appeals from Judge McGeehan's decision could be taken to the Appellate Division, La Guardia effectively abolished Russell's post at City College by striking its $8,000 salary from the city budget, greatly distressing CCB and others by acting as if the case were decided when it was still before the courts. In May the Appellate Division rejected the appeal without giving an opinion, and normally the city's next step would have been to petition the Court of Appeals in Albany, which, being removed from the scene, would offer a chance for a fresh look at the issues free of the passion of the city's contending groups.

CCB wrote to La Guardia:

> I strongly urge you to direct [corporation counsel] Chanler to consent to appeal. I seriously doubt his right to tell the Board of Education they cannot appeal and I regard this refusal . . . as high-handed.
>
> You know how foolish I think the Department of Philosophy and the Board of Higher Education were in nominating and appointing Russell, and how abhorrent Russell's doctrines are to me. But why should a man with your record in a free country do to the CCNY what the Nazis have done to Heidelberg and Bonn?
>
> Your attempts to dispose of the case while it was in the courts was bad enough; but to prevent the Board appealing to higher courts is far worse . . .
>
> It is not like *you*.[73]

The appeal was never taken. La Guardia personally blocked it with an order to corporation counsel Chanler. He evidently had decided that the thousands—students, academics, and liberals—who thought Russell should be allowed to teach, were less important to his political future than the million or more who found the man's views offensive. CCB attempted by a backhand route to encourage Chanler to stand up to the mayor,[74] but after Chanler protested to La Guardia and suggested actions that could be taken to placate the liberals, he received a note from the mayor ending: "I fear you are under a misapprehension as to the duties of your office and the responsibilities which go with these duties. Further correspondence will not be helpful; nor is it desirable."[75]

La Guardia's failure to lead in the Russell affair seemed to CCB and others who admired the mayor a distressing shift in character, a sign perhaps of worse to come, an omen of deterioration. La Guardia, using words that might apply better to himself than to CCB, replied to the latter's criticism: "The pressure groups are certainly bearing down on you." Then he added tartly, "A lawyer [the corporation counsel] has advised his client (the mayor) not to appeal, and the client has accepted . . . That is all there is to that."[76] But not quite. Russell, instead of City College, went to Harvard and a post at the Barnes Foundation, and New York was left with a stain on its reputation for tolerance. Unhappily, as La Guardia probed for a high post in Washington, even a chance to be president, such behavior seemed increasingly like him.

One biographer of La Guardia has suggested that Chanler, not notably timid, in this instance gave way because of La Guardia's quite evident exhaustion from overwork.[77] The mayor's energy and speed of work were remarkable, but in his desire to raise standards he tried to run every city department. In the Parks Department he constantly fought over aesthetics and priorities with Robert Moses, a man of equally large ego and furious rhetoric. Their battles in the mayor's office, easily overheard, were awesome, and after six years of argument La Guardia was tired. Yet he refused to take a break. In December 1939 Geoffrey Parsons, editor of the *Herald Tribune*, had warned CCB that La Guardia's bad temper was a cancerous flaw.[78] And three months later the mayor's exhaustion was greater, his temper worse, and his abuse of those close to him abhorrent. Possibly Chanler thought this was not the moment for an open split in the mayor's team. Everyone in his administration worried about him.

In May 1940 La Guardia's doctor, George Baehr, urged him to enter a hospital for a week of rest, and CCB wrote Baehr an account of the mayor's most recent bad behavior and obvious need of vacation. CCB's letter is lost, but Baehr, after showing it to La Guardia, told CCB: "Your medicine was rather bitter, but it is just the kind which the patient requires."[79] La Guardia thought otherwise, and mocked CCB with a letter mimicking the old man's style.

I feel that I must write to you because I am so worried that you are not taking proper care of yourself. Here you are, when you should be resting, in so many activities and giving so much of yourself to each of them, from the eugenics of Bertrand Russell to the breeding of horses . . .

Yesterday, when I was talking, I purposely shouted into the microphone in order to make sure that you would hear me. What you need is to take it easy for a while and be guided entirely by your friends. Change is good even if you have to fire a few people around you. So I strongly recommend my remedy.

I am going to see you real soon and in the meantime be good to yourself and know that I am always thinking of you.[80]

CCB, as he sometimes did to soothe a critic, replied with a bit of apologetic doggerel.

> In Baghdad there dwells an M.D.,
>   Whose duty it is for to see
> That La Guardia, the Mayor,
>   Has the very best care,
> And is always quite fit for his job.
>
> This medico's name is George Baehr,
>   He's supposed to control the Lord Mayor,
> But that's all in your eye,
>   He might as well try
> To tame a wild man-eating beast.
>
> There's a foolish old man called C.C.,
>   Who is awfully fond of LaG.,
> He wrote Baehr a letter—
>   He should have known better—
> And urged him to tell
>   His patient august
> That he'd better pipe down
>   Or he'd certainly bust.
>
> Forgetting his oath Hippocratic,
>   Or thinking it more democratic,
> The letter Baehr showed to LaG.
>   Whereupon Fiorello

> Who's quite a smart fellow
>   Turned the tables on C,
> And said: "Dr. B.
>   You've got the wrong party,
> Myself, I am hearty,
>   The man you should see
> Is that ancient C.C.,
>   Whose letters and notes—
> They get me no votes—
>   Diverting my fine Nordic trends
> Set me quarrelling with my best friends.[81]

The outcome? No change on either side: La Guardia continued to overwork and lose his temper, and CCB to make suggestions—some of which, of course, the mayor liked. Yale, at its June 1940 commencement, awarded him an honorary degree, arranged by Thacher, a member of the Yale Corporation, who had the idea from CCB.[82]

Nevertheless, June 1940, the month when Italy invaded France and France collapsed, was an unhappy month for La Guardia in domestic politics. Throughout the spring he had reason to believe he would be Roosevelt's choice to replace Secretary of War Harry Woodring, an isolationist whom FDR was forcing to retire. CCB opposed the idea. He wrote to Seabury, "I have had bad times and good times with F.H. I hope he will not be such an ass as to go into Roosevelt's cabinet. He would only be a tool." And one time he said to La Guardia, "You won't get anything by cuddling up to Franklin. He doesn't give a damn for you. I'm perfectly sure of that."[83] On 20 June, FDR named Henry Stimson as secretary of war and as secretary of the navy Frank Knox, two Republicans who supported his foreign policy but who, unlike La Guardia, often had opposed him on domestic issues.

A few months earlier CCB had assured the Hirsts that Roosevelt could not "say the Lord's Prayer without political implications. Even his highest and most idealistic aspirations are not free from political, party and personal considerations."[84] Stimson's appointment was an example. Though he was, in CCB's opinion, "the best man in America for the post," still, FDR in the choice had "a mischievous purpose," for by announcing it on the eve of the Republican presidential convention, he threw his opponents into confusion. In creating a bipartisan national cabinet for the war he saw coming, he doubtless figured he would gain more politically in appointing the staunch Republican Stimson than the maverick La Guardia.[85] So the loyal La Guardia was passed over. In August Roosevelt appointed him to a joint U.S.-Canadian board to coordinate defense of North America. With New York City the biggest port on the East Coast and New York State sharing a long stretch of the St. Lawrence River with Canada, the appointment was appropriate—but not a call to higher office.

Meanwhile, at the Republican convention in Philadelphia in June 1940, to almost everyone's surprise, Wendell L. Willkie, a Wall Street lawyer, defeated the three leading candidates for the presidential nomination. The losers were Senator Robert A. Taft of Ohio, Senator Arthur Vandenberg of Michigan, and District Attorney Thomas E. Dewey of New York, all of whom in foreign policy were to some degree isolationist. Willkie, however, favored intervention. He had been a Democrat to start with, voting in 1932 for Roosevelt, but had become a major critic of New Deal programs affecting business, in particular speaking for and representing the utility industries. He was articulate and, despite his Wall Street polish, had a rugged charm that bespoke his birth and boyhood in Indiana. And because he supported aid to Britain and arming the United States, his nomination all but removed these issues from debate in the coming campaign, regardless of whom the Democrats nominated.

Announced contenders in the Democratic convention in Chicago, in mid-July, were Secretary of State Cordell Hull, Postmaster General James A. Farley, Vice President John Nance Garner, Senator Millard E. Tydings of Maryland—and, most important, an undeclared Roosevelt, maneuvering to have the convention draft him. La Guardia stood aside. As a Republican and scourge of Tammany, he had no chance for the nomination, not even if he had received a public blessing from the president as chosen successor— a possibility Roosevelt, as chief contender for the nomination, never for a moment considered.

Five days before the balloting, CCB wrote to an English friend: "I am one of the very few who think F.D.R. will not accept a nomination. It is strange that he should have kept silent so late. It was proper enough and wise to say nothing before the R.'s named Willkie, but I think it unfair to aspirants to wait until the Convention meets. Perhaps he thinks that he can name the candidates himself. The latest guess is Hull (old for America, 68) and Farley . . ." In this instance, CCB underestimated Roosevelt's willingness, in order to gain a third term, to wrestle in the mud of politics.[86]

Roosevelt won the nomination on the first ballot, but not without a bitter fight with Farley and a rigged fifty-three-minute demonstration on the floor orchestrated by Chicago's Mayor Kelly, with Kelly's henchmen parading the aisles and a voice "from the sewers" continually booming over the hall's loudspeakers, "WE WANT ROOSEVELT!" Later, as president and chosen candidate, Roosevelt forced the convention to nominate Secretary of Agriculture Henry A. Wallace for vice president. The delegates, infuriated by Roosevelt's tactics, during the balloting whistled, booed, and cat-called at every mention of Wallace's name, while on the stage, close to the front and beside Mrs. Roosevelt, sat Mrs. Wallace, visibly "reeling" under the hour-long hail of abuse. Mrs. Roosevelt took her hand and held it. So virulent was the delegates' anger that when the deed was done and the nomination secured, the convention's leaders forbade Wallace to offer an acceptance speech or even to show himself. Thus, instead of the friendly draft the president had tried to manipulate, he, Mayor Kelly, and the leaders had produced what FDR's speechwriter Robert Sherwood described as "this dreadful display of democracy at its tawdriest."[87]

The convention set the tone for the campaign. Willkie soon was prophesying that Roosevelt would drag the country into war "by April 1941," and Roosevelt, in order to win isolationist votes, promised Americans (in a speech of which Sherwood was deeply ashamed), "I have said this before, but I shall say it again—and again—and again. Your boys are not going to be sent into any foreign wars."[88]

In September La Guardia, though still nominally a Republican, joined Senator Norris to lead an Independent Committee (not tied to the Democratic National Committee) for Roosevelt. And despite his ban on city employees taking an active part in politics, he campaigned vigorously in all the bigger Northern cities. In his usual rough style, made rougher by exhaustion, he spoke like the demagogue many thought him to be and frequently slandered Willkie, appalling the Republican Windels and Thacher as well as the nominal Democrat Seabury, all of whom favored Willkie. And La Guardia did more for Roosevelt, though he denied it. To help the president win votes in the New York City Democratic organization he appointed Tammany's ex-mayor Jimmy Walker, who had returned from Europe, to a job as "czar" of industrial and labor relations to the women's coat-and-suit industry—at a salary of $20,000 a year with $5,000 more for expenses. This rich plum for Walker so angered Seabury that in a radio address for Willkie, he charged that La Guardia had "stepped down from his position of political leadership among those who are striving for decent municipal government in the United States," and he applied to La Guardia the sharpest lines of Robert Browning's poem "Lost Leader," in which Browning wrote of Wordsworth: "Just for a handful of silver he left us, / Just for a riband to stick in his coat." La Guardia, Seabury told his radio audience, had "adopted the tactics of his ally in the present campaign, Boss Flynn."[89] When a bystander in Detroit, one Benjamin H. Owens, asked La Guardia if he was taking orders from Flynn, La Guardia seized the man's necktie, tore his collar, and had to be pulled off him. Back in New York, he said that Owens, a bus company employee, was "drunk," but Owens turned out to be a total abstainer, and New York had a mayor being sued for assault and slander.[90]

In late October the *Times* published a column-long letter from CCB discussing two points: the issue of a third term for any president, and the qualities of leadership in the two candidates. He dismissed the third term as "not a real issue," historically ill founded—Grant had tried for a third term in 1876 but lost the Republican nomination to Rutherford B. Hayes—and used mainly by those wanting to charge Roosevelt with aiming at dictatorship. He quoted Willkie on the founders' intent: "They left it for the people to decide." More important, "the paramount issue," was: "Which of the candidates is best fitted to conduct our foreign relations?" And here CCB concluded: "We know Mr. Roosevelt's faults . . . [but] we know his virtues and his qualities . . . Mr. Willkie is a man of character and ability, but he has neither knowledge nor experience in public affairs . . . He would, no doubt, make an admirable President in normal times; but these times are not normal." Roosevelt's knowledge, experience, courage, resourcefulness, political wisdom, and "high standing and influence with the peoples of Europe, give assurance of a better administration and leadership than Mr. Willkie or any other untested man can have in this critical period of our history. This is why millions of us are supporting him."[91]

Amid an angry campaign in which isolationists and interventionists seemed at times at the verge of violence, such calm talk was striking. To Frank MacKinnon, uninvolved and overseas, CCB confessed that the letter had been written on Roosevelt's request: "Confidentially I may tell you that I wrote it on a tip from the All Highest himself." Nevertheless, CCB's opinions were not thereby tailored. They repeated what he was writing daily to friends in America and abroad.[92]

At some point toward the end of the campaign at least six Fusion leaders, including Windels and Thacher, issued a statement in support of Willkie. It apparently was not published in a newspaper, perhaps was mailed only to friends and persons interested, and beyond what appears in its first two paragraphs, has no reference to La Guardia. It began:

> Seven years ago we joined in a non-partisan effort to free New York City from political machine rule. This resulted in the election of a fusion city

administration headed by Mayor La Guardia and its re-election four years later.

It is therefore with regret that we differ with Mayor La Guardia in the present campaign and record our profound disagreement with his support of President Roosevelt.

Thousands of our fellow citizens throughout the country who are interested in municipal government must be greatly disturbed, as are we, by one outstanding fact of the present campaign, that is the prominence and malign influence of corrupt municipal political machines in the third term campaign.

President Roosevelt was not drafted by his party. He succeeded in forcing himself on a sullen and unwilling Convention by his alliances with Boss Flynn and his machine in New York City, Mayor Hague's vote-stealing and book-burning machine in Jersey City, the Kelly-Nash racketeer infested machine in Chicago, the Crump machine in Memphis, what is left of the notorious Prendergast machine in Kansas City and the remains of the Huey Long boodle organization in Louisiana . . .

The community of interest between national bureaucracy and local political gangs is an axis all too familiar to the subjugated peoples on the continent of Europe . . . The immediate and supremely important duty before us is to defeat the alliance between this national administration with its definite trend toward autocracy and the corrupt political gangs which control some of our large cities.

We are therefore supporting, and urge our fellow citizens to support, Wendell L. Willkie for President . . .[93]

Three weeks after Roosevelt won the election, thirty-eight states to ten, La Guardia replied to this statement. He wrote on his official stationery to seven Fusion leaders: Paul Windels, Williams [sic] Chadbourne, Victor Ridder, Henry C. Turner, Charles E. Hughes Jr., Thomas C. [sic] Thacher, and Samuel Seabury. La Guardia perhaps typed the two-page single-spaced letter himself, but in any case it was sloppily edited. Among other defects, besides adding an incorrect s to Chadbourne's first name and mistaking Thacher's middle initial, it included Seabury, who had not signed the statement in support of Willkie.

My dear Friends:

I have purposely waited for sufficient time to elapse since the election to refer to the unjustifiable and unnecessary statement signed by you during the campaign . . . that filthy statement . . . Did not every one of you cooperate and help the so-called Democrats for Willkie? Why was that right not accorded to me?

I understand the high esteem my administration has won in this county . . . Some of you wanted to make it appear that you owned me body and soul . . . Most of you have been grouped together before but you have never been able to have clean, efficient, decent City government in New York City until I ran and gave it to the people of this City . . .

I will not again run for the office of the Mayor of the City of New York . . . There is no one for whom I had greater affection than the Judge [Seabury]. To have a group—a small group—for whom I had such affection, resort to such unbelievable, political tactics hurts more than I can tell. I forgive every one of you, but please don't ask me to forget.

Timothy II, 4:7*

Sincerely,
F. H. La Guardia[94]

His Fusion friends apparently put the letter aside as yet another sad example of temperament and exhaustion. But Seabury discussed it with CCB, who then wrote to "Dear Fiorello."

I wish you had a secretary or friend who had the courage or the sense to tell you not to send a letter which you should destroy before you sign it. The Bishop [Seabury] showed me such a letter addressed to a number of your friends, which he answered immediately.

If you were well and courageously served you would have been told that S.S. was not one of the signatories of the document which you described as filthy, and you would have kept your letter on a higher plane or better still would have given it to the flames. Of course, you had a right to vote and speak and work for F.D.R. I cannot remember the statement signed by Windels, etc. I thought your attacks on Willkie might help F.D.R. in the Middle West. I don't think they had any material effect in New York City or State.

In your letter you say that you expect soon to issue a statement that you will not "again run for the office of Mayor."

I hope that on further reflection you will do nothing of the kind. No one knows what the situation will be in New York or the U.S.A. six or

---

*"I have fought a good fight. I have finished my course. I have kept the faith."

eight months from now. You may be needed in New York as much as
F.D.R. was and is in the U.S.A. Next to the Presidency, the Mayoralty of
New York is the most important office in the U.S.A.—certainly far more
important than any cabinet post, even the highest. So I beg you to keep
your shirt on and give out no statements. The less talk, the more do.

Your old friend,[95]

Perhaps CCB's letter, followed by morning talks in the limousine driving downtown, calmed the mayor's spirit, for the following month La
Guardia declined a post in Washington, though not revealing to CCB
what he had been offered. But his decision had CCB's approval: "If the
post tendered was one of four to which later a lame-duck Senator was
appointed, you were wise to refuse it, and if it is for a more independent
post, you would do well to refuse it. It is extraordinary how impossible it
seems to resist the blandishments of our Good and Great Friend. I am
told that H.L.S. [Stimson] now not only admires but loves him."[96]

By January 1941, as La Guardia started the final year of his second
term, he seemed more content in his job than he had been for many months.
He was already the best mayor the city had ever had—rebuilding it with
new parks, bridges, and highways, upgrading its bureaucracy through civil
service, fighting crime and corruption in the police, wiping out the worst
of patronage and graft, and transforming charitable relief into a system
that could cope (or almost) with the size of its problems. If he occasionally
stumbled, failing to provide leadership when it seemed needed, his accomplishments still greatly outweighed his failures. Even fifty years later
he consistently won polls as the greatest mayor in the country's history.[97]

Though Roosevelt's run for a third term had denied La Guardia a
chance at the presidency, CCB urged the mayor to take heart and not to
burn any bridges to the future: "No one knows what the situation will be
in New York or the U.S.A. in the next six or eight months." At eighty-
three, CCB may have doubted he would live to see the war's end, but La
Guardia, fifty-nine, surely would. Meanwhile, if this year La Guardia
couldn't have the White House or a cabinet post, there was New York's
City Hall—to CCB, "Next to the Presidency . . . the most important
office in the U.S.A."[98]

22

New York City in Wartime

THROUGHOUT THE WINTER of 1940–41, a sense of imminent war smoldered in New York City, and nowhere more strongly than around its harbor and in every sort of business that touched on maritime affairs. Roosevelt interpreted his reelection as an endorsement of his aid-to-Britain policy, and in January 1941 proposed the Lend-Lease Act to Congress. Isolationists protested, debate was fierce, but the act passed in March and authorized the president to "sell, transfer, exchange, lease, lend" any defense articles "to the government of any country whose defense the president deems vital to the defense of the United States." It also opened to such nations the use of American shipyards, and New York's facilities were unrivaled. The port not only had an inner harbor, the Upper Bay, a space of seventeen square miles, but in 1940 it offered some nine hundred piers, the Brooklyn Navy Yard, two commercial dry docks, four navy dry docks, and had begun construction on a dry dock to accommodate a 45,000-ton battleship. It also had fifty floating docks for unloading cargo or making repairs above the waterline, some floating grain elevators that could moor alongside a ship and unload tons of grain in minutes, some two thousand barges, freight-car lighters (twenty-four cars to a barge), and tugs to move them, more mobile derrick equipment and other freight-handling machinery than any port in the world, and finally railroad connections with fast-freight schedules leading directly to the country's important cities. Naval business of all kinds boomed as ships came in for repairs, convoys gathered in the harbor, and food and arms were shipped to Britain. And as refugees from Europe arrived, many of them professors, doctors, lawyers, and distinguished artists, their stories and speeches daily added certainty to the sense that war was inevitable.[1]

La Guardia continued to divide his attention and hopes between New York City and Washington. In New York, besides the daily crises of administration, budget, schools, snow, and garbage removal, he now faced, in his eighth year as mayor, increasing opposition in the City Council and Board of Estimate. In addition, two long-term problems without easy solutions loomed increasingly large: the city's inadequate tax base and its impoverished transit system. The tax base, levied chiefly on real estate, could not sustain the social services the city now offered, a situation worsening as Washington directed its subsidies away from schools, highways, and bridges toward the needs of defense. And the transit system, largely private until unified under city ownership in June 1940, was crippled financially by its long-held five-cent fare. This famous "nickel ride" created an annual deficit of some $40 million, not including costs of delayed maintenance on cars, rails, and tunnels. But raising the fare was something most politicians were unwilling to do.

New York City's transit system, with 30,000 employees, was the largest municipal enterprise in America. Its many subway and bus lines carried two billion passengers a year, five times the number carried by all the country's railroads. Besides problems of maintenance—tunnels, rails, streets, subway cars, and buses—that of personnel was immense. On what basis were the employees, whose contract rights widely differed, to be taken into the city's civil service?[2] Several times strikes were averted, but in March 1941 employees of the bus lines shut down service for eleven days, and their leader, Michael J. Quill, threatened to halt the subways in June. La Guardia managed to prevent the June strike, but in a manner that left many workers angry. Opposition to the mayor, perhaps unavoidable after eight years in office, was stiffening, and no doubt he saw in a cabinet post in Washington—new faces, overtones of national defense—an appealing alternative. Frequently in the winter of 1941, he warned of a sudden departure for Washington, even on such municipal occasions as his annual address to the City Council.[3]

Newspapers continually reported him a candidate for this or that federal post—after the president and first lady he was the most likely source for a story—but the appointment, when it came, on 18 May 1941, was for a wholly new position (without pay): director of the Office of Civilian Defense.[4] No one at the time, not even the president, could fully define the job. In England, at war, the analogous post of home secretary had considerable power. During the Blitz, for example, the secretary ordered compulsory night fire-watch on buildings heretofore left unguarded, organized the local volunteer fire brigades into a National Fire Service, and then "froze" the volunteers into their jobs. Though civilians, by law they could not resign. And further, the home secretary sat in Churchill's "war cabinet." What La Guardia might make of a similar post in a country at peace, where night bombing seemed impossible, was unclear. Still, he asked for and received a place in Roosevelt's cabinet and set to work with his usual vigor, traveling to all the bigger cities to speak on dangers if war should come and to organize plans for defense.

New Yorkers soon felt neglected by their mayor. By summer his typical pattern was to spend Tuesday, Wednesday, and Thursday in Washington, staying over Friday if there was a cabinet meeting. The balance of the week he was in New York—except that he was constantly flying to meetings elsewhere. In December 1939 the greatly enlarged North Beach Airfield in Queens County had reopened as "La Guardia Airport," giving the city one of the country's most modern and busiest airfields.[5] Journalists continually were there to interview the arriving or departing mayor—a routine CCB lamented as La Guardia shooting "off his mouth as he hops into a plane at *HIS* field."[6]

Throughout June 1941 a question much put to the mayor was: Will you seek a third term? Often followed by: If so, will you continue as director of civilian defense? On both questions La Guardia was coy, even as civic groups, doubtless with his approval, began to call for him to run again. And on 21 July Seabury and Thacher announced, as patriarchs of the Fusion Party, that they would work through the already formed Citizens Non-Partisan Committee to Re-elect La Guardia. The next week Tammany picked its candidate, William O'Dwyer, a Brooklyn district attorney of good reputation. This left La Guardia to gather, if he could, the nominations of the Republican and Fusion Parties and of the new American Labor Party (formed in 1936 by leaders of the garment trades unions).[7]

CCB, now eighty-three and deaf, had a lesser role than eight years earlier but one that still was crucial. Of the city's five Republican county organizations, two, Queens and the Bronx, refused to nominate La Guardia. Their leaders protested that he had denied Republicans patronage in the city and had campaigned across the country against Willkie. The result was a party divided and a primary fight in which La Guardia was opposed by an old-line Republican, John R. Davies, an elderly respected conservative who was strongly isolationist and anti–New Deal.

Many New York Republicans waited for their most prominent leader, Tom Dewey, to take a stand. Having lost the party's presidential nomination in June 1940 to Willkie, Dewey recently had decided not to seek reelection as county district attorney but to wait until 1942, when he could run again for governor, a race he had lost in 1938 to Lehman. Meanwhile, in the summer of 1941, Davies gathered support with his argument that Tammany now was less of a danger to the city than the New Dealers and left-wingers flourishing under La Guardia. What New York needed, Davies insisted, was a true Republican, not a member of Roosevelt's cabinet. Thrice president of the city's National Republican Club, Davies was popular with party regulars, and an endorsement by Dewey seemed certain to give him the Republican nomination in the September primary. In that case, La Guardia would have the backing of only the American Labor and Fusion Parties, and the race for mayor would be three-way: Republican, Democrat, and American Labor–Fusion, with Tammany's O'Dwyer the assured winner.

The prospect worried CCB. According to Reuben A. Lazarus, then assistant to the president of the City Council, one day late in the summer CCB drove "all about the town" with Dewey in the latter's limousine. His purpose was to win Dewey's support for La Guardia in the primary, a hard task, for La Guardia in 1938 had supported Lehman for governor, and Dewey was not one to forget. According to Lazarus:

> Dewey had been plagued by everyone in the Republican organization not to endorse Mr. La Guardia, because all La Guardia did after being elected was to endorse Roosevelt and make trouble for every Republican candidate. Getting out of the car in front of the National Republican Club, Mr. C. C. Burlingham, who is a very persuasive man, a very old man, and a very wise man, finally got this out of Dewey: "C.C., I shouldn't do this for the son-of-a-bitch, but we're going to give him the endorsement again!"[8]

In addition, La Guardia received important last-minute primary endorsements from Moses and Willkie, two others who might have expressed a personal disregard in similar terms but instead chose, on the mayor's record, to support him publicly.[9] With such backing, La Guardia perhaps should have won the primary more decisively than he did, 63,246 to 43,426. (Davies took two of the city's five counties, Queens and the Bronx, a defeat for La Guardia which CCB later ascribed to the population, at least in Queens, being largely "German and Isolationist.")[10] And the citywide turnout was low, suggesting that La Guardia's aloofness, his policy of letting his record speak for him, was not exciting voters. So, with the Republican nomination secured and seven weeks to the final election in November, he turned to O'Dwyer and began to campaign hard.

Though the Fusion Party gave La Guardia a line on the ballot and the support of many distinguished citizens, its role in this third campaign was less than in the previous two. To a friend in England, CCB described his own part as "trivial," saying he, Seabury, and Thacher had merely "started the nominating machine." To another friend he wrote, "For me, it is the last kick of an old horse, and I enjoy it."[11]

This time, Fusion did not organize its own campaign committee, raise money, and send out speakers; most of that work was handled by the Republican and American Labor organizations or by the mayor's own team at City Hall. This suited La Guardia, for he wanted to be free of what he saw as Fusion domination. In previous campaigns, the Fusion Party had brought him workers in its local clubs throughout the city. But these clubs had atrophied, in part because their main purpose seemed achieved by eight years of honest city government, and in part because of La Guardia's rule (from which he excused himself) that anyone joining his administration had to cease work for a political party.[12] The clubs thereby had lost into city jobs many of their leaders. By 1941 Fusion was becoming a group of elderly men and women without troops to command. Yet these elderly cadres, surviving in power as the war began to drain away the best of the next generation, still had influence, and in some troublesome situations could be extremely useful. One such involved the Manhattan borough president Stanley Isaacs, who sought renomination but La Guardia wanted him off the ticket.

Isaacs, an honest, courageous, competent Republican, was one of the city's most valued officials, but over the past three years he had become entangled in a controversy. In February 1938 he had appointed to a low office in his department a young man whom he found bright and articulate, Simon Gerson, a reporter for the *Daily Worker* and a Communist. In neither 1938 nor 1941 was membership in the Communist Party a bar to government service, and the party often ran its own candidates for office. Nevertheless, objections to Gerson gradually mounted. Isaacs, wanting to be fair and believing on principle that until the country outlawed the Communist Party he should not bar the man, refused to dismiss Gerson. No one familiar with Isaacs or his work could imagine him as a Communist or even a Communist sympathizer, but his reluctance to dump Gerson, even refusing the man's offer to resign, promised to give Davies an issue for the Republican primary and, more important, the Democrats an issue for the November election.

To get Isaacs off the ticket, La Guardia first tried to bully him. Calling Isaacs to a supposedly private meeting to discuss some school construction on which they disagreed, he had reporters on hand and, in front of them, threatened "to break" Isaacs if the latter persisted in opposition. Isaacs, though shaken by the temper and rhetoric, refused to yield. His resignation, he told his wife, was the real purpose of the ambush: the mayor "wants to get rid of me because he thinks the Gerson matter will hurt his chances of election." Sometime later La Guardia invited Isaacs and his wife to dinner and offered him a judicial appointment, which Isaacs declined.[13]

In early August, fearing that the rising furor over Communism imperiled the La Guardia ticket, Fusion leaders sent CCB to urge Isaacs to withdraw. CCB reported to Thacher, "I rehearsed our meeting of Monday and put the case as strongly as I could." Still, Isaacs stood firm, though CCB believed "he will wash out soon."[14] Meanwhile, the leaders had recruited Edgar J. Nathan Jr. as a substitute candidate, though he agreed to run only with Isaacs's approval. So, a day or less before the last hour when a withdrawal could be legally effective, CCB and Nathan visited Isaacs in his house on East Ninety-sixth Street. CCB later explained, "We talked it out, and I made it clear to Isaacs that it would be a heavy burden and he consented to our naming Nathan."[15] Whereupon, with only an hour and a half to the deadline, Isaacs announced he would not seek reelection as borough president but instead would run on his own for the City Council. The next morning in the newspapers, Seabury and CCB hailed his decision as a noble sacrifice to keep Tammany out of office. CCB stated frankly that Isaacs's record of accomplishments in office were "so great that he deserved renomination and re-election." The charge of Communist sympathy was "preposterous . . . Nothing could be more false, but falsehoods are not unknown in our democracy, particularly at election time."[16]

About his decision to run for the City Council, Isaacs told his wife the post was "a comedown from the Borough Presidency," but it would give him a forum. "I could fight there for the things I believe in." Putting himself on the ballot without the nomination of any party and without a word of support from La Guardia, he ran and was elected. In votes received, he ranked second among the six councilmen elected from Manhattan. As a Republican on the council, sometimes the only one, he served as its minority leader from 1941 until his death in 1962, making of his lonely pulpit an outstanding career of sense, reason, and integrity.[17] CCB greatly admired him, and the two were constantly in touch. Before the election, Isaacs wrote him a letter of thanks for the "generous contribution . . . to my campaign fund." Then he added:

I want you to know I have been far more influenced than you realize throughout this year's discussions by your point of view and your attitude. There were times when I had to say "no" to your direct requests for practical reasons, but nevertheless I never intended to take any attitude which you could justly have criticized as disloyal to the cause of good government, and it means a great deal to me to have your confidence and your continued support—and I hope to continue to deserve it.[18]

Ten days before the election, CCB also undertook to elicit for La Guardia a helpful word from President Roosevelt. PLEASE TELL SKIPPER FROM ME, he wired to Frankfurter, RARE OPPORTUNITY FOR STATEMENT. THAT IN PRESENT EMERGENCY HONEST EFFICIENT AND SMOOTH RUNNING CITY GOVERNMENT SHOULD BE CONTINUED REGARDLESS OF STATE POLITICS. THIS IS THE VERY BASIS TO NEW YORK CONSTITUTIONAL PROVISION FOR MUNICIPAL ELECTION IN OFF YEARS.[19]

At a press conference the next day, Roosevelt said: "I am not taking part in the New York City election but . . . I do not hesitate to express the opinion that Mayor La Guardia and his administration have given to the City the most honest and, I believe, the most efficient municipal government of any within my recollection." The city election had no relation to national policies, he added, as was "attested by the fact that the Constitution of the State provides for the municipal election in off years." Thus, La Guardia finally had some reward for his support of FDR in the 1940 campaign against Willkie, and CCB telegraphed Roosevelt: SPLENDID. YOU HAVE STIMULATED GOOD GOVERNMENT IN EVERY AMERICAN CITY.[20]

Just when every political domino seemed to fall into place (including an ecclesiastical endorsement by Bishop Manning)[21] La Guardia made a clumsy mistake. Governor Lehman, who always supported the city Democratic organization, in a speech in the Bronx had given a somewhat tepid endorsement to O'Dwyer, while extolling many of La Guardia's achievements. But he questioned whether La Guardia was "superman" enough to fill two full-time jobs, and insisted that the mayor resign his city post if he continued to be director of civilian defense.[22] La Guardia disliked Lehman, took offense, and found, or so he thought, in a minor matter of state administration a chance to mock the governor and his brother Irving Lehman, chief justice of the Court of Appeals.

The arcane situation concerned the governor's temporary appointment of a successor to the state comptroller, who had died. Irving Lehman was involved because the state's attorney general had challenged the governor's appointment, arguing that the post required an immediate special election, and the Court of Appeals had nonetheless ruled that the temporary appointment was valid and that the election could be held the following year. La Guardia professed to see in this episode an effort to support O'Dwyer that had backfired. His version of events and motives had the governor making the appointment, changing his mind by using the attorney general to attack the appointment, and then changing his mind again by using his brother's court to reject the attorney general's argument. In the final week of the campaign La Guardia made this convoluted scenario the center of his standard stump speech. He then was speaking some thirteen times a day, and in high school auditoriums he would roam the stage, making big gestures, his voice high with excitement as he recounted: "I think it's the funniest thing that has happened in American politics . . . It's the first time a man [the governor] has hit himself on the jaw and knocked himself out . . . You've heard of goniffs [Yiddish for thieves] stealing from goniffs. Well, you're now hearing of double-crossers double-crossing double-crossers." At the Seth Low High School, while imitating Lehman striking himself on the jaw, La Guardia had nearly knocked himself down. And at that school and others, audiences found their Fiorello and his antics extremely comic. But the governor, when he heard of it, was not amused, nor were many others. They saw truth in Lehman's indignant response that La Guardia had accused him "of being a thief and a double-crosser, and a fixer . . . [and] the Court of Appeals of being corrupt and taking orders from me." They agreed, "New Yorkers are sick and tired of Mr. La Guardia's unbridled tongue." Suddenly the mayor's personality was the main issue: was he fit for office?[23]

Fusion leaders urged La Guardia to apologize, but he would not, and on Election Day the vote, though in his favor, was closer than expected: 1,186,301 to 1,054,175, a margin of only 132,126. In 1937 the margin had been almost four times larger and he had carried every borough, where now he failed in two of the five (Queens and Staten Island). Estimates of the votes lost by his crude assault on Lehman ranged from 25,000 to ten times higher.[24] Had a mere 70,000, roughly 3 percent of those cast, gone the other way, Tammany would have won, in which case, the *Times* suggested in an editorial, "we suspect that many who voted for O'Dwyer, including Lehman himself, would have read the news with a chilly feeling."[25]

Whereas La Guardia's first two terms had been dominated by the Depression, his third was dominated by the war. Thirty-three days after the election, the Japanese attacked Pearl Harbor, and the next day, 8 December, the United States declared war on Japan. Three days later Germany and Italy, as required by their pact with Japan, declared war on the United States. In New York all work on such projects as the Brooklyn-Battery Tunnel promptly stopped as steel went into battleships and guns. The city's civil service was hard hit: many of the promising younger men and women entered the armed services or took war-related jobs in Washington or in industry. The number of resignations in fiscal year 1941–42 was 7,358, and the next year 15,712. Similarly, older workers retired early to take higher-paying jobs in industry; and the number of retirements jumped about 50 percent.[26] The replacements often were less competent, even as the city faced such additional wartime duties as organizing a system of air raid wardens, interning some 2,500 Japanese on Ellis Island, and taking measures against sabotage of railways, bridges, and tunnels.

When a newspaper photographer congratulated the mayor on winning reelection, La Guardia replied, "Thanks, but the next four years will be hell."[27] In that spirit he started his third term, and typically he refused to take any vacation, or even a day off.

At the end of his first month, in an extraordinary display of temper, he forced the resignation of William Fellowes Morgan Jr., one of his ablest commissioners. Morgan, a quiet-spoken man who had been commissioner of markets from the first day of La Guardia's first term, had protested three appointments La Guardia had made to the commissioner's staff without consultation and chiefly for political reasons. When he asked to see the mayor, Morgan was fobbed off with "out of town" or "too busy." Then La Guardia ordered him to fire a staff member, a respected volunteer, again for political reasons. Morgan refused. The mayor, calling him to a meeting, repeatedly screamed, "Fire that dame, fire that dame." Morgan offered his resignation, which was taken. La Guardia later dismissed a reporter's question by saying, "Commissioners never have disputes with the mayor—You should know that."[28]

But Morgan was not an unreasonable man, nor was his complaint: no commissioner of quality would accept such abuse and interference in his department, and Morgan's successor was not his equal. Worse yet, when Morgan explained to the press the political pressures applied to him and his staff, La Guardia sought revenge by ordering an investigation of "irregularities" in the department. The issue was fake, and the probe soon dropped. CCB wrote the mayor in disapproval: "Am I glad I am your friend. I should not like to be investigated *dum vivo* or *post mortem*."[29]

Yet the mayor did not moderate his behavior. Before the Morgan episode was finished, he started a similar one with Paul Kern, chairman of the Civil Service Commission, trying to force onto the chairman's staff, over Kern's objections, four Tammany stalwarts. Refusing to accept the men or to resign, Kern defended his position in the press and in the courts, causing a bitter public rift in the administration. During the controversy, La Guardia briefly suspended the entire commission—much to the joy of Tammany, which saw a thousand doors opening to jobs for its members. The commission's powers soon were restored, and Kern ultimately was dismissed—yet not before his defense had gone up to the state Supreme Court, Appellate Division, which held that the mayor had acted within his powers. Whether he had or not, his reputation for bullying his commissioners, and for opening positions to Tammany, was growing. Most newspapers and citizens ascribed such uncharacteristic behavior to the pressure of two full-time jobs, and were unsympathetic. People began to question his readiness to always blame others for his problems, a trait seeming at times to veer toward paranoia. His popularity began to slip.[30]

Before the election, CCB in serious discussion twice, and doubtless more often in passing, had urged La Guardia to announce at once that in any conflict between his double duties he would resign as director of civilian defense.[31] Many others—Seabury, Thacher, Windels, editorial writers, citizens' groups, and not least Governor Lehman—had urged the same. Early in February 1942, when La Guardia finally bowed to the pressure, CCB wrote: "Dear Fiorello: Believe it or not, I feel a little shy of saying anything to you about your resignation as Director, but I don't think it would be friendly of me not to tell you how pleased I am with your decision, and it would not be frank not to say that I was most anxious to have you resign on December 8th [the morning after Pearl Harbor], if not earlier."[32] Even now La Guardia's resignation, by refocusing his attention on the city, brought a surge of hope and vitality to reform groups and his administration.

CCB's unofficial role in La Guardia's administration continued much as before. He joined Thacher and Windels in an effort to persuade the mayor, in the flush of election victory, to tackle the problem of the five-cent subway fare, which contributed so largely to the city's annual deficit. Early in La Guardia's perilous first term, when New York in the depth of the Depression had faced bankruptcy, he had solved the crisis in part by educating the public to accept three new taxes, on sales, cigarettes, and public utilities. Now, urged the Fusion leaders, was the moment to persuade the people once again to face necessity and pay more. According to CCB, however, La Guardia "thought he would lose votes," and refused to act. The moment passed, and at the term's end the fare still stood at five cents, its inadequacy still boosting the city's annual deficit.[33]

As usual, some of CCB's deeds were done behind the scenes and sometimes without La Guardia's knowledge. One such act concerned the country's strategy for fighting the war: should the United States put its primary effort into Europe, bolstering Britain and so keeping Hitler at bay, or into the Pacific, where Japan now held most of Southeast Asia and the Philippines? The country's citizens debated the issue, their opinions sometimes reflecting prejudices buried in their ethnic backgrounds, but unknown to most, Roosevelt, his cabinet and military advisers were already agreed on a strategy of Europe first, and then Japan. With Germany occupying half of France and its submarines operating out of French Atlantic ports, the German threat to Britain and the United States was the more immediate, and Germany, with a larger industrial plant than Japan and better access to oil, was potentially the greater threat. In April 1942, presumably on a tip from someone in the mayor's office, CCB wrote to Stimson at the War Department:

> Fiorello is going to make a speech at the annual convention of the Veterans of Foreign Wars on May 3rd in Detroit. Somebody tells me that F. has said that he is going to tell them what's what, which, being interpreted, means that the Veterans should not play second fiddle to Britain. I hope he is not of the same mind as McCook, J[udge], who told me the other day that he did not think it would be wise or safe for us to join Britain in a European expedition, but that we should direct our offensive against Japan. I told him that my view was absolutely contrary to this; and I was delighted with your press statement the other day when you said we were nearly ready for an offensive, from which I infer that you prefer that to defending here, there and everywhere.
>
> It will be a very serious thing if F.H. should get off any such bunk in Detroit. I don't feel that I am the man to tell him so, but I don't know who is, and it occurs to me that if you agree with my sentiments and should write me a letter in which you say that you had heard an almost unbelievable rumor that La G. might make such a speech, I could use that with him with great effect. Is it too much to ask you to write me such a letter, and, if not you, will someone else do so?[34]

At the same time, CCB wrote a similar letter to La Guardia, but in a more chatty style: "The other day I had a talk with the warlike McCook, J. He said to me, sez he: 'I don't think it wise or safe for us to join England in a European expedition. We should direct our offensive against Japan.' I replied . . ."[35]

Stimson, already involved in plans for an Allied invasion of Europe, seized on CCB's scheme, writing at once: "Dear Charles, An unbelievable rumor has come to my ears . . . I have always thought highly of our Mayor . . . He must also know better than even you and I know the latent possibilities for prejudice and dangerous cross currents which exist in our population . . . It would be a dire calamity if he should lend his great influence to light such dangerous fires . . . The foundations of victory have now been pretty well laid."[36]

CCB passed on the letter to the mayor, who thanked him for the chance to read it. Later La Guardia denied to CCB that his Detroit speech was yet written, and protested he had intended to confer "with General Marshall [chief of the army general staff] before speaking." Filling two single-spaced pages, he repeated much of what Stimson had said, but in a tone of self-importance: "By that time [1943] no force on earth can stop us if—with a great big if—we do not dissipate our forces or consume our energies, equipment and men for local detached victories that have no decisive value in the ultimate winning of the war. The Secretary will understand this. We are not concerned with headlines or political situations anywhere . . . I will be glad to confer with General Marshall and General Arnold [head of the air force]."[37]

In November 1942 an anxious CCB listed for the mayor what he thought were the latter's chief problems of the moment. He began with the statement: "I am not a disciple of Freud, but I think I could make a pretty good psychoanalysis of you if it would do any good. I won't do that, but I will enumerate a few things that I wish were not so." These were: (1) bad relations with the press, (2) exaggerated criticisms of civil and military defense personnel in the city, (3) a charge that Moses had stopped work on the Battery Tunnel out of "revenge," supposedly because of threatened cuts in the Parks Department's budget, and:

> (4) This is what I feel strongest about: You don't seem to appreciate that your post as Mayor of the City of New York is one of the greatest in the United States. I put the President first, then the Secretary of War, then the Secretary of the Navy and, fourth, the Mayor of New York. It is still true that with all your faults you are the best Mayor New York has had in my lifetime . . .
>
> Lastly, I know what you need, though you will laugh me to scorn: (1) a vacation once in a while of a week or two; (2) somebody near you who will say, as Paul Windels used to say to you, "Don't."
>
> Like Roosevelt, you are surrounded almost completely by yes men. Yours are made by fear, his by charm. But he has the good fortune to have in his cabinet one man who knows no fear, Henry L. Stimson. You have one, Robert Moses, but he is a wild man, and his comebacks are very like your own.
>
> Affectionately yours,[38]

Befriending La Guardia without fear, CCB not only wrote him letters of criticism but on some issues confronted him in person. Records of such meetings do not survive, as CCB intended, but occasionally a trace may be found. One day in December 1942, following a dinner meeting with the mayor, Thacher, and Seabury at the latter's house on East Sixty-third Street, CCB wrote to Thacher: "Did you think me too violent—you should have heard me the day before in the City Hall alone with F.H. for ½ hour, after which I told him I had spilled my bile and would be nice at the Bishop's [Seabury]. Wasn't I?"[39]

At the same time, of course, there were issues that went smoothly. One was the replacement for corporation counsel Chanler, who resigned in December 1942 to enter the army and go to Europe. (Chanler had arranged for a lieutenant colonel's commission through Stimson, a route into the army that La Guardia hoped to follow himself.) CCB's candidate, suggested to him by Windels, was Tom Thacher, distinguished, competent, and only sixty-one, but likely to be reluctant. CCB did not hesitate to spoil Thacher's vacation, writing to him in South Carolina: "I'm very glad you're taking a little vacation, and I hope and pray that you are taking it wisely and playing nine holes and not eighteen or thirty-six, and lying about and loafing a lot. You see how mild my hortatory style has become." Then he struck:

> Words would not express the strength of my feeling that you should consent to be what I have been since 1858, *C.C.* It is an office of great importance at this critical period in our history. No one, not even the Bishop, has as much influence with F.H. as you, and no one is more respected by him than you. You are such a selfless creature that it would not add force to my persuasions if I told you that this would put you on the way to the Chief Magistracy.

The idea of Thacher succeeding La Guardia as mayor was one to which CCB would cling.[40]

In January 1943 Thacher did indeed become corporation counsel, and his presence in the city's government heartened everyone. He was a Republican, and La Guardia had appointed only a few; he was an outstanding lawyer, former judge, and former solicitor general of the United States; he had been chairman of the mayor's Charter Commission that in 1936 had restructured the city's government. Few in New York knew more about its city government than Thacher. The city's pleasure in him, however, was cut short. Dewey, who had defeated Lehman in 1942 and was now governor, wanted a respected Republican for the state's Court of Appeals, and he appointed Thacher, who departed in May for Albany. CCB rejoiced for the court but felt keenly the loss of Thacher both as a colleague for reform and as a friend. Without Thacher close by, life would be lonelier.[41]

To fill the vacant post, he suggested that the mayor ask Seabury, for whom the job would be "a sacrifice no doubt, but *pro bono publico*; and the office is in good shape and the first Asst. would relieve the Judge of detail. What a boon it would be to you!" But if La Guardia proposed the idea, Seabury refused. He was seventy, starting to slack off his law practice in favor of his farm in East Hampton. (The man ultimately appointed, Ignatius M. Wilkinson, on leave as dean of Fordham Law School, though honorable was not the equal of his predecessors.)[42]

In the spring of 1943, La Guardia suffered his greatest disappointment of the war years. As Allied armies in North Africa, fighting along the Mediterranean shore from the east and west, boxed the Germans and Italians in Tunisia, an Allied invasion of Sicily, and then mainland Italy, seemed certain. At this prospect La Guardia's desire for a military role in the war steadily increased. Because he was a well-known figure in Italy and spoke the language fluently, he and others imagined a use for him there in a top administrative post as the country was gradually liberated. On 3 February he wrote to Roosevelt, "I still believe that Genl Eisenhower can *not* get along without me and am awaiting your order (but as a soldier) . . . Let me know . . . *Con amore*, Fiorello."[43]

By mid-March he felt sure of the appointment, probably as a brigadier general. He scheduled a physical examination, was measured for a uniform, and began to acknowledge the congratulations of friends. On 27 March White House press secretary Stephen Early "confirmed reports" that La Guardia would join the army, and in anticipation of the event the *Herald Tribune* had a front-page picture of him in his World War I major's uniform, looking very fit and spruce.[44]

In Albany, meanwhile, at La Guardia's behest the state legislature considered a bill formally titled "Absence from Office for Military Duty." Probably most legislators did not understand the bill, for it was seventy-odd pages long and deliberately misleading. It was introduced by Harold C. Ostertag, assemblyman from Attica, in Wyoming County, a western upstate village with a voting population of 1,492, and it seemed on its face not to apply to New York City, but to be merely a technical wartime measure about succession of village officials leaving office. Both the Assembly and the state Senate passed it, without debate or hearing, and the governor signed it.

Yet by backward internal reference on its thirty-sixth page, the Ostertag bill applied only to New York City, and it allowed its mayor to leave the country without resigning his office. Under the old procedure the president of the City Council in such circumstances became the acting mayor until a special election could be held. This was the procedure followed when Mayor Walker resigned in September 1932; McKee became acting mayor for four months, and John O'Brien took office as winner of the special election. Under the Ostertag bill, La Guardia could appoint a deputy of his choosing, thus changing the order of succession, and there would be no special election, merely the next regularly scheduled mayoralty election in November 1945. If the mayor returned before then, he could retire his deputy and resume office. There were other clever touches. A provision gave the mayor, though absent, a hand in voting within the Board of Estimate. Conversely, another provision, usual in most emergency wartime legislation—the law to expire automatically after a year in force—was missing. CCB, on hearing of the bill, wrote instantly to La Guardia:

> What is this political streptococcus that is biting you? Are you sick of your job? Well, why did you take it? Do you really think you can serve your country better running about in a jeep in North Africa than attending to the affairs of the biggest City in the World? . . . You owe it to this City to stay right here and do your job.[45]

La Guardia denied the bill was "smart" legislation:

> Am I sick of my job? Yes. Why did I take it? Because I wanted it the first and second time, and the third time you asked me to. Do I really think I can serve my country better in running about in a jeep . . . Yes . . . I am not concerned about rank. I would take an assignment as a cook . . . The general mass of the people are all right. I have not lost confidence in them. I have lost confidence in people who pretend to be for good government but who are sometimes very selfish . . . Do write to me, please, as I do need help at this moment.[46]

Many people, on studying the Ostertag bill, were appalled. CCB wrote to Seabury that it was "undemocratic and smart aleck. The Court of Appeals might easily hold it unconstitutional."[47] At very least the provisions for the change in succession, the lack of a special election, the lack of an expiration date, and the votes retained on the Board of Estimate were questionable. As La Guardia's biographer Thomas Kessner concluded, "Something had happened to La Guardia's relationship to his office. Once he had thought of it as a trust. Now he viewed it as a private possession, something for him to pass around or keep at his own pleasure."[48]

On 31 March, in the midst of the uproar over the bill, CCB, claiming to be not yet recovered from the flu, excused himself from an afternoon meeting with La Guardia, Seabury, and "the Brethren" (probably Windels and Thacher). By now most people believed the city was about to lose its mayor to the army, but CCB still opposed the plan, and sent a note with his views to Seabury: "I cannot hurrah for FH's warlike spirit. It is infantile and shows no true sense of proportion. Patriotism for him is here, not in N. Africa. I could name 100 men as fit as he to be a Proconsul or Procurator. I could not possibly name more than 2 or 3 as fit as he to be Mayor."[49] The next day Seabury, who had been "very much surprised" to hear of CCB's sudden attack of flu, reported to him: "We had our interview. It was not important. My own judgment is that the Mayor has made up his mind to take a commission, but I think the arrangements are far from settled."[50]

CCB knew more than he let on, however. Several days earlier, acting on his own, he had written a letter in his unique scrawl to Secretary Stimson. That letter is lost, but some of what it must have said can be gleaned from Stimson's response and a second CCB letter. To the first Stimson had replied, the day *before* the Brethren's meeting with the mayor:

Dear Burly:
Your letter came this morning, and I deciphered its chorography just in time to show it and its enclosures to Marshall who in turn used it to prevent the President from giving the little Mayor the rank of Brigadier General which I think had been suggested by the "All Highest."
The "All Highest" took this whole action while I was away at Yeamans [a private club in South Carolina]. I think he knows I have been particularly careful to hold down civilian appointments and this was his easy way out. So you probably saved your country a little money and the Army some prestige by writing me. Eternal vigilance is the price of efficiency in this curious Administration, but it is very wearing on an elderly gentleman who has to exercise it.

I am very sorry to hear of your illness but delighted that you pulled through with such resilience.

When all is said and done, I like the Little Flower and think that he would not make a bad soldier if he was young enough and was not given too high rank. I think he has a hereditary sense of devotion to the Army which will tend to keep his mouth shut more when in uniform than when in politics.

Faithfully yours,[51]

Besides his letter, CCB had sent enclosures. What were they? Newspaper clippings? A letter from Dr. Baehr about La Guardia's health? Did CCB now attempt a Freudian analysis of La Guardia's recent behavior? In an immediate typed reply to Stimson's note he wrote:

You can't imagine what a grim satisfaction I got from your letter. The grave could not be more silent than I . . . While LaG insists that he would not accept anything but a military office, he really wants to shoot with his mouth and call all his enemies "bastardi" in all the languages he knows. He has acted so badly this past year that the foolish real estate men and taxpayers would really be glad to see him out of the mayoralty—fools and blind, they do not appreciate their blessings—nine years in office and not a financial scandal.[52]

Whatever CCB's first letter and its enclosures, they were enough to deny La Guardia the commission. On 6 April, President Roosevelt, in answer to a planted question at a press conference, said he had no plans to make Mayor La Guardia a brigadier general. The press corps was dumbfounded; for days they had been filing stories that an appointment was imminent.[53] The next day Stimson confirmed that the mayor had offered his services to the army but that no position could be offered to match the importance of his post as mayor of New York. For days the story with its "slightly baffling developments," as the *Herald Tribune* called the strange twist of events, made front-page headlines. For La Guardia, the disappointment was very great, the humiliation very public.[54]

A week later a letter appeared on La Guardia's desk addressed "To His Honor the Mayor of the Greatest City in the World: Some Thoughts on our Present Discontents." In considerable detail CCB discussed seven of the major problems the city faced: (a) the subway fare, (b) department store branches opening in the suburbs, (c) preparation for a special session of the state legislature, (d) the assessments for real estate taxes, (e) the bloated budget allocations to Moses for the parks and to the Board of Education, (f) how to deal with Ellsworth Buck, president of the Board of Education, "(z) and lastly" the problems of the wartime blackout at night and crime. His effort to refocus the mayor on the city was "Respectfully submitted."[55]

La Guardia wrote angry comments all over the letter and sent it back: "So What?"—"Look up your press clipping"—"I will call names when NY City is injured or doublecrossed"—"I am reconciled to getting credit in history and reward in Heaven." Yet at the letter's end, as if recognizing CCB's kindly purpose, he signed, "Lots of love, C.C.—I still like and love you. Fiorello!"[56]

Was Burlingham's role in the denial of La Guardia's army commission an act of friendship or betrayal? And if a bit of both, how does the balance tip? CCB himself saw ambiguity in it. After La Guardia's death, in recording his act for the Columbia Oral History project, he said: "I did him a disservice once; or rather, he thought it was a disservice, but I didn't. He wanted to give up the mayoralty . . . So I stepped in . . . I don't believe he suspected me, because he cursed out Frankfurter for it. I was quite disgusted with that . . . got hold of Fiorello, and I said, 'You're absolutely wrong' . . . But he never forgave Stimson, of course."[57]

On the side of betrayal, the act was done behind La Guardia's back; it hurt him deeply; and he was never told the truth of it. On the side of friendship, it was not a secret switch of policy but consistent with CCB's view of duty long urged on La Guardia by letter and in person. It played to La Guardia's strength, for he was truly a great mayor, irreplaceable, but with some qualities—temper, self-pity, depression, unwillingness to delegate authority—that forecast failure as a political general. Lastly, by the deed CCB gained nothing personal, but acted, at least in his view, for the good of La Guardia and the city. About CCB's love for New York, with its conjoined sense of duty owed the city, there is no doubt: citizens and officials alike were constantly impressed by it, and in his dealings with them it was a source of his influence.

Thereafter La Guardia, often to the despair of those "for good government," continued his third term much as he had begun it. He conducted a long, abusive fight with the Board of Education, interfering in much the way he had in the Bertrand Russell affair, and similarly earning reprimands from CCB.[58] But he was less interested now in what his friends had to say, and though he answered CCB's notes, his replies increasingly were politely dismissive. Their artery of communication was congealing, cooled less by the old man's age than by the younger man's decline in temperament.

Paradoxically, many New Yorkers now felt closer to their mayor than ever before. La Guardia often had turned to radio to explain the city's needs and his policies, and starting on 18 January 1942 he began regular Sunday broadcasts over the city's station, WNYC. He talked on anything, from politics to life, even advising people, when it was raining, to take an umbrella. During a newspaper strike, he read the comics aloud so that the city's children could keep abreast of Dick Tracy and other favorite characters. His talks were popular, the kind of theatrical gesture that showed him at his best, warm and caring. And in a time of war, when civil unrest was feared, they bound the city's diverse and sometimes hostile groups together. With La Guardia chronicling the city's daily life, like a Father Knickerbocker and often just as comic, it was easy to feel a member of the family. He helped to make New York a city to be proud of, to make it seem, as he once had promised, a bit like Heaven and Home. Privately, however, he continued to hope for a Washington or army position, and wrote letters of appeal to the president, whom he rightly felt was more sympathetic to him than Stimson.

In February 1944 the dissatisfaction of many of those "for good government" was expressed by the American Civil Liberties Union, then led by Roger Baldwin and the Reverend John Haynes Holmes. They published a Letter of Complaint signed by many reformers, which after listing a number of La Guardia's recent shortcomings, particularly having to do with police violence, ended with an appeal to the mayor that he "desist from arbitrary and lawless short-cuts which defy established rights. The temptation to do good, as you see it, by extra-legal means—natural doubtless to a man of your temperament—will we hope, be resisted in the interest of the larger democratic purposes which you have so long professed to serve."[59]

CCB, like a number of others close to the Mayor, had refused to sign the letter because, as he told Holmes, "the Mayor should not be wounded publicly, especially now when the war had laid such a heavy burden on him."[60] But he did not argue that the mayor had not earned the reprimand. La Guardia ignored the letter, confirming for many that the breach between him and most of the city's reform groups was now unbridgeable.

Early in 1945, when the question of a fourth term for La Guardia began to cloud the political horizon, it soon became clear that the Republican Party would not give him its nomination and that what remained of the Fusion Party was equally disinclined to endorse him. The double re-

jection left him only the possibility of the American Labor Party, which
was split between a Communist wing, led by his former protégé Vito Marcantonio, and a liberal wing, led by officers of the garment workers' union.
No group by itself could elect him, and no fusion among them seemed
likely. In matters of patronage he always had treated the Republicans badly,
and more recently, also the Fusionists. In place of both he had tried to
substitute the liberal wing of the American Labor Party, but even the
latter might not support him, for with his intemperate statements he had
offended its leaders. Paul Windels thought that this effort to substitute
the American Labor for the Fusion Party

> was a mistake because they were organized on a class-interest basis.
> That was not the kind of vote or organization or platform on which he
> should have stood for the perpetuation of good government in this city.
> Good government wasn't based on that kind of issue. That is precisely
> the point where he finally failed politically . . . The whole effort got too
> personal—based entirely on La Guardia's name, prestige and record.[61]

In this way, La Guardia became his own victim. CCB, attempting to
rescue the mayor from himself, considered the possibility of a fourth term:
"What you need [if you decide to run] is an issue . . . There is one issue on
which you can win beyond doubt—the Subways." La Guardia wrote a
contentious reply, and they exchanged several more letters on the subways. But to no purpose.[62]

By now even the mayor saw that the considerable support he still had
was not enough. And his position worsened on 12 April 1945, when Roosevelt, who might have helped him, died. Only a few weeks later, in his
May 6th Sunday broadcast, La Guardia announced in a frequently self-
pitying, self-righteous speech, "I am not going to run for Mayor this year."[63]
The almost certain winner of the race then became the nominee of the
regular Democratic organization, Tammany's William O'Dwyer. As spring
turned to summer, twelve years of reform government in New York, of the
best municipal administration in American history, drew to a close.

Meanwhile, as the war in Europe came to an end with Germany's un-
conditional surrender on 7 May, there were many great occasions in the
city, and none greater than the reception at City Hall on 19 June to greet
General Dwight D. Eisenhower (supreme commander of the Allied forces
in Europe), which was followed by a motorized cavalcade through the five
boroughs with La Guardia at his side.

The victorious general came to New York after addressing Congress and a similar popular celebration in Washington. At City Hall, before a huge crowd standing and sitting in the streets and park, he was welcomed by La Guardia, made a short speech, and was cheered by the crowd. The General Electric Company, with a noise meter on hand, reported the decibels were equal to "3,000 peals of thunder at the same time."[64] CCB, always one for an historic occasion, especially one in New York and at City Hall, was on hand, in a seat presumably given him by the mayor. The following week he described the occasion for the Hirsts in England:

Before I finish dictating this letter let me tell you my amusing experience at the Eisenhower celebration. I went to the City Hall and had a good seat and a fine view of the General. His speech was admirable . . . The Police Commissioner told me he thought there were about forty thousand people seated in City Hall Park, and as I drove down with a public official two hours before the cavalcade, the sidewalks along the whole route from the 70s to City Hall were crowded with people three deep—later six and eight deep. When I tried to get out of the City Hall I was pushed and shoved as in the subway and finally found myself on the steps at the rear, on the north side of the building, when suddenly La Guardia and the General emerged. La Guardia introduced me to the General, whose firm hand-clasp and charming smile quite thrilled me. One of our stenographers discovered in one of the evening papers a picture of this very scene, and I sent to the newspaper to get a print, and if I can, I will send you one for your amusement. Telling a friend of my happy fortune I recalled that eighty years ago at the Astor House I presented a bouquet to General Grant![65]

23

The Theory and Practice of

Judicial Appointments

IN THEORY, under the federal constitution (and most state constitutions), the government's judicial arm is equal in strength and importance to the legislative and executive. In practice, it is the weakest of the three—in part because Article III of the Constitution, the judiciary article, which establishes the Supreme Court, is notably inexplicit: it leaves to Congress the creation and jurisdiction of lower federal courts, and subjects the Supreme Court's appellate jurisdiction to "such Exceptions, and under such Regulations as the Congress shall make." It does not set down, as Roosevelt made clear, the number of judges for the Supreme Court, and it does not prescribe—what many consider the Court's greatest power and distinction—a right to review the constitutional validity of federal or state legislation.

Moreover, selection of judges for the Court is covered not in the judiciary article but in Article II, section 2, concerning executive powers: the president, "by and with the Advice and Consent of the Senate, shall appoint . . . Judges of the supreme Court." But their tenure is set by Article III, "The Judges, both of the supreme and inferior Courts, shall hold their Offices during good Behaviour." Thus, in the federal system—for Congress in creating lower courts followed the pattern set for the Supreme Court—the judges always have been chosen by the leader of the currently most powerful political party, i.e., the president, with confirmation needed by the Senate. All those involved in the appointment are active politicians, and among them only rarely is one found who views the judiciary as an equal partner in government. For the great majority of politicians, the court systems (federal, state, and city) are primarily bins of patronage where are stored rewards for those who support the party. What the legal profession—judges, lawyers, bench, or bar associations—may think of the judicial nominations counts for little.

Burlingham, like many who watched the courts, ranked Roosevelt low on the quality of his appointments: "He certainly never knew or at least never acted as if it made any difference what sort of a man was put on the bench so long as his views were satisfactory."[1] Despite the fact that Roosevelt was himself a lawyer and even had practiced briefly in New York,[2] his lack of concern for the judiciary as an equal arm of tripartite government continually hindered CCB and others in their efforts to improve the quality of appointments. In the mid-1930s CCB and Roosevelt had a correspondence on the subject, on both sides pleasant but provoking.

Early in February 1936, "more in sorrow than in anger," CCB wrote to Roosevelt—"Dear Governor"—to protest the rumored choices for new judges on the Southern and Eastern District Courts in New York. After reviewing with disapproval the men as individuals, he stated some general principles:

> I am one of those who think that political experience is a valuable asset for a judge, but it is not the principal asset. Character comes first, ability second, learning third. Our judges in the District Court are not Marshalls or Mansfields, but they are men of high character and keep their offices clear of politics.
>
> If you are really interested in getting the best judges on the Federal bench, we [the City Bar Association, which had "disapproved" several of the men] can help you, and we are keen to do so; but if the chief considerations are political, you might as well count us out.
>
> If you knew how I *felt*, you would regard this letter as a fine example of moderation and understatement.[3]

The president replied to "Dear C.C.":

> You are right—and you are wrong! I know how you feel, and I go along with you a long part of the way. On the other hand, for years—four years at Albany and then before that—I got rather fed up with the consistent and unimaginative type of Bar Association suggestions. They never, under any circumstances, suggested a "man of the people." Always someone from a big law firm, all of which did and do the same type of legal business . . . Dig me up fifteen or twenty youthful Abraham Lincolns from Manhattan and the Bronx to choose from. They must be liberal

from belief and not by lip service. They must have an inherent contempt both for the John W. Davises and the Max Steuers. They must know what life in a tenement means. They must have no social ambition.[4]

Roosevelt's criteria are rhetorically fine but essentially meaningless. Men like Abraham Lincoln are not found "fifteen or twenty" at a time. And if to be a "man of the people" is important for a judge, that standard surely also should apply to the office of president. Yet Roosevelt himself, a patrician graduated from Harvard and Columbia, with an estate on the Hudson and married to Theodore Roosevelt's niece, was proof that, in CCB's words, an "open mind and sympathetic heart" could surmount differences of class and origin. As for Roosevelt's scorn for Davis and Steuer, at least as regards Steuer CCB swiftly pierced the president's screen of half-truth. He wrote:

> But let me tell you something funny now. Maxie has come out for the Child Labor Amendment; so I wrote thanking him, which led to correspondence, and Tuesday I had him at the Down Town Club for lunch and showed him off with pride to my conservative and respectable friends. After talking Child Labor for a bit, we got round to politics, and he told me of his call on you. He could not imagine why you should speak to such a humble private citizen as if he had influence with Tammany Hall! . . . What made it so funny was that I had in my pocket your letter, and there it reposed.[5]

So in the very week that Roosevelt wrote to CCB expressing contempt for Steuer, he had consulted him in the White House about Tammany's wishes! Further, FDR had bent the truth about the bar association: as CCB reminded him, "Please don't forget that when you were Governor, the Bar Association did not suggest names. All they did was to pass on the names [whether or not qualified] you sent them."

This riposte led to a further exchange, mainly on how the bar association should act. "I bother you with a reply," CCB wrote to "Dear Franklin," "only because I feel so strongly that there is little that you do as important as the selection of judges."

> For the asking you could get from the Bar Association Committees all the facts as to the ability, experience and character of any lawyer whose name is before you; and they would *suggest* names if you *requested*, which I have never known you to do as Governor or as President. They hesi-

tate, properly so, to volunteer names unasked . . . You seem to divide lawyers into those connected with the big firms and the people's friends. To my mind it is not so simple as that. The big law offices are full of young men who have no part or lot with Liberty Leaguers or Max Steuers. Many of the best young lawyers in the Departments in Washington came out of those offices. But no matter—avoid the big firms if you will; the important thing is to leave no stone unturned until you find the best men available.[6]

But when Roosevelt made his appointments to the Southern and Eastern District Courts, CCB felt he had made little effort to consult anyone other than the leaders of Manhattan and Brooklyn Democratic clubs. One man named for the Eastern District was Matthew T. Abruzzo, a business colleague of Judge Manton's who had been strongly recommended by the Brooklyn leaders and presumably also by Steuer. Following the appointment CCB wrote to Roosevelt in June 1936:

I should be lacking in friendliness, if I failed to express frankly my deep regret at your recent judicial appointments . . . I have recently read an opinion of Abruzzo's, a model of ignorance and illiteracy . . . *I am not taking a walk* [in the upcoming presidential election]; but I have a Hell of a time to defend your judicial appointments. In my opinion the only defense is political necessity. You may need New York and the support of the County Organizations of the City. It is a pity that you have to pay so high a price, giving life appointments to inferior men.[7]

To Frankfurter, he wrote, "The most degraded specimen is Abruzzo in the E.D." Two weeks later he erupted again, "You should see an admiralty opinion of Abruzzo's—illiterate and too ignorant to copy a brief! . . . F.D. has certainly discredited the appointive system. One of the most sickening things is to hear it said that F.D. as a New York lawyer knows the N.Y. bar."[8]

In the Southern District Court as well, some of Roosevelt's appointments seemed exceptionally bad. In that same year, 1936, he put on the bench Samuel Mandelbaum, a Polish immigrant who had, indeed, grown up in the tenements of the Lower East Side, worked his way through law school, and made an honorable career out of representing the people of the tenements, chiefly in the city's lower courts. As a loyal member of his Manhattan Democratic district club, he had become an assemblyman, then a state senator, had worked in Albany with both Franklin and Eleanor Roosevelt, and gradually become a leader in the Tammany hierarchy. According to the lawyer Milton Gould, who has reported all the good that can be said of Mandelbaum as a judge, he was modest, charming, tenderhearted, well intentioned, and knowledgeable in certain areas of New York life. Yet at the time of his appointment Mandelbaum had never tried a case in federal court and, in Gould's opinion, "was 'unqualified' by any standards." When the judge died after ten years on the bench, "there were no tributes to his scholarship, but many references to his heart." But Mandelbaum's virtues could not make of him the judge he was not. On the bench, in CCB's opinion, he was "a travesty," and brought the court into disrepute.[9]

Roosevelt, explaining his choice to CCB, wrote: "Well, in regard to Mandelbaum you can put it down to personal prejudice in his favor by me, I having seen him and worked with him for four years during my term as Governor." Gould, however, adds a gloss, reporting the setting and manner in which the appointment was made: at the White House, Roosevelt is with Mandelbaum, and the latter, told of his appointment, is modest and unsure of the president's wisdom; Roosevelt, calling in some staff to make an audience, revels in Mandelbaum's lack of qualification, seemingly eager by the appointment to mock all those—editorial writers, CCB, the city and county lawyers' associations—who had proclaimed him unqualified.[10]

In May 1942, when Roosevelt nominated Thomas F. Meaney to the district court in New Jersey, he aroused even more opposition than he had with Abruzzo or Mandelbaum because his choice seemed more sinister. Meaney was a protégé of Mayor Frank Hague of Jersey City, a Democratic boss in the style of Croker or Curran. A *Times* editorial described him as standing "for nearly everything, including the suppression of civil liberties, against which the New Deal is supposed to be fighting."[11] In a letter to the *Times*, CCB explained for laymen the background of the appointment:

> The record seems to be plain. A judge of the [New Jersey] Court of Errors and Appeals was induced [in 1940] to resign to make way for Hague's son; then Meaney was induced to resign as [New Jersey] Common Pleas judge of Hudson County to make way for that judge; and then Meaney was rewarded by being appointed counsel in a bankruptcy case from which he has recently been removed on the ground that his fees and expenses were excessive and that he did not do the work for which he was paid.[12]

Yet Roosevelt sent Meaney's name to the Senate even as Governor Charles Edison of New Jersey appealed publicly to the Senate Judiciary

Committee to deny confirmation. The *Washington Post* commented: "The President has allied himself with the evil forces in New Jersey which Governor Edison is seeking to overthrow . . . He [Hague] is the prime exhibit of what Bryce called the blot on our democracy, namely, our city machines."[13] Other papers had similar editorials. In a letter in the *Times*, CCB urged rejection of Meaney, who had "lent himself to one of the most shameful and high-handed pieces of nepotism by resigning his judicial office at the behest of Hague and thus proved himself unfit for the Federal or any bench."[14]

As seldom happened, CCB was challenged by another letter writer, Francis Hackett, to prove either that Meaney "has lent himself to shameful nepotism" or to withdraw the charge "with apology."[15] CCB replied, "I relied on the statements in the Governor's letter to the Senate Judiciary Committee and on the fact that no one disputed their accuracy . . . I suggest that Mr. Hackett disclose the 'very different version of Mr. Meaney's resignation,' which he says he 'heard many months ago.'"[16] Hackett did not respond.

The editor of the *Times*, before sending CCB's rebuttal of Hackett to the printer, phoned to say that he had forgotten to sign the letter and to warn that it might be libelous. "Print it," said CCB, "I will stop in and sign it in my own blood in the a.m."[17] In addition, CCB wrote directly to Attorney General Francis Biddle, who replied soothingly, "Meaney seemed to us a much better man than C. Jones." CCB wired back: THANKS. WHETHER M. OUTRANKS J. SEEMS IRRELEVANT TO THE ISSUE, WHICH IS H.[18] Protest proved vain. The president and a Democratic senator from New Jersey facing reelection wanted the appointment, and the Senate confirmed it. On 16 July, Meaney was sworn in, ending what the *Times* called "a nation-wide controversy" over the naming of a henchman of Hague.[19] From a Chicago lawyer CCB had a letter of condolence: "I am sorry that your sabre wasn't as effective as it should have been in the Meaney case. Still there are many such cases out here—possibly not quite so bad. The appointing power does not seem to give a hang about who goes on the Federal bench."[20]

Regardless of political party, many who worked to improve the federal judiciary would have agreed. Biddle ruminated on the problem in his autobiography:

I had to learn by experience when and how far to oppose the President when he wanted to make a bad political appointment. There were times when one could insist on a better man: and he liked to have the satisfaction of supporting one, not so much, I think, because he was concerned with putting men of professional competence on the bench, but rather that, surrounded by the plaudits of the hungry office seekers who favored and flattered, and lay on the threshold of his door, he responded happily to the applause of those of his friends who really counted—Felix Frankfurter and Charles C. Burlingham and George W. Norris—men who were devoted to the necessity of the best, not only from the professional angle, but from the deeper consideration of a humane and broadly liberal approach to life, of which the law was so important an expression.[21]

A danger in playing gadfly to the powerful is that one may grow tiresome, always buzzing, buzzing in disapproval. With Roosevelt, CCB by wit, charm, and perhaps by keeping a certain distance (not "lying on the threshold") managed to survive without being shut out or sacrificing his integrity. Possibly his outspoken support of the president's foreign policy and his willingness in areas of agreement to aid at any time, in any way he could, without seeking any reward, helped to insulate him from a break with his mighty friend. When, on 12 April 1945, Roosevelt died suddenly of a cerebral hemorrhage, their long relationship ended still strong and friendly. With La Guardia, events unfolded differently.

Though by 1945, the last year of La Guardia's third term, CCB could see that his influence with La Guardia was waning, he could see also that the mayor needed fearless, friendly advice more than ever. So, despite increasing rejection, CCB continued with his notes, letters, and limousine conferences. There was the question of the mayor's fourth term. Would he run in November? In May he announced he would not, and immediately a scramble for support began among possible successors.

Two Fusion stalwarts, hoping to combine Republican and Fusion elements, were eager for the nomination: Newbold Morris, the City Council president, and Joseph McGoldrick, the city comptroller. Of the two, McGoldrick was the stronger personality, the more competent, and therefore the better candidate, but for just those reasons he was less appealing to La Guardia. CCB wrote to the mayor in June:

You don't answer my letters, so I'll write you another one. I respectfully suggest that you keep your hands off the nominations. It is not for you to decide between Morris and McGoldrick. I suppose it is too much to ask you to tell the Republicans and the Fusionists—if there are any— that you will deal out even-handed justice to both these honorable men without discrimination ... I think you have a great influence with Labor, and I hope you will use it to persuade the rank and file of Labor to support the anti-Democratic [anti-Tammany] ticket, whatever it is.[22]

La Guardia scrawled on the bottom: "I will support only an honorable man. If [Tammany] control is the issue—nothing will suit me better." But he dithered, playing politics, while Tammany nominated William O'Dwyer. The Republicans, seeking Fusion and Jewish votes (and with the approval of Republican governor Dewey), also nominated a Tammany Democrat, General Sessions judge Jonah J. Goldstein.

With the Fusion votes in mind, Goldstein phoned CCB and suggested a chat. CCB replied by letter:

> I am taking no part in the mayoralty campaign. So you must not waste your time on me. As we are old friends, it is only fair that I should speak frankly to you. I am disappointed that both candidates are Organization Democrats, neither of whom, so far as I have observed, has ever shown any sympathy with non-partisanship in municipal affairs . . . I shall watch this campaign as the old men watched the Trojan War from the city wall . . . and hope that the best man will win."[23]

La Guardia, however, meddled. In early August he decided to back Morris, who had left the Republican Party when it nominated the Democrat Goldstein, and together Morris and La Guardia formed a new group, the No Deal Party.[24] By doing so, they fragmented still further the Republican and Fusion vote, ensuring a three-way race that Tammany would win. In November the vote put a decisive end to twelve years of reform government. The tally was O'Dwyer, 1,125,357; Goldstein, 431,601; and Morris, 408,348, with O'Dwyer's plurality of 700,000 the largest till then in the city's history. If La Guardia had been willing—as was Dewey—to back Goldstein wholeheartedly, if he had persuaded Morris not to run, and if he had tried to energize the Fusion and Republican ranks, then just possibly the slightly less Tammany-dominated ticket, led by Goldstein, might have won. At least reform government would have had a chance to win some of the more important municipal offices. Instead, Tammany all but swept the board, electing in addition to the mayor the city comptroller, the president of the City Council, and four borough presidents (all except Staten Island). Many people, regardless of party, felt that La Guardia, in his exit from office, had played "the spoiler" out of petulance and frustration in his failure to advance to president or brigadier general.[25]

CCB, though disappointed in the mayor's performance, wrote him friendly squibs, and in one to the *Herald Tribune* rejoiced in La Guardia's sixty-third birthday, 11 December 1945. Noting that "by old Spanish custom" a Spanish official, to mark the sixty-third birthday, resigned all offices and retired "to some place of Devotion," whereas an Englishman by custom "loves not to pull off his Clothes 'til he goes to bed," he concluded: "Despite his Latin origin it seems probable that Hizonner will follow the English rather than this 'old Spanish custom.'"[26]

La Guardia, however, though no one yet knew it, had pancreatic cancer and only twenty months to live. He sorely needed a rest, but instead of taking a vacation he contracted to write an autobiography, to deliver two weekly radio programs (one on national, one on municipal topics), and to provide a periodic column for the afternoon daily paper, *P.M.* To stay abreast of his deadlines, he hired an office at Rockefeller Center and six assistants. His column and broadcasts were popular, in part because of his belligerent style, which often swerved close to libel. In this vein, on 10 February, over the air, he castigated the bar association for its feeble efforts to improve the city's judiciary. Many lawyers, startled by his harsh language, saw this as a personal assault on the man who more than any other in this pursuit personified the Association—CCB.

> Now here is something . . . I note that the Bar Association is protesting the appointment of two district leaders as secretaries to two newly elected judges. Now what hypocrisy, what sham, what pretense! So the Bar Association . . . is waking up now . . . Say, Bar Association, why didn't you protest the selection of these two judges by these same two district leaders? You didn't peep then, did you? No, the Bar Association never peeps. It will send out a release once in a while, but did you, who are listening to me—did I—did anybody else have anything to say in the selection of these judges or any other judges? These same district leaders handpicked these judges, and the Bar Association knows it, and doesn't dare peep about it . . . Do you remember some years ago when there was some scandal about the selection of some judge, and the Bar Association was going to do something about changing the method? Did they do anything? They did not . . . So don't expect any help from the Bar Association of the City of New York. The people of this State should do something about changing the system of selection of judges and the removal of judges when found to be incompetent or dishonest.[27]

La Guardia often had attacked the condition of the courts, most notably in April 1938, in a speech at the bar association. But his speech then had been a detailed two-hour examination of a difficult, complicated problem, with charts and figures to show how ridiculously expensive were the state and city judicial systems. (The city courts, with overpaid judges, clerks, and secretaries, cost more than the entire federal system, including the Supreme Court.) Whereas the radio speech, in its heat, sarcasm, and misstatements, struck many who heard or read it as another sad example of how much, in twelve years as mayor, La Guardia had diminished in character, been damaged by power.[28]

The Association's president, Harrison Tweed, consulted CCB on how to respond, and CCB wrote La Guardia a private letter chronicling some of the Association's recent efforts and suggesting that the ex-mayor might, in his next broadcast, correct his misstatements. La Guardia replied:

> It was nice to get your letter, even though I do not agree with you . . . Sincerely, I do not believe that the Bar Association of the City of New York, which might have a tremendous influence for good, has used its influence, its effort, its time, its mind or its heart in purifying and cleansing our courts. It has made a gesture, a slight motion now and then and let it go at that. That permits reference to feeble efforts never followed through.[29]

La Guardia in his broadcasts offered no corrections, and Tweed then wrote to him defending the Association and mentioning CCB indirectly: "When a good friend of yours wrote giving you the facts and an opportunity to correct your misstatements, you refused." Point by point he refuted La Guardia's statements. For example:

> One of the things that you *have not done* in connection with the New York courts has been to consult with the Bar Association during your mayoralty in connection with the appointment of judges. This you refused to do. One result was the appointment by you of a man who it turned out was entirely unfit. The scandal was sufficient to impel you to the statement "when I make a mistake, it is a beaut."[30] This is the only reported instance when you have admitted a lack of omniscience, but it is not the only instance of a "beaut" of a mistake . . .
>
> Another of the things that you *have not done* was to oppose the Democratic and American Labor Party candidate for a Supreme Court judgeship last Fall, Samuel Dickstein, whose lack of qualification was well known to everybody and was conspicuously pointed out in the press as a result of Bar Association action.
>
> Two more things that you *have not done* . . .[31]

And the list went on, focusing chiefly on "the hand-picking of judges by the district leaders which is what you particularly object to." Tweed's final sentence, however, alluded to a difficulty that hobbled the Association's response to the attack: "Since I have no radio sponsor I am sending a copy of this letter to the New York Times." But the *Times* declined to publish it, whole or in part, making of it merely a four-paragraph news item on page 27, "La Guardia Assailed by Head of City Bar."[32] Selection of judges apparently was not an important issue, not "news." Only when the Association could ally itself to a major scandal or politician could it project its views and actions into headlines.

CCB's response to the episode was characteristic. He brushed aside as unimportant whatever may have been personal in La Guardia's speech. He wanted Tweed to meet with La Guardia, presumably in CCB's apartment, and work out ideas together that might advance the cause for better judges. Tweed refused. "I didn't want to get into that." La Guardia, in his present discontent, was too unstable.[33]

Still, La Guardia's attack and Tweed's defense, published in the bar association's *Record*, helped to fix in the collective mind of the city's bench and bar the already well-formed idea that no lawyer in the first half of the twentieth century had fought more frequently than CCB to improve the judiciary. Just as Seabury, even today, comes to mind in connection with the exposure of Tammany and Mayor Walker's corruption, so does Burlingham in connection with attempts to improve the quality of judges in all courts.

In an exchange of letters on the subject with Roosevelt in June 1937, CCB received a short one that closed with a question in which the president clearly delighted: "Finally, ask yourself what Christ would say about the American Bench and Bar were he to return today?"[34] In replying to this mischievous request, CCB expressed his principles in broader, more general terms than usual, buttressing them with a parade of learned references.

> 1. I confess that I cannot understand why you are so hard on the lawyers. True, only a remnant seek to improve the law; but are the physicians any better? Witness their attitude toward health insurance and public medicine, and it was the same in England 30 years ago. Do bankers reform themselves? Witness their fight against S.E.C. Is it not the prophets and saints—the Wilberforces, the John Howards, the Elizabeth Frys and the never say die-ers, like Rowland Hill and Samuel Plimsoll—who brought things to pass?[35]

2. The reforms in English procedure in 1873–5 were the work of few men, not all lawyers by any means. The Royal Commissions have done wonderful work over there. Every so often an enlightened Law Chancellor or law officer or judge works some reform . . .

3. You ask me what Christ would say about the American Bench and Bar were he to return today. That is not a hard question to answer. After he had castigated the Pharisees, you remember that a lawyer said to him: "Master, in saying this thou reproachest us also." And Jesus said: "Woe unto you lawyers also, for ye lade men with burdens grievous to be borne, and ye yourselves touch not the burdens with one of your fingers." And again: "Ye took away the key of knowledge: ye entered not in yourselves and them that were entering in ye hindered." But let us never forget that it was the questioning of our Lord by a lawyer that brought from him the parable of the Good Samaritan.[36]

Yes, I think He would have had something to say about our judges, for He would surely have known that it was not reformed procedure and new laws that we needed so much as better judges. A Mansfield, a Jessel, a Hough, a Holmes, a Cardozo, a Hand needs no new system of law or procedure.[37]

But this all too long letter should "to the barber's" with Polonius's beard.[38]

CCB in his answer—"He would surely have known that it was not reformed procedure and new laws that we needed so much as better judges"—turned the president's question back on him. What would Christ say about Roosevelt's choices for the federal bench? The president was magnificent in selecting his deputies to conduct the war; regardless of party, he would have none but the best—Stimson, Knox, Marshall, King, and Eisenhower. But when it came to the government's judicial arm, politics at its tawdriest often ruled; more often than not he preferred the bad to the better and even, at times, appointed the worst. He had no sense of law as an institution, a source and triumph of civilization. Yet he was president, so CCB kept trying.

In the 1930s a layman might have had a hard time defining the source of CCB's reputation, in part because he had been important in so many areas—the Welfare Council, civil service reform, St. George's Church, Fusion politics, City Hall, the bar association. Most people might have said simply that he was an old man who wrote letters to newspapers on public issues and whose ideas usually seemed sensible. The *Herald Tribune*, in an editorial honoring him as New York's First Citizen on his eighty-fifth birthday

(1943), mentioned many of his projects but put first in importance "the Fusion movement." For lawyers his reputation lay more in his work to improve the judiciary. His place was somewhere behind, but in sight of those other "prophets and saints" who had sought to improve the dispensation of justice. He was not a political philosopher like Bryce or Tocqueville, but he believed passionately that the government's judicial arm should be as strong as the other two. When it wasn't, corruption followed.

Everyone agreed in admiring the spirit and skills he had brought to his work, and perhaps, too, the humor in which he clothed his moral tone. As the *Herald Tribune* said,

> He has exhibited remarkable qualities—diplomacy and immovable firmness, humor and the spirit of the quiet crusader. A little at a time, with infinite patience, he has helped to bring New York along the right path, and is undisturbed by the thought that Utopia still lies beyond the horizon. His best employment has been as learned counsel to our better selves.[39]

In New York CCB could deploy his qualities and political skill in person, willing to talk with anyone, and able to enhance his call "to our better selves" with personal charm. In attempting to influence Roosevelt in Washington, however, he was at a disadvantage. After his sudden deafness in the summer of 1938, following his son's suicide, his heart attack, and his eightieth birthday, he no longer went to Washington, and except for a rare phone call from the president, he had to ply his wiles entirely through other people or by his letters. Yet these years were the most important in the saga of appointments to the federal bench, for in Roosevelt's last eight years in office he had the chance to appoint nine judges to the Supreme Court, more than any other president except George Washington.[40]

As might be expected, the "Roosevelt Court" survived its creator by many years, in part because, breaking with the then current tradition, he put on it younger men. Hugo Black, his first appointee, lived to serve thirty-four years, 1937–71; his second, Stanley Reed, nineteen, 1938–57; his third, Frankfurter, twenty-three, 1939–62; and his fourth, William O. Douglas, with the longest service of any justice on the Court, thirty-six, 1939–75.[41] Nine years after Roosevelt's death, when the school integration case of *Brown v. Board of Education* (1954) was decided (9 to 0), perhaps the century's most important case, five of the justices were Roosevelt appointees.

Starting with the first appointment, of Hugo Black in 1937, many people worried that Roosevelt, despite the rebuke he had received on his Court-packing plan, still cared too little about preserving the Court's standing with the public. He named Senator Black, of Alabama, aged only fifty-one, because Black was an outspoken supporter of New Deal legislation (including the defeated Court plan) and seemed sure to continue his support on the Court. And also, as a senator, Black was assured of Senate confirmation. Some lawyers were distressed by Black's lack of judicial experience: only eighteen months in the far past as a police court judge in Birmingham. Others worried that his harsh, self-assured, and combative style as a lawyer and senator was suited more to a prosecutor than to a judge. And still more were affronted by his rumored membership in the Ku Klux Klan.

This secret organization, founded after the Civil War to maintain white supremacy throughout the South, was infamous for terrorizing and lynching Negroes. After World War I, the Klan spread to the North, adding to white supremacy strains of anti-Semitism and anti-Catholicism. Roosevelt had not discussed his choice of Black with any bar group, congressional leader, or his cabinet, and had sent the nomination to the Senate outside of regular channels. According to Postmaster General James Farley, whom FDR usually consulted about appointments (though not this one), Roosevelt intended it to be a "surprise."[42]

As was their custom, the senators did not call Black to testify before their Judiciary Committee, which recommended confirmation, nor did they question him when debate began on 17 August in the full Senate. When one senator asked about Black's connection to the Klan, another, William E. Borah of Utah, while acknowledging the country's interest in the issue, dismissed it out of hand: "There has never been at any time one iota of evidence that Senator Black was a member of the Klan." Thus assured, the Senate voted to confirm, 63 to 16.[43]

Four weeks later, after Black had taken his seat on the Court, the *Pittsburgh Post-Gazette* started a series of six articles that established the truth of what had been rumored: Black in 1923 had indeed joined the Klan, which three years later had helped him to defeat Alabama's anti-Klan senator Oscar W. Underwood. The facts, spread across the country in newspaper headlines, caused a national revulsion, and many people, not only Catholic and Negro leaders, called for Black to resign (Klan membership was not an impeachable offense). Black, in Paris, refused to talk to reporters, and later, in London, barricaded himself in his hotel and refused all calls. Roosevelt, in Washington, denied any knowledge of Black's Klan connection (though he apparently had known of it) but, alarmed by the intensity of the disapproval, told reporters that nothing could be said until Black's return and then left on a Western tour.[44]

Meanwhile, Black, though booked for New York on the liner *Manhattan*, before its departure snuck out the back door of his London hotel, drove to Southampton, and boarded the Baltimore Mail Line's small 8,400-ton *City of Norfolk*, which landed in Baltimore on 30 September. The next day he made an eleven-minute radio speech, heard by perhaps fifty million people and read by millions more in the country's newspapers. He confessed he had joined the Klan, insisted that he had resigned soon after, claimed to have many friends who were Jews, Catholics, and Negroes, praised his own congressional record on civil rights legislation, and warned those who were questioning his fitness not to fan the flames of prejudice. He did not condemn the Klan or its activities, or explain why he had remained silent about his membership throughout the Senate hearings and debate. As Farley observed, "For an Associate Justice to broadcast on any controversial subject was unusual enough, but for a Justice to defend himself, as Black did, was sensational."[45]

Many people, disgusted by the sight of a former Klansman on the Court, blamed Black less than Roosevelt. CCB wrote to Senator Borah:

> My view of the matter was that at his first interview with the President, Senator Black should have said to him, "Mr. President, you know, I was a member of the Klan." Also . . . when Black's name was before the Senate, he should either have made a statement of the facts on the floor, or should have offered to go before the Judiciary Committee and state the facts and answer any questions that might be asked.[46]

In a postscript CCB concluded: "I need hardly tell you how deeply I feel the humiliation to the Country and Court that any man should be appointed as Justice who is guilty of *suppressio veri*."

Besides Black's shameful behavior in Paris and London, he brought to the Court a new, demeaning morality—deceive by silence, confess the fraud, but keep the prize. Yet behind Black was Roosevelt, who, with his cavalier attitude toward the judiciary, had made himself peculiarly responsible for the nomination. Many lawyers and newspapers saw in it a deliberate slap at the Supreme Court. And adding to their distress, Black in his first year as associate justice, when he might have been expected to tread lightly and avoid the spotlight, wrote nine lone dissents to majority opinions. He seemed eager to spike the Court's harmony and its ability to speak with a clear, unambiguous voice.[47]

Roosevelt's second appointment, of Stanley F. Reed in 1938, was far less controversial. Though never having served as a judge, Reed had a career in government and law that seemed fit to end in a position on the Court. A lifelong Democrat, after nineteen years of private practice he had been appointed by Republican President Hoover as counsel to the Federal Farm Board and then to the Reconstruction Finance Corporation. Roosevelt had retained him at the latter, and in 1935 had named him a special assistant to the attorney general, and later that year solicitor general. The last was a position that by statute required the holder to be "learned in the law," and because he so often appeared before the Court he had an office in the Court's building. Reed, soft-spoken, competent, mild in manner, seemed suited to the Court, and his appointment, after Black, came as a relief.

Then, in January 1939, Roosevelt nominated Frankfurter to succeed to Cardozo's seat. CCB, on news of it, wired the nominee: "The spirits of Holmes and Cardozo rejoice with us, Love, CCB." To the president he wrote: "I shall be very happy to see Felix on the Supreme Court, and it is a joy to have the appointment so universally praised." But even while delighting in Frankfurter he could not forgo a regret: "Counsels of perfection after the event are futile, I know, but I had hoped that if you disregarded geography, you would have put Learned Hand on the S.C. and let Felix succeed Isaiah [a common epithet for Brandeis, who was expected soon to resign]."[48]

Though the Senate had a tradition that a nominee for the Supreme Court need not appear in person before its Judiciary Committee, he often was represented by a lawyer, and Dean Acheson, a friend and former undersecretary of the Treasury, appeared for Frankfurter. For the third day of the hearings, however, the committee, perhaps chastened by its failure to have questioned Black directly, asked for Frankfurter to appear in person. Acheson agreed, but on three conditions: that the committee formally request Frankfurter's appearance; that he not be asked how he would rule on cases coming to the Court; and—neatly dodging a contentious subject—that he not be questioned about Roosevelt's Court-packing plan because "he had meticulously refrained from expressing any views."[49]

Frankfurter, in answering questions, charmed most of the senators, won rounds of applause from an audience full of admirers, and was extolled in newspaper editorials around the country. And on 30 January he took his seat on the Court. Acheson's third condition, however, confirmed for some that Frankfurter, like Black, had won his seat by keeping silent when he should have spoken up. Some portion of the country's lawyers felt that he, like Black, demeaned the Court, but most thought that in his unmatched learning he was a worthy addition. One of his biographers summarized the general feeling: "With Frankfurter's knowledge of the

Court and the Constitution, his strong analytic powers, his energy and political savvy, he was expected, and he expected himself, to dominate the 'Roosevelt Court.'"[50]

Two weeks later, on 13 February, Brandeis resigned, and to replace him Roosevelt appointed William O. Douglas, a former professor at Columbia and Yale Law Schools and presently chairman of the Securities and Exchange Commission. Douglas, a lanky "outdoors" man, had grown up in Yakima, Washington (later falsely claiming to have triumphed as a boy over polio in his legs),[51] worked his way through college, and then taught for two years in Yakima High School before going East to enter Columbia Law School. Only forty-one, and the second youngest appointee in the Court's history, he was a startling choice.[52] Unlike Cardozo or Holmes, he had no judicial experience, and compared to Brandeis, Reed, or even Frankfurter, very little as a practicing lawyer—and he had never argued a case before the Supreme Court. His chief qualification, many lawyers felt, was an assiduous polishing of his friendship with Roosevelt, in whose poker games he was a regular player. Though CCB seems not to have written Roosevelt about Douglas, on other occasions he had stated strongly that the best judges for appeals courts were those with considerable experience as trial judges or at least as courtroom lawyers. Douglas, however allegedly brilliant as a professor and chairman of the SEC, seemed less qualified than many federal judges or more experienced lawyers.

Eight months later, in November 1939, Justice Pierce Butler died, giving Roosevelt his fifth appointment within two and a half years. Butler had distinguished himself by voting to hold invalid most New Deal legislation to come before the Court, and his replacement seemed to ensure an easy "Roosevelt majority" for any important decision. CCB, on hearing rumors that FDR was thinking of naming Attorney General Frank Murphy to succeed Butler, promptly wrote to Roosevelt in a light vein to suggest that, with the politics of the Court now in hand, the time had come for Roosevelt to put on its bench another top-notch legal mind. In that respect, CCB wrote, Murphy was lacking. The attorney general had many achievements to his credit, but not legal learning.

Murphy had been an outstanding mayor of Detroit through the Depression's worst years, and before that a judge (1924–30) on a Detroit municipal trial court. Earlier still, he had briefly been an assistant U.S. attorney. He had also served as high commissioner in the Philippine Islands for three years, 1933–36, and then, 1937–38, as governor of Michigan. Failing to win reelection, he became a distinguished "lame-duck" Democrat to whom the party owed allegiance, and Roosevelt had made him attorney general. Murphy was a Midwesterner and a Catholic, and those who liked to believe that certain religious denominations were entitled to a seat on the Court considered that Butler had held the "Catholic seat." Geographic and political reasons for Roosevelt's choice were clear.

CCB approached his point obliquely, in the midst of a gossipy letter: "Well, I am working up to my point rather dodderingly on the A.G. He is no doubt a choice spirit and he is a true son of the Church and he is a Mid-Westerner and he is a New Dealer, but I can't abear to think of so slight a lawyer on the S.C. . . . So I hope the A.G. will not be appointed to the Court and will devote his powers to executive, administrative or legislative duties."[53]

He did not reveal that behind his letter was a visit to him in New York, on 24 December, by associate justice Harlan Fiske Stone. He and Stone had discussed several problems in the federal courts, among them the rumored appointment of Murphy. That afternoon, CCB wrote to Learned Hand: "H.F.S. says the A.G. is reported as not wishing to go on the S.C. Possibly he knows what a heavy job it would be with his light equipment." Then he added, "It has been *very* amusing to get inside dope from F.F. [Frankfurter] and S.—very different."[54] After brooding for three days on what he had heard, he wrote to Roosevelt.

Believing that religious and regional diversity gave strength to the Court, CCB did not urge on him an Eastern or Protestant candidate, but merely suggested that Murphy was not a man for the Supreme Court. In some respects Murphy seemed to many people more like a secular priest than a lawyer. He was tall, spare, unmarried, and devout, and because of poor circulation in his hands had a characteristic gesture of rubbing his fingers to keep the blood flowing.[55] In his career, particularly as mayor, he had demonstrated some great qualities, especially a sympathy for people; but in these he was primarily a humanist, not a legal scholar or craftsman. CCB probably also had heard, from either Frankfurter or Stone, that another reason for moving Murphy to the Court was that Roosevelt was eager to make his solicitor general, Robert H. Jackson, the attorney general. But then, what could FDR offer to the loyal Murphy? Well, the Court.

Murphy initially told reporters congratulating him on the appointment that he had not yet decided to accept it. But with no other government post likely, he soon did, and served until his death nine years later. Douglas thought him "a great Justice," though lacking "the technical competence of either Frankfurter or Reed or Stone," and observed, "He longed, I think, for an executive job, probably as Secretary of War." Francis Biddle, who succeeded Jackson as solicitor general and later as attorney general, was harsher: "His opinions evinced moral conviction on a high level of indignation. But the man saw always in values of black and white, knew no intervening shades, disentangled none of those perplexities and balanced values the discovery of which distinguishes the searching mind of a useful judge."[56]

Roosevelt's next two appointments struck many people as better. First, in July 1941, to replace Hughes as chief justice, he advanced Stone, who after sixteen years of preparation on the Court as an associate became the first (and so far the last) professor to serve as chief justice. Though he had voted on occasion to uphold New Deal legislation, he was a Republican, and his promotion to the top post of the government's judicial arm in mid-June 1941, when the country seemed to be edging closer to war, soothed Republicans angry at Roosevelt for snatching the presidency for a third term.

To Stone's place as associate justice, Roosevelt named James Byrnes, a Democrat from South Carolina who had served as a congressman from 1911 to 1925, and ten years, from 1931, as a senator. Like Black, he had been a strong New Deal supporter, but without arousing anger or fear in his opponents. He was popular and admired, but he served on the Court only sixteen months, and for ten of those was on leave of absence to work with the president on the war effort. In all, Byrnes wrote for the Court sixteen majority opinions and none concurring or dissenting. His talents were more executive than judicial, and at Roosevelt's request he resigned from the Court in October 1942 to become director of economic stabilization and then of the War Mobilization Board. "I'm sorry to lose you," Chief Justice Stone told him, "but I'm glad you can make up your mind whether you want to be a judge or something else."[57] Though the Court sorely needed the geniality and skill at compromise that distinguished Byrnes, Roosevelt's appointment of him had not been helpful. The Court was ill served by a judge who, at the president's call, treated the job as part-time work and within eighteen months resigned.

In the same month Roosevelt appointed Byrnes to the Court, he also nominated Solicitor General Jackson to take the place of James C. McReynolds, the last of the four justices who had voted consistently against the validity of any New Deal legislation. Jackson certainly would be more sympathetic. Taking his seat in July 1941, he served thirteen years, dying of heart failure in 1954, at age sixty-two. He is well remembered for two nonjudicial episodes of his career: when, at President Truman's request in 1945, he took a leave of absence from the Court to act as chief counsel for the United States in the prosecution at Nuremberg of Nazi war criminals; and in 1946 when he and Justice Black quarreled in public.[58]

During Jackson's fifteen-month leave of absence at Nuremberg, the

Court had only eight justices, and many people, including Chief Justice Stone, questioned if that reduction to an even number was wise or proper. Would not Truman have done better to send over, say, the nation's solicitor general or some specially appointed prosecutor? Justice Douglas later wrote: "I thought at the time he accepted the job that it was a gross violation of separation of powers to put a Justice in charge of an executive function. I thought, and I think Stone and Black agreed, that if Bob did that, he should resign."[59]

Roosevelt's final appointment, to fill the seat vacated by Byrnes in October 1942, was of yet another relatively young professor and dean of a law school, Wiley B. Rutledge, of Iowa. He was only forty-eight, and after admission to the bar in 1922 had practiced for two years and then begun to teach law, ultimately becoming dean of the law schools at Washington University, St. Louis, and then at the University of Iowa. He had spoken out frequently in favor of New Deal legislation, and Roosevelt in 1939 had appointed him to the Court of Appeals for the District of Columbia. His years as a judge therefore were only four, and as a practicing attorney, only two. According to Attorney General Biddle, who informed him of his nomination, "he really believed he was not up to it."[60]

CCB's distress with the "Roosevelt Court" steadily mounted, especially as its harmony visibly shattered and the number of dissents and concurring opinions soared. Even before Byrnes resigned, he characterized the Court to his English friend MacKinnon, a judge, as "a thing of shreds and patches torn by intellectual dissensions, and Stone, C.J., a fine judge and a grand person, doesn't seem able to knock their heads together and produce judicial harmonies . . . Why should there be concurring opinions for slight differences? Well, no more of this."[61] But the question bothered him, and he returned to it often. When he heard the rumor that Rutledge would replace Byrnes, he rushed a letter to "Dear Franklin."

> Let me suggest for the Supreme Court the one man who would be acclaimed by the entire Bar as Cardozo was when president Hoover appointed him, LEARNED HAND. He is 70 and from New York. But he is an ox for work, and he is far and away the best judge on any Circuit Court of Appeals, learned as his name, liberal, wise . . . Except for Wilbur of California, who doesn't count, Hand has served on the Federal bench longer than any judge . . .
>
> The S.C. needs strengthening; Byrnes is a great loss; Murphy is out of place. Douglas as smart as Berle or Laski would like to succeed you [i.e. as president]. Not one Justice has been promoted from Federal

bench or any bench except Black, who served as a police judge for 18 months in Birmingham (and they say he is making one of the best Justices of the S.C.).

There is political and poetical justice in promoting Hand; he will fit into the Court instanter without apprenticeship, continuing the work he has done so grandly for 33 years.

You are on top of the World and can do anything. The regional representation on the Court is enough—two from the South, Black and Reed; Murphy from the Mid-West, and Douglas from the Coast.

As I began, so I end. Hand would be as good and as well received as Cardozo was and would add as much weight to the Court as he did.[62]

He telegraphed a similar message to Chief Justice Stone, and also to his Black Point neighbor Lloyd K. Garrison, then dean of the Wisconsin Law School, suggesting that he might rally support in the Midwest; and he reported to Frankfurter what he had done. Stone, meanwhile, had replied to his letter: "Inquiry has been made of me. I stated very emphatically my view that the appointment in which you and I are interested would greatly strengthen the Court . . . I suspect, however, that the age question stands in the way."[63] CCB guessed, apparently correctly, that the "inquiry" had come from the attorney general, and so he wrote to Biddle, too, remarking about Hand's age: "To appoint a man of 70 may seem inconsistent with F.D.R.'s position in '37 on aged judges; but L.H. is an exception . . . As for consistency, *vide* Emerson's Self-Reliance on that hobgoblin of little minds."[64]

Not having heard from Roosevelt, CCB wrote to him again:

> I have long favored voluntary retirement at 70 and compulsory at 75. But the critical period is *before* not *after* 70. The grand Climacteric of the Romans was 63 (9 x 7). The survivors are tough. And this is especially true of judges, who usually lead regular and cloistered lives . . . [As for] Consistency "that hobgoblin of little minds." In '37 you conceded there were exceptions. L.H. is one. His appointment would be an outstanding confirmation of your own open-mindedness.[65]

Roosevelt replied: "I love especially your remark about 'judges who usually lead regular and cloistered lives.' Thank God, Q.E.D., that you were never a judge! There never would have been a C.C.B. if you had ever led a regular or cloistered life." But this was one of Roosevelt's charming evasions, dashing hope. CCB already had despaired to Frankfurter, "The longer F.D. delays, the less chance."[66] Nevertheless, early in December he sent a humorous note on Hand's age to the president, and on Christmas Eve a letter enclosing a copy of Hand's speech at the memorial service for Brandeis. Later he told Frankfurter: "I sent B.'s [LH] speech to F.D. and am sorry I did because I think it is too highbrow for him. But I sent a low-brow letter with it, anyway."[67]

When he heard from Frankfurter that the nominee would be Rutledge, CCB mourned: "Sad, and oh, so foolish! . . . But a professor, if not a dean, must, unlike the proverbial stone (no pun), gather some mossy law!"[68] Biddle, in his autobiography, reported that he heard later that Roosevelt named Rutledge because "he resented what he called the 'organized pressure' in Hand's behalf." This is the generally accepted view of what happened, and Frankfurter usually is blamed for irritating the president with too much importuning. But CCB perhaps deserves some of the blame for his haranguing letters and the imposition of a "highbrow" speech.[69]

He was disgusted. "What is it," he wrote to Stone, seeming to forget Stone's twenty-five years at Columbia Law School, "that makes F.D.R. so partial to professors?" "Professor folks are all right," Stone replied, "but we don't need too many of them, at least unless they have been seasoned by some of the hard knocks that one gets out of the practice of the legal profession or the business of judging."[70] (Earlier CCB had written to Roosevelt about law professors: "Their weakness is that they have never had to come up against reality. They can think and say one thing this term and the contrary the next term or the next week. They are freed from responsibility for the consequences of their preachments. In a Trial Court they go to school and learn to be judges; on an Appellate Court they are a real danger.")[71]

Hand, though privately disappointed, was probably less upset than his supporters,[72] and perhaps saw more deeply than they into Roosevelt's lack of enthusiasm for him. It was not so much a question of age as of personality. Roosevelt liked fawners—Frankfurter, who applied adulation with a trowel; Douglas, who came to the White House to swap stories and to play poker; and to a lesser extent, Reed, Jackson, Rutledge, and Murphy. Roosevelt liked to feel that he had made their careers. In Hand's case that could never be true. And there was another irritant. As Hand wrote to CCB after learning of Rutledge's nomination:

Dear Charlie,
    I never had more than the faintest notion that you and Gus and Felix could get F.D.R. to appoint me. I think that there was a deeper difficulty than age, though that was enough. Probably I would have voted as he

would have liked, but not for the reasons he would have liked, if he had ever known them, which he never would. He has a sensitive nose for people, and my ways of going at things are so different from his that he may well have felt me alien; I fancy he did.

All this is not important; what I am writing for is to let you know that your interest in me and my appointment has moved me very much. I know you don't do such things from affection; but affection had a share in it and that was the share which meant the most to me. I do not want to have the whole thing pass into limbo without telling you how I felt about it.[73]

After all the talk about age, the younger Rutledge served only six years on the Court before dying in 1949, whereas the elderly Hand stayed active on the Second Circuit Court of Appeals until his nominal retirement in 1951, continuing for ten years thereafter to decide a limited number of cases each year until his death at eighty-nine (1961). In all, he served fifty-two years as a federal judge—none has served longer—and he and his colleagues, chiefly Judges A. N. Hand and Thomas Swan, made the Second Circuit for a quarter of a century one of the best-regarded courts in the country.

Meanwhile, in Washington, by the end of 1942 the "Roosevelt" Supreme Court, with eight of its nine judges appointed by him (all except Owen J. Roberts), was proving extremely fractious and divided. The open quarreling tormented CCB, who began to receive letters from lawyers around the country lamenting the behavior of the Roosevelt appointees. He himself wrote many letters on the subject, and none sharper than those to Frankfurter. These reveal not only something about the Court's rulings, legal trends, and personal feuds, but also a remarkable friendship, able to absorb harsh words and disagreements.

Though Frankfurter had been a professor for twenty-five years, CCB wrote bluntly of his dislike of professors on the bench. On 11 December 1942, after hearing that Roosevelt might appoint Rutledge to the Court, an exasperated CCB wrote to Frankfurter, "Well, without offense may I suggest that the Court doesn't need another Professor. You & Dean Stone & Professor W.O.D. [Douglas] are enough." Two weeks later, on Christmas Eve, he was still more forceful: "I think it would be a public calamity to have another professor on your Court unless he was seasoned by experience."[74] CCB's reasons for thinking professors did not make good judges were well known, because frequently expressed, and they were strengthened now, as Frankfurter knew, by reports of his own professorial behavior on the bench and in the Court's weekly conference. He knew because

CCB had written him scolding letters, and sometimes Frankfurter had accepted the censure and sometimes stoutly protested. He was, after all, by 1942, fifty-nine and a man of great learning and wide experience, while his would-be tutor had never been a judge and was a Methuselah of eighty. Their disagreements, vigorously expressed, sometimes required a truce, and for weeks at a time they would not discuss the Court.[75] Then CCB would break out again.

On the bench Frankfurter's professorial habits had shown themselves at once. Solicitor General Biddle recalled that in 1940–41

> on the average I argued a case every two weeks. I had to work through long evenings to master the records, to be ready to answer Mr. Justice Frankfurter's questions—he had the ability to swallow records like oysters . . . [He] liked to pick out some obscure morsel not referred to in the briefs—which became horribly relevant if the Solicitor General missed it—darting down into the record apparently at random and pulling out and holding up the telling bit. A suspended and involuted question would then emerge, as if Henry James had been dictating *The Wings of the Dove* to a new amanuensis. Do you see what I mean, Mr. Solicitor? The answer need not be simple, he seemed to indicate, sitting back to watch the government lawyer's reaction.[76]

For lawyers less polished than Biddle, Frankfurter's interruptions and questions often were unnerving, throwing the lawyers and their arguments "off track" so that sometimes the case never got a full and proper statement. Meanwhile, he also irritated his colleagues on the bench, who wanted to get on with the case.

In conference with his fellows, he could be similarly schoolmarmish. One time when Earl Warren was chief justice (1953–69) and had the misfortune to say that he was unfamiliar with some point, Frankfurter had the Library of Congress send over five or six books. Into each, before passing the books on to Warren, Frankfurter inserted a memo on what to read. Warren, new to the bench, had his own insecurities, but Frankfurter was insensitive to them.[77] He was used to dealing with students and seemed unable to treat colleagues as equals. Douglas, who had little love for Frankfurter (though "he was probably the best conversationalist that my generation knew"), wrote:

> He was . . . a proselytizer, and every waking hour vigorously promoted the ideas he espoused. Up and down the halls he went, pleading, needling,

nudging, probing. He never stopped trying to change the votes on a case until the decision came down . . . [He] also indulged in histrionics in Conference. He often came in with piles of books, and on his turn to talk, would pound the table, read from the books, throw them around and create a great disturbance. His purpose was never aimless. His act was designed to get a particular Justice's vote or at least create doubts in the mind of a Justice who was thinking the other way. At times, when another was talking, he would break in, make a derisive comment and shout down the speaker.[78]

Harvard Law students in class, knowing they could not match wits with the professor, had sat back and enjoyed his show. But his colleagues on the bench increasingly ignored him. And as his influence waned in personal relations, so, too, it waned in legal thought.

His increasing isolation can be seen in three wartime cases involving First Amendment rights. In the first, the *Gobitis* case (1940), two Jehovah's Witness children, Lillian Gobitis (aged twelve) and her brother William (ten), were expelled from a Pennsylvania public school for refusing to salute the flag, which they had been taught (Exodus 20:4–5) was "a graven image." The children's lawyers sought to have the state law declared an unconstitutional infringement of their First Amendment rights. Frankfurter wrote the majority opinion (8 to 1), speaking for all the Court except Chief Justice Stone. The state had a right to determine "the appropriateness of various means to evoke" a unifying sentiment of patriotism. At times, even First Amendment guarantees had to give way to the needs of the state—in this case, the need to strengthen patriotism as a prop to national security in a hostile world. As the law then was, the decision clearly was correct, but many newspapers and liberals lamented what they thought an unnecessary, wrongful start of wartime repression of liberties.[79]

A second Jehovah's Witness case, *Jones v. Opelika* (1942), upheld a city ordinance requiring a license to sell religious material on the street. In this 5-to-4 decision, Justices Black, Douglas, and Murphy joined Stone in the dissent, announcing tangentially that they had changed their minds about *Gobitis*: "Since we joined in the opinion in the *Gobitis* case, we think this is an appropriate occasion to state that we now believe that it also was wrongly decided." Such a statement, an open invitation to litigation, was without precedent in the Court's history. To many in the older generation of lawyers, it seemed a bad departure from tradition.[80]

The next year the Court decided the *Barnette* case (1943), in which a West Virginia Jehovah's Witness challenged the state's flag-salute law, and the Court, 6 to 3, with Frankfurter one of the three dissenters, overruled *Gobitis* and held the state law unconstitutional. Thus he who in the 1920s had seemed the radical defender of Sacco and Vanzetti against the state now found himself labeled a conservative defender of the state against the appeals of "outsiders" like Jehovah's Witnesses. Instead of leading the Court in its thinking, Frankfurter now frequently found himself in the minority, and along with him his beliefs in judicial self-restraint.[81]

This doctrine of self-restraint, with which Frankfurter became closely associated, embraces a range of ideas, but they may be summarized as saying that except in clear cases the Supreme Court should not substitute its ideas of what is constitutional for those expressed by the Congress or state legislatures; that it should declare what the law is, not what a majority of the judges think it should be; that the embodiment of new ideas in the law is a legislative, not a judicial, function. Underlying the doctrine, however stated, is a deference to the Constitution's separation of powers, executive, legislative, and judicial, and to the theory of republican government: primarily the people's elected representatives make the law; primarily the courts expound it.

For many people, the Roosevelt Court was beginning to seem just as much a usurping second legislature as the anti–New Deal Court had seemed a decade earlier. Moreover, its nine judges increasingly argued their different views aloud in concurring and dissenting opinions, with the Court's majority now led by Black, Douglas, and Murphy (the last having shifted allegiance from Frankfurter to Black).[82] This three-man nucleus was often able to win over two colleagues and by a 5-to-4 decision proclaim new rights (most often civil rights) just discovered in the Constitution. Many people approved of what they considered a fresh wind clearing the Court of musty doctrines; and many were distressed not so much by the close decisions as by the many concurring opinions which deprived the law of certainty. Laymen as well as lawyers wrote to CCB hoping that since he knew well Frankfurter, Stone, and Roberts, he might influence the Court's behavior.

One of the first of such letters came in November 1939 from the editor of the *Harvard Alumni Bulletin* asking about Frankfurter's likely position on a university problem. CCB, in reply, remarked on how "F's mind works. It never works very calmly. Passion soon intervenes. He starts meaning to be judicial and almost immediately becomes an advocate and often a passionate one." An advocate, not a judge. As Augustus Hand was to observe to CCB in 1943, "F.F. is the best educated and most intellectual man on the Court, but he is restless, divisive and has always been so. He is not and cannot be a judge . . . The present Court has lots of able men in it but no cohesion and no conception of what a workable judicial tribunal must be."[83] Courts, unlike the executive or legislative arms of government, must reach decisions, and these should be clear and firm.

After receiving more letters about Frankfurter, CCB evidently wrote to him directly, for he described the result in September 1943 in a letter to his English friend S. K. Ratcliffe:

> I am sorry I inflicted the Supreme Court opinions on you, but you should not have waded through them. I thought it was about time that F.F. was told what the Bar thought of him, and as I couldn't think of anybody else to do the telling, I did it myself. They think he behaves on the Bench like a schoolmaster, questioning his pupils and interrupting and argifying [sic] with them. I went so far as to send him an extract from a letter I received from a very wise and distinguished person about the Court and his own behavior, not only to the Bar, but to his brethren. F. came back with a very lovely, there is no other word for it, letter thanking me for my frankness and promising to profit by it. (This of course is all very confidential.)[84]

But habits of a lifetime, cemented into a personality, are not easily changed. Moreover, the Court's conferences by then were so contentious that all positions seemingly had to be defended in public, usually in concurring or dissenting opinions. On 10 January 1944, CCB published in the *Herald Tribune* a letter he signed only as "A member of the Bar of the Supreme Court."

> On January 3rd the Supreme Court of the United States handed down thirteen opinions in twenty-one cases. In four of these the Court was unanimous; in nine there were dissents as follows: three 5 to 4, two 6 to 3, one 5 to 3, one 7 to 2, two 8 to 1. The Justices who dissented and the number of their dissents were Murphy 5, Black, Reed and Frankfurter 4 each, Roberts 3, Douglas 2 Stone C.J. 1, Rutledge 1.
>
> It is not to be expected that the Justices will always agree, but there seems to be a growing tendency to disagree; and if this is not checked, the effect on the public will be unfortunate, making for doubt and uncertainty and lack of respect and a loss of confidence in the Court.
>
> It is one of the essential functions of a Chief Justice to persuade his associates not to insist on differences which can be adjusted. One of the notable accomplishments of Justice Cardozo when he was Chief Judge

of the N.Y. Court of Appeals was his success in bringing harmony out of differences which seemed essential but were not so actually.

A Court of last resort, whether in a State or in the Federal system, exists for the purpose not merely of determining the rights of the parties, but in order to settle the law, so that the whole body of citizens may know what it is and what it will continue to be. The turn-about of the Supreme Court in the case of Jehovah's Witnesses is a glaring instance of uncertainty. Two Justices [Black and Douglas] reversed themselves within two and a half years. One would think that in cases involving the Bill of Rights a judge would know his own mind in 1940 as well as in 1943.

Where there is a fundamental difference on a Constitutional question, we cannot ask or expect Judges who have settled in their own minds the principles which they believe the Court should follow, e.g., with regard to the powers of Congress and of the States, they should not be reproached for adhering to these principles. Justice Sutherland [1922–38] is entitled to the respect of the Bar and of the People as much as Justice Holmes or Justice Brandeis.

One of the least desirable practices that has grown up in the Supreme Court in recent years is the *concurring opinion* in which a Justice who agrees with the decision but is dissatisfied with the language of the opinion or its implications insists on expressing himself in his own words.

In this last batch of decisions two of the Justices have indulged themselves in concurring opinions criticizing the approach and attitude if not the character of one of their colleagues [Black and Murphy criticizing Frankfurter]. This break of judicial propriety is in violation of the high traditions and the dignity of the Court.

The Supreme Court is not a mere judicial tribunal of Nine Men, it is a coordinate branch of our Government charged with grave responsibilities and endowed with great authority and power. Personal differences should be confined within the Council Chamber and not proclaimed from the bench.[85]

Chief Justice Stone wrote directly to the anonymous author, whom he recognized was CCB: "I read your piece in the *Herald Tribune* about the unhappy state of the Court, and found myself in substantial agreement with it." He took exception only to the idea that Cardozo on New York's Court of Appeals could serve as a model for himself on the Supreme Court. "I doubt if Cardozo ever did more than to encourage proper judicial self-restraint in the matter of dissents, or that he would have gotten very far with some of my associates. Our trouble really comes from the persistent use of the concurring opinion."[86]

CCB in reply agreed. "But while I had my pen in hand I thought I'd express a few other prejudices. I have a strong aversion to Black because he sat silent in the Senate and permitted Borah to state that he had never had anything to do with Ku Klux Klan. I am told he is very smart and very diligent. Maybe so! I was vexed by the two concurring opinions *slating* Felix. It may be that he has brought it on himself by previous opinions prevailing, dissenting, or concurring."[87]

Unhappily, the Court's many disagreements, as well as Frankfurter's share in them, did not ease, and CCB continued periodically to receive letters from lawyers outside New York who hoped he might be able to moderate the behavior of some of the judges. One such came in January 1944 from Benjamin V. Cohen, a close friend of Frankfurter and one of the best-liked and most admired of New Deal lawyers in Washington, a selfless, soft-spoken, shy man and a fine legal draftsman. At the time he was chief assistant to Byrnes at the Office of War Mobilization.

> Dear Uncle Charlie:
>
> Is there anything we can do to save Felix from himself. He feels so very strongly he is writing for history. He may be right and I may be all wrong, but I am afraid that he has become so emotionally involved that his work on the Court and his opinions will be historically judged far different from what he now fervently believes.
>
> In answer to a note of mine he sent me copies of his letters to you of January 11 and 12. I gathered from these that you, too, have been trying to help him. That is why I feel free to write to you without mentioning to him that I am doing so . . . I hope that you will keep up the work on your side because he cannot suspect that your head has been turned by the wave of the present.[88]

In a chatty letter to Frankfurter the following week, CCB returned to concurring opinions: "In none of your letters have you said a word about them . . . I have a notion there are mighty few concurring opinions *ante adventum* F.F." (CCB had asked a young lawyer in his firm to count the number of concurring opinions in the Supreme Court Reports, volumes 306 to 320 [roughly, five years]: the score, with the Court's three professors leading, was: Frankfurter 12, Douglas 11, Stone 6, and Black, Jackson, and Murphy 5 each.) "Maybe you will like to know," CCB continued, "what the lawyers say here in the Metropolis about the Court. They are all disgusted with Black and Douglas, but they think that you brought it on yourself in part by your schoolmaster's ways in open court and, they suspect, still more in conference."[89]

This time, Frankfurter met the charge head-on. In a long reply he set forth a historical background to concurring opinions and countered CCB's figures with one from the pre–New Deal Court: In the four years 1926–29, then associate justice Stone had written eight. Frankfurter, perhaps suddenly recalling that Stone was another professor, went on to a more important point: "When the course of decisions is as much under critical scrutiny as it is in our time, there are likely to be more dissenting and concurring opinions. It is for that reason—for purpose of justifying differences of opinion and not letting them be *ipse dixits*" that he wrote concurring opinions. As for his "schoolmaster's ways in open court," he had been a schoolmaster for twenty-five years and was appointed because as a professor he presumably had "some learning in the law and not because I was either a leader of the bar or a senator or other statesman." He thanked CCB for the critique, for "I deem it a true kindness of friendship to tell me of things that are within the remedial possibilities of my temperament."[90]

A year later CCB tried to explain the Court's difficulties to an English friend: "It isn't properly pulled together." The fault perhaps lay with Stone, but "perhaps nobody could control individualists like Black and Douglas." Then he added, "I made what I thought was an amusing suggestion to F.F., that every one of the nine Judges should write in every case—and let the lawyers find out what the decision is. This, I said, would make for business. Apparently he didn't think it very funny for he made no response."[91]

Perhaps only lawyers and those who read the opinions were fully aware of the intellectual hostilities roiling the Court. But laymen read of them frequently in news reports and saw the public behavior of several justices, which often seemed questionable. Douglas, for one, from the moment he came on the Court abandoned its tradition that its judges, to avoid any appearance of partiality or bias, should stay aloof from public life. "I took a different course . . . I would fight to raise the level of public schools . . . I would become immersed in conservation . . . I would travel and speak out on foreign affairs." (In 1951, for example, he announced in a public interview that the United States should recognize Communist China, causing cries of rage in Congress and in newspapers across the country. Frankfurter's complaint to CCB on the incident was relatively mild: "Judges shouldn't express views as to matters that may come before the Court . . .

The Court should be enveloped in security not in agitation." Privately, President Truman advised Douglas to pay attention to his duties on the Court and to "let the President of the United States run the political end of foreign and domestic affairs.")[92]

Douglas also publicly treated his seat on the Court as a mere stepping-stone to other office. In 1940 and again in 1944, he allowed his name to be put forward as a vice presidential candidate to run with Roosevelt. In 1948 he allowed himself to be considered a possible candidate for the Democratic nomination for president. Though nothing came of these plans, he plainly enjoyed the publicity and continued to dangle himself before politicians as a possible candidate. He declined Truman's offer to appoint him secretary of the interior, but then suggested himself as secretary of state.[93] CCB and many others, not necessarily lawyers, feeling that a seat on the Supreme Court was the profession's highest honor, resented such behavior.

Even more damaging to respect for the Court than Douglas and his hankering after celebrity was a feud that burst into the headlines soon after the death of Chief Justice Stone in April 1946. It originated in a disagreement between Justices Jackson and Black over law and behavior in the *Jewell Ridge Coal* case, decided in 1945. Black angered Jackson when he refused to disqualify himself from sitting on a case in which Black's former law partner was chief counsel for a labor union. The decision in favor of the ex-partner's client was 5 to 4, with Murphy writing the majority opinion, and Jackson the dissent. Because Black voted with Murphy, he could be said to have cast the deciding vote.[94]

When Chief Justice Stone died and President Truman debated his choice for Stone's successor, Black and Jackson seemed the leading candidates, with Jackson the favorite. But the Court's frequent displays of bad temper disgusted Truman, and rather than promote any associate justice he appointed Fred M. Vinson to be chief justice (1946–53). Vinson, a lawyer with experience in all three branches of the government, had a reputation for knocking heads together and working out compromises.

While Vinson's appointment awaited Senate confirmation, Jackson, at the war trials in Nuremberg, cabled a public letter to the chairmen of the House and Senate Judiciary Committees. In it he severely criticized Black for not withdrawing from the *Jewell* case and threatened that if a similar situation should arise, his future castigation of Black would "make my Jewell Ridge opinion look like a letter of recommendation." The *Times* in an editorial the next day spoke for many: "It seems to us that Justice Jackson has committed an error in taste and that Justice Black has committed the worse offense of lowering judicial standards."[95]

CCB wrote to Geoffrey Russell, in London:

We all are shocked by Jackson's statement—foolish and worse! . . . It is hard to see how he can sit on the same Bench with Black . . . Black himself is smart and hard working, but he is a skunk and I can prove it—but I won't trouble to do that now. He will never resign! These quarrels have lowered the prestige of the Court greatly. Our people are not much interested in courts or judges, but the Supreme Court is an exception as it represents the third estate.[96]

A week later, in a letter in the *Times*, he tried to prescribe for the Court's troubles in an unprovoking manner by quoting Chief Justice Morrison R. Waite (1874–88):

In the confusion of voices as to the Supreme Court, its prestige, and especially the Jackson-Black episode, it may be well to go back seventy years and read what Chief Justice . . . Waite wrote to his nephew . . . a member of the House of Representatives from Connecticut, in 1876, when he was asked to permit his name to be used as a candidate for the Presidency.

When I accepted it [his judicial appointment], my duty was not to make it a stepping-stone to something else . . . Ought not the Constitution to have provided that a Chief Justice should not be eligible to the Presidency? If such ought to have been the Constitution, can I with propriety permit my name to be used for the formation of political combinations? If I do, can I remain at all times and in all cases an unbiased judge in the estimation of the people? If I am not, shall not I degrade my office? Put these things in your pipe and smoke them and then tell me if you think I ought to permit my name to be used.[97]

Though CCB cited no sitting justice in his letter, his complaint clearly was aimed at Douglas and those other Roosevelt appointees in the federal court system who seemed inclined to treat their judicial posts as simply a means to a political end. The Jackson-Black episode was disgraceful, but an aberration. The constant political play of Douglas, and to a lesser extent of Black and Murphy, was the greater threat to the Court's reputation for impartiality.

In a letter published in 1951 regretting the decline of the Court's prestige, CCB put the blame "chiefly on the bar and the press, but somewhat on the court itself." The bar was at fault because lawyers had too often abandoned civility for partisan politics: Roosevelt's Court-packing scheme had "opened the floodgates to a deluge of bitterness." The press was at fault because newspapers filled their columns "with comment, ignorant and shameless, on courts and judges, on witnesses and parties in cases on trial and on appeal, and especially where civil rights are involved; and this has shaken the confidence of the people in the administration of justice." For his example of a justice who had manifested "prejudices and personal antipathies" on the bench, CCB was careful to choose from among the dead, citing McReynolds, 1914–41, appointed by President Wilson. In closing, he returned to a constant theme of American legal thought since the Revolution: the desire to have a government of laws, not of men. And this required that judges, as much as possible, be kept out of, and keep themselves out of, politics.

> Political experience is an asset for a judge provided he abjures politics on ascending the bench. Many of us go further and think that the justices of the Supreme Court should abandon all political ambition. Many lawyers think that Chief Justice Hughes should not have left the bench to be a candidate for the Presidency; certainly every right-minded lawyer condemns political maneuvering by speeches or silences by justices while on the court.[98]

But by 1951 CCB's views carried less weight. What Justice Holmes once had called "the felt necessities of the time"[99] were turning in other directions, shifting opinions, changing agendas and priorities. Many people thought that the Court, despite its acrimony and dissension, was performing better than in the past. The influential columnist Max Lerner, for one, rejoiced "to have Justices on the Supreme Court who pretend to no Olympian infallibility and who can stick their necks out of their enfolding robes." A professor at the New School for Social Research, speaking for many in the emerging fields of social science, he wrote triumphantly: "Law is too serious a business to be left to lawyers. While there are legal questions and legal problems, there are no legal answers or solutions. The greatness of the Court is manifested in its growing awareness that the issues which confront it, no matter how legal, must of necessity find a composition social, economic, or political in nature."[100]

Many others now admired judicial activism—judges boldly making new law rather than interpreting the old—and judicial restraint was increasingly thought to be old-fashioned and inadequate to the issues of the day. Yet, of course, a court can be active in one field and restrained in another, and most courts over periods of time swing back and forth, depending on the exigencies of the particular political and moral struggle. Nevertheless, in typical fashion, those people propelling the new ideas and riding them to positions of power and prestige believed that their legal theories were more universal, permanent, and morally worthy than any put forward by the older generation.

In March 1947 Frankfurter, speaking for restraint, delivered at the City Bar Association a lecture, "Some Reflections on the Reading of Statutes." To begin, he stressed how much practice in the Supreme Court had changed, though "broadly speaking, the number of cases disposed of has not changed." In 1875 more than 40 percent turned on common law; in 1925, 5 percent; "while today cases not resting on statutes are reduced almost to zero." Later on he urged:

> In those realms where judges directly formulate law because the chosen lawmakers have not acted, judges have the duty of adaptation and adjustment of old principles to new conditions. But where policy is expressed by the primary law-making agency in a democracy, that is by the legislature, judges must respect such expressions by adding to or subtracting from the explicit terms which the lawmakers use no more than is called for by the shorthand nature of language.[101]

Though a major effort, the speech did not turn the tide of opinion. Seven years later he returned to many of the same ideas in a more popular style in "The Job of a Supreme Court Justice," an article for the *Times* Sunday magazine section. As if in answer to CCB's continuing complaints about concurring opinions, he quoted former chief justice Hughes:

> How amazing it is that, in the midst of controversies on every conceivable subject, one should expect unanimity of opinion upon difficult legal questions! In the highest ranges of thought, in theology, philosophy and science, we find differences of view on the part of the most distinguished experts—theologians, philosophers and scientists. And when we deal with questions relating to principles of law and their application, we do not suddenly rise into a stratosphere of icy certainty.[102]

The quotation was apt, but in suggesting that the Supreme Court presently was ruffled mainly by philosophical differences, debated at a high level of civility, it touched CCB's complaints at only one point. There remained the dissatisfaction of many lawyers with the men Roosevelt had appointed to the Court, chiefly with a group Frankfurter was not likely to criticize: the professors. From a lawyer in Louisville, Kentucky, CCB had a letter lamenting: "The most pitiful thing about the Supreme Court is that substantially not a one of them has ever had any kind of a reputation as a lawyer . . . I doubt very much if, prior to their appointment to the Supreme Court, Rutledge, Murphy or Douglas ever argued a case, or even were admitted to the Supreme Court . . . Black perhaps only had one case . . . Rutledge, Douglas and Frankfurter were college professors. In short, not a single person on the Supreme Court had, prior to his appointment, acquired any outstanding position as a lawyer, even in his own narrow community, to say nothing of his state, section of the country, or the bar as a whole."[103] Roosevelt, himself a lawyer of little experience or learning, in his appointments had disconnected the Court from its professional base. The consequences, because the new justices were mostly so much younger than those traditionally appointed, stretched far into the future. Wailed the Louisville lawyer, "What a change has taken place!"

24

The Last Decade

BY THE SPRING OF 1946, at age eighty-seven, CCB was ready to admit that his eyesight was failing. Asked to speak at a memorial service for Chief Justice Stone, he afterward confessed to a friend he had been unable to read his notes and had been forced "to shoot my mouth off," forcefully adding, "This is the end of my jawing!" But not of his energy or courage. About this time, crossing Park Avenue one day, he terrified a slightly younger friend by propelling the elderly man into traffic, saying cheerfully, "Have you ever noticed how seldom they hit two old men at once?"[1]

A year later, though a cataract in each eye was starting, CCB undertook to lodge a seven-year-old grand-nephew for two nights. The boy, raised on a New Hampshire farm, was Lawrie Taylor's son, the eldest grandchild of Louie's sister Grace, and on his way to Washington, D.C., to visit an aunt. Entertainment for the two evenings was easy: backgammon, talk, and for young and old, early to bed. But between the nights stretched the day. At the breakfast table, the boy faced the old man, expectant. CCB pondered, and then decreed a walk to Grant's Tomb, across Central Park, then north and west to the river at 122nd Street, a round-trip of some seven miles. That would fill the morning. The boy recalled:

After breakfast we went down on the elevator and out onto the street. I recall it being a very bright, mild and breezy day. We walked a considerable distance. He would take my hand crossing streets, but would allow me to roam ahead and then wait for him to catch up at the curbs. At the tomb he gave me a little lecture about Grant. I can't recall the details, but I distinctly recall him talking about Grant as President of the United States, about Grant as a great general in the Civil War, and about how he had been there when Grant was brought there to rest . . . Then there was a little quiz at the end, and I recall I managed to answer his questions to his satisfaction. What is much more vivid is that on the walk back to his apartment he tested my sense of direction at the turns, asking me each time which way we should go. I can see him peering down at me, hands clasped behind his back.[2]

Because of the tomb the lecture and quiz were on Grant, but that did not mean that CCB had changed his ranking of Civil War leaders. Once when the skeptical Hand, always in doubt, wrote to CCB: "Way down in the bottom of my belly I have always just wondered about Lincoln. I know my father, who had more sense than I, although somewhat partisan, no doubt, always felt that Lincoln was somewhat overrated." By return mail he was told, "Now, don't get woozy on A. Lincoln. Let us have one H E R O." And at Black Point, every day at his desk CCB sat down under the sepia reproduction of Saint-Gaudens's memorial to Robert Gould Shaw and the Massachusetts Fifty-fourth Regiment.[3]

That winter of 1946, CCB's oculist told him that his sight was improving and was actually better than four years earlier. Hence no operation needed. CCB thought otherwise. Reading "those capital letters" had been a mere "tour de force," and he sent his son Charles to confer with the doctor. But Charles brought back the same report. So in the spring CCB, as he had done the previous year, went to Cambridge to join his surviving classmates for commencement. At the morning ceremony, as the representative of the Class of 1879, the oldest class present, he led the alumni procession. In the afternoon, in the alumni march from the Yard into Sever Quadrangle, CCB and classmate Jabish Holmes started off together in the lead. But as they passed Thayer Hall, from between it and University Hall emerged Dr. Alfred Worcester, Class of 1878, who took first place. And another jolt that day: English supplanted Latin in the commencement program.[4]

By 1948 CCB's class had shrunk to six, and lost another at that year's commencement when Jabish Holmes, who had driven CCB to Cambridge, died there of a heart attack. In 1949 CCB's family opposed his going. Later he told his nephew, "I attended in the face of almost universal opposition. Charles thought me a silly old man, but my answer to them all was that I was an addict, and it was too late for me to reform."[5] In 1950 Young Charles spoke still more bluntly: CCB was "too old, too deaf, and too blind to go to Cambridge alone." To which CCB suggested that his son carry him on his back, as Aeneas had his father. Said Charles, "Your antics worry me." So CCB offered what he thought a practical solution: Augustus Hand, a youngster of eighty-one, would accompany him. At the station as Charles put the two on the train, CCB asked: "Do you still think me an ass?" Said Charles, "No comment."[6] Both CCB and Hand missed the morning proceedings, but in the afternoon, as CCB and his classmate Frank Crawford headed the alumni procession, for the final yards entering the quadrangle Dr. Worcester of 1878, as before, emerged from between buildings to take the lead. Worcester, though a class ahead of CCB, was a year younger, only ninety-one, yet needed a young man at his side to support him, whereas CCB and Crawford, however perilously, skipped along unaided. Still, this was the last Harvard commencement CCB attended.[7]

He continued to write Harvard letters, however, becoming increasingly obsessed with obtaining an honorary degree for Frankfurter and one for a woman, never yet granted. For the latter he had a number of candidates but lobbied hardest for Eleanor Roosevelt. In January 1954 he was taken to the New York Harvard Club's annual dinner to hear Harvard's new president, Nathan M. Pusey, and before the evening's speeches, CCB, as the oldest graduate present, was led onto the floor to a hand microphone, through which he delivered a one-sentence blast—"It's a scandal that Harvard still has not given an honorary degree to a woman"—and with a violent gesture of reproval thrust the microphone from him.[8] The younger members of the 484 diners whooped and hollered, the dignitaries on the dais smiled, and the next year the university awarded an honorary degree to a Radcliffe graduate, Helen Keller. An instance, said CCB, of *post hoc*, not *propter hoc*.

Meanwhile, in October 1952, he had undergone an operation on his right eye. From the hospital he dictated a note to Frankfurter: "Your delightful letter was read to me by Charles in the tumbrel in which I was driven to the execution that was as painless as the Guillotine." The next day, again to Frankfurter, he reported, "I'm where I started." Charles explained to family and friends, "The operation itself was perfect," but because of CCB's "hard arteries" and his difficulty in lying still (he had sat up in bed to dictate letters), "the results were not." CCB recited factually to any who asked, "The hemorrhage that followed the operation on the cataract on my right eye blinded that orb for good and all."[9]

In the spring of 1954, an operation on his left eye also failed, leaving him wholly blind, and more than ever dependent on old friends and his family, Charles and Cora, Nancy, Robert's children, his niece and nephews, and their children. Most of his legal and church friends saw him in New York, but every summer Frankfurter would come to Black Point for several days, sit on the porch with CCB, and discuss the world's affairs. Surely such loyalty to an old friend in decline was a most attractive quality.[10] Customarily, in July and August at Black Point, CCB's family gathered round him, and one September, mimicking the prophet Jeremiah, he reproached his nephew Lawrie, "The summer is past, and the harvest is ended, but your long-hoped for visit is not made." As friends died, his focus on his family increased. The intensity of his attention had always been a mixed blessing for those close to him, and his love of family now became, in a grandchild's word, "ferocious." His demands, his bossiness, his urge to criticize and to correct—no doubt strengthened by frustration at being blind and deaf—were at times hard to bear. But out of respect, though one sharp tongue hones another, sparks seldom flew. No one doubted the love was real, and the bad days were few. One good day, he expressed his appreciation for his son Charles by writing a poem he titled

SPOTS!

My beloved son Charles is my joy and my pride.
He's as patient as Job, and a whole lot beside,
But there's one thing in life that he cannot abide,
SPOTS!
If by an ill chance he finds spots on my pants,
Potatoes or what not on my coat or waistcoat,
He loses at once his air serene and cries aloud for
ENERGINE!
Or other cleansing fluid like a veritable Druid.
As for me—I'm almost in a coma
When I think of Oklahoma
And the poor spotted leopard who couldn't change his
SPOTS![11]

In winter, from his New York apartment, CCB kept a hand in city, law firm, church, and bar association affairs. To most of the people he met he appeared cheerful, energetic, and full of wisdom. He was admired as a model of old age, and perhaps he was. At that time few lived into their eighties, and those who continued into their nineties, in good health and still fun to talk to, were revered as demigods of some past era. Among those younger, only a few saw the effort it took. On Stimson's death in 1950, when CCB had been a widower for thirteen years, he warned Mrs. Stimson that even "precious memories" could not ease "the loneliness." He seldom talked of being lonely, except perhaps to his sister-in-law

Grace, for by his code, as he wrote to his nephew Lawrie, "an old fellow, I think, has a right to be gloomy, but not to talk gloomy."[12] Yet even in old age he lost none of his intensity. In the early 1950s Bethuel Webster, president of the bar association, after a chat about its affairs with CCB at 860 Park Avenue, let himself out of the apartment. Then, discovering he had forgotten his umbrella, he let himself back in (the door was seldom locked) and saw CCB crash his cane on a table in a fury of frustration. Similarly, CCB's grandson, a naval officer going overseas, having kissed his grandfather good-bye, let himself back into the apartment and saw the old man sobbing violently. And Phil Taylor, entering the apartment one evening to spend the night with Uncle Charlie, discovered him in the midst of a St. George's vestry meeting. Taylor gave a loud "hello" to identify himself and went directly to the guest room. When the rector and the vestry had gone, he met CCB in the hallway, and CCB asked, "How did I do? Did you hear me?" Taylor was startled by the anxiety and the vanity. How much of the grand old man was charade?[13]

CCB's ties to his law firm continued strong. Every new associate was brought to the apartment for a meeting, and if one became engaged to marry, then he had to return with his betrothed. One of the latter had a job at the Carnegie Endowment for Peace, and she asked CCB if upon marriage she should give it up. "Of course not," he replied. "You can't just sit around the apartment waiting for Richard to come home." She was charmed. She also was impressed by CCB's quickness to urge—and to help—young people to join the bar association, the maritime association, St. George's Church. He was "more than just talk."[14]

Frequently, on a Sunday afternoon, Roscoe Hupper would stop in for tea and bring his young son. CCB and the son would play backgammon while over the boy's head the men talked. On these occasions, CCB often asked gossipy questions about the firm, and the boy saw that these irritated his father. Yet the friendship was firm, and Hupper regularly continued to drop in. Meanwhile, the boy became convinced that CCB sometimes cheated at backgammon, which indeed he did—but not always to win. One day at Black Point, his grandson, with his pieces far behind on the board, announced, "You win. I quit." CCB, in a spasm of rage, shouted, "No Burlingham ever quits," hurled the cup to the floor, ordered his grandson to pick it up, and then, with the game resumed, cheated to lose.[15]

During the winter, when the weather was good, CCB would go twice or thrice a week to the office, accompanied usually by his son Charles. He would dictate his letters, and unaware of how loudly he spoke, he frequently shouted, sending away the stenographers with their ears ringing.

After dictating letters and planning for the next day's batch, he might do some research in the library, sending the younger men (some of them in their seventies) up the ladder to pull a book from the top shelf. Thereafter he would walk, usually accompanied by Charles or some other partner, to the Downtown Club, where he would lunch with friends, one of whom might shepherd him home.[16]

One day at the office, speaking to a newly hired law school graduate in the library, CCB asked aloud in one breath: "Can you write a bully letter? Are you a Democrat?" The first question, though seemingly trivial, goes to the heart of daily law practice. Letters are important, for besides setting agendas and priorities, they can frame the issues of a case, determining how the lawyer and judge will view it. The young man, aware of others in the library listening, softly replied that he hoped he could write a good letter. CCB, plainly dissatisfied with soft hopes, repeated loudly, "Are you a Democrat?" This time, the associate, now slightly peeved at the public examination, loudly said, "Yes." CCB broke into a smile. In a voice that brought everyone in the room to attention, he announced, "Good. You make three: Me, Charles, and you. The rest"—with a wave of dismissal— "are Republicans." Having sparked laughter all around, he shuffled out, keeping a hand to the wall.*[17]

At the bar association, whose officers often arranged for him to be present at meetings, he was treated as a sage. Young lawyers were brought up to him for a few words of wisdom and led away. CCB did not enjoy the role. He took no pleasure in his age, did not like references to it, and preferred to meet people one or two at a time, for a real conversation. He found the Association's large receptions difficult and soon gave them up.[18] Moreover, the Association had changed, and though he was in part responsible, he was beginning to question whether all of the changes were entirely for the better.

In 1945, with the war coming to an end, he had forced his choice for president on the nominating committee. He had been sure that Harrison Tweed was the man to revive an association that during the war had lost members, income, and even, to some extent, its purpose.[19] Tweed, energetic, democratic in thought and manner, and supported generously by his

*The Burlingham firm, last titled Burlingham Underwood, stopped the practice of law and disbanded on 31 August 2002. At the time it had four partners, two associates, and two of counsel. The partners donated all of the firm's historical data to the Harvard Law School Library, along with all of the bound appellate briefs, which went back almost a century.

firm in his charitable work, devoted three years full-time to the job and introduced many changes. Most important, he hired a lawyer to act as executive secretary, to run the building, coordinate the Association's many committees, and publish a new periodic journal, *The Record*. To accommodate members who lived in the suburbs, evening meetings were scheduled for 8 p.m. instead of 8:30 and dinner jackets were no longer worn. Purely social functions designed to draw lawyers into the building were scheduled throughout the winter: smokers, dinners, buffet lunches, plays, and art shows (Tweed painted oils), and membership mounted, from roughly 3,800 in 1944 to 6,100 by 1956.[20]

For the social activities, the wives of members and guests were encouraged to come and, in another break with custom, alcohol and hors d'oeuvres were served. City and state judges began to show up, which before the war had been unusual and even discouraged. Some lawyers liked to be seen with judges and brought pocket cameras so that they could be photographed talking to them. Using a word from Trollope's novels, CCB complained of "tufters," lawyers who were using the Association to climb socially and politically. Though the wider membership seemed good to him in some ways, it was bad in others, particularly as it introduced city and state politics into a professional group which, to be effective, needed to stay clear of them. To the dismay of more than just the older generation, the Association now had examples of "packed" meetings on the qualifications of judges. The relevant committee would bring in its report (the nominee "qualified" or "not") to a meeting of the full Association, and with many otherwise inactive members on hand and voting, the report would be rejected. With the larger membership, district clubhouse politics increasingly invaded the Association, changing what had been a small, like-minded group, sometimes useful as a tool, into a larger, blunter instrument that was more unwieldy and less effective.[21]

The practice of law, too, was changing in ways that distressed CCB and others in the profession. Many deplored what they saw as the gradual substitution of business practices and ethics for traditional legal independence and integrity. Lawyers in large corporate firms increasingly served as directors on the boards of commercial enterprises. CCB called them "green-goods" lawyers, lamenting that they spent more time shuffling dollars in commercial deals than in the practice of law. Concurrently, it became fashionable, in a first step toward advertising one's self or firm, to list all the corporations with which one had a connection. (An example in the decade following CCB's death occurred in the Association's printing of its 25th Annual Benjamin Cardozo Lecture, delivered in March 1968.

The introduction to "The Obligations of the Lawyer to His Profession" lists the speaker as a trustee or director of twenty-two organizations.) By the mid-1970s a profession that long had forbidden advertising, as an unethical form of stirring up litigation, had embraced it.[22]

Lastly, there were signs of the coming surge of egalitarianism that would give "inclusion" and "diversity" top priority in the Association's aims. Increasingly, in the quarter century after CCB's death, the Association's attention turned inward, leading to a quip, variously worded, that the Association was now so keen to achieve "proper diversity" on its committees that it had no time left for improvement of justice throughout the courts. Though exaggerated, the statement had a seed of truth. In the coming years, as CCB in his last decade sometimes worried, the Association seemed to grow complacent and to forget the purpose for which it was founded.[23]

He would not live to see the extent of the coming changes in the profession. But he saw enough to sense their beginnings and to feel that the law and the bar association as he had known them were passing. Even admiralty practice seemed to be dying, given the postwar decline of shipping in New York Harbor. In the early 1950s, partly because of labor troubles and racketeering on the docks, New York was losing its position of leadership to other ports. In a rare day of sourness on the city, CCB advised an associate in his law firm (and a future president of the Maritime Law Association) to get out of admiralty and into some other kind of practice.[24]

Though becoming in his final decade increasingly an observer in most legal and political matters, at St. George's Church CCB continued remarkably active. One reason perhaps was that the church, more easily than the legal profession or the city's political reform groups, found ways to accommodate old age. He had been elected senior warden of St. George's in 1936, and had tried to resign eight years later because the job required "vigor, energy and hard work, which old age cannot give." His plea for release was refused. But soon afterward the vestry shifted regular meetings from the parish house to CCB's apartment, and on Sunday mornings a parishioner who kept a car would pick him up at 860 Park Avenue, take him to church, and sometimes deliver him home. He seldom was accompanied by any member of his family. St. George's was still *his* project.[25]

One church activity for which he had always assumed a personal responsibility was the combined medical and dental clinic, known in the neighborhood simply as "St. George's Clinic." From its founding in 1920, it had expanded its services rapidly, and by 1933 the two clinics annually had about 17,000 calls. During the Depression and the war, however, when the church's income declined, the number of calls also dropped, partly because of improvement under La Guardia in the city hospitals and public health department. In 1942 St. George's, having made a survey, published a report on "Why a Clinic?" It had discovered, perhaps to its own surprise,

> many single self-supporting people as well as families in our Parish who hesitate to accept the free service of the city hospitals, and yet can barely meet the fees of a private doctor. Also there are many health situations closely linked with other problems of so personal a nature that the Church is peculiarly fitted to be of help; for the church alone among modern institutions, is interested in the "whole man"—his body, his mind and his spirit.[26]

Accordingly, St. George's continued its clinic, which charged a moderate fee (often waived), but with reduced hours, fewer staff, and a greater reliance on volunteers. Finally, in 1949, the vestry closed the clinic, chiefly because the number of hospital and dental facilities in the neighborhood had increased, and with the funds released founded an experimental school for three- to five-year-olds which soon proved a success in drawing children and parents to the church.

St. George's rector, throughout the war years, had been Elmore M. McKee, an exceptional leader in parish activities but who probably is best remembered because he was a pacifist. He had never made a secret of his belief, preaching his first sermon on pacifism four weeks after coming to St. George's in 1936, but as war approached, many parishioners wondered how he could continue as rector. CCB put his thoughts on the issue in a letter to Allen Wardwell, a vestryman.

> I was not impressed by Elmore's letter to you. It seemed to me rather muddy. His pacifism, he says, is not a philosophy; it comes from his idea of *relationship* as distinguished from values, which in turn comes from his understanding of the meaning of the Incarnation.
>
> I am no philosopher and need to be taught the meaning of the term. His concrete illustration of the parachutist in his backyard I can understand. He would spare his life for the possibility of a future relationship and would not kill him for the sake of Liberty, an "abstraction." Well, I would spare the fellow unless I thought he was about to kill my wife or child or do some mortal injury to my country.[27]
>
> I suppose these religious pacifists take our Lord's words literally.

I don't. I think He laid down principles. To love one's enemies and resist no evil do not seem to me inconsistent with killing a man who is seeking to kill innocent children, women and men for his own selfish purposes.

But enough of this. I tell Elmore that the pacifists love peace no more than we do, that as we respect his opinion so he should respect ours. He is a true Christian and no fanatic. Your attitude toward him I share.[28]

In St. George's tradition of mutual respect for different views, McKee continued as rector, though the vestry did not allow him to use the church for a meeting of the Episcopal Pacifist Fellowship, a group of which McKee was a vice president. The vestry feared that such a gathering, sure to be reported by newspapers, would suggest to the public that St. George's, its vestry, and parishioners were all pacifists—when the great majority were not. On the other hand, given St. George's tradition of a "free pulpit," McKee could continue to preach as he wished. Even shortly before the Japanese attack on Pearl Harbor, according to a later *Herald Tribune* report, he "opposed such preparatory measures as the establishment of air raid precautions, on the ground that they tended to create a receptive attitude toward war. He argued that we should exert our efforts in the other direction, toward bringing about reconciliation among nations." After Pearl Harbor, McKee offered his resignation to the vestry, but it asked him to stay on.[29]

Though supporting McKee's right to preach pacifism, CCB worked actively for those who believed differently. In these years a custom of St. George's pulpit was that annually, on the second Sunday of January, Reinhold Niebuhr would preach and afterward lunch with the senior warden. Niebuhr, then a professor of ethics and theology at the nondenominational Union Theological Seminary, New York, opposed pacifism, and in November 1940 he and other church activists had founded a journal, *Christianity and Crisis*, its purpose being, in CCB's words, "to express the attitude of the Christian Church toward the war." In asking a friend to help with the cost of "a new little paper of eight pages to be published fortnightly," CCB explained:

The idea we have is to publish four pages of news from Europe, such for instance as a talk by the Archbishop of York, or a report of the state of the Lutheran Church in Germany, etc., which would not be likely to appear in the daily press or in religious papers . . . [W]e expect to send out through the country several thousand to clergymen on the list of the

Federal Council of Churches in order to enlighten them on the issues and tell them what's what. The Pacifists are a very small body, but they make an awful noise and have done a lot of harm with young people. No one who hasn't had a good deal to do with the clergy knows how ignorant they are.[30]

In seeking subscribers, *Christianity and Crisis* described its purpose more formally:

To present the bearing of Christian faith upon the international and so-cial issue of our day. While its columns will welcome pacifist contribu-tions, its own view-point will dissent from Christian pacifism. Rather, it will elaborate the historic Protestant faith which holds that in history men must choose between relative goods, and even insists that only such relative choices are possible. Therefore, it will refute pacifist interpreta-tions of our faith which seek, vainly we believe, to practice an absolute perfection in historic decisions, and thereby are betrayed into submis-sion to tyranny . . . This position compels us to advocate that Christians enlist their resources in defense of democratic civilization, despite its obvious imperfections, against the totalitarian menace which imperils all Christian as well as all humanistic values.[31]

The statement, probably drafted by Niebuhr and worked over by others (including CCB), certainly expressed CCB's views. As he wrote to the Hirsts in England, "The head and front of Xianity and Crisis is Reinhold Niebuhr . . . He is reputed very able. He is too deep for me and his style is *deep* and Germanic." CCB modestly told the Hirsts that he was a "merely nominal" editor of the paper, but Niebuhr evidently thought him more than that, and five years later CCB still edited material for him. Though its circulation was small, initially about 10,000 and never more than 13,000, *Christianity and Crisis* helped many Protestants to sort their beliefs on right and wrong about World War II and the conflicts that followed. (Typical of its species, it was always in need of support, yet survived fifty-two years, closing only in 1993. In those years it opposed anti-Communist "Mc-Carthyism," supported the civil rights movement, and opposed the Viet-nam War.) CCB's part in its founding no doubt was minor. Still, as was his way, when he saw the need, he did more than write a check.[32]

In 1946, when McKee resigned from St. George's, his main reason was fatigue. The parish was big—its Sunday school, for instance, enrolled more than 2,000 children—and exhausting. The vestry, eager to have him stay, offered him a year's leave of absence. He pointed out, however, that he had come to the church at age forty, was now fifty, and the job was growing larger, not smaller. In a year or two, new housing in the neighborhood, mostly the Stuyvesant Town and Peter Cooper Village projects, would bring some 50,000 new residents into the parish. To CCB he confessed: "With steady fatigue has come a decline in zest and the ability to give the steady stimulus needed. The Stuyvesant Town era literally appalls me. It is for a man nearer thirty than fifty, who knows the 'young marrieds' and their children." As CCB knew, the rector in the 1880s, William S. Rainsford, had come to the church in his thirties and had retired after twenty-two years, physically and spiritually worn out. St. George's was an exciting place to work, but it drained its clergy of energy, health, and sometimes even of their calling. CCB admired McKee and regretted his going, but he began a search for a younger man.[33]

The vestry screened a list of more than a hundred candidates and gradually settled on Edward O. Miller, then assistant minister at Christ Church, Cincinnati. Miller, a tall, athletic, intense man in some ways reminiscent of Rainsford, had felt called to the ministry because of an increasing belief that the world's illness needed a solution more profound than legal revisions or treaties. He was an exceptionally good preacher, and he was somewhat familiar with St. George's because, while a divinity student, he had worked for three years as a part-time assistant to McKee. Knowledge of what the post required, however, led him to tell CCB in an interview that he was too young; St. George's needed someone older, wiser. "Nonsense," said CCB. "I am 88 and you are 30. That makes an average of 59. What's so young about that?" And on 1 December 1946, Miller at age thirty-one became rector.[34]

Aware of life expectancy tables, CCB in 1946 must have believed that each year would be his last. Yet the partnership of age and youth, wisdom and energy, continued at St. George's for another thirteen years. One accomplishment that gave both men particular pleasure was their leadership in a ten-year campaign in the diocesan conventions to have women serve on the vestry, and in 1957, with the election of Mrs. Henry Hill Pierce, St. George's became the first church in the New York Episcopal Diocese to elect a woman to its vestry. And in the next three years the parishioners added two more.[35]

A problem of discrimination in a very different form faced the Episcopal church in New York in the spring of 1957. The American evangelist Billy Graham announced a "Crusade" in the city, and St. George's, though an evangelical church, was unsympathetic. In this, it was out of step with the majority of the diocese, and CCB turned to Niebuhr for help:

> I have a very faint recollection—if I can call it that—that you wrote something about Billy Graham a few months ago. If I am right, will you tell me where I can find it . . .
>
> Billy is coming in May, and one vestryman of St. George's, a rather rich banker, has contributed to a fund for Billy. Miller has read to our Vestry passages from a book by Billy, which shows him as an extreme fundamentalist. I think we ought to make plain to the members of our parish why we cannot support Billy in any way. I do not want to get us into open conflict with him, but I wish we could make a moderate statement exclusively for members of our parish—reasons why we cannot back him . . .
>
> Billy's appeal at present is to the rich. They hear that he has reformed drunkards and whoremongers. That is enough for them. Billy's appeal to the churches is chiefly to get from them ushers for the big meetings in Madison Square Garden, etc.
>
> It has got around that Miller is strongly opposed to Billy, and several clergymen have agreed with him, but they do not wish to get into a row with Billy.[36]

Niebuhr's article, "Proposal to Billy Graham," had appeared in the August 1956 issue of *Christian Century*, and in it he had expressed what bothered many people in Graham's message. After stating his admiration for Graham's "modesty and sincerity in the Christian community," Niebuhr proposed that Graham should incorporate into his message that among the "fruits meet for repentance" should be "a whole-souled effort to give the Negro neighbor his full due as a man and brother." Graham, Niebuhr wrote, "is 'enlightened' on the race issue. He does not condone racial prejudice. But neither does he incorporate the demand of love transcending racial boundaries into his evangelistic appeal. He does not suggest that the soul, confronted with the judgment and the forgiveness of Christ, should regard racial prejudice as an element in the 'life of sin' from which the conversion experience redeems."

Why not? Because Graham's form of evangelicalism "relies on an oversimplification of the issues in order to create the 'crisis' which prompts conversion and the acceptance of the Christian faith. The best way of inducing this crisis is to call attention to some moral dereliction of the person, in which some accepted moral norm has been transgressed and the conscience is consequently uneasy." The accepted moral norms are most easily found in the Ten Commandments, which list sins we do as individuals, not as communities. Graham's technique, said Niebuhr, "requires the oversimplification of moral issues and their individualization for the sake of inducing an emotional crisis. Collective sins are therefore not within the range of a revival."[37]

St. George's parishioners had no difficulty in loving the exceptional Negro whom they had known well, Harry T. Burleigh, who had sung in the choir and been an outstanding member of the church for fifty-two years. More complicated were the issues of segregation in New York's public housing, schools, and neighborhoods. Niebuhr's article became CCB's touchstone for a Christian's duty on the most profound moral issue of the final decade of his life. Through him, and through the rector, Niebuhr's ideas passed into the parish and became, however poorly understood or articulated, the majority view of St. George's vestry and parishioners.

As important as any philosophic idea a man may hold is the example he sets to others in daily life. And here, too, CCB, though blind, deaf, and old, was conspicuous in his church. On Sundays, when in the city, he would come to the morning service and sit in "Deaf Man's Corner," the front right-hand pews directly beneath the pulpit. There he usually was joined by a vestryman or, for a number of years, by Morgan Jones, the retired head usher. On communion Sundays, the other deaf parishioners and their families sitting close by watched Jones help CCB up to the communion rail and back into the front pew. It was a contest. Jones believed he gained credit with God if he assisted the old man; CCB gained credit if he could contain his anger over the unwanted "fussing." For CCB, the greatest danger lay in the return to the pew at the step down. At that moment Jones, for extra credit with the Lord, would pluck assiduously at CCB's sleeve, hand, and arm. If CCB could get back into the pew without pushing Jones away, he would sit straight, triumphant. If he had broken down, brushing off Jones in anger and striking at the unwanted hand or arm, he would sit slumped, defeated. In his last years, CCB took to bringing a box of cornflakes to the pew, to provide "sustenance" for the trip to the communion rail and back. By then a more sensitive vestryman, John Hazard, had succeeded Jones, and CCB never lost his temper.[38]

The Sunday "battle" with Jones was visible only to a few. What most of the parishioners saw was described by one in the months after CCB's death.

I never had the privilege of meeting Mr. Burlingham, but in the ten years that I have attended St. George's—and with no idea of who he was—his example of devotion has left an impression upon me that I'll never forget. Certainly his steadfastness has done much toward the stiffening of my spine in many ways.[39]

In Harvard affairs CCB still had one distinction to strive for, that of oldest living graduate, and his friend Joe Hamlen at the *Alumni Bulletin* kept him advised of how those in the lead were dropping. In the spring of 1953, there were eight ahead of him, and by the fall of 1956 only one, who, though a member of the Class of 1889, was 101 to CCB's 98. Then, in 1957, CCB was the oldest. Though he pooh-poohed the distinction, he was pleased.[40]

A St. George's vestryman who was also a graduate of Harvard, in an article on CCB for the college *Bulletin*, expressed the general feeling of the alumni: "Mr. Burlingham is in his ninety-ninth year, and has accomplished more important things in his long life than the attainment of this particular prominence; but it is a matter of satisfaction to the rest of us that our senior graduate is a man who brings luster to Harvard."[41]

On 31 August 1958, he turned 100. Besides a nice letter in the *Times* from Frankfurter, there were the usual editorials and news stories about the city's First Citizen. In April of the following year, an hour's ceremony at the federal courthouse in Foley Square was held to commemorate Learned Hand's fifty years on the bench. CCB felt the event would be too much for him, but that evening he went to a dinner for Hand at the Century Club, where Chief Justice Earl Warren sat on Hand's right and CCB on his left. On CCB's other side was Frankfurter. With animation, CCB poked his hearing aid left, right, and across Hand at Warren. After dinner, a younger lawyer took CCB home. Asked in the car if he'd had a good time, CCB replied, "Yes, but I had hoped to meet some new people."[42]

In the midst of a heat wave on 28 May, while CCB was still at 860 Park Avenue, his kidneys began to fail. Thereafter he was increasingly unhappy and sometimes muddled. For ten days, while he was dying, he made a great deal of noise, groaning, roaring, wheezing, gasping, sighing, calling aloud, giving every indication he was loath to let life go. Yet he had always said that he looked forward to the first thirty minutes after death as life's most interesting.[43]

He died at home on 6 June. As he had requested, he had no funeral or memorial service. His body was cremated and his ashes buried next to his wife and close to his parents and son Robert in the Kensico cemetery. Just before becoming ill, he had dictated to his rector what was probably his last letter, his thoughts on a vestry meeting the night before:

Dear Ed,

Last night I did not hear well except what Harvey [Pike] said. I do not think a church should ask a foundation for contributions. If Protestants do it, Catholics will. If a church like ours renders public service such as combating Juvenile Delinquency in Stuyvesant Square such a request might be proper, but to ask a foundation to help make up a church deficit seems to me highly improper.

I heard nothing last night of wiping out our deficit. Is that not our immediate duty?

I need not tell you that I should be ashamed if we gave up any of our activities.

Ever thine,
C.C.B.[44]

EPILOGUE

An American Life

IN THE YEARS after CCB's death, those who recalled him spoke of him mostly as he had been in his last ten years—a fragile sage, with freakishly bushy white eyebrows, nearly wholly deaf and later wholly blind. Yet from his eyrie on the thirteenth floor of 860 Park Avenue, peering into the present and future, he often saw more than most and delighted in talking over his views with any who sought them. His experience was vast, his memory good, and he had known, and still knew, many important and interesting men and women. An English friend, the journalist Molly Hamilton, described him in the 1940s as being one of "the most completely European Americans I know." If it was natural for an Englishwoman to claim his virtues as European, his American friends saw those same virtues as peculiarly American.[1]

He was, after all, only one generation removed from the frontier. His father, like the fathers of many of his contemporaries, was a Baptist preacher, and if the family never knew poverty, it also never knew wealth. For example, CCB's friend and fellow New Yorker Grenville Clark, as a baby in 1882 was carried to Grace Church for baptism in a carriage, with a family coachman up front and a footman on the box behind. He wore a long white christening gown, and at the family buffet of rich, heavy food that followed he was presented by his godfather with a large silver cup. In CCB's background, in his boyhood, and in the life that he fashioned for himself, there was nothing so grand. He did not start in rags, but neither did he end in riches. Yet in America's essentially classless society he was able to rise and make of himself what he wanted.[2]

He also, to American eyes, seemed very American in his continual turning to what Tocqueville called "Public Associations." Tocqueville has much to say about the American habit of citizens coming together in voluntary political or civil associations to solve a problem: "Every new want instantly revives the notion. The art of association then becomes . . . the mother of action, studied and applied by all." In this art CCB was a master.[3]

He made no claim to be a scholar or an intellectual, and he shared the American prejudice against ideology and abstract ideas. As Tocqueville observes, "The spirit of the Americans is averse to general ideas; and it does not seek theoretical discoveries." CCB in his reform work was usually pragmatic, willing to make deals and to compromise. When he chose to stand firm, he typically saw in the issue some clear moral principle that overrode convenience.[4]

In one respect, he may have seemed to differ from most Americans. Tocqueville remarks on the difficulty of achieving distinction in a society where all the usual distinctions—birth, condition, education, profession—are held in disregard. In such democratic societies, "the distinction originating in wealth is increased . . . When all the members of a community are independent of or indifferent to each other, the co-operation of each of them can only be obtained by paying for it: this infinitely multiplies the purposes to which wealth may be applied, and increases its value."[5]

CCB, however, never sought wealth beyond what was necessary to sustain his moderate tastes and habits. When he felt he had enough, he stopped amassing more, and he did not consider wealth in itself a distinction. And while this may seem contrary to American habits, it is not so rare as often stated. Any honest lawyer who becomes a federal judge, for example, knows that he is trading the possibility of wealth in favor of an important job to be done. What mattered to CCB about wealth was not its quantity but how it was used. And contrary to Tocqueville's statement, he never used wealth to buy cooperation. He won that in other ways.

In this attitude, his classical education supported him. The Greeks had considered that virtue, or *areté*, lay in an ability to put one's self to use, especially in the service of the city or state. The *areté* of the body lies in its strength and health; of the mind, in its cleverness and insight. In the first, CCB thought himself weak, but in the second, as he must have realized, he was remarkably strong. He had, as a grandson said, "a towering intelligence, and an uncanny understanding of what makes people tick . . . [which] in the end, is so much *more* valuable." After CCB's death, a contemporary said of him, with a mixture of relief and appreciation, "He was always trying to make me do what I didn't want to do."[6] And in doing so he treated all alike. Roosevelt, La Guardia, Frankfurter, all might have said the same, and though he occasionally lost a friend because of his nagging, he managed to keep most of them, even men and women of vast egos and difficult temperaments. He had a gift for friendship.

Finally, he was always optimistic in his view of life, deeds, and continual attempts at reform, a quality Lord Bryce, in writing of the United States as it was in the early years of CCB's generation, described as peculiarly American:

> They are a hopeful people . . . And this sanguine temper makes them tolerant of evils which they regard as transitory, removable as soon as time can be found to root them up. They have unbounded faith in what they call the People and in a democratic system of government . . . And if you ask an intelligent citizen why he so holds, he will answer that truth and justice are sure to make their way into the minds and consciences of the majority. This is deemed an axiom, and the more readily so deemed, because truth is identified with common sense, the quality which the average citizen is most confidently proud of possessing.[7]

Could any man or woman today, acting like CCB, as a private citizen without public office, exert a similar influence for good on a community as large and varied as New York? Possibly. He in his optimism would think so. Though he in his self-made role relied largely on print, newspapers, journals, and church bulletins to reach the community, there are other options. He lived into the era of radio and to a small extent used it. Television, with its sound bites, seems quite unsuited to his type of reasoned discourse, but the Internet seems ideal for it. Not only can the message be held in abeyance until convenient to summon it up, but once on the screen it can be held there, and it can be printed out for later consideration. Tomorrow's replica of CCB may well be a blogger, posting his personal, frequently updated Web pages (blogs) on Web sites set up by others or even on one of his own.[8]

Moreover, the sources of CCB's influence are just as available now and just as powerful as in his era. A lawyer who had seen much of CCB at bar association affairs remarked of him in a tone of disapproval, "He was very opinionated." But then added with a smile, "It didn't matter." It didn't matter because CCB was always aboveboard. Though he sometimes made outrageous statements, they weren't malicious, and he accepted reproof. He might be quick with his judgmental "Nonsense," but he was always willing to listen. In any public statement he usually was exceptionally well prepared in his thoughts and presentation, and the well-known fact that he wanted nothing for himself moved others to listen. Once entered into a conversation or debate he became a dangerous opponent, for he then asked men and women to do their best, not their best in self-interest but for the community, their moral best. Many people found this moral tone and re-quest disturbing, but many also, however reluctantly, responded to it.[9]

That strong moral tone was always present in what Burlingham said and did, and it was a source of strength. He could walk into Tammany Hall and talk with corrupt officials and by appealing to their better selves (or offering them a sensible compromise) sometimes persuade them to do what was right. That perhaps was his most attractive quality: he believed that in every group, regardless of ethnic, religious, political, or cultural background, there were men and women of goodwill, waiting to be found and motivated. The publisher of *The Nation*, the first to name CCB as New York's First Citizen, observed, "Isn't it wicked that when there are Americans of this admirable type we get so damnably few of them into our public life?"[10]

APPENDIX:

The Burlingham Children and Anna Freud

NOTES

A SHORT BIBLIOGRAPHY

ACKNOWLEDGMENTS

INDEX

APPENDIX

The Burlingham Children and Anna Freud

The later lives of Dorothy Burlingham's four children raise questions about Anna Freud and her practice that her biographers, in varying degree, seem reluctant to consider. When Anna Freud wrote her *Introduction to the Technique of Child Analysis*, for example, she had six American children in analysis, which made up two-thirds of the cases on which she based her recommendations (see Elisabeth Young-Bruehl, *Anna Freud: A Biography*, 187). Today, most psychoanalysts likely would agree that the sample is too small to support the theories drawn.

Four of the Americans were the Burlingham children and of these the only one who in youth became what most laymen would call "well adjusted" was the youngest, Michael, who rejected the technique of analysis and its practitioner. His nearest sister in age, Katrina, who likewise showed opposition to it (though not so strongly), eventually also was able to develop a relatively happy, long life. But neither of the two eldest, Bob and Mabbie, the two longest in analysis with Anna Freud, were so fortunate, although their shorter lives were in many ways rich and full. Their psychological problems, of course, may have been vastly more complicated and difficult, and perhaps only because of Anna Freud's help did they survive into middle age, yet when an analyst adds to the role of doctor that of surrogate parent, as did Anna Freud, to most laymen's eyes she or he becomes peculiarly responsible for the patient/child. With Bob and Mabbie, Anna Freud, some people would say, failed. Others, going further, would say she interfered in their lives to their disadvantage. And for these people her alleged failure or interference calls into question the validity of her work.

The novelist and literary critic George Steiner, in reviewing Young-Bruehl's biography of Anna Freud, raised questions that she seems reluctant to pose: "Deep ethical and social questions arise from the very idea of child-analysis, from the violations of privacy, from the stage-managing of incipient singularities and possible fertile tensions which analysis inevitably comports. Imagine a Lewis Carroll, a Proust, a Nabokov being made naked and 'more normally functional' by child-analysis. But imagine also, the possible waste of the unknown in the unknown. One cries out: 'By what right?'" (*Sunday Times*, London, *Books*, 11 June 1989, 1).

Among some of CCB's descendants, emotions over what happened to Bob and Mabbie still run strong. The Freuds, father and daughter, are seen as wrongfully coming between wife and husband in at least three cases. The first, described in Chapter 15, concerns the marriage of Robert and Dorothy. The second and the third, both outside the scope of this biography, concern the marriages of Bob (the eldest child) to Mossik Sorenson and of Mabbie (the elder daughter) to Simon Schmiderer. In each case the spouse as well as the children believed that Anna Freud was partially responsible for the breakdown or difficulties of the marriage. She also is blamed for keeping Bob, Mabbie, and to some extent Katrina in a state of dependency—to herself and to psychoanalysis. She did not show them the way to adult independence.

Dorothy Tiffany Burlingham, too, is held responsible for injury to the family, for putting her own self-fulfillment ahead of the good of her children. Her husband, Robert, suffering from a manic-depressive illness, posed problems for her that she could not handle, and for her response to those problems—flight—her descendants are inclined to be forgiving. Also, they are aware that Dorothy, as the motherless child of an unsympathetic father, undoubtedly carried some scars and fears into her adult life, and for these, too, the family is inclined to be forgiving. But they are far less sympathetic to her treatment of her children. Still, she is judged less harshly than Anna Freud because she was the latter's student and deferred to the older, better-educated woman.

Even outside the family the saga resonates. A Californian, Robert Katz, wrote a three-act play on it, *In the Best Interest of Anna Freud*, in which the characters, besides the two Freuds, are Robert, Dorothy, Mabbie, and CCB. The second act takes place in CCB's law office, with him as the voice of common sense. The play, which had several performances at Berkeley in the spring of 1993, was Katz's revenge for a child custody decision that deprived him of his son, and Katz was harsh in his condemnation of the Freuds (review in *The Oakland Tribune*, 21 March 1993).

For their part, two biographers of Anna Freud, Young-Bruehl and Robert Coles (*Anna Freud: The Dream of Psychoanalysis*), write as if nothing serious happened—Young-Bruehl being the more nuanced in her views. Coles simply ignores the fate of Robert, Bob, and Mabbie Burlingham, and discusses Anna Freud's work (and Dorothy's) without any Burlingham family context. It may be fair for Coles to leave aside Robert's suicide, for Robert was never a patient of Anna Freud, and Dorothy had left Robert five years before meeting the Freuds in Vienna, but the Burlingham children are a different case. Bob and Mabbie entered Anna Freud's care in their childhood, returned to her as adults, and both were in her care at the time of their deaths. Yet for Coles, their fates raise no questions. They do not exist, even as names.

Young-Bruehl begins in much the same way. In her "Acknowledgments and Notes on Sources," she lists many doctors, child psychologists, and families whom she consulted, but of Burlingham family members and spouses, she interviewed only Katrina. She did not talk to Dorothy's son Michael, to Bob's first wife, Mossik, or to Mabbie's husband, Simon Schmiderer. For her, too, the patients are unimportant. Theory is all. In discussing Anna Freud, however, she well displays the ambiguity in Anna's position as doctor and surrogate parent to the children and mentor to Dorothy. But then, she skims by the conflict of interest and ambiguity as merely an immaturity of the science and its practice (and abjured by practitioners today). Though she devotes considerable space to discussing Mabbie's problems as an adult (420–22), she does not reach Steiner's question of "By what right?" and does not discuss the effect of Anna Freud's analysis on the four Burlingham children. She does not question Dorothy's right to self-fulfillment and exclusive custody of the children, and dismisses Robert out of hand as "quite opposed to psychoanalysis" (132)—despite his recourse to Dr. Amsden. She also does not consider the possibility that Robert's problems might have eased had he been allowed to play a greater role in his family's life. As for CCB, besides having his middle name misspelled and Black Point located on Long Island, he is described as wanting "to draw the children away from Dorothy, from psychoanalysis, and from the Jewish Freuds" (132). This seems unfair.

Michael John Burlingham, in *The Last Tiffany* (1989), has written a summary of how events were viewed thirty years after CCB's death by many in the Burlingham family:

> The deaths of Bob and Mabbie severely strained Dorothy's relationships with some of her grandchildren in the last decade of her life. Amidst the shambles, Bob's and Mabbie's children particularly found it hard to see Dorothy and Anna Freud in a positive light. When the turbulence subsided, what remained was a nagging image: that instead of, or perhaps in addition to, having received a golden key, Bob and Mabbie had been loaded with an enormously heavy cross and bear it they did, to the very altar of psychoanalysis. There remains the ironic conclusion that psychoanalysis had been foisted upon them unnecessarily, and when dependent upon it, had not helped them. Then, when they had really needed help, Freudian ideology had discouraged them from seeking it, for example, in the realm of pharmacology.

This account may place too much responsibility on Anna Freud, though it is undeniable that she offered treatment to children (and to these children grown to adults) at the same time that she became personally and professionally involved with their mother. Yet Bob and Mabbie had in their Lawrence family ancestry a genetic predisposition to severe depression; they had a father who was severely mentally ill and could function only intermittently; they had a mother who had suffered as a child from a notoriously self-centered father, and who, finally given a chance to develop a life of her own, put that interest ahead of her husband and even of her children. Given these circumstances in the 1930s, when so little was known about manic depression, possibly not even the best psychiatric treatment could have kept the patients in a state of health.

The saga of these two families, Burlingham and Freud, so unhappily entwined, is inherently dramatic, and what balance to strike between the competing interests and actions of the players is the author's choice. The story, like a Greek myth, lends itself to interpretation: events and persons are fixed, but the dramatist (or reader), by emphasis, can distribute rewards and penalties, praise and blame, as he or she wishes. The role of one player, however, should not be misconstrued. Throughout four decades of turmoil, until his death in 1959, CCB was the voice of reason, sympathy, and disinterest. His restraint in action and in tone, considering his emotional intensity and the influence he had to wield, was remarkable.

NOTES

In most cases, full titles for the works cited are given in the Bibliography.

In addition to the abbreviations used for manuscript collections, explained in the first section of the Bibliography, others frequently used for individuals are:

For the BURLINGHAM family

CCB: Charles Culp Burlingham
LLB: Louisa Lawrence Burlingham, his wife
AHB: Aaron Hale Burlingham, his father
ESB: Emma Starr Burlingham, his mother
ASB: Albert Starr Burlingham, his brother
CB: Charles Burlingham, his elder son
CB Jr.: Charles Burlingham Jr., his grandson
Nancy: Anne Hoe Burlingham, his daughter
RB: Robert Burlingham, his younger son
DTB: Dorothy Tiffany Burlingham, RB's wife
RTE: Rosamond Taylor Edmondson, CCB's niece
LHT: Lawrence Hoe Taylor, CCB's nephew
PLT: Philip Longley Taylor, CCB's nephew
KBV: Katrina Burlingham Valenstein, CCB's granddaughter

For FRIENDS and ACQUAINTANCES

GC: Grenville Clark
SCC: Samuel C. Coleman
CPC: Charles P. Curtis
TED: Thomas E. Dewey
FF: Felix Frankfurter
MAH: Mary Agnes Hamilton
ANH: Augustus Noble Hand
LH: Learned Hand
FWH: Francis Wrigley Hirst
HH: Helena Hirst
ACH: Annie Corbin Hoe (later Mrs. Charles Platt)

CEH: Charles Evans Hughes
RMH: Richard March Hoe
SMI: Stanley M. Isaacs
CRL: Carlotta Russell Lowell
FHL: Fiorello H. La Guardia
JSL: Josephine Shaw Lowell
FDM: Frank D. MacKinnon
SKR: Samuel Kerkham Ratcliffe
FDR: Franklin D. Roosevelt
TR: Theodore Roosevelt
GWR: Geoffrey W. Russell
HLS: Henry L. Stimson
SS: Samuel Seabury
HWT: Henry Waters Taft
WHT: William Howard Taft
TDT: Thomas D. Thacher
VVV: Van Vechten Veeder
PW: Paul Windels
PW Jr.: Paul Windels Jr.

For INSTITUTIONS and INSTITUTIONAL JOURNALS

ABCNY: Association of the Bar of the City of New York
DAB: *Dictionary of American Biography*
HAB: *Harvard Alumni Bulletin*
ST. GCB: *St. George's Church Bulletin*

Prologue: New York's First Citizen

Unless otherwise stated, throughout the Notes all communications between people are letters, and all newspapers are New York City papers.

Notes to many of the generalized statements about the 1933 Fusion campaign are in Chapter 16, where the statements are more detailed.

1. CCB-HLS, 1:10, CCB to Charles H. Strong (secretary of ABCNY), 21 Jan. 1932: "I like to butt in, but I don't like to be known to do so." See also ibid., CCB to John McKim Minton Jr., 10 Feb. 1932.

2. "Wisest." Mann, *La Guardia Comes to Power* (1965), 82, quoting Richard Welling letter, 22 July 1933, to Ben Howe, director of organization of the newly formed City Party, later called the City Fusion Party. For its formation, see Garrett (1961), 96–97.

3. "Steadies." CCB-HLS, 4:11, CCB to FF, 8 Nov. 1933.

4. FDR-FDRL, PPF, 1169, CCB file, CCB to FDR, 25 Oct. 1933. He sent it to FDR's secretary, Marvin H. McIntyre, "the *via directa*," in CCB's phrase, to the president. Other documents in the file show that FDR acted on the idea at once, and had cleared it with the State Department by 28 October, ten days before the election.

5. *Times*, 26 Jan. 1934, 15:5.

6. *World-Telegram*, 4 Nov. 1933, 14:1. See Welling (1942), 85–86, and n. 18 below.

7. CCB-HLS, 6:2, LH to CCB, 8 Nov. 1933.

8. Ibid., CCB to LH, 11 Nov. 1933.

9. Ibid., 6:1, CCB to Emory Buckner, 15 Aug. 1933.

10. Ibid., CCB to F. Quattrone, 15 Aug. 1933.

11. Ibid., 4:11, CCB to FF, 29 Nov. 1933.

12. "Hat." Heckscher (1978), 160. "Scolding." Garrett (1961), 127.

13. E.g. and famously, Bryce (1891), 1:608: "There is no denying that the government of cities is the one conspicuous failure of the United States."

14. GM interview with Brownell, 5 Aug. 1992, and Brownell to GM, 9 Sept. 1992. See also Greenbaum (1967), 116–17: "To me, Charles C. Burlingham embodied the highest values in our profession." Also SMI-COH, 27.

15. E.g., Kessner (1989), 257. "Patrician," 291. "Caste mark." 446–49.

16. *The Nation* 137:3556 (30 Aug. 1933): 231.

17. Other journals. E.g., *United States Law Review* LXVII: 9 (Sept. 1933): 484, quoting Villard at length; and again more briefly, LXX:2 (Feb. 1936): 60. CCB-HLS, 13:13, CCB to the editors of the *Times*, 5 Sept. 1938.

18. CCB-HLS, 4:4, CCB to Abraham Flexner, 5 Sept. 1948.

PART ONE: AS THE TWIG IS BENT . . .

1. A Boy's View of the Civil War

Chief sources for this chapter, other than the Burlingham collections, are: Whitney R. Cross, *The Burned-Over District: The Social and Intellectual History of Enthusiastic Religion in Western New York, 1800–1850* (New York: Harper Torchbook, 1965); Iver Bernstein, *The New York City Draft Riots: Their Significance for American Society and Politics in the Age of the Civil War* (New York: Oxford University Press, 1990); Timothy J. Reese, *Sykes' Regular Infantry Division, 1861–1864: A History of Regular United States Infantry Operations in the Civil War's Eastern Theater* (Jefferson, N.C.: McFarland, 1990); and James McCague, *The Second Rebellion: The Story of the New York City Draft Riots of 1863* (New York: Dial Press, 1968); information on AHB in Special Collections Division, Case Library, Colgate University; and clippings in an album about AHB preserved in a trunk owned by CCB's eldest great-grandchild, Timothy F. Schmiderer, and denoted throughout as CCB-TFS.

1. "Born cheap." E.g., CRB&M, Belmont Collection, CCB to Eleanor Belmont, 9 June 1950; and *The New Yorker*, "Nonagenarian," 27 Sept. 1952. The church was at 147 West Twenty-fifth St.; the house, at 221 West Twenty-seventh St.; *New York City Directory*, 1863. CCB in old age frequently confused the streets. In Plainfield. CCB-HLS, 20:1, "II—Childhood," 2. His mother's elder sister Mary Starr was married to Dr. Charles H. Stillman. CCB-HLS, 1:18, CCB to Van Wyck Brooks, 14 Dec. 1951, describing his uncle's home. See also BUL, CCB to "Anita," 18 June 1958.

2. CCB-HLS, 20:3, CCB to SCC, 24 Feb. 1959; also ibid., 3:2, CCB to Gherardi Davis, 7 June 1933; also ibid., 9:1, CCB to FWH, 9 June 1933. The *Columbia Alumni News*, 9 June 1933, reports him "a native of Plainfield, N.J."

3. Name. CCB-HLS, 20-3, CCB to SCC, 24 Feb. 1959. See also CCB-TFS, CCB to ESB, 13 Jan. 1878, describing a call on a Mrs. Culp, a friend of the family; and CCB to AHB, 8 Jan. 1878.

4. "Weak man." CCB-HLS, 20:3, CCB to SCC, 24 Feb. 1959. "Axe work." CCB-HLS, 2:1, Benjamin Burlingham autobiography.

5. CCB-HLS, 20:9, AHB autobiography (ed. CCB). In another account, written by CCB 15 July 1943 and sent to Colgate University for its records of AHB, CCB stated: "When Aaron was ten, his father turned him over to his elder brothers for whom he had to work until he was 21." Special Collections Department, Case Library, Colgate University.

6. Cross (1965), 89–92.

7. Definition. Ibid., 3–4. Credulity. Ibid., 80, 287, 304. Alertness. Ibid., 103.

8. CCB-HLS, 20:9, AHB autobiography.

9. Ibid.

10. On Hamilton and Madison University. Archivist, Special Collections Department, Case Library, Colgate University, to GM, 3 Aug. 1995.

11. CCB-HLS, 20:9, AHB autobiography.

12. Ibid. See also CCB-TFS, Scrapbook, account of AHB, clipping from *The Gospel Age* 1:9 (June 1887). Family history. CCB-HLS, 20:9, from CCB's appendix to AHB autobiography: CCB's parents married on 11 Nov. 1851; his elder brother, Albert, was born in Boston, 15 Apr. 1854. On Emma Burlingham (born 7 Oct. 1829): very few of her letters survive, indicating perhaps that few were written. In one to Albert, CCB-TFS, 17 May, with year unspecified but whose contents imply he was an adult, her style suggests a limited education. Though her thought is expressed clearly, her writing is ungrammatical, shy of capital letters, with full stops used sparingly and commas not at all. For birth dates of her siblings, see BUL, CCB to "Anita," 18 June 1958.

13. CCB-TFS, Scrapbook, 71. The article, unsigned and clipped from an unspecified paper, runs fifteen inches and presumably was cut from a local Pike or Wyoming County news or church paper. And another similar and to the same effect.

14. CCB-HLS, 3:15: typed sermon, "The Law and Measurement of Christian Growth." According to a schedule on the title page, delivered at Second Baptist Church, St. Louis, Missouri, 8 Oct. 1876; Broad Street Baptist Church, Elizabeth, New Jersey, 3 Dec. 1876; First Baptist Church, Paterson, New Jersey, 15 Apr. 1877; and Gethsemane Church, Brooklyn, 19 May 1878. The sermon's preacher is nowhere named, but churches and dates fit AHB's movements, and the location of its preservation suggests he is the preacher.

15. CCB-TFS, Scrapbook, 66–67, article clipped from an unidentified newspaper recounting at length a speech delivered by AHB to an audience in an unspecified First Baptist Church.

16. CCB-TFS, Scrapbook, on AHB, clipping from *The Gospel Age* 1:9 (June 1887): "He has a peculiarly sensitive nature, and while he is one of the most genial and sympathetic of men, he is especially hostile to anything ungenerous or mean."

17. Bernstein (1990), 18–24; Strong (1914), 3:334–43; *Times*, 14 and 15 July 1863, 1. For a passionate denunciation of the rioters, see Carl Sandburg, *Abraham Lincoln: The War Years* (New York: Harcourt, 1939), 2:361–67. For a display of contemporary Yankee Protestant prejudice against Irish Catholic immigrants, failing to recognize the courage of the city's Irish-born police and firemen, see Strong (1914), 3:342–43.

18. Bernstein (1990), 18, 56. Reese (1990), 285–86, quoting the report of Colonel Robert Nugent, from the Army's Official Records: "There is no doubt that most, if not all, of the Democratic politicians are at the bottom of the riot, and that the rioters themselves include not only the thieves and gamblers that infest this metropolis, but nearly everyone of the vast Democratic majority . . . I would advise the proclamation of martial law, and the presence of an adequate force here, before any steps are taken to enforce the draft." Nugent, a former colonel of the Irish Sixty-ninth Regiment of New York, had been appointed to command the federal troops detailed to the city.

19. Bernstein (1990), 21, 27. Cook (1974), 77. See McCague (1968) for a narrative account with considerable detail. Note: In keeping with the conventions of the times, "Negro" is used in place of African American throughout the text.

20. Reese (1990), 279–81, gives an account of this battle as well as reproducing an illustration of it from *Leslie's Illustrated*, 1 Aug. 1863.

21. The dead. Bernstein (1990), 5, 288 n. 8; Cook (1974), 194, 217; and McCague, (1968), 178–79. Reese (1990), 284. Five regiments. Bernstein (1990), 3; Strong (1914), 3: 340–41; and McCague (1968), 173. Most estimates hover around 125 dead.

22. CCB on the Draft Riots, with year of recall (if not a dated letter) in parentheses. CCB-HLS, 17:1, CCB to SS, 24 May 1940; ibid., 14:7, CCB to SKR, 4 Mar. 1946; CCB-COH, 1; CCB-HLS, 20:1, "II—Childhood," 3; and CCB-HLS, 20:3, CCB to SCC, 24 Feb. 1959.

23. CCB-HLS, 20:1, "II—Childhood," 4.

24. Poe, *Broadway Journal* 1:1 (4 Jan. 1845).

25. Werner, *Barnum* (1923), 43, 50, 64; and *The 1866 Guide to New York City*, a reprint of *Miller's New York as It Is* (New York: Schocken, 1975), which reproduces an advertisement for the museum, with admission fees; another may be seen at *Times*, 21 Apr. 1865, 7:5. The museum burned.

26. CCB-HLS, 20:1, "II—Childhood," 3. Werner, *Barnum* (1923), 291.

27. Werner, *Barnum* (1923), 292, 294.

28. CCB-HLS, 15:6, CCB to SKR, 14 Mar. 1952; ibid., 20:1, "II—Childhood," 3; ibid., 20:3, CCB to SCC, 24 Feb. 1959. On AHB as "a strong Union man" and his work for U.S. Sanitary Commission, CCB to Colgate University Archives, 15 July 1943.

29. Strong (1914), 3: 583.

30. David B. Chesebrough, *Phillips Brooks: Pulpit Eloquence* (Westport, Conn.: Greenwood, 2001), the sermon complete, 125–37.

31. *Times*, 25 Apr. 1865, 1:3; Clark (1890), 134–37; see also Sandburg, *Abraham Lincoln*, 3:395–400.

32. GM interview with CB Jr., 14 July 1995.

33. Ibid.

34. Clark (1890), 136–37, the weather was "bright and beautiful"; *Times*, 26 Apr. 1865, 1:1: Spectators stood "in a dense human hedge fifteen feet deep along the curb stones."

35. GM interview with PW Jr., 8 June 1995.

36. CCB and the Shaw family, see Chapters 5 and 7.

37. From the fourth verse of "The Battle Hymn of the Republic," by Julia Ward Howe, 1862. On the hymn's meaning and significance, see Wilson (1994), 91–96.

2. A Spirit Open to Stimulus

A chief source for this chapter, other than the Burlingham collections, is Neola McCorkle Koechig, *The Story of Second Baptist Church of Greater St. Louis* (St. Louis: privately printed, 1982). Also WPA (Works Projects Administration), *A Maritime History of New York* (Garden City, N.Y.: Doubleday, 1941), hereafter cited as WPA-Maritime. On Colonel R. M. Hoe, his company, and Brightside: Frank E. Comparato, *Chronicles of Genius and Folly: R. Hoe & Company and the Printing Press as a Service to Democracy* (Culver City, Calif.: Labyrinthos, 1979); J. Henry Harper, *The House of Harper: A Century of Publishing in Franklin Square* (New York: Harper, 1912); *Hoe Family and Collateral Lines of Mead-Lawrence-Harper*, ed.

Alexander Dubin (New York: New York Genealogical Society, 1940); and Michael John Burlingham, "Richard M. Hoe's Brightside and the Development of Hunts Point," *Westchester Historian* 69:4 (Fall 1993): 73–80.

1. CCB-HLS, 20:1, "II—Childhood," 3; also ibid., 20:3, CCB to SCC, 24 Feb. 1959; and Michael Burlingham Collection, CCB to his great-grandson Robert Burlingham, 14 June 1955. Probably AHB negotiated the family's fare with the line. But almost surely it was less than fifty dollars. In the 1880s, on a steamship, typical fares were: first-class passengers, sixty dollars; steerage, twenty dollars for adults, ten dollars for children, three dollars for infants. See WPA-Maritime (1941), 205–6.

2. WPA-Maritime (1941), 142–48. Returning, against the wind, took forty-four days.

3. CCB-HLS, 20:2, "A Lawyer," 2, describing the start of his admiralty practice: "Although I had crossed the Atlantic twice in sailing vessels, I had no interest in the sea or ships."

4. Ibid., 20:1, "II—Childhood," 5, besides Spurgeon names the English Baptist Hugh Stowell Brown; also ibid., 20:3, CCB to SCC, 24 Feb. 1959. Spurgeon's collected sermons, titled *The Tabernacle Pulpit*, ran to fifty or more volumes.

5. Ibid., 20:1, "II—Childhood," 5; also ibid., 20:9, CCB appendix to AHB autobiography, 1. The donkey. Michael Burlingham Collection, CCB to great-grandson Robert Burlingham, 14 June 1955.

6. AHB revisited the chapel in September 1892 and wrote an article about it, giving a bit of its history and naming some of its ministers; in CCB-TFS, Scrapbook, 86, clipping from unidentified journal. CCB-HLS, 20:1, "II—Childhood," 5.

7. CCB-HLS, 20:1; ibid., 20:3, CCB to SCC, 24 Feb. 1959. The journalist, "Mons. Blum," lived "near the Champs Élysées and Rond Point." Lions. Ibid., 20:9, CCB appendix to AHB autobiography, 1.

8. CCB-HLS 20:9; CCB appendix to AHB autobiography, 1–2. When not a diplomat, Bigelow (1817–1911) was the owner and editor, with William Cullen Bryant, of the *New York Post*. He also had an important role in creating the New York Public Library. His sons were John and Poultney.

9. Jeanne d'Arc. Ibid., 3. Sightseeing with parents. CCB-DFT, CCB to LHT, 21 Dec. 1950.

10. Tuileries. CCB-HLS, 20:9, 2; ibid., 20:1, "II—Childhood," 7.

11. Pinkney (1958), 104. For CCB's fights for and against Moses, see Chapters 17 and 20.

12. CCB-HLS, 20:9, CCB appendix to AHB autobiography, 2; also ibid., 20:1, "II—Childhood," 6.

13. CCB-HLS, 20:1, "II—Childhood," 7. ST. GCB 9:10 (5 Mar. 1950): 2.

14. CCB-HLS, 20:1, "II—Childhood," 7; ibid., 20:3, CCB to SCC, 24 Feb. 1959.

15. Osgood Pierce. CCB-HLS, 20:9, AHB autobiography, 11. Also AHB autobiographical sketch, Special Collections Department, Case Library, Colgate University, 2–3; and Koechig (1982), 23–27.

16. *The Examiner.* CCB biography of AHB in letter to Colgate University Archives, 15 July 1943; also CCB-HLS, 20:1, "II—Childhood," 5. AHB "called" 2 Nov. 1866. CCB-HLS, 20:9, Second Baptist Church to CCB, 31 Dec. 1952. "Cracker Castle." Ibid., CCB appendix to AHB autobiography; also ibid., 20:1, "III—Education," 7.

17. CCB-HLS, 20:3, CCB to SCC, 24 Feb. 1959.

18. Koechig (1982), 18–22.

19. Ibid. Also CCB-TFS, article on AHB, *The Gospel Age* 1:9 (June 1887).

20. CCB-HLS, 20:1, "III—Education"; ibid., 16:5, CCB to GWR, 2 Apr. 1947; and CCB-DFT, CCB to LHT, 21 Dec. 1950.

21. Visits East. CCB-HLS, 20:2, "The first time I ever say my Louie . . . ," 3; and ibid. 20:1, "III—Education," 9. Church affairs. CCB-TFS, ESB to ASB, 17 May (year unspecified). See also CCB-TFS, CCB to ESB, 10 Feb. 1878, on the sinfulness of working on Sunday; and CCB-HLS, 20:2, "Where and How we lived," on her being "a strict Sabbatarian."

22. According to Washington University's registrar to CCB, 12 May 1941, in CCB-HLS, 20:1, he attended the preparatory academy, 1870–74, and the college, 1874–76. CCB is nowhere clear on which schools he attended previous to the academy. See ibid., 20:1, "III—Education," 7. Recorded memory begins with the academy in 1870.

23. Obit of ASB. *Times*, 18 Oct. 1934, 23:3. Baptism on 25 Feb. 1872. CCB-HLS, 20:9, Second Baptist Church to CCB, 31 Dec. 1952. "Nice man." CB to CB Jr., GM interview with CB Jr., 14 July 1995.

24. Pony. Michael Burlingham Collection, CCB letter to great-grandson Robert Burlingham, 14 June 1955.

25. Guignols. CCB-HLS, 20:9, CCB appendix to AHB autobiography, and ibid. 20:1, "II—Childhood," 6. Smalley (1833–1916), often called "the dean of American correspondents." He had created the European Bureau of the *Tribune* in 1866 and served as its head until 1895, gaining early fame by going to "the front" to gather news on the Franco-Prussian War. He liked the theater and admired Irving. See his obit, *Times*, 5 Apr. 1916, 13:7.

26. CCB-HLS, 20:2, "CCB and the Stage," 1. Crunden, later librarian of the St. Louis Public Library. CCB-HLS, 20:2, "CCB and the Stage," 1.

27. Alexander C. Flick, *Samuel J. Tilden* (New York: Dodd, 1939), 286–91; CCB-HLS, 21:1, CCB speech at ABCNY 75th Anniversary, 16 Mar. 1946, 16–17.

28. *Times*, 28 June 1876, 1:1.

29. CCB-TFS.

30. CCB-COH, 1.

31. McFeely (1981), 404–16, 441–43; also Morison, Commager, and Leuchtenburg (1980), 1:780.

32. CCB-TFS, E. W. Gurney (dean of Harvard College) to CCB, 18 Jan. 1876, discussing CCB's qualifications for Harvard's sophomore class. CCB-HLS, 5:1, CCB to FF, 18 Dec. 1952, names some of his teachers and courses at Washington University.

33. Greek historian Polybius, book 29, 20:4.

34. GM interview with PW Jr., 8 June 1995. Yelping. CCB may have echoed William James, who, according to S. E. Morison, *Three Centuries of Harvard* (1936), 413, used the expression to end a lecture at Harvard, urging his students not to be stampeded by William Randolph Hearst and Theodore Roosevelt into approval of the Spanish-American War. Einstein, see Prologue at n. 4.

35. Carl J. Richard, *The Founders and the Classics* (Cambridge: Harvard University Press, 1994), 55, 71, 160.

36. Ibid., 26, 28, 61. Aristotle, *Nichomachean Ethics*, 1166a19–1166b28. A professor at Yale Law School, Kronman (1993), 74–87, discusses this idea with reference to lawyers.

37. CCB-HLS, 20:2, "CCB and the Stage," 1; also ibid. 20:3, CCB to SCC, 24 Feb. 1959.

38. Ibid., 20:1, "III—Education," 8.

39. "Colonel." CCB-HLS, 19:8, CCB to Cornelius Wickersham, 28 Mar. 1956, and Harry Disston to Cornelius Wickersham, 5 Apr. 1957; also Comparato (1979), 161, 640; and DAB IX (orig. ed.): 104. Summer visits. CCB-HLS, 20:1, "III—Education," 9; and CCB-HLS 20:12, typescript "Aunt Annie," 2–3.

40. M. J. Burlingham, "Richard M. Hoe's" and Frank E. Comparato, "Brightside: A Busy Inventor's Return to Nature," *Bronx County Historical Society Journal* XV:1 (Spring 1978).

41. Dubin, ed. (1940), 33–43. According to family genealogy and to the New York Stock Exchange Archives, as well as to newspaper obituaries of the Lawrence brothers, three reached maturity: DeWitt Clinton, born 1830; Cyrus J., born 1832; and Darius Weed, born 1837. DeWitt and Cyrus J. formed a partnership for brokerage business in 1864 or possibly earlier. The firm's name was Lawrence Bros. & Co., and Darius, the youngest brother, had joined by 1873. This firm dissolved on 15 March 1888, three years after the death of Darius and during the illness of DeWitt. On that same day was founded Cyrus J. Lawrence & Sons, with Cyrus the senior partner and his two sons, Richard H. and Henry C., juniors. The firm continued under that name, recruiting new members during CCB's life mostly from within the Lawrence family.

42. CCB-HLS, 20:12, CCB pamphlet *Aunt Annie, Annie C. Hoe Platt, 1852–1887, Sketch* (privately printed, 1957).

43. Son-in-law and author. Harper (1912), 559.

44. David Dempsey, "Dodd, Mead & Company, A Commentary," *Saturday Review*, 12 Dec. 1964; Comparato (1979), 229, 629–33. Carl L. Cannon, *American Book Collectors and Collecting from Colonial Times to the Present* (New York: Wilson, 1941), chap. XIV, "Robert Hoe III, 1839–1909," 157–69: "Mr. Hoe had a rough and unpleasing exterior and an overbearing manner, but back of that and back of the restless, energetic businessman there was the true collector, the true bibliophile." Also Lee Edmonds Grove, "Robert Hoe III," *Grolier 75: A Biographical Retrospective to Celebrate the Seventy-fifth Anniversary of the Grolier Club in New York* (New York: Grolier Club, 1959), 24–26; Comparato (1979), ix, 660–64, 670–73; and DAB IX (orig. ed.): 105–6. The colonel and daughters as book collectors. Comparato (1979), 647–49; M. J. Burlingham, "Richard M. Hoe's," 75: "Each daughter had her own private library, with its leather-bound printed catalogue." See CCB-TFS, CCB to LLB, 9 Sept. 1887. Music. M. J. Burlingham, "Richard M. Hoe's," 75.

45. ASB and R. Hoe & Co. CCB-TFS, CCB to ACH, 5 Apr. 1877; CCB to AHB, 31 Aug. 1877; CCB to ESB, 26 May 1886; and CCB to Robert Lawrence, 14 June 1886. Also ASB obit, *Times*, 18 Oct. 1934, 23:3. CCB's address. His entry in *Harvard College Class of 1879, First Report*, 1879.

46. Comparato (1979), chap. 5, "The Incredible Lightning Presses," 261–303; Moran, (1973), 178.

47. Comparato (1979), 415. American machines selling in Europe. Ibid., 417. Others were McCormick's reaper, Colt's revolver, and Hobbs's unpickable lock. *Lloyd's Weekly*. Ibid., 423.

From the *Encyclopaedia Britannica* (1946 ed.), the entry on "Printing": "[In Hoe's press] the type cylinder was placed in a horizontal position and the type secured in cast-iron beds by special locking up apparatus. Each bed represented one page of a newspaper. Grouped around the type cylinder were four, six, or ten impression cylinders, each of which had feeders laying on sheets of paper. As the main cylinder rotated, the type was inked by a roller, the sheets as they were fed in being taken by grippers to receive the inked impression of the type. In this instance, the sheets were delivered by means of 'mechanical flyers' . . . The first machine was erected in London in 1856; it had six cylinders and was installed to print *Lloyd's Weekly Newspaper*."

48. Harper (1912), 559. Privy Council. Quoted in Dubin, ed. (1940), 36. Burlingame (1938), 398. On printing's importance to New York's intellectual life, see Bender (1987), 156–57. Also Jan Morris (1987), 239–43. And Tocqueville (1946), "Public Associations," 381, on the importance of newspapers to American democracy.

49. This aspect of the high-speed press is a theme of Gurstein (1996); see esp. 6, 32, 173. For what the faster presses meant in 1861 to James Gordon Bennett Sr. (1795–1872), publisher of the *Herald*, see Comparato (1979), 284.

50. CCB-HLS, 20:2, "The first time I ever saw my Louie . . . ," 1. Conceivably the festivity was part of the marriage of the colonel's daughter and J. Henry Harper, 5 June 1873. Red-haired. GM interview with CCB's niece, RTE, 3 Oct. 1993. By the 1920s LLB's hair was graying, and in the next decade became white. She was named after her grandmother Louisa Maria Weed, second wife of Cyrus Lawrence. The first had died in childbirth, with her child. When LMWL died in 1837 she left five children, DeWitt, seven years old, Cyrus J., four and a half, Mary Louisa, three and a half, Edward, two, and Darius Weed, one day old.

51. "No impression." CCB-HLS, 20:1, "III—Education," 13. Photograph. CCB-TFS, CCB to ACH, 15 Jan. 1877. Birthday. CCB-TFS, CCB to ACH, 5 Apr. 1877. "Baptist pup." GM interview with RTE, 15 May 1993.

52. Reverend Huckle. CCB-HLS, 20:11, CCB to Fletcher Harper, 22 Nov. 1941. On RMH. M. J. Burlingham, "Richard M. Hoe's," 75; Comparato (1979), 563–71; Bernstein (1990), 172–73.

53. CCB-HLS, 20:2, "The first time I ever saw my Louie . . ." suggests that when the boys came East with only their mother, they visited relatives; but when their father joined them they visited the Hoes. And when one of CCB's parents wrote to ACH about CCB, it was the father, in CCB-TFS, AHB to ACH, 20 Nov. 1876. Pallbearer. Comparato (1979), 649.

54. CCB-HLS, 20:1, "II—Childhood," 5–7; and CCB-TFS, Scrapbook, 67, unidentified newspaper report of AHB speech "Atmospheres"; see Chapter 1, n. 16. Collapsible chair, Comparato, "Brightside," 37; Comparato (1979), 646–49.

55. Comparato (1979), 29–30, 33–34, 53–54, 62–63, 66.

56. Maid and coachman. Harper (1912), 59–60. Shared coach. Comparato (1979), 67, quotes James H. Collins, "The Story of the Printed Word," *A Popular History of American Invention*, ed. Waldemar Kaempffert (New York: Scribner, 1924), 1:221–61. Murray Hill. roughly Twenty-seventh to Forty-second Street and Third to Sixth Avenue.

57. Burgeoning Murray Hill. The Church of the Incarnation (Madison Avenue and Thirty-fifth Street), which the Hoes and CCB and his family would later join, was founded in 1850 as a mission chapel of Grace Church (Broadway and Ninth Street). Then, in 1852, as families continued to move into the area, the church was built. Brothers aghast. M. J. Burlingham, "Robert M. Hoe's," 73.

58. J. C. Derby, *Fifty Years Among Authors, Books and Publishers* (New York: Carleton, 1884), 106–7. According to Harper (1912), 120, the brothers started to keep double-entry accounts only about 1857 and only upon their accountant's impassioned pleading.

59. RMH whistling. *Harper* (1912), 120. Helping employees. Comparato (1979), 648–49; also DAB, Hoe, IX (orig. ed.): 104–5. Poodles. Grove, "Robert Hoe III," 24. Firing employees. Comparato (1979), ix, xii.

60. GM interview with PW Jr., 21 Oct. 1993.

3. Harvard and Phillips Brooks

Chief sources for this chapter, other than Burlingham collections, are: Horace E. Scudder, "Harvard University," *Scribner's Monthly*, vol. 12, no. 3 (July 1876): 337–59; *The Development of Harvard University since the Inauguration of President Eliot, 1869–1929*, ed. Samuel

Eliot Morison, Class of 1908 (Cambridge: Harvard University Press, 1930), the "official" history; *Three Centuries of Harvard, 1636–1936*, by S. E. Morison (Cambridge: Harvard University Press, 1936), an "unofficial" history; *Glimpses of the Harvard Past*, by Bernard Bailyn, Donald Fleming, Oscar Handlin, and Stephan Thernstrom (Cambridge: Harvard University Press, 1986). Also M. A. DeWolfe Howe, *Phillips Brooks* (Boston: Small, Maynard, 1899); William Lawrence, *Phillips Brooks: A Study* (Boston: Houghton, 1903); William Lawrence, *Life of Phillips Brooks* (New York: Harper, 1930); John F. Woolverton, *The Education of Phillips Brooks* (Urbana: University of Illinois Press, 1995); and David B. Chesebrough, *Phillips Brooks: Pulpit Eloquence* (Westport, Conn.: Greenwood, 2001).

1. CCB-HLS, 20:1, "III—Education," 8; and 10:8, CCB to William James Jr., 3 Dec. 1940; TDT-YSML, 1:65, CCB to TDT, 12 Nov. 1940; HAB 43:5 (30 Nov. 1940): 263. CCB-COH, 1. Frank William Taussig. DAB, supp. 2, 650–52.

2. CCB-HLS, 20:1, "III—Education," 10; CCB-TFS, CCB to ACH, 16 Oct. 1876; HAB 43:5 (30 Nov. 1940): 263.

3. CCB-TFS, Harvard's dean E. W. Gurney to CCB, 18 Jan. 1876; Harvard's dean Charles F. Dunbar to CCB, 19 July 1876; registrar of Washington University to CCB, 24 Aug. 1876; and CCB to ACH, 16 Oct. 1876. CCB-HLS, 20:1, letter of registrar of Washington University to CCB, 12 May 1941, showing CCB and Taussig completed sophomore year. In CCB-COH, Addendum (recorded and revised by CCB in 1949, or later), 2, he states the fact correctly.

4. CCB-HLS, 20:1, "III—Education," 10; CCB-TFS, CCB to ACH, 16 Oct. 1876. With his brother. CCB-HLS, 203, CCB to SCC, 24 Feb. 1959.

5. College totals. Harvard University Archives. University figures, 112 faculty, 1,278 students, Scudder (1876), 346, citing the "latest catalogue."

6. Scudder (1876), 353. Morison, *Three Centuries of Harvard* (1936), 267, states Gore Hall opened in 1841, with 41,000 volumes and a life expectancy of seventy-five years; by 1863 it was full; and by 1912, when work began on its replacement, Widener Library, Gore housed (after expansion by "a series of wings, stacks, and additional floors") half a million books. See also Morison, ed., *The Development of Harvard* (1930), 623–28. On breakdown of the "alcove" system by 1876, see description by F. W. Taussig, Morison, ed., *The Development of Harvard* (1930), 187 n. 1; library's main reading room, Scudder (1876), 353; on "open" stacks, Morison, *Three Centuries of Harvard* (1936), 396.

7. Memorial Hall. Scudder (1876), 337, 357–59. According to S. E. Morison, *Three Centuries of Harvard* (1936), 303 n. 1, of Harvard students and graduates 1,311 fought for the Union, with 138 dead, 257 for the Confederacy, with 64 dead, almost a third of Harvard's total. To date, the Confederate dead are uncommemorated despite much debate, beginning soon after the war's end, on how to honor them. Because of restrictions put on the funds to build Memorial Hall, the Southerners cannot be joined with their classmates in that building; see *Harvard Magazine*, May–June, 1995, 62–63.

8. McShane (1994), 55. Following the introduction of the "safety" model, the decade of the bicycle was the 1890s, of which a memento is "Daisy" and her bicycle built for two, by Harry Dacre, published in 1892. CCB-TFS, CCB to ACH, 16 Oct. 1876.

9. Polluted river. Scudder (1876), 343. "Bridge" and "horse-car." Ibid., 337.

10. On TR. Miller (1992), 65, 69, 71–72, 90, 93, 95; E. E. Morris (1979), chaps. 3 and 4, 81–133; and Welling (1942), 33.

11. HAB 43:5 (30 Nov. 1940): 263. Taussig's father, William Taussig, DAB. XVIII (orig. ed.): 311–12, was a prominent physician and businessman in St. Louis. The account of F. W. Taussig, DAB, supp. 2, 650, incorrectly states that he transferred to Harvard after one year

at Washington College. See CCB-HLS, 20:1, registrar of Washington University to CCB, 12 May 1941.

12. CCB-HLS, 20:3, Dean C. F. Dunbar to AHB, 6 Sept. 1876. Bailyn et al. (1986), 123.

13. CCB-HLS, 20:3, Dean C. F. Dunbar to AHB, 6 Sept. 1876.

14. CCB-TFS, CCB to AHB, 8 Sept. 1877.

15. Average award. Bailyn et al. (1986), 123. CCB-TFS, CCB to AHB, 15 May 1877. Notice of election to Phi Beta Kappa. CCB-TFS, CCB to AHB, 25 Feb. 1879.

16. CCB-HLS, 20:1, autobiographical account, 5, and "At Harvard," 1; and ibid., 20:3, CCB to SCC, 24 Feb. 1959.

17. CCB-TFS, CCB to ACH, 10 Nov. 1876. Ibid., CCB to ACH, 14 Dec. 1876.

18. Ibid., CCB to ACH, 10 Jan. 1877. His "route" would have been via Hartford and Springfield, for the swifter "shore line" did not open until 1889, see WPA-Maritime (1941), 219.

19. Brethren. CCB-HLS, 21:9, notice of election, 23 Feb. 1877. S. E. Morison, *Three Centuries of Harvard* (1936), 368, states the Society by 1890 had "died"; and even in CCB's day it seems to have been moribund. Crew race. CCB-TFS, CCB to AHB, 15 May 1877. Eames. CCB-TFS. CCB to AHB, 13 Apr. 1877; also CCB to AHB, 26 Sept. 1877, 13 Oct. 1877, and CCB to ESB, 10 Feb. 1878.

20. HAB 43: 5 (30 Nov. 1940): 263; CCB-HLS, 20:1, "III—Education," 11.

21. Bathing. Bailyn et al. (1986), 81. CCB-TFS, CCB to AHB, 15 May 1877; also CCB to AHB, 4 Nov. 1877, and CCB to ESB, 14 Nov. 1877.

22. Quotation. CCB-HLS, 20:1, autobiographical account, 2. Works studied. FF-LOC, container 35, CCB to FF, 5 Mar. 1943.

23. CCB-HLS, 20:1, autobiographical account, 2–3; ibid., "At Harvard," 1; ibid., "III—Education," 11; also S. E. Morison, ed., *The Development of Harvard* (1930), "The Classics," 38–39. CCB-TFS, CCB to ACH, 14 Dec. 1876.
Note: George Martin Lane, Ph.D., Göttingen University, 1851, was a professor of Latin at Harvard for almost a half century, 1851–94. He wrote a number of scholarly books of which perhaps the most influential was *Latin Pronunciation* (1871). But his most enduring work is one for which he seldom receives credit: "The Lay of the One Fish Ball." First published in 1857, it is the original of the song still sung, "One Meat Ball," and has as its punch line: "We don't give bread with one fish ball!" Until at least 1888 it was included in Harvard College songbooks, and given pride of place as second only to "Fair Harvard." Today the university has a George Martin Lane Chair, tied to classical studies but not necessarily to the teaching of Latin. The present holder, Christopher P. Jones, is "the Lane Professor of Classics and of History," whereas his predecessor was "of Philosophy and the Classics"—the variety of pursuits allowed to the holder reflects the ranging interests and enthusiasms of the chair's progenitor.

24. Scudder (1876), 355; Bailyn et al. (1986), 60, 101, 105; Morison, *Three Centuries of Harvard* (1936), 357, 370.

25. On James (1842–1910). CCB-HLS, 7:5, CCB to Ralph Barton Perry, 23 Oct. 1929. Also Townsend (1996), 162, citing George Santayana; and see Morison, ed., *The Development of Harvard* (1930), "Philosophy," 1–9, 5, and Bailyn et al. (1986), 87. Great years roughly 1885–1909; in 1891 he published *The Principles of Psychology*. See Townsend (1996) for an account of his beliefs and influence.

26. Norton (1827–1908) quoted in Gurstein (1996), 23; and see Gurstein's account of his thought, 19–28, 39–42, and its influence reaching down the years to Lionel Trilling, 255. See Bender (1987), 172–73. S. E. Morison, Commager, and Leuchtenburg (1980), 2:153, quotes Norton on the ideal community: "New England during the first thirty years of the century, before the coming of Jacksonian Democracy, the invasion of the Irish, and the establish-

ment of the system of Protection." And Morison, ed., *The Development of Harvard* (1930), "The Fine Arts," 130–32. CCB-TFS, CCB to ACH, 10 Nov. 1876 and 16 Feb. 1879. CCB's interest in Norton and his ideas, in addition to his books and articles, was refreshed periodically by Norton's presence in the summer at Ashfield, Massachusetts, where CCB, sometimes renting a house in the years 1890–1906, knew him personally and heard him lecture.

27. CCB-HLS, 20:1, autobiographical account, 4, and CCB-COH, 2.

28. CCB-HLS, 20:1, autobiographical account, 4. CCB probably heard the story from the son Henry James, a friend in later years.

29. HAB 43:5 (30 Nov. 1940): 263; also DAB, supp. 2, 650–52. Walking. Welling (1942), 27–28. Years later another of CCB's friends, John H. Finley, walked from Princeton to New York City, starting after an evening meeting that broke up shortly before midnight, Finley Memorial, *Century Association Yearbook 1941*, 26–28; and *Herald*, 24 May 1906, 4:4, reporting a man of sixty-eight walking one hundred miles from City Hall, Philadelphia, to City Hall, New York, in 23 hours 25 minutes.

30. Emerson. CCB-HLS, 20:1, "III—Education," 12, and CCB-COH, Addendum, 2–3.

31. Signet. William James Jr. Collection, Houghton Library, Harvard, CCB to W. James Jr. 25 Jan. 1955. Also CCB-HLS, 20:1, autobiographical account, 5; CCB-HLS, 2:8, memorandum of 19 Mar. 1941 on James Byrne; and CCB-HLS, 20:3, CCB to SCC, 24 Feb. 1959. Morison, *Three Centuries of Harvard* (1936), 427: Signet "occasionally elects the unclubbed intelligentsia . . . and is still one of the pleasantest societies in College." On CCB's speech. CCB-TFS, CCB to ESB, 10 Feb. 1878. Ruskin's political and economic ideas entered the Protestant churches, contributing to the rise of their Social Gospel movement, in which CCB later had a part; see Hopkins (1940), 28 n. 9, 284–86.

32. On the college clubs generally, Scudder (1876), 343–44; Morison, *Three Centuries of Harvard* (1936), 420–28; CCB-HLS, 20:1, autobiographical account, 5.

33. Sunday school. Edward S. Martin Collection, Houghton Library, Harvard: TR to Martin, 26 Nov. 1900. TR published his first two works while still an undergraduate, *The Summer Birds of the Adirondacks in Franklin County, N.Y.* and *Notes on Some of the Birds of Oyster Bay, Long Island*, as well as starting *The Naval War of 1812* (1882). See Miller (1992), 74, 99, 115–16.

34. Edward S. Martin (1856–1939) later cofounded and for many years wrote the editorials for the satiric magazine *Life* (1883–1936) and from 1920 to 1935 wrote "The Easy Chair" at *Harper's Magazine* with sensible observations on public affairs, charmingly expressed. See memorial pamphlet published by the Class of 1877, ESM Collection, Houghton Library, Harvard. Also DAB, supp. 2, 434–35. Morison, *Three Centuries of Harvard* (1936), 430; Harper (1912), 647–48; and Mott (1957), chapter on *Life*, 556–68, "not a comic paper, but a gently satirical observer." See Welling (1942), 34, for Martin on the clubs and their members.

35. On TR. Miller (1992), 69, 71, 85. Welling (1942), 28, and HAB 43:5 (30 Nov. 1940): 263. Welling states that this small informal club eventually became the still-existing Fly Club, whose most famous member is Franklin D. Roosevelt.

36. CCB-TFS, AHB to ACH, 20 Nov. 1876.

37. Best preacher. Ibid., CCB to ACH, 18 Mar. 1877. Influence. CCB-HLS, 20:1, autobiographical account, 6; and CCB-HLS, 3:13, CCB to Bishop William Lawrence, 17 Nov. 1930: "Although I really never knew him, no one has had a greater influence in my life."

38. *Atlantic Monthly: A Magazine of Literature, Art, and Politics* II:XI (Sept. 1858): 496–97. The magazine had been founded the previous year, with James Russell Lowell as editor. The poem was reprinted in editions of Holmes's collected pieces, *The Autocrat at the Breakfast Table*, and in many anthologies. Howe, in *Holmes of the Breakfast Table* (New York:

Oxford University Press, 1939), 9, 117–18, first suggests that the poem's readers did not realize it was a parable on the death of Calvinism until roughly 1900. But then, almost immediately, he offers reasons why the date might be as early as 1859. Among others: "The conflicts of theological belief were matters of intense interest—to him [Holmes] and to the whole society of which he was a part." Surely, even in 1859 people realized the poem was about something more than the collapse of a carriage.

39. Lawrence, *Phillips Brooks* (1903), 6–7. Cf. Lawrence, *Life of Phillips Brooks* (1930), 91–92: Woolverton (1995), 43, 49, 110.

40. Lawrence, *Phillips Brooks* (1903), 26–27, 85.

41. Chesebrough (2001), 6, 110.

42. Quoted in Lawrence, *Phillips Brooks* (1903), 25, citing Phillips Brooks, *Lectures on Preaching* (New York: Dutton, 1877), 5. Cf. Woolverton (1995), 108. In the fall of 1878, while CCB was a senior at Harvard, the first volume of Brooks's sermons was published, *The Purpose and Use of Comfort.* Chesebrough (2001), 83.

43. Quoted by Woolverton (1995), 97, citing Alexander V. G. Allen, *Life and Letters of Phillips Brooks* (New York: Dutton, 1900), 2:349–50.

44. CCB-TFS, CCB to ACH, 16 Feb. 1879. One college mate not yet ready for the "broad liberality" of Brooks was William Welling, see Welling (1942), 30–31. By the 1890s probably most of the progressive theologians in American churches had accepted the probability of Darwin's theories; see Hopkins (1940), 123.

45. Placement of altar. Lawrence, *Life of Phillips Brooks* (1930), 90; also Woolverton (1995), 109.

46. Lawrence, *Life of Phillips Brooks* (1930), 107.

47. Woolverton (1995), 41, 85, discusses this historical background. The English Civil War (1642–60), besides its role in church reform, through its battles over the constitutional rights of Parliament and king left a strong imprint on American law and government. Its events and personalities were familiar to most educated Americans of the nineteenth century.

48. Sunday sermons. Lawrence, *Life of Phillips Brooks* (1930), 86, 109.

49. CCB-TFS, CCB to ACH, 18 Mar. 1877.

50. Brooks's speech "Orthodoxy," delivered before the Clericus Club, Cambridge, 2 June 1890. Quoted by Chesebrough (2001), 6.

51. Lawrence, *Life of Phillips Brooks* (1903), 28–29.

52. CCB-TFS, CCB to ACH, 11 Apr. 1879.

53. Lawrence, *Life of Phillips Brooks* (1930), 96.

54. Ibid., 106–7. See also Howe (1899), 63–65, who estimated that "the average speaker gives forth about 120 words to the minute; from 190 to 215" was said to be the speed with Brooks. CCB-HLS, 9:14, Howe to CCB, 25 Feb. 1957: "I came under his influence much as you did—first at Harvard, then as a member of the unvested Trinity choir through the last three years of his rectorship, when I used to hear him both morning and afternoon every Sunday." And an account of Brooks preaching by Lord Bryce quoted without citation in A.V.G. Allen, (1907), 581. Sermons written out. Woolverton to GM, 2 Nov. 1993.

55. CCB-HLS, 3:13, CCB to William Lawrence, 17 Nov. 1930.

56. Brooks's sermon "The Candle of the Lord," quoted in Chesebrough (2001), 148; complete sermon, ibid., 139–50.

Note: On the idea of going out to do God's work, see Kronman (1993), 370: "Behind the original Protestant idea of a calling there lay a whole complex of religious ideas (the inscrutability of God's will, the need for human beings to help complete the work of creation through their own productive labor, and so on). This religious background is now gone. But the idea of a calling, of salvation through work, did not disappear with the religious beliefs that brought it into being. For a time at least, it outlived them as a secular ideal that could survive without religious supports." GM: Setting a date for the decline or death of an idea—the Christian life expressed in daily work—cannot be exact, but I would guess that in the decade after World War II, from 1945 onward, even of those children educated in Episcopal church schools the great majority no longer thought of work as informed by a religious purpose.

57. Chesebrough (2001), 139; and the sermon, ibid., 140.

58. Quoted by Chesebrough (2001), 119.

59. Woolverton (1995), 94. Woolverton is a minister, scholar, and historian of the Episcopal church, and editor of the quarterly journal *Anglican and Episcopal History.* "Incarnation," ibid., 38, 66–67. Cf. Lawrence, *Phillips Brooks* (1903), 13: "The truth of the Incarnation was the central truth of his life, thought, and preaching. For him it solved the pressing problems of life and nature, and knit the universe, God, and his creation into living unity." "Conversion," Woolverton (1995), 83. "Sanctification," Woolverton (1995), 84. "Metaphors," Woolverton (1995), 105 and 110.

60. The Gospel According to St. John, 14:6. CCB-HLS, 12:11, CCB to Father Gordon Wadhams, 21 Mar. 1944. Wadhams was "high church," hence the title "Father," whereas CCB was "low." "Thank you, also for your Lenten pamphlet, which I read and marked but neither learned nor inwardly digested, I fear. Possibly it may interest you to know how the book affected a layman of another school of thought—although I hesitate to call my impressions thoughts. (1) I was struck by the omission of references to our Lord, except in the Sections on the Holy Communion. The Church seemed to take His place, yet for most of us it is through Christ that we come to know God as our Father . . ."

61. GM interview with Susan and John Hazard (vestryman of St. George's Church), 10 June 1993: and with CB Jr., 14–15 July 1995. CB Jr., however, was certain CCB believed in the divinity of Christ and the concept of the Trinity.

62. Joining wife in death. CCB-HLS, 9:7, CCB to HH, 21 Feb. 1947. On entering the afterlife. E.g., Susan and John Hazard, GM interview, 10 June 1993. E. O. Miller (rector of St. George's Church), "*C. C. B.*" *As We Knew Him,* in ST. GCB, Aug. 1959.

63. Audible prayer. Lloyd K. Garrison, "C. C. Burlingham, 1858–1959," ABCNY, *Record* 14:9 (Dec. 1959): 10. Belief in God. GM interview with PLT, 11 Sept. 1993. Also Hamilton (1944), 231: "Being a Christian in C.C.B. is quintessential. It is not a thing he speaks about; it directs his action, and that action is persistent."

4. Slouching into the Law

Chief sources for this chapter, other than the Burlingham collections, are: Julius Goebel Jr., *A History of the School of Law, Columbia University* (New York: Columbia University Press, 1955); Arthur E. Sutherland, *The Law at Harvard: A History of Ideas and Men, 1817–1967* (Cambridge: Harvard University Press, 1967). And CCB memorial pamphlet, *Joe Evans, 1857–1898* (privately printed, 1949). Also Theron G. Strong, *Landmarks of a Lawyer's Lifetime* (New York: Dodd, 1914); CCB, *Notes on the History of Burlingham, Veeder, Clark & Hupper* (privately printed, 1946); Walter K. Earle, *Mr. Shearman and Mr. Sterling and How They Grew, Being annals of their law firm, with biographical and historical highlights* (New Haven: Yale University Press, 1963), and *Hubbell's Legal Dictionary for Lawyers and Business Men,* beginning with the years 1873–74.

1. CCB-TFS, CCB to ESB, 13 Jan. 1878.

2. Ibid., CCB to ESB, 10 Feb. 1878.

3. Ibid., CCB to ACH, 5 May 1878.

4. CCB-HLS, 20:3, Harvard College transcript, with notes by CCB; CCB-TFS, CCB to AHB, 4 Nov. 1877, describing forensic themes.

5. CCB-TFS, CCB to ACH, 2 Mar. 1879.

6. Family tradition. If CCB wrote to his father, the letter is lost. GM interview with CB Jr., 14 July 1995.

7. Albert. CCB-TFS, CCB to ACH, 5 Apr. 1877, and CCB to AHB, 31 Aug. 1877. On AHB. Ibid., CCB to AHB, 31 Aug. 1877: "A bankrupt church is not a cheerful prospect . . ." CCB to AHB, 8 Jan. 1878, talks of "hard times" for AHB; and CCB-HLS, 20:3, CCB to SCC, 24 Feb. 1959: AHB on leaving St. Louis, "for a time had no salary." (This letter quoted more fully in n. 22 below.) On AHB's poor health. CCB-TFS, CCB to ESB, 7 Oct. and 2 Nov. 1877, and 13 Jan. 1878.

8. Number of law schools. Sutherland (1967), 181, quoting a report (1879–80) of Harvard's President Eliot. Indiana was perhaps the least demanding state. Its constitution from 1851 to 1933 stated: "Every person of good moral character, being a voter, shall be entitled to admission to practice law in all courts of justice." No examination or study required, see Hurst (1950), 250, 272, 277.

9. On Harvard Law School, see Sutherland (1967), chap. 6, "The Langdell Era: 1870–1895," 162–205; Morison, *Three Centuries of Harvard* (1936), 336–38; Morison, ed., *The Development of Harvard* (1930), chap. 30, "The Law School, 1817–1929," by Roscoe Pound.

10. On Columbia Law School and Theodore W. Dwight, see Goebel (1955), 75–92; also on Dwight, see Strong (1914), 252–55. From 1859 to 1873, the law school was at 37 LaFayette Place; 1873 to 1883 on Great Jones Street in the Schermerhorn house, a four-story corner building plagued by street noises making it difficult to hear in lecture halls when windows were open; and 1883 to 1897, at Madison Avenue at Forty-ninth Street. Thereafter the school was at Columbia's present campus in Morningside Heights. Like CCB, TR, Harvard College 1880, preferred Columbia's law school to Harvard's. Dwight quoted in *The Oxford Dictionary of American Legal Quotations*, ed. Fred R. Shapiro (New York: Oxford University Press, 1993), 29, citing Dwight, "What Shall We Do When We Leave the Law School?," *Counsellor* 1 (1891): 63–64.

11. "Spoon-fed," CCB-HLS, 21:1, a brief account titled "abc" in the upper left-hand corner. Ibid., 20:1, CCB speech at dedication of memorial to Dwight, 3 Oct. 1932. Dicey and Bryce on Dwight are both in *Macmillan's Magazine* 25 (1871): 127 and 209; and quoted in Goebel (1955), 63.

Note: On Dwight and his method for teaching law. The law school's historian, Julius Goebel Jr., writes of Dwight: "That the newly launched Columbia Law School remained afloat was due almost entirely to the efforts of the man whom the Trustees selected to put at the helm . . . [He] got the School well under way and kept it going almost singlehanded for thirty-three years" (33). For example, from 1864 to 1872 "it is no exaggeration to say that the School was Dwight. As professor of Municipal Law, Dwight personally gave all the required instruction. As Warden, Dwight directed the administration of the school and its students. [By the] regulations of February, 1864, Dwight controlled the School's finances and pocketed most of the income" (62). Yet this lawyer's lawyer died intestate because in signing his will, he got only part way through the "g" in his last name when he fell back dead (132). In 1891, when an academic reorganization at Columbia forced the aging Dwight to retire, the law school broke in two. About half its students and faculty, wanting to continue with his methods, withdrew and founded a new school. Those that remained adopted Harvard's case system. The departing faculty and students, led by Professor George Chase, founded the New York Law School, unaffiliated with any college or university and which by 1906 had 1,000 students, more than any other law school in the country. It closed in 1941 but reopened in 1947. In 1991 it had a faculty of fifty full-time, fifty-five part-time, and 913 students full-time, 468 part-time. See *The Encyclopedia of New York City* (1995).

12. Rise of social sciences in law. E.g., Morris R. Cohen (1880–1947), legal philosopher at City College of New York, see letters to Roscoe Pound and FF quoted in Lash (1975), 10–11.

13. For an account of these years, see his reminiscences in CCB-HLS, 21:1. Metropolitan Museum. Ibid., 11:9, CCB to FHL, 20 Jan. 1936. CCB misremembers the event's date, placing it in Dec. 1876. Held in the museum's main hall, it was one of the decade's great occasions, to which 3,500 of the city's leading citizens, among them Colonel Hoe, had been invited. The museum, after a nomadic decade, finally had a home. The ceremonies opened with a prayer, continued with a speech by Joseph Hodges Choate, and closed when President Hayes declared, in toto, "I have now the honor to make the formal announcement that the Metropolitan Art Museum is open to the public." See Winifred E. Howe, *A History of the Metropolitan Museum of Art with a chapter on the Early Institutions of Art in New York* (New York: Metropolitan Museum of Art, 1913), 189ff.

14. CCB-HLS, 21:1, an account of these years. Also DW-PW Jr., CCB to PW, 18 May 1947. See Baldwin's obit, *Times*, 19 May 1947, 21:14. Recommendations. CCB-TFS, Eliot letter, 26 July 1879; also letters of C. F. Dunbar (political economy), 26 June 1879, of W. W. Goodwin (Greek), 24 Apr. 1879, and F. Bowen (philosophy), 25 Apr. 1879. CCB-TFS Clement L. Smith, professor of Latin, to CCB, 6 Feb. 1880.

15. CCB-HLS, 20:2, "The first time I ever saw my Louie . . . ," 4; ibid., 21:1, an account of these years. Sea travel. *Times* index, Jan. through June 1880: for the six months the entry "Marine Intelligence" lists thirty-four ships "lost," eleven more in collision, as well as others involved in mutiny, scuttling, burning, and running aground.

16. CCB-HLS, 21:1.

17. Ibid.

18. CCB-TFS, CCB, *Joe Evans* (1949). Also CCB-HLS, 21:1 and ibid., 20:2 "The first time I ever saw my Louie . . . ," CCB tells more about the family in his memorial letter to the *Herald Tribune*, 9 Feb. 1945, 16:4, on the death of Joe's sister Anna Evans.

19. CCB-TFS, CCB, *Joe Evans* (1949), 3.

20. WPA-Maritime (1941), 203. Typical fares for a one-way crossing in these years: first-class passengers, sixty dollars; steerage, twenty dollars for adults, ten dollars for children, three dollars for infants, ibid., 205–6.

21. White (1951), 10. The biography has a photograph of Thayer's portrait of Joe Evans.

22. CCB and theater. CCB-HLS, 20:3, CCB to SCC, 24 Feb. 1959, states: "When I got to Cambridge, I was free and could go to the theatre without let or hindrance. Meanwhile my father had resigned his pastorate in St. Louis and came East and for the time being had no salary, and I did not feel it right to use his money for the theatre. In my junior and senior years I earned considerable money by tutoring, and then I began to go to the theatre." (GM: More likely the theater-going began in 1879–80, his first year at law school and the year his father settled securely in a job with the Baptist Missionary Society. There is no record of his tutoring anyone until the first year of law school.)

23. CCB-HLS, 20:2, "CCB and the Stage," 3. On the cut *Merchant of Venice* and *Iolanthe*, see Laurence Irving, *Henry Irving* (London: Faber, 1951), 356–57, 706. *The Merchant of Venice*, including its fifth act, had entered Irving's repertory the preceding November and played with its fifth act until *Iolanthe* came on in May 1880. The season ended on 31 July, so

CCB saw the double bill toward the end of its run. Purists criticized Irving for cutting Shakespeare, but he evidently wanted to give Terry a chance to play Iolanthe, a part in which she was sure to shine. Tchaikovsky based his final one-act opera, *Iolanta*, on the play.

24. For a summary history of New York's requirements for admission to the bar, see Martin, *Causes and Conflicts* (1970), Appendix B, 385–87, and 136–38; also Goebel (1955), 51–53, and 104–8.

25. GM interview with Elliott B. Nixon (a member of CCB's law firm), 18 Feb. 1992; CCB-HLS, 3:1, CCB to Thomas O'Gorman FitzGibbon, 5 May 1958, and CCB to Grayson Kirk, 8 Sept. 1957; also CCB-HLS, 21:1, a brief account titled "abc" in the upper left-hand corner. Figures on the law school Class of 1881. *Catalogue of Officers and Graduates of Columbia University*, 15th ed. (New York: privately printed, 1912). The class was initially larger than 123; CCB speaks of several good students who withdrew, see CCB-HLS, 20:1, "III—Education," 14.

26. CCB-HLS, 3:1, CCB letter to Thomas O'Gorman FitzGibbon, 5 May 1958.

27. *In the Matter of Lewis S. Burchard, An Attorney, et al.*, June 1882, 34 Hun 429–39. The petitioning lawyer was Lewis L. Delafield, chairman of the bar association's committee on admissions. But the Association, where Dwight was popular, dithered; see Martin, *Causes and Conflicts* (1970), 135–39.

28. "Shameful." CCB-HLS, 20:1, "III—Education," 15. Spelling of name. Ibid., 3:1, CCB to Grayson Kirk, 8 Sept. 1957.

29. Bangs & Stetson. CCB-HLS, 20:2, "A Lawyer," 1; CCB, *Notes*; TDT-YSML, 2:15, Alexander Gilchrist Jr. to CCB, 8 July 1941, and CCB to Gilchrist, 12 July 1941. After six more changes of name Bangs & Stetson emerged in 1925 as Davis Polk Wardwell Gardiner & Reed. Mount Vernon. It is not clear when the family moved to Mount Vernon, but in CCB-TFS, ACH to CCB, 6 Oct. 1882, refers to his mother entertaining there in her home all the young Lawrences, including Louie. AHB's obituary in *Herald*, 2 Mar. 1905, 12:6, states he had lived there "for twenty-three years." Mount Vernon was easily reached by the New Haven railroad, or by the elevated lines on Third or Second Avenue to 129th Street followed by a long walk.

30. TDT-YSML, 2:15, CCB to Alexander Gilchrist Jr., 12 July 1941.

31. Hascall's new partner was Herbert H. Taylor, see *Hubbell's Legal Dictionary*, 1883–84.

32. Strong (1914), 358, 359.

33. Root & Strong. Ibid. Strong left the firm after five years, and it became Root & Clarke, which, after another change in name, became in 1901 Winthrop & Stimson. "Paramount meanness": TDT-YSML, 2:15, Alexander Gilchrist Jr. to CCB, 8 July 1941; and CCB-HLS, 10:2, CEH Jr. to CCB, 17 Nov. 1948, suggests CCB's salary may have been less even than $10 a week, the sum CCB mentions as the maximum for clerks in his speech to the ABCNY on its seventy-fifth anniversary, 16 Mar. 1946, CCB-HLS, 21:1. Hughes added another $500 to his $1,500 by tutoring two nights a week at Columbia Law School, a prize fellowship awarded to an outstanding scholar, see Pusey (1951), 1:73, 75, 82. CCB-HLS, 10:2, CEH Jr. to CCB, 17 Nov. 1948, recalling a story of AHB telling CEH's parents of "the very low salary you were working for in a law office. Perhaps that is the one you referred to in your letter."

34. Complaint against CCB. By Eugene Underwood, interview on tape, 25 Oct. 1993, recorded by EU Jr. Pay for starting lawyers has always been troublesome. E. E. Morison (1960), 64, suggests that until the mid-1890s most firms did not pay clerks; see also Mayer (1968), 20. If so, Strong in paying CCB anything in 1881 was generous. On the other hand, CCB states, in CCB-HLS, 20:1, "The New York Bar 75 Years Ago," 4: "Clerks in law offices in the last century were known, not as associates or assistants, but as law clerks . . .

[Walter S.] Carter . . . got the pick of the [Harvard Law School] . . . The salary was small, not more than $25 or $30 a week." See Pusey (1951), 1:70, for a description of CEH going to work for Carter in 1883, and the terms of employment, 75, 77.

35. Strong (1914), 384–85; Earle (1963), 26.

36. Strong (1914), 396; Earle (1963), 26; Pusey (1951), 1:90.

37. Strong (1914), 397; Earle (1963), 25; Pusey (1951).

38. Gilmartin (1995), 47, makes the comparison. He gives as some of the costs: Carpets, window shades, and curtains, $675,534.44; plasterwork, $531,594.22; "repairs" to plasterwork, $1,294,684.13; "repairs" to woodwork, $750,071.92; and "brooms, etc.," $41,746.83.

39. Decline of courtroom eloquence. Strong (1914), 361; CCB-HLS, 20:1, "New York Bar 75 Years Ago," 4; Botein (1952), 106, 212.

40. Evarts. CCB-HLS, 20:2, "A Lawyer," 4, and Taft (1941), 190–92.

41. Choate. CCB-COH, 4.

Note: A friend of CCB who may have shared his view of Choate was Edward S. Martin, commissioned by the Choate family to write the great man's biography: *The Life of Joseph Hodges Choate, As Gathered Chiefly from his Letters, Including his own Story of his Boyhood and Youth* (New York: Scribner's, 1920). Edward S. Martin, according to Martin family tradition, was chosen chiefly because as an editorialist he had supported the Allied cause in World War I (being made a *chevalier de la légion d'honneur* by France for his support), and because he was known to admire greatly Choate's work as ambassador in strengthening Anglo-American relations before the war. In other respects, however, Martin inclined toward CCB's feelings about Choate's moral center, or lack of it, and planned to portray Choate as gaining, in his later life, greater moral stature. The Choate family forbade any such appraisal. Though Choate was five years dead and the world after the war quite different from the world before, family piety demanded that the distinguished ancestor be portrayed without blemish, start to finish. This may explain the book's structure and Martin's surprising but accurate opening sentences: "The reader will promptly discover that this life of Mr. Choate is not so much a biography after the manner of Plutarch as a compilation. The chief contributor, by far, is Mr. Choate himself, whose writings, public and private, make up four-fifths, or more, of the book." And further, after quoting many memorial eulogies, Martin concluded with another odd sentence: "Having lived long as life goes, and done what he could and got what he might, he felt that what he had got and done and been was not enough, and that further adventures lay before him." For belief in Choate's "complacent arrogance," see Hurst (1950), 371, and Welling (1942), 63; for examples of it, Goldmark (1953), 154, and Rainsford (1922), 321. Most people, however, considered him outstanding in every way. Stanley M. Isaacs, of a younger generation and with a different background and religion, thought him "a fine person" and "the first citizen of New York"; SMI-COH, 27. See also Taft (1941), 192–94, and CEH, in Pusey (1952), 1:93. This division in opinion on Choate possibly reflects a division in types of lawyers, and their admirers, which recurs in each generation. For example, in the 1930s and 1940s John W. Davis, in many ways the Choate of his day, would be accused by some of too often putting his exceptional skills at the service of bad causes. Mayor La Guardia, for example, disliked the frequency with which Davis defended Tammany politicians whom La Guardia considered "crooks," and he frequently referred to Davis in such cases as "the Little Weeper," PW Jr. to GM, interview 8 June 1995. Though FHL's view was too simple a judgment on a complex personality, others shared it, particularly in the later years of Davis's career, see Harbaugh, *Lawyer's Lawyer* (1973), 354–56.

42. CCB-TFS, "McCutcheon" box.

43. CCB-TFS, ACH to CCB, 4 Sept. 1882.

44. CCB-TFS, "McCutcheon" box.

45. WPA-Maritime (1941), 208, 212. Bone, ed. (1997), 239, states that before bridges and tunnels, the number of ferry lines operating around New York City reached 125.

46. WPA-Maritime (1941), 209. Ice. Bone, ed. (1997), 27, 155. Shift to Hudson. Bone, ed. (1997), 116, and see 97, and 155: The first pier in the Hudson was begun in 1771; in the East River, completed in 1659.

47. Strong (1914), 381; Earle (1963), 27.

48. TDT-YSML, 2:15, CCB to Alexander Gilchrist Jr., 12 July 1941.

49. Ibid. Also CCB-HLS, 13:5, CCB to Robert Moses, 13 Dec. 1954. CCB's weekly salary. TDT-YSML, 2:15, CCB to Alexander Gilchrist Jr., 12 July 1941.

50. The building. CCB-HLS, 21:1, CCB, *Notes,* 9; Earle (1963), 125–26. In BUL History Files, *Red Shield News* 7:12 (July 1976): 6, a publication of Royal Globe Insurance (merged with L&L&G in 1919) has an article "Wall to William—New York Offices of Royal-Globe."

51. On Hill. CCB, *Notes, 9* On Shoudy. Ibid., 4. On Wing. Ibid., 3.

52. Ibid., 5.

53. First case. *The Exile, Her Tackle,* etc., District Court, D. New Jersey, 5 July 1884, 20 Fed. Rep., 878–80. Before John T. Nixon, district judge; Beebe & Wilcox for libelants; Wing & Shoudy, for claimants. In later years CCB's memory may have confused two cases. In TDT-YSML, 2:15, CCB to Alexander Gilchrist Jr., 12 July 1941, he argues his "first case," which he names "The bark *Exile,* before Judge Benedict in the Eastern District of New York." He states, "Judge B. sustained the libel." But no record of such a case has been found.

5. Three Women: Louisa Lawrence, Ellen Terry, and Josephine Shaw Lowell

The chief sources for marriage and theater are the various Burlingham collections and the author's interviews with family members. For Josephine Shaw Lowell: doctoral thesis of Joan Waugh, *Unsentimental Reformer: The Life of Josephine Shaw Lowell* (submitted to the University of California, Los Angeles, 1992); Robert H. Bremner, *The Public Good: Philanthropy and Welfare in the Civil War Era* (New York: Knopf, 1980); George M. Fredrickson, *The Inner Civil War: Northern Intellectuals and the Crisis of the Union* (New York: Harper, 1965); Gordon Milne, *George William Curtis and the Genteel Tradition* (Bloomington: Indiana University Press, 1956); remarks by Homer Folks and CCB at the "100th Anniversary Ceremony of the Birth of Josephine Shaw Lowell, 16 December 1943," CRB&M, Community Service Society Collection, box 143; Edward T. Devine, *When Social Work Was Young* (New York: Macmillan, 1939); and an unpublished six-page typescript, "Carlotta Russell Lowell, 1864–1924," written by CCB in August 1949, Michael John Burlingham Collection.

1. CCB-HLS, 20:2, "The first time I ever saw my Louie . . . ," 9.

2. Adeline Lawrence died on 17 October 1882, "at her residence in this city," *Times,* 18 Oct. 1882 5:6; and 20 Oct. 5:6: services at her home, 135 East Thirty-ninth Street, with burial in Woodlawn cemetery. She left a journal now possessed by her great-granddaughter, Helen Taylor Davidson.

3. On Mariella. Margaret Day Broussard Collection, Cyrus J. Lawrence to his father, 17 Oct. 1882. CJL was DeWitt's younger brother. Adeline's son Rob, away at the time, was hurrying to his mother's bedside when she died. The letter does not mention Mariella's four younger sisters.

4. CCB-HLS, 20:2, "The first time I ever saw my Louie . . . ," 9.

5. Annie, rent. Ibid., 20:2, "Where and How we lived," 1; CCB-TFS, "McCutcheon" box, CCB to CB, 8 June 1941, and CCB to LLB, 12 Aug. 1884. Wedding presents. CCB-TFS, CCB to CB, 8 June 1941.

6. The cook. CCB-TFS, CCB to CB, 8 June 1941. Also CCB-HLS, 20:2, "Where and How we lived," 2. The constant immigration to the city, whether from Europe or American farms, kept women's wages low, and since domestic service was one of the few jobs open to them, except for occasional weeks in the summer, CCB and Louie were never without "help" in the house.

7. "Happy?" CCB-TFS, "McCutcheon" box, CCB to CB, 8 June 1941. "Kiss." CCB-HLS, 20:2, "Where and How we lived," 2.

8. CCB-HLS, 20:2, "Where and How we lived." 2–4, 6. Also ibid., "The first time I ever saw my Louie . . . ," 6, and "CCB and the Stage," 3. The games were simple. In "poise" someone would perform a trick, such as balancing a cane on his chin, that others would then try to imitate, or players, seated in a circle on chairs, would bat balloons back and forth, with the loser perhaps sent to the lowest position.

9. Ibid., "Where and How we lived," 4; and ibid., 1:18, CCB to Van Wyck Brooks, 14 Dec. 1951, on observing the Sabbath in the homes of his uncle, Dr. Charles Stillman, and of his parents: "Sunday when we read nothing more worldly than the *Youth's Companion*." And see CCB-TFS, "McCutcheon" box, CCB to LLB, 15 July 1888, at Mount Vernon with his parents: a Sabbath spent "in true Sunday fashion."

10. Barbara Belford, *Bram Stoker: A Biography of the Author of Dracula* (New York: Knopf, 1996), 50.

11. CCB-HLS, 20:2, "Where and How we lived," 2. Ibid., 9:9, CCB to Edwin H. Cassels, 8 July 1941. The Star, with a capacity of 1,600, was by then one of the city's older theaters, built in 1861, before steel construction made protruding balconies possible, so that its galleries were narrow and clinging to the walls.

12. Ibid., 20:2, "The first time I ever saw my Louie . . . ," 7; ibid., "CCB and the Stage," 4; CCB-TFS, CCB, *Joe Evans* (1946), 4. Description of Arnold. *Herald*, 31 Oct. 1883, 3:6, and *Times*, 31 Oct. 1883, 5:5.

13. CCB-HLS, 20:2, "Where and How we lived," 3; ibid., "The first time I ever saw my Louie . . . ," 7–8, and "CCB and the Stage," 4. Terry did not create the role of queen in *Charles I*; that was done by Isabel Batemen, at the premiere in the Lyceum Theatre, London, 28 Sept. 1872. The play has a place in English theatrical history because, in an age dominated by French styles of drama, it was one of the first to hark back to Elizabethan models, with a subject from English history, presented in an English form of verse.

14. CCB-HLS, 20:2, "CCB and the Stage," 4. The company's repertory in New York for this first tour, 1883–84, was: *Merchant of Venice, Much Ado About Nothing, Richard III, The Bells, The Belle's Stratagem, Charles I, Louis XI,* and *The Lyons Mail.* In Philadelphia, Irving performed *Hamlet.*

15. Ibid., 5.

16. Ibid. Repertory in New York for the tour, 1884–85: *Hamlet, Twelfth Night, Much Ado About Nothing, Louis XI,* and *The Lyons Mail.*

17. CCB-HLS, 2:9, Ten Eyck R. Beardsley to CCB, 31 Aug. 1957.

18. Ibid., 20:2, "CCB and the Stage," 6. Ibid., 16:6, CCB to GWR, 29 Jan. 1948, specifies the shop, Robinson & Cleaver.

19. The Evans drawing of Terry as Portia (see illustration) is brown ink on paper over pencil indications, 7¼ by 3¼ inches. It is presently owned by CCB's grandson, CB Jr., son of the drawing's one-year-old donee.

20. Putnam. CCB-HLS, 2:9, CCB to Ten Eyck R. Beardsley, 6 Sept. 1957.

21. Ibid., Beardsley to CCB, 31 Aug. 1957. The reference to General Cronjie (1835–1911) almost surely dates the incident to "Black Week" for the British, in December 1899, when the Boers defeated three separate British forces. Cronjie's victory, at Magersfontein on 11 December, cost the English 950 men. "Put." ibid.

22. CCB-HLS, 2:9, CCB to Beardsley, 6 Sept. 1957.

23. CCB-TFS, "McCutcheon" box, CCB to LLB, 2 Sept. 1884. Ibid., LLB to CCB, and CCB to LLB, both 16 Apr. 1893.

24. Ibid., CCB to LLB, 19 Aug. 1894.

25. Ibid., CCB letter to CB, 8 June 1941.

26. CCB-TFS, CCB to ACH, 6 Aug. 1884.

27. GM interview with RTE, 15 June 1993.

28. The school. CCB typescript on CRL, 2. CCB-HLS, 20:2, "Where and How we lived," 5, describing friendship with Mrs. Ireland, "Iley," who had taught LLB mathematics at Miss Brackett's. See CCB letter memorializing Mrs. Ireland, *Herald Tribune*, 22 Aug. 1934, 16:6. On W. T. Harris, *Herald*, obit, 6 Nov. 1909, 7:2; see also DAB VIII (orig. ed.): 328–30, which states: "Hardly any American philosopher was more widely acclaimed in his own time; hardly any is so little read today." True, also, of his role as an educator. He was superintendent in St. Louis 1868–80 and federal commissioner of education, 1889–1906.

29. Waugh (1992), 29, 32, 36. Francis Shaw was strong for women's rights.

30. Ibid., 39–40, 41, 70, 255.

31. Milne (1956), 95, 96, 109, 111, 150–56. Waugh (1992), 71–79. Fredrickson (1968), 209. For a disparaging view of Curtis, see Bender (1987), 177–81.

32. Waugh (1992), 254; Child. Quoted by Waugh (1992), 41. Child in 1833 had written and published *An Appeal in Favor of That Class of Americans called Africans*, one of the earliest books to attack slavery. She also wrote what now is probably better known, "The New England Boy's Song About Thanksgiving Day," which begins: "Over the river, and through the wood,/ To grandfather's house we go."

33. Waugh (1992), 171–78. Milne (1956), 119.

34. CCB-TFS, CCB to LLB, 5 and 10 Sept. 1895.

35. Waugh (1992), 252, 256; CRB&M, CSS Collection, Box 143: CCB, Remarks at 100th Anniversary, 3.

36. Barlow, the Union army's "boy-general," commissioned at age thirty-one, had been left for dead on the field at Gettysburg, but was saved by the care of a Confederate officer. He was a Republican and abolitionist. Later, as a reformer, he had an important role in New York in 1870 in breaking Tammany's "Tweed Ring."

37. Quoted by Waugh (1992), 138, from William James's memorial address. The other speaker was Booker T. Washington. See ibid., 568–72; Fredrickson (1968), 161, 233; Burke Wilkinson, *The Life and Works of Augustus Saint-Gaudens* (New York: Dover, 1992), 274–88; and David W. Blight, *Race and Reunion: The Civil War in American Memory* (Cambridge: Harvard University Press, 2001), 338–45, with profuse citations.

Fredrickson (1968), 153, 162, 165, offers two views of Shaw's death: (1) as an icon of abolitionist martyrology—he gave his life for Negro freedom; and (2) as a symbol that the aristocratic class still had vigor, still could produce heroes. CCB's view was wholly the first.

Sarah Shaw said of the sculpture: "Saint-Gaudens has immortalized my native city, he has immortalized my dear son, and he has immortalized himself"; see Wilkinson, *The Life and Works*, 286.

38. On Charles R. Lowell. Fredrickson (1968), 29–31, 172; and Waugh (1992), 67, 69, 87–95, 149–51. He married on 31 Oct. 1863; he died 19 Oct. 1864.

39. Face to the wall. CRB&M, CSS Collection, box 2: CCB to Clare Tousley, 30 Nov. 1943. Bonnet, ibid., box 143, CCB, Remarks at 100th Anniversary, 5.

40. Ibid., box 143, CCB, Remarks at 100th Anniversary, 4, where according to CCB, "She was brought up a Unitarian of the strictest sect. There was nothing narrow about her. When she went off to the country, she always went to church, no matter what church it was . . ."

41. Milne (1956), 233.

42. My summary owes much to conclusions reached by Bremner (1980), xviii, and Waugh (1992), introduction, 143–44, 150–51, 169, 175, 263. And to accounts of JSL by contemporaries such as Homer Folks, CCB, and Joseph Devine.

Note: Fredrickson (1965) and Boyer (1978) both judged JSL harshly, especially Boyer. He concluded, 148, that her charitable works allowed her "to sublimate her bitterness and perhaps even hatred toward the urban poor who had behaved so ignobly [as in the draft riots] during her own and the nation's great ordeal." (GM: I believe, however, that bitterness and hatred are easy to recognize and hard to conceal. That none of her contemporaries, friends or enemies, accuse her of either during her forty-year career refutes the charge. Bremner, I think, is correct, xviii: "Men and women like Samuel Gridley Howe and Josephine Shaw Lowell certainly hoped and intended that the reforms they initiated and policies they advocated would influence people's conduct in ways beneficial to society and advantageous to individuals. Perhaps they were presumptuous in thinking they knew what was good for others, but that fault is not peculiar to them or their class. However harsh they sometimes sounded, the ultimate control they sought to impose on people was self-discipline; instead of subjecting the poor to rigid authority, they proposed to put them on the path to self-help and independence.")

43. Waugh (1992), 6; Fredrickson (1968), 213.

44. Waugh (1992), 260, and Bremner (1980), 10, 144–45. See Bender (1987), 203–5, who has an interesting comment on the rewriting of her memorial tablet, presently placed in Bryant Park.

45. Bremner (1980), 202; Devine (1939), 49, 67, 118; and Hammack (1982), 77–78.

46. CRB&M, CSS Collection, box 143, CCB, Remarks at 100th Anniversary, 3.

47. Dinners, Chinese Theatre. Ibid. Singing. CCB typescript on CRL, 4.

48. CRB-M, CSS Collection, box 143, CCB, Remarks at 100th Anniversary, 4.

49. Pamphlet. *Workingmen's Rights in Property Created by Them: Letter from Josephine Shaw Lowell* (New York: Farmington, 1893). In the *Tribune* the letter was titled "The Rights and Wrongs of Strikers," and was written 15 July 1892, in Geneva, Switzerland. The pamphlet's brief introduction, by Erastus Wiman, begins: "The strength of thought and expression in the following letter is a justification for its reproduction. The novelty of the view taken by Mrs. Lowell, the fact that it is so pronounced and vigorously stated by a woman, deserves the production should have some permanent shape . . ."

50. CRB&M, CSS Collection, box 143, Homer Folks, Remarks at 100th Anniversary, 3.

51. Paul B. De Witt, executive secretary of the Association of the Bar of the City of New York, 1945–79. Remark to GM, circa 1969.

52. CRB&M, CSS Collection, box 143, Homer Folks, Remarks at 100th Anniversary, 2. Devine (1939), 23–24.

53. GM interview with Herbert M. Lord, 20 Oct. 1994.

54. Fredrickson (1968), 212, states of JSL: "She soon became recognized as a representative figure of the war generation." Figures. Hopkins (1940), 79–81, 98–102. Hopkins gives as sources for his facts and summaries many of the books and articles that CCB, increasingly

active in the neighborhood programs of St. George's Church, must have read. Even if he had not discovered them for himself, the church's rector, William S. Rainsford, would have urged them on him, for by 1890 Rainsford was the leading Episcopal minister in New York in that church's Social Gospel movement, and St. George's Church, with its huge number of programs, the country's outstanding example of the movement in action. See 284–86, 296.

6. The Lawrence and Hoe Families in the 1880s

Chief sources for this chapter, other than the Burlingham collections, are: Frank E. Comparato, *Genius and Folly: R. Hoe & Company and the Printing Press as a Service to Democracy* (Culver City, Calif.: Labyrinthos, 1979), and Michael John Burlingham, "Richard M. Hoe's Brightside and the Development of Hunts Point," *Westchester Historian* 69:4 (Fall 1993): 73–80. On Grant, St. George's Church, and the district courts: William S. McFeely, *Grant: A Biography* (New York: Norton, 1981); C. Vann Woodward, "The Lowest Ebb: Grant's Sorry Administration," in *Times of Trial: Great Crises in the American Past*, ed. Allan Nevins (New York: Knopf, 1958); Elizabeth S. Moulton, *St. George's Church* (New York: privately printed, 1964); CCB, *Notes on the History of Burlingham, Veeder, Clark & Hupper* (privately printed, 1946), found in several Burlingham collections, including CCB-HLS, 21:1; and *United States Courts in the Second Circuit: A Collection of History Lectures Delivered by Judges of the Second Circuit* (New York: Federal Bar Foundation, 1992).

1. CCB-TFS, CCB to LLB, 3 Sept. 1884. The earliest note found of odd behavior. Ibid., ACH to CCB, 6 Oct. 1882, remarking on an overeffusive letter to her parents.

2. Darius W. Lawrence. *Herald*, 4 Apr. 1885, 5:3; *Times*, 4 Apr. 1885, 1:6; *Tribune*, ibid., 5:5.

3. CCB-TFS, Rob Lawrence to CCB, 6 Sept. 1887, and CCB to LLB, 3 Sept. 1887.

4. CCB-TFS, CCB to LLB, 3 Sept. 1887.

5. Colton, marriage. CCB-HLS, 20:2, "Where and How we lived," 5; also Mrs. Benjamin Day (married to Cyrus J. Lawrence's great-grandson) to GM, 8 June 1996. Charles Lawrence. GM interview with CB Jr., 14 July 1995.

Note: Mrs. Colton and her sons, Colton and Lawrence, are elusive. CCB-TSF, "McCutcheon" box, CCB to LLB, 27 Apr. 1893, writes: "I am sorry to see that young Colton is dead. I hope some of you can go to the funeral. It is pretty hard for Mrs. L., isn't it?" The *Times*, 27 Apr. 1893, 5:7, had a death notice: "G. Q. Colton, Jr., of consumption on 24 April. Friends invited to funeral service at his residence, 141 East 39th St., Thursday April 27th, 1 p.m." CCB at the time was on Staten Island recuperating from a long illness and could not go. Whether any members of his family went is not known.

According to M. J. Burlingham (1989), 139, and also a GM interview with RTE: DeWitt had disgraced the family by "walking off with the French widow down the block"— evidently the family's view of what happened. It can be seen in CCB-TFS, CCB to LLB, 10 Sept. 1887, in which he remarks: "So perhaps Mrs. Lawrence is painted blacker than she is." Also CCB-TFS, CCB to LLB, 7 Sept. 1887. Mrs. Colton's origins and social position, however, are unknown.

6. Mariella. CCB-TFS, CCB to ACH, 9 July 1886: "It is very sad for her to be alone without members of her family by her—sadder perhaps because she wants it so." Niece. GM interview with RTE, 3 Oct. 1993.

7. CCB-TFS, CCB to LLB, 7 Sept. 1887.

Note: The Capen School was founded by Mary A. Burnham in 1877 as a "Classical School" to prepare girls to enter neighboring Smith College. In 1880 Bessie Capen, a chemistry professor at Smith and formerly at Wellesley, began teaching at the school, and after Burnham's premature death in 1885, Capen was its headmistress until she died at eighty-two in 1920. Thereafter the school went through several transformations, emerging in 1967 as part of the Stoneleigh-Burnham School, Greenfield, Massachusetts, which continues. Under Miss Capen the school developed a loyal band of distinguished alumnae and a reputation for placing its girls in the leading women's colleges. Apparently records do not survive, but presumably both Grace and Edith graduated, with neither going to college, though Edith for a time considered Bryn Mawr. Grace, an excellent pianist, profited from the school's music curriculum.

8. CCB-TFS, "McCutcheon" box, CCB to Rob Lawrence: "You must stop looking for a boarding place. We have all piled into 449 before now"; and ibid., CCB to Lawrence, 14 June 1886.

9. Ibid., CCB to ACH, 1 Jan. 1885.

10. No present. CCB-TFS, CCB to ACH, Christmas 1885. Cordial relations. Ibid., CCB to ACH, 13 Jan. 1886. Ibid., ACH to CCB, 17 June 1886. The Tabers had three daughters, Dorothea, Frances, and Carlotta Lowell, none of whom saw much of their Burlingham aunt and uncle. The contrast with the children of Louie's younger sister Grace is marked.

11. Park Avenue became fashionable only in the early 1920s, when electric engines had replaced steam and it became possible to cover the railroad tracks. By then, too, steel stilts could support heavier apartment houses free of the vibrations of trains passing beneath. The present Grand Central Terminal opened in 1913. Until the building of bridges in 1909 across the railroad's open cut up the center of the avenue, most side streets did not cross it. The Burlingham apartment, at 449 Park Avenue (Fifty-sixth Street), was probably in a row of houses called "twenty-foot flats," i.e., four- or five-story houses twenty feet wide. CCB in his letters constantly referred to the apartment as a "flat."

12. CCB-TFS, CCB to Rob Lawrence, 12 Sept. 1889. Ibid., Rob Lawrence to Grace and Edith, 31 July 1889. CCB-HLS, 20:2, "Where and How we lived," 5. CCB-TFS, "McCutcheon" box, CCB to LLB, 16 Aug. 1894, admiring an article Rob hoped to publish, "A Year in the Olympic Forests." (No record of publication found.) Mariella. CCB-TFS, CCB to LLB, 29 Aug. 1897, in which Mariella makes a rare appearance in the family's correspondence. CCB, visiting the family plot in Woodlawn Cemetery (the Bronx), reports on Rob's grave and states, "The sweet briar, or rose bush, that Mellie sent has grown well." Naming of son Robert. GM interview with KBV, 7 Oct. 1997.

13. Lines drawn, but not by CCB. See n. 5 above. On Charles Lawrence. GM interview with CB Jr., 14 July 1995, who recalled being introduced by his father one day on the street to "Uncle Charles," who was "short, and pleasant."

14. GM interview with RTE, 3 Oct. 1993. It is perhaps an example of the Victorian ability to ignore unpleasant incidents that in interviewing CCB's descendants and discussing suicides in subsequent generations of the family, none had heard of Darius Lawrence.

15. CCB-TFS, CCB to ACH, 9 July 1886, referring to her letter to him, 3 Mar. 1886, announcing the engagement. CCB-HLS, 20:2, typescript, "Aunt Annie," 5. Platt reported to his parents that Annie "is not exactly pretty although she has a most charming face, extremely interesting and a smile that is quite impossible to resist"; quoted in Keith N. Morgan, *Charles A. Platt: The Artist as Architect* (Cambridge: MIT Press, 1985), 21.

16. CCB-TFS, CCB to Rob Lawrence, 14 June 1886. Ibid., ACH to CCB, 17 June 1886.

17. Ibid., CCB to LLB, 6 Sept. 1886.

18. CCB-HLS, 20:2, typescript, "Aunt Annie," 5. ACH died 18 March 1887. Twin daughters. See Morgan (1985), 22 n. 21, citing a manuscript by CCB, "Reminiscences of Charles Platt," Platt Office Papers, with wording almost identical to the passage quoted.

19. CCB-TFS, CCB to LLB, 16 Sept. 1886. CCB-HLS, 20:2, typescript, "Aunt Annie," 6. This typescript, dated August 1953, apparently is the original version of the pamphlet, *Aunt Annie, Annie C. Hoe Platt, 1852–1887, Sketch*, which CCB had privately printed in 1957. There are many revisions in the latter, arguably not all for the better. It does not include the quoted line—William Wordsworth, "She was a Phantom of Delight"—but ends: "She was deeply religious and loved the services of the Church."

20. Funeral. Comparato (1979), 649. Tablet. Ibid., 751, and see n. 24, below.

21. Ibid., 649. CCB-TFS, CCB to LLB, 9 Sept. 1887.

22. Comparato (1979), 650.

23. M. J. Burlingham, "Robert M. Hoe's" 79–80.

24. CCB-HLS, 20:11, CCB to Fletcher Harper, 22 Nov. 1941; *Herald Tribune*, 27 Oct. 1941, 7:1, reporting the dedication of the tablet with a picture of it.

25. Comparato (1979), 649. GM interviews with PLT, 11 Sept. 1993 and 3 Oct. 1994: PLT believes that by the mid-1920s his mother, Grace, and his Aunts Edith and Louie each had annual unearned incomes of between $8,500 and $10,000, having gained by inheritance funds then worth at least $100,000. In each case, he surmised, this "was essentially Hoe money." Presumably the fourth sister, his Aunt Fanny, whom he knew less well, had an equal inheritance.

26. Woodward (1958), 174. Also Wilson (1962; repr., 1994), 166: "Under Grant's two administrations, there flapped through the national capital a whole phantasmagoria of insolent fraud, while a swarm of predatory adventurers was let loose on the helpless South." For CCB and the "Whiskey Ring Trials," see Chapter 2.

27. McFeely (1981), 492–93, quoting as contemporary opinion C. W. Moulton to W. T. Sherman, 9 May 1884, and for a later view, Karen A. Wendell, "Grant & Ward: The Anatomy of a Fraud" (seminar paper, History Department, Smith College, 1977). Also Wilson (1962; repr. 1994), 167. For an account of the sentimentalizing of Grant, see David W. Blight, *Race and Reunion: The Civil War in American Memory* (Cambridge: Harvard University Press, 2001), chap. 7, 210–54.

28. *Personal Memoirs of U.S. Grant*, 2 vols. (New York: 1885–86).

29. CCB-TFS, "McCutcheon" box, CCB to LLB, 9 Aug. 1885.

30. McFeely (1981), 493, Grant "had an exceedingly limited moral sense." And on Grant and the bankruptcy: "To him, the man who won—who got rich and stayed rich—was the one who was moral and could make the judgments. All that mattered was success." This was never CCB's belief.

31. Woodward (1958), 174; also Wendell, "Grant and Ward," n. 27 above: "The matter of General Grant was one of cognitive dissonance—Americans *wanted* to see Grant as a truly great hero, so they blocked out any conflicting information." Also Blight, *Race and Reunion*, n. 27 above.

32. Arthur Brooks (1845–95). Under his leadership, 1875–95, Incarnation, with Murray Hill as its neighborhood, became a rich, prominent parish. See Brooks's obit, *Tribune*, 17 July 1895, 7:1; *Herald*, 17 July 1895, 12:1; and *Times*, 17 July 1895, 5:6. The parish was founded in 1850 as a mission of Grace Church, Broadway and Ninth Street; the church was built in 1852; architect, E. T. Little, and builder, Marc Eidlitz. It is now a New York Community Landmark.

33. CCB-TFS, ACH to CCB, 26 Jan. 1887.

34. Reverend J. Douglas Ousley, rector of the church, to GM, 3 Mar. 1994; and CCB-TFS, ACH to CCB, 17 June 1886.

35. CCB-TFS, CCB to ESB, 26 May 1886.

36. Ibid., "McCutcheon" box, CCB to LLB, 15 July 1888.

37. The Reverend Ousley to GM, n. 34 above.

38. *Family Record, St. George's Church, vol. 1, 1886–1896.* In a space at the entry for "Remarks" is noted "also sister Miss Lawrence." But which of the four is not specified.

39. Moulton (1964), 49.

Note. St. George's was founded in 1752, on Beekman Street, as a chapel of Trinity Church. During the Revolution, according to Moulton, both "Trinity and St. George's were smug and Royalist, undisturbed by Methodist fervor or Calvinist preoccupation with sin." St. George's Chapel, with the aid and blessing of Trinity, separated in 1811, becoming St. George's Church, and its rectors in the coming years were always "low church." By 1846 the church was facing increasing financial trouble as much of its congregation moved farther uptown, and the vestry at first planned to open a chapel at Fourteenth Street. Hearing of the plan, Peter G. Stuyvesant, who recently had given a four-acre park, Stuyvesant Square, to the city, offered a plot overlooking the square to the vestry. The church, in accepting it, decided to make the new building the main church. This building, designed by the architectural firm of Blesch and Eidlitz, was consecrated in December 1849. It burned in 1865, and was rebuilt by Leopold Eidlitz alone. From 1845 to 1878 the rector was Stephen H. Tyng, one of the great preachers of his generation. He was confident, quick, decisive, and had a temper. Moulton reports, "When one parishioner taxed him with this, he replied: 'My dear Sir, I have restrained more temper in half an hour than you ever did in your whole life.'"

40. The Reverend Stephen Garmey, "St. George's Church: An Evangelical Bulwark," *Tidings: The Newsletter of the Parish Calvary/St. George's,* Summer 1994.

41. GM interview with the Reverend Thomas F. Pike, rector of Calvary/St. George's, 15 Feb. 1994.

42. Moulton (1964), 80. ST. GCB IV:10 (25 Dec. 1915); and a memorial volume presented to H. H. Pike for "35 years of faithful service," 1884–1919.

43. For general background, see Gilmore and Black (1975) chap. 1.

44. Court founded on 5 October 1678. See Gordon W. Paulsen, *The Silver Oar of the Vice-Admiralty Court of the Province of New York,* MLA, Doc. 735, 1 May 1998, 10672; and the "Introduction" to Hough (1925).

45. Paulsen, *The Silver Oar;* Hough (1925); *The Encyclopedia of New York City* (1995), see "Courts, (3) Federal." On the silver oar, see Chapter 19.

46. Hough (1925) and Paulson (1998), see n. 44 above.

47. Act of 9 Apr. 1814, 3 Stat. 120–21. Judicial disagreement on "Mother Court," *United States Courts in the Second Circuit* (1992), 42, 69–70.

48. Act of 25 Feb. 1865, 13 Stat. 438. Eastern District waterfront, see *United States Courts in the Second Circuit* (1992), 24, 26, Harbor waterfront, Bone, ed. (1997), 19.

49. Pedestrian toll. *The WPA Guide to New York City* (1982), 313.

50. Gilmartin (1995), 69: "At the turn of the century the post office building was universally regarded as an eyesore." Gunther (1994), 139: "The building had been unattractive even when it opened in 1875." Gould (1979), 73–74.

51. Admiralty suits in Eastern District. *United States Courts in the Second Circuit* (1992), 28. Gunther (1994), 144, 705 n. 173, gives some figures for the Southern District Court. The 1920s figures: 1,503 bankruptcy cases; 7,620 for the rest, including 1,904 admiralty cases, 2,620 law and equity, and 2,740 criminal—admiralty being slightly less than a fifth of the total.

52. CCB-HLS, 3:5, CCB to Paul D. Cravath, 27 Jan. 1920. CCB's essay on admiralty practice: in *A Treatise on Federal Practice in Civil Causes*, by Roger Foster, 2nd ed. (1892). It was reprinted in the 3rd ed. (4th not seen). By the 5th, it had been dropped. For a letter of admiration at the time, CCB-TFS, "McCutcheon" box, George H. Eilman to CCB, 22 Sept. 1892.

Note: According to Gilmore and Black (1975), 2: "Until 1966, each federal district court had an admiralty 'side,' with a separate docket and rules of procedure peculiar to admiralty cases. In 1966 the separate 'sides' were merged, the admiralty 'suit' became a regular 'civil action,' and the Federal Rules of Civil Procedure were made generally applicable, with some special rules for certain cases heard under the 'admiralty' jurisdictional grant. Despite this 'unification,' the admiralty power remains a separate and independent *ground of jurisdiction*, both constitutional and statutory." The authors continue their discussion of "unification," and its effect on admiralty cases, procedures, and terminology, on pp. 19ff. But as the new rules did not come into existence until seven years after CCB's death, they are not important here.

53. CCB, *Notes*, 6, 8.

54. Ibid. Robert D. Benedict's firm, Benedict, Taft & Benedict, was a principal admiralty firm in 1883; and RDB, who retired in 1907 and died in 1911 (*Times*, 30 July 1911, 9:5), was "the leader of the admiralty bar." He was "a man of learning and ability, although technical and inclined to argue any and every point. He was of high character." On "B. Lincoln" Benedict. CCB, *Notes*, 8.

Note: The three Benedict brothers were nephews of Erastus C. Benedict (1800–1880), author of the honored treatise *The American Admiralty: Its Jurisdiction and Practice, with Practical Forms and Directions* (1850), popularly known as *Benedict on Admiralty*. His firm, Benedict, Burr and Benedict, was for many years a leader in admiralty law, and both nephews Robert and Charles started practice with him. See DAB II (orig. ed.): 176–77, and *United States Courts in the Second Circuit* (1992), 26.

See *United States Courts in the Second Circuit*, 27, citing *Times*, 10 June 1897, 2:4, and speculating that Judge Benedict may have delayed his retirement until 1897, despite thirty-two years on the bench, ill health, and increasing criticism, to preserve for his brother, B. Lincoln, the latter's lucrative position.

55. Judge Choate: "forbad brother." CCB, *Notes*, 8.

56. Choate's resignation. *Times*, 14 Mar. 1881, 8:5; *Tribune*, editorial, 15 Mar., 3:2; and see *Annals of the Harvard Class of 1852*, by Grace Williamson Edes (Cambridge: privately printed, 1922), on resignation and character: quiet, retiring, kindly. Choate founded and endowed the boys' boarding school "Choate," in Wallingford, Connecticut, in 1896. It prepared boys for college, and its most famous graduate became the thirty-fifth president of the United States, John F. Kennedy. In 1974 the school joined Rosemary Hall, a girl's boarding school in Wallingford, to form the present Choate Rosemary Hall, which takes both day and boarding students.

57. On Brown. CCB, *Notes* (1946), 7; *United States Courts in the Second Circuit* (1992), 16; and J. B. Morris, (1987), 83.

58. CCB-HLS, 6:9, CCB to New York *Law Journal*, memorializing Alexander Gilchrist Jr., 26 Nov. 1948, 4:3.

59. Initials in ink. TDT-YSML, 2:15, copy of Alexander Gilchrist Jr. to CCB, 2 July 1941. Brown's business deals. CCB *Notes*, 7: Brown "had made quite a fortune by investments in real estate and the purchase of second mortgages."

60. Addison Brown (1830–1913). He was a founder in 1891 of the New York Botanical Garden, and in 1896–98, with Nathaniel Lord Britton, its director, published the three-volume *Illustrated Flora of the United States and Canada*, with 4,000 illustrations. Brown also

published *The Elgin Botanic Garden* (1908), an account of the country's first botanical garden open to the public. It was established in 1801 by David Hosack, a professor of botany at Columbia College, on twenty acres in mid-Manhattan, a site now part of Rockefeller Center. See *The Encyclopedia of New York City* (1995), 130, and Brown's obit, *Times*, 10 Apr. 1913, 11:5. CCB *Notes*, 7.

61. CCB, *Notes* 7. "Spot a liar," CCB-HLS, 3:3, CCB to CPC, 18 Mar. 1952.

7. *Breakdown and Rescue*

Chief sources for this chapter are CCB's letters and memorandums in the various Burlingham collections and author's interviews.

1. CCB-TFS, "McCutcheon" box, CCB to LLB, 23 Aug. 1890.

2. Percentage of fees. CCB-HLS, 20:2, "Where and How we lived," 6. See CCB-TFS, "McCutcheon" box, CCB to LLB, 29 June 1890. Quotation. CCB-TFS, "McCutcheon" box, CCB to LLB, 29 June 1890.

3. Rent. CCB-HLS, 20:2, "Where and How we lived," 6. His article for the handbook on federal practice (see Chapter 6, n. 52) may have started as a way of increasing income and originally been intended to be a book. See CCB-TFS, "McCutcheon" box, CCB to LLB, 29 June 1890: "I made good progress with my book last night. I have written nothing yet, and I shall not till I have got the plan perfected."

4. CCB-HLS, 3:5, CCB to Paul D. Cravath, 27 Jan. 1920.

5. Gilmore and Black (1975), 3. These two Yale professors, seemingly as fearful as CCB of appearing sentimental about the history of admiralty law, title their review of it "The Rhodian Law and All That."

6. Nelson, ed. (1983), 41. The clerk was Joseph Barbash.

7. Hough (1925), "Introduction," xxiv. *The Maritime Law Association of the United States, Annual Book, 1995–1996*, sec. II, 1, 7. Although MLA members practice in every state and territory of the United States where maritime activity exists, most of them are in New York, Louisiana, Texas, and California.

8. Quotation. CCB-HLS, 20:1, "Clerks in law offices . . .," 4. Also ibid., 20:2, "A Lawyer," 3: "I have enjoyed the practice of law, and especially admiralty."

9. CCB-HLS, 20:2, "Where and How we lived," 6.

10. CCB-TFS, "McCutcheon" box, Sarah B. Shaw to CCB. Envelope postmarked 11 a.m., 7 Oct. 1892.

11. CCB-HLS, 20:2, "Where and How we lived," 7. The son's school. In ibid., 5–6, Charles attends an elementary school run by Miss Miller and Miss Small, both former teachers at Miss Brackett's school. Their building faced Bryant Park, where the boys had their sports. In these years the park was still cut off from Fifth Avenue by the Croton Reservoir (replaced by the New York Public Library, 1911). In some year, perhaps 1895, CB transferred to the Cutler School, which prepared him for Harvard College. See Chapter 10, n. 8, and CB's *Harvard College Class of 1906, 3rd Report*.

12. CCB-HLS, 20:2, "Where and How we lived," 7.

13. Ibid.

14. Michael John Burlingham Collection, CCB typescript on Carlotta Russell Lowell, 5.

15. CCB-HLS, 20:2, "Where and How we lived," 7.

16. CCB-TFS, "McCutcheon" box, CCB to LLB, 14 Apr. 1893.

17. CCB-TFS, CCB to ESB, 30 Aug. 1893.

18. Faint. CCB-HLS, 20:2, "Where and How we lived," 7–8. CCB-TFS, "McCutcheon" box, CCB to LLB, 10 Oct. 1893.

19. CCB-TFS, W. S. Rainsford, rector of St. George's Church, to CCB, 15 Nov. 1893, addressed to CCB at Thirty-eighth Street (whence he had received a note from CCB): "I am so glad you're slowly winning your way back to health." Ibid., CCB to ESB, 7 Aug. 1894.

20. "Nervous prostration." CCB's autobiographical entry for *Harvard Class of 1879, Report IX, Fiftieth Anniversary*, 78. Overwork. CCB-HLS, 20:2, "Where and How we lived," 8, and Michael John Burlingham Collection, typescript on CRL, 5. Declining bench appointment. GM interview with Herbert M. Lord (CCB law partner), 20 Oct. 1994; and see LH-HLS, 100:26, CCB to LH, 2 Apr. [1918]: "I am at present hoping to get relieved of my job as chairman of Local Board Div. 8 as it has proved rather more than I can stand . . . [I]n fact my doctor told me if I did not quit there was danger of a complete break up again."

21. "Never to eat." CCB-HLS, 20:2, "Where and How we lived," 8. A better son. CCB-TFS, CCB to ESB, 30 Aug. 1893.

22. Rent. CCB-TFS, "McCutcheon" box, CCB to LLB, 12 Aug. 1884.

23. CCB, "Memorial of Henry Galbraith Ward," ABCNY *Yearbook, 1934*. Helping the young. E.g., when his young partner William J. Dean suddenly died in 1936, leaving a widow and daughter, with the widow pregnant, CCB was "remarkably kind and helpful" to the widow. GM interview with William J. Dean Jr., 22 May 1995. Also GM interview with Nancy Shaw Palmer, 16 Oct. 1994.

24. CCB-TFS, "McCutcheon" box, CCB to LLB, 9 Sept. 1890, on new stationery, and CCB to LLB, 11 Sept. 1890 on old.

25. "Slummish slopes." CCB-HLS, 20:2, "Where and How we lived," 6.

26. The *Silvia*, 171 U.S. 462 (1898), 463.

27. The *Silvia* in circuit court, 35 U.S. App., 395; and in district court, Southern District, New York, 64 Fed. Rep. 607 (24 Nov. 1894), Wing, Shoudy & Putnam (CCB, of counsel) for libelant.

28. The *Silvia*, 171 U.S. 462, 464. Justice Horace Gray (1828–1902) was appointed an associate justice of the U.S. Supreme Court in 1882. After his death in 1902, TR appointed Oliver Wendell Holmes Jr. (1841–1932) to Gray's seat.

29. Ibid., 465.

30. The income tax case. *Pollock v. Farmers' Loan & Trust Co.*, 157 U.S. 429 (1895), was won by Joseph Hodges Choate, whose highly emotional argument—though the judges were hardly less emotional—was considered by many to be the apex of a long and distinguished career.

31. The *Silvia*, 171 U.S. 462, 465–66. The court's decision posed a problem for some admiralty suits, and CCB in a letter to a colleague in a Boston firm, Dodge & Dodge, wrote: "I send you by this mail a copy of the opinion in the *Silvia*, which you may not have seen. We must get round the word 'management' as defined in that case." HLS, Dodge & Dodge Collection, 4:3, CCB to E. S. Dodge, 26 Nov. 1898.

32. Shoudy, only briefly ill, died at home in Brooklyn 11 Aug. 1894. See CCB-HLS, 21:1, CCB, *Notes on the History of Burlingham, Veeder, Clark & Hupper* (privately printed, 1946), 4; obits, *Herald*, 12 Aug. 1894, 11:6, and *Times*, 12 Aug. 1894, ibid., 5:7. For changes in the firm name on its stationery. E.g., CCB-TFS, "McCutcheon" box, CCB to LLB, 20 Sept. 1895.

33. CCB-TFS, "McCutcheon" box, CCB to LLB, 20 Sept. 1895, on stationery with new firm name and list of partners. But in his *Notes*, above, 10, CCB states: "Masten was taken into the firm at the same time as I was; and James Forrester somewhat later." GM: I have

followed the contemporary letterhead. In ibid., 9, CCB mistakenly puts the cause of the new firm, Shoudy's death, in 1898.

34. Masten. CCB-HLS, 21:1, CCB, *Notes*, 8. CCB-HLS, 2:9, Ten Eyck Remsen Beardsley to CCB, 31 Aug. 1957; and GM interview with John R. Hupper, 2 Aug. 1994.

35. Forrester. CCB-HLS, 21:1, CCB, *Notes*, 8–9. LH-HLS, 100:24, CCB to LH, 16 Aug. 1910 and 6 Sept. 1911; in the second letter CCB has crossed out Forrester's name in the letterhead. On Forrester's name stricken from the roll. BU History Files, clerk of the New York Court of Appeals to the firm, 2 June 1943.

36. Cowen. CCB, *Notes*, GM: CCB's year, 1899, for Cowen joining the firm is incorrect. Its stationery in the fall of 1896 shows Cowen present, see CCB-TFS, "McCutcheon" box, CCB to CB, 20 Aug. 1896; also HLS, Dodge & Dodge Collection, 4:3, correspondence with CCB; and CRB&M, Seth Low Collection, CCB to SL, 4 Mar. 1897. Regarding Cowen's importance to the firm, it is perhaps significant that Beardsley (see n. 39, below), in describing the partners in these years, does not mention him. Also Cowen's "Memorial," ABCNY *Reports* 9 (*Yearbook*, 1901), 104–7, was written by a man outside the firm. See also obit, *Tribune*, 5 Jan. 1900, 7:5. Cowen died of apoplexy while at Troy, New York.

37. CCB-TFS, "McCutcheon" box, CCB to LLB, 10 Aug. 1890.

38. CCB-HLS, 2:9, Ten Eyck Remsen Beardsley to CCB, 31 Aug. 1957: "My dear Old Friend and former Boss . . ."

39. Ibid.

40. Ibid., 20:2, "A Lawyer," 3.

41. On Marlowe and Taber. CCB-TFS, "McCutcheon" box, CCB to LLB, 15 Sept. 1891. John D. Barry, *Julia Marlowe* (Boston: Richard G. Badger, 1899), 52–59, and on her "decision to star alone," 79–80. See also Charles Edward Russell, *Julia Marlowe: Her Life and Art* (New York: Appleton, 1926), 270.

42. CCB-HLS, 20:2, "CCB and the Stage," 3. *Times*, 7 Jan. 1900, 1:6. Though the court sustained the charge of "intolerable severity," it dismissed two others of desertion and refusal to support. Taber did not oppose the suit, and Marlowe was granted $3,000 a year alimony. The decision was reported in less detail in the *Herald*, 7 Jan. 1900, sec. VI, 5:1: "The case was very quietly heard." CRB&M, Belmont Collection, CCB to Eleanor Belmont, 21 Jan. [1958]: "He was my intimate friend, and I knew Julia Marlowe well. I knew her maid Mary, too, and when Herbert Satterlee and I arranged for the divorce of Julia and R.T. in Vermont, Mary was sent to be a witness. She thought she would help things along and told a cock and bull story of R.T.'s habit of physically bashing Julia."

43. Advising Taber. CCB-HLS, 20:2, "CCB and the Stage," 4. See also Michael John Burlingham Collection, CCB, *Joe Evans, 1857–1898* (privately printed, 1949), 9. According to CCB typescript on Taber, CCB-HLS, 17:16, Taber acted with success in England until he fell ill with pneumonia, "was stricken with tuberculosis in the throat, and was brought home by his dear friend, Edward Knoblock to die. After a few days in New York City at the house of his sister, Mrs. Henry Holt, he was taken by his mother to Saranac, where he died 8 March 1904."

44. The source of Grace and Edith's income in these years before they received Colonel Hoe's legacies, following the death of his widow in 1901, is not clear. From hints in CCB's correspondence with LLB and her brother Rob Lawrence it would seem that DeWitt Lawrence had provided some money in trust for the education and support of his two youngest children by his first wife. See CCB-TFS, CCB to LLB, 7 Sept. 1887; ibid., "McCutcheon" box, Rob Lawrence to Grace and Edith, 31 July 1889; and ibid., CCB to LLB, 11 Sept. 1892: "We have lots of money—*we* have. But Grace and Edith haven't, for the Trust Co., has no funds, it writes."

45. CCB-TFS, from the ledger titled "Invoices," a clipping 31 Oct. 1901 from *The Examiner*, a Baptist weekly paper.

46. "Weepy." CCB-TFS, "McCutcheon" box, CCB to LLB, 29 Aug. 1897. Ibid., CCB to LLB, 8 Sept. 1897.

47. Ibid., CCB to LLB, 26 Aug. 1897, 29 Aug. 1897, and 21 June 1903; and CCB to CB, 11 July 1897, with an anecdote on Dickens's burial in Westminster Abbey.

48. Ibid., CCB to CB, 20 Aug. 1896.

49. Ibid., CCB to Nancy, 2 Aug. 1891.

50. Ibid., CCB to LLB, 10 Oct. 1893.

51. Ibid., CCB to LLB, 15 July 1888.

8. Taking on Tammany Hall

Chief sources for this chapter, other than Burlingham collections, are: On tenements: Jacob A. Riis, *How the Other Half Lives: Studies among the Tenements of New York*, ed. Sam Bass Warner Jr., (Cambridge: Harvard University Press, 1970); and Edward T. Devine, *When Social Work Was Young* (New York: Macmillan, 1939).

On Tammany Hall: William L. Riordon, ed., *Plunkitt of Tammany Hall*, with an Introduction by Arthur Mann (New York: Dutton, 1963); Lothrop Stoddard, *Master of Manhattan: The Life of Richard Croker* (New York: Longmans, Green, 1931); M. R. Werner, *Tammany Hall* (Garden City, N.Y.: Doubleday, 1928), which extensively quotes sources; and Leo Hershkowitz, *Tweed's New York: Another Look* (Garden City, N.Y.: Anchor, 1977), which attempts to rehabilitate Tweed.

On the Department of Education: David C. Hammack, *Power and Society: Greater New York at the Turn of the Century* (New York: Russell Sage Foundation, 1982; repr., New York: Columbia University Press, 1987); Diane Ravitch, *The Great School Wars: New York City, 1805–1973* (New York: Basic Books, 1974); Herbert Shapiro, *Reorganizations of the New York City Public School System, 1890–1910* (Ph.D. thesis, Yeshiva University, 1967); Sol Cohen, *Progressives and Urban School Reform: The Public Education Association of New York City, 1895–1954* (New York: Teachers College, Columbia University, 1964); and A. Emerson Palmer, *The New York Public School* (New York: Macmillan, 1905).

1. Bryce (1891), 1:608. Hammack (1982), in his opening chapter, "Contemporary Perceptions, Historical Problems," discusses the different views, then and later, of what was happening in the city and why; and touches on these again in his fourth chapter, "Tradition and Reality." In this biography I hew to the traditional view, presenting reality much as CCB and most of his contemporaries saw it. Hammack states his view at 111 (and differently phrased at 103 and 316): "The great theme of the period [1886–1903] was not the static battle between bosses and reformers, but the increasing diversity of the political organizations that could influence mayoral elections."

2. Bryce (1891), 1:613.

3. Riis (1970), 188 15–17,. "Brother's keeper." In 1938, in part because of Mayor La Guardia's urgings, voters in New York amended the state's constitution (Article 17:1) to read: "The aid, care and support of the needy are public concerns and shall be provided by the state and by such of its subdivisions, and in such manner and by such means, as the Legislature may from time to time determine." There is no such provision in the federal constitution. Lowell on laboring classes. Waugh (1992), 462, citing William Rhinelander

Stewart: *The Philanthropic Work of Josephine Shaw Lowell*, 371. Lowell made the remark, which caused laughter, in a debate at the 25th National Conference of Charities and Correction held in New York City in May 1898. At issue was an amendment to the state constitution about the uses of prison labor. She was speaking in support of labor unions.

4. Conflict on Croker's birth year. Werner (1928), 303, Stoddard (1931), 3, and DAB, vol. 2, part 2, 558, all state that Croker arrived at age three, putting his birth in Ireland, 24 Nov. 1843, two years later than *The Encyclopedia of New York City* (1995), and the *Times*, obit, 30 Apr. 1922, 1:1, which states he died at age eighty. Crowded classrooms, Ravitch (1974), 89. The gun and musical salutes, Stoddard (1931), 194; gun, Werner (1928), 464; "Hail to the Chief" for Croker on another occasion, *Tribune*, 20 Oct. 1898, 2:4. The song had become associated with the president of the United States by 1845, see Elise K. Kirk, *Music at the White House: A History of the American Spirit* (Urbana: University of Illinois Press, 1986), 56.

5. Figures differ slightly among sources. Riis (1970), in his appendix, 201–5, gives census and Health Department reports through 1890, showing the density of the population in the city's Tenth Ward in 1890 to be 334,080 per square mile. For a discussion of the comparisons among cities of density per acre, see Sam Bass Warner Jr.'s introduction to Riis (1970). *The Encyclopedia of the City of New York* (1995), "Immigration," has some tables; and see Cohen (1964), 5–6; Ravitch (1974), 173–77, 190; and Waugh (1992), 260. On limiting immigration. Ravitch (1974), 123, citing Riis "The Problem of the Children," *The Children of the Poor* (1892). See also Devine (1939), 67. Hammack (1982), 141, quotes a private letter of Bryce about tenement crowding: "I wish it were possible to stop all Italian and Jewish immigration into the U.S. for the next ten years, if that could be done without hardship to the poor people. For your country is not getting a fair chance."

6. Huthmacher (1968), 12.

7. Devine (1939) has a chapter on the history of tenement house reform, 67–80; on the exhibit, ibid., 75. On its national importance. Allen F. Davis, *Spearheads for Reform: The Social Settlements and the Progressive Movement, 1890–1914* (New York: Oxford University Press, 1967), 68–69. See also Waugh (1992), 400.

8. Devine (1939), 77. The commission was led by Robert W. de Forest, with Lawrence Veiller as secretary, and it published a two-volume report *The Tenement House Problem* (in New York City and Buffalo), generally agreed to be the most exhaustive and constructive investigation ever made of tenement conditions. See Devine's chapter "Tenement House Reform," 67–80.

9. Figures on the number of jobs Tammany controlled, if it won the election, vary widely. Waugh (1992), 248, adopts for the late 1880s (i.e., before the creation of Greater New York on 1 January 1898) the largest number seen, 40,000, citing Steven P. Erie, *Rainbow's End: Irish-Americans and the Dilemmas of the Urban Machine Politics, 1840–1895* (Berkeley: University of California Press, 1988), 5. Erie makes the statement without citation. Arthur Mann, in his introduction to Riordon (1963), states 12,000, the lowest figure seen, and makes the comparison to Carnegie. In the early twentieth century (i.e., after the creation of Greater New York), Mann notes, xii, that Tammany had 32,000 committee men in the five boroughs. Eisenstein (1966), 18, 25, 28, 35, gives a clear personal account of how low-level city jobs and favors were distributed. The *Herald*, 9 Nov. 1906, 5:5, had an article on the amount of state patronage Tammany won in that month's elections, despite losing the governorship to Republican Charles Evans Hughes: "$1,000,000 spoils in state offices."

10. Mann's introduction, Riordon (1963), x. Others, citing mayors who showed some independence of Tammany, might put the years of reform at thirteen or even fifteen, but the

ratio remains greatly in Tammany's favor. For a brief history of Tammany, see Garrett (1961), 6–11, 38–41.

11. For a brief statement of Tammany's inherent conservatism and lack of any vision of what the city might be other than a source of personal wealth, see Daniel P. Moynihan's article, "When the Irish Ran New York," *Reporter*, 8 June 1961, 32–34. See also Mann's introduction, Riordon (1963), and Garrett (1961), 6–11, 38–41. In contrast, Eisenstein (1966), 11, 15, 16, 25, extols Tammany's service to the poor: Its job "has since been taken over by bureaucratic agencies at perhaps two or three times the expense—and probably with half the efficiency." On "repeaters." Stoddard (1931), 45–46, and Werner (1928), 305.

12. Ballots. Welling (1942), 54, and Hammack (1982), 128. "Big Tim" Sullivan. Stoddard (1931), 232. Loyalty. Eisenstein (1966), preface.

13. Quoted by Werner (1928), 446–50, and Stoddard (1931), 77–80. The article, "Richard Croker," was by William T. Stead, editor, *Review of Reviews*, Oct. 1897. Stead (1849–1912) in 1893, after visiting the Chicago Columbian Exposition, on the request of a citizens' committee wrote an exposé of the city's social conditions. His book, *If Christ Came to Chicago!* (1894), was unsparing in its realistic account of civic corruption and became the chief text in a campaign for reform. Though the corrupters managed to keep copies out of many Chicago stores, the book was widely read there, elsewhere in the country, and in England. Stead drowned in the *Titanic* sinking.

14. Bryce (1891), 1:609–10. For the effort to exonerate Tweed, see Hershkowitz (1977), on the rise in debt and taxes, 170, and, in summary, his epilogue.

15. Sheriff. Werner (1928), 318–24. Judge. Mann's introduction, Riordon (1963), 74. "Honest graft." Mitgang (1963), 26, and Riordon (1963), 3–6.

16. Werner (1928), 424–26; Stoddard (1931), 214. On the significance of ice to the tenements. Eisenstein (1966), 7.

17. Stoddard (1931), 233.

18. Werner (1928), 348–56.

19. The Lexow Committee, led by state senator Clarence Lexow of Rockland County, because of its sensational findings has always been one of the most famous in the history of New York State. It was composed of five Republicans and two Democrats, all state senators.

20. CRB&M, Community Service Society Collection, box 143, CCB, Remarks at the "100th Anniversary Ceremony of the Birth of Josephine Shaw Lowell, 16 December 1943."

21. Welling (1942), 66, 69.

22. Ibid., 72.

23. Mann's introduction, Riordon (1963), 11.

24. CCB-COH, 5.

25. CCB-HLS, 15:16, TR to CCB, 16 May 1900; ibid., TR to Silas W. Burt, 16 May 1900. See also ibid., Burt to CCB, 17 July 1900.

26. Notice of appointment. CCB-HLS, 13:9.

27. Wards and school. *Times*, 1 Apr. 1893, 9:5. Hammack (1982), 277, citing Good Government Club E, Pamphlet 9, states: "By 1895 Ward 2 had only 112 school-age children, while Ward 22 had 32,741, Ward 19 had 46,797, and Ward 12 had over 70,000. Yet each ward had one and only one board of five school trustees."

28. Joseph Mayer Rice, "The Public School System of New York City," *Forum*, Jan. 1893, 616–30, quoted by Ravitch (1974), 129, who states, 156, that the article "launched the drive for school reform."

29. CCB-HLS, 2:7, CCB to Butler, 12 July 1945. Without humor. CRB&M, Belmont Collection, CCB to Eleanor Belmont, 9 June 1950. "Very stuffy." CCB-COH, 17; and gen-

erally on Butler and the campaign for school reform, 14–19. Hammack (1982), 279–84, describes Butler and some who worked closely with him. One of the latter to whom Hammack grants influence, 281, 293, was the Reverend William S. Rainsford, rector of CCB's St. George's Church, of which Butler's predecessor at Columbia, Seth Low, was a vestryman, 1893–1916. On Butler versus Low on the development of Columbia, and the role of the Episcopal church, and of Jewish groups, see Bender (1987), 284–90, 292–93.

30. Nicholas Murray Butler, *Across the Busy Years: Recollections and Reflections* (New York: Scribner's, 1939, 1940), I:311.

31. Good Government Club E and the PEA are described in Cohen (1964): club, 3, 19–20, 25–27, 31, and PEA, 27, 32–33, 37–38, 45–46, et seq. See also Hammack (1982), 280–83. Ravitch (1974), 144.

32. Palmer (1905), 193. On appointments, see *Harvard College, Class of '79, Sixth Report, 1900*, and *Seventh Report, 1905*.

33. Palmer (1905), 286.

34. CCB-HLS, 13:9. The appointment by Strong, on 12 September 1895, to the ward trustees ran to 1 January 1900. But before it expired, Strong appointed CCB, in 1897, to the Board of Education. The new appointment by Van Wyck, starting 1 January 1901, was for three years but ended with CCB's resignation in the fall of 1901. The appointment by Seth Low started 20 January 1902 and CCB's election to president followed in 2 February. It is not clear whether CCB was "off" the board for the year 1900 or received some sort of temporary reappointment by Van Wyck. Palmer, the Board's secretary, in Palmer (1905), lists 431 board members for each year, and shows CCB "off" for 1900, but in an earlier biographical description, 365, states that CCB "was re-appointed in 1900." CCB's statements, in his *Seventh Harvard Class Report* and COH, 3, 14, suggest some sort of temporary reappointment.

35. CCB-HLS, 3:1, CCB speech on "The Department of Education," at Columbia University, on 25 Mar. 1904, 1: "I think it may fairly be said that the school boards have not been partisan bodies . . . [T]he fact is that when a man has once taken his seat in the Board there seems to be something in the nature of the work which makes him put away partisanship, and devote himself with the best light he has to the welfare of the children. I attribute this largely to the fact that we have had unpaid boards." On Jasper. How he dominated the board, *Times*, 18 Jan. 1891, 14:1, and 1 Feb. 1891, 10:3. Jasper and Maxwell feuding. *Tribune*, 23 Sept. 1899, 7:6. Resumption of feud. *Times*, 30 Jan. 1901, 6:6. Jasper obit. *Times*, 8 Feb. 1915, 7:4. Apportionment of commissioners. CCB-HLS, 3:1, CCB speech on "The Department of Education," 3.

36. Shapiro (1967), 167, quoting Board of Education *Journal*, 3 Feb. 1902, 221–22, CCB's speech on accepting office of president.

37. CCB-HLS, 13:9, clipping from Board of Education *Journal*, 25 May 1896. On Gilman and Jasper, see Hammack (1982), 295–96; also *Times*, 29 May 1896, 8:4.

38. Tribune, 23 Sept. 1899, 7:6, and *Times*, 30 Jan. 1901, 6:6.

39. Palmer (1905), 365, ignores the row with Jasper and cites this extracurricular use of school buildings as CCB's main accomplishment. And CCB, in "Socialization of the School," *Ethical Record*, Jan. 1903, 43–44, in CCB-HLS, 13:9, stresses the importance of this development. Yet in CCB-COH, 3, he stated: "My whole mission on the Board was to get John Jasper kicked out of it." Also CCB-HLS, 13:9, CCB to William McAndrew, 28 Aug. 1922. Letter of resignation. CCB-HLS, 13:9, CCB to Low, 2 Feb. 1903. See also CCB-HLS, 13:9, letter of appreciation to CCB from Dr. Ernest F. Lederly, commissioner of health, 2 Feb. 1903.

40. Quotation from CCB-HLS, 21:6, unidentified clipping (circa 28 May 1902). On Jasper's resignation. *Times*, 29 May 1902, 1:3–4, *Tribune*, 29 May 1902, 1–4, and *Herald*, 29 May 1902, 3:5.

41. CCB-HLS, 13:9, William McAndrew to CCB, 30 July 1920. Ibid., William McAndrew to CCB, 21 Jan. 1924. There is much about W. McA. in Welling (1942). His *Times* obit, 29 June 1937, 21:1, and see *Times*, 29 June 1937, editorial, 20:3.

42. *Herald*, 27 Nov. 1902, 10:4. In 1897, as a reform measure, the Board of Education had established on East Twenty-first Street a special school for truants. See Palmer (1905), 194.

43. *Herald*, 28 Nov. 1902, 5:1.

44. *Tribune*, 24 Dec. 1902, 2:4. See also *Herald*, 24 Dec. 1902, 4:1, and *Times*, 24 Dec 1902, 9:2.

45. CCB-HLS, 3:1, CCB speech on "The Department of Education," 13.

46. "Smoothly." Ibid., 13:9, CCB to Mayor Low, 2 Feb. 1903. "Without being spoiled," ibid., E. J. Goodwin, principal of Morris High School, to CCB, 5 Feb. 1903.

47. Ibid., Low to CCB, 3 Feb. 1903. Hammack (1982), 263, quoting Butler editorials in the *Educational Review*, Jan. 1898, 15, and Mar. 1898, 95.

48. CCB-HLS, 13:9, John Dwyer, district superintendent, to CCB, 3 Feb. 1903.

49. Figures for 1903–4. Palmer (1905), 316. Later figures, variety of programs. Cohen (1964), 86.

50. CCB-HLS, 13:9, Jacob W. Mack to CCB, 4 Feb. 1903. Mack firmly supported a program of centralization but was not blind to the virtues of individual trustees, see Hammack (1982), 274, and 372 n. 23. CCB-HLS, 13:9, Mack to CCB, 5 Feb. 1903. *Tribune*, 15 Feb. 1903, 8:8.

9. Improving the Bench

Chief sources for this chapter, other than Burlingham collections, are: Richard W. G. Welling, *As the Twig is Bent* (New York: G. P. Putnam's Sons, 1942); George Martin, *Causes and Conflicts: The Centennial History of the Association of the Bar of the City of New York, 1870–1970* (Boston: Houghton, 1970; repr. New York Fordham University Press, 1997); Gerald Gunther, *Learned Hand: The Man and the Judge* (New York: Knopf, 1994); Joan Waugh, *Unsentimental Reformer: The Life of Josephine Shaw Lowell* (Ph.D. thesis submitted to University of California, Los Angeles, 1992); Clay McShane, *Down the Asphalt Path: The Automobile and the American City* (New York: Columbia University Press, 1994); and Documents of the Maritime Law Association of the United States (presently stored on microfiche in the Burlingham Underwood firm, New York City).

1. Daniel P. Moynihan, "When the Irish Ran New York," *Reporter*, 8 June 1961, 32–34.

2. Martin (1970), 167–68; Stoddard (1931), 202–4; and Werner (1928), 468–69. For Croker's "aversion" to Daly, see *Herald*, 10 Oct. 1898, 4:5; 11 Oct., 7:1; 15 Oct., 4:5. Also Matthew P. Breen, *Thirty Years of New York Politics Up-to-Date* (New York: privately printed, 1899), 774ff.

3. *Herald*, 15 Oct. 1898, 4:5.

4. On the source of Root's special relationship with TR, see Jessup (1938), 1:198. There are many references in Jessup's two-volume biography to Root's character, and a summary, based chiefly on Jessup, appears in Martin (1970), 180–83.

5. For ABCNY's role, see Martin (1970), 167–68, and *Tribune*, 16 and 17 Oct. 1898, 1:6. CRB&M, Shepard Collection, CCB to Edward M. Shepard, 27 and 29 Oct. 1898, make clear that Taft was ABCNY's candidate, adopted by the Republicans.

Note: Henry Waters Taft (1859–1945) mostly practiced law alone until 1900, when he joined the firm of Strong & Cadwalader as partner. He remained there for the rest of his life, with the firm name in 1914 becoming Cadwalader, Wickersham and Taft. The DAB, supp. 3, 758, states that he "at first had doubts of his ability to succeed in the law, in part at least shared by his family, who considered him moody and nervous. He enjoyed New York, however, and ultimately was to have a most successful career there." He was president of the State Bar Association (1919–1920), one of the better presidents of the ABCNY (1923–25), and a founder and later president (1930–32) of the New York County Lawyers' Association. In addition, he was a good golfer, an active member of the Wine and Food Society, and a president of the Japan Society of New York, traveling in Japan and writing books about it. In all, he published ten books on a variety of subjects, and in one, *A Century and a Half at the New York Bar*, he rescued George Templeton Strong's diary from obscurity. Only a year younger than CCB, he was a major figure in the city's legal and cultural circles in CCB's generation.

6. Carnegie Hall meeting, 21 Oct. 1898. Martin (1970), 167–68; Stoddard (1931), 202–4; and Werner (1928), 468–69; and *Times*, 22 Oct. 1898, 1:6 and *Herald*, 22 Oct. 1898, 3:3. Root was the chief architect of the "Committee of Fifty," see Jessup (1938), 1: 200–1. See also CRB&M, Shepard Collection, CCB to Edward M. Shepard, 27 Oct. 1898, seeking support for Taft as "one of the best men."

7. On Tammany's victory. *Herald*, 9 Nov. 1898, 3:1, and 5:1. Quoting Root. *Herald*, 9 Nov. 1898, 5:2.

8. *Herald*, 9 Nov. 1898, 3:1.

9. Martin (1970), 169–71, quoting *Report of Counsel to the Honorable Robert Mazet, Chairman of the Special Committee of the Assembly*, etc., 22 Dec. 1899, 79–80.

10. Welling (1942), 78. See *Herald*, 16 May 1906, 3:6. There were fifteen new Supreme Court judgeships, eight in New York County (Manhattan) and seven in Kings (Brooklyn). Tammany and the Republicans were planning to divide these in both counties, with Tammany taking six in Manhattan and four in Brooklyn. In mid-May the Citizens Union seemed the only group disturbed at that prospect; but within a fortnight the Nominators revealed their organization and opposition, see *Herald*, 26 May 1906, 6:6. On CCB. See Welling (1942), and also CCB-HLS, 6:4, Raymond B. Fosdick to CCB, 31 Jan. 1959. CRB&M, Shepard Collection, letters between CCB and Edward M. Shepard, July–Aug. 1906, with a copy of a letter from Root, U.S. secretary of state, to CCB, 30 June 1906, with suggestions on how to proceed.

11. See *Herald*, 4 June 1906, 6:5: "A self-constituted committee of lawyers of which Joseph Hodges Choate is a conspicuous member. Another movement has been begun by the Citizens Union. The lawyers committee was first in the field, and it may make public today its list of selections for the Bench." It did not. CRB&M, Shepard Collection, CCB to Edward M. Shepard, 11 Sept. 1906: "I saw Mr. Choate in Stockbridge, but got no suggestions re judges. I suppose we can't expect much political interest until after the primaries." Choate was the principal speaker at meetings in Cooper Union and Carnegie Hall, see *Herald*, 17 Oct. 1906, 5:6, and 24 Oct. 1906, 5:7. Also *Times*, 24 Oct. 1906, 1:1. By Election Day the Nominators had their headquarters in the Union Square Hotel, see *Herald*, 5 Nov. 1906, 5:2, and Welling (1942), 79, who reproduces the Nominators' letterhead.

12. On candidates. CRB&M, Shepard Collection, CCB to Edward M. Shepard, 3 July 1906; *Herald*, 26 June 1906, 6:5.

13. Pusey (1951), 1:178. The *Times* strongly supported the Nominators' ticket; see its editorials on 3 Oct. 1906, 10 Oct. 1906, and 18 Oct. 1906, 8:2. The *Herald* had fewer stories.

14. Hughes, Pusey (1951), 1:178. *Times*, 10 Oct. 1906, 8:2.

15. *Times*, 7 Nov. 1906, 8:2, and 8 Nov., 8:2, "a pitiful showing." *Herald*, 7 Nov. 1906, 4:2: "The men nominated by the Judiciary Nominators, while doing a good run, did not post as heavy a vote as was expected. Their defeat was a big surprise as well as disappointment to the men who had brought about their nomination."

16. Welling (1942), 79. He recalled how among his speakers had been John Cadwalader, newly elected president of the ABCNY, who in addressing voters on the Lower East Side had pitched his speech "far over the heads of the audience"; see *Herald*, 19 Oct. 1906, 6:1. On Tammany's likely analysis of the election, *Times*, 8 Nov. 1906, 8:2.

17. "Greatest." Wyzanski (1965), 79, republishing his article "Learned Hand," *Atlantic Monthly*, Dec. 1951.

18. "Legacy." Gunther (1994), xvii.

19. "Outsider." Gunther (1994), 26, 27, 73, 152, 154, and 260, where Hand so describes himself in a letter to FF. "Dig out." Ibid., 46.

20. Kathryn Griffith, "Learned Hand," Nelson, ed. (1983), 13, citing Philip Hamburger's "The Great Judge," *Life*, 4 Nov. 1946.

21. Gould & Wilkie. Gunther (1994), 102–6.

22. LH-HLS, 100:24, CCB to LH, 16 July 1904.

23. He was christened Billings Learned Hand, with the two given names being surnames from his mother's family. According to Gunther (1994), 4–5: "The women in his family usually addressed him as "Bunny" or "Bun," a nickname that evolved into a simple "B," by which he was known to close friends throughout his life." In letters, however, his family always referred to him as "Learned." His mother's maiden name was Lydia Coit Learned.

24. LH's response to *Lochner v. New York*, 198 U.S. 45 (1905) was "Due Process of Law and the Eight-Hour Day," *Harvard Law Review*, May 1908, 495–510.

25. Gunther (1994), 122.

26. Ibid., 130.

27. CCB-HLS, 6:16, LH to CCB, 23 Mar. 1947; similarly, ibid., 22 Sept. 1942 and 21 June 1951. Corlear's Hook is the bump on lower Manhattan that projects east, toward Brooklyn, causing the East River to make a large bend; its northern boundary is Delancey Street, where the Williamsburg Bridge (1903), rising in the northwestern section of Brooklyn, debouches onto Manhattan.

28. LH-HLS, 100:24, LH to CCB, 8 June 1909.

29. Aaron H. Burlingham. CCB-TFS, ledger titled "Invoices," clipping from *The Examiner*, 31 Oct. 1901. Partial paralysis. CCB-TFS, CCB to CPC, 29 Jan. 1951; also ibid., public letter by AHB, 1 Oct. 1897, on American Baptist Missionary Union stationery to contributors. Obits. *Times*, 2 Mar. 1905, 9:6, and *Herald*, 2 Mar. 1905, 12:6. Emma Starr Burlingham died in October 1906 and was buried on 23 October beside AHB in Kensico Cemetery in the plot CCB had bought at his father's death.

30. Albert S. Burlingham. Died 15 October 1934; *Times*, obit, 18 Oct. 1934, 23:3. He and his widow, Martha Jackson Burlingham (died Nov. 1943), are both buried in the Burlingham plot at Kensico Cemetery.

31. Waugh (1992), 585–86, citing Jacob Riis in "Lowell, Josephine Shaw, Memorial Meeting, 1905," Community Service Society Records, Butler Library, Columbia University.

32. Stanley Karnow, *In Our Image: America's Empire in the Philippines* (New York: Random House, 1989), 167–95. The fighting started in February 1899 and ended officially on 4 July 1902. Waugh (1992), 583, gives higher figures of dead, citing Charles DeBenedetti, *The Peace Reform in American History* (Bloomington: University of Indiana Press, 1980), 75. Yet *The World Almanac*, 2002, 209, does not list the war among those fought by the United

States, though in battle deaths it outranks four for which figures are given: the War of 1812, the Mexican War, the Spanish-American War, and the Persian Gulf War.

33. On Roosevelt. Harbaugh (1966), 138–40; Miller (1992), 412; Fredrickson (1968), 224–25, 233–34. On Root. Jessup (1938), 1:337: "Did [Root do] everything possible to check the atrocities? Stated so broadly, the answer is probably 'No.' His attitude was rigorously correct . . ." Hodgson (1990), 50–52. TR on JSL, Waugh (1992), 588, citing TR to John Hay, 22 July 1902, in Elting E. Morison, ed., *The Letters of Theodore Roosevelt*, vol. 3, *The Square Deal* (Cambridge: Harvard University Press, 1951), 300. On JSL. Waugh (1992), 585, citing Lowell to Edward W. Ordway, 22 Sept. 1905, in Edward W. Ordway Papers, New York Public Library. CCB on committee, Waugh (1992), 584, and 598 n. 43.

34. On Charles R. Lowell and the "useful" life, see Fredrickson (1968), 29–31, 172; and Waugh (1992), 67, 69, 83–95, 141–51. On Lowell as the ideal's embodiment, see Fredrickson (1968), 212.

35. GM interview with CB Jr., 14 and 15 July 1995; CB Jr. to GM, 23 June 1997.

36. Daniel P. Davison, "Yale's Naval Air Force," *Social Register Observer*, Winter 1997, 57.

37. Frederick G. Howes, *History of the Town of Ashfield, Franklin County, Massachusetts, from its Settlement in 1742 to 1910* (published by the town) tells much about the summer residents and programs. The Burlinghams were at Ashfield for most of the summers of 1890, 1894, 1896, and 1906, and for shorter visits in other years. Ashfield's great years ended in 1903, with the twenty-fifth and last of the Ashfield Academy dinners that Charles Eliot Norton had organized annually, attracting an outstanding roster of speakers (see Howes, 197–98). Norton died in 1908.

38. GM interview with CB Jr., 14 and 15 July 1995.

39. Bryan. McShane (1994), 131. TR and Taft. Miller (1992), 17, 493, 495.

40. Driscoll. McShane (1994), 173.

41. Bliss. Ibid. *Times*, 14 Sept. 1899, 1:2; see also *Times* 6 Aug. 1999, F1:1, describing plans for a centennial commemoration on the site, with descendants of Mr. Bliss expected to attend. In 1991 Ralph Nader, the consumers' advocate, presented an "H. H. Bliss award" to eleven inventors who helped to develop the air bag.

42. Camille. McShane (1994), 176.

43. NYC. Ibid., 198–201. Michigan. Theodore Kaghan, "Edward Hines, Father of the White Line," *Detroit News*, 25 Dec. 1938. Connecticut. Robert Zearfoss, "Fresh Guidelines," *Crosslands Chronicle*, Sept. 1994, 4.

44. MLA-BUL, Doc. 1, Bylaw 2, adopted at the adjournment on 28 June, at the ABCNY, of the 21 June meeting. Bylaw 3 states: "Membership in the Association shall not be confined to the legal profession." And over the years there have always been some members who are not lawyers.

Note: MLA Doc. 717, Sept. 1995, reports that the association "has about 3,600 members. Of these, some 3,200 are lawyers in maritime law, including approximately 225 judges and law professors. The rest are non-lawyers selected because they hold responsible positions in the maritime field. MLA members are found in all states and territories of the United States where there is maritime activity, the heaviest concentrations being in New York, Louisiana, California and Texas."

The association has many committees continually at work on aspects of the sea and seaborne trade, and once every two years holds a four-day meeting. As its booklet states: "It can be said that active membership in the MLA is a professional 'must' for any lawyer engaged in the practice of maritime law."

Despite this growth, the MLA continues to be a remarkably informal, even impromptu organization, sustained chiefly by its members' enthusiasm. It has no headquarters or permanent staff, and the business of its committees and organization is run out of its members' offices. Hence the loci, as lawyers would say, of its activities and documents periodically shift. In 1996 the membership secretary was Lizabeth L. Burrell, a partner at the Burlingham Underwood firm, and her office housed copies (on microfiche) of documents of the past.

45. "Apparently." It is not *absolutely* clear whether CCB was at the 21 June meeting, though his name appears on the MLA 28 June list of 106, the first such list and often taken to record the "founders." But an account of the 21 June meeting (MLA, Doc. 1) states, somewhat in passing, that on that day 12 New York City lawyers were present, as well as Frederick Dodge of Boston and Daniel N. Hayne of Baltimore. Of New York's 12, 5 *seem* to have been Benedict, Putnam, Ward, Mynderse, and J. H. Choate; the other 7 are not named; and there is no statement that *only* 12 were present. In the next few years CCB is recorded present at most meetings. *Times*, 2 Apr. 1899, magazine, 5:4. MLA-BUL, Doc. 7, 15 Nov. 1901, divides members into "active" and "associate" categories. CCB and Henry T. Wing are "associate"; Putnam, "active." CCB in 1910 served on a five-man committee to revise the Pilot Rules for Inland Waters, MLA-BUL, Docs. 33 and 37; and 1918–20, on the executive committee. Similarly, with the American Bar Association CCB seemed content to be a relatively inactive member. He joined in 1910 and continued a member until his death. He served on its Committee for Admiralty and Maritime Law for five years, 1922–26, the last four as chairman. But he never sought office in the organization and generally worked through others, particularly John W. Davis and Charles Evans Hughes.

46. LH-HLS, 100:24, CCB letter to LH [n.d.], Sept. 1909. Noyes (1865–1926), after six years on the court, resigned in 1913, publicly stating that his annual judicial salary of $7,000 was too small to support his family and educate his children. His remarks, as he no doubt intended, caused a flurry of newspaper editorials across the county. In general his gesture was admired and supported; see DAB XIII (orig. ed.): 591–92. The other two delegates to the conference were A. J. Montague and Edwin W. Smith.

47. Expense money. LH-HLS, 100:24, CCB letter to LH (n.d.), Sept. 1909. *The Mauretania* was for many years one of the most popular liners on the "north Atlantic ferry run," earning the title "the Grand Old Lady" and staying in service until the *Queen Mary* was launched in 1934. Her sister ship, sunk by a German U-boat in World War I, was the *Lusitania*.

48. CCB-TFS, "McCutcheon" box, CCB to LLB, 24 Sept. 1909.

49. Ibid., 29 Sept. 1909.

Note: The troubles of this branch of the Hoe family, including courtroom exposure of a son's sexual escapades, continued for years. Robert Hoe III, however, is most often recalled today for the sale of his library, starting in 1911. He had been collecting with intelligence and taste for more than fifty years, and by his death he had assembled one of the most distinguished libraries in the world. Two years later, in New York, the auction of it began, drawing many European collectors and dealers for the first time to the United States. The collection was divided into four parts with their sales scheduled at intervals of several months. The auction of the first part, which included a Gutenberg Bible on vellum and the rarest of William Blake's books with plates colored by him, began on 24 April 1911 and ended on 5 May, with many of the volumes entering the collections of H. C. Folger, J. P. Morgan, and Henry P. Huntington (who won the Gutenberg with a bid of $50,000). The auction of the second part was in January 1912; of the third, with bidding depressed by news of the *Titanic* sinking, in April; and of the fourth, in November. The total of the bids for the 14,558 lots offered was $1,932,056.60, a fantastic sum for its day. See Carl L. Cannon, *American Book Collectors and Collecting, from Colonial Times to the Present* (New York: Wilson, 1941), 157–69.

50. CCB-TFS, "McCutcheon" box, CCB to LLB, 5 Oct. 1909. "Old Fool." Ibid., CCB to LLB, 6 Oct. 1909. "Goat." Ibid., CCB to RB, 9 Oct. 1909.

51. CCB best describes the work of the conference in CCB-TFS, "McCutcheon" box, CCB to CB, 28 Sept. 1909; to LLB, 1 and 5 Oct. 1909; and LH-HLS, 100:24, CCB to LH, 12 Oct. 1909. For a brief summary report of it, see MLA-BUL, Doc. 29. In MLA-BLU Doc. 30, 28 Jan. 1910, the MLA approves the conventions on collision and salvage and recommends approval by the U.S. government. On ratification and significance of salvage convention, see Gilmore and Black (1975), 534: "Except for the conforming statutory changes, the Convention has played little part in the development of American salvage law and has rarely been construed, discussed or cited."

52. CCB-HLS, 21:2, typescript dated 16 Apr. 1931. Why the speech was not delivered is not known. But the statement that it was not is in CCB's hand.

53. CCB-HLS, 4:16, CCB wrote to FF, 12 January 1938: "I was in Washington Monday appearing before a Committee on the Collision Convention, of which I was one of the signers in Brussels in October 1910. They have at last waked up to it, and the President sent it to the Senate April 29 . . ." See Gilmore and Black (1975), 490–91.

54. See n. 52 above.

55. CCB-TFS, "McCutcheon" box, CCB to Nancy, 9 Oct. 1909.

56. Ibid., CCB to LLB, 5 Oct. 1909; and CCB to CB, 28 Sept. 1909.

57. CCB-TFS, LLB undated letter to CCB, but circa 1907–9.

58. Ibid., "McCutcheon" box, CCB to Nancy, 9 Oct. 1909.

59. Ibid., LLB undated letter to CCB, but circa 1907–9.

60. Trees. Gilmartin (1995), 50, citing *Municipal Art Society Bulletin*, no. 12 (25 Apr. 1904).

61. CCB-TFS, "McCutcheon" box, CCB to LLB, 19 Oct. 1909.

62. For the Brussels Conference in 1910 he crossed with LLB and Nancy but went alone to the conference, where he enjoyed last year's friends. His sons, crossing on their own, met him briefly in Paris. See LH-HLS, 100:24, CCB to LH, 16 Aug. and 22 Sept. 1910.

10. Building a Law Firm

Chief sources for this chapter, other than interviews, the Burlingham collections, and contemporary city newspapers, are: CCB, *Notes on the History of Burlingham, Veeder, Clark & Hupper*—hereafter CCB, *Notes*—CCB-HLS, 21:1; Raymond B. Fosdick, *Chronicle of a Generation: An Autobiography* (New York: Harper, 1958); CCB, *Nomination of John Purroy Mitchel for Mayor of the City of New York in 1913* (privately printed pamphlet, 1943)—hereafter CCB, *Nomination of JPM*—CCB-HLS, 21:1; CCB and Stanley M. Isaacs, Oral Histories, Columbia University; Allan Nevins and John A. Krout, eds., *The Greater City: New York, 1898–1948* (New York: Columbia University Press, 1948); Edwin R. Lewinson, *John Purroy Mitchel: The Boy Mayor of New York* (New York: Astra Books, 1965), and Andrew L. Kaufman, *Cardozo* (Cambridge: Harvard University Press, 1998).

1. CCB-HLS, 21:1, CCB, *Notes*, 11.

2. Ibid.

3. Putnam slow. CCB-TFS, undated clipping from the *Sun*, in which Mayor Gaynor recommends the renomination of Putnam, "an independent Democrat," and discounts charges of slowness. The walk. CCB-HLS, 21:1, CCB, *Notes*, 20.

4. CCB-HLS, 21:1, CCB, *Notes*, 12. "I formed." *Harvard Class of 1879, Eighth Class Report, 1914.*

5. CCB-HLS, 21:1, CCB, *Notes*, 12.

6. E.g., Thomas B. Fenlon, *The Emmet Firm* (New York: privately printed, 2001), 211.

7. On Clark. BUL, "Further Notes on the History of the Burlingham firm," by Eugene Underwood. Best "oral advocate" and "You're late." GM interview with Herbert M. Lord, 20 Oct. 1994. Lord was a partner of the firm, 1954–92. And see Hupper's obit, *Times*, 10 May 1967, 47:1.

8. The Cutler School, founded in 1873 by Arthur H. Cutler, Harvard Class of 1870, had its first home on Forty-second Street near Sixth Avenue, moved several times through the West Forties, always staying between Fifth and Sixth Avenues, and then about 1895 settled at 20 East Fiftieth Street, where it stayed until 1914 and where CB would have known it. For its last four years, until Cutler's death in June 1918, it was at 49–51 East Fifty-first Street. Cutler, who had personally tutored TR and climbed mountains with him, shared TR's ideas of rugged sportsmanship, and the school's teachers were men. See Miller (1992), 62, Dunne (1986), 8, and Cutler's obits in *Herald*, 22 June 1918, 6:2, and *Times*, 22 June 1918, 9:6.

9. GM interview with Herbert M. Lord, 20 Oct. 1994. Also Nicholas Kelley-COH, 54, 71–72. And CCB-HLS, 17:12, CCB to HLS, 31 May 1911, discouraging the application to the firm of a Harvard Law School graduate "because we are full up."

10. GM interview with John R. Hupper, 2 Aug. 1994, and Herbert M. Lord, 20 Oct. 1994.

11. Ibid., both interviews. Also GM interview with Eugene Underwood Jr., 25 Oct. 1993, who recorded on tape remarks of his father, Eugene Underwood, who was with the firm 1922–72, becoming a partner in 1936.

12. GM interview with Herbert M. Lord, 20 Oct. 1994.

13. Election. *Tribune*, 3 Nov. 1909, 1:7: Every Tammany nominee for borough president was defeated, and on the Board of Estimate Tammany had 3 votes, Fusion, 12, and Independents, 1. See also *Herald*, 3 Nov. 1909 and *Times*, 3 Nov. 1909. Nevins and Krout (1948), 73–77. "Crumb." Welling (1942), 80; also Raymond B. Fosdick, who was Gaynor's commissioner of accounts, Fosdick (1958), 89. "Kind words." Quoted by Nevins and Krout (1948), 80. Told at greater length by Mortimer Smith, *William J. Gaynor, Mayor of New York* (Chicago: Regnery, 1951), 83, and by Lately Thomas, *The Mayor Who Mastered New York: The Life and Opinions of William J. Gaynor* (New York: Morrow, 1969), 204.

14. *Herald*, 10 Aug. 1910, 7:7. Nevins and Krout (1948), 77, and Fosdick (1958), 92–93, quote the usually hostile *Evening World* on Gaynor's six-month administration: "No other man ever accomplished so much in so little time. He has revolutionized the spirit of the city government. The power of his precept and example has spread throughout the public service." See summary of the change in view of Gaynor, Smith, *William J. Gaynor*, 97, and Thomas, *The Mayor Who Mastered New York*, 225–26. Fosdick, a commissioner of accounts in Gaynor's administration, writes of what it was like to work for him, 90–121. CCB thought Fosdick's description of Mitchel and Gaynor accurate. CCB-HLS, 6:4, CCB to Fosdick, 29 Jan. 1959.

15. The *Kaiser Wilhelm der Grosse* was not only famous for its speed. It was the first liner to have four stacks, and the first to install a wireless radio (which initially in 1900 had a range of twenty-five miles).

16. The would-be assassin was James J. Gallagher, who, discharged from the Dock Department, had been "haunting" City Hall hoping to retrieve his job. *Herald*, 10 Aug. 1910, 1:7 and 5:1; *Times*, 10 Aug. 1910, 1:7, 3:4, and 6:2; also Nevins and Kraut (1948), 81; and Fosdick (1958), 114.

17. The libeled chairman of the investigating committee was Judge Henry H. Curran. See Smith, *William J. Gaynor*, 131–32, and Thomas, *The Mayor Who Mastered New York*, 438–40.

18. CCB-HLS, 21:1, CCB, *Nomination of JPM*, 1. CCB admired Price. See letter in memoriam, *Times*, 20 May 1949, 20:6; and Price's obit, *Times*, 14 May 1949, 13:3. Lewinson (1965), 84, making use of the Joseph R. Price Papers, Columbia University, has the meeting in the Imperial Hotel.

19. CCB-HLS, 21:1, CCB, *Nomination of JPM*, 1. Also Lewinson (1965), 84.

20. Viz. Raymond V. Ingersoll, one of the original ten, was not one of the committee of twenty or of 107, yet served on CCB's subcommittee to select judges.

21. *Herald*, 20 Mar. 1913, 7:1; CCB-HLS, 21:1, CCB, *Nomination of JPM*, 2–3.

22. CCB-HLS, 21:1, CCB, *Nomination of JPM*, 2.

23. *Tribune*, 25 Apr. 1913, 4:4, listing the 107-man committee, composed of representatives of the city's four anti-Tammany parties, roughly gauged to be Republicans, 30; Anti-Tammany Democrats, 31; Progressives, 31; and Independents, 15. CCB-HLS, 21:1, CCB, *Nomination of JPM*, 2. CCB-HLS, 21:2, a speech for 1949 municipal campaign with its audience not stated. Note: another typescript of the speech, with a word substitution in CCB's hand, has been incorrectly dated by someone else "1945."

24. Besides *Encyclopedia*. Nevins and Kraut (1948), 69, 73; and among contemporary newspapers, *Herald*, 6 Nov. 1901, 5:1. Conversely, Gunther (1994), 109, refers to the Mitchel campaign as "the city's first anti-Tammany 'Fusion' movement." CCB, in a letter to the *Times*, 24 June 1953, 24:6, notes the confusion and regrets that a group calling itself the City Fusion Party has a line on the ballot. Though this book hews to CCB's definition, the meaning does vary, especially in quoted matter.

25. CCB-HLS, 21:2, speech for 1949 municipal campaign. See n. 23 above.

26. *Tribune*, 2 May 1913, 5:5. The executive committee had twenty-three members, exclusive of seven officers of its parent committee.

27. CCB-HLS, 21:1, CCB, *Nomination of JPM*, 2.

28. The executive committee had created a subcommittee, the Committee on Candidates, *Tribune*, 22 May 1913, 4:5. According to CCB-HLS, 21:1, CCB, *Nomination of JPM*, 3, this subcommittee held eleven meetings between 17 June and 23 July. It heard the opinions of forty-four delegations, see Lewinson (1965), 85. For the sentiment on candidates, see *Times*, 9 July 1913, 3:7. According to CCB-HLS, 21:1, CCB, *Nomination of JPM*, 3: "It was conceded that if Whitman were nominated there should be a preponderance of Democrats in the rest of the ticket and *vice versa* if Mitchel were nominated." See CCB-HLS, 10:5, SMI to CCB, 24 Jan. 1950, suggesting CCB in *Nomination of JPM* missed the significance of the Progressive Party in dividing Republican support for Whitman.

29. *Herald*, 1 Aug. 1913, 1:4; *Times*, 1 Aug. 1913, 1:8, 2:2; and CCB-HLS, 21:1, CCB, *Nomination of JPM*, 4.

30. CCB-COH, 5–6. Straight later served Mitchel as chairman of the Mayor's Committee for Defense, see Nevins and Kraut (1948), 86–87.

31. LH-HLS, 100:25, CCB to LH, 8 Aug. 1913.

32. *Herald*, 1 Aug. 1913, 1:4; Lewinson (1965), 86. These laconic words are CCB's description, in *Nomination of JPM*, 5, of an event the *Herald* was headlining "All Night Fight" and "Mutiny Confronts Fusion [as] Republicans are Resentful." See CCB-HLS, 21:1, CCB, *Nomination of JPM*, and *Herald*, 1 Aug. 1913, 1:4 and 2 Aug. 1913, 4:2.

33. Fusion nominees. *Times*, 14 Sept. 1913, II, 2:6. There was trouble also in Brooklyn with Progressive leaders and with Republican rank and file in Manhattan, but these potential revolts were contained; see *Herald*, 1 and 2 Aug. 1913, 4:2, 17 Aug. 1913, 3:7, 20 Aug. 1913, 7:1, 21 Aug. 1913, 5:3, and 27 Aug. 1913, 4:3.

34. *Herald*, 6 Nov. 1913, 4:4; *Times*, 6 Nov. 1913, 1:8; *Tribune*, 6 Nov. 1913, 3:1.

35. CCB-HLS, 21:1, CCB, *Nomination of JPM*, 8.

36. Nevins and Kraut (1948), 84. See Fosdick (1958), 86–88: "Never again . . . would the handling of the city's affairs sink to the levels of Tweed and Croker and Murphy."

37. Members of the committee apparently were William H. Hotchkiss, Raymond V. Ingersoll, Darwin H. James, and William H. Schiefflin. See CCB quoted by *Times*, 25 May 1930, 15:1. In CCB-COH, 10, CCB substitutes Philip J. McCook for Hotchkiss, but speaks then in 1949 when memory may have been less sure. *Herald*, 3 Aug. 1913, 4:2, is the first reference found in a newspaper to CCB's subcommittee, but evidently Price had appointed it earlier, for CCB mentions its work in a letter to LH on 31 July, LH-HLS, 100:25.

38. LH-HLS, 100:25, CCB to LH, 31 July 1913. On Nott. Ibid. Hand had recommended him to CCB, an act CCB called "taking coals to Newcastle." Steuer (1950), 47, on Nott: "He was the most dreaded man on the bench. This was not because he was overbearing, harsh, or satirical. It was the opposite. He was so scrupulously fair, so protective of the defendant's rights, that when the trial was over the prisoner had nothing to complain of and the issue went to the jury in its most unsympathetic light."

39. On Wadhams. CCB-COH, 10, and LH-HLS, 100:25, CCB to LH, 8 Aug. 1913.

40. On Frank. CCB-COH, 10. According to the city directory, 1913, Frank's office address was 52 William Street, not No. 58, as CCB recalls it in COH.

41. E.g., CCB-HLS, 10:2, CCB to CEH (newly appointed chief justice, U.S. Supreme Court), 4 Mar. 1930: "More and more, as I consider the various questions that arise in our Special Calendar Committee and elsewhere, it seems to me that good administration is far more important than changes in the law. Even with a complex and wretched system of procedure, a good judge is able to cut right through to the heart of things and work out swift and certain justice." And CCB-HLS, 20:1, CCB speech at dedication of memorial to T. W. Dwight, 30 Oct. 1932: "It is not methods but men, that make a law school."

42. Moskowitz on Cardozo. CCB-COH, 10. The conversation was likely at Black Point, for CCB's letter to LH, 8 Aug. 1913, LH-HLS, 100:25, which has the first discovered mention of Cardozo for the court, was written while Moskowitz was in the house. The *Herald*, 3 Aug. 1913, 4:2, lists men being "considered" for the court: Bartow S. Weeks, Frank Moss, George W. Alger, Gilbert E. Roe, Charles H. Strong, Eugene Philbin, and W. H. Wadhams. LH-HLS, 100:25, CCB to LH, 8 Aug. 1913, also mentions Isidor Wasservogel. Felix Adler, according to Hopkins (1940), 58, "chose a platform of 'natural ethics,' holding that true religion is based upon the moral life and that the moral law 'has an immediate authority, not contingent on the truth of religious beliefs or philosophical theories.'" A motto of Adler's Ethical Culture Society was "Not the creed but the deed," and he and his followers were leaders in programs of social and civic reform.

43. Martin (1970), 70–84.

44. The most recent and fullest biography of Cardozo is Kaufman (1998), forty-one years in the writing. Also recent is Polenberg (1997). Shorter and specialized is Posner, *Cardozo* (1990). There are also numerous law review articles on his judicial opinions and thought as well as his own *The Nature of the Judicial Process*.

45. CCB-COH, 9. CCB's memory goes awry here, having Michael H. Cardozo live to be defeated in the election. But see Cardozo's obit, *Times*, 20 July 1906, 7:6, which states, however, that he had been "selected last week by the lawyers committee of 35 as a candidate for the Supreme Court Bench." Most likely CCB would have been the one to inform him of the selection and so had an opportunity to witness his pleasure. Cardozo's great-grandson Michael A. Cardozo was president of the ABCNY, 1996–98.

46. Both quotations, CCB-COH, 9.

47. Ibid.

48. SMI-COH, 26–27.

49. "Too late." CCB-COH, 8. Republican efforts to substitute one of their candidates for Cardozo, in *Herald*, 15 Aug. 1913, 6:1; 16 Aug. 1913, 4:3; 17 Aug. 1913, 3:7; 20 Aug. 1913, 7:1; and 27 Aug. 1913, 4:3, when Republicans ratify Fusion ticket. See also *Times*, 21 Aug. 1913, 3:1 and 8:5, and *Herald*, 21 Aug. 1913, 5:1, for the Progressives endorsing Philbin and Cardozo for the Supreme Court.

50. *Times*, 15 Aug. 1913, 1:3.

51. SMI's nominating speech is quoted in part in George S. Hellman, *Benjamin N. Cardozo, American Judge* (New York: Whittlesley, 1940), 53–54.

52. The *Sun*. Ibid., 56. The sponsors. Ibid., 55.

53. Cardozo's remark (which seems to have no single source) is made frequently by others, in words that differ though the point is constant. E.g., CCB-HLS, 22:2, CCB to Benjamin N. Cardozo, 13 Nov. 1933: "Considering that you owe your own judicial life to some 1200 Italians in the Bronx . . ." Even more specifically than perhaps CCB or Cardozo seemed to realize, in Italy it is roughly true that proper names ending in *i* bespeak a northern origin; in *o*, a southern. Thus, Verdi and Puccini are from the north; Gesualdo and Leoncavallo, from the south. And most Italian immigrant voters in the Bronx and Manhattan were from the south. See also CCB-COH, 11. Election returns. *Tribune*, 6 Nov. 1913, 3:1, and *Times*, 6 Nov. 1913, 1:1. Kaufman (1998), 125 and 613–14 nn. 37–41, suggests, with figures and analysis, that Cardozo's remark is a misleading "legend": the crucial vote, the important defection from Tammany loyalty, was among Irish-American Democrats. He can be correct, however, without disproving the "legend," for without the healthy margin in Bronx votes that Cardozo won (roughly 38,100 to 33,500 for Weeks), he might have lost. And legends, widely held, often have some basis in fact.

54. The bar greeted him to the bench with enthusiasm. *Times*, 6 Jan. 1914, 22:3.

55. *Times*, 4 Feb. 1914, 8:3. Greenbaum (1967), 39; Kaufman (1998), 127–28.

56. Kaufman (1998), 128, citing Irving Lehman, *Benjamin Nathan Cardozo: A Memorial* (1938), 7, and quoted also in Greenbaum (1967), 40.

Note: CCB, in his oral history (1949), tells a tale about this temporary appointment that Cardozo's most recent biographer, Kaufman (1998), 615 n. 57, has shown cannot be true. It seems that CCB, in recalling the incident in 1949, attached to Cardozo a story about Glynn's appointment of William B. Hornblower—signed on the same day as Cardozo's, 2 February 1914—to fill a regular seat on the court. In 1946, however, in a letter to the *Herald Tribune*, 13 Apr., 12:4, CCB tells the same story, though more briefly, and though he does not mention Hornblower by name, seems to have had him in mind, for the appointment under discussion was not temporary. CCB's letter, titled by the editors "Naming a Judge: Consideration of Religion or Race Unwise," states: "What we need on our high court is not that the judges should hold certain political, economic or religious views, but should be men of character, learning and experience, fair and open-minded."

57. Bergan (1985), 248.

58. The judgment of most writers on Cardozo. E.g., Bergan (1985) 248; Posner, *Cardozo* (1990), 93–94, 96.

59. SMI-COH, 27. Isaacs continues: "Burlingham is one of the great people of the city. He's done things in the background for a great many years, and I regard him as our number one citizen today." See also George W. Alger-COH, 287, and John Lord O'Brian-COH, 384.

60. CCB-HLS, 4:10, FF to CCB, 15 Feb. 1932.

61. Four judges. E.g., Henry J. Friendly, a judge of the Second Circuit Court of Appeals (1959–71) and chief judge (1971–73), wrote in 1962: "When the history of American law in the first half of this century comes to be written, four judges will tower above the rest—

Holmes, Brandeis, Cardozo and Hand." Quoted in J. B. Morris (1987), 141, citing Friendly, *Benchmarks* (Chicago: University of Chicago Press, 1967), 309.

PART TWO: A LEADER OF THE BAR

11. Defending the White Star Line

Chief sources for the *Titanic* are: Robin Gardiner and Dan van der Vat, *The Riddle of the Titanic* (London: Weidenfeld and Nicolson, 1995); John P. Eaton and Charles A. Haas, *Titanic: Triumph and Tragedy* 2nd ed. (New York: Norton, 1995); Walter Lord, *The Night Lives On* (New York: Morrow, 1986); and *A Night to Remember* (New York: Holt, 1955); and Wyn Craig Wade, *The Titanic: End of a Dream* (New York: Rawson, Wade, 1979). Also United States Senate, "*Titanic* Disaster: Hearings before a Sub-committee of the Committee on Commerce" (Doc. 726, Government Printing Office, Washington, D.C., 1912); and Steven Biel, *Down with the Old Canoe: A Cultural History of the Titanic Disaster* (New York: Norton, 1996). (Biel's Notes are very detailed.) Chief sources for the judiciary are: Gerald Gunther, *Learned Hand: The Man and the Judge* (New York: Knopf, 1994), and two interviews by GG with CCB and a memorandum by CCB, mostly on the federal judiciary, cited here as in the Gerald Gunther Collection. Also Jeffrey B. Morris, *Federal Justice in the Second Circuit: A History of the United States Courts in New York, Connecticut and Vermont, 1787 to 1987* (New York: Federal Bar Council Foundation, 1987); *United States Courts in the Second Circuit: A Collection of History Lectures Delivered by Judges of the Second Circuit* (New York: Federal Bar Council Foundation, 1992); *The Remarkable Hands: An Affectionate Portrait*, ed. Marcia Nelson (New York: Federal Bar Council Foundation, 1983); and Charles E. Wyzanski Jr., *Whereas—A Judge's Premises: Essays in Judgment, Ethics, and the Law* (Boston: Little, Brown, 1965).

1. TDT-YSML, 17:337, TDT to John Lord O'Brian, 29 May 1942, recommending Nathan A. Smyth.

2. Ibid., 18:357, TDT letter to Captain D. Karlen, 18 July 1945. Another judge who shared Thacher's views on luck in legal reputation was J. Edward Lumbard, chief judge of U.S. Court of Appeals, Second Circuit, 1959–71; GM interview with Lumbard, 14 Dec. 1995. See also Posner, *Cardozo* (1990), 123; FF (1960), 10–11; and Fosdick (1958), 78–79, 89.

3. North versus Hudson River. The name "North" is the older. According to WPA-Maritime (1941), 11–12: "Hudson's charts refer to the river that now bears his name as the Great River of the Mountains." Subsequently Dutch traders called it the North River "because it marked the northern limit of the Dutch territorial claims in America. This name distinguished it from the South or Delaware River. It was not until fifty years later that the name Hudson's River was first used on the charts of the encroaching English. The North River designation still holds for the lowermost reaches of the Hudson." In shipping circles, and in others historically minded, that name is still in use. See Bone, ed. (1997), 21: "The North River . . . may be defined as the stretch extending from the southern tip of Manhattan Island to the Piermont Marshes of the Tappan Zee, several miles north of New York City. These marshes represent the northern extent of the marine-rooted aquatic vegetation of the New York–New Jersey Harbor Estuary, and the southern extent of freshwater-submerged aquatic vegetation in the Hudson River."

4. The six partners: CCB, Montgomery, Norman B. Beecher, Everett Masten, George H. Emerson, Morton L. Fearey; the three associates, Chauncey I. Clark, Roscoe H. Hup-

per, and Charles Burlingham (CCB's son). CCB-HLS, 21:1, CCB, *Notes on the History of Burlingham, Veeder, Clark & Hupper* (privately printed, 1946) 6, 12.

5. Figures on the number of passengers, crew, and survivors vary slightly depending on the source. The differences occur partly because of stowaways, errors of listing, and confusion in classification of certain groups such as musicians, postal clerks, and wireless operators, all of whom technically were neither crew nor passengers. The totals here are taken from Gardiner and van der Vat (1995), 69, 127, but see 265, 282; and Wade (1979), ix, 26, 63. For seventy-five years the *Titanic* set the record for lives lost in a peacetime disaster, until in 1987 a ferry in the Philippines surpassed it with 4,375.

6. On the search for bodies and their burial, see John P. Eaton and Charles A. Haas, *Titanic: Destination Disaster* (New York: Norton, 1987), 97–105.

7. The Senate committee's report is summarized in Gardiner and van der Vat (1995), 202–3; also in Lord, *The Night Lives On* (1986), 203–5.

8. *Times*, 20 Apr. 1912, 1:4, and Wade (1979), 62–63. See Biel (1996), 72–73, and 253 n. 24, for condemnations culled from newspapers around the country.

9. On Smith. Wade, (1979) 75–87, 330–31.

10. Senate hearings (1912), 2–18. Besides Smith, the committee had six members: Senators Jonathan Bourne Jr., Oregon; Theodore Burton, Ohio; Duncan U. Fletcher, Florida; Francis G. Newlands, Nevada; George C. Perkins, California; and Furnifold M. Simmons, North Carolina. According to Eaton and Haas, *Titanic: Triumph and Tragedy* (1995), 220: "Senator Smith had a personal axe to grind. He was a vehement opponent of the Morgan interests—the very J. P. Morgan whose International Marine owned the White Star Line . . . But throughout the hearing Smith maintained an air of objectivity which made the summary of his findings acceptable to many." "Grievous mistake." Quoted in Lord, *The Night Lives On* (1986), 205.

11. Whitewash. E.g., *Times*, editorial, "Nobody to blame, as usual," 31 July 1912, 8:3, called the report "preposterous." "Grievous mistake." Quoted in Lord, *The Night Lives On* (1986), 205.

12. On Ismay. Gardiner and van der Vat (1995), 244.

13. *American*, 19 Apr. 1912, 10; and see Biel (1996), 72–73, and 253 n. 24.

14. During the period 10 June–12 July 1955, Walter Lord had an interview and exchanged several letters with CCB about the *Titanic*, and gave me copies of his notes and letters. One incident CCB recalled for Lord from his preparation of Ismay: CCB, trying to soften Ismay's probable answer, if asked by Smith, proposed, "But you wouldn't have entered the lifeboat if you had seen women in it?" To which Ismay replied, "And why not?" GM interview with Walter Lord, 24 Mar. 1993.

15. Senate Hearings (1912)., 118–19, 166. For crew subpoenaed and sailing of *Lapland*, see *Times*, 21 Apr. 1912, 6:1; *Herald*, 21 Apr. 1912, 6:4; *Tribune*, 21 Apr. 1912, 3:3; Wade (1979), 135–36. Most of the 170 returning to England lived in Southampton.

16. Senate Hearings (1912), 930–31; Wade (1979) has a photograph of CCB and Ismay arriving in Washington for the hearings. Eaton and Haas, *Titanic: Triumph and Tragedy* (1995), 279, has portrait photographs of CCB (as he was in 1936), Judge Julius M. Mayer, and Senator Isidor Raynor.

17. Senate hearings (1912), 928. On Ismay and the lifeboat, see n. 14 above.

18. Biel (1996), 135, 144–45, 183, has an account of the unveiling of the Women's *Titanic* Memorial in Washington, D.C., in May 1931 and some speculation on its meaning for women then and now.

19. Lord, *The Night Lives On* (1986), 205–9.

20. Figures are taken from the Final Decree in "the *Titanic* case," District Court of the United States for the Southern District of New York, file A55–279, National Archives, NARA—Northeast Region (New York City); see n. 26 below.

21. The suit, 209 Fed. 501, was titled *The Titanic*, with the decision on 21 April 1913, to which a very brief "additional opinion" was added on 19 May 1913. Mellor (sometimes spelled Meller, or Mellors) was a passenger in second class. Eaton and Haas, *Titanic: Triumph and Tragedy* (1995) has some discussion of the court case, with documents reproduced, in its chap. 19, "Limitation of Liability," 277–90.

22. In the second CCA the suit still was titled *The Titanic*, and the decision, 209 Fed. 513, issued on 14 Nov. 1913. In the Supreme Court, 233 U.S. 718–34, the title was *Oceanic Steam Navigation Company, Limited, as Owner of the Steamship* Titanic, v. *Mellor.*

23. GM interviews with Herbert M. Lord, in later years a partner of CCB, 20 Oct. and 13 Dec. 1994. Another partner, Eugene Underwood, suggested its wide application: "A signal victory for the White Star Line and all other foreign shipowners who need to have recourse to our courts in cases appropriate for limitation of liability." In his notes for a firm history, BUL.

24. E.g., the firm of Harrington, Bigham & Englar, in advising a potential claimant against the line, stated that the suit should "be instituted in a Court other than the admiralty in order to have the benefit of a jury trial upon all disputed questions of fact." The opinion letter to Messrs. F. Herrmann & Company, 23 Aug. 1912, courtesy of the present successor firm, Bigham Englar Jones & Houston.

25. How far negotiations proceeded is not known, but *Times*, 18 Dec. 1915, 7:4, refers to them. The Burlingham firm's files for the case, along with those for many other old cases, were destroyed sometime in the 1950s to save space and the cost of storage.

26. Although this suit was treated by the court as merely a continuation of the first, of 1912, with papers continuing to be filed in A55–279, the title now is *In the Matter of the Petition of the Oceanic Steam Navigation Company, Ltd., for limitation of its liability as owner of the steamship Titanic*. The file, at NARA–Northeast Region (New York City), 201 Varick Street, consists of ten boxes with many folders in each; its papers, open to the public and much scrutinized, are now thoroughly mixed.

27. On Mayer. Gerald Gunther interview with CCB, 18 Mar. 1957, Gerald Gunther Collection. CCB's comment on Mayer was made without reference to the *Titanic* case. See CCB-HLS, 3:1, CCB to Julius M. Mayer, 19 Nov. 1921, for ease of relationship.

28. CCB-HLS, 2:6, Chauncey I. Clark to CCB, 8 Sept. 1944, recalling the remark.

29. *Herald*, 3 July 1915, 15:2, and *Times*, 3 July 1915, 9:5. Ballard (1995; orig. ed., 1987), 245, states: "The tragedy should not be allowed to overshadow the fact that the *Titanic* was a relatively safe ship, not only according to the standards of her time but of ours."

30. *Herald*, 4 July 1915, III, 5:4; *Times*, 4 July 1915, III, 4:2; and *Tribune*, 4 July 1915, 5:8. The lawyer stating the issue was Roger Foster.

31. Won the case, and reason for settlement. CCB-HLS, 20:2, "A Lawyer," 3. Settlement announced. *Times*, 18 Dec. 1915, 7:4. According to the court's Final Decree the agreement was dated 20 Dec. 1915.

32. The Final Decree was not published but the original is in NARA–Northeast Region (New York City), file A55–279, see n. 26 above. Also, see *Times*, 29 July 1916, 9:5.

33. Note: The *Florida-Republic* collision and the sinking of the *Republic*. The immensity of the *Titanic* disaster, with its eagerly awaited lists of passengers and crew saved, drowned, and missing, lists constantly changing with each report by wireless from the scene, has erased from public memory, though not from that of the admiralty bar, what was truly the first sea disaster in which radio played a crucial part: the collision, in fog, twenty-six miles

off Nantucket Island, on 24 January 1909 of the *Florida* and the *Republic*. In that instance the *Florida*, a small steel screw steamer (3,231 tons) with schooner rigging rammed the *Republic* (15,400 tons) amidships at 3:30 a.m., when most passengers on both ships were asleep. The bow of the *Florida* was badly damaged, but the ship would float; the *Republic*, however, was left without power and evidently in time would sink. So an orderly transfer began of passengers and crew, some 750, to the *Florida*, already crammed with 850 immigrants sailing from Italy to New York. The small ship had no room for more, and those coming aboard had to stand on deck in freezing weather. The *Florida* had no wireless, but the *Republic* did, and its operator, John R. Binns, remained at his post in the dark and cold, his hand all but frozen to the key, guiding the *Baltic* and other ships to the scene. Ultimately only a half a dozen people died, all from the impact of the collision, and some 1,500 passengers and crew were saved almost entirely by the work of Binns. After the survivors reached New York, Binns, a twenty-six-year-old bachelor, received a ticker-tape parade, was kissed by chorus girls, became the subject of a popular song, and was pursued by reporters for weeks. He testified before Congress, urging that all ships be required to carry a wireless and man it twenty-four hours a day. But many laymen and politicians failed to grasp its significance until the *Titanic*. Binns, a reserved young man who had disliked the publicity, had been scheduled by the White Star Line to sail as wireless operator on the *Titanic* but for love of a woman had turned down the assignment.

Admiralty lawyers do not forget this earlier disaster, and in CCB-HLS, 2:6, Chauncey I. Clark, in writing to CCB, 8 Sept. 1944, recalled: "You will remember that the *Florida-Republic* collision was the first one which gave publicity to the wireless."

34. On these questions, see Ballard (1995), chap. 10, "*Titanic* Reconsidered," and "Epilogue."

35. "Foundation." The word used by Eugene Underwood, eldest of the partners surviving to be interviewed (died in 1996, aged ninety-nine). He joined the firm as an associate in 1922 and as partner in 1936. Interview tape-recorded by Eugene Underwood Jr., 20 Aug. 1993. See also Underwood (circa 1972), in "Further Notes on the History of the Burlingham Firm," 1, BUL. All the firm's lawyers interviewed confirmed the importance of the case to the firm's development. CCB-HLS, 2:9: CCB in letter to Ten Eyck Beardsley, 6 Sept. 1957, remarked, "It is rather odd that we had the *Stockholm-Doria* case just as we had the *Titanic*—the two admiralty cases of highest values in my lifetime." It is not clear from the context whether he meant financial rewards, interesting legal issues, or boosts for reputation. Perhaps all three. See also CCB-HLS, 20:2, "A Lawyer," 3. "Dean of your admiralty bar," CCB-HLS, 10:10, John Crosby, of Washburn-Crosby Company, Minneapolis, to Pierre Jay, chairman, Federal Reserve Bank, 3 Aug. 1922.

36. London *Times*, 9 June 1959, 14c.

37. *Harvard College Class of 1879, Ninth Report*, 1929.

38. Ibid., *Eighth Report, 1914*. Second illness. "I worked so hard, or so unwisely, that I worked myself out," *Ninth Report, 1929*.

39. LH-HLS, 100:26, CCB to LH, 13 Apr. 1916. ST. GCB, 4:27, 23 Apr. 1916, "Personal Notes": "Mr. and Mrs. Charles C. Burlingham will be in Bermuda over Easter and both are greatly improved in health."

40. LH-HLS, 100:26, CCB to LH, 6 June 1916.

41. Ibid., CCB to LH, 13 Apr. 1916: "powerful thro' repose."

42. In his *Harvard College Class of 1879, Ninth Report, 1929*, CCB states: "I had a good deal to do with shipping during the war," but does not specify his duties. Presumably these were connected with his position at Local Board Division 8, from which he felt forced to retire. LH-HLS, 100:26, CCB to LH, 2 Apr. 1918.

43. GM interview with Herbert M. Lord, 20 Oct. 1994, and see nn. 37 and 38 above.

44. Various reports of the Harvard College Class of 1879. From the accounts of class meetings it appears that the first reunion he attended was the twenty-fifth, in 1904; the first at which he spoke or in any way appeared on a program was the thirtieth in 1909; and first humor in self-description occurred in a report for the thirty-fifth, in 1914.

45. CCB-HLS, 18:2, CCB to W. H. Taft, 2 Apr. 1924. Judge William James Wallace (1837–1917), DAB XIX (orig. ed.): 378, was appointed to the Northern District Court bench in 1874 and to the Second Circuit Court in 1882, where he served until retirement in 1907. He had been mayor of Syracuse and was a protégé of the U.S. senator and Republican state boss Roscoe Conkling. CCB thought Wallace "a very able lawyer and judge," see Gerald Gunther Collection, Gunther interview with CCB, 18 Mar. 1957, 1. See n. 66 below.

46. On Hough. From Gerald Gunther Collection, Judge Charles E. Clark to Gunther, 11 Oct. 1957, with a memorandum (1957) on Hough by CCB, and Gunther interview with CCB, 18 Mar. 1957, 8–9. Also CCB-HLS, 20:1: "The New York Bar 75 Years Ago," 5; Gunther (1994), 279–82; J. B. Morris (1987), 97–98, and DAB IX (orig. ed.): 249–50.

47. See CCB-HLS, 19:1, Van Vechten Veeder to CCB, 18 Sept. [1916], on Hough's "hearty tribute of friendship" for CCB. Hough's sentimentality, Gerald Gunther Collection, CCB memorandum (1957), and Gunther interview with CCB, 18 Mar. 1957.

48. Telegram. Gerald Gunther Collection, Gunther interview with CCB, 18 Mar. 1957. Also CCB-COH, 41. *Herald*, 21 June 1906, 4:4, and *Tribune*, 21 June 1906, 2:3. The *Herald*, describing the appointment as "a genuine sensation," stressed Hough's reputation as an admiralty lawyer; the *Tribune*, mentioning the objection to him as counsel for the Pennsylvania Railroad, called the campaign on his behalf "spirited." Both stressed the support of Parsons.

49. Colonel E. M. House. LH-HLS, 100:25, CCB to LH, 31 July 1913; and CCB to Colonel House, 6 Mar. 1918. McReynolds. Ibid., CCB to LH, 31 July 1913, in which he lists McReynolds's reasons as: "(1) He [Hough] is not a real Democrat; (2) He is sick; (3) If he is appointed, another man will have to be appointed in his place," i.e., to the Southern District Court. On Rogers. After five years of Rogers, CCB described him to Colonel House as "a justifiable error, as he was Dean of the Yale Law School, but an old Dodo, dilatory, long-winded, without force or ability"; see LH-HLS, 100:29, CCB to Colonel House, 6 Mar. 1918. See also Gunther (1994), 282, and J. B. Morris (1987), 97, both more charitable.

50. See n. 46 above. Hough took the seat formerly held by Emile Henry Lacombe.

51. Figures. DAB IX (orig. ed.): 249–50. Velocity of "his mind." Ibid., 249, written by Van Vechten Veeder.

52. Figures. See n. 49 above. Commercial cases. J. B. Morris (1987), 97, citing dedication of Karl L. Llewellyn, *The Common Law Tradition: Deciding Appeals* (Boston: Little, Brown, 1960). For an interesting account of Llewellyn and his thoughts on the process of judging, see Kronman (1993), 210–25. Hough's works: *The United States District Court for the Southern District of New York—Its Growth, and the Men Who Have Done Its Work*. Written in 1923, it was published in 1934, after his death, by the Maritime Law Association. The *Reports of Cases in the Vice Admiralty . . .* was completed in 1924 and published by Yale University Press, 1925. It saved from oblivion much of the old court's history. CCB on Hough, J. B. Morris (1987), 97, citing "A Memorial from Bench and Bar to Charles Merrill Hough," 13 (minutes of the United States Circuit Court of Appeals for the Second Circuit and the United States District Court for the Southern District of New York, May 2, 1927). FF's fears. FF-LOC, container 36, FF to CCB, 3 Oct. 1952.

53. Ward memorial. By CCB, ABCNY, *Yearbook, 1934.* For a sample of CCB's continuing affection for Ward, see CCB-HLS, 19:3, CCB to Ward, 11 July 1922. Impatient. Gerald Gunther Collection, Gunther interview with CCB, 18 Mar. 1957, 13.

54. CCB on A. N. Hand. William James Jr. Collection, Houghton Library, Harvard, folder 4, CCB to WJ Jr., 18 Nov. 1954. Hand is well described in a memorial address at ABCNY delivered by Charles A. Wyzanski Jr. and republished in Wyzanski (1965), 65–78. See also Wyzanski's tribute published in *Harvard Law Review* 61:4 (Apr. 1948): 573. Its closing quoted in *The Remarkable Hands* (1983), 63. Wyzanski began by quoting CCB on ANH in "Judge Learned Hand," *Harvard Law Review* 60:3 (Feb. 1947): 330–31. And J. B. Morris (1987), 142.

Follow Gus. Often thought to have been said first by U.S. Supreme Court Justice Robert H. Jackson in an address at a New York State Bar Association dinner; see J. B. Morris (1987), 142. But Gunther (1994), 647, states that Jackson "once related that as a young country lawyer in upstate New York, he had been taught 'to quote Learned, but cite Gus.'" So presumably Jackson was at least the second to say it.

55. Wyzanski (1965), 68. Hand's grandson Arthur V. Savage knows no reason to doubt the statement and, in view of Hand's intimacy with Wyzanski, believes it true; telephone to GM, 13 May 1997. FF, "A Legal Triptych," *Harvard Law Review* 74:3 (Jan. 1961): 436. The first portrait of the triptych purports to reprint FF's article on CCB, ABCNY, *Memorial Book, 1960*, but the later piece is considerably longer and more detailed.

56. Wyzanski (1965), 76; the quotation, 302.

57. On Veeder. LH-HLS, 100:24, CCB to LH, 16 Aug. 1910, enclosing a copy of CCB to Wickersham, 12 Aug. 1910. Memorial by CCB and ANH in ABCNY, *Yearbook, 1944,* 445–49. Veeder died 4 December 1942.

58. LH-HLS, 100:24, CCB to LH, 16 Aug. 1910. For some of Veeder's publications, see CCB and ANH memorial to him, ABCNY, and ANH, *Yearbook, 1944,* 446–47.

59. LH-HLS, 100:24, CCB to LH, 16 Aug. 1910, enclosing CCB to Wickersham, 12 Aug. 1910.

60. CCB-HLS, 21:1, CCB, *Notes,* 13–14.

61. Gunther (1994), 257–61; LH-HLS, 100:26, CCB to LH, 24 June 1917; Attorney General Gregory to CCB, 21 July 1917; and CCB to LH, 8 Oct. 1917.

62. LH-HLS, 100:26, CCB to Gregory, 28 Nov. 1917, in which, attempting to meet an objection that promoting L. Hand would require the appointment of a successor to the district court, he recommends for that post Francis G. Caffey, U.S. attorney for the Southern District, who later served on the court, 1929–47; see Caffey obit, *Herald Tribune,* 21 Sept. 1951, 16:6, and *Times,* 21 Sept. 1951, 24:2 (with a mistake in years served). Caffey's best-known decision (overruled in 148 F.2nd 416 [2nd Cir. 1945]) was the Aluminum Company of America monopoly case, in which, over a period of ten days, he dictated from the bench an opinion of 170,000 words. Also LH-HLS, 100:29, CCB to Colonel E. M. House, 6 Mar. 1918.

63. *Masses Publishing Company v. Patten,* 244 Fed. 535 (S.D.N.Y., 1917), reversed, 246 Fed. 24 (2nd Cir. 1917). Gunther (1994), 151–61, and J. B. Morris (1987), 118–20.

64. LH-HLS, 100:26, LH to CCB, 6 Oct. 1917.

65. Gunther (1994), 151. The Supreme Court case, *Brandenburg v. Ohio,* 395 U.S. 444 (1969). See Holmes dissent in *Abrams v. United States,* 250 U.S. 616 (1919).

66. Gunther (1994), 226–39. There was precedent. In 1897 Judge William J. Wallace, while on the federal Second Circuit Court, had run for chief judge of the New York Court of Appeals and been defeated, but had continued on the circuit court until retirement in 1907; see J. B. Morris (1987), 74, 137–38. On Ward. His wife had predeceased him and he

lost both his sons in World War I. After retirement from the Second Circuit Court he continued for several years to sit in the district court, where he heard many admiralty cases.

67. Gunther (1994), 231.

68. Mason, *William Howard Taft* (1965), 171, Taft to Harding, 4 Dec. 1922: ". . . Roosevelt man and a Progressive, and though on the bench, he went into the campaign . . . If promoted to our Bench, he would most certainly herd with Brandeis and be a dissenter. I think it would be risking too much to appoint him." See also Gunther (1994), 274. For Mason's summary of Taft's view of his role in selecting judges, 173–74. Mason, *William Howard Taft* (1965), 182, Taft to H. F. Stone, 1 Aug. 1924; also J. B. Morris (1987), 138.

69. Quoted by Harrison Tweed in memorial address on CCB at ABCNY in Oct. 1959. Published in ABCNY, *Record* 14:9 (Dec. 1959), and then in a reprint. See also J. B. Morris (1987), 136, citing "In Commemoration of Fifty Years of Federal Judicial Service by the Honorable Learned Hand, New York, 10 April 1959." LH-HLS, 100:27, CCB to LH, 13 Aug. 1924, and ibid., 24 Dec. 1924.

70. Gunther (1994), 259, quoting LH to wife, 16 July 1917.

12. Religion, Social Justice, and Brotherhood

Chief sources on the church are: Henry Anstice, *History of St. George's Church in the City of New York, 1752–1811–1911* (New York: Harper, 1911); William S. Rainsford, *The Story of a Varied Life: An Autobiography* (Garden City, N.Y.: Doubleday, 1922); Elizabeth Moulton, *St. George's Church, New York* (New York: privately printed, 1964); Charles Howard Hopkins, *The Rise of the Social Gospel in American Protestantism, 1865–1915* (New Haven: Yale University Press, 1940); and various records of St. George's Church, such as *Parish Register, Church Bulletin,* and *Minutes of the Vestry.* Sources for the family and the decade, other than interviews with family members and CCB papers, are: *The Last Tiffany: A Biography of Dorothy Tiffany Burlingham,* by Michael John Burlingham (New York: Atheneum, 1989), and *Only Yesterday: An Informal History of the Nineteen-Twenties,* by Frederick Lewis Allen (New York: Blue Ribbon Books, 1931).

1. *Records of St. George's Church, City of New York, 1892–1918,* 385.

2. Gospel According to St. Mark, 12:28–34.

3. Anstice (1911), 271, 284, 286–87; Rainsford (1922), 198, 200; Moulton (1964), 57–61.

4. Hopkins (1940), 250, citing Charles Stelzle, *Christianity's Storm Center* (New York: Revell, 1927), 22.

5. The soiled park. Rainsford (1922), 210–11. Anstice (1911), 281, 287.

6. WSR to NY, Anstice (1911), 288. New bishop. Rainsford (1922), 196–98. Morgan. Anstice (1911), 288–91; Rainsford (1922), 199–202; Moulton (1964), 67–68; and on Rainsford, DAB, supp. 1, 618–19.

7. Pew rentals. Anstice (1911), 292–94; Rainsford (1922), 212; Moulton (1964), 68, 74. For the notice "All Seats Free," see successive Saturdays in the *Herald* and *Times,* starting 13 Jan. 1883. The Westminster Presbyterian Church, at Twenty-second Street between Sixth and Seventh Avenues, also advertised "Seats free." Apparently the only other Episcopal "free" church was the much smaller Holy Communion, which seems not to have advertised its services in newspapers, see Anstice (1911), 309.

8. Anstice (1911), 293, 353.

9. House calls. Anstice (1911), 298. Croker. Rainsford (1922), 210–11.

10. Rainsford (1922), 235–36.

11. Sunday school. Ibid., 238. Kindergarten. Ibid., 243. "Suffer . . ." Gospels of Matthew, 19:14; Mark, 10:14; and Luke, 18:16. Enrollment. Anstice (1911), 378; Rainsford (1922), 249. Sunday school. Anstice (1911), 295, 353.

12. Burleigh (1866–1949), DAB, supp. 4, 125–26; Rainsford (1922), 267; Moulton (1964), 87–88; and *Episcopal Life* (4 Nov. 1994), 6:1.

Note: According to *Episcopal Life*, Burleigh, who lay "in an unmarked grave" in West-chester County, was reburied in the summer of 1994 in a cemetery in Erie, Pennsylvania, his birthplace. As a boy he had "accompanied his grandfather, a lamplighter, on his nightly rounds. As they walked, the grandfather, a former slave, sang spirituals to him." The rein-terment followed a funeral service at St. Paul's Episcopal Church. The eight-paragraph ar-ticle, with a photograph of the procession to the cemetery led by two Episcopal bishops, omits any mention of Burleigh's tenure at St. George's. Twenty-three of Burleigh's original songs, in the romantic style of his day, have been recorded and issued on a compact disc, Centaur CRC 2252. A critical biography of him appeared in 1990: *Hard Trials: The Life and Music of Harry T. Burleigh*, by Anne Key Simpson (Metuchen, N. J.: Scarecrow Press). For a discussion of the biography, stressing the importance of Burleigh in American musical life, see *American Music* 12:2 (Summer 1994): 197–200.

13. Rainsford "drew us." ST. GCB 9:10 (5 Mar. 1950): 2.

14. Rainsford (1922), 240, states emphatically, in italics: "*A down-and-out man, a bum, a drunkard, these are the very last who should be pushed to their feet to tell to others a religious expe-rience that they have had or suppose themselves to have had.* To do so is to strike strings already out of tone, and none I think can attend such services and listen for long to the experiences they produce and attach real importance in permanent value to the one or the other." A somewhat related point of conflict between Rainsford and his conservative critics arose over German-style beer gardens. Instead of forbidding them, he wanted them available for recreation, and open on Sundays, see Rainsford (1922), 337–38. Hopkins (1940), 49, states the Social Gospel movement's strongest claim to realism "lies in the fact that it continued to regard the relations of labor and capital as the sore spot of modern machine civilization." For an example of conflict on this point, see Rainsford's ultimately effective criticism of Trinity Church drawing income from a brothel, Rainsford (1922), 242.

15. Hopkins (1940), 318.

16. Rainsford (1922), 241: "Men outside her [the church's] fold were crying not for *rescue* but for *justice*," and 243, brotherhood.

17. William H. Allen-COH, 71; CCB's friend Robert Shaw Minturn was treasurer. In 1939 the Community Service Society was formed by the merger of the Charity Service So-ciety and the Association for Improving the Condition of the Poor, the society sponsoring CCB's committee. Traces of his work can be found in CRB&M-Community Service Soci-ety Collection, box 2, correspondence between CCB and Edward Devine, John Kingsbury, and Bailey B. Burritt, 1908–19. See Hammack (1982), 281–82.

18. *Times*, 28 June 1906, 4:3; *Herald*, 28 June 1906, 7:5; and *Tribune*, 28 June 1906, 14:1.

19. *Times*, 29 June 1906, 9:1; *Herald*, 29 June 1906, 8:3; and *Tribune*, 29 June 1906, 8:3.

20. See n. 18 above.

21. Anstice (1911), 297: In the first ten months (1883) there were 1,140 house calls and 1,000 prescriptions. Hospital. Moulton (1964), 79, 110, and plaques on building.

22. Rainsford's successor was Hugh Birckhead (1906–12). Anstice (1911), 385; Moulton (1964), 176, "the first attempt by a church to reduce the high tuberculosis rate." Volunteers. ST. GCB, 7:23, 23 Mar. 1919. *Minutes of the Vestry*, 10 Feb., 10 Mar., and 14 Apr. 1919.

23. CCB-HLS, 16:11, CCB to Dr. George E. Rice, 3 Jan. 1920.

24. ST. GCB, 18 Apr. 1920.

25. Moulton (1964), 111; *Times*, 20 Apr. 1920, 1:8, and *Tribune*, 19 Apr. 1920, 1:8; *Times*, 20 Apr. 1920, 1:4, and *Tribune*, 20 Apr. 1920, 3:1. The "tacklers" were G. Morgan Jones and Dr. George Emerson Brewer. The assassin was Thomas W. Simpkins, who had escaped several times from asylums. Committed again, he was sent to Matteawan State Hospital, where he died four years later.

26. CCB-HLS, 16:11, CCB to William Fellowes Morgan, 8 Dec. 1926.

27. Ibid., CCB to R. Fulton Cutting, 20 Oct. 1925.

Note: The Reverend Edwin Augustine White, *American Church Law: A Guide and Manual for Rectors, Wardens and Vestrymen of the Church Known in Law as the Protestant Episcopal Church in the United States of America* (New York: James Pott, 1898), states at 299: "With very few exceptions the various Dioceses require that a person must be a communicant to be eligible for the office Warden," and at 145, "Only communicants should ever be chosen as Wardens of a Church." And on vestrymen, at 301, "Vestrymen shall be chosen by the Congregation. Both Wardens, and a majority of the vestrymen, shall be recognized Communicants of the Parish"; and at 146, "Only a qualified voter is eligible for the office of Vestryman . . . In New York State the law requires that a Vestryman must be a qualified voter and have been baptized." (The trend, as noted, was to require all vestrymen to be communicants.)

28. *Times*, 10 May 1922, 21:8, and 11 May 1922, 3:1; *Tribune*, 10 May 1922, 8:1, and 11 May 1922, 1:4; and *Herald*, 10 May 1922, 7:1, and 11 May 1922, 10:6.

29. *Times*, 10 May 1922, 21:8. and 11 May 1922, 3:1.

30. *Minutes of Vestry*, 8 Oct. 1934, Wickersham elected senior warden, and committee to nominate a junior warden; ibid., 13 Nov. 1934, CCB elected junior warden; ibid., 6 Apr. 1936, CCB, senior warden. As a vestryman CCB was senior to Wickersham by two years. The Reverend White (1898), see n. 27 above, Appendix D: Form of Certificate of Lay Deputies to Diocesan Conventions, ". . . and that each of said Deputies (or Delegates) so elected is a communicant of the Church of this Parish." If CCB was confirmed privately, no record has been found.

31. M. J. Burlingham (1989), 127–33.

32. Ibid., 120–23, 127–33, and photograph of the Tiffany mansion, 140ff.

33. Ibid., 135. *Times*, 11 July 1914, 7:3, in announcing the engagement, reports that Robert "became ill almost a month ago." *Tribune*, 11 July 1994, 7:1, states "the wedding will take place within a year." The illness seemingly did not cause Dorothy to hesitate.

34. M. J. Burlingham (1989), 146.

35. Ibid., 143, 144, 147, 150.

36. Ibid., 140. According to CB's autobiographical entries in the *Harvard College Class of 1906* Reports, issued in 1907, 1916, 1921, and 1926, he lived with his parents after graduation from law school (1908) until marriage, in 1929.

37. M. J. Burlingham (1989), 143.

38. Ibid., 140–41.

39. Ibid., 146. See the summary of his career through 1934 that Robert wrote for his *Harvard College Class of 1910, Seventh Report, 1935*, 94–95. Though he does not mention breakdowns, his posts of employment and dates reveal gaps when he presumably was too ill to work. See also CCB-TFS, LLB to CCB, n.d., about taking RB to Harvard and recording a breakdown either during his years there, 1906–10, or, more likely from the context, just before entering his first year. Also CCB-TFS, Nancy to CCB, 4 Oct. 1909, saying, "Robert is here now as you know, but he seems pretty well, nevertheless." He had been confirmed at a service in St. George's in 1905, *St. George's Church Confirmation, 1883—*, 110, and *Year Book Easter, 1905*, 24.

40. RB's sexuality. GM interview with PLT, 11 Sept. 1993. When PLT tried to warn his mother, Grace Taylor, that RB, who was recuperating at her house in Williamstown, was making his female nurses nervous, Grace left the room, refusing to discuss the problem. But it may have underlain CCB's decision to hire a male nurse-companion, Archie Sinclair, who for a number of years reappeared whenever RB was ill; PLT to GM, 5 Feb. 1994, and GM interview with RTE, 3 Oct. 1993. For RB's gentleness, see his obituary in *Harvard College Class of 1910, Eighth Report, 1940,* 30–32: "His diffident manner and quiet smile . . . his unfailing kindliness; the fact that he never hurt anyone . . . [He] yearned for love from his family and friends." See also CCB-TFS, HH to CCB, n.d., and to LLB, 1 June 1930.

41. CCB acting on RB's behalf. E.g., CCB-HLS, 3:11, CCB to Dr. W. H. Doughty Jr., University Hospital, Augusta, Georgia: "I appreciate very much your kindness in taking Robert in. I know he will enjoy the association and the work. He probably won't tell you very much about himself, so I venture to say that he had been under a good deal of strain and was not very well when he went South . . . It was very good of Dr. Flexner to write to you and still better of you to grant his request."

42. M. J. Burlingham (1989), 150.

43. Ibid., 152.

44. Dr. George S. Amsden was the first psychiatrist-in-chief (1932–35) at the 104-bed Payne Whitney Psychiatric Clinic at New York Hospital. Previous to that he had been a physician at the Bloomingdale Insane Asylum. He became a member of the New York Psychoanalytic Society in 1930.

45. Cars. F. L. Allen, *Only Yesterday* (1931), 6–7. Colored. Ibid., 160–64. Closed. Ibid., 100. And see McShane (1994), 127.

46. Ibid., 288; Gilmartin (1995), 83, 136, 165, 192.

47. F. L. Allen, *Only Yesterday* (1931), 89, 103–6.

48. GM interviews with RTE, 15 May and 3 Oct. 1993.

49. Ibid. GM interview with Mrs. Robert Burlingham Jr. (now Mrs. Malcolm Sheldrick), 1 June 1993.

50. On Edith. Like her oldest sister Mellie and her mother, Adeline Hoe Lawrence, Edith left only dim memories among her surviving relatives. None could say how or why she died, though only fifty-five, nor had anyone an anecdote about her. On Grace. GM interview with PLT, 11 Sept. 1993, and PLT to GM, 5 Feb. and 22 Dec. 1994. See also her biography, 240–42, in an account (1996) about the Cornish (New Hampshire) Colony, *Footprints of the Past,* ed. James Atkinson and Carrie Brown from interviews by Virginia Reed Colby. And also CCB-TFS, closing page of CCB to RB, [4 Mar.] 1932: "As a family the Ts are not very sensible in respect of finance." Taylor descendants, however, generally hold CCB responsible for the railroad bonds held by or for Grace that proved all but worthless in the Depression. E.g., Stephen Howard Taylor (Lawrie's eldest son) to GM, 15 Nov. 1997, and GM interview and letters with PLT.

Note: The Plainfield property. It is possible that Grace and Edith, both unmarried in 1892, paid the $2,000 for the farm's original seven acres and used CCB merely as the owner of record on the town's tax rolls. Grace's grandson, Stephen H. Taylor, points out that in 1893, "when New Hampshire real estate law scarcely recognized females as human beings," the tax rolls list not a single property owned outright by a woman. "All properties were assessed to males alone or to male executors, guardians or other agents of females." Additional purchases in 1902 and 1907 brought the total acreage to 146, with CCB remaining the owner of record until Grace's death (1940), when he transferred it "for $1 and other valuable consideration" to family members. Stephen H. Taylor to GM, 15 Nov. 1997.

51. On Lawrence. See CCB-HLS, 12:8, CCB to Albert H. Licklider (professor at Williams), 21 Apr. 1927 and 12 June 1941. David Fairbanks Taylor (Lawrie's second son) has a collection of letters between his father and CCB, most of them written between February 1941 and June 1956.

52. GM interview with PLT, 11 Sept. 1993; and PLT to GM, 5 Feb. and 22 Dec. 1994. On Lindbergh. PLT to GM, 5 Feb. 1994. Charles A. Lindbergh, *The Spirit of St. Louis* (New York: Scribner's, 1953), which publishes the plane's log, shows a flight from Concord, New Hampshire, to Springfield, Vermont, on 26 July 1927, 2 hours, 10 minutes, and from Springfield to Albany, 27 July, 2 hours, 45 minutes.

53. GM interview with PLT, 11 Sept. 1993. The Hoosac School. The founder was the Reverend Edward Dudley Tibbits, and the school every year performed (and still does) a Christmas pageant, "The Boar's Head and Yule Log," dating back to fifteenth-century England.

54. The Lenox Academy, near Williamstown. GM letter from Exeter archivist, 4 Aug. 1997; and phone interview with college registrar, 4 Dec. 1997.

55. GM interview with PLT, 11 Sept. 1993. While in college PLT considered joining the air force, but was not encouraged in the idea by CCB, who commented in a letter to LHT, CCB-DFT, 19 Mar. 1934: "I should think in Hartford or Springfield some mechanical work about motors might help towards aviation. What I fear is that his years of unthoroughness would make it hard for him to keep up to the Army standards." PLT continued briefly at Williams.

56. Young Charles showed more understanding of Phil than did CCB, and arranged for himself and Phil, then ten or eleven, to ride in the cab of a New York Central Railroad steam engine from Albany to Harmon, New York. Phil recalled it was "a noisy, rough ride. At speed the locomotive swayed from one side to the other. There were two crew, the engineer and the fireman; the coal was automatically stoked into the firebox." PLT to GM, 22 Dec. 1994.

57. An example occurred in the educational career of Lawrence H. Taylor, the schoolteacher. CCB used to lament, in a scolding tone, that LHT had not obtained a Ph.D. This caused LHT, who would have liked the greater opportunity the degree would have offered, sometimes to grumble: It was the Depression. There was no money. If CCB thought the degree important, why didn't he put up the money to make it possible? LHT apparently was too diffident to propose some workable plan, and CCB either too busy with other matters or too unimaginative to suggest one. GM phone interview with LHT's son, Stephen Howard Taylor, 27 Aug. 1997. CCB lamenting the lack of the degree in a letter to Albert H. Licklider, 15 July 1958, CCB-HLS, 12:8.

58. GM interviews with RTE, 15 May and 3 Oct. 1993.

59. Ibid. The Harvard College Class Reports for CB (1905, 1916) and RB (1910, 1921) record that CB prepared for Harvard at the Cutler School in New York City, a day school (see Chapter 12, n. 12), and RB at the Middlesex School, in Concord, Massachusetts, a boarding school for boys.

60. CCB-HLS, 19:3, CCB to Henry Galbraith Ward, 11 July 1922.

61. CCB-TFS, n.d., partial handwritten memorandum.

62. GM interview with PLT, 11 Sept. 1933, and PLT to GM, 5 Feb. 1994.

63. M. J. Burlingham (1989), 142.

64. CCB-HLS, 10:10, CCB to Pierre and Loulie Jay, 28 Mar. 1929. Mrs. Jay, "Loulie," was a daughter of Ellen Shaw (Sarah Shaw's youngest daughter) and Francis Channing Barlow and hence a first cousin of CRL, May Minturn, and Lizzie Curtis. CCB-TFS, CB Jr., speech at his mother's memorial service, 17 Dec. 1986.

65. CCB-TFS, CB Jr. speech at his father's memorial service, Aug. 1979.

66. CCB-HLS, 10:10, CCB to Pierre and Loulie Jay, 28 Mar. 1929, and see n. 64 above.

67. CCB-TFS, CCB 2 Apr. 1929, to someone addressed by an indecipherable initial that may be "G."—perhaps Grace Taylor, whom he does not list among the family attending the wedding.

13. CCB as Public Sage

Chief sources for this chapter, other than daily newspapers and the Burlingham papers, are: *Causes and Conflicts: The Centennial History of the Association of the Bar of the City of New York, 1870–1970,* by George Martin (Boston: Houghton, Mifflin, 1970; repr., New York: Fordham University Press, 1997); *Albany: The Crisis in Government,* by Louis Waldman (New York: Boni & Liveright, 1920); *Charles Evans Hughes,* 2 vols., by Merlo J. Pusey (New York: Macmillan, 1951); *Lawyer's Lawyer: The Life of John W. Davis,* by William H. Harbaugh (New York: Oxford University Press, 1973); *Cardozo,* by Andrew L. Kaufman (Cambridge: Harvard University Press, 1998), and Richard A. Posner, *Cardozo: A Study in Reputation* (Chicago: University of Chicago Press, 1990); *Brandeis and Frankfurter: A Dual Biography,* by Leonard Baker (New York: Harper, 1984); *From the Diaries of Felix Frankfurter: with a Biographical Essay and Notes,* by Joseph P. Lash (New York: Norton, 1975); *Felix Frankfurter Reminisces,* recorded and edited by Harlan B. Phillips (New York: Reynal, 1960); and *Felix Frankfurter: A Tribute,* ed. Wallace Mendelson (New York: Reynal, 1964).

1. See CCB-HLS, 21:1, CCB, *Notes on the History of Burlingham, Veeder, Clark & Hupper,* (New York: privately printed, 1946), 6.

2. Beecher, who had "a highly nervous temperament," left private practice for a quieter life as a counsel to the Shipping Board, in Washington. Ibid., 12.

3. See Chapter 11, and its nn. 57–60. The lesser of the two judges, in CCB's opinion, was Thomas Chatfield, a Columbia Law School graduate and the first graduate of a law school to sit in the district. He was appointed in 1907, and was its sole judge until joined by Veeder in 1911.

4. CCB-HLS, 19:1, VVV to CCB, 13 July, 26 July, 24 Aug., and 18 Sept. 1917. Using Charles. Ibid., 13 July and 24 Aug. 1917.

5. Ibid., 18 Sept. 1917. A decision on the firm's name was left until after the partnership shares were settled.

6. "No money." CCB-HLS, 3:5, CCB to Paul Cravath, 27 Jan. 1920. On earnings of other lawyers. Davis and Steuer, this chapter; Emory Buckner, see Mayer (1968), 245, 253; William D. Guthrie, see Martin (1970), 219.

7. CCB-HLS, 21:1, CCB, *Notes,* etc., 23–27, being an article on VVV prepared by CCB and ANH for ABCNY *Memorials.* In it they list some of VVV's legal articles, mentioning that among readers impressed by them was Sir Frederick Pollock. VVV in his letters often comments on his reading. Hardy is "one of my hobbies. But I do not fail to observe his limitations . . . The truth is that in all his five volumes of verse there is only one piece of real poetry, 'The Darkling Thrush.'" And he sends CCB a book by Conrad. CCB-HLS, 19:1, VVV to CCB, 18 Sept. 1917. See obits, *Herald Tribune,* 5 Dec. 1942, 10:1, and *Times,* 5 Dec. 1942, 15:1.

8. CCB-HLS, 3:5, CCB to Paul Cravath, 27 Jan. 1920: "Now I find that every other man from the law schools wants to go into the Admiralty."

9. See Chapter 10, and its nn. 9–11; CCB-HLS, 21:1, CCB, *Notes*, 13.

10. TDT-YSML, 2:13, 5 Aug. 1918. The man was W. H. McGrann, a former partner of J. Parker Kirlin. He had graduated from the Naval Academy at Annapolis and after serving some years in the navy had retired to practice admiralty law.

11. CCB-HLS, 21:1, *Proceedings . . . to Commemorate the Seventy-Fifth Anniversary* of ABCNY, 13, 14; also in ABCNY *Reports* 90, 730.

12. Martin (1970), 143–57.

13. James C. Carter, "The Proposed Codification of Our Common Law," ABCNY *Reports* 3, 36, quoted in Martin (1970), 154. For summary of debate, see Horwitz (1992), 117–21; for an account of Carter, see Taft (1941), 194–95.

14. CCB's focus on the practical. See Greenbaum (1967), 196: "He was always working on ideas of his own for court reform." Defeating the codes. ABCNY *Reports* 23, 83, 226; quoted in Martin (1970), 155.

15. Martin (1970), 183–86. Women in the County Lawyers' Association. See Taft (1941), 67. CCB joined the NYCLA in 1909, serving on the Federal Courts Committee, 1912–20, and as chairman, 1921–27; on the Discipline Committee, 1930–38; and on the Law Research Committee, 1935.

Note: CCB on the County Lawyers' Association. In a letter to FDR, 6 Dec. 1929, when Roosevelt was governor of New York, CCB sent some "pensées re judges." In the course of the letter he compared the two associations: "I appreciate how slight the influence of the Bar Association is. A nomination being equivalent to election, everything depends on John F. Curry [boss of Tammany] . . . I am speaking only for the Association of the Bar. It is in no sense an aristocratic body, but its membership includes the best men at the Bar. The New York County Lawyers Association is a fine body, very active, but somewhat more closely allied with the Hall [Tammany]; sometimes I think the only difference between the two associations is that there are a few members of the New York County Lawyers Association who could not possibly be elected to the Association of the Bar, and also that some of these same gentlemen, who, though they may have a bad reputation, are men of ability, are members of important committees in the County Lawyers Association." FDR Personal Papers as governor, box 11, C. C. Burlingham folder, FDR Library, Hyde Park, New York.

16. Martin (1970), 206–13. Waldman (1920), 1–13.

17. The speech in full. Waldman (1920), 3–7.

18. *World*, editorial, "A Legislative Outrage," 8 Jan. 1920, 22:3, reprinted in full, Waldman (1920), 21–22. *The World* also published a collection of articles on Article I of the U.S. Constitution, Sunday, second news section, 18 Jan. 1920, 1:1–8.

19. Pusey (1951), 1:391–93. Also *Herald*, 10 Jan. 1920, 1:2, and *Times*, 10 Jan. 1920.

20. Waldman (1920), 43. Waldman was admitted to the bar in 1923 and became a member of ABCNY in 1940.

21. *Times*, 13 Jan. 1920, 1:6–8, and *World*, 13 Jan. 1920, 1:7–8.

22. Martin (1970), 210–11; 8 ABCNY *Minutes*, 13 Jan. 1920, 97–103. John Lord O'Brian-COH, 313–17.

23. Stone. *Proceedings . . . to Commemorate the Seventy-Fifth Anniversary* of ABCNY, 5–6, in ABCNY *Reports* 90, 730, and also in CCB-HLS, 21:1.

24. Waldman (1920), 225. The speaker was Assemblyman Marty McCue, former prizefighter and saloonkeeper. According to Waldman, "None of the following orators could approach his effort in abuse or indecency." But Waldman, who was on first-name terms with McCue, was ready to take the personal abuse with a grain of salt—but not the expulsion of duly elected assemblymen.

25. *Times*, 2 Apr. 1920, 14:1; and *Herald*, 2 Apr. 1920, 8:2: "The sentiment of honest, intelligent patriotism which animates a great majority of the people of this state, found adequate expression." But see *Tribune*, 2 Apr. 1920, 12:2: "A lynching has occurred."

26. Martin (1970), 213. "Bearded iceberg," Pusey (1951), 1:336. CCB-HLS, 5:11, CCB to FF, 21 Feb. 1952: "Any attempt to humanize the Chief is futile. I don't believe he had a single intimate friend outside his family."

27. Timothy N. Pfeiffer, *Law Practice in a Turbulent World: An Informal Narrative of Four Decades, 1921–1963, of Milbank, Tweed, Hadley & McCoy* (New York: privately printed, 1965), 14–15. Also Greenbaum (1967), 42–45, and Botein (1952), 216, 219. For an astonishing example of M. D. Steuer's preeminence as a trial lawyer, in which he received a retainer of $10,000, nonrefundable, in case a will is contested, see A. Steuer (1950), 17–18. And for a fiery attack on M. D. Steuer by FF, see Freedman (1967), 318–19.

28. Greenbaum (1967), 42–45; Steuer (1950), 25; and R. O. Boyer (1932), 29ff.

29. Harbaugh (1973), 183–84. On M. D. Steuer, R. O. Boyer (1932), 16–17: "For the last ten years Steuer has earned more than $1,000,000 annually." And A. Steuer (1950), 16–17: "From about 1918 he adopted a flat charge of $1,000 a day for each court appearance, plus a retainer in consonance with the difficulty or importance of the matter. This was always payable in advance and was not dependent on the outcome of the litigation . . . In later years the daily fee became $1,500."

30. Mason, *William Howard Taft* (1965), 168.

31. Salary. Harbaugh (1973), 191–92, and 572 n. 33, in which he estimates the salary to have been the equivalent in 1970 of about $60,000 before taxes. Vows. CCB-HLS, 4:8, CCB to FF, 23 Oct. 1924.

32. Mason, *William Howard Taft* (1965), 172, citing W. H. Taft to CCB, 16 Jan. 1923; also Harbaugh (1973), 193, citing same and quoting Henry F. Pringle, *The Life and Times of William Howard Taft*, (New York: Farrar, 1939), 2:1058.

33. CCB-HLS, 4:8, FF to CCB, 4 Feb. 1924, and ibid., 5:8, FF to CCB, 23 Nov. 1948. Also FF (1960), 4.

34. On FF, see Mendelson, ed. (1964), 38, 56–57, 83. "Head, eyes, and glasses." Lash (1975), 18, quoting a reporter for *The Nation*. Baker (1984), 42ff., citing on public school, FF to CCB, 23 Nov. 1948, Library of Congress-FF Papers: Correspondence File. See also FF (1960), 3–5; at City College, 11, and Harvard Law School, 16–33. And see Mendelson, ed. (1964), 28, 56, 83.

35. CCB-HLS, 4:8, CCB to FF, 7 Feb. 1924.

36. Practical. CCB-HLS, 4:8, CCB to FF, 13 Feb. 1924; ibid., FF to CCB, 14 Feb. 1924.

37. Harbaugh (1973), 201–2, and 574 n. 19. FF's position at *The New Republic*. FF (1960), 93: "I became associated with, though I was not an editor of, the *New Republic*. I was one of the trustees, technically speaking. I was with them and sat with the editorial board all through the early stages before the child was born. When the child was born, I was kind of a godfather, or perhaps godcousin is better."

38. CCB-HLS, 4:8, CCB to FF, 20 Oct. 1924.

39. CCB-HLS, 4:8, FF to CCB, 21 Oct. 1924, enclosing copy of FF to LH, 3 Oct. 1924. FF on influence of elder lawyers on law students. FF (1960), 190–93.

40. CCB-HLS, 4:8, CCB to FF, 23 Oct. 1924. For Davis's account of how and why he joined the Stetson firm in 1921, see Davis-COH (recorded in 1953–54), 155–56: "After my ambassadorship I was busted. This happens quite frequently to public servants." And he recounts how all the old partners in his new firm died "as soon as they heard I was coming."

41. Harbaugh (1973), 200.

42. Quoted in ibid., 201, citing Hocking, "Leaders and Led," *Yale Review* XIII (July 1924): 637.

43. Court-packing. See Chapter 18 and notes. On FF's possible envy. Harbaugh (1973), 201. On FF's lack of money sense. Baker (1984), 493. FF on it. FF (1960), 195; and see Mendelson, ed. (1964), 46. Further, not long after Frankfurter died in 1965, it became known that although he and his wife had been childless, he had left her so ill provided that his former law clerks were having to share the cost of some of her nursing home expenses. CCB, and most others in his generation, would have been both saddened and shocked: A husband's first duty was to provide for his wife. For CCB, and Hughes and Davis, that was an honorable part of being "practical."

44. This is a recurring theme in Kronman (1993). E.g., at 232, quoting Richard Posner, he writes: "The lawyer-economist is not at all concerned, in short, 'with being thought sound by judges and practicing lawyers; nor is he concerned with writing in a language they understand or with using concepts familiar to them. He is not one of them. He is part of the scholarly rather than the legal community.' To the extent that he sees himself in this . . . [he will] give no weight to the claims of practical wisdom." See also 315–16 and 362–64.

45. Bender (1987), 295, discusses an article in *The New Republic* by Morris R. Cohen, in 1914, in which "with unconcealed enthusiasm he [Cohen] explained that the clergy and the legal profession had deservedly lost their claims to intellectual leadership. His appreciation for—and identification with—the 'growing influence of the university professor' was equally clear."

46. LH-HLS, 100:27, CCB to LH, 24 Dec. 1924.

47. LH (1974), 211, being a reprint of his article on Swan first published in *The Yale Law Journal*, LVII (Dec. 1947): 167–72.

48. On Manton, see Chapter 19 and its n. 61. On ANH. CCB-HLS, 4:8, CCB to FF, 12 June 1926.

49. Mason, *William Howard Taft* (1965), 187.

50. CRB&M-CEHughes Collection, CCB to CEH, 2 Aug. 1925.

51. On Caffey. CRB&M, CEH Collection, CCB to CEH, 8 and 11 Feb. 1929, and ibid., CCB to CEH, 15 Feb.: "If Caffey should be thought too old—nearly sixty. Then as Democrats I suggest in addition Walter H. Pollak, Michael Cardozo, of Nathan & Cardozo, who, A. N. Hand tells me, has an intellect worthy of his cousin." (This Michael H. Cardozo, 1881–1951, was a first cousin once removed of Benjamin Cardozo and grandfather of Michael A. Cardozo, president of ABCNY, 1996–98.)

52. CCB-HLS, 18:2, CCB to WHT, 30 June 1925.

53. CRB&M, CEH Collection, CCB to CEH, 3 Aug. 1925.

54. Thacher. CCB-HLS, 17:14, CCB to H. F. Stone, 30 Apr. 1929. In TDT-YSML, 14:201, CCB letter to Senator Robert F. Wagner, 26 Feb. 1930, of which CCB sent a copy to LH, who forwarded it with notes of his own to TDT.

55. On Chase. Gunther (1994), 286.

56. On Mack. Barnard (1974), 118, 137–39; and Gunther (1994), 285. CCB admired Mack, Barnard, (1974), 125, 319.

57. See Chapter 10.

58. Quoted by Bergan (1985), 252. Cardozo. "The Home of the Law," address at the dedication of the New York County Lawyers' Association, 28 May 1930.

59. Taft (1941), "Jewish Lawyers in New York," 75–85, and Appendix, 211–12. At 77, "In 1885 there were approximately 5,000 lawyers in the then City of New York [Manhattan and a small part of the Bronx], of whom about 400, or 8%, were Jews; in 1939, in the same area, the entire bar consisted of approximately 19,000 lawyers, of whom about 9,467, or

49.8%, were believed to be Jewish." And at 82, "In 1882, the City Bar Association had 657 members, of whom only 31 were Jews, that is about 4¾% of the entire membership. In 1939, the membership had increased to 3,841 (honorary and associate members included) and the Jews to 430, or about 11%." After discussing posts held by Jews in the Association, he similarly analyses the numbers of Jewish lawyers on the bench.

Note: In these years the problem of anti-Semitism in the city was not so simple as later generations are often inclined to assume. Cardozo's twin sister, Emily, married a Christian, Frank Bent, and within the extended family there seems to have been objection to Frank and to her apostasy, although not on Cardozo's part. Stephen Birmingham, *The Grandees: America's Sephardic Elite* (New York: Harper & Row, 1971), 299, tells a lurid story of her rejection by the family, which Cardozo's biographer, Kaufman (1998), 65–66 and 600–601 n. 50, treats as "utterly unreliable" although, on 65, stating that there was "some strain" in accepting the Christian into the family and, in n. 50, agreeing that Bir-mingham's story had "some currency" among the "more distant" family members. In another Jewish family, the Loebs, young James Loeb, founder of the Loeb Classical Library, had his engagement to a Christian broken by family pressures, and his brother-in-law Jacob Schiff in his will threatened to disinherit any child who married a Christian. See S. Birmingham "Our Crowd" (New York: Harper & Row, 1967), 255, and Andrea Olmstead, "The Toll of Idealism: James Loeb—Musician, Classicist, Philanthropist," *Journal of Musicology* (University of California) XIV:2 (Spring 1996): 241–42. And the prejudices were not just between Gentile and Jew. The German Jewish men's club, the Harmonie, would not admit Sephardic members, while the latter's Sephardic Beach Point Club barred German Jews. Among Christians there were many Protestant clubs that balked at electing a Roman Catholic, and Roman cemeteries that would not bury a Protestant wife beside her Catholic husband. It was an era of discrimination, softened occasionally by moderates on all sides, and to some extent by professional organizations, such as the ABCNY, the political clubs, or the Municipal Art Society. See Gilmartin (1995), 36.

60. CCB-HLS, 22:1, CCB to John C. Milburn, 5 June 1925.

61. Chapter on "Committee on Admissions," by George W. Martin, in *The Century, 1847–1946* (New York: Century Association, 1947), and subsequent talks by GM with members of the committee.

62. On the peculiar difficulty of cutting short an American bore, see Tocqueville (1946), 440. On LH interrupting bores, "Memorial on Learned Hand," 1962, reprinted in *The Century at 150: Excerpts from the Archives*, ed. James Duffy (New York: Century Association, 1997), 133.

63. CCB was quoted briefly on the "long table" in Martin, *The Century, 1847–1946*, 267–68. He was proposed for the club by George William Curtis and elected in 1893, continuing a member until his death in 1959.

64. Poll of committee. CCB-HLS, 22:1, CCB to John C. Milburn, 5 June 1925; and CRB&M, CEH Collection, CCB to CEH, 11 June 1925. Martin, "Committee on Admissions," 232.

65. CCB-HLS, 22:1, CCB to John C. Milburn, 5 June 1925: "I asked Mr. Root to propose him, but he thought it better to second him, on the ground that if by any chance the candidate were rejected, the President would have to resign. That is an extreme view, but there is force in it, no doubt." For an account of Milburn, with an appraisal by BNC, see Martin (1970), 202–3; also Taft (1941), 195–96.

66. CCB-HLS, 22:1, CCB to Elihu Root, 24 June 1925; and CRB&M, CEH Collection, CCB to CEH, 11 June 1925.

67. LH-HLS, 100:28, CCB to LH, 11 June 1925. CCB also suggested to CEH what might be said: "The personality of the man and his modesty and charm are, of course, not

known to the Centurions. If they can be made known, we can do the trick," CRB&M-CEHughes Collection, CCB to CEH, 11 June 1925.

68. CCB-HLS, 22:1, Benjamin N. Cardozo to CCB, 26 June 1925.

69. Kaufman (1998), 169–71, calls Cardozo's decision to join the club "controversial," and Cardozo's willingness to leave the election process to CCB "problematic." He then quotes his interview with FF to the effect that Cardozo should not have joined a club where anti-Semitism existed. It is probably true, of course, that even today among such a large group as the Century's 2,300 resident and nonresident members, there are some anti-Semites, but a policy such as FF's, which leaves the club to them—or other associations to such—seems self-defeating.

70. For a summary of this, see Moscow (1948), 148–65, 155. CCB, in a letter on "Appointed Judges," *Times*, 25 Mar. 1930, 28:8, offered this example: "When a vacancy occurs through death or resignation, the Governor has an opportunity to select a judge to serve until the end of the year, and the man selected by a Democratic Governor is almost invariably nominated by the convention. Thus Governor Smith appointed Judge Proskauer, and he was nominated in the fall."

71. Posner, *Cardozo* (1990), 131.

72. CRB&M-CEHughes Collection, CCB to CEH, 3 Aug. 1925. See George Hellman, *Benjamin N. Cardozo, American Judge* (New York: Whittlesey House, 1940), 144–45, for others urging the appointment, and Kaufman (1998), 178–82.

73. September shuffle: *Herald Tribune*, 22 Sept. 1926, 11:1; 23 Sept. 1926, 8:2; and 15 Sept. 1926, 2:3; also *Times*, 22 Sept. 1926, 12:4; and 23 Sept. 1926, 1:5. Hellman (1940), Cardozo (1940), 149, offers an account of why Governor Smith appointed O'Brien: "Cardozo told me to."

74. CCB-HLS, 4:8, CCB to FF, 27 Sept. 1926.

75. On the good and bad of assignment by rotation, see Posner, *Cardozo* (1990), 145–48. For an example of assignment by prerogative on the U.S. Supreme Court, in which Chief Justice Hughes possibly was unfair to Cardozo, see Mason, *Harlan Fiske Stone* (1956), 459–60. And also CCB-HLS, 22:2, CCB to Benjamin N. Cardozo, 9 Jan. 1934: "You ought to have written that opinion yesterday instead of the C.J., but it is interesting to see the C.J. coming along." The case was *Home Building and Loan Association v. Blaisdell*, 290 U.S. 398 (1934), upholding 5 to 4 the Minnesota Mortgage Moratorium Law of 1933; for discussion, see Mason, *Harlan Fiske Stone* (1956), 360–66, and Kaufman (1998), 499–503, who discusses Cardozo's unpublished concurring opinion and its probable influence on the thinking of CEH.

76. Posner, *Cardozo* (1990), 6–9, 130–31. See Hellman, Cardozo (1940), 57, 66–67, and Kaufman (1998), 157–60. Kaufman (1998), 136–40, recounts how Cardozo ran the court, and at 143 ascribes its collegiality directly in part to the formal courtesy of the judges: they addressed one another as Judge X and Judge Y. No first names.

77. Posner, *Cardozo* (1990), 74–91, using various measures to determine importance.

78. Ibid., 41: At the time Posner wrote, circa 1989, *MacPherson* had been cited 381 times by state courts outside New York, 179 within, and 267 by federal courts.

79. *MacPherson v. Buick Motor Co.*, 217 N.Y. 382 (1916), 391. Case discussed by Bergan (1985), 295–98, and Kaufman (1998), 265–85.

80. Posner, *Cardozo* (1990), 109. Kaufman (1998), 113, 165, 401.

81. CCB signed the letter merely "A member of the U.S. Supreme Court," *Herald Tribune*, 10 Jan. 1944, 16:4. But his style was unmistakable, and on 15 January the court's chief justice, Harlan Fiske Stone, wrote directly to him, with CCB replying on 18 January. For an account of this incident, with long quotations from the letters, see Mason, *Harlan Fiske Stone* (1956), 606–11, and this book, Chapter 24.

82. CCB-COH, 13.

83. *Hess v. Rath*, 249 N.Y. 436 (1928), 438. Chalcedon: Herodotus, *History*, Book 4, 144. See Posner, *Cardozo* (1990), 55–57, analyzing how a single sentence of Cardozo, by the use of a single word, "constable" instead of "policeman," achieved brilliance.

84. Kaufman (1998), 455.

85. TDT-YSML, 4:38A, LH to TDT, 27 Feb. 1932.

86. Memorial on Cardozo, 1938. Reprinted in *The Century at 150*, 126. Kaufman (1998), 204, states that *The Nature of the Judicial Process* sold 24,805 copies between 1921 and 1960, and 156,637 between 1960 and 1994.

87. CCB-HLS, 22:1, Benjamin N. Cardozo to CCB, 14 Mar. 1932.

88. No part of the money was ever recovered.

89. FF, *The Case of Sacco and Vanzetti: A Critical Analysis for Lawyers and Laymen* (Boston: Little, Brown, 1927). See FF (1960), 213–15, for his account of the article and book's origin. The article, *Atlantic Monthly*, Mar. 1927, 409–32.

90. Governor Fuller released the letter, one of hundreds received. See *Times*, 19 Apr. 1927, 28:2. CCB-HLS, 16:10, copy of letter to governor, 12 Apr. 1927, signed by Lawrence, Taussig, Curtis, Roland W. Boyden, and Heman M. Burr.

91. *Times*, 20 Apr. 1927, 24:8, and *Herald Tribune*, 20 Apr. 1927, 22:5.

92. CCB-HLS, 16:9, CCB to editor of *World*, 20 Apr. 1927, and the reply, signed "WL," to CCB, CCB-HLS, 16:9. Editorial, *World*, 21 Apr. 1927, 14:2.

93. CCB-HLS, 16:9, CCB to F. W. Taussig, 19 Apr. 1927. Ibid., CCB to George R. Nutter, 19 Apr. 1927, Ibid., Taussig to CCB, 20 Apr. 1927.

94. CCB-HLS, 16:9, CCB to William Lawrence, 22 Apr. 1927. Lawrence (1850–1941) retired officially on 30 May 1927, having been consecrated on 5 October 1893, as the successor to Phillips Brooks (died 23 January 1893)—a term of thirty-three and a half years. He was succeeded by Charles L. Slattery (1867–1930).

95. Ibid. CCB to FF, 22 Apr. 1927. CCB mailed the letter to FF in Cambridge, suggesting that FF did not spend the night in New York.

96. *World* editorial, 14 May 1927, 12:2. The group, numbering thirty, seems merely to have been a list of distinguished names whose views were thought to be known. CRB&M, Robert Lee Hale Collection, CCB to Robert Lee Hale, 17 May 1927, in response to a letter from Hale wanting New York lawyers to speak out.

97. *World*, 18 May 1927, 12:4. Reference to Buckner, see *New Republic* 50 (27 Apr. 1927): 278–79, and Mayer (1968), 245.

98. Lash (1975), 38. *World*, 19 Aug. 1927, 12:1–6, analysis of the Lowell Report. It is presented as an unsigned editorial. *Times*, 20 Aug. 1927, 14:8, CCB analyzing Lowell Report. In two private letters CCB states that he wrote at the newspaper's request: CCB-HLS, 10:10, CCB to Loulie (Mrs. Pierre) Jay, 14 Sept. 1927, and CCB-HLS, 16:9, CCB letter to Louis Stix, 22 Oct. 1927. CCB-HLS, 16:9, CCB to F. W. Taussig, 29 Aug. 1927. Greenbaum (1967), 78: "Al Smith once . . . told me I was unfair to criticize this report because they were honest men and made what they believed was an honest report. He added, 'What did you expect? If the Governor had appointed Lillian Wald [Henry Street Settlement], Norman Thomas [Socialist Party leader], and me, what do you think we would have done?'" CCB-HLS, 16:9, CCB to FF, 13 Sept. 1927.

99. CCB-HLS, 16:10, an undated typescript of the appeal, which had been circulated by Paul U. Kellogg, editor of *The Survey*. The appeal was issued initially in New York and Boston "by a group of well known professional men and women, lawyers, university men, editors, physicians and social workers." Ultimately it was signed by hundreds, in twenty-two states; see *Times*, 21 Aug. 1927, 3:3.

100. CCB-HLS, 16:9, CCB to Bishop Slattery, 17 Aug. 1927. Slattery. See n. 94 above, and DAB XVII (orig. ed.): 206–7.

101. CCB-HLS, 16:9, CCB to Slattery, 29 Aug. 1927, thanking him for his reply and stating that the bishop's reasoning "does not appeal strongly to me." Date of execution. Though some works state that the men were executed on 22 August and by hanging, the men died in the first hour of 23 August, by electric chair. See Greenbaum (1967), 75, and Sutherland (1967), 261. Also the latter, 261–62, for reaction within Harvard circles to Frankfurter's actions: "At one time President Lowell was seriously concerned about clamor for Frankfurter's dismissal, but Lowell stood firm for Frankfurter . . ."

102. CCB-HLS, 12:12, CCB to Justice MacKinnon, 29 Aug. 1927.

103. The earliest reference found to *The Transcript*, when only an idea, occurs in CCB-HLS, 16:9, CCB to FF, 5 Oct. 1927: "What you said last night went to the heart of the business. Perhaps there is very little we can do, sodden in prosperity as we are. But we must not lie down—the Record must be printed and the Report must be shown up. Who can do it?" CCB suggests "old Father Fabian" Franklin, a writer, journalist, and mathematician, "who knows how to write and he has little to do." Franklin (1853–1939), DAB, supp. 2, 206–7, had published a long letter, with complimentary references to CCB, in the *Times*, 27 Apr. 1927, 24:7, recommending a full inquiry of the case by Governor Fuller. But CCB's proposal of Franklin died at birth.

104. The cost. Joughin and Morgan (1948), 318. The sponsors. Ibid., and *World*, 24 June 1928, editorial section, 2:3. Also CCB-HLS, 16:9, CCB to Elihu Root Jr., 27 Mar. 1928, naming Rockefeller and Rosenwald. But see Mendelson, ed. (1964), 110, who states that FF "raised part of the money . . . This massive contribution to history is almost entirely due to the foresight and initiative of Felix." (GM: In my opinion the assertion is unpersuasive. More likely, I think, the sponsors would have asked FF to stay out of the project in order to avoid charges of bias. Also, if there was truth to the assertion, I think CCB at some point, perhaps to MacKinnon in England, would have let the cat out of the bag. He liked to relay this sort of secret. Also, I think he would not have written to FF about it in this manner: "When [James] Byrne died, I asked B. Flexner whether he knew him. B.F. said that he saw him only once. J.B. had written that he wished to call on him, and instead, he called on Byrne. He found him very angry. 'You are one of the sponsors of the volumes of evidence in the *Sacco-Vanzetti* case. Why was I not asked to be a sponsor and why was I not asked to contribute to the expense. I suppose, I should not be angry with you; but Burlingham, he was one of the sponsors, and he never said a word to me about it! Outrageous!'" FF-LOC, container 35, CCB to FF, 31 Dec. 1942. And see n. 108 below.

105. "Cold, unemotional preface." CCB-HLS, 16:9, CCB to Elihu Root Jr., 27 Mar. 1928.

106. *The Sacco-Vanzetti Case: Transcript of the Record of the Trial of Nicola Sacco and Bartolomeo Vanzetti in the Courts of Massachusetts and Subsequent Proceedings, 1920–1927*, 6 vols. (New York: Henry Holt, 1928). From the Prefatory Note: "Misspelt words and errors in punctuation which occur in the record are reprinted without change, as we were unwilling to make any corrections whatsoever."

107. E.g., William Young and David E. Kaiser, *Post-mortem: New Evidence in the Case of Sacco and Vanzetti* (Amherst: University of Massachusetts Press, 1985); and Francis Russell, *Sacco and Vanzetti: The Case Resolved* (New York: Harper, 1986). The former concludes that both men were innocent of the crime; the latter that Sacco was guilty and Vanzetti, though innocent, willing to die a martyr for the cause of anarchism.

108. CCB-HLS, 11:1, CCB to G. Louis Joughin, 28 Dec. 1948: "As you write, I had a great deal to do with the publication of the record." See also CCB-HLS, 4:8, FF to CCB,

12 June 1928: Brandeis enthusiastic "about your share in securing the sponsorship and publication."

109. CCB-HLS, 11:1. On Bishop McConnell (1871–1951), see DAB, supp. 5, 445–46. He had "Social Gospel" views, which became important nationally through his writings and reports on labor confrontations. He was much admired in New York and other centers of liberalism but much disliked by the conservative wing of his church.

110. Greenbaum (1967), 75–78. The plaintiff dropped his suit before trial. And see Baker (1984), 269–70. On Fuller. CCB-HLS, 16–9, F. W. Taussig to CCB, 20 Apr. 1927. FF on Fuller. FF (1960), 206. Also FF's description, 214–15, of Ellery Sedgwick, editor of the *Atlantic Monthly*, turns sneering; also of Lowell, 217 (on which, see Mendelson, ed. [1964], 40–41). On Sedgwick, see Bender (1987), 247–49.

111. LH (1974), 138. His speech was made upon the award by the university of an honorary degree. It was published in HAB (7 July 1939): 1129–31.

112. CCB's burgeoning reputation as a writer on public issues. The request in August from the *Times* for a letter on a prescribed subject, the "Lowell Report," seems to have been the first such CCB received, see n. 98 above. For the inquiry from a lawyer in Ohio, see CCB-HLS, 16:9, CCB to Louis Stix, 22 Oct. 1927. On the Dec. request from the dean of Harvard Law School, see ibid., Roscoe Pound, dean, to CCB, 9 Dec. 1927. Pound writes of a recent report of the Massachusetts Judicial Council that sustains FF's position in a controversy on evidence in the case: "If you could find time to write a letter to the *Times* about this matter, I believe it would do much toward setting the public mind in right channels about an important feature of this controversy." On letting the controversy die, see ibid., CCB to Slattery, 29 Aug. 1927.

14. CCB as Bar Association President

Other than the Burlingham collections and newspapers the chief source for CCB as president of ABCNY is George Martin, *Causes and Conflicts: The Centennial History of the Association of the Bar of the City of New York* (Boston: Houghton, 1970; repr., New York: Fordham University Press, 1997). And of the Tammany investigations and the Judges Party: Herbert Mitgang, *The Man Who Rode the Tiger: The Life and Times of Judge Samuel Seabury* (Philadelphia: Lippincott, 1963); George Martin, *Causes and Conflicts*; Bernard Bellush, *Franklin D. Roosevelt as Governor of New York* (New York: Columbia University Press, 1955; repr., New York: AMS Press, 1968); Warren Moscow, *Politics in the Empire State* (New York: Knopf, 1948; repr., Westport, Conn.: Greenwood, 1979); Gene Fowler, *Beau James: The Life and Times of Jimmy Walker* (New York: Viking, 1949); Norman Thomas and Paul Blanshard, *What's the Matter with New York?: A National Problem* (New York: Macmillan, 1932); Association of the Bar of the City of New York, *Clippings, 1928–1931* and *1931–1934*.

1. *Herald Tribune*, 15 May 1929, 21:1, and *Times*, 15 May 1929, 34:8.

2. *Herald Tribune*, 15 May 1929, 21:1 and *Times*, 15 May 1929, 34:8. On the ambulance-chasing, see Martin (1970), 374–77, and nn.; also ABCNY *Year Book* 37, 151–52. On bankruptcy. Martin (1970), 226–27, and nn; also ABCNY *Year Book* 42, 354–57.

3. CRB&M, CEH Collection, CCB to CEH, 15 Feb. 1929, recruiting for the special committee; CCB to CEH, 9 Mar. and 9 Apr. 1929, reporting its activities.

4. FDR Library, Hyde Park, N.Y., FDR New York state senator, 11:85, CCB to FDR, 15 Mar. 1912.

5. FF, who knew Mrs. Kelley well and had often served as counsel for the Consumers' League, states in FF (1960), 95–96, that after Mrs. Kelley was turned down by Joseph Hodges Choate for the *Muller v. Oregon* case, she went for advice to CCB, who suggested a lawyer in Boston named Louis D. Brandeis; and thus CCB had a hand in the birth of the "Brandeis brief." GM: Maybe, but Brandeis was married to Alice Goldmark, Josephine's sister, and it seems unlikely Mrs. Kelley needed to hear about Brandeis from CCB—and yet she may have wanted CCB's opinion. Though CCB discusses Brandeis and mentions the "brief" in his oral history, he does not mention this incident, CCB-COH, 31.

6. CCB-HLS, 3:1, CCB to Julius M. Mayer, 19 Nov. 1921.

7. For a history of the steps by which Columbia opened its school to women, see CCB-HLS, 3:1, James P. Gifford to CCB, 7 Apr. 1954. Gifford taught at Columbia Law School 1930–61, and was its associate dean 1946–52. See obit, *Times*, 17 Sept. 1961, 87:1.

8. CCB to HAB, 20 June 1942, 514, and republished, though much cut, in *Harvard Magazine*, May–June 1998, 42. In HAB the letter gives facts about the history of women in the Yale and Columbia law schools.

9. James McCauley Landis Papers-HLS, 5:9, CCB to Landis, 14 Jan. 1939, 15 Oct. 1943, and 17 Mar. 1945.

10. James McCauley Landis Papers-HLS, 5:9, Landis to CCB, 20 Mar. 1945.

11. Ibid., CCB to Landis, 26 Mar. 1945. GC-DCL, ser. 4, box 1, GC to CCB, 19 Oct. 1949. GC was a member of the Corporation, 1931–50. Yale admitted women beginning in the autumn of 1919. See Taft (1941), 72–73, for a brief summary.

12. Sutherland (1967), 319–20.

13. Taft (1941) 64, gives the language.

14. This summary is taken from a report prepared by the ABCNY secretary, Charles H. Strong, for CCB as president, see CCB-HLS, 1:9, Strong to CCB, 27 Feb. 1930. On the vote adopting the resolution, see ABCNY executive committee minutes, 6 Jan. 1926, 165. Also a summary in Taft (1941), 65–67, and an account of "The Situation in England" in 1925, 67–72.

15. CCB-HLS, 1:9, Charles H. Strong to CCB, 27 Feb. 1930.

16. *World*, 11 Feb. 1931, 1:6, reported 275 members present, three times the usual number, of which on the vote 26 abstained. See also *Times*, 11 Feb. 1931, 1:4–5, and *Herald Tribune*, 11 Feb. 1931, 3:5, which gave the initiation fee at ABCNY as $75 for those being members of the bar ten years or less, and $100 for those over ten years. The day after the meeting an assistant district attorney, a woman, lamenting for herself and her fellows the continued denial of access to the best law library in the city, and possibly in the country, blamed the amendment's failure on the inability of women to stand together and make a movement, see *World*, 12 Feb. 1931, 15:1.

17. Taft (1941), 67.

18. Estimate of women lawyers. *Times*, 11 Feb. 1931, 1:4–5. Number in the NYCLA. *Herald Tribune*, 11 Feb. 1931, 3:5.

19. *Times*, 12 May 1937, 8:4, and *Herald Tribune*, 12 May 1937, 23:7; also Martin (1970), 244–45; Taft (1941), 66–67; and ABCNY *Minutes*, 13 Apr. 1937, 31, and 11 May 1937, 40–41. In CCB's firm a woman was not hired as an associate lawyer until relatively late, 1974, and a woman was not made partner until 1988. Emmet, Marvin & Martin, a small firm of roughly the same size but with a different practice, mostly trust, estates, and bank work, had its first woman partner in 1944. Reportedly many of the Emmet firm's clients who were women preferred to have their wills written by a woman. See the entries for Elizabeth M. Graham in Thomas B. Fenlon, *The Emmet Firm* (New York: privately published, 2001).

20. Riordon, ed. (1963), ix.

21. Martin (1976), 99–100, 179; Matthew and Hannah Josephson, *Al Smith: Hero of Cities* (Boston: Houghton Mifflin, 1969), 139, 222, 352; Huthmacher (1968), 23–31, 35–37.

22. Josephson (1969), 189.

23. Nevins and Krout, eds. (1948), 90.

24. Mitgang (1963), 162: $2,170,761.

25. Riordon, ed. (1963), ix, 3–6.

26. Plunkitt. Ibid., 41. O. Henry (W. S. Porter), in "Innocents of Broadway," commented on the provincialism of Manhattan New Yorkers generally: "He hadn't been above Fourteenth Street in ten years"; "His cousin is coming over from Brooklyn that evening and they are going to see the sights of Broadway"; and "He's lived twenty years on one street without learning as much as you would in getting a once-over shave from a lock-jawed barber in a Kansas crossroads town." And perhaps most famously in "The Pride of the Cities," in which he has a Manhattanite say: "I was never farther west than Eighth Avenue. I had a brother who died on Ninth, but I met the cortege at Eighth. There was a bunch of violets on the hearse, and the undertaker mentioned the incident to avoid mistake. I cannot say that I am familiar with the West."

27. Foley. Besides good decisions, he did much to bring state laws on surrogate matters up to date, such as revising the law on dowry to give widows more protection in a nonagricultural age. See obit, *Times*, 12 Feb. 1946, 25:1. Moscow (1948), 160: "Probably the most effective, learned, and nationally respected jurist ever to spend his legal career on a purely local court."

28. Flynn (1947), 49.

29. Olvaney. For a summary of how he profited, see Thomas and Blanshard (1932), 52–54. Mitgang (1963), 163. His $2 million, *Times*, 10 Nov. 1931, 1:1.

30. Fowler (1949), 151–52, has a brief account of the campaign, not entirely to the credit of "Beau James."

31. According to Fowler, ibid., 153, before Walker ninety-six mayors had been elected and three had succeeded to office to fill a vacancy. Not quite so, as *The Encyclopedia of New York City* (1995) makes clear. Walker was the hundredth to be sworn in, but from 1665 to 1820 the colonial or state governor appointed the mayor, and direct election to the office began only in 1834.

32. Flynn (1947), 52.

33. *Brooklyn Daily Eagle*, 24 May 1925, 4:3. In 1924, according to Thomas and Blanshard (1932), 125, quoting the *Eagle*, 19 May 1925, the prominent Brooklyn lawyer and Republican leader Meir Steinbrink said of calendar congestion in the state Supreme Court: "The majority of Supreme Court judges do not really work. Some of them are lazy . . ." In 1931, however, as part of an unsavory deal for posts on the Supreme Court, Second Judicial District, Steinbrink put himself on the court. See Mitgang (1963), 232–34; also Thomas and Blanshard, 94–103, which closes by blaming, in part, Governor Roosevelt for assisting "a corrupt bargain" despite warnings by civic leaders that one "was in the making."

34. *Brooklyn Daily Eagle*, 26 May 1925, 2:6, presents the quoted passage in a box on the page.

35. R. O. Boyer (1932), 91.

36. Ibid., 92.

37. Ibid., 78–82, 107.

38. Curry. See Mitgang (1963), 163–65; Moscow (1948), 21, 160; Josephson (1969), 423, 442. For some years Smith, Wagner, and Foley were so "out" with Boss Curry that they did not enter Tammany Hall until after his ouster in 1934. See Foley's obit, *Times*, 12 Feb. 1946, 25:1. See n. 66 below.

39. At greater length in Mitgang (1963), 166–67.

40. *Times*, 20 Dec. 1929, 1:6, gives the full text of CCB's letter and presiding justice Victor J. Dowling's reply. ABCNY, *Clippings, 1928–1931*, 97–99.

41. Vitale to chief magistrate. Quoted in Martin (1970), 229.

42. Steuer. *Times*, 9 Jan. 1930, 1:1. Court decision. *Herald Tribune*, 14 Mar. 1930, 1:8. *Times*, 14 Mar. 1930, *Evening Post*, 14 Mar. 1930, 12:2, and 13 Mar. 1930, 1:8. The Spence committee's report to ABCNY's executive committee is ABCNY *Reports* 42, 325; its pleadings before the Appellate Division, ABCNY *Reports* 42, 326. Spence argued the case. Steuer's simple question. R. O. Boyer (1932), 38. ABCNY, *Clippings, 1928–1931*, 111.

43. Martin (1970), 229. CCB, speaking for ABCNY, protests De Luca's appointment, *Times*, 21 May 1930, 1:2. Vitale, *Times*, 25 June 1930, 17:3. ABCNY, *Clippings, 1928–1931*, 70, 128.

44. *Herald Tribune*, 7 Mar. 1930, 20:1, and *Times*, 7 Mar. 1930, 20:1.

45. *Herald Tribune*, 7 Mar. 1930, 20:1, and *Times*, 7 Mar. 1930, 20:1.

46. *Herald Tribune*, 14 May 1930, 6:1, and *Times*, 14 May 1930, 18:4.

47. CCB's annual report, May 1930, ABCNY *Yearbook* 42, 157.

48. Ewald. Thomas and Blanshard (1932), 107–9. ABCNY, *Clippings, 1928–1931*, 140.

49. At FDR Library, Hyde Park, N.Y., in Personal Papers as Governor, box 11, folder "Burlingham, C. C."

50. *Herald Tribune*, 19 Aug. 1930, 2:3.

51. CCB used "perfunctory" in his article discussing the Ewald case, *Times*, 24 Aug. 1930, sec. IX, 1:1. For view that FDR, by limiting the probe to two boroughs, had done "the least that he could do." See Thomas and Blanshard (1932), 111.

52. *Times*, 24 Aug. 1930, sec. IX, 1:1.

53. Ibid. CCB was careful, even in the use of a transparent subterfuge. On 24 March 1930 he wrote a long letter to FDR about filling a Supreme Court vacancy but had Grenville Clark, a member of the ABCNY Judiciary Committee, sign it. Why? Probably because he already had written much the same letter to the *Times*, published on 25 March 1930, 28:8; and, not surprisingly, the substance, syntax, and diction of the two were similar. Presumably he did not want Roosevelt to receive a letter supposedly private and read one all but identical to it the next day in the *Times*. But he would not have cared if FDR saw through the charade (which Roosevelt most likely would have, knowing Clark's heavier style as well as CCB's lighter), for CCB by his maneuver allowed the governor honestly to deny to reporters receiving any correspondence on the matter from the president of the bar association. CCB's copy of the letter is in CCB-HLS, 1:9.

54. CCB-HLS, 4:9, CCB to FF, 24 Sept. 1930.

55. CCB quoted by Mitgang (1963), 171, who describes CCB as "the most respected civic leader in the city."

56. Ibid., 65, and GM interview with Herbert Brownell, 5 Aug. 1992.

57. District leader James W. Brown. See Mitgang (1963), 195.

58. Norris had been a co-leader of a Manhattan Democratic assembly district and in 1919 was appointed magistrate by Mayor Hylan. She quickly earned a reputation for harshness, particularly to women. In one case she had changed the court record to conceal her judicial mistreatment of a woman and the woman's lawyer; she held stock in a bond company whose bail bonds she approved as magistrate; and she posed in judicial robes for commercial advertisements for Fleischmann's Yeast, taking a fee of $1,000, see *Times*, 28 Feb. 1931, 2:1. The five Appellate Division judges voted unanimously to remove her for conduct unworthy of a judge. See Mitgang (1963), 191–93.

59. Ewald, case dismissed. See *Times*, 23 Jan. 1931, 1:6, and *Herald Tribune*, 23 Jan. 1931, 1:4. Also Thomas and Blanshard (1932), 107–9.

60. CCB as the "principal mover" behind the City Club's petition. See *Evening Post*, 21 Mar. 1931, 1:8; also *Herald Tribune*, 21 Mar. 1931, 1:7, and *Times*, 22 Mar. 1931, 1:1. Crain confers with Steuer. *Times*, 10 Mar. 1931, 1:8.

61. Mitgang (1963), 222.

62. Moscow (1948), 223, states that Roosevelt in removing Sheriff Farley "laid down a new rule . . . that a public official was obligated to give the public a reasonable explanation of money he had amassed during his term of office." Thomas and Blanshard (1932), 187, quote FDR's statement in part and comment: "There, for once, spoke a man and not a politician!" For FDR's full text, see *Times*, 25 Feb. 1932, 4:3. See Mitgang (1963), 241. But then he spoiled his good deed by appointing as Farley's successor John E. Sheehy, a personal friend of Boss Curry and a Tammany district leader; see Bellush (1955), 281 and n. 47.

63. Marriage licenses. A Tammany assembly district leader appointed deputy city clerk banked about $500,000 in six years; see Mann (1965), 53–54. The unemployment fund, Garrett (1961), 74; Mitgang (1963), 228.

64. Editorial, "Open letter to Samuel Seabury," *The Nation* 134:347 (13 Jan. 1932): 32.

65. Mitgang (1963), 252–53, 259–60. For a full transcript of Walker's testimony, see *Times*, 26 and 27 May 1932.

66. Thomas and Blanshard (1932), in Appendix I, offer "A Calendar of Scandals during the Walker Administration," and in Appendix II, in full, "The Seabury Charges against Mayor Walker." Of the fifteen, the shortest is No. 14: "That the Mayor neglected his official duty in permitting his Corporation Counsel to designate, in City compensation cases, doctors who split their fees with the Mayor's brother [a doctor]." For assorted reports and in general on the investigations, see ABCNY, *Clippings, 1931–1934*.

67. Mitgang (1963), 293.

68. Note: Assessments of Roosevelt's actions throughout the investigations vary. Many biographers, admiring him, praise his political skill and tend to ignore his moral ambiguity. On the political right, however, Republicans incline to the reverse, and on the left, likewise the two Socialists, Thomas and Blanshard. Perhaps the best summary is by Bellush (1955), 279–81, who displays the ambiguity by noting how FDR, in "a grave political error," mocked two leading clergymen, the Reverend John Haynes Holmes and Rabbi Stephen S. Wise, who asked for the removal of Mayor Walker; how he continued until 1932 to designate Tammany nominees to the city's judiciary, preferring to Al Smith's recommendation of Bernard L. Shientag for the Supreme Court Boss Curry's friend Joseph F. Crater, famous soon for vanishing without a trace; and how, upon removing Sheriff Farley from office, despite reformers' protests, he then appointed another Tammany district leader and close friend of Curry. Throughout, Bellush concludes, "He followed public opinion instead of leading and educating it."

CCB expressed his view in a letter to his English friend Francis Hirst, prophesying FDR's election in a week's time to a second term as governor. "Roosevelt will be re-elected with a fine majority. But he has done himself great injury in the eyes and minds of independents by failing to hit Tammany hard. T. resents a tap on the wrist as much as a blow in the face. I hoped, and I urged him, that when he opened his campaign down here he make some statement which would show his independence. But he failed to do so, and yesterday Stimson hit him hard in a vulnerable point. Roosevelt . . . fails to appreciate that Tammany's support is a millstone round a candidate's neck. It is good politics to hit them hard, and then give them all you can in the way of patronage. That is the way T.R. did with the Republican Organization. He was continually slamming them, but appointed Organization men whenever he had a chance—O.K. if they are up to the standard one sets." CCB-HLS, 8:10, CCB to Francis Hirst, 29 Oct. 1930.

Eisenstein and Rosenberg (1966), 71–75, offer an account of Walker sending a Tammany leader to FDR to learn his probable fate. FDR states that his mind is made up: he will have to remove Walker, if not for malfeasance, then for nonfeasance. Hence Walker's sudden resignation. See Rosenman (1952), 83.

69. CCB, 31 Jan. 1931, to FDR, Personal Papers as Governor, box 11, folder "Burlingham, C. C." Bellush (1955), 325 n. 10, remarks that the record of a Seabury hearing of one day before a grand jury, typically eighty pages of transcript totaling 15,000 words, was the equivalent to four months of a similar hearing conducted by Crain.

70. The resolution, *World-Telegram*, 12 May 1932, 22:2. Offered by George W. Wickersham, it called the obstructive tactics "unprofessional and contrary to good morals," and pledged support to the Hofstadter Committee and its counsel. For CCB's speech, see *Times*, 13 May 1931, 1:4, and editorial, 14 May, 22:3; editorial, *Herald Tribune*, 14 May, 18:2, and *World-Telegram*, 14 May, 28:2.

71. FDR, 19 Jan. 1931, to CCB, Personal Papers as Governor, box 11, folder "Burlingham, C. C."

72. CCB-HLS, 10:15, CCB to Judge Irving Lehman, 4 Jan. 1940: "I am devoted to F.D.R., but I never knew a man so politically-minded. Even the finest things he does have almost invariably a political edge." And LH-HLS, 101:2, CCB postcard to LH, 22 June 1940, referring to FDR's cabinet appointment of two Republicans, Henry L. Stimson as secretary of war (replacing Harry Woodring) and Frank Knox as secretary of the navy (replacing Charles Edison): "To F.D.R. *nihil sine animo politico est*, but what of that? He has replaced 2 dubs by able and experienced men." See Rosenman (1952), 84: "[FDR] was most generous and forgiving about human weakness; but he was implacable and vindictive toward those who deliberately were unfair to him, especially in political matters." For an example of FDR being vindictive, see Rosenman (1952), 105.

73. CCB to FDR, 21 July 1930, in Personal Papers as Governor, box 11. See CCB-HLS, 10:16, CCB to Arthur Ballantine, 4 Apr. 1952, "I myself favor deals if they are wise and will carry through. That is the only way [Charles O.] Breitel could continue on the bench." On Seabury, Mitgang (1963), 153: "His anti-Tammany stand was not merely a cause; it was a mania that prevented him from reaching any accommodation with the New York county leaders." Heckscher (1978), 28, "[His] hatred of the Tiger was almost pathological."

74. Rosenman (1952), 83–84. On hearing the news FDR wired Rosenman, "You will remember that I have a long memory and a long arm for my friends." And within less than a year the succeeding Democratic governor, Herbert H. Lehman, had appointed Rosenman to the first vacancy on the court; Mitgang (1963), 302. On appointments to vacancies, see Moscow (1948), 155 ff.

75. For the resolutions in full, with CCB's comments, see his speech, 3 Nov. 1932, at Town Hall, CCB-HLS, 10:14.

76. *Herald Tribune*, 10 Nov. 1932, 6:3.

77. Radio speech, over WRNY, on 29 Oct. 1932, text in CCB-HLS, 10:14; see *Times*, 30 Oct., 16:1.

78. ABCNY *Yearbook* 51, 145.

79. Election eve speech. Town Hall, 3 Nov. 1932, text in CCB-HLS, 10:14; see *Times*, 4 Nov. 1932, 9:2.

80. CCB on election. *Times*, 9 Nov. 1932, 1:2.

81. Quoted at greater length in Martin (1970), 241–42, citing ABCNY *Reports* 49, 354, 3–4. For other reports, notices, clippings, etc., on the campaign, see ABCNY *Folio Pamphlets* 87, and "Greenbaum Scrapbook of Alger-Deutsch Election Materials."

82. Smith, as usually quoted. *Times*, 2 Dec. 1932, 16:1, reported a less succinct version: "No man sitting on the bench should feel that he has to owe anything to anybody to continue in his job. He should feel that he owes it to the people of the city or the state of New York and to nobody else. I think that important." The remark drew applause.

83. *Herald Tribune*, 10 Nov. 1932, 6:3.

84. CCB to TDT, 12 Nov. 1932, TDT-YSML, 2:13. For Thomas and Blanshard (1932), 123, the bar was "timid to the point of cowardice in criticizing incompetent judges and correcting inefficient practice."

85. For example of Surrogate Foley supporting the anti-Curry faction in Tammany by patronage appointments in his court, see Eisenstein and Rosenberg (1966), 63, and Moscow (1948), 160. See n. 27 above.

86. Size of party. Moscow (1948), 54–56, 149. Its organization in the early 1930s, Mann (1965), 50, 125, 132: Greater New York's five counties, or boroughs, were divided into sixty-two assembly districts for the state legislature (twenty-three each in Manhattan and Brooklyn, eight in the Bronx, six in Queens, and two in Staten Island). These, in turn, contained some 4,000 election districts, each with about 600 voters. At each level, there was a leader assisted by a committee, and they numbered roughly 32,000. According to the census of 1930, the city had a population of 6,930,446, of which in 1933 2,324,289 registered as voters. Of these only 435,966 registered as Republicans. ABCNY, *Clippings, 1928–1931*, 116.

87. CCB-HLS, 1:10, CCB to Lucille Hollis, 16 Mar. 1931.

Note: On 8 November 1977, voters in New York, by a margin of 200,000, approved an amendment to the state constitution that provided for a nonpartisan committee of lawyers and nonlawyers to recommend candidates to the governor when vacancies on the seven-judge Court of Appeals, the state's highest court, occur. As of the year 2000, this procedure of appointment, rather than election, is still in effect.

CCB, as he surely was aware, in his opinion on appointment versus election of judges was reflecting the views of both Tocqueville and New York's great jurist James Kent. See Tocqueville (1946), 1:256 and 2:458–59. In the former passage Tocqueville quotes Chancellor Kent: "It is indeed probable that the men who are best fitted to discharge the duties of this high office would have too much reserve in their manners, and too much austerity in their principles, for them to be returned by the majority at an election where universal suffrage is adopted." Added Tocqueville, "Such were the opinions which were printed without contradiction in America in the year 1830!" In the second passage, he remarked: "The judiciary . . . is the true moderator of the American democracy."

15. Contesting the Freuds

Chief sources for Robert, Dorothy, and the Freuds: interviews with the family, letters in the various Burlingham collections, and also *The Last Tiffany: A Biography of Dorothy Tiffany Burlingham*, by Michael John Burlingham (New York: Atheneum, 1989); *Anna Freud: The Dream of Psychoanalysis*, by Robert Coles (Reading, Mass.: Addison-Wesley, 1992); *Anna Freud: A Biography*, by Elisabeth Young-Bruehl (New York: Summit Books, 1988); and *Sigmund Freud: Life and Works*, 3 vols., by Ernest Jones (London: Hogarth; vols. 1 and 2, "new" ed., 1954, 1958, and vol. 3, 1957). Sources for CCB and Louie: chiefly family interviews and the Burlingham collections; for the law firm, the Burlingham collections, interviews with partners of the firm, and the firm's history files.

For an account of Robert and Dorothy's early years of marriage, see Chapter 12.

1. *Harvard Class of 1910, Eighth Report, 1940*, 32, written by Arthur Lawrence Washburn, a physician living in New York and working at Bellevue Hospital.

2. M. J. Burlingham (1989), 185.

3. Jones (1958), 2:219, citing Sigmund Freud's paper "A Difficulty in the Path of Psycho-Analysis."

4. Jones (1954), 1:15, 265, 436, and (1958), 2:240. In 2:240 Jones writes: "Freud considered there were two principal intellectual difficulties in the way of accepting psycho-analytical findings. One was that we were not accustomed to apply the laws of strict determinism to mental process in the way any scientific investigation of them must. The other was the fear, just alluded to, that the admission of unconscious process might lower our cultural standards."

5. Coles (1992), 108–10, including a complaint by the poet and pediatrician William Carlos Williams about how cultists in Manhattan made a God of Freud. See F. L. Allen, *Only Yesterday* (1931), 98–99. Another poet, W. H. Auden, in his poem "In Memory of Sigmund Freud" (1939), summed up Freud's influence: "If often he was wrong and at times absurd,/To us he is no more a person/Now but a whole climate of opinion/Under whom we conduct our different lives."

6. Young-Bruehl (1988), 136, and M. J. Burlingham (1989), 192.

7. "Mad Dorothy," heard by GM as a boy; "beyond the reach of reason." GM interview with RTE, 15 May 1993. On custody, see CCB-TFS, HH to LLB, 1 June 1930: "She cannot be normal, it seems to me, to think she is the only possessor [of the children]." And see ibid., undated letter (probably Jan. 1930) of HH to CCB: "Also your quite amazing patience and even understanding (for R's sake) of her."

8. See RB's summary of his career in *Harvard Class of 1910, Seventh Report, 1935*, 94–95. In Albany, at this time, he officially worked for the Department of Medicine, Albany Medical College.

9. Amsden. He became the first psychiatrist-in-chief (1932–35) of the Payne Whitney Clinic at New York Hospital. Young-Bruehl (1988), 190. For mention of Amsden by CCB, and Amsden's plans for Robert, see CCB-HLS, 12:8, CCB to Albert H. Licklider, 21 Apr. 1927.

10. M. J. Burlingham (1989), 203.

11. CCB-TFS, "McCutcheon" box, four letters, two dated 6 and 19 May 1932; the box also has letters from CCB to RB.

12. CCB-HLS, CCB to Pierre and Loulie Jay, 28 Mar. 1929.

13. M. J. Burlingham (1989), 197.

14. Ibid., 199.

15. Ibid. The appointment books are in CCB-HLS, Paige box 1.

16. M. J. Burlingham (1989), 203–4.

17. Ibid., 203.

18. Ibid., 208.

19. Young-Bruehl (1988), 190, states: "The Freuds pressured both Amsden and Ferenczi [psychoanalysts in Budapest] to do their best to convince him [RB] not to sue for custody of his children." If true, it seems unlikely that RB, CCB, or perhaps even Dorothy knew of this.

20. GM interview with KBV, 2 Oct. 1997.

21. Ibid. And M. J. Burlingham (1989), 234.

22. M. J. Burlingham (1989), 234.

23. Ibid., 235.

24. Ibid., 236.

25. GM interview with KBV, 2 Oct. 1997; and M. J. Burlingham (1989) 237.

26. CCB-HLS, 9:1, CCB to FWH and HH, 30 Mar. 1933. This English couple, and especially Helena, were the friends to whom CCB wrote most often and freely about his family problems.

27. TDT-YSML, 2:13, CCB to TDT, 5 Apr. 1933.

28. Ibid., 15:236, TDT to CCB, 13 Apr. 1933.

29. CCB-HLS, 9:1, CCB to HH, 21 June 1933.

30. Ibid.

31. M. J. Burlingham (1989), 245–46.

32. CCB-HLS, 13:3, George S. Messersmith to CCB, 24 Apr. 1934.

33. Ibid., Messersmith to CCB, 7 Nov. 1935. For DB making use of Messersmith for Anna Freud, see Young-Bruehl (1988), 219.

34. CCB's parents. CCB-TFS, clipping from unidentified newspaper.

35. See Chester L. Burrows, *William M. Evarts: Lawyer, Diplomat, Statesman* (Chapel Hill: University of North Carolina Press, 1941), 486–88.

36. CCB-HLS, 20:2. His list of where he spent the summers 1884–1914 shows six in Cornish, 1892, 1893, 1894, 1895, 1903, 1904.

37. Ibid., 9:1, CCB to FWH, 26 Sept. 1933.

38. Ibid., CCB to HH, 17 Aug. 1932. Evidently Molly [Mary Agnes] Hamilton (see Chapter 21, n. 21) had written in a recent book of a political friend's marital indiscretion and HH had brought the passage to CCB's attention. He replied: "I must say that marital episodes in the lives of the great are always interesting and throw a light on their character . . . It would have been better if M. had said *l'on dit*, but she didn't, and probably having led so public a life and been so knocked about in political campaigns she does not have quite the same 'delicatessency' of nature as you have. A close friend of Hoover's [who recently had entertained HH in the White House] told me the other day that at last he had become inured to criticism, whether fair or unfair. I doubt it, but that is what he said. Of course, F.D.R. wouldn't care a single damn what appeared in the book."

39. GM correspondence and phone interviews with all three children of this marriage: Stephen Howard Taylor, David Fairbanks Taylor, and Helen Taylor Davidson.

40. CCB-HLS, 2:3.

41. GM interview with Eugene Underwood (by a tape recording made by EU Jr.), 25 Oct. 1993.

42. GM interviews with Herbert M. Lord, 20 Oct. and 13 Dec. 1994. According to HML, the Burlinghams, though only two of the eleven partners, took almost 50 percent of the firm's profits.

43. *Harvard College Class of 1879, Ninth Report, 1929,* 79: Concerning the firm's new name, CCB wrote: "Four names are bad enough, but, as Dogberry [*Much Ado About Nothing*] would say, Five are 'tolerable and not to be endured.'—Burlingham, Veeder, Fearey, Clark & Hupper."

44. CCB, *Notes on the History of Burlingham, Vedeer, Clark & Hupper* (privately printed, 1946) 10.

45. GM interview with John R. Hupper (eldest son of RHH), 2 Aug. 1994. Another gardener among the partners was Burton H. White, who joined the firm in 1924, became a partner in 1946, and in the 1950s was president of the North American Lily Society.

46. B-U History Files, Norman M. Barron, letter to Elliott B. Nixon, 4 Feb. 1984. NMB joined the firm in 1924 and became a partner in 1943. EBN joined in 1948 and became a partner in 1956. He was for many years the firm's unofficial archivist and a good friend of Charles and Cora Burlingham. Judge Francis A. Winslow, see Chapter 19.

47. WPA-Maritime (1941), 263–65.
48. The liners compared to the *Titanic*—year built, gross tonnage, length in feet:

Normandie	1935	France	83,423	981
Queen Mary	1936	Britain	81,235	975
Bremen	1929	Germany	51,731	899
Rex	1932	Italy	51,062	879
Titanic	1911	Britain	46,329	880

49. WPA-Maritime (1941), 264–65.
50. GM interviews with Herbert M. Lord, 22 Oct. and 13 Dec. 1994.
51. Unpublished memoir of Morton Lazell Fearey by his wife, Julia L. Fearey, Sept. 1958, 18, 20, 41. Courtesy of granddaughter Caroline Fearey Schimmel.
52. GM interviews with Herbert M. Lord, 22 Oct. and 13 Dec. 1994.
53. CCB, *Notes*, 13–14. Veeder died 4 December 1942. Obits: *Herald Tribune*, 5 Dec. 1942, 10:1; *Times*, 5 Dec. 1942, 15:1. See ABCNY *Memorials* of Veeder by CCB and ANH, included in copies of CCB, *Notes*.
54. "Rich wife." GM interviews with Herbert M. Lord, 22 Oct. and 13 Dec. 1994. "Hard lot." This opinion was widely held.
55. Roscoe H. Hupper was president of MLA, 1940–42; he served on its executive committee, 1924–26, 27–30, 34–35, and 37–40. He died 9 May 1967; *Times*, obit, 10 May, 47:1.
56. CCB-HLS, 9:2, CCB to HH, 24 Apr. 1934. *Matter of Ridley*, Surrogate's Court, New York County, 2 May 1934, before Surrogate Foley, 151 Misc. Reports, 474–79. Edward Albert Ridley, over eighty and with eyesight "extremely defective," was murdered on 10 May 1933, leaving an estate valued at $3 million. CCB and his firm's youngest partner, John L. Galey, tried the case.

PART THREE: BLOOMING IN OLD AGE

16. La Guardia's Fusion Campaign

Chief sources for this chapter are CCB's pamphlet, *Nomination of Fiorello H. La Guardia for Mayor of the City of New York in 1933* (1943), cited hereafter as *Nomination of FHL*. Also Charles Garrett, *The La Guardia Years: Machine and Reform Politics in New York City* (New Brunswick, N.J.: Rutgers University Press, 1961); Arthur Mann, *La Guardia Comes to Power, 1933* (Philadelphia: Lippincott, 1965); August Heckscher with Phyllis Robinson, *When La Guardia Was Mayor: New York's Legendary Years* (New York: Norton, 1978); and Thomas Kessner, *Fiorello H. La Guardia and the Making of New York* (New York: McGraw Hill, 1989).

This chapter recounts in greater detail some events briefly treated in the Prologue. Nevertheless, the notes to the Prologue contain a number of citations, in particular to personal letters of CCB, that are not repeated here.

1. Figures are taken from Bellush (1955), 126–49.
2. CCB-HLS, 21:1, CCB, *Nomination of FHL*, lists the fifty members (himself included) of a reform group, the "Independent Fusion Committee," organized by Joseph M. Price, chairman, in November 1932 (see Garrett [1961], 98). Price, a businessman, and CCB had worked together in the past for reform, notably in the 1913 election. Later, in 1932–33, several more reform groups organized, such as the City Party, the Republican Mayoralty Committee, the Municipal Affairs Committee of the New York State Chamber of Commerce, and the anti-Tammany Knickerbocker Democrats. In the background were older civic

groups like the City Club, of which Price was chairman of the board, and the Citizens Union. Some persons were members of several groups, and some important reformers, members of none. Membership in all groups seems to have been fluid, and their meetings, singly or together, open often to any person or group inclined to attend, or to send a representative.

The Fusion Conference Committee, recruited in April 1933 by Price, its chairman, gathered leaders of the various groups, hoping to agree on a candidate for mayor; see Garrett, (1961), 98. For a list of persons to whom the nomination by mid-July had been offered, Garrett (1961), 99; Kessner (1989), 241; and Caro (1974), 352–53, and n, 1198.

3. Medalie, like Seabury, knew CCB well from work together at the City Bar Association; Howard's *World-Telegram*, in these years, was the paper most enthusiastic for reform. None of the three was a member of Price and CCB's Independent Fusion Committee, or perhaps even of the Fusion Coordination Committee; yet they were among the most important of those working for reform. CCB-HLS, 21:1, CCB, *Nomination of FHL*, 3, tells of the lunch, Medalie's proposal, and the creation of the Harmony Committee.

4. Mitgang (1963), 112–18; and Mann, *La Guardia Comes to Power* (1965), 42, quoting Walter Chambers, *Samuel Seabury: A Challenge* (New York: Century, 1932), 180.

5. "The Inside of the Banking Investigation," *Liberty* 10: 19 and 20 (13 and 20 May 1933): 6, 22.

6. Mann, *La Guardia Comes to Power* (1965), 323–26.

7. This seems to have been Berle's pattern. Mann, *La Guardia Comes to Power* (1965), 323, dates the start of Berle-FHL friendship to a dinner in Berle's house on East Nineteenth Street. Also, at home, over dinner, Berle introduced FHL to Newbold Morris, see N. Morris (1955), 71–72. Mann, *La Guardia Comes to Power* (1965), 74, who interviewed Berle in 1960, states that Berle "arranged" CCB's meeting with FHL. Vos (1983), 15, states that the first meeting was at Berle's "house," and though his citation to CCB's COH does not confirm the claim, he may have had other sources. Seabury seems to have met La Guardia, probably through Berle, earlier than CCB. See Mitgang (1963), 316–17.

8. *Herald Tribune*, 10 Feb. 1939, 22:3, editorial, "The Welfare Council." CCB was president of the council 1931–39. See other editorials on his retirement, in *Sun*, 9 Feb. 1939, 20:2, and *World-Telegram*, 9 Feb. 1939, 22:2. "Own eyes." CCB speech at Town Hall, 28 Apr. 1932, CCB-HLS, 21:2. He spoke as president of the Welfare Council on "relief of the unemployed and . . . how much money is needed to carry on the work for the next six months." CCB-HLS, 21:2, his radio speech, WJZ, 4 Mar. 1932, describing conditions in the city and discussing the state's obligation for unemployment relief. His feature article, *Times*, 23 Oct. 1933, VIII, 3:1. For St. George's Church and CCB's part in its social programs, see Chapter 20.

9. Seabury. Mitgang (1963), 313, 317–18; Mann, *La Guardia Comes to Power* (1965), 83. The unfortunate host was Maurice Davidson, chairman of the City Fusion Party, see Caro (1974), 1198 n "Seabury-Davidson lunch."

10. *Herald Tribune*, 28 July 1933, 1:8. *Times*, 27 July 1933, 1:5. See also Mann, *La Guardia Comes to Power* (1965), 83.

11. "Trumpet blast," Mann, *La Guardia Comes to Power* (1965), 84, quoting CCB to Richard Welling, 19 Aug. 1933. *Herald Tribune*, 1 Aug. 1933.

12. CCB-HLS, 21:1, CCB, *Nomination of FHL*, 3, 4. Of the eight invited to the meeting, seven were able to attend; and the eighth, J. Barstow Smull, representing the Chamber of Commerce, "authorized" CCB "to say that he joined in this letter."

13. CCB-HLS, 5:18, CCB to Geoffrey Parson, 2 Aug. 1933.

14. *Herald Tribune*, 3 Aug. 1933, 14:1.

15. *Times*, 3 Aug. 1933, 16:1, and *World-Telegram*, 3 Aug. 1933, 18:1.

16. CCB-HLS, 21:1, CCB, *Nomination of FHL*, 4, names the fourteen present: CCB, Berle, Maurice P. Davidson, James E. Finegan, Robert McC. Marsh, Medalie, Newbold Morris, J.G.L. Molloy, Price, Seabury, J. Barstow Smull, Charles H. Tuttle, Mrs. Rosalie Loew Whitney, and Mrs. George Wyeth.

17. "Bust." Mann, *La Guardia Comes to Power* (1965), 72, citing an interview (29 Mar. 1960) with Berle, who was present; also Mitgang (1963), 319. "Sit down." Mitgang, (1963), 319. CCB-HLS, 21:1, CCB, *Nomination of FHL*, 4, describes the meeting as "a frank and not too mild discussion."

18. CCB-HLS, 21:1, CCB, *Nomination of FHL*, 4.

19. *Times*, 4 Aug. 1933, 1:8; *Herald Tribune*, 4 Aug. 1933, 1:8.

20. Mann, *La Guardia Comes to Power* (1965), 100. On Chadbourne. CCB-HLS, 4:11, CCB to FF, 8 Nov. 1933, "So far as I can see, W.M.C.'s little gray cells have been washed out. He preserves the syllogistic forms and his thoughts are numbered 1,2,3, but they are unrelated and sequential." And Herbert Brownell to GM, 9 Sept. 1992: "He had a good heart but was able to contribute little of practical value."

21. On additions to the breakfast committee. CCB-HLS, 4:11, CCB to FF, 8 Nov. 1933. On Windels. ABCNY *Memorial Book, 1968*. PW-COH, "Additional Material," 1. GM interviews with PW Jr., 29 Sept. 1992, 8 June 1995; and PW Jr., to Harold R. Tyler Jr., 21 July 1992. Also CCB-COH, 33.

22. Brownell managed T. E. Dewey's first successful campaign for governor in 1942 and TED's two unsuccessful presidential campaigns, 1944 and 1948. He was chairman of the Republican National Committee 1944–46. In 1952 he helped to manage Eisenhower's campaign for president of the United States; and 1953–57 he served as Eisenhower's U.S. attorney general. In 1932 he became a partner in the law firm Lord, Day & Lord, and was president of ABCNY 1962–64. He died 1 May 1996. Brownell to GM, 9 Sept. 1992, following interview.

23. Mann, *La Guardia Comes to Power* (1965), 102; PW-COH, "Additional Material," 4.

24. Languages. La Guardia (1948), 35, states: "I never could [master Hungarian], or even seriously tried." But biographers list it as one he spoke, e.g., Heckscher (1978), 161, 247. Picking up a phrase. Speech at opening of Vladeck Housing Project. CCB-COH, 33–34. TDT-YSML, ser. 1, 2:13, CCB to TDT, 27 Nov. 1939, referring to story in *Herald Tribune*, 23 Nov., 44:1. Baruch Charney Vladeck (1886–1938). A Russian Jewish immigrant, he came to the United States in 1908. He was for many years the general manager of the *Jewish Daily Forward*. Elected to the City Council as a candidate of the American Labor Party, he supported FHL, and because of his interest in public housing, a housing project in the Lower East Side was named after him.

25. PW-COH, "Additional Material," 4.

26. On judicial candidates. CCB-HLS, 6:1, Max Herzfeld to CCB, 17 Aug. 1933; and ibid., 5:18, W. H. Seligsberg to CCB, 7 Aug. On balancing the ticket. Ibid., 5:18, A. A. Berle Jr., telegram to CCB, 8 Aug.

27. Quoted in Vos (1983), 29.

28. FDR and McKee. Flynn (1947), 133–38; and Farley (1948), 43.

29. PW-COH, "Additional Material," 2. Newspapers. Mann, *La Guardia Comes to Power* (1965), 106.

30. Herbert H. Lehman Papers, CCB to Lehman, 19 Oct. 1933. And see CCB-HLS, 4:3, CCB to H. V. Evatt, 15 Nov. 1945, expressing much the same view of Seabury's hurt in old age.

31. PW-COH, 15–17. "Low blow." Mann, *La Guardia Comes to Power* (1965), 29. Untermeyer. *Times*, 16 Oct. 1933, 8:1, "a gross libel on 30 percent of the population of this

city and sounded like a reverberation of Hitlerism." On Untermeyer, FHL, and McKee. Flynn (1947), 137.

32. Flynn (1947), 138; and Farley (1948), 43: "The promised administration help did not materialize." The Prologue of this biography quotes a letter CCB wrote to FDR and speculates on its influence on FDR's behavior. See Prologue, nn. 4, 5.

33. Wall Street and T. W. Lamont. CCB-HLS, 4:11, CCB to FF, 8 Nov. 1933. Rockefeller family. Ibid., 6:2, CCB to Arthur Woods, 26 Dec. 1933. Campaign cost. PW-COH, "Additional Material," 4: "It was a very conservatively managed campaign so far as money was concerned. My impression is that we didn't go over $150,000." He points out, 5, that the Republican side of the campaign "had its own headquarters and its own campaign fund."

34. CCB-HLS, 6:2, CCB to David M. Heyman, 19 Oct. 1933. PW-COH, 3–4.

35. Loan. CCB-HLS, 6:2, CCB to D. M. Heyman, 19 Oct. 1933. Gifts. Ibid., CCB to Maurice P. Davidson, 13 Dec. 1933, and D. M. Heyman to CCB, 12 Dec. 1933. "Vocative." Ibid., CCB to Thomas M. Debevoise, 26 Oct. 1933.

36. Rally. *Herald Tribune*, 3 Nov. 1933, 1;8; *Times*, 3 Nov. 1933, 1:8, and 4 Nov. 1933, 10:1. CCB's speech. In CCB-HLS, 2:12.

37. CCB-HLS, 6:3, CCB to Arthur Woods, 26 Dec. 1933.

38. Ibid., Thomas W. Lamont to CCB, 27 Nov. 1933, and CCB to Woods, 26 Dec. 1933. Note: Lamont was an unusual bank executive. Like CCB, he was the son of a Protestant minister. He had started life poor, working as a reporter for the *Tribune* and retaining for life an interest in politics and the press, at one moment buying the *Evening Post* in order to prevent it turning into a tabloid. A letter from CCB to La Guardia, CCB-HLS, 6:2, 21 Sept. 1933, recounts at length an effort of Lamont on that day to persuade the editor of the *Sun* to endorse La Guardia.

CCB nowhere states what scruples prevented him from accepting Lamont's gift when first offered, but presumably he felt Lamont should make the gift directly to the campaign. Whereas Lamont, on his side, probably felt awkward in offering such a sum to La Guardia, the scourge of bankers. CCB's fullest explanation is in his letter to FF, 8 Nov. 1933, CCB-HLS, 4:11: "I was offered $4,000, which was later raised to $5,000, and then to $6,000, to do with as pleased me. I refused to take it, but said that if there was a deficit I might call on them. So I took a chance and lent the Fusion Campaign Committee $4,500 [*sic*] of my own, and perhaps I'll get it back." La Guardia probably never knew it, but ironically to some extent his campaign was rescued financially by one of his hated "banketeers."

39. "First Citizen," "the bunk." See Prologue, n. 18. All debts paid. CCB-HLS, 6:2, D. M. Heyman, treasurer of Fusion Campaign Committee, to CCB, 22 Dec. 1933.

17. CCB as Mentor to La Guardia

Chief sources for this chapter, other than the Burlingham collections, are: Thomas Kessner, *Fiorello H. La Guardia and the Making of Modern New York* (New York: McGraw Hill, 1989); August Heckscher with Phyllis Robinson, *When La Guardia Was Mayor: New York's Legendary Years* (New York: Norton, 1978); Charles Garrett, *The La Guardia Years: Machine and Reform Politics in New York City* (New Brunswick, N.J.: Rutgers University Press, 1961); and Columbia Oral Histories for Paul Windels and Justine Wise Polier. Also Robert A. Caro, *The Power Broker: Robert Moses and the Fall of New York* (New York: Knopf, 1974), particularly useful for Caro's interviews with Paul Windels; *The WPA Guide to New York City: The*

Federal Writers' Project Guide to 1930s New York, with a new Introduction by William H. Whyte (1939; repr., New York: Pantheon, 1982).

Note: In keeping with the conventions of the times, "Negro" is used in place of African American throughout this chapter and book.

1. Some biographers of La Guardia, e.g., Kessner (1989), 253, 257, state that he was the city's ninety-ninth mayor, apparently deleting from their count the four "acting" mayors who merely completed the terms of others. But these four, though not elected to office, nevertheless were sworn into it. Further, if election is to be the standard, then the first direct election was not until 1834, making FHL the city's thirty-ninth elected mayor. See Chapter 14, n. 31, and *The Encyclopedia of New York City* (1995), entry on mayors.

2. Others present included: Supreme Court justice Philip J. McCook, who delivered the constitutional oath; Vito Marcantonio, political leader in East Harlem and later a congressman; and Republican leaders W. Kingsland Macy and Charles H. Tuttle. Also a number of elected reform candidates, future commissioners in La Guardia's administration, and their wives. But even on such an occasion as this, Mrs. Burlingham stayed home.

3. *Times*, 2 Jan. 1934, 1:6.

Note: The "Oath of the Ephebes [young men] of Athens," though unfamiliar to most laymen, is well known to classicists. In the 1930s it was recorded in two post-classical reports, of which the more familiar appeared in a collection made by Stobaeus (early fifth century A.D.), 43, 48. This read: "I shall not disgrace the holy armor nor abandon the comrade beside whom I stand. I shall defend the holy and sacred rites both alone and with many. I shall hand over the city not smaller but greater and more beautiful than I received it. I shall listen to those who judge wisely, and I shall obey the established laws as well as whatever other laws the people unanimously lay down. If anyone tears down the laws or does not obey them, I shall not give in but offer a defense both alone and with everyone. I shall honor the city's sacred rites."

In 1932 an inscribed stela from the fourth century B.C. was discovered at Acharnae in Greece with the oath's full text, confirming the approximate accuracy of the post-classical reports. And although the contemporary stela's text was not published until 1938, it may be that La Guardia (or his immediate source) had heard of the excitement the find had stirred among classicists. In any case, he was remarkably up to date in "evoking one of the hottest topics in Greek epigraphy at the time." (Professor Glen W. Bowersock, Institute for Advanced Studies, Princeton University, to GM.)

4. FHL statement. *Times*, 2 Jan. 1934, 1:6.

5. See Kessner (1989), 262–64; Garrett (1961), 142–52; and Heckscher (1978), 37–47.

6. See Kessner (1989), 262–64; Garrett (1961), 142–52; and Heckscher (1978), 37–47.

7. See Moscow (1948), 216–24, for a brief account of the complex relations between city and state.

8. The "Economy Bill." See n. 5 above. CCB-HLS, 11:8, CCB to FHL, 19 Feb. 1934: "I thoroughly approve your not informing [John J.] Dunnigan [Democratic state senator] and [Irwin] Steingut [Democratic Assembly minority leader] et al., what you intend to do if the Economy Bill is passed." See also CCB-HLS, 11:8, CCB to FHL, 16 Apr. 1934. Dunnigan, an architect from the Bronx, was a Flynn stalwart, and Steingut represented the Brooklyn equivalent of Tammany. For a strong anti-Steingut statement, see *World-Telegram* editorial, "Steingut Statesmanship," 1 Feb. 1934, 20:2, which closes: "No wonder Mayor La Guardia has to turn from the Legislature and appeal to the people!"

9. *Times*, 6 Jan. 1934, 1:8, *Herald Tribune*, 6 Jan. 1934, 1:8, both with text of Lehman's letter. FHL's reply. *Times*, 8 Jan. 1934, 2:2, and *Herald Tribune*, 8 Jan. 1934, 1:8.

10. Kessner (1989), 268. Governor Lehman takes Dunnigan and Steingut to Washington to see FDR. Heckscher (1978), 45–46; see n. 8 above.

11. Heckscher (1978), 47, reports that "as a result of the Economy Bill . . . roughly half of the city's $30 million deficit was made up." See Kessner (1989), 269.

12. E.g., the growing enthusiasm of *Daily News* editorials: 26 Jan. 1934, 29:1: "You're turning out to be too good a Mayor to lose." On 2 Mar. 1934, 33:1: "We did not support La Guardia for Mayor, but we are glad he won. What a fire he is building under the chair warmers and parasites." And 8 Mar. 1934, 29:1, after the Economy Bill's "third knockdown in the Assembly" and FHL's confrontation with Farley: "The people know he is doing the best he can."

13. CCB-HLS, 4:12, CCB to FF, 10 Jan. 1934, and CCB-COH, 35. See PW-COH, 107–10, on FHL: "He was not, however, a good administrator in the sense of being able to establish an effective organization and tradition which could operate without his personal direction. His idea of good administration was largely a matter of his personal direction [107] . . . He was not an administrator, because he attempted to assume too much responsibility for too many details of administration in all the city departments [110]."

14. PW-COH, 56, 81.

15. CCB-HLS, 4:12, CCB to FF, 10 Jan. 1934; and see PW-COH, 108–9.

16. PW-COH, 84–85. See FHL's Report to the Public on the year 1934, *Times*, 11 Jan. 1935, 2:6, and his four-year summary of the work of the corporation counsel, given in a speech in Brooklyn, 24 Oct. 1937, 4:3. In the latter he gives a detailed example of how, in reversing a condemnation award to a Tammany stalwart, the counsel's office had saved the city $3.2 million. FHL estimated that the $50 million recovered was "more than enough to pay the whole cost of the Holland Tunnel."

17. PW-COH, 82–83.

18. CCB-HLS, 4:12, CCB to FF, 10 Jan. 1934: "I gave him five good men. *Te absente*, I have resorted to Dean Smith of Columbia for men. I got a very able one in Joseph L. Weiner." PW-COH, 85.

19. Three of PW's chief assistants were Edmund L. Palmieri, who soon detached to become FHL's law secretary and later became a federal judge; William C. Chanler, who in FHL's second term succeeded PW as corporation counsel; and Frederick van Pelt Bryan, who, though slated to succeed Chanler, instead left for World War II.

20. PW-COH, 84. "I laughed." Ibid., 82. But CCB recalls that "at times" PW "wasn't on speaking terms" with FHL. CCB-COH, 35.

21. At this time there were six vice presidents. Besides CCB, Henry DeForest Baldwin (tutored as a boy by CCB), Richard S. Childs (president of the City Club, 1926–38), George McAneny, William Church Osborn, and Mrs. Everett P. Wheeler. The executive secretary, much admired by CCB, was H. Eliot Kaplan.

22. Kessner (1989), 210–13; Garrett (1961), 132–36; and for the most details, Thomas and Blanshard (1932), 34–43.

23. CCB-HLS, 11:8, CCB to FHL, 16 Feb. 1934. For an account of Finegan's efforts to improve the Brooklyn judiciary in 1931, an attempt in which neither SS nor CCB are reported to have been helpful, see William H. Allen-COH, 465–66. CCB-HLS, 11:8, CCB to FHL, 19 Feb. 1934; also CCB-HLS, 11:8, CCB to FHL, 16 Apr. and 25 May 1934; and 29 May 1936. William H. Allen-COH, 465–67: Allen was a director of the Institute for Public Service and (1934–37) the secretary of the New York City Municipal Civil Service Commission, and he has interesting views of Finegan, La Guardia, Seabury, CCB, and the Fusion movement. He is harsh on Seabury and states that the "basic force" in the Fusion movement and La Guardia's election "was rather Charles C. Burlingham, a man whom the

community did know and respect, who voted in New York as Seabury did not, and who had a right to play a strong hand in New York." Leaving aside the comparison of Seabury and CCB, Allen does suggest how CCB's long association with the civil service movement made him a familiar and popular figure with others involved in it.

24. Kessner (1989), 287–90; Garrett (1961), 132–36. See FHL's Report to the Public on the year 1934, *Times*, 11 Jan. 1935, 2:2.

Note: CCB, in a memorial for Charles W. Watson, a member of the Civil Service Reform Association from 1884 to 1917, published in *Good Government* (journal of the National Civil Service Reform League) 34:10 (Nov. 1917): 76, some interesting figures on the movement's early success and failure during and after the administration of reform mayor William L. Strong, Republican, 1894–96. "In 1895 Mayor Strong appointed him [Watson] a Municipal Civil Service Commissioner . . . The administration of the civil service law under Mayor Gilroy [Tammany Democrat] had been very lax . . . The classified service, which at the beginning of the Strong administration consisted of 7,897 persons, was increased in one year to 13,603, of which only about 250 were exempt from competition. Within eighteen months 170 of these exempt positions, many of them of great administrative responsibility, were subjected to competition. Although much of the work of this commission was undone during the Van Wyck [Tammany Democrat] regime, this record remained a high example for succeeding administrations." Like CCB, Watson was recruited to civil service reform by George William Curtis.

25. Plunkitt, enraged, on civil service. Riordon, ed. (1963), 18–19, 89; also 11–16, 38–40, 55–56, 60, 69, 72, 75, 78, 83.

26. Bryce (1891), 2:608: "There is no denying that the government of cities is the one conspicuous failure of the United States . . . The commonest mistake of Europeans who talk about America is to assume that the political vices of New York are found everywhere. The next most common is to suppose that they are found nowhere else. In New York they have revealed themselves on the largest scale." Cuneo (1955), vii, on FHL: "No man in American history had done more to erase what Lord Bryce called America's worst stain, municipal corruption."

27. Cuneo (1955), 5; La Guardia (1948), 91.

28. Herbert H. Lehman Papers, CCB to Lehman, 26 Dec. 1933. The opinion that CCB cited as revealing O'Brien's incompetency as a judge is *Matter of Erlanger* (1932), 145 Misc. Reports, 1–267.

Note: The case was a skirmish in the thirty-year struggle between Max D. Steuer and Isidor J. Kresel, two of the leading trial lawyers of the day, to have the other disgraced and disbarred. The battles began in 1912 with an earlier Erlanger case in which a faded burlesque queen sued the theatrical agent for money promised in return for favors. This part of the story is amusingly told in R. O. Boyer (1932), 58–77. Middle parts of the saga, with fortune wavering between the opposing lawyers, can be found in Mayer (1968), 269–77, and Mitgang (1963), 172–75, 180–91. The final cantos in which John W. Davis in 1934, like a St. George to the rescue, saves Kresel from a total smashup contrived by Steuer, is best told by Harbaugh (1973), 303–13. Because of the eminence and qualities of the men involved, including an overeager prosecutor and a fool of a judge, lawyers in the city for years followed it closely.

29. Hartman. Kessner (1989), 447. CCB may have thought Hartman unsuitable because of the sensational failure in 1930 of the Bank of the United States, which had injured many New Yorkers and revealed that a number of judges, including Hartman of the City Court, had borrowed heavily from the bank to conduct private business activities.

30. GM interviews with PW Jr., 27 Sept. 1992 and 8 June 1995. See La Guardia (1948), 91.

31. CCB-HLS, 11:9, FHL to CCB, 21 Jan. 1936. To which CCB instantly replied: "Thank you for your charming but ridiculous letter. You gave yourself away completely by one word—'I have *practically* made up my mind on appointments to the bench.'" A week later he wrote: "Dear F.H.: Despite your repulses, I humbly suggest that you might do worse than talk with me about the successor to Casey." On the letter sheet's large white blank space is scrawled: "Yes indeed, F.H."

32. Ibid., 11:8, CCB to FHL, 26 Apr. 1934.

33. Ibid., 10:15, CCB to Roy W. Howard, 6 Sept. 1939.

34. La Guardia (1948), 91. FHL, like CCB, thought changes in structure, by themselves, did not long preclude corruption, see ibid., 137. Institutions and their rules required constant revival by infusions of men and women of character or they became archaic and easily manipulated for the worse. CCB to Howard, see n. 33 above.

35. Kessner (1989), 356–58; Heckscher (1978), 109–10; and Garrett (1961), 138, 162.

36. CCB-HLS, 11:8, CCB to FHL, 28 Nov. 1934.

37. Ibid., FHL to CCB, 28 Nov. 1934.

38. Ibid., CCB to FHL, 30 Nov. 1934.

39. Ibid., CCB to FHL, 10 Dec. 1934.

40. Ibid., CCB to FHL, 16 Feb. 1934. Kessner (1989), 399, calls the appointments "an example of exquisite cultural symmetry."

41. CCB-HLS, 11:8, CCB to FHL, 30 Apr. 1935.

42. Ibid., CCB to FHL, 13 June 1935.

43. Ibid., 11:9, CCB to FHL, 11 Apr. 1936.

44. On Paige. *Herald Tribune*, 2 Sept. 1936, 8:3, and 3 Sept. 1936, 7:2; *Times*, 2 Sept. 1936, 22:1, and 3 Sept. 1936, 12:1, and editorial, 20:2. On Rivers. *Times*, obit, 29 July 1975, 32:2.

45. Toney obit. *Times*, 23 Mar. 1951, 21:6; and Watson obit, *Times*, 10 May 1952, 21:2. Like Rivers, Watson joined the ABCNY.

46. Justice Wise Polier-COH, 161–64. See also William Manners, *Patience and Fortitude: Fiorello La Guardia* (Boston: Houghton, 1976), 177–81, and Vos (1983).

47. Besides recommending and disapproving choices for judges, at some time in the mid-1930s CCB became chairman of a Public Relations Committee of the Domestic Relations Court, whose members were Charles E. Hughes Jr., David T. Leahy, George Mac-Donald, George Z. Medalie, and Adrian Van Sinderen. On 24 August 1937 it submitted a report, (written by CCB on his office stationery) "To His Honor, the Mayor," emphasizing "the very real need of additional probation officers and professional and clerical assistants in the Court and strongly urges that the 1938 budget provide for additional personnel." The report cites facts in support of its plea, including the progress made in collecting support payments from those in arrears. La Guardia, in reply, wrote, "I am most unhappy about the Domestic Relations Court and would like a conference with your Public Relations Committee sometime when you get back [from Black Point, where CCB's wife was ill]." After this exchange, CCB-HLS, 11:9, CCB report to FHL, 24 Aug. 1937, and FHL reply, 3 Sept. 1937, the committee sinks from view, suggesting that any ideas it may have had were put to the mayor in some other fashion.

48. WPA-Maritime (1941), 196, 202: The last sailing packet especially built for North Atlantic trade, the Black Baller *Charles H. Marshall*, was launched in 1869. The last passenger-carrying packet sailed in 1873, and the last freight in 1883. Melville was a customs inspector on the Gansevoort Street piers (Greenwich Village) 1866–85. An occasional wooden whaler could be found on South Street long after the turn of the century.

49. See Washington Irving's comic caricature *Diedrich Knickerbocker's History of New-York*, Book III, "in which is recorded the Golden Reign of Wouter Van Twiller." For a more

factual account of him, see Edward Robb Ellis, *The Epic of New York City* (New York: Coward-McCann, 1966), 31–33. For a comment on Irving's "history" and an anecdote involving Van Twiller, see Carl Carmer, *The Hudson* (New York: Holt, 1939), 33, 38–39.

50. CCB-HLS, 19:6, "Remarks," 5 Oct. 1937.

51. The plan laid out city streets on undeveloped land as a grid with fixed block and lot sizes. The width of the east-west streets was set at sixty feet between building lines with the roadway in the center roughly thirty-four feet, leaving space for sidewalks and trees. The north-south avenues, which the planners mistakenly thought would be less used for trade and therefore were more widely separated than the streets, were to be a hundred feet between building lines. The widths were generous compared to medieval cities, but proved a straitjacket as buildings grew taller, traffic heavier, and horse-drawn vehicles were replaced by cars. Then, to widen the roadways, sidewalks were narrowed, trees cut down, stoops chopped off, and even fronts of buildings removed. See Gilmartin (1995), 101, on the sad fate of Delancey Street.

52. The city's Department of Plants and Structures was in charge of most bridges.

53. RM thought this the worst example of poor planning he ever encountered, Caro (1974), 390. As early as the 1890s the need for ramps and approaches had been proved by the Brooklyn Bridge, which had been built without any. By 1901 the "Bridge Crush" on the Brooklyn Bridge was a common newspaper story and sight for visitors. Half a million people a day on the bridge, and at the rush hours, chaos. See Gilmartin (1995), 77.

54. Caro (1974), 360–62, 368–72. See FHL's Report to the Public, 2:1, 3.

55. Caro (1974), 386–95. On the need for a cleanup and reorganization of the Tammany-dominated Triborough Authority, see *World-Telegram* editorial, 1 Feb. 1934, 20:1.

56. PW-COH, "Additional Material," 17–19. "Something permanent." Hence the title of Thomas Kessner's (1989) biography of the mayor, *Fiorello H. La Guardia and the Making of Modern New York*.

57. CCB-HLS, 11:8, CCB to FHL, 16 Feb. 1934.

58. Caro (1974), 426–27, 1172. Caro's quotations come from his three interviews with PW, 8, 9, and 10 November 1967. PW died the fifteenth of the following month.

59. Animosity between FDR and RM, see Heckscher (1978), 87–93. For greater detail, see Davis (1972), 790–92, and Frank Freidel, *Franklin D. Roosevelt*, vol. 2, *The Ordeal* (Boston: Little, Brown, 1954), 219–20.

60. CCB-HLS, 11:8, CCB to FHL, 16 Apr. 1934. Berle. Caro (1974), 428.

61. Caro (1974), 428.

62. Ibid., 402–5. Moses was so little a Republican that in 1928, when he thought he had a chance to be the Democratic nominee for governor (ultimately FDR), he had registered as a Democrat, which he remained until switching back in 1934, when he briefly thought he might be the Fusion-Republican candidate for mayor (ultimately La Guardia). For the latter episode, see Chapter 16.

63. Ibid., 412.

64. Ibid., 413–18. Court of Claims corruption. *Times*, 26 Oct. 1934, 10:2.

65. Caro (1974), 418. Flynn's speech. *Herald Tribune*, 4 Nov. 1934, 28:1, and *Times*, 4 Nov. 1934, 34:1.

66. *Herald Tribune*, 8 Nov. 1934, 1:5. In its editorial, 7 Nov. 1934, 26:1, the paper stated that Moses "was defeated because he was too good a man, too honest and too fearless."

67. Text in Caro (1974), 430.

68. *Herald Tribune*, 4 Jan. 1935, 1:3, *Times*, 4 Jan. 1935, 1:4, both with RM's reply to Ickes.

69. CCB-HLS, 11:8, CCB to FHL, 4 Jan. 1935.

70. Ibid., 4:13, CCB to FF, 9 Jan. 1935. Even now CCB, like many others, seems not to have grasped the strength of FDR's dislike of RM, for after the sentence quoted, he added: "It may be Ickes, it may be Farley, it may be F. himself, and it may be Lehman who must resent R.M.'s calling L. a liar."

71. Twenty-three groups. *Times*, 15 Jan. 1935, 20:1. Guthrie's opinion, too long in preparation to have much impact, concluded that Order 129 was "an arbitrary and capricious fiat without any authority in law." The group responsible for the report included the Chamber of Commerce of the State of New York, the Merchants Association of New York, the New York Board of Trade, the Citizens Union, and the City Club. Also the Brooklyn Chamber of Commerce and the Chamber of Commerce of the Borough of Queens. See *Herald Tribune*, 12 Mar. 1935, 2:4.

72. CCB-HLS, 11:18, CCB to FHL, 14 Feb. 1935; the text, also in full, in Caro (1974), 436.

73. Lippmann. *Herald Tribune*, 24 Jan. 1935, 19:1. On CCB's role with FHL, Kessner (1989), 447.

74. Caro (1974), 437–38.

75. Ibid., 439.

76. Ibid., 440. *Daily News*, 12 Mar. 1935, 2:1; *Herald Tribune*, 12 Mar. 1935, 16:1. *Times*, editorial, 12 Mar. 1935, 20:2, was headed "The Mayor Wins."

77. CCB to FDR, 18 Mar. 1935, FDR Library, Hyde Park, N.Y., Personal Papers as President, box 1169, folder "Burlingham, C. C."

18. Harvard and FDR

Chief sources on Harvard activities are the Burlingham collections, *The Harvard Alumni Bulletin*, and CCB's College Class Reports; on the Court-packing bill, other than the Burlingham collections, William E. Leuchtenburg, *The Supreme Court Reborn: The Constitutional Revolution in the Age of Roosevelt* (New York: Oxford University Press, 1995); *Roosevelt and Frankfurter: Their Correspondence, 1928–1945*, annotated by Max Freedman (Boston: Little, Brown, 1967); the Grenville Clark Papers, Dartmouth College Library, Hanover, N.H., and *Memoirs of a Man: Grenville Clark*, collected by Mary Clark Dimond, edited by Norman Cousins and J. Garry Clifford (New York: Norton, 1975).

1. CCB's name well known on country's "East Coast." See *Boston Transcript* editorial, 21 June 1934, clipping, CCB-HLS, 7:8, and *Herald Tribune*, 21 June 1934, 11:6.

2. Letters to and from Albert H. Licklider. See CCB-HLS, 12:8, notably AHL to CCB, 6 Dec. 1941, responding to CCB's remarks on Judith Anderson's *Macbeth*, which had provoked CCB. AHL taught at Williams 1914–41. On *Macbeth*. Also ibid., 18:15, CCB to Professor Mark Van Doren (Columbia), 23 Nov. 1941, written in flush of indignation over the production and critical response to it.

3. CCB-HLS, 21:2, speech at Williams College, 15 June 1931, 6:9; see *Williams Alumni Review*, "The Commencement Story," 407–8. Alfred Zimmern, *The Greek Commonwealth: Politics and Economics in Fifth-Century Athens* (London: Oxford University Press, 1911; 5th ed., 1931; repr. 1944), 63, a book widely read for many years. Edmund Burke, *Thoughts on the Cause of the Present Discontents*, 23 Apr. 1770. Dr. Samuel Johnson. Recorded by Boswell in the *Life*, 21 July 1763. Johnson was then fifty-four years old. CCB "flattered" the young by cutting Johnson's final sentence, "but then the dogs are not so good scholars."

4. Reorganizing Columbia Law School Alumni Association. See CCB-HLS, 17:4, CCB to Harlan Fiske Stone, 23 Oct. 1932, and ibid., 21:2, CCB speech at the association's annual meeting, 8 May 1934. CCB was its president for the academic years 1932–34. For notice of degree, see ibid., 2:7, N. M. Butler to CCB, 6 Mar. 1933.

5. CCB was president of the Harvard Alumni Association 21 June 1934 to 20 June 1935. For letters about the 1934 and 1935 commencements to and from CCB, see CCB-HLS, 6:18, 7:5, and 7:8; for an account of the 1935 commencement afternoon meeting, see HAB 37:35 (Friday, 5 July 1935): 1119–38.

6. CCB-HLS, 7:5, CCB to Conant, 27 June 1934.

7. Ibid., Conant to CCB, 29 June 1934.

8. Told in both *George Bellows, Painter of America*, by Charles H. Morgan (New York: Reynal, 1965), 189–95, with photograph of portrait; and in *From the Age That Is Past: Harvard Club of New York City; A History*, by Ormonde de Kay (New York: Harvard Club, 1994), 114, 124–25.

9. *Harvard College Class of 1879, 50th Anniversary Report, 1929.*

10. CCB was not the first in his class to receive an honorary degree; the statesman George von Lengerke Meyer had been given one in 1911, and Frank Taussig in 1916. After Taussig, Meyer was probably the best known of the class. Besides doing good works for the university, he had served as TR's ambassador to Russia during the Russo-Japanese War and later as his postmaster general; and then, 1909–13, as secretary of the navy for Taft.

11. The ritual: The chief marshal, advancing to the center of the dais, requests: "Mr. Sheriff, pray give us order"; and the sheriff demands of the crowd, "The meeting will be in order." When one sheriff said "The meeting will please come to order," he was reproved by President Eliot: "The statement is a command, not a request." See *The Tercentenary of Harvard College*, by Jerome D. Greene (Cambridge: Harvard University Press, 1937), 193.

12. CCB-HLS, 6:18, Henry C. Clark to CCB, 9 Oct. 1934.

13. Ibid., Harper Woodward to CCB, 23 May 1935; CCB to HW confirming phone call, 24 May 1935.

14. Ibid., CCB to J. D. Greene, 29 May 1935. Of the twelve, the eight not yet mentioned are: Walter Prentice Bowers, physician and general practitioner; Norman H. Davis, statesman, ambassador; Waldemar Lindgren, geologist; John Campbell Merriam, paleontologist and president of the Carnegie Institution of Washington, D.C. (1920–38); George Sarton, historian of science; Albert Sauveur, metallographer; Charles Schuchert, paleontologist; and William Allen White, editor and publisher of the Emporia, Kansas, *Gazette*.

15. CCB-HLS, 7:1, CCB to Conant, 11 June 1935.

16. Ibid. The congressmen were Chester Bolton, Harvard '05, and Richard Wigglesworth, '12, see Joseph R. Hamlen to CCB, 3 June 1935, and CCB's reply, 4 June.

17. Ibid., Hamlen to CCB, 12 June 1935.

18. Ibid., CCB to Hamlen, 4 and 11 June 1935.

19. James B. Conant, *My Several Lives: Memoirs of a Social Inventor* (New York: Harper, 1970), 147.

20. CCB-HLS, 7:1, CCB to Hamlen, 4 June 1935; and see CCB to Conant, 11 June.

21. Ibid., CCB to Henry A. Wallace, 14 June 1935; and to Wallace, 15 May.

22. CCB's "Introductory Remarks," in full. HAB see n. 5 above, 1120–23. To meet requests for copies CCB had the "Remarks" privately printed (4 pages), copy in CCB-HLS, 7:1. See CCB-HLS, 19:1, CCB to VVV, 28 June 1935.

23. CCB-HLS, 7:1, J. P. Morgan (the son) to CCB, 2 July 1935.

24. Ibid., 19:1, CCB to VVV, 28 June 1935.

25. Neilson's speech and all others are in HAB, see n. 5 above.

26. Ibid., 1117.

27. CCB-HLS, 7:5, Hamlen to CCB, 1 Dec. 1939.

28. LH-HLS, 100:30 Hamlen to CCB, 22 Jan. 1936, sent with CCB handwritten note to LH, 24 Jan. 1936; CCB-HLS, 8:3, Hamlen to CCB, 27 Jan. 1936, and four more, through 13 Feb. 1936; another (n.d.) Hamlen to CCB; CCB to Hamlen, 22 Apr. 1936; J. D. Greene to CCB, 4 May 1936; and Hamlen to CCB, 28 Sept. 1936.

29. A more serious disagreement arose in 1939 between Conant and the faculty over salaries and retirements. See CCB-HLS, 7:1, Hamlen to CCB, 9 Nov. 1939; CCB to Hamlen, 10 and 30 Nov. 1939; Hamlen to CCB, 1 Dec. 1939.

30. Besides Attorney General Cummings, those who prepared the bill were Solicitor General Stanley Reed; former counsel and head of the NRA Donald Richberg; and former FDR speechwriter and adviser Judge Samuel I. Rosenman (New York Supreme Court, First District). Note that FDR did not include FF in the bill's preparation. On this point, see Lash (1975), 60–61. Rosenman (1952), 140–62, recounts the bill's drafting. For a different view, see Leuchtenburg, *The Supreme Court* (1995), 82 and n. 1.

31. The *Times*, 6 Feb. 1937, 1:4, gave the story five of its eight front-page columns, and at 10:3 published a roundup of editorial views across the country: Of the twelve newspapers quoted, none favored the bill and most strongly opposed it.

32. In 1789 the Court started with six judges; in 1801 reduced to five; in 1802 restored to six; in 1807 increased to seven; in 1837 increased to nine; in 1863 increased to ten; in 1866 reduced to seven; in 1869 increased to nine. Most of the early increase in numbers was a result of the country's Western expansion.

33. Bryce (1891), 1:268–69.

34. FDR, Fireside Chat, 9 Mar. 1937, in *Nothing to Fear: The Selected Addresses of Franklin Delano Roosevelt, 1932–1945* (Boston: Houghton, 1946), 92–104, 99.

35. *Herald Tribune*, 6 Feb. 1937, 6:7; *Times*, 6 Feb. 1937, 8:4.

36. *Times*, 6 Feb. 1937, 9:2.

37. CCB-HLS, 4:15, CCB to FF, 7 Feb. 1937.

38. Ibid., 18:13, CCB to Senator Wagner, 8 Feb. 1937.

39. CCB-DFT, CCB to Grace Taylor, 14 July 1937. Copeland. *Times*, 21 Feb. 1937, 24:1. He claimed to have received some 30,000 messages opposed and only a few hundred in favor of the plan.

40. ABCNY *Yearbook* 64, 287–90.

41. ABCNY actions. Ibid., 148–49; and ABCNY *Yearbook* 67, 149–50. On Court not behind, see Rosenman (1952), 149, 157.

42. *F.D.R.: His Personal Letters, 1928–1945* (New York: Duell, Sloan, 1950), 1:661–62, FDR to CCB, 23 Feb. 1937.

43. FDR, Fireside Chat, 9 Mar. 1937, in *Nothing to Fear*, 98.

44. CCB-HLS, 18:3, Radio Speech on WEVD, 28 Mar. 1937.

45. Ibid. See *Herald Tribune*, 31 Mar. 1937, 16:2, which picked up the phrase "the King's men" and built an editorial on it. CCB sent a copy of the speech to Cardozo, who wrote him on 2 April: "Dear CCB. Fragments of your radio address came to me through the newspapers. Now I have it complete. You hit the nail on the head unerringly." In CCB-HLS, 22:3.

46. CCB-HLS, 4:15, CCB to FF, 8 Mar. 1937. Ibid., FF to CCB, 16 Mar. 1937.

47. Dunne (1986), 86. For a lengthy list of FF's writings on the Supreme Court, see Mendelson, ed. (1964), 232–34.

48. Dunne (1986), 87.

49. Lash (1975), 49: "His general preference for the amendment route and his opposition to 'packing' were well known." For the *Encyclopedia of Social Sciences* (1934) FF had written: "There is no magic in the number nine, but there are limitations to effective judicial action . . . Experience is conclusive that to enlarge the size of the Court would be self-defeating."

50. FF-LOC, GC to FF, 19 Mar. 1937, copy in CCB-FF Correspondence on microfilm at HLS, container 34.

51. *Times*, 6 Mar. 1937, 2:6. Among those signing were many of the faculty's best-known names: Samuel Williston, Joseph H. Beale, Erwin N. Griswold, Warren A. Seavey, and Sheldon Glueck. See Austin W. Scott Collection-HLS, 8:13, Scott to CCB, 8 Mar. 1937, who did not sign; he opposed the bill but thought a group protest inappropriate. Austin W. Scott Collection-HLS, 8:13, CCB to Scott, 4 Mar. 1937: "More or less confidentially, which means that you do not reveal the source of your information, the vote in Columbia of the full time professors was passed seventeen against and six for, but it shifted later to fourteen against and nine for." And in Austin W. Scott Collection-HLS, 8:13, CCB to Scott, 9 Mar. 1937, he said: "I am amazed at the difficulty of making the laity understand how strongly we lawyers feel about the independence of the Judiciary. They seem to consider it merely a question of method."

52. CCB-HLS, 4:15, CCB to FF, 12 Mar. 1937. Freedman, ed. (1967), 392: "It was his usual performance—very explicit on the background to the crisis, very vague on the President's plan."

53. Freedman, ed. (1967), 372. Freedman's suggestion that FDR in his phone call referred to the situation as "a mess" seems incorrect. By all reports, FDR in the days immediately following the launching of his plan was quite euphoric about it and his cleverness. The "mess" sounds more like what FF might have called it at the start and even more surely in his interviews with Freedman many years later.

54. Ibid., 400–401; also Lash (1975), 61–62.

55. Dimond, Cousins, and Clifford, eds. (1975), 59–60. Averell Harriman's description of the Plattsburg movement: "Early in 1915 Grenville Clark came to the conclusion that the United States would have to come to the aid of the Allied forces in Europe. (At that time sentiment in America was strongly against preparation for such action.) Realizing America's lack of trained officers, Clark formed a group which proposed to the War Department that military training be offered to business and professional men, in order to have ready a pool of officer candidates if and when America would be required to enter the war. The War Department agreed, only on condition that Clark would assume the task of finding volunteers who would, at their own expense, report for training at an army post in Plattsburg, New York. Clark then began an intensive campaign to recruit and train volunteers, under which 29,000 officers and 130,000 technicians were readied. A French military historian said for the United States to have raised so quickly an armed force of two million men was not remarkable, but to have produced the officers to command them was 'a military miracle.' It was in large measure a personal contribution by Grenville Clark to Allied victory. In 1921 Clark was awarded the Distinguished Service Medal." See also Dunne (1986), 43–45.

56. Dimond, Cousins, and Clifford, eds. (1975), 85. See the excerpt from Vandenburg's diary quoted in Leuchtenburg, *The Supreme Court* (1995), 140. CCB joining the committee. GC-DCL, ser. 7, National Committee for Independent Courts, box 1, GC to CCB, 12 Mar. 1937, and GC to CCB, 27 Mar. 1937. The earliest letter to CCB, plainly following conversations, is 12 March 1937; and by 27 March CCB was fully involved.

57. CCB-HLS, 18:13, CCB speech to the Committee on the Judiciary of the U.S. Senate, 6 Apr. 1937. For the response to CCB's radio speech by Walter Brower, special assistant

to the U.S. attorney general, see *Herald Tribune*, 29 Mar. 1937, 1:2, and *Times*, 29 Mar. 1937, 4:3. Brower's argument was the one commonly put forward by administration speakers: "The president seems to have discovered a way around technical obstructions" to legislation "overwhelmingly voted by Congress. Therefore why should there be any quarrel about making use of this means to a most desirable end?'"

58. *Herald Tribune*, 7 Apr. 1937, 13:1; clipping in CCB-HLS, 20:6.

59. Ibid. And U.S. Senate Judiciary Committee Hearings on S. 1392, 6 Apr. 1937, 1063, recording Nebraska senator Edward R. Burke's enjoyment in the quotations. Part of the record excerpted in CCB-HLS, 5:9, CCB to FF, 14 Dec. 1949.

60. *National Labor Relations Board v. Jones and Laughlin Steel Corporation*, 301 U.S. 1 (1937), 43. See also 36: "Burdens and obstruction [on interstate commerce] may be due to injurious action springing from other sources. The fundamental principle is that the power to regulate commerce is the power to enact 'all appropriate legislation' for 'its protection and advancement.'" The decision reversed 83 F.2nd 998, Fourth Circuit Court of Appeals.

61. *Steward Machine Company v. Davis*, 301 U.S. 548 (1937), and *Helvering v. Davis*, 301 U.S. 619 (1937).

62. The number steadily rose. On 19 April 1937 GC wrote CCB that it was "about 40 members from 23 States"; on 11 May 1937 he wrote to Congressman Charles F. McLaughlin that it was "approximately 110 men of outstanding influence from 33 States"; and in a memorandum of 16 August 1937 to officers of the committee, "The total membership is 230 from 42 States." All documents in GC-DCL, ser. 7, box 1.

63. Ibid., GC to Congressman Charles F. McLaughlin, 11 May 1937.

64. Dimond, Cousins, and Clifford, eds. (1975), 85.

65. The committee, for instance, was strong in Louisiana, where its local leader was Monte M. Lemann, a Harvard Law School graduate, a close friend of Frankfurter, and one of New Orleans's most distinguished lawyers. Dunne (1986), 81–82, recounts how the South was organized.

66. Senate Report 711, 75th Congress, 1st session, 23.

67. Leuchtenburg, *The Supreme Court* (1995), 147–48, gives a summary of the Jefferson Island "frolic" and newspaper reports of it.

68. Ibid., 149.

69. *Times*, 6 July 1937, 18:6. *Times*, 11 July 1937, IV, 8:5.

70. *Boston Herald*, 12 July 1937; clipping in CCB-HLS, 18:13.

71. The appointment of Laporte was by the Association's new president, Henry L. Stimson (1937–39), but in Dimond, Cousins, and Clifford, eds. (1975), 86, Laporte states it was on CCB's "suggestion." Freedman, ed. (1967), 400, FDR to CCB, 27 May 1937.

72. The upright men who resigned were chief counsel Morrison Shaforth and assistant chief counsel Russell J. Ryan. See *Times*, 17 Sept. 1937, 1:7, and Dunne (1986), 94. The resignations were dated 28 June 1937, but they were not accepted until 16 September. The Treasury Department did not explain why.

73. Dunne (1986), 91.

74. *Times*, 2 July 1937, 22:1.

75. *Times*, 16 July 1937, 7:5.

76. *Times*, 17 July 1937, 4:3: "This bill constitutes the most serious threat to the independence of the judiciary which has occurred in the history of this nation . . . The true purpose of the bill remains clear. It is an effort to force the court to accede to the views of the Executive on constitutional issues." Laporte has an interesting story about the distribution of the Report to Washington Senators, see Dimond, Cousins, and Clifford, eds. (1975), 86–87.

77. *Times*, 20 July 1937, 1:8.

78. Ibid., 3:4.

79. Freedman, ed. (1967), 403, FF to FDR, 20 July 1937.

80. *Times*, 23 July 1937, 1:6.

81. Wagner's reply to Lehman. *Times*, 22 July 1937, 1:7, with his letter's text in the story. Although Wagner's part in this episode was often on front or editorial pages of newspapers, his biographer, Huthmacher (1968), does not discuss it.

82. *Times*, 26 Aug. 1937, 1:3.

83. GC-DCL, ser. 7, box 1, CCB to GC, 30 Aug. 1937.

84. Ibid., memorandum, 16 Aug. 1937.

85. FDR's appointments to the Court, with dates of taking oath: Hugo L. Black, 19 Aug. 1937 (replacing Van Devanter, retired); Stanley F. Reed, 31 Jan. 1938 (replacing George Sutherland, retired); Felix Frankfurter, 30 Jan. 1939 (replacing Benjamin N. Cardozo, died); and William O. Douglas, 17 Apr. 1939 (replacing Louis D. Brandeis, retired).

86. Initially, the defeat was often compared to President Wilson's experience with the Senate, e.g., *Times*, 23 July 1937, 1:3; and *Times*, 25 Aug., 1:3: "the most decisive legislative defeat dealt to a Chief Executive since the Senate, twenty years ago, blocked Woodrow Wilson's dream of American participation in the League of Nations."

87. Leuchtenburg, *The Supreme Court* (1995), 156–61.

88. E.g., Burns (1956), 298, who is more expansive than many: "Patriotic groups moved quickly into action. New England town fathers called mass meetings. Bar associations met and denounced. Mail flooded congressional offices." Senator Copeland, *Times*, 21 Feb. 1937, 24:1, claimed to have received some 30,000 messages opposed and only a few hundred in favor of the plan. Clark's biographer, Clifford, ranked it as "perhaps the most formidable adversary that the Roosevelt administration had to face in 1937." Perhaps an exaggeration. See Dimond, Cousins, and Clifford, eds. (1975), 15.

19. Family Deaths and Sorrows

Chief sources for Louie are interviews with the family and letters in the Burlingham collections; for Robert, Dorothy, and the Freuds, in addition to the former, also *The Last Tiffany: A Biography of Dorothy Tiffany Burlingham*, by Michael John Burlingham (New York: Atheneum, 1989); *Anna Freud: The Dream of Psychoanalysis*, by Robert Coles (Reading, Mass.: Addison-Wesley, 1992); *Anna Freud: A Biography*, by Elisabeth Young-Bruehl (New York: Summit Books, 1988); and *Sigmund Freud: Life and Works*, 3 vols., by Ernest Jones (London: Hogarth; vol. 1 and 2 "new" ed., 1954, 1958, and vol. 3, 1957). For an account of Robert and Dorothy's early years of marriage, see Chapter 12. On Nancy's decline in health, the Burlingham collections and interviews with family members. On the law firm, the Burlingham collections, interviews with partners of the Burlingham firm, and the firm's history files. On a corrupt judge, other than contemporary newspapers: John C. Knox, *A Judge Comes of Age* (New York: Scribner's, 1940); Joseph Borkin, *The Corrupt Judge: An Inquiry into Bribery and Other High Crimes and Misdemeanors in the Federal Courts* (New York: Clarkson N. Potter, 1962); Milton S. Gould, *The Witness Who Spoke with God and Other Tales from the Courthouse* (New York: Viking, 1979). On the silver oar: Charles M. Hough, *Reports of Cases in the Vice Admiralty of the Province of New York and in the Court of Admiralty of the State of New York, 1715–1788*, with an Historical Introduction and Appendix (New Haven: Yale University Press, 1925); Gordon W. Paulsen, "The Silver Oar of the Vice-Admiralty

Court of the Province of New York," Maritime Law Association, Document 735, 1 May 1998, 10672. For general background, see chap. 1, *The Law of Admiralty*, 2nd ed., by Grant Gilmore and Charles L. Black Jr. (Mineola, N.Y.: Foundation Press, 1975).

1. Bronchitis. CCB-HLS, 9:2, CCB to HH, 24 Apr. 1934. Ibid., 22:3, Benjamin N. Cardozo to CCB, 11 Aug. 1937.

2. La Guardia committee. *Times*, 23 July 1937, 1:2. Attends meeting. *Times*, 27 July 1937, 1:7. Plain people. CCB-HLS, 4:15, CCB to FF, 19 Oct. 1937.

3. "Irregular at the office." GC-DCL, ser. 7, National Committee for Independent Courts, box 1, CCB to GC, 9 Sept. 1937. Church affairs. *Times*, 13 Sept. 1937, 20:6. CCB-HLS, 4:15, CCB to FF, 19 Oct. 1937. Dewey. *Times*, 5 Oct. 1937, 6:6.

4. CCB-HLS, 22:3, CCB to Benjamin N. Cardozo, 10 Nov. 1937.

5. Ibid., 12:13, CCB to Frank MacKinnon. See n. 11 below.

6. Ibid., 2:3, CCB to Tucker Burr, 17 Dec. 1937. Stimson. Ibid., 17:12, HLS to CCB, 9 Dec. 1937. Stimson was one of the few who sometimes addressed CCB as "Burley." Another was A. N. Hand, though he spelt the name "Burleigh," see ibid., 6:13, ANH to CCB, 26 Dec. 1937.

7. Ibid., 2:3, CCB to Tucker Burr, 17 Dec. 1937.

8. *Times*, 8 Dec. 1937, 25:3, and *Herald Tribune*, 8 Dec. 1937, 16:4.

9. FF-LOC, container 34, CCB to FF, 23 Dec. 1937.

10. CCB-HLS, 10:2, CCB to CEH Jr., 13 Dec. 1945. A letter to the son on the death of his mother.

11. Ibid., 12:13, CCB to Frank MacKinnon, 15 Dec. 1937. MacKinnon, a Kings Bench judge in this year became a lord justice of appeal. He was the author of *On Circuit, 1924–1931* (1940), a book CCB thought "a mine of curious and out-of-the-way learning and information, containing besides much outspoken criticism of the circuit system and practical suggestions for its reform." See CCB's letter on MacKinnon following the latter's death, in January 1946, *Times*, 5 Feb. 1946, 22:7. CCB-HLS, 9:7, CCB to HH, 21 Feb. 1947. Blessed. CCB-HLS, 12:13, CCB to Frank MacKinnon, 15 Dec. 1937.

12. Burlingham (1989), 255–57. Mossik Sheldrick to GM, 6 Oct. 1997: "When Bob came home to Vienna, Summer 1937, he—or I think, rather his mother and Anna Freud— decided that Harvard was not the right place for him."

Note: CCB's letter to Bob, about the decision, is not in the HLS Collection, but a copy of it can be found in FF-LOC, box 38, 11 Sept. 1937:

Dear Bob:

Well, we have had quite an interchange of cables, and you have made your decision and that settles it . . .

I tried to omit from my cables any reference to the personal disappointment that I had in your decision. I should not really have minded if you had come to the conclusion that it was on the whole wise for you to give up the thought of college and go to work. I have seen a good many cases where men went into business for a year or two and then went back to college, but I had supposed that your experience with the Antioch system had made that unnecessary in your case. Apparently you feel that you need psychoanalysis for whatever you do and that is a matter which of course you will have to decide for yourself. You know much more about analysis than I do. I regard Professor Freud as a great man who has made very real contributions to the sum of human knowledge. I have assumed that you think that by being analyzed again you will develop powers of will and concentration which will be of great value to you. My own feeling is that you have shown capacity at various times, and I have assumed that you had enough self knowledge and power to accomplish whatever you might seek.

I am under no illusions as to the value of a college education. Some men don't need it, some men are the worse for it. What I regret most is that you came in contact with so few teachers at Harvard who made an impression on you, but that is not to be wondered at in such a big place where the element of chance is so strong. As I look back sixty years I think of only six or eight who made a deep impression on me, and that is a good many . . .

13. M. J. Burlingham (1989), 249–51, and see long note for 251, at 338. Young-Bruehl (1988), 128, 133, 187, 421.

14. Coles (1992), 10–11.

15. M. J. Burlingham (1989), 251.

16. Ibid., 306; and GM interview with Michael Burlingham, 19 Feb. 1993.

17. GM interview with Michael Burlingham, 19 Feb. 1993.

18. M. J. Burlingham (1989), 304–5.

19. CCB-HLS, 9:3, CCB to HH, 20 Oct. 1936: "I have had very intimate talks with Mabbie who is mature and wise far beyond her years. We talked of D.'s coming over, and I told her to talk to R. and make it perfectly plain to him that D. would not come if he was going to bother her. And M. did this. At first it was a blow to R. because she accompanied it by saying that they could *jamais vivre ensemble* again. But it was necessary to make it clear to him."

20. GM interview with KBV, 2 Oct. 1997, and with Dorothy Schmiderer Baker (phone), 15 Oct. 1997. Sleeping pill. M. J. Burlingham (1989), 265.

21. *Times*, 29 May 1938, I, 7:1. *Herald Tribune*, 29 May 1938, 2:7, also published CCB's statement.

22. *Harvard Class of 1910, Eighth Report, 1940*, 32, written by Arthur Lawrence Washburn, a physician living in New York and working at Bellevue Hospital.

23. *Times*, 29 May 1938, I, 7:1.

24. *Confrontation in Vienna*, by Leopold Bellak (Larchmont, N.Y.: CPS, Inc., 1993), chap. 7. Dorothy's son Michael offered the incident as an example of his grandfather's sense of family obligation, even at a difficult time. Bellak's description of his attempt to repay the loan is amusing.

25. Sister's letter. M. J. Burlingham (1989), 266. Freud's letter. Young-Bruehl (1988), 238.

26. M. J. Burlingham (1989), 303. He was told of the statement by Annelisa (Mrs. George F.) Kennan, Mossik Sheldrick's sister, Michael Burlingham to GM, 12 Aug. 1997. GM interview (phone) with RTE, 6 Aug. 1997.

27. CCB-DFT, CCB to Grace Taylor, 5 Apr. 1940.

28. CCB-HLS, 9:6, CCB to HH, 11 Aug. 1941.

29. Ibid., 2:4, CCB to DTB, 3 Feb. 1947; CCB-HLS, 9:12, DTB to CCB, 17 Dec. 1952; M. J. Burlingham (1989), 304. Appendix, "The Burlingham Children and Anna Freud."

30. FF-LOC, container 34, CCB to FF, 23 Dec. 1937. See also CCB-HLS, 12:13, CCB to Frank MacKinnon, 15 Dec. 1937.

31. GM interview with KBV, 3 Oct. 1997.

32. Ibid., and on 7 Oct. 1997.

33. GM interview with RTE, 3 Oct. 1993.

34. GM interviews with CB Jr., 14 and 15 July 1995, and with Mossik, Mrs. Malcolm Sheldrick (formerly Mrs. Robert Burlingham Jr.), 1 June 1993.

35. TDT-YSML, 2:13, CCB to TDT, 12 Nov. 1940. See also CCB-HLS, 10:8, CCB to

William James, 3 Dec. 1940: "My darling daughter has had a nervous breakdown, and we have been and still are in Portchester."

36. CCB-HLS, 9:6, CCB to HH, 11 Aug. 1941.

37. GM interview with RTE, 15 May 1993.

38. GM interviews with KBV, 3 and 7 Oct. 1997, and with Mossik, Mrs. Malcolm Sheldrick (formerly Mrs. Robert Burlingham Jr.), 1 June 1993.

39. CCB-HLS, 6:14, ANH to CCB, 13 Aug. 1942.

40. TDT-YSML, 2:15, CCB to TDT, 30 Aug. 1942.

41. CCB-HLS, 9:6, CCB to FWH and HH, 1 Dec. 1942.

42. Ibid., CCB to HH, 7 May 1943. See also ibid., 14:13, CCB to SKR, 25 May 1943.

43. Ibid., 9:7, CCB to FWH and HH, 23 June 1945.

44. Ibid., CCB to HH, 21 Feb. 1947; and CCB-TFS, CCB to FWH and HH, 20 Nov. 1950.

45. CCB-TFS, CCB to FWH and HH, 23 Apr. 1951.

46. GM interviews with TFS, 22 May 1995, and with CB Jr., 14 and 15 July 1995.

47. GM from PLT, 14 Feb. 1994.

48. GM interview with CB Jr., 7 Oct. 1992.

49. *Paradise Lost*. GM interview with CB Jr., 22 Aug. 1997.

50. CCB-HLS, 21:3. The typed poem is dated 22 May 1950.

51. B-U History Files, Grace Stanley to Elliott B. Nixon, 19 Mar. 1984.

52. Ibid.

53. GM interview (phone) with Dr. Daniel W. O'Connor Jr., 24 Apr. 2000.

54. GM interview with Herbert M. Lord, 20 Oct. and 13 Dec. 1994, and interview with John R. Hupper, 2 Aug. 1994.

55. Underwood. GM interview with Richard W. Palmer, 16 Oct. 1994. Underwood died 1 Jan. 1996, at age ninety-nine, *Times*, obit, 5 Jan. D21:1. Palmer was an associate with the firm 1948–58, when he left to become a partner in a Philadelphia firm later titled Palmer, Biezup & Henderson.

56. Hupper's party. CCB-HLS, 2:6, Harold M. Kennedy to CCB, 14 Mar. 1958.

57. Botein (1952), 294–95, records a countrywide Gallup poll taken in 1939, soon after Manton's conviction, on belief in the honesty of judges: 72 percent thought municipal or local judges honest; 76 percent, state judges; and 86 percent, federal judges. The local and municipal judges were thought to be too closely tied to politics; and except for the recent example of Manton, faith in federal judges might have been still higher.

58. Gould (1979), 189. Starting with the trial judge at sentencing (see *Times*, 21 June 1939, 1:3), the comparison has been made by many: e.g., Borkin (1962), 80, and Botein (1952), 293, but it is not exact: Bacon, when he pled guilty to accepting bribes, was James I's lord chancellor, the highest-ranking judicial figure in England; Manton at most ranked tenth, after the Supreme Court justices.

59. On Winslow. See CRB&M, Charles Evans Hughes, CCB to CEH, 9 Mar. 1929. The scandal shook New York's bench and bar, and can be followed in *Herald Tribune*, 2 Apr. 1929, 1:3, and *Times*, 2 Apr. 1929, 1:6, 3 Apr., 2:4, and 7 Apr., 6:4, in a story captioned "Legal Comment of Current Events." For summaries of the scandal, see Borkin (1962), 32 and 255; Knox (1940), 203, with greater detail and not always in sympathy with CCB; Martin (1970), 226–27; and feature report in *Times*, 20 Jan. 1929, IX, 10:1. CCB expressed his feelings in a letter just before Winslow's resignation, CCB-HLS, 10:10, CCB to Pierre and Loulie Jay, 28 Mar. 1929: "We federal lawyers have been having a wretched time here on account of the disgrace that has come to the bench through the improprieties, to say the

least, of Judge Winslow, U.S. District Judge. Everybody thinks that he will resign despite the fact that that will be interpreted as an admission of guilt. His conduct has injured the whole bench in the mind of the plain people."

60. See Chapter 11 and Gunther (1994), 260–61.

61. For a brief account of Manton's judicial career, see J. B. Morris (1987), 133–34; for a longer one, Borkin (1962), 25–31; and for one longer still, Gould (1979), 189ff.

62. Dewey's letter to Congressman Hatton W. Sumners. *Herald Tribune*, 30 Jan. 1939, 1:1, estimated money received from litigants at $439,481; and *Times*, 30 Jan. 1939, 1:8.

63. See *Times*, 30 Mar. 1939, 10:3. To the charges Manton pled "not guilty." The indictments, starting on 1 Mar. with the "Schick case" (see *Times*, 3 Mar., 1:4), came down one by one, and ultimately were superseded on 26 April by a single indictment charging Manton and four others with conspiracy to obstruct justice, etc.

64. Chesnut's charge to the jury. Quoted from the trial record by Borkin (1962), 79–80; and *Times*, 4 June 1939, 1:7. Manton's appeals are: *United States v. Manton*, 107 F.2nd 834 (2nd Cir. 1939), and cert. denied 309 U.S. 664 (1940).

65. Manton sentenced on 20 June. *Times*, 21 June 1939, 1:3. Dishonored. Gould (1979), 244. Manton goes to prison. *Times*, 8 Mar. 1940, 10:4.

66. Borkin (1962), 25–26.

67. TDT-YSML, 2:13, CCB to TDT, 12 Nov. 1932.

68. On Manton's wealth and the loss of it. See Borkin (1962), 40–41. Judge Chesnut, in sentencing Manton, said: "In the attempt to save this fortune he violated the most fundamental feature of his judicial office, which requires absolute impartiality and personal disinterestedness in the performance of official duties." See *Times*, 21 June 1939, 2:3.

69. The summary. Gould (1979), 192–93. Gould's opinion continues: "Soon one of them [the two receivers] died; the other 'moved down to Virginia and asked to resign.' In their place, in 1934, this judicial Pooh-Bah [Manton] appointed Milton C. Weisman and Kenneth Steinreich. Five years later, we learned that Weisman's law firm acted as Manton's lawyers in 'settling' claims against him, and handled large amounts of cash for him. And we learned that Steinreich had a number of personal transactions with Manton; he obtained loans for Manton and guaranteed some of his debts. Manton was tireless in milking the Fox receivership." And about Manton's corruption of Judge Edwin S. Thomas, of the U.S. District Court, Connecticut, who "was destroyed after a comic-opera effort to avoid subpoenas, including pell-mell flight to Panama, barricading himself in his New Haven chambers against federal marshals, and, finally, taking refuge in a mental hospital"; see ibid., 188–89. Like *The Mikado*. TDT-YSML, 2:13, CCB to TDT, 7 Sept. 1932.

70. On CCB's warning Hughes against Manton. See reference in FF-LOC, container 33, FF to CCB, 26 Sept. 1933. CCB's letter to CEH not found.

71. CCB to Roosevelt is cited in CCB to John W. Davis, 8 June 1939, quoted in Harbaugh (1973), 314. CCB-HLS, 4:16, CCB to FF, 1 Apr. 1938. Also CCB-HLS, 8:2, CCB to Professor Jesse S. Reeves, 3 Mar. 1939: "I have long known that M. was devoid of moral sense."

72. See n. 59 above. Borkin (1962), 28, quoting Representative Hatton Sumners, chairman of the Judiciary Committee: "Why kick at the place where the fellows used to be."

73. CCB-HLS, 13:7, CCB to Manton, 1 Feb. 1939.

74. Coleman, a retired City Court judge who had been selected by CCB to be his biographer—but to publish only after CCB's death—wrote his queries on the copy of the letter. Coleman, who gathered material but never started writing, raises another important question: To what extent may a biographer assume that copies of letters, saved as a normal practice, indicate that the original was sent? I have made that assumption, as I think most biog-

raphers do when writing of persons living in the post-typewriter age. To work only from originals, where these can be found, is too limiting. Coleman's comment, I feel, expresses surprise at any sympathy for Manton as much as questioning whether the letter was sent.

75. CCB-HLS, 3:3, CCB to Charles P. Curtis Jr., 10 Apr. 1952.

76. Timothy N. Pfeiffer, *Milbank, Tweed, Hadley & McCloy, Law Practice in a Turbulent World: An Informal Narrative of Four Decades, 1921–1963* (New York: privately printed, 1965), 195. Pfeiffer and his firm were counsel for the City Bar Association in a disbarment proceeding against Louis Levy which arose out of Manton's trial. "Manton, before going to prison, was a witness. It was fascinating to observe, in conversation with him before he testified . . ." LH-HLS, 101:1, CCB to Fanny (Mrs. Learned) Hand, 9 June 1939, three days after the trial concluded: "The Interboro receivership stank. But I did not think he would commit a crime"; and see n. 71, CCB to Reeves, 3 Mar. 1939. For general opinion, see *Times*, editorial, 5 June 1939, 16:1: "It is not difficult to understand the reluctance of citizens to accept Manton's guilt as a fact."

77. CCB-HLS, 18:11, Julius L. Goebel Jr. to CCB, 30 Nov. 1940.

78. On the silver oar. Its history may be found in Hough (1925), Introduction, particularly p. xxviii; in Paulsen (1998); and CCB-HLS, 18:11, Julius L. Goebel Jr. to CCB, 30 Nov. 1940 and 16 Jan. 1942, and Robert Ensko, Inc., to CCB, 18 Jan. 1941.

79. CCB-HLS, 18:11, CCB to Julius L. Goebel Jr., 24 Jan. 1941: "From the former Clerk of the Court, Alex Gilchrist Jr., I learned that there was a duplicate of the Oar in the Clerk's office, and I looked it up and found a discolored black brute of a model, lead, silver plated, with the plating worn off, weighing 40 oz. plus as against 12 oz. 17 dwt. for the Oar. I am having it plated and shellacked, for the judges are afraid that the original will be stolen, as a lot of overcoats have been from the C.C.A. lately." No trace of this "brute of a model," if it was replated and shellacked, has been found.

80. CCB-HLS, 18:11, Julius L. Goebel Jr. to CCB, 30 Nov. 1940.

81. Ibid., TDT to CCB, 16 Dec. 1940.

82. Ibid., CCB to TDT, 16 Dec. 1940.

83. Ibid., Arnold W. Knauth to CCB, 8 Jan. 1941; CCB to Knauth, 13 Jan. 1941; and ibid., 21:1, pamphlet recounting the proceeding at which the oar was presented to the court. The Maritime Law Association published the account as a pamphlet in March 1941, a project to which the MLA's printer, the Hecla Press, donated its costs.

84. CCB-HLS, 18:11, Letter of Appeal, 30 Dec. 1940.

85. Ibid., Loomis, Williams & Donohue to CCB and TDT, 31 Dec. 1940. CCB letter to Arnold W. Knauth, 14 Feb. 1941, states that the author of the letter, "which neither I nor Thacher answered," was "the ineffable Loomis [Homer L. Loomis]."

86. Ibid., secretary of the MLA, George C. Sprague, to CCB, 9 Jan. 1941. Hupper to CCB, 13 Jan.

87. Ibid., CCB to Alexander Gilchrist Jr., 14 Jan. 1941. Gilchrist was clerk of the court from 1912 to 1930, having started work there in 1883 under Samuel H. Lyman, clerk from 1878 to 1901.

88. Ibid., Harrison Tweed to CCB, 17 Jan. 1941.

89. Ibid., CCB to TDT, 21 Jan. 1941; Ensko to CCB, 18 Jan. 1941; and TDT-YSML, 17:323, TDT to CCB, 22 Jan. 1941.

90. CCB-HLS, 18:12, to Julius L. Goebel Jr., 24 Jan. 1941.

91. Ibid., CCB to TDT, 4 Feb. 1941; and TDT to CCB, 5 Feb.

92. Account of proceeding. Ibid. *Times*, 13 Feb. 1941, 21:3, also 15 Feb., 16:3. *Herald Tribune*, 15 Feb. 1941, 8:3, has a three-column picture of CCB presenting the oar to Judge Knox, with TDT looking on.

Note: The court's judges continue to feel warmly about their oar even though they now sit "in admiralty" without it before them, for it is held in safekeeping by the Museum of the City of New York. In 1999, at the opening of the Blue Ribband Exhibit, evoking the gracious and luxurious era of the Transatlantic liner, Charles S. Haight Jr., senior United States district judge, Southern District of New York, remarked as follows on the court's silver oar:

> Lastly I invite you to consider the shape of the Admiralty Oar, the beauty of its utilitarian simplicity.
>
> We live in an age when the latest, most expensive Silicon Valley device becomes obsolete in twelve months. The oar has never changed. You sit in your ship, grasp the oar's handle, place its blade in the water, pull, and the ship moves through the water; and so humankind has been progressing since the beginning of recorded time. This sophisticated audience is surely aware that at the battle of Salamis, in the Aegean Sea in the year 480 B.C., when the Greek fleet defeated the Persian fleet under Xerxes the Great, the principal warship was the trireme: 150 feet long, 18 foot beam, drawing 4 feet, equipped with a bow ram, and powered by three banks of oars, port and starboard, manned by 200 rowers. These ships were built not just before the age of steam, they were built before the age of sail; and I do not doubt that their oars looked just like this one.
>
> So there is something eternal about the oar; and it is wholly fitting that the oar is a symbol of the law of the sea: for the sea itself is eternally fascinating, and so are ships and those who go down to the sea in ships, who by their daring or timidity, courage or cowardice, foresight or foolishness, triumphs or tragedies of navigation, give employment to admiralty lawyers and judges, thereby generating that equally fascinating body of law that we call admiralty. (Maritime Law Association of the United States, Doc. 744, 15 Oct. 1999, 11698–700.)

20. Moses, Roosevelt, and CCB

Chief sources for this chapter, other than the city newspapers and the Burlingham collections, are: Thomas Kessner, *Fiorello H. La Guardia and the Making of New York* (New York: McGraw Hill, 1989); August Heckscher with Phyllis Robinson, *When La Guardia Was Mayor: New York's Legendary Years.* (New York: Norton, 1978); Charles Garrett, *The La Guardia Years: Machine and Reform Politics in New York City* (New Brunswick, N.J.: Rutgers University Press, 1961); and Robert A. Caro, *The Power Broker: Robert Moses and the Fall of New York* (New York: Knopf, 1974).

1. CCB-HLS, 9:3, CCB to HH, 25 Feb. 1936.

2. FHL to Senator James F. Byrnes, 5 Apr. 1939, La Guardia MSS, quoted in Leuchtenburg, *Franklin D. Roosevelt* (1963), 263.

3. *The New Yorker*, 3 June 1933, 13. CCB-HLS, 9:5, CCB to FWH and HH, 17 Feb. 1940. Also CCB-HLS, 8:2, CCB to Jesse S. Reeves, 8 Feb. 1939, "All Roosevelts (except Eleanor) are more or less inclined to suppress or twist the truth when hard pressed."

4. CCB-HLS, 3:8, CCB speech for TED's election: "The people—the plain people—average men and women know what sort of men La Guardia and Dewey are." And ibid., 10:10, CCB letter to Pierre and Loulie Jay, 28 Mar. 1929: "[Judge Winslow's corrupt] conduct has injured the whole bench in the mind of the plain people."

5. See *Times*, 1 Jan. 1938, 1:4, and *Herald Tribune*, 1 Jan. 1938, 1:1.

6. CCB-HLS, 11:9, SMI to CCB, 7 Jan. 1937. The meeting of support for La Guardia that SMI proposed was held by the City Fusion Party at the Hotel Astor on 31 March; see *Times*, 1 Apr. 1937, 2:2. CCB-HLS, 6:3, telegram inviting membership on the Citizens Committee, 21 July 1937. Creation of the committee. *Times*, 23 July 1937, 1:2. CCB-HLS, 3:8, CCB telegram to SS on FHL and the primaries, 11 Aug. 1937; CCB-HLS 6:3, CCB to Thomas W. Lamont, 9 Sept. and 22 Oct. 1937; CCB-HLS, CCB to Geoffrey Parsons of *Herald Tribune*, 26 Oct. 1937. Letters and statements on the post-election debts. CCB-HLS, 3:8 and 6:3.

7. PW-COH, 86–88; see Heckscher (1978), 164–72; Garrett (1961), 259–62; and Kessner (1989), 414.

8. See refs. in n. 7 and CCB-HLS, 6:3, Kenneth F. Simpson to CCB, 17 Aug. 1937.

9. CCB-HLS, 3:8, CCB telegram to TED, 15 Aug. 1937; ibid., Clarence J. Shearn to CCB, 7 Sept.; ibid., CCB to Victor F. Ridder, 20 Sept.; and *Times*, 5 Oct. 1937, 6:6. On Berle speaking to TED on behalf of Fusion and TED's demands, see Mitgang (1963), 348.

10. CCB-HLS, 3:8, CCB speech, Nov. 1937.

11. Ibid., 11:9, CCB to FHL, 9 Nov. 1937.

12. Ibid., CCB to FHL, 8 June 1938.

13. See *Times*, 31 July 1938, 2:5. Report on reduction of number of political jobs in the city. *Times*, 1 Aug. 1938, 15:5. Morton's obit. *Times*, 9 Nov. 1949, 27:5. For a CCB letter on the Civil Service Reorganization Bill, see *Herald Tribune*, 2 Apr. 1938, 10:4, and CCB-HLS, 21:4.

14. CCB-HLS, 11:9, CCB to FHL, 20 July 1938.

15. Ibid., FHL to CCB, 23 July 1938.

16. Ibid.

17. Ibid., 6:13, ANH to CCB, 21 Aug. 1938.

18. Ibid., 11:9, CCB to FHL, 20 July 1938.

19. Ibid., FHL to CCB, 7 Aug. 1938.

20. TDT-YSML, 2:13, CCB to TDT, 24 Oct. 1938.

21. Mendelson, ed. (1964), 36.

22. *Times*, 31 Aug. 1938, 36:2, and *Herald Tribune*, 31 Aug. 1938, 2:5. Resolution. It was also without his son's knowledge, for CB, on his father's behalf, would have stopped it, see CCB-TFS, H. Eliot Kaplan to Charles Burlingham (the son). For CCB's letter of acknowledgment to Kaplan, CCB-HLS, 3:4, 3 Sept. 1938.

23. *Herald Tribune*, editorial, 10 Feb. 1939, 22:3; *Sun*, 9 Feb. 1939, 20:2; *Times*, 9 Feb. 1939, 20:2, and *World-Telegram*, 9 Feb. 1939, 22:2, and a news story, 8 Feb. 1939, 12:1.

24. CCB-HLS, 19:6, CCB to Schoellkopf, 20 Jan. 1939.

25. Sherwood (1948), 23–34, in describing the early career of Harry Hopkins, working in New York for the AICP and other relief groups, writes of the increasing arrogance of the professional "welfare worker" and the skirmishing with "the voluntary civil servant" (26): "Both were commercially unselfish, animated by public spirit and reconciled to careers uncomplicated by the profit motive. It was therefore not unnatural that both should strive to be paid off in the currency of increased authority and opportunity to extend influence. This ambition led to competitive struggle which inevitably produced endless jurisdictional disputes—and the border warfare between one charity organization and another was much the same as between one government agency and another." See Schlesinger (1960), 3:416, on the "New Dealers" as a class.

26. *Sun*, editorial, 9 Feb. 1939, 20:2, on CCB's retirement from the Welfare Council.

27. CCB-HLS, 6:16, 2 Nov. 1940, LH to CCB.

28. The most detailed description of this battle over the Brooklyn-Battery Tunnel is in Caro (1974), 639–77; also Kessner (1989), 454–59; and Heckscher (1978), 221–28.

29. The figures continually change, depending often on what parkways and approaches are included and the source of the money. But $30 million is roughly what was needed, see Caro (1974), 660: "If the Mayor could grab off a $30,000,000 piece of that action for a tunnel, the cooperative Tunnel Authority instead of arrogant Triborough could build the Crossing."

30. Traffic on the Triborough Bridge. *Times,* 22 Jan. 1938, 17:5.

31. Caro (1974), 607–8.

32. On completion of the Bronx-Whitestone Bridge. *Herald Tribune,* 5 Feb. 1939, II, 1:3.

33. Caro (1974), 641–44.

34. Ibid., 641, and see 1213 nn.

35. *Times,* 23 Jan. 1939, 15:1, *Herald Tribune,* 23 Jan. 1939, 5:2, both with pictures of the bridge, as if seen from an airplane, and *World-Telegram,* 23 Jan. 1939, 11:3.

36. *Times,* 26 Jan. 1939, 23:4.

37. Caro (1974), 657. This figure of $39 million seems more accurate than the $18 million which is often given, e.g., *The WPA Guide to New York City* and *The Encyclopedia of New York City.*

38. Ten-story building. *Times,* 26 Jan. 1939, 23:4. Drawings of bridge. *Herald Tribune,* 6 Feb. 1939, 13:2, and *Times,* 26 Jan. 1939, 23:4.

39. Caro (1974), 661, and 1214 n. Bard already had written a letter opposing the bridge, *Times,* 10 Mar. 1939, 22:7.

40. Caro (1974), 662, and see 1214 n.

41. Ibid., 663.

42. Account of RM. *Times,* 28 Mar. 1939, 1:2, and *Herald Tribune,* 28 Mar. 1939, 1:4.

43. Caro (1974), 668. The response of Moses to a question by a councilman.

44. Votes in Albany. See *Times,* 30 Mar. 1939, 1:3. Moses moving ahead. Ibid., 16:1.

45. Caro (1974), 671, citing his interviews with PW.

46. Eleanor Roosevelt, "My Day," *World-Telegram,* 5 Apr. 1939, 21:1.

47. *Herald Tribune,* 6 Apr. 1939.

48. FDR-FDRL, PPF 1169, CCB to FDR, 10 Apr. 1939. Except for the scrawl at the top, typed, on office stationery.

49. Ibid., FDR to CCB, 12 Apr. 1939.

50. Ibid., CCB to FDR, 13 Apr. 1939. Scrawled on scratch paper, to "Dear Franklin."

51. Heckscher (1978), 226, quoting CCB to FHL, 10 Apr. 1939.

52. FDR-FDRL, PPF, 1169, FDR Memorandum for Harry Woodring, 12 Apr. 1939; and ibid., Edwin M. Watson Memorandum for Major General J. L. Schley (chief of engineers, War Department), 26 Apr. 1939: "At the direction of the President I am forwarding the attached correspondence to you and ask that you speak to the President before you make any report on the subject."

53. *Herald Tribune,* 2 June 1939, 24:5; Moses reply. *Herald Tribune,* 5 June 1939, 14:4.

54. Secretary Woodring's decision. *Herald Tribune,* 18 July 1939, 1:4, and *Times,* 18 July 1939, 1:8.

55. PW-PW Jr., CCB to PW, 19 July 1939.

56. Caro (1974), 674–75.

57. Heckscher (1978), 228.

58. Caro (1974), 669–70, 676–77, and Starr (1985), 203. Starr wrote from a varied background, as a businessman, a professor, a writer, and even a city housing commissioner. In 1977 he published *America's Housing Challenge,* and in 1975 *Housing and the Money Market.*

21. War and Presidential Politics

Chief sources for this chapter are contemporary news reports and letters in the Burlingham collections. Also, for several of CCB's friends in England: Ruth Dudley Edwards, *The Pursuit of Reason: The Economist, 1843–1993* (Boston: Harvard Business School, 1994); and Mary Agnes Hamilton, *Remembering My Good Friends* (London: Jonathan Cape, 1944). And on La Guardia's second term: Thomas Kessner, *Fiorello H. La Guardia and the Making of New York* (New York: McGraw Hill, 1989); August Heckscher with Phyllis Robinson, *When La Guardia Was Mayor: New York's Legendary Years* (New York: Norton, 1978); Charles Garrett, *The La Guardia Years: Machine and Reform Politics in New York City* (New Brunswick, N.J.; Rutgers University Press, 1961). Caroline Moorehead, *Bertrand Russell: A Life* (New York: Viking, 1992); Ronald W. Clark, *The Life of Bertrand Russell* (London: Jonathan Cape, 1975; New York: Knopf, 1976); and John Dewey and Horace M. Kallen, eds., *The Bertrand Russell Case* (New York: Viking, 1941).

1. Collision treaty. For CCB's feelings about the Senate's failure to ratify the collision treaty, see Chapter 9 and its nn. 50–54.

2. On the research project, see correspondence in CCB-HLS, 7:9, e.g., Manley O. Hudson letter to members of the advisory committee, 12 Jan. 1940, and Hudson, DAB, supp. 6, 307–8.

3. *Harvard College Class of 1879, Ninth Report, 1929.*

4. Chairman. See correspondence in CCB-HLS, 7:9 and 8:2. Deafness. Ibid., 8:2. On the creation and early years of the postwar International Court of Justice, see letters in 19:11 and CCB-HLS to *Times,* 21 Jan. 1946, 22:6.

5. CCB-HLS, 8:2, Hudson to CCB, 21 Jan. [1940].

6. Ibid., 9:1, CCB to FWH and HH, 27 Oct. 1932.

7. Ibid., CCB to FWH and HH, 30 Mar. 1933.

8. Morison, Commager, and Leuchtenberg (1980), 2: 432.

9. CCB-HLS, 9:1, CCB to FWH and HH, 14 Apr. 1933.

10. Ibid., 14 Apr. and 17 May 1933.

11. CCB-HLS, 9:3, CCB to FWH, 22 Sept. 1936.

12. Ibid., 12:13, CCB to FDM, 18 Jan. 1940: "I dislike our form of neutrality intensely. It is humiliating to me that we do not take the same position as Norway, Sweden, Holland and Belgium, and sail our ships at the owner's risk. Of course, I would personally prefer to go further and have Congress declare that while they would send no expeditionary force, they would repeal all the prohibitions, including the prohibition of loans, etc., etc. . . . A phrase has been trying to break into my memory about filthy rags of righteousness. I thought it was in Bunyan, but it is in Isaiah, 64:6."

13. *Times,* 31 Jan. 1939, 2:2.

14. CCB-HLS, 8:2, CCB to Jesse S. Reeves, 3 Mar. 1939.

15. *Times,* 11 Aug. 1940, IV, 8:5, and CCB-HLS, 9:5, CCB to FWH, 9 Sept. 1940.

16. Senator Lee. See *Times,* 16 Aug. 1940, 6:3. Stimson. CCB-HLS, 17:12, HLS to CCB, 25 Aug. 1940.

17. *Times,* 29 May 1933, 5:1. Other signers were Samuel Seabury, George W. Wickersham, Henry W. Taft, Grenville Clark, and Roscoe H. Hupper.

18. CCB-HLS, 9:1, CCB to FWH and HH, 17 May 1933; see also ibid., 14 Apr. 1933, "The other day I drafted a protest against the action of the German Government toward the bench and bar of Germany."

19. Ibid., CCB to FWH, 9 June 1933.

20. "Closed mind." Edwards (1994), 465; on economic theory, 462. Meeting Smith and Simon. CCB-HLS, 17:11, CCB to Simon, 20 May 1941. Sailing to New York with Smith on the *Olympic* and hosting a lunch for him with New York lawyers and judges—among them Cardozo, Thacher, Davis, Cravath. See CCB-HLS, 16:1, CCB to GWR, 17 and 26 Sept. 1929. F. E. Smith (from 1922, Lord Birkenhead) was lord chancellor, 1919–22; secretary of state for India, 1924–28; and John Simon (from 1940, Viscount Simon), home secretary, 1915–16 and 1935–37; foreign secretary, 1931–35; and chancellor of the Exchequer, 1937–40.

21. Edwards (1994), 498.

Note: Mary Agnes [Adamson] Hamilton, 1883–1966, had joined the Labour Party in 1914, was a Socialist, and had served on the London County Council. She had been a contributing editor to *The Economist* (1912–16) and then to *Common Sense* (1916–20). In these years she is described by the historian of *The Economist*, Edwards (1994), 498, as "the epitome of the then modern woman: cigarette-smoking, opinionated, committed to her career, absorbed in politics, and separated from her husband." After three years in Parliament, 1929–31, she served four on the board of the British Broadcasting Company. She wrote novels, biographies, and essays, the latter two usually in a chatty, name-dropping, superficial style. Before and during World War II she often reported to the British public on American affairs, and sometimes the reverse. After the war she became head of the Bureau of British Information in America and made a tour to inspect its offices and to cement relations with the American press. In these years, when in the United States, she always stopped to visit CCB and sometimes put up in his apartment. She met CCB, possibly not for the first time, during her first visit to New York, in 1923, Hamilton (1944), 230. She died in London on 10 February 1966. See *Times*, obit, 12 Feb. 1966, 25:2.

22. Hamilton (1944), 80–81.

23. CCB-HLS, 15:1, CCB to SKR, 4 Mar. 1948: "The Hotel Burlingham is about to change its name to L'hôtel des Veuves. I've had two here and now only one, but another, Mary Taussig Henderson, will come next week to take the place of Mrs. Platt."

24. Edwards (1994), 504–5.

25. CCB-TFS, CCB to LLB, 24 Sept. 1909.

26. Edwards (1995), 543: "The first had been during the South African war [1899–1902] and the second at the height of the suffragette militancy [1912–13]. (The fourth was to be during the 1956 Suez invasion, which [Donald] Tyerman's *Economist* opposed.) Francis Hirst's moral courage [in the second and third episodes] is one of the great legacies he left the paper."

27. CCB-TFS, from a memorial for FWH that CCB wrote and titled "A Victorian Liberal." It seems not to have been used, for CCB's letter to the *Times*, 27 Feb. 1953, 20:7, memorializing Hirst, is quite differently worded.

Note: On Helena Hirst. Despite having two intelligent sisters and an intelligent wife, Francis Hirst believed that women were fundamentally irrational and therefore should be denied the vote. His wife disagreed, but they had a pact that neither would take a public stand on the issue. But in private the disagreement sometimes boiled to the surface. See CCB-HLS, 9:4, A. Lawrence Lowell to CCB, 6 Dec. 1939: "I first knew them at the time she was a suffragette; and far from being suppressed by him, he seemed to be a little afraid of her breaking loose on the subject, and asked us not to refer to it at a dinner he was giving—which did not prevent somebody else doing it, and getting some lively expressions of opinion from her. And I remember the amazement, to say the least, when she admitted that she should prefer to avoid burning the house of an anti-suffragette friend, but would do so if necessary."

Later, in the excitement of a demonstration in London in 1913, she broke loose, threw a stone at a cabinet minister's window, and was arrested. The act and the publicity deeply upset FWH, who felt she had betrayed his trust. According to Hamilton (1944), 82, "Poignant at the time, this rift in the end, deepened their unity." But it required John Simon, at FWH's suggestion, to mediate between them. For CCB's recollection of this incident, see CCB-HLS, 5:12, CCB to FF, 3 Mar. 1953.

28. On 26 Sept. 1938, in a speech in Berlin, Hitler had said, referring to the Sudeten problem: "This is the last territorial demand I have to make in Europe . . . We do not want any Czechs." Text of the speech, *Times*, 27 Sept. 1938, 17:1.

29. CCB-TFS, HH to Nancy, 20 Mar. [1939].

30. CCB-HLS, 9:4, CCB to A. Lawrence Lowell, 21 Nov. 1939.

31. Ibid., FWH to CCB, 6 Sept. 1939.

32. Ibid., FWH to CCB, 23 Nov. 1939.

33. See ibid., 9:5, letters of CCB, John Stewart Bryan, president of the College of William and Mary, Nicholas Murray Butler, ex-president of Columbia, and A. Lawrence Lowell, ex-president of Harvard.

34. CCB-HLS, 9:4, CCB to FWH, 6 Dec. 1939.

35. Ibid., HH to CCB, 20 Dec. 1939.

36. Ibid., FWH to CCB, 22 Dec. 1939.

37. Ibid., 9:5, CCB to FWH, 7 Feb. 1940.

38. Ibid., copy of portion of HH letter to her daughter Gertrude, 15 Sept. 1940, sent to CCB. Doormat. Edwards (1994), 461.

39. LH-HLS, 101:3, CCB to LH, 22 Aug. 1944.

40. CCB-HLS, 14:15, SKR to CCB, 17 Dec. 1944. Hamilton was referring to her own speaking tour, but SKR was angered for the craft. See FF-LOC, container 35, CCB to FF, 23 Jan. 1945: "This got under S.K.'s skin, and his letter to me was violent."

41. CCB-HLS, 9:7, CCB to FWH and HH, 9 Jan. 1945. In May 1949, however, MAH stayed "at the Hotel Burlingham, which will be her h.q. during her visit," ibid., 15:3, CCB to SKR, 24 May 1949.

42. CCB-HLS, 14:4, SKR to CCB, 23 Feb. 1944.

43. Ibid., 16:1, GWR to CCB, 15 Oct. 1939.

44. Ibid., GWR to CCB, 26 Nov. 1939.

45. "Arrogance." Ibid., 2:14, Edwin H. Cassels to CCB, 3 Sept. 1942. Frankfurter. FF-LOC, container 34, FF to CCB, 11 Mar. 1941: "The important thing to do about the Holmes Letters is to whet the reader's appetite and make him go to the Vols. That's what your piece has done, and adequately. The only thing that I miss is a paragraph at the end conveying in your own spontaneous way the feelings aroused in you by the quality of Holmes and Pollock and more particularly the sense that the Letters gave you of Holmes that you didn't have before you read them." "Superficial." CCB-HLS, 6:17, CCB to Arthur L. Goodhart, 25 Mar. 1941.

46. CCB-HLS, 16:3, GWR to CCB, 10 Nov. 1942.

Note: On the reputation of Oliver Wendell Holmes Jr. The interest in Holmes, who in thirty years on the U.S. Supreme Court wrote more opinions, 837, than any other justice, was strengthened in 1944 with the publication of a biography, *Yankee from Olympus: Justice Holmes and His Family*, by Catherine Drinker Bowen. CCB initially was mild in his objection to the book, wondering where Bowen had discovered some facts and opinions she had put into dialogue. Thus he wrote to FF, 29 May 1944, CCB-HLS, 5:5, "I hate fictional biographies. However, it's quite entertaining." Two months later, in a letter to SKR, 18 July, ibid., 14:15, he apparently was willing to accept Bowen's unflattering portrait of Holmes's vanity, for he concluded: "Her serious offenses were (1) making out a jealous feud between O.W.H. Sr. and the judge, and (2) making Mrs. Holmes a dull person when in fact she was brilliant." Yet as the months passed, his view against the Bowen biography hardened; and in coming years he was apt to say, as he wrote to Learned Hand, "I think that the life of a Judge should be written by a lawyer or by someone who knows something of the Law," LH-HLS, 101:6, CCB to LH, 6 Nov. 1957. By then the Holmes-[Harold]Laski letters had begun to be published (1952), distressing further many who admired Holmes. CCB found the letters "over-affectionate." And his friend Mark A. DeWolfe Howe quoted with approval to him the opinion of federal district judge Charles Wyzanski that "neither Holmes nor Laski was lifted in his estimation, by these letters, from one so lavish of praise to another so obviously battening on it." See letters between Howe and CCB, CCB-HLS, 9:12, 1 and 3 Oct. 1952.

In the years 1941–57, largely because of the Holmes-Pollock letters, Bowen's biography, the Holmes-Laski letters, and the partial biography of Holmes (1957) by Mark DeWolfe Howe (son of the Howe above), the portrait of Holmes as a man, and even to some extent as a jurist, began to change—a fact causing much discussion among lawyers on both sides of the Atlantic, and one to which the elderly, like CCB, had a hard time adjusting. And with each new publication the round of letters and comment revived. What CCB, who died in 1959, might have thought of the portrayal of Holmes the man in the years following is hard to conceive. By 1989 a Holmes biographer, Sheldon M. Novick, in his preface to *Honorable Justice*, could write: "Holmes proved to be a shadowed figure, marked by the bigotry and sexism of his age, who in personal letters seemed to espouse a kind of fascist ideology. He was a violent, combative, womanizing aristocrat whose contribution to the development of law was surprisingly difficult to define." And in 1995 Leuchtenburg in his chapter "Mr. Justice Holmes and Three Generations of Imbeciles" summarized: "In truth, *Buck* v. *Bell* shows the revered 'Yankee from Olympus' at his worst: his disdain for facts (he made a point of never reading newspapers), his contempt for views divergent from his own, his indifference to citing legal precedent, his reliance on quips, and his allegiance to elite attitudes." See Leuchtenburg, *The Supreme Court* (1995), 3–25.

For other letters in CCB-HLS on this aspect of Holmes, see 19:15, CCB to Alfred North Whitehead, 19 Mar. 1941; 2:7, Nicholas Murray Butler to CCB, 25 Mar. 1941; 14:11, SKR to CCB, 19 Sept. and 4 Oct. [1941]; 9:15, CCB to Mark DeW. Howe, 15 June 1942; and 1:14, CCB to Douglas Arant, 25 Mar. 1947.

47. CCB-HLS, 16:5, CCB (after FDM's death) to GWR, 4 Feb. 1946, in which he quotes the statements from an earlier letter to him from FDM, 14 Mar. 1935. See also ibid., 17:11, CCB to Simon, 20 May 1941.

48. Ibid. 16:5, GWR to CCB, 3 Nov. 1946, suggesting "self-protective" was originally CCB's phrase.

49. Ibid., 12:13, FDM to CCB, 27 Sept. 1940. The *Jarndyce* case is the nub of Charles Dickens's novel *Bleak House*, a satire on the abuses of the old court of Chancery. After years of delay, the case, a family quarrel over the distribution of a deceased's estate, ends only after the lawyers discover their costs and fees have exhausted the estate's funds, leaving none for the heirs. Dickens's famous statement "The law is a ass, a idiot" is said by Mr. Bumble in *Oliver Twist*, chap. 51.

50. Ibid., FDM to CCB, 27 Sept. 1940.

51. Ibid., FDM to CCB, 28 Oct. 1940. For a later summary of the damage, which CCB forwarded to TDT, see TDT-YSML, 3:19, FDM to CCB, "My dear Charles," 19 May 1941. For a more detailed summary account of the damage to the Inns, see *A History of the Inns of Court*, by W. C. Richardson (Baton Rouge, La.: Claitor's Publishing Division, 1975), 472. Lincoln's Inn library was the only one of the four to survive the war intact; Gray's Inn library had the most damage.

52. CCB-HLS, 12:13, FDM to CCB, 17 Feb. 1941. His signature on this and other letters raises a question. He signed "FDMacKinnon," whereas CCB and most others apparently wrote the surname without capitalizing the *k*. See CCB's memorial tribute, *Times*, 5 Feb. 1946, 22:7. In a postscript to a letter to TDT, 19 May 1941, CCB was able to give further details about MacKinnon's loss. The son-in-law, an officer in the British air force, had been posted to Trinidad, sailed with wife and child on a merchant vessel, which had been "sunk and burnt by a German U boat." TDT-YSML, 2:9.

53. CCB-HLS, 10:1, CCB to Manley O. Hudson, 20 June 1941: See also ibid., 9:5, CCB to FWH and HH, 12 Nov. 1940: "Now we can go ahead [after reelection of FDR]. First, we must repeal the Johnson Act, which prohibits loans to debtors; next, the Cash and Carry, and then we must convoy our own ships to you, and I hope our Navy will ultimately help you directly too." And ibid., 2:16, CCB to Tuan-Sheng Chien, 13 Jan. 1941.

54. CCB-HLS, 16:2, CCB to GWR, 3 Sept. 1941. CCB had joined the ABA in 1910. See also FF-LOC, container 34, CCB to FF, 22 Sept. 1941, and CCB to FF, 23 Sept., and FF to CCB, 2 Oct. For John W. Davis's part in the resolution, see CCB-HLS, 16:2, CCB to GWR, 7 Oct. 1941. For Davis's love of England and eagerness to support it, including its empire, see Harbaugh (1973), 423–28. The rebuilding of the Inns. ABA *Annual Report, 1942*, 349; and *Annual Report, 1945*, 210; and *Annual Report, 1946*, 38. See also *Times*, 14 Mar. 1947, 21:1, reporting Davis appointed "chairman of the Association Committee on Restoration of Libraries of Inns of Courts." The committee raised a total, after expenses, of $41,107.82. See ABA *Annual Reports, 1950*, 489. Reasons for why the amount was so small are speculative, but five seem likely: (1) The destruction at the Inns of Court was more gradual and less dramatic than the torching of the Louvain library in World War I; (2) the destruction of other buildings in England, such as the cathedral at Coventry, seemed even more barbaric; (3) many American lawyers, their careers interrupted by three or four years of armed service, had less in hand to give; (4) inflation was ravaging the value of money; and (5) the huge amount of statutory law passed in the New Deal and war bills dwarfed the importance of common law and its hereditary tie to England.

55. CCB-HLS, 17:6, CCB to SS, 24 May 1940.

56. Heckscher (1978), 212, thinks FHL would have liked the post; although see 215; but Kessner (1989), 462, thinks not, and gives examples of FHL eyeing more national positions.

57. Conference of Mayors. A leading founder was Frank Murphy, mayor of Detroit (1930–33), governor of Michigan (1937–38), and associate justice, U.S. Supreme Court (1940–49). La Guardia's national celebrity while mayor greatly increased the status and influence of the conference.

58. On FDR. Farley (1948), 152. On FHL, see summary in Garrett (1961), 267.

59. SMI-COH, 144, 161; PW-COH, "Additional Material," 7; CCB-COH, 36.

60. News story of the appointment, with no hint of the storm to come. *Times*, 27 Feb. 1940, 19:2. The hostile *Sun* editorial, 28 Feb. 1940, 22:1. Bishop Manning's letters to newspapers. *Times*, 1 Mar. 1940, 23:6, 13 Mar. 1940, 20:2. Sermons, in St. Bartholomew's Church, *Times*, 11 Mar. 1940, 17:4, and in Cathedral of St. John the Divine, *Times*, 25 Mar. 1940, 18:5. Manning is echoed by Monsignor Francis J. Walsh, speaking to the city police force, *Times*, 11 Mar. 1940, 17:4.

61. Bertrand Russell, *Marriage and Morals* (New York: Liveright, 1929), 58, 106.

62. "Companionate marriage." Ibid., 163. "University life." Bertrand Russell, *Education and the Modern World* (New York: Norton, 1932), 119–20. "All sex relations." Russell, *Marriage and Morals* (1929), 165. Christianity. 48.

63. In 1929 Manning had persuaded President Butler of Columbia to withdraw an invi-

tation to Russell to lecture, see R. W. Clark (1976), 432. Manning quoted, *Times*, 1 Mar. 1940, 23:6. FF's opinion was that Russell was "an extinct volcano, so far as responsible and stimulating thought goes . . . [F]or the last few years he has lived off his old fat and most of it has turned into rancid butter . . . But of course, when Manning raises the issue that he does raise, it's a horse of a different color and no concession can be made to him on his obscurantist line." See FF-LOC, container 34, FF to CCB, 12 Mar. 1940.

64. CCB to FHL, and FHL to Manning, quoted in Heckscher (1978), 272.

65. *Herald Tribune*, 15 Mar. 1940, 26:4; PW-PW Jr., CCB note to PW, 15 Mar. 1940.

66. E.g., some Russell views in *Marriage and Morals* that Manning did not quote: "I believe marriage to be the best and most important relation that can exist between two human beings," 143; "I do not recognize in easy divorce a solution to the troubles of marriage," 142; "But in this [the "gospel of work and economic success"] as in all human matters a balance is necessary," 120; "The threats of parents and nurses as to the bad consequences of masturbation have been shown by psycho-analysis to be a very frequent cause of nervous disorders," 103; "There exists a vast mass of knowledge on homosexuality obtained by students in continental countries . . . not allowed to be disseminated in England," 110; on "free love": "When people no longer feel any moral barrier against sexual intercourse . . . they get into the habit of dissociating sex from serious emotion and from feelings of affection," 127.

He expressed his views on masturbation and homosexuality in *Education and the Modern World*, 120: "Masturbation after puberty, while it does not do as much harm as conventional moralists pretend, undoubtedly has certain grave evils. It tends to make a man self-centered and unadventurous, and sometimes it makes him incapable of normal intercourse. It is possible that homosexual relations with other boys would not be very harmful if they were tolerated, but even then there is the danger lest they should interfere with the growth of normal sexual life later on."

Manning's letter to the *Times*, 1 Mar. 1940, 23:6.

67. CCB-HLS, 11:10, CCB to FHL, 25 Mar. 1940.

68. Moorehead (1992), 432, notes that what prompted Mrs. Kay's suit is not clear. Mrs. Kay acted with notable speed and was ready to start her suit by mid-March, later explaining, "I don't want the minds of my children contaminated." At the time many persons thought her an agent for others. If so, the principals have never been revealed. Moorehead also states, 430, "For years he [Russell] had been allowed to pronounce more or less unchallenged, on the faults of American capitalism, and the stranglehold of business interests over the universities . . . It was now the turn of all those who had felt impotent before his mockery and criticism to fight back."

69. Expunging Martin Luther. R. W. Clark (1976), 471–72. *Matter of Kay v. Board of Higher Education, N.Y. City*, 173 Misc. Reports, 943–53; 259 Appellate Division, 879, 1000. "Most compelling." 947, 953.

70. See Dewey and Kallen, eds. (1941), 79. From the chapter "Trial by Ordeal, New Style," by Walton H. Hamilton: Judge McGeehan "sat as a judge to hear motions, not to conduct a trial. Before him was only one motion—to dismiss an action against the Board of Higher Education. Without further ado, he reserved the motion, held trial, rendered judgement, and closed the case. Lost was the immemorial right to answer charges filed; ignored were objections to irregularities of process. The urge against free thought left no time for the etiquette of stately adjudication."

Judge McGeehan's view of the action was different: "The court has afforded the respondent [corporation counsel] an opportunity to interpose an answer, but the respondent has declined . . . [informing] the court that its defense is to be limited to the question of law raised by the cross-motion to dismiss the petition." In addition, the court allowed three briefs to be filed as *amici curiae* in support of the appointment. These, according to McGeehan, argued that "citizenship was not an issue and the appointment should not be disturbed because it would be an interference with 'academic freedom,'" *Matter of Kay v. Board*, 944.

Russell silent. Moorehead (1992), 433–34.

71. On the decision. Alan Ryan, *John Dewey and the High Tide of American Liberalism* (New York: Norton, 1995), 308. CCB-HLS, 11:10, CCB to FHL, 17 May 1940.

72. Stimson. E. E. Morison (1960), 202. FHL. Heckscher (1978), 271, and Kessner (1989), 288. CCB, GC-DCL, Ser. 4, box 1, CCB to GC, 20 Sept. 1931: "It would be well for you to look into his present outlook on life so far as sex is, and it is, a big part of life. I fancy he is in the dangerous 'fifties,' *not 40s* . . ." The applicant of dubious reputation, E. F. Gay, was not hired.

73. Heckscher (1978), 274.

74. CCB in a longhand memorandum he handed to Grenville Clark on 11 April 1940, see GC-DCL, ser. 4, box 1, typed copy prepared by GC. Presumably CCB hoped to encourage Chanler by reaching him through a lawyer Chanler greatly respected and whose firm was becoming involved in the case (see n. 76 below).

If I were a member of the Board of Higher Education I should insist on appeal unless Russell should withdraw (as he should to save the College of the City of New York from a continuing and recurring stench).

I tried to prevent W.C.C. [Chanler] from saying that he had control of case to extent of determining whether it should be appealed.

Also I think he should not prophesy result of appeal for his own reputation.

And I wish to protect him from charge that he is the Mayor's tool.

75. Heckscher (1978), 274.

76. Ibid., 273, quoting CCB to FHL, 18 Apr. 1940. In several respects, however, the case did not end so neatly or promptly as the mayor implied. Students had protested his actions, distinguished men and women had criticized him, and there had been a meeting at Carnegie Hall urging him to restore the post's salary to the budget. Further, the bizarre episode and court case made finding a new president for the college difficult, for candidates feared political or ecclesiastical interference. See CCB-HLS, 11:10, Morris R. Cohen to CCB, 7 Jan. 1941, and CCB to FHL, 22 Jan. 1941.

Also, the Board of Education, dissatisfied with the corporation counsel's refusal to appeal, chose to oppose the mayor's wish and to be represented by lawyers from the firm Root, Clark, Bushby, and Ballantine, who had agreed to serve without charge. But this effort was dropped when it became clear that even if the Court of Appeals agreed to hear the case, it could not be decided in time for Russell to take up the post.

77. A biographer. Hecksher (1978), 274; but Kessner (1989) 475, ascribes FHL's actions wholly to politics.

78. CCB-HLS, 11:10, Geoffrey Parsons to CCB, 11 Dec. 1939.

79. Ibid., Dr. George Baehr to CCB, 18 May 1940.

80. Ibid., FHL to CCB, 16 May 1940.

81. Ibid., CCB verses to FHL, 16 May 1940. "Nordic." The mayor often joked that despite his heritage and tantrums he was at heart "a cool calm Nordic."

82. TDT-YSML, 2:13, CCB to TDT, 23 Mar. 1939; TDT's reply, ibid., 24 Mar., "I believe the list is made up for this year." CCB repeats suggestion, ibid., to TDT, 27 Nov. 1939. Several years earlier, after FHL's landslide reelection as a reform mayor, CCB had suggested to Grenville Clark, then a member of the Harvard Corporation, that Harvard

award an honorary degree to La Guardia. See GC-DCL, ser. 4, box 1, CCB to GC, 5 Dec. 1937. But no action followed.

83. CCB-HLS, 17:6, CCB to SS, 24 May 1940. "Cuddling up" to FDR. CCB-COH, 38.

84. CCB-HLS, 9:5, CCB to FWH and HH, 17 Feb. 1940.

85. On Stimson's appointment, for which Grenville Clark was the moving force, see E. E. Morison (1960), 479–86; also Hodgson (1990), 213–24, on HLS's record as "the American Churchill," 220. "Best man . . . mischievous," CCB-HLS, 16:1, CCB to GWR, 16 July 1941.

86. CCB-HLS, 16:1, CCB to GWR, 10 July 1940.

87. The amplified voice shouting into a microphone in the hall's basement came from Mayor Kelly's superintendent of sewers, "a leather-lunged, pot-bellied little man." See description in Burns (1956), 427–30. On Ilo B. Wallace's ordeal, see Martin, *Madam Secretary* (1976), 549 n. 25, citing Frances Perkins-COH book 7, 464. Sherwood (1948), 179.

88. Sherwood (1948), 201: "I burn inwardly whenever I think of those words 'again— and again—and again.'"

89. *Times*, 1 Nov. 1940, 19:4, and see Mitgang (1963), 354–55. FHL, "pained" by the speech, replied that SS was motivated by "obsessive hatred" of FDR, and denied that Walker was an issue in the campaign, *Times*, 2 Nov. 1940, 8:6. CCB expressed his view of the Walker appointment and SS's reaction to it in a letter, 3 Nov. 1940, to Raymond Daniels, a writer for the *Times*: "The Bishop (Seabury) is still fiercely angry with LaG. for appointing Jimmie Walker, and has come out with a blast against both F.D.R. and LaG. I tell him that as both Dubinski [labor union leader] and the employer asked for J.W. (no doubt at F.D.R.'s suggestion) that is enough; but that doesn't go down with S.S. He never forgets or forgives wrong doing or doers. I fancy F.D.R. suggested the appointment to please Farley, who doesn't forget that Jimmie made him a Boxing Commissioner."

90. Assault, on steps of the Detroit City Hall. *Times*, 22 Oct. 1940, 1:4. Owens sued for $350,000, *Times*, 2 Nov. 1940, 8:6. Presumably the suit was either settled or dropped, for it disappears from view.

91. *Times*, 21 Oct. 1940, 10:8; letter questioning CCB's opinion, *Times*, 29 Oct. 1940, 16:6; his reply, *Times*, 31 Oct. 1940, 22:6. CCB-HLS, 12:13, CCB to FDM, 25 Oct. 1940.

92. E.g., CCB-HLS, 11:3, CCB to Raymond Daniels of *Times*, 3 Nov. 1940: "The best reason for giving FDR another term is that nobody knows whether W. can lead his Party, or Congress." LH-HLS, 101:2, CCB to LH, 23 Sept. 1940: "[B]ut the other kind of defense, thro' aid to England I'm sure F.D.R. is better at than W. as a leader of opinion and a shrewd politician." And still earlier, CCB-HLS, 6:12, CCB to Joseph R. Hamlen, 14 Dec. 1939: "I certainly am against a third term for F.D.R., or anybody else, and I would not vote for Roosevelt if he were nominated *if I could avoid it*. But I feel confident that F.D.R. will not seek or accept a nomination."

93. TDT-YSML, 5:48. This copy of the statement is typed, two-page, double-spaced, without addressees, date, or signatures. By what means and how widely the statement was distributed is not clear. Heckscher (1978), 288, refers to La Guardia's letter to the Fusion leaders: "It was a sad, unnecessary communication, at once defensive and provocative, the outpouring of a mind brought to the edge of despair." The despair was occasioned by La Guardia's increasingly isolated political position in city and national politics.

94. TDT-YSML, 5:48, FHL to Fusion leaders, 26 Nov. 1940.

95. CCB-HLS, 11:10, CCB to FHL, 5 Dec. 1940. FF-LOC, container 34, CCB to FF, 20 Dec. 1940, states: "LaG's letter to Thacher, et al, was quite a blackguardly piece. He included S.S., who was not signatory of the document."

96. CCB-HLS, 11:10, CCB to FHL, 22 Jan. 1941.

97. See tables in Melvin G. Holli, *The American Mayor: The Best and The Worst Big-City Leaders* (University Park: Pennsylvania State University Press, 1999). By polls taken of "scholar-experts" in 1985 and 1993, La Guardia in both, by a large margin, ranked first for the periods 1820–1985 and 1820–1993, New York's only mayor to place among the ten best. Among the ten worst in the 1993 survey New York had three: number 3, James Walker, 1926–32; number 6, A. Oakey Hall (Boss Tweed's mayor), 1868–72; and number 9, Fernando Wood, 1855–58 and 1860–62. In the 1985 poll, they had ranked, respectively, fourth, third, and ninth.

98. CCB-HLS, 11:10, CCB to FHL, 22 Jan. 1941.

22. New York City in Wartime

Chief sources for this chapter other than contemporary newspapers and the Burlingham collections are: Thomas Kessner, *Fiorello H. La Guardia and the Making of New York* (New York: McGraw Hill, 1989); August Heckscher with Phyllis Robinson, *When La Guardia Was Mayor: New York's Legendary Years* (New York: Norton, 1978); Charles Garrett, *The La Guardia Years: Machine and Reform Politics in New York City* (New Brunswick, N.J.; Rutgers University Press, 1961); Edith S. Isaacs, *Love Affair with a City: The Story of Stanley M. Isaacs* (New York: Random House, 1967), and Stanley M. Isaacs, Oral History, Columbia University; Warren Moscow, *Politics in the Empire State* (New York: Knopf, 1948; repr. New York: Greenwood, 1979).

1. WPA-Maritime (1941), 297–303.

2. For summaries of transit unification and fare problems, see Garrett (1961), 210–18 and its nn; Kessner (1989), 459–61; and Heckscher (1978), 264–69, 377–79. See n. 60 below.

3. *Times*, 9 Jan. 1941, 1:6, with headline "Hints He May Not Finish Term."

4. Without pay and description of the job. See Kessner (1989), 491–95, 492.

5. Dedication of the airfield. *Times*, 5 Jan. 1941, 1:2.

6. PW-PW Jr., CCB to PW, 27 Sept. 1941.

7. Fusion leaders declare. *Times*, 22 July 1941, 1:1. Tammany. *Times*, 30 July 1941, 11:1.

8. Reuben Lazarus-COH, 206. Moscow (1948), 220, considered Lazarus the "leading expert on home-rule questions." TED announces. *Times*, 14 Sept. 1941, 1:1; *Herald Tribune*, 14 Sept. 1941, reporting La Guardia's comment, "I am just too busy running the city to think about it."

9. Moses. *Times*, 16 Sept. 1941, 1:1, and text of speech; 24:2; *Herald Tribune*, 16 Sept. 1941, 15:1. He twitted La Guardia on his "cussedness." Willkie. *Times*, 16 Sept. 1941, 1:1; and *Herald Tribune*, 16 Sept. 1941, 1:2, recording FHL comment, "This is the most generous and sporting attitude taken in politics for a long while."

10. CCB-HLS, 2:11, CCB to Kenneth Dayton (FHL's budget director), 7 Nov. 1941; and FF-LOC, container 34, CCB to FF, 5 Nov.

11. "Trivial." CCB-HLS, 16:2, CCB to GWR, 20 Dec. 1941. "Old horse." Ibid., 9:6, CCB to FMH and HH, 11 Aug. 1941. In a letter to TDT, 7 Aug. 1941, TDT-YSML, 2:2, CCB wrote as a postscript: "It is pretty good fun to be triumviring with you and the Bishop, a last kick of a dying horse."

12. For some accounts of the decline of the Fusion organization and power, see Garrett (1961), 268, 314–19, and Kessner (1989), 393–98.

13. Isaacs (1967), 46–53. This is Mrs. Isaacs's account. SMI's appears in SMI-COH, 92–95: Gerson "seemed to be particularly able and was willing to come to one of the jobs in

my office at a very low salary, so I decided to take him. He was a Communist—a member of the Communist Party. This was in 1937. I didn't regard that as a disqualification. I mentioned all my appointments before I made them in final form to Kenneth Simpson [Republican New York County leader]. He saw no objection to it. I mentioned all my appointments at one time or another to Mayor La Guardia, and he made no objection to it. Nobody raised any objection to that appointment. When it was made, however, both the *World Telegram* and the *Journal* began to attack me . . . I felt that, until membership in the Communist Party was proved actually subversive and while it was recognized as a legal party, membership in that party had no right to bar a man. So I stood firm."

Note: CCB has considerable correspondence on "Gerson," starting with CCB-HLS, 22:3, CCB to B. N. Cardozo, 4 Mar. 1938: "Our friend, Stanley Isaacs, has got himself into a bad box appointing a Communist. Grenville Clark and I are trying to persuade him to appoint a committee to find out whether it is possible to be a member of the Communist Party and yet take, without reserve, the oath of allegiance to the U.S.A." But nothing seems to have come of this. In 1941 CCB corresponds with TDT, see below, and in CCB-HLS, 2:11, has telegrams to Joseph M. Price, 6 Aug., and from SS, 16 Aug; and ibid., 10:5, CCB to William H. Allen, 9 Nov. 1949.

Heckscher (1978), 305, states: "One cannot altogether lack sympathy for the mayor, though his manner of dropping Isaacs seemed unnecessarily harsh. Mrs. Isaacs, whose account is understandably biased . . ." Yet Heckscher quotes it, seemingly with approval. She ends it with a long quotation from George Britt's much read article "What Has Happened to La Guardia," *New Republic*, 9 Mar. 1942, 342: "When the slate of his running mates was being made up for the last election, the Mayor permitted the dropping of Isaacs without lifting a finger in his defense—a surrender to his enemies which, in retrospect, appears as needless as it was costly . . . The Mayor's present position in local politics is a headache, and perhaps not primarily to himself . . . If his grip is weakened for any reason . . . it is the tragedy of New York and the dimming of a hope given to decent government in every city. La Guardia will have only himself to blame, the least sturdy and mature elements in his own character, if he does not look squarely at himself as others see him, if he does not hear the pleading of his best friends, and reoccupy a position in harmony with his past."

Britt states that the removal of Isaacs was unnecessary; and CCB, in CCB-HLS, 2:20, letter to SS and TDT, 15 Aug. 1941, reports as Isaacs's opinion: "If you two, I [CCB] and the Mayor had worked as hard to get him nominated as we have worked to get him to withdraw, he would have won out in both primaries." The foundation of that support, however, needed to be the mayor, who seems to have been unwilling to make the fight. Perhaps La Guardia was politically wise, for even with Isaacs off the ticket, in the last week before the election James Farley, the New York State Democratic chairman, was calling the mayor "Red La Guardia," and in a radio speech said, "La Guardia is completely dominated by Communists, reds, and promoters of subversive activities." See *Herald Tribune*, 2 Nov. 1941, 1:2, and *Times*, 2 Nov. 1941, 46:3, and 3 Nov. 1941, 13:1. Also Heckscher (1978), 308; and Farley (1948), 363.

14. TDT-YSML, 2:2, CCB to TDT, 7 Aug. 1941.

15. CCB-HLS, 10:5, CCB to William H. Allen, 9 Nov. 1949. Ibid., 17:33, TDT to CCB, 16 Aug. 1941: "I think you must have done the trick with Isaacs. Certainly everything indicated he would not withdraw when I left town at four on Thursday. My efforts were to keep Nathan from withdrawing. He will thank us for our advice, but I'm afraid Isaacs will never do that . . . I'm sorry for that because I think he is a fine man and sincerely resolved to do the right regardless of consequences to himself or anyone else. I do hope he will be of great service to the City in the future and that the Mayor will wish to have his aid."

16. SMI's withdrawal statement only an hour and a half before the deadline. See *Times*, 16 Aug. 1941, 1:3. SS and CCB's on the withdrawal. *Times*, 17 Aug., 24:1. "Falsehoods . . . at election time." Perhaps Farley's in the campaign's final week were the worst, see n. 13 above.

17. Isaacs (1967), 51, and LH's tribute, 163: "I think I need not tell you how much I have admired your public career, especially the incorruptible courage with which you faced abuse and misunderstanding."

18. CCB-HLS, 10:5, SMI to CCB, 22 Oct. 1941. See also SMI to CCB, sometime during the election campaign, quoted in Isaacs (1967), 51.

19. FDR-FDRL, PPF, 1169, Presidential Memorandum for the Press Conference 24 Oct. 1941, with copy (now missing) of telegram CCB to FF, 23 Oct. Original in FF-LOC, container 34.

20. Ibid. Also CCB telegram to FDR, 25 Oct. 1941.

21. Bishop Manning's endorsement. *Herald Tribune*, 31 Oct. 1941, 21:3.

22. Governor Lehman's speech in the Bronx. Text in *Times*, 28 Oct. 1941, 20:2.

23. FHL's mockery of Governor Lehman, *Herald Tribune*, 28 Oct. 1941, 12:2. Lehman's response, closing a Democratic rally at the Brooklyn Academy of Music, "Regardless of any other considerations," Mayor La Guardia "has shown himself unworthy of being Mayor of New York," *Herald Tribune*, 1 Nov., 1:2. CCB-HLS, 16:2, CCB to GWR, 20 Dec. 1941, refers to the episode as La Guardia's "vulgar outburst." See Kessner (1989), 498–99.

24. CCB-HLS, 2:11, CCB to Kenneth Dayton, 7 Nov. 1941, suggests that the "unbridled tongue" cost FHL only 5,000 votes. In FF-LOC, container 34, CCB to FF, 5 Nov. 1941, he writes: "I don't think LaG's vulgarity played a very large part, but it hurt him with *nice* people a good deal." CCB's estimate of 5,000 votes is by so much the lowest, it seems possibly a typographical error. Geoffrey Parsons of the *Herald Tribune* suggests "tens of thousands," ibid., Parsons to CCB, 17 Nov. 1941. Garrett (1961), 273, was able to interview Louis Weintraub and Joseph D. McGoldrick, both members of La Guardia's administration. Weintraub told of Fusion leaders' efforts to persuade La Guardia to apologize, and McGoldrick believed "that La Guardia easily lost a quarter of a million votes by his remarks and that he could have lost the election had they been made earlier in the campaign." See also Moscow (1948), 235. On FHL's relations with the press, see Heckscher (1978), 334–37.

25. *Times*, Nov. 1941, quoted in Heckscher (1978), 312–13.

26. People leaving civil service and the city's workforce. See Garrett (1961), 281, citing Civil Service Commission Report, 1 July 1942 to 30 June 1943, 3.

27. Heckscher (1978), 312.

28. Morgan. Ibid., 322–23; Garrett (1961), 280–81; Kessner (1989), 503–4. Morgan's successor was Daniel P. Wooley, a retired vice president of Standard Brands. See *Times*, 27 Jan. 1942, 10:8.

29. CCB-HLS, 11:10, CCB to FHL, 13 Feb. 1942.

30. Kern. Heckscher (1978), 325–30; Garrett (1961), 286–90; and Kessner (1989), 487–89, 506–9. In the course of "the Kern affair" FHL, as in the Bertrand Russell case, ordered corporation counsel W. C. Chanler not to take an appeal; see Kessner (1989), 507.

31. TDT-YSML, 2:14, CCB to TDT, 15 Oct. 1941. PW-PW Jr., PW to CCB, 30 Sept. 1941, "The Directorship, I believe, is now an embarrassment to him and will become increasingly so." CCB-HLS, 16:2, CCB to GWR, 20 Dec. 1941: "We [SS, TDT, PW, CCB] are now urging LaG. to resign the Directorship of Civilian Defense."

32. CCB-HLS, 11:10, CCB to FHL, 13 Feb. 1942.

33. CCB-COH, 40. On the subway unification and fare. Heckscher (1978), 377–79; Garrett (1961), 210–19; and Kessner (1989), 459–61. See CCB-HLS, 17:12, CCB to FHL, 31 Mar. 1945, 5 Apr., and FHL to CCB, 2 Apr.

34. CCB-HLS, 17:12, CCB to HLS, 21 Apr. 1942.

35. Ibid., 11:10, CCB to FHL, 21 Apr. 1942.

36. Ibid., 17:12, HLS to CCB, 23 Apr. 1942.

37. Ibid., 11:10, FHL to CCB, 25 Apr. 1942.

38. Ibid., 11:10, CCB to FHL, 9 Nov. 1942.

39. TDT-YSML, 2:14, CCB to TDT, 10 Dec. 1942.

40. Windels suggests TDT. FF-LOC, container 35, CCB to FF, 25 Jan. 1943. TDT-YSML, 2:14, CCB to TDT, 16 Dec. 1942. FHL mentions TDT as a desirable candidate for mayor. See *Times*, 14 May 1945, 1:2.

41. TDT appointed to court. *Times*, 13 May 1943, 23:6. CCB thought the appointment "the best imaginable." See FF-LOC, container 35, CCB to FF, 13 May 1943. TDT was elected to a full term on the court in November 1943, serving until he resigned in 1949 and returned to his law firm in New York, Simpson, Thacher & Bartlett.

Note: TDT's first wife, Eunice, whom CCB knew well, had died suddenly of a stroke in January 1943 (*Times*, obit, 20 Jan., 19:2), and two and a half years later TDT married a widow from Philadelphia, Eleanor M. Lloyd (*Times*, 21 July 1945, 8:8), whom CCB did not know and whose interests seem not to have included him. So even when TDT resigned from the court and returned to New York City, CCB's friendship with him was not so close as before. On CCB's liking of the first wife and Thacher family, see CCB-HLS, 12:14, CCB to Frank MacKinnon, 20 Jan. 1943.

TDT died 12 November 1950, and his second wife and widow arranged a funeral service for him that in its grandeur, while possibly appropriate, struck some of his closest friends as uncharacteristic of the man. The service, in St. James Episcopal Church, New York, had three presiding clergy, some fifty honorary pallbearers, including ex-president Herbert Hoover, FF, the two Hands, and Swan, and such a collection of distinguished judges as is seldom seen in one place; also many of the city's leading lawyers, including CCB. The great names, announced in advance, drew a crowd of more than a thousand. See *Herald Tribune*, 14 Nov. 1943, 21:4, and 15 Nov. 1943, 33:6.

Perhaps what attracted CCB and others most in TDT was best expressed by the Century Club memorialist: "But he was more than a successful publicist and jurist. He was an entirely reliable man. When there were heads to be broke he was never afraid, and when there were defeats to be taken he was never wanting. He had a capacity to inspire confidence that was entirely out of this world. Men would follow him, confide in him, and work and fight for him in the happy and unquestioning assurance that they were doing right. And he never let them down." *Century Yearbook 1951*, 89–91.

42. CCB-HLS, 11:11, CCB to FHL, 17 May 1943. Wilkinson sworn in. *Times*, 8 June 1943, 9:5, and 16 July 1943, 19:3.

43. Quoted in Kessner (1989), 542, citing PPF 1376, FDR Papers-Hyde Park, FHL to FDR, 3 Feb. 1943.

44. *Herald Tribune*, 28 Mar. 1943, 1:4. See ibid., 29 Mar., 6:2, "Mayor Teases Public on Plan to Enter Army," and editorial that same day, 12:2, "Enough is enough." The coyness at City Hall and in Washington was beginning to hurt the city.

45. Ostertag bill. See *Herald Tribune*, 16 Mar. 1943, 12:1, and Garrett (1961), 282–83; Kessner (1989), 542–43; and CCB-HLS, 11:11, CCB to FHL, 15 Mar. 1943. Moscow (1948), 205–6: The bill "was a conspiracy, participated in by the Mayor, Governor Dewey, and three principal leaders of the Legislature, to keep the fusion administration in control in New York City. The purpose was admirable, and the methods rotten. No one, not even the members who voted for the bill, had an inkling of what was going on until, weeks after the Governor had signed the measure, his press secretary let the story out so that the pub-

lic mind would be somewhat prepared for the expected events. La Guardia's commission never came through . . ."

46. CCB-HLS, 11:11, FHL to CCB, 17 Mar. 1943.

47. Ibid., 17:6, CCB to SS, 31 Mar. 1943.

48. Kessner (1989), 543.

49. CCB-HLS, 17:6, CCB to SS, 31 Mar. 1943.

50. Ibid., 17:6, SS to CCB, 1 Apr. 1943.

51. Ibid., 17:2, HLS to CCB, 30 Mar. 1943. The letter's date suggests that CCB wrote to HLS at least as early as 29 March and apparently had done so without informing SS or any of "the Brethren." He knew TDT's view, however, for TDT had written him on 10 March: "He [FHL] asked me if I would write to Stimson and ask him to do something for him, to which I replied that if he was looking for a job I would write Stimson and tell him not to give it to him." TDT-YSML, 18:346, TDT to CCB, 10 Mar. 1943.

For FF's view from Washington of what happened—HLS simply told FHL to go back to City Hall and govern the country's most important city—see CCB-HLS, 5:11, FF to CCB, 29 Sept. 1952. In stating that, however, FF asked CCB if he had anything to do with the episode, and CCB admitted only that he had written HLS, with nothing about what he had said or his enclosures. FF-LOC, container 36, CCB to FF, 1 Oct. 1952.

52. CCB-HLS, 17:12, CCB to HLS, 2 Apr. 1943.

53. See *Herald Tribune* stories, 27 Mar. 1943, 1:6. FDR press conference, "baffling." *Herald Tribune* 7 Apr. 1943, 1:4. FHL trying to be lighthearted. 10 Apr. 1943, 12:7. Similarly in *Times*, chiefly 7 Apr. 1943, 1:6.

54. Stimson. *Herald Tribune*, 9 Apr. 1943, 1:5; and *Times*, 9 Apr. 1943, 1:6.

55. CCB-HLS, 11:11, CCB to FHL, 13 Apr. 1943.

56. Ibid.

57. CCB-COH, 38.

58. CCB-HLS, 11:11, CCB to FHL, 22 Apr. 1943; and FHL's reply, 14 May; and CCB's to FHL, 17 May.

59. Letter of Complaint issued February 1944. Discussed and quoted in Kessner (1989), 546–48.

60. CCB and others refuse to sign. See Kessner (1989), 547, citing CCB to John Haynes Holmes, 24 Sept. 1943.

61. PW-COH, "Additional Material," 10–11.

62. CCB-HLS, 11:11, CCB to FHL, 31 Mar. 1945.

63. Speech. *Times*, 7 May 1945, 1:1. Biographers disagree on its tone. Heckscher (1978), 397, quotes the *Herald Tribune* with approval: it was "annoying, gracious entertaining, and courageous." Kessner (1989), 569, calls it "a sad, silly, troubling broadcast, especially for those who remembered a different La Guardia." On FHL's lack of support in any party, see Garrett (1961), 291–94. Though FHL was elected mayor three times on the Republican ticket, he never supported a Republican candidate for top state or national office, see Moscow (1948), 27–28.

64. Kessner (1989), 566.

65. CCB-HLS, 9:7, CCB to FWH and HH, 23 June 1945.

23. The Theory and Practice of Judicial Appointments

Chief sources for this chapter, other than contemporary newspapers and the Burlingham collections, are the Franklin D. Roosevelt Papers, in the FDR Library, at Hyde Park, New

York. On Mandelbaum, Milton S. Gould, *The Witness Who Spoke with God and Other Tales from the Courthouse* (New York: Viking, 1979). On nomination of Black, William E. Leuchtenburg, *The Supreme Court Reborn: The Constitutional Revolution in the Age of Roosevelt* (New York: Oxford University Press, 1995). On nominations of Murphy and Rutledge, Francis Biddle, *In Brief Authority* (Garden City, N.Y.: Doubleday, 1962). For much relating to associate and later Chief Justice Stone, Alpheus Thomas Mason, *Harlan Fiske Stone: Pillar of the Law* (New York: Viking, 1956); and for much on Douglas, his two books, *Go East, Young Man: The Early Years; The Autobiography of William O. Douglas* (New York: Random House, 1974) and *The Court Years, 1939–1975; The Autobiography of William O. Douglas* (New York: Random House, 1980), and Bruce Allen Murphy, *Wild Bill: The Legend and Life of William O. Douglas* (New York: Random House, 2003).

1. CCB-HLS, 16:4, CCB to GWR, 17 Apr. 1945. CCB wrote this opinion five days after FDR's death, and went on to say of him: "But he was a great man all the same, and his instincts and hunches were worth all the reasoning of a wilderness of philosophers." Others disappointed in FDR's judicial appointments: e.g., Thomas and Blanshard (1932), 103, 178, and Bellush (1955), 154–55: "Shortly thereafter, when respected Joseph M. Proskauer retired from the State Supreme Court bench, Roosevelt designated Joseph F. Crater, another Curry choice, to the vacant post. Crater's appointment was an affront to Al Smith, who had originally suggested the highly esteemed Bernard L. Sheintag, deemed by many liberals as the best choice the Governor could have made. Roosevelt had again selected a relatively unknown member of the Bar, unknown except to Tammany." Also Bellush (1955), 281: "Until 1932 he designated Tammany nominees to the judiciary in New York City." See Hurst (1950), 99–100; Burns (1956), 120–21; Freidel (1956), 91; and Schlesinger (1960), 3:447–49, on FDR's difficulties with federal district judges enjoining officials from executing federal laws. Aside from FDR's effort to pack the Supreme Court, there is remarkably little discussion of his judicial appointments, an indication perhaps of how low most scholars and the public have ranked the subject. Hurst (1950), 334, lays the difficulty of tracing individual creativeness in attempts to improve the judiciary partially to the subject's lack of general interest.

2. FDR's early years practicing law in New York. He passed the bar examination in 1907 without having completed the requirements for a degree from Columbia Law School, and entered the office of Carter, Ledyard, and Milburn, a Wall Street firm, as an unpaid clerk. After a year he was given a salary and worked mostly for the firm's partner, Edmund Baylies, on admiralty matters. At that time CCB first met him, while taking depositions in a case in which FDR represented the opponents. Years later, on a visit to FDR in the White House, as CCB related to a friend, the president recalled the incident: "Do you remember once you said to me, 'You like ships and sailors. Why don't you come over with us and be a real admiralty lawyer?'" Whereupon FDR "let out a loud guffaw and said, 'That might have changed my career, don't you think so?'" But, added CCB, "he wasn't much interested in the law." CCB-HLS, 16:4, CCB to GWR, 17 Apr. 1945, and Davis (1972), 208–14.

In 1910 FDR left the Carter firm to run on the Democratic ticket for New York state senator in his home district, Dutchess County. Though the county was predominantly Republican, it had a Democratic majority in the city of Poughkeepsie upon which to build, and somewhat to everyone's surprise, he won the election. Shortly thereafter his friend Langdon P. Marvin invited him to join the firm of Marvin and [Henry] Hooker, a two-partner firm on Wall Street. Though FDR worked only part-time (when he was not in Albany or otherwise politicking), the firm became Marvin, Hooker, and Roosevelt. In 1912 President Wilson appointed him assistant secretary of the navy (serving under Josephus Daniels), and though he was barred from the practice of law while holding the federal office, his name could remain in the firm while he was on leave of absence, which it did.

Meanwhile, in 1916 Hooker resigned from the firm to join the army, and Marvin, left without an active partner, merged with Emmet and Parish, from which Parish was withdrawing to practice alone. The new firm became Emmet, Marvin & Roosevelt, with FDR a partner in name only. Following the election of Harding in November 1920 and the defeat of the Cox-[F. D.] Roosevelt ticket, FDR returned to New York, starting work for the first time in January 1921. He still, however, worked only part-time, generally in the afternoon and exclusively on work that he brought to the firm. In the mornings he worked for the Fidelity and Deposit Company of Maryland, of which he was a vice president. That summer he contracted polio, and for several years thereafter was mostly at home or in Warm Springs, Georgia, doing little or no legal work; he formally resigned from the firm in September 1924, after which it became Emmet, Marvin & Martin. That firm's historian, Thomas B. Fenlon, has concluded that during FDR's "membership in the Emmet firm there was no legal matter of importance conducted by FDR either by himself or by his partners for him." Further, "in the fourteen years during which FDR was a name partner of those [Marvin] firms he had been able to practice law actively only for a period less than a year," in 1921. Thomas B. Fenlon, *The Emmet Firm* (privately printed, 2001); Davis (1972), 220–24, 603, 626–27, 697–98, 767.

Starting New Year's Day, 1925, FDR and D. Basil O'Connor announced a new law firm of Roosevelt and O'Connor. The latter had a practice specializing in contracts between crude oil producers and refining companies; FDR advised a few personal clients on legal matters, continued to work for the Fidelity and Deposit Company, and spent most of his time on political affairs. Davis concludes of FDR, "The law per se had no interest for him whatever." Davis (1972), 698.

3. FDR Papers, Hyde Park, President's Secretary's File, box 97, CCB to FDR, 4 Feb. 1936.

4. Ibid., FDR to CCB, 6 Feb. 1936. CCB sent a copy of this letter to FF, who commented in reply 11 Feb., CCB-HLS, 4:14: "I think F.D.R.'s letter to you is handsome and human and candid. It's now up to you really to put up names, say half a dozen." CCB responded 13 Feb., CCB-HLS, 4:14, the "letter was human and candid, but not handsome . . . And what about Abruzzo for the E.D.?" For more on Abruzzo, see n. 8 below.

5. FDR Papers, Hyde Park, President's Secretary's File, box 97, CCB to FDR, 13 Feb. 1936.

Note: CCB and the Federal Child Labor Amendment. In the years 1934–37 CCB was a leader in the movement urging ratification by the states of a federal constitutional amendment to prohibit child labor, generally defined as under "eighteen years of age." Initially he was chairman of a [New York State] Non-Partisan Committee for Ratification of the Federal Child Labor Amendment (see *Evening Post*, 15 Mar. 1934, 7:3, accepting chairmanship), and with three others in April published a thirty-three page "Argument for Ratification" of the proposed federal amendment, for which Joseph P. Chamberlain, professor of public law, Columbia, probably was chiefly responsible. The following year CCB became chairman of a National Non-Partisan Committee urging the ratification by all states which had not yet done so. Sixteen more were needed, including New York, see *Times*, 7 Jan. 1935, 10:3, and *Evening Post*, editorial, 7 Jan. 1935, 12:1. And in April 1935 he published in the *American Bar Association Journal*, "The Need for a Federal Child Labor Amendment." His article countered the opinion officially adopted by the ABA, was widely read, and issued as a reprint (copy in CCB-HLS, 13:8). By the end of the 1936 legislative session in Albany, however, neither the Senate nor Assembly had brought the amendment up for a vote, despite its support by Governor Lehman. Chiefly to blame, in CCB's opinion, were the Democratic members of the Senate's Judiciary Committee, and he excoriated them in a letter to the *Times*, 16 May 1936, 14:6. By the winter of 1937, the proposed amendment to the federal constitution still lacked eight of the thirty-six states needed for adoption by Congress, and in May national attention began to shift to the Fair Labor Standards [Wage and Hours] Act that Roosevelt had sent to Congress, and which would achieve by one of its clauses at least some of what the amendment sought. When the House failed to act on it, Roosevelt called Congress back into session in November, still without success. In January 1938 FDR urged the new Congress to adopt the bill, which finally passed in May and was signed by the president in June. The act did not cover children in agriculture, but it did prohibit the employment of children under sixteen in factories. The Supreme Court, in *United States v. Darby Lumber Co.*, held it constitutional in 1941, allowing expansion for the protection of children to continue under the act, and the movement for a constitutional amendment, already in suspension, came to an end.

6. FDR Papers, Hyde Park, President's Secretary's file, box 97, CCB to FDR, 18 July 1936.

7. Ibid., CCB to FDR, 26 June 1936, see also ibid., FDR to CCB, 2 July 1936.

8. CCB-HLS, 4:14, CCB to FF, 11 Feb. 1936, on Abruzzo: "[He] succeeded Manton as an ambulance-chaser. It is said that his appointment depended on whether Tammany would put a Coney Island politician, Kenneth Sutherland, in as assistant to the President of the Board of Aldermen. That was done and Abruzzo's name went in. It is a purely political appointment." See also FF-LOC, container 33, CCB to FF, 10 Jan. 1936, and CCB to FF, 19 Mar. 1936. *Times*, 5 Jan. 1936, 22:3, and 4 Feb. 1936, 11:4, state that F. V. Kelly, the Democratic leader in Brooklyn, had been called to the White House and the naming of Abruzzo was the "first major recognition" for Kelly. "Degraded specimen." FF-LOC, container 34, CCB to FF, 8 June 1937. Abruzzo "illiterate." CCB-HLS, 4:14, CCB to FF, 23 June 1936. See also a CCB-FDR exchange the following year in FDR Papers, Hyde Park, President's Secretary's File, box 97, CCB to FDR, 25 May 1937; FDR to CCB, 27 May 1937; and CCB to FDR, 14 June 1937.

9. Gould (1979), 134–57, quotations, 135, 157. A "travesty." CCB-HLS, 10:13, CCB to Owen J. Roberts, 31 Mar. 1947. CCB-HLS, 4:14, CCB to FF, 23 June 1936: "It is hard to understand [the choice of Mandelbaum] save on the theory that F.D. doesn't know the qualities needed for a judge and/or doesn't care or knows that the public doesn't care, or thinks that the opinion of the Bar is negligible. Of Mandelbaum it might be said that a fair record in the Assembly and Senate is equivalent to learning in the law or experience."

10. FDR Papers, Hyde Park, President's Secretary's File, box 97, FDR to CCB, 2 July 1936. Gould (1979), 141–42.

11. *Times*, 20 May 1942, 18:2: "Mr. Meaney was one of four men recommended to the President by Senator [William H.] Smathers . . . Mr. Roosevelt passed over the other three and chose Hague's man."

12. *Times*, 30 May 1942, 14:6.

13. *Washington Post*, editorial, 21 May 1942, 14:2.

14. *Times*, 26 May 1942, 20:6. *Herald Tribune*, 26 May 1942, 13:4: Senator W. Warren Barbour, Republican from New Jersey, promised to vote against confirmation: "Mr. Meaney can never escape being always viewed as a pawn of Mayor Hague."

15. *Times*, 28 May 1942, 16:6; *Herald Tribune*, editorial, 28 May 1942, 18:3. "The issue . . . is that Mr. Meaney is Boss Hague's henchman."

16. *Times*, 30 May 1942, 14:6.

17. CCB-HLS, 3:11, CCB to Raymond Daniell, 9 June 1942.

18. Recounted by CCB in letter to TDT, TDT-YSML, 2:14, 25 June 1942.

19. *Times*, 16 July 1942, 38:2. Despite the backing of Hague's machine, Senator Smathers was defeated easily by Albert W. Hawkes, see *Times*, 5 Nov. 1942, 30:6.

20. CCB-HLS, 2:14, E. H. Cassels to CCB, 3 Sept. 1942.

21. Biddle (1962), 201.

22. CCB-HLS, 11:11, CCB to FHL, 4 June 1945.

23. Ibid., 19:10, CCB to Jonah J. Goldstein, 15 June 1945.

24. N. Morris (1955), 202–11: "When I put the proposition up to La Guardia, the Machiavellian flavor of it warmed his soul. His eyes flashed . . . [and] he put his whole heart and soul into the fight. Every morning during the campaign he had breakfast with me and my running mates." See Heckscher (1978), 398–400: "But the mayor could never wholly dispel the impression that he had fabricated the Morris movement either in self-interest or in a last gesture of pique against the Republicans."

25. See Garrett (1961), 295–301, on FHL's destructive role in the election. For CCB's views, see CCB-HLS, 4:3, CCB to H. V. Evatt, 15 Nov. 1945: "[FHL] should have been nominated as an Independent. He would have had Hillman's enthusiastic support and the rank and file of Labor would have been for him despite Dubinsky and Rose [the split in the American Labor Party] . . . Dewey is responsible for the nomination of Goldstein. He didn't suggest it, but he approved it when he could have vetoed it . . . The next step was LaG's. He persuaded Morris to run as an Independent—a nice gentleman, whose ancestor signed the Declaration of Independence . . . If the Republicans had taken Morris and Mc-Goldrick they might have won, but LaG. had had a petty quarrel with McGoldrick and refused to support him. Well, we'll get along somehow or other. O'Dwyer is starting well but he will be absolutely controlled in the end by the Democratic bosses."

26. *Herald Tribune*, "A Mayor's Climacteric," 1 Jan. 1946, 20:4.

27. FHL's broadcast. ABCNY, *Record* 1:2 (Mar. 1946): 54–55.

28. FHL speech at ABCNY, *Times*, 20 Apr. 1938, 1:1; *Herald Tribune*, 20 Apr. 1938, 1:3; see Heckscher (1978), 199, where in his discussion he includes a quotation from a CCB letter written fifteen months later as if it were CCB's comment on the speech. HLS introduced La Guardia, and CCB was present for the speech, as were SS and PW.

La Guardia pointed out that it was costing nearly $4 million more to maintain the courts in New York City for 1938 than it was to maintain the federal courts. The causes were many, but chiefly three: (1) an archaic system, in which court salaries were not controlled by the city, which had to pay them; (2) payrolls loaded with political appointees; and (3) lack of any single administrative head or office keeping records on the courts, their expenses, and their 3,600 employees.

Comparative salaries for the U.S. Supreme Court and the Supreme Court of New York, First Department (inferior to the state's Court of Appeals) were:

POSITION	U.S. SUPREME COURT	FIRST DEPT. SUPREME COURT, N.Y.
Chief justice	$20,000	$25,000
Associate justice	$20,000	$25,000
Law clerk	1 @ $4,200	36 @ $7,500
Librarian	1 @ $4,500	1 @ $9,500
Associate librarian	1 @ $2,900	1 @ $6,500
Chief clerk	1 @ $4,200	1 @ $10,000
Attendant in courtroom	1 @ $2,030	136 @ $3,000

29. CCB-HLS, 11:11, FHL to CCB, 20 Feb. 1946.

30. La Guardia's most famous remark. It was uttered while testifying before the U.S. Senate Foreign Relations Committee in support of FDR's Lend-Lease Bill in February 1941. He was questioned about the statements of a New York Domestic Relations judge, Herbert A.

O'Brien, who had predicted that the passage of Lend-Lease would so stir ethnic hatreds in the city that there would be civil war. When asked if he had not appointed O'Brien to his position as judge, La Guardia replied: "I have made some excellent appointments in my time and I think I am good, but Senator, when I make a mistake, it's a beaut." Hecksher (1978), 432, states, "The correspondence in the [city] Archives indicates that the man [O'Brien] (besides being a sympathizer with totalitarian regimes) was a colossal bore." See *Times*, 12 Feb. 1941, 9:3. For O'Brien's testimony, see *Times*, 8 Feb., 1:2. La Guardia had announced he would appoint O'Brien, *Times*, 25 Jan. 1936, 16:2, and had sworn him in three days later, *Times*, 28 Jan., 5:6.

31. ABCNY, *Record* 1:2 (Mar. 1946): 56–58.

32. *Times*, 26 Feb. 1946, 27:6.

33. GM interview with Harrison Tweed, 12 Sept. 1967 (notes taken for the centennial history of ABCNY) see Martin (1970).

34. FF-LOC, container 34, FDR to CCB, 10 June 1937. FDR sent a copy of his letter to FF for praise.

35. William Wilberforce (1759–1833) led the movement in England to abolish slavery throughout the British Empire, and Parliament passed a bill doing so a month after his death, thus anticipating the United States by many years. John Howard (1726–90), English prison reformer responsible for improving sanitary conditions and treatment of prisoners in much of Europe. Elizabeth Fry (1780–1845), English Quaker prison reformer who improved conditions for women prisoners in England, particularly in Newgate Prison. Sir Rowland Hill (1795–1879), English educator, inventor, and postal reformer. Introduced self-government into schools, invented a rotary press, and developed a system of prepaid postage that was adopted in 1839. Samuel Plimsoll (1824–98), "the sailors' friend," Liberal member of Parliament who sought to require of British merchant shipping (mostly owned by Conservatives) what now almost universally is called "the Plimsoll mark," the short horizontal lines seen close to water level on the bow of ships. These lines, first adopted in legislation by Parliament in 1875, determine the depth to which the hull may be submerged (depending on season and particular sea) by the weight of the cargo. Overloading had led to many ships foundering and the loss of sailors' lives. In the United States the Plimsoll mark is required by the "loadline statute," adopted in 1929. Centuries earlier the Venetian republic had adopted such statues. The English shipowners, powerful in Parliament, had long opposed any such legislation, and to win it Plimsoll stage-managed a famous outburst in the House of Commons, which set an example of winning by creating disorder, still cited today by those who think good motives justify bad behavior. Today, in London, a statue of Plimsoll overlooks the Thames.

36. Gospel According to St. Luke 11:45, 46, and 52. The Good Samaritan. Luke 10:25–37. CCB jests, for in the context of the story the lawyer does not shine. Apparently CCB dictated the letter without looking up the biblical quotations, for while almost exact (King James Version), they are not.

37. William Murray Mansfield (1705–93), lord chief justice of Britain, 1765–88, who did much to modernize and humanize the law. Sir George Jessell (1824–83), master of the rolls (1873–83), and solicitor general for Gladstone, 1871–73. He worked to advance English court reform, but perhaps is best known for driving the freedom of contract to its limits. In *Bennet v. Bennett* (1876), he upheld a loan assumed at 60 percent by an alcoholic on the ground that "a man may agree to pay 100 percent if he chooses." Why CCB chose to include Jessel in his list is unclear.

38. *Hamlet*, Act II, scene 2, line 499. Polonius complains that Hamlet's preceding speech is too long, to which Hamlet replies: "It shall to the barber's, with your beard." FDR Papers, Hyde Park, President's Secretary's File, box 97, CCB to FDR, 14 June 1937.

39. *Herald Tribune*, editorial, "Citizen First," 1 Sept. 1943, 18:3.

40. Washington made fourteen nominations of eleven men, of which ten served. The Senate confirmed twelve, of which two declined their appointments; but one was an associate justice, William Cushing, who declined to become chief justice. Another recess appointment of a retired associate justice to chief justice, John Rutledge, was rejected by the Senate, and a nomination for associate justice of William Paterson was withdrawn by Washington, but later remade and confirmed.

41. Before Douglas, the four judges with longest tenure, tied at thirty-four years, were John Marshall, Joseph Story, John Marshall Harlan, and Stephen J. Field.

42. Farley (1948), 97–98; see Leuchtenburg, *The Supreme Court* (1995), 180–84; and see *Times*, 2 Oct. 1937, 3:6.

43. Borah's speech, *Times*, 18 Aug. 1937, 1:1, and quoted 13 Sept. 1937, 2:6. Borah voted against confirmation, though on different grounds. In August Borah had written to a friend that Black had continually denied the charge, see Leuchtenburg, *The Supreme Court* (1995), 302 n. 27. And see FF to CCB, in n. 46 below. For Black confirmed, see *Herald Tribune*, 18 Aug. 1937, 1:8.

44. *Pittsburgh Post-Gazette*, 13–18 Sept. 1937. Other papers, picking up story. E.g., *Times*, 13 Sept. 1937, 1:6. Black "silent" in Paris, "barricaded" in London. *Times*, 13 Sept. 1937, 2:5, and 16 Sept. 1937, 14:6. Opinion has varied on FDR's knowledge of Black's Klan connection. E.g., Burns (1956), 312, states FDR did not know of it; but Leuchtenburg, *The Supreme Court* (1995), 208 and 308 n. 78, concludes, after presenting considerable evidence: "There is every reason to assume that when he made the appointment Roosevelt had knowledge of Black's KKK past."

45. The *Manhattan* and *City of Norfolk*. *Times*, 22 Sept. 1937, 2:5, and *Herald Tribune*, 22 Sept. 1937, 1:4. Radio speech. *Times*, 2 Oct. 1937, 1:6–9, and *Herald Tribune*, roundup of editorials, 2 Oct. 1937, 2:5. Farley (1948), 98.

46. FF-LOC, container 34, copy of CCB to Borah, 6 Oct. 1937, with postscript in a second letter that same day. See CCB-HLS, 4:15, FF to CCB, 1 Sept. 1937, citing "the full debate on Black's confirmation," and Borah's statement that Black "had several times, long before the present matter came up, denied he was a member of the Klan." FF, eager to support FDR, dismisses objections to Black, ending: "The fundamental fact that is too widely forgotten is that the Supreme Court of the United States is, in everything that matters about it, not like unto other courts." Presumably he meant that FDR's effort to control the politics of the Court, primarily its decisions on economic legislation, was justified, a point CCB would not have contested—though he might have replied that Roosevelt could control the Court's politics with better men than Black.

47. Black's appointment. Leuchtenburg, *The Supreme Court* (1995), 210: "Roosevelt wanted to make clear that he was as committed to the New Deal as ever, and his selection of Black was a symbolic and defiant act." For newspaper reaction, see ibid., 185–87. For views on Black's dissents, see ibid., 201: "Even Max Lerner acknowledged, 'Black has become a judicial crusader before he has come to maturity as a judge.'" See also Baker (1984), 423–24.

48. CCB-HLS, 5:1, CCB telegram to FF, 5 Jan. 1939. FDR-FDRL, PPF 1169, CCB to FDR, 9 Jan. 1939. FF was the fourth justice in the Court's history born outside the United States and the first whose childhood language was not English.

49. For the Senate tradition, not always observed, and the FF hearing, see Baker (1984), 365–68. In September 1937 the American Bar Association had passed a resolution urging the Senate to adopt a rule requiring public hearings (with questions by the public) upon the fitness and qualifications of nominees for judicial office. The Senate ignored the

suggestion. Following the Black hearings and the revelations that followed, the American Bar Association again passed the resolution, in October 1941. See ABA *Annual Reports*, vol. 66, p. 121.

50. Lash (1975), 67. Douglas, *Go East* (1974), 324, complains of FF's failure to tell the truth about his role in the Court-packing plan. For Douglas's animosity toward FF, see nn. 55 and 69 below.

51. Douglas, as revealed in a recent biography by Murphy (2003), was a great liar, e.g., on his claimed polio, 282–86; on his alleged service in the army during World War I, 32–33 and 509–10; and on his supposedly standing second in his law school class, 473–74.

52. Douglas, *Go East* (1974), opening chapters. Joseph Story (1779–1845) in 1811 was appointed an associate justice by President Madison at age thirty-two. He served until his death in 1845 and generally is counted among the greatest of the Court's judges.

53. FDR-FDRL, PPF 1169, CCB to FDR, 27 Dec. 1939.

54. LH-HLS, 101:1, CCB to LH, 24 Dec. 1939. The primary point of Stone's visit, and of CCB's letter to LH, was to discuss the appointment of a new marshall [a sort of head policeman and a patronage post] in the federal court building in New York, a problem on which LH and CCB had been working. LH had given CCB examples of misbehavior by the recently resigned marshall, some of which suggested an intimacy with criminal leaders in the city. CCB had then written to the president suggesting that the next marshall should be better than average in order to clean up a bad situation. Stone proposed that LH write to him, and then he would speak to the president, hoping in turn to stir him to speak to the attorney general, who would make the appointment. See CCB-HLS, 6:16, LH to CCB, n.d. [Oct. 1939], and LH-HLS, 101:1, copy of CCB to FDR, 24 Oct. 1939.

55. Douglas, *The Court Years* (1980), 25: "Murphy was a special target of Frankfurter . . . Frankfurter pilloried Murphy for the habit [rubbing his fingers], whispering that Murphy was so distraught that he was trying to solve legal problems by wringing his hands." And see Douglas on FF, ibid., 23, 33. These stories, written after FF had died, may be exaggerated. At the very least they seem incompatible with Douglas's statement, 37, "The Court in my time always had amicable personal relations." Cf. Jackson's contrary opinion, n. 59 below. On the bad relations between FF and Douglas, see Baker (1984), 419–22; and Lash (1975), 77–78.

56. Douglas, *The Court Years* (1980), 25, 26. On Murphy's reluctance, see J. Woodford Howard Jr., *Mr. Justice Murphy: A Political Biography* (Princeton, N.J.: Princeton University Press, 1968), 214–28. Biddle (1962), 92–94; at 93, "It was a bad appointment, and Murphy knew it, and everyone knew it. I suspect that he might have resisted and argued had he been consulted. But he was not consulted, and woke up one morning to find himself thrown at the bench, part of a shuffle that put Jackson in his place, and Biddle [the writer] in Jackson's."

57. Ten months. Biddle (1962), 192. Stone. Mason, *Harlan Fiske Stone* (1956), 713. After the war, from 1945 to 1947, Byrnes was Truman's secretary of state, and from 1951 to 1955 governor of South Carolina, where, perhaps more conservative with age and regional pressures, he supported segregation in schools, but also pushed through the state legislature a bill to outlaw the Ku Klux Klan. Few of his generation held so many important executive offices.

58. Robert H. Jackson, despite a year at Albany Law School, qualified for the bar, to which he was admitted in 1913, by "reading law" in a single practitioner's office in Jamestown, New York. He is the last member of the Court to have entered the bar in this older way rather than from a law school. CCB knew Jackson well enough to address him as "Dear Bob," see PW-PW Jr., CCB to Jackson, 13 Mar. 1940, proposing a man for federal district judge in Maine; and to receive a letter from him, 9 Sept. 1938, about a meeting of the Supreme Court bar and proposing a visit to CCB in New York, see TDT-YSML, 2:15.

59. Douglas, *The Court Years* (1980), 28–29. Difficulties caused by the eight-man court, see Mason, *Harlan Fiske Stone* (1956), 717–18 and n: "For Stone, Justice Jackson's participation in the Nuremberg trials combined three major sources of irritation: disapproval in principle of non-judicial work; strong objections to the trials on legal and political grounds; the inconvenience and increased burden of work entailed." Jackson, according to Mason, 716 n, thought Stone correct about the impropriety of off-Court duties for justices, and told Mason in an interview in April 1953: "I feel that he was right about it. I was entirely willing to quit the Court if this was the price. In those days this wasn't a pleasant place to be." Jackson was appointed to be the United States' representative in setting up the International Military Tribunal and, with that accomplished, chief counsel for the prosecution. Biddle accepted from Truman the post of voting American member of the International Military Tribunal that was to try the major German war criminals; Judge John J. Parker, of the Fourth Circuit Court of Appeals, was his nonvoting alternate. Each of the four powers occupying Germany had a voting member and an alternate. Biddle (1962), 367–487, has an account of the trials.

CCB's English friend GWR went to Nuremberg to observe the trials and wrote him a description, see CCB-HLS, 16:5, GWR to CCB, 8 June 1946.

60. Biddle (1962), 94; on Rutledge, 193–94: "His views were sound, carefully reasoned, and lawyerlike. He was long-winded, suffering from a sense of obligation to answer everything in the case." Ten years later, after meeting Hand on an Atlantic crossing, Biddle "came to believe that his appointment would have been more suitable, and that I should have urged the President to appoint him in spite of his age."

61. CCB-HLS, 12:14, CCB to FDM, 1 May 1942. "Shreds and patches." Most immediately from Gilbert and Sullivan, *The Mikado*, Act I, entrance song of Nanki-Poo, the wandering minstrel. And behind that, *Hamlet*, Act III, scene 4, Hamlet to the Queen, scorning his stepfather Claudius as "a king of shreds and patches."

62. FF-LOC, container 35, copy of CCB to FDR, 6 Nov. 1942; copy of telegrams to Stone and Garrison, 11 Nov. 1942; and CCB to FF, 12 Nov. 1942.

63. Ibid., copy of Stone to CCB, 14 Nov. 1942.

64. Biddle (1962), 193, consulted Stone in "early November." FF-LOC, container 35, copy of CCB to Biddle. Emerson, *Essays: First Series*, "Self-Reliance": "A foolish consistency is the hobgoblin of little minds, adored by little statesmen and philosophers and divines."

65. FF-LOC, container 35, copy of CCB to FDR, 18 Nov. 1942.

66. Ibid., CCB to FF, 20 Nov. 1942; also copy of FDR reply to CCB, 20 Nov. 1942.

67. Ibid., copy of CCB to FDR, 23 Nov. 1942; also copy of CCB to FDR, 8 Dec. 1942; copy of CCB to FDR, 24 Dec. 1942; and CCB to FF, 29 Dec. 1942. The 8 Dec. note to FDR joked about changing LH's year of birth in a parish register. CCB wrote as one senior warden in an Episcopal church to another.

68. Ibid., CCB to FF, 9 Dec. 1942. On background to Rutledge's appointment, see Fowler V. Harper, *Justice Rutledge and the Bright Constellation* (New York: Bobbs Merrill, 1965), 38–43.

69. Biddle (1962), 94–95, 194. See Douglas, *Go East* (1974), 331–32, who reports a conversation with FDR at a poker party during which FDR stated who he was *not* going to appoint in place of Byrnes. "Learned Hand is *not* going to be appointed . . . This time Felix overplayed his hand." LH's biographer, Gunther (1994), 561–62, feels "this tale is somewhat suspect. By the time Douglas wrote, he looked back across years of service with Frankfurter on the Court marked by a mounting, increasingly intense animosity. Casting clouds on Frankfurter's reputation must have had special appeal."

70. Quoted in Mason, *Harlan Fiske Stone* (1956), 593, citing CCB to Stone, 23 Dec. 1942, and Stone's reply to CCB, 4 Jan. 1943.

71. FF-LOC, container 35, copy of CCB to FDR, 24 Dec. 1942. For LH's private estimate of Rutledge: CCB-HLS, 6:16, LH to CCB, 15 Jan. 1943: "Rutledge is well enough if you go on past averages; but not considering the set-up there just now."

72. LH's disappointment. His sense of being "an outsider," is a minor theme in Gunther (1994), 27, 87, 88, 152, 154, 294, 408, and perhaps this streak of insecurity fed Hand's characteristic uncertainty. One time LH, musing on his temperament, said of himself: "I'm in some doubt; I'm always in doubt." CCB, describing him, remarked of Hand's perpetual doubt that except for the requirement that a judge decide the case, "not a few of Hand's opinions might well end with a question mark." See CCB, "Judge Learned Hand," *Harvard Law Review*, vol. LX, 1946–47, 330. In an interview with Gunther on 18 March 1957, CCB, remarking on LH's readiness always to see another side to any question, said of him: "Learned is willing to discuss everything. He would discuss his mother's chastity."

73. CCB-HLS, 6:16, LH to CCB, 12 Jan. 1943. See Gunther (1994), 568: "This comment ranks among those with greatest insight. Roosevelt was not acquainted with Hand, but he knew enough about him to recognize that he was no ideological crusader. Hand was a probing skeptic, a judge committed to independent, reasoned decision making; and these traits were indeed 'alien' to the president."

74. FF-LOC, container 35, CCB to FF, 11 and 24 Dec. 1942.

75. CCB-HLS, 2:10, CCB to Marshall Bullitt, 31 July 1946: "Felix and his wife spent a weekend with me here [Black Point] a fortnight ago, and I got all the dope; but before F. left, he said, 'We haven't talked about the Court, have we?' 'Not a word!'"

76. Biddle (1962), 98. Biddle in 1911–12 had been a clerk for Justice Holmes. He practiced law in Philadelphia 1917–34, when he went to Washington and held a succession of New Deal jobs. Roosevelt appointed him to the Third Circuit Court of Appeals in 1939, but Biddle resigned after a year because "the court work bored me," 96, and thereafter he consistently declined to be considered for various judicial posts, 194–195 (except for the Nuremberg Trials, see n. 59 above). He liked best the work of solicitor general, 97–99. Cf. Biddle's description of FF on the bench to LH's of Swan, chap. 13 (at n. 47).

77. GM interview with Gunther, 4 Oct. 1994. Gunther at the time of the incident was one of Warren's three clerks. Warren, at the time, was new to the bench and had just returned to law after several nonlegal decades of politics.

78. "Best conversationalist." Douglas, *The Court Years* (1980), 21. For FF in conversation, see Isaiah Berlin, *Personal Impressions* (London: Hogarth Press, 1981), 83–90, "Felix Frankfurter at Oxford." "Proselytizer." Douglas, *The Court Years* (1980), 22. According to Douglas, 18, the other two active proselytizers on the Court were Stone and Black.

79. *Minersville School District v. Gobitis*, 310 U.S. 586–607 (1940).

80. *Jones v. Opelika*, 316 U.S. 584–624 (1942), 623–24.

81. *Board of Education v. Barnette*, 319 U.S. 624–71 (1943), 646–71. FF's dissent was very personal, beginning, "One who belongs to the most vilified and persecuted minority in history is not likely to be insensible to the freedoms guaranteed by our Constitution," and both Justices Roberts and Murphy urged him to drop his initial paragraphs, or rewrite them. His personal history and feelings were, or should be, irrelevant to the law of the case. The dissent has always been one of FF's most controversial. See Baker (1984), 405–9. For further battles between FF, Black, and Murphy, see *Herald Tribune*, 5 Jan. 1944, 6:3.

82. Howard, *Mr. Justice Murphy*, 263: The justice "found himself veering from the leadership of Felix Frankfurter, whom he had assumed would be his spiritual and intellectual knight, to that of Hugo L. Black." Many, including CCB, thought that Black also dominated the mind of Rutledge, see CCB-HLS, 2:10, CCB to Marshall Bullitt, 31 July 1946.

83. CCB-HLS, 7:5, CCB to Joseph Hamlen, 30 Nov. 1939. Ibid., 6:14, ANH to CCB, 15 Aug. 1943. See also ibid., LH to CCB, 15 Jan. 1943: "He [FF] doesn't like Biddle much now, and he is getting a little out with the New Hampshire Farmer [Stone]; he has great possibilities where he is, and is somewhat—indeed a good deal—injuring them by talking too much and misbehaving on the bench. I wish he wouldn't . . . he is really the best."

84. Ibid., 14:14, CCB to SKR, 30 Sept. 1943.

85. *Herald Tribune*, 10 Jan. 1944, 16:4, "Danger in Dissent."

86. Quoted in Mason, *Harlan Fiske Stone* (1956), 609.

87. Ibid., citing Stone to CCB, 15 Jan. 1944; CCB reply, 18 Jan. In *Barnette*, Black and Douglas filed a special statement explaining their change of view.

88. CCB-HLS, 2:19, Ben V. Cohen to CCB, 28 Jan. 1944. The "Dear Uncle Charlie" does not state a blood relationship but affection and respect. CCB-DFT, CCB to "Lawrie," 3 Jan. 1945: "I know B.V.C. very well—he calls me 'Uncle Charlie,' and he is one of the ablest and finest men I know." According to Lash (1975), 52, Cohen was said to be "the most brilliant man who had ever attended the University of Chicago Law School . . . [and] the best legal draftsman in New Deal Washington." (GM: I did not find the two letters referred to by Cohen, but in CCB-HLS, 5:5, there is a short one from CCB to FF, 21 Jan., that refers to another from FF, 18 Jan. 1944, also not discovered. Evidently after CCB's letter in the *Herald Tribune* there was a flurry of correspondence.

89. CCB-HLS, 5:5, CCB to FF, 4 Feb. 1944. Rutledge, the fourth professor on the Court, was too recently appointed to be included in the count.

90. Ibid., FF to CCB, 8 Feb. 1944.

91. Ibid., 16:4, CCB to GWR, 21 Mar. 1945.

92. Douglas, *Go East* (1974), 466–67. His statement on China, in an interview in San Francisco, front-page headline story, *Times*, 1 Sept. 1951, 1:5. FF on the statement. ANH-AVS, copy of FF to CCB, 17 Sept. [1951]. The president's private rebuke, see Murphy (2003), 108: "Since you are on the highest Court in the land it seems to me that the best thing you can possibly do would be to give your best effort to that Court and let the President of the United States run the political end of foreign and domestic affairs."

93. As nothing came of his efforts, Douglas treats them in his autobiography as of no account, but at the time they loomed large. E.g., *Times*, 24 Feb. 1946, IV, 3:1; and for Truman's offer of secretary of interior, *Times*, 15 Feb. 1946, 28:2. On secretary of state, see Douglas, *The Court Years* (1980), 289, 290, for the continuing movement after 1948 "to make me the Democratic nominee for President." For the 1944 near-nomination as vice president, see Rosenman (1952), 446ff.

94. *Jewell Ridge Coal Corp. v. Local No. 6167, United Mine Workers of America*, 325 U.S. 161 (1945). Black's ex-partner, Crampton Harris, represented the respondents.

95. In his cable to the congressional committees, the newspapers' lead story on 11 June 1946, Jackson said: "I do not want it inferred that I charge that Justice Black's sitting in the Jewell Ridge case involved lack of 'honor.' It is rather a question of judgment as to sound judicial policy. There may be those who think it quite harmless to encourage the employment of Justices' ex-law partners to argue close cases by smothering the objections which the bar makes to this practice. But in my view such an attitude would soon bring the Court into disrepute." The full text in *Times*, 11 June 1946, 2:3, and *Herald Tribune*, 11 June 1946, 16:3. Douglas, *The Court Years* (1980), 32, who had little sympathy with Jackson, quotes parts of the letter and concludes, "But his ambition to be Chief Justice truly poisoned his judicial career." *Times*, editorial, 12 June 1946, 26:3; *Herald Tribune*, editorial, 12 June 1946, 28:1: "It hardly seems possible that Justice Black, a man whom many believe should never have been appointed in the first place, can survive the accusations brought against him."

96. CCB-HLS, 16:5, CCB to GWR, 18 June 1946.

97. *Times*, 27 June 1946, 20:7. See C. Peter Magrath, *Morrison R. Waite: The Triumph of Character* (New York: Macmillan, 1963), 276–96, quotation at 281–82. Waite wrote to his nephew John T. Wait [sic], Republican congressman from Connecticut. The original, November 1875, is in the Library of Congress, M. R. Waite Letterbooks, 1875. Pressure was put on Chief Justice Waite (1874–88) because he seemed the Republican Party's best successor to the morally repugnant Grant.

98. *Times*, 17 Sept. 1951, 23:6.

99. Holmes. "The life of the law has not been logic: it has been experience. The felt necessities of the time, the prevalent moral and political theories, intuitions of public authority, avowed or unconscious, even the prejudices which judges share with their fellow-men, have had a good deal more to do than the syllogism in determining the rules by which men should be governed." From the opening paragraph of *The Common Law* (1881).

100. Lerner quotation and following in *Law and Social Action: Essays of Alexander H. Pekelis*, ed. Milton R. Konvitz (Ithaca, N.Y.: Cornell University Press, 1950), 200. On FDR's appointment of professors, Douglas, *The Court Years* (1980), 42, concluded: "There was great merit in FDR's predeliction for offbeat law professors and lawyers. It produced unique and outstanding federal judges: Charles E. Clark [and] Jerome Frank of the Second Circuit Court of Appeals; Henry Edgetron of the Court of Appeals of the District of Columbia; and Felix Frankfurter, to name only a few. These men were not bar association prototypes and might not have passed muster there." Gunther (1994), 521–35, discusses Clark and Frank and their relations on the court with LH. Clark, before his appointment in 1939, had served for ten years as dean of Yale Law School and for the ten years previous, as a professor at the school. See also J. B. Morris (1987), 143–48, "The New Deal Appointees." Edgetron had taught at Cornell Law School. Frank had practiced in Chicago and New York firms and held various New Deal posts, succeeding Douglas as SEC chairman.

101. FF, "Some Reflections on the Reading of Statutes," the Sixth Annual Benjamin N. Cardozo Lecture delivered before the Association of the Bar of the City of New York, 18 Mar. 1947. Published in ABCNY, *Record* 2:6 (1947): 213–37. And republished in *Columbia Law Review* 47:4 (May 1947): 527–46.

102. FF, "The Job of a Supreme Court Justice," *Times Magazine*, 28 Nov. 1954, 14. Until CCB died in 1959, he and FF continued to wrangle about the need for concurring opinions. For one of the last letters, see CCB-HLS, 5:17, FF to CCB, 12 Nov. 1958. An earlier one, CCB-HLS, 5:10, FF to CCB, 2 July 1951.

103. CCB-HLS, 2:10, Marshall Bullitt to CCB, 10 Aug. 1946. Bullitt analyzed the advantage of appointing men in their sixties, rather than younger, to the Court, which then, through earlier retirement and death, could more easily make readjustments in its views. But another problem on which he and CCB agreed was that with the rise of the corporate office-lawyer the number of first-rate courtroom lawyers had declined. CCB reported, "A Chicago lawyer said to me the other day that there were not more than three lawyers in Chicago known outside of Cook County." As for New York, he challenged Bullitt to add to the six that came first to mind: "John W. Davis, William Mitchell, Joseph Proskauer, Nathan L. Miller, Whitney North Seymour, and Charles Evans Hughes, Jr." The solution, wrote CCB, was to train judges on the federal district courts and then to promote them.

24. The Last Decade

Chief sources for this chapter, other than the Burlingham collections, the author's interviews, and contemporary newspapers, are: Elizabeth Moulton, *St. George's Church, New York* (New York: privately printed, 1964); Charles P. Curtis, *Law as Large as Life: A Natural Law for Today and the Supreme Court as Its Prophet* (New York: Simon and Schuster, 1959); *"C. C. B." As We Knew Him*, a collection of short notes, editorials, and articles about CCB, published in *St. George's Bulletin*, Aug. 1959.

1. Stone memorial. CCB-HLS, 16:5, CCB to GWR, 18 June 1946. The younger man was Walter Binger.

2. Stephen H. Taylor to GM, 15 Nov. 1997.

3. LH-HLS, 100:26, LH to CCB, 6 Oct. 1917. Ibid., CCB to LH, 8 Oct. 1917.

Note: The Lincoln Memorial in Washington, completed in 1922, greatly impressed many of those who thought highly of Lincoln. A Greek temple, entered untypically from its side, it contains only a single figure, Lincoln seated and brooding. The concept is striking in part for what is not portrayed: the log cabin, the law office, the debates with Douglas, the great moments before Congress or in his cabinet, or the assassination. Instead the whole is directed toward an aspiration, an effort to find some meaning, some hope in what had happened. Individual suffering was subsumed in an idealization of purpose, and this was increasingly how CCB thought of the Civil War, extracting from its events and actors values by which he attempted to live.

4. CBS-TFS, Dr. John H. Dunnington to CB, 29 June 1948. Commencement 1946. CCB-HLS, 7:3. CCB and Holmes's joint report on it to surviving classmates, 10 June 1946. English had displaced Latin in the program in 1944.

5. Holmes. CCB-HLS, 7:3, CCB letter to Mrs. Edgar Felton, a classmate's widow, 25 June 1948. Nephew. CCB-DFT, CCB to LHT, 24 June 1949.

6. CCB-HLS, 7:3, CCB to surviving classmates, 27 June 1950. The Burlingham family were not the only ones to worry. ANH's clerk, Weaver W. Dunnan, on hearing that his elderly mentor planned a trip to Cambridge, inquired delicately if the judge would be traveling alone, intending for safety's sake to offer to accompany him—until hearing that ANH was going only to support CCB, who was ninety! Nelson, ed. (1983), 46.

7. CCB-HLS, 7:3, CCB to surviving classmates, 27 June 1950.

8. GM present at the dinner. About that same year, at the law firm CCB showed a list of recipients for Harvard honorary degrees to his associate Richard W. Palmer, barking, "Read that list!" Said Palmer, "A distinguished roster." Said CCB, slamming his hand on the table, "A disgrace. There's not a woman on it." GM interview with Richard W. Palmer, 16 Dec. 1994.

9. FF-LOC, container 36, CCB to FF, 9 and 10 Oct. 1952. "Hard arteries." CCB-DFT, CB to LHT, 11 Dec. 1952. "For good and all." Hamilton Family Papers, Schlesinger Library, Harvard, CCB to Alice Hamilton, 16 Jan. 1953.

10. Frankfurter. GM interview with CB Jr., 14 and 15 July 1995. Frankfurter liked his cocktail before dinner, but CCB did not serve hard liquor, so for the hour before dinner Frankfurter would walk up the street to visit Charles and Cora, have his drink along with a chat, and then return to the old man.

11. Mimicking Jeremiah, 8:20. CCB-DFT, CCB to LHT, 5 Sept. 1952. "Ferocious." GM phone interview with CB Jr., 22 Aug. 1997; CCB-HLS, 21:3. CCB poem, 6 Aug. 1950. Printed in *"C. C. B." As We Knew Him*, in EOM's sermon on the Sunday after CCB's death.

12. CCB-HLS, 17:3, Mabel Stimson to CCB, 17 Nov. 1950, quoting CCB to her. On missing Louie. CCB-DFT, CCB to Grace Taylor, 6 Apr. 1940. "Gloomy." CCB-DFT, CCB to LHT, 14 Apr. 1951.

13. GM interview with Bethuel M. Webster, 1967 (in connection with GM, Martin [1970]). GM interview with CB Jr., 14 and 15 July 1995; GM interview with PLT, 11 Sept. 1993.

14. GM interview with Nancy Shaw Palmer, 16 Dec. 1994.

15. GM interview with John R. Hupper, 2 Aug. 1994; interview with CB Jr., 14 and 15 July 1995.

16. GM phone interview with Dr. Daniel W. O'Connor Jr., son of stenographer Emma O'Connor, 24 Apr. 2000.

17. GM interview with Elliott B. Nixon, 18 Feb. 1992.

18. GM interview with Herbert M. Lord, 13 Dec. 1994.

19. At greater length in Martin (1970), 247–50. Also a letter to GM from Thomas B. Fenlon, 18 October 1996. Fenlon was a member of the nominating committee, and he leaves no doubt that CCB had picked Tweed before the committee members gathered to vote. In ABCNY, *Record* 10 (1955), 261, Tweed states that CCB put him in as president. Tweed was open and emphatic about his gratitude to his partners at Milbank, Tweed for their financial support over many years for his work *pro bono publico*. Before his three years as president of the Association, he was president of the Legal Aid Society (1936–45), and for five years thereafter (1953–58), chairman of the state legislature's Temporary Commission on the Courts, popularly known as "the Tweed Commission to Reform the Courts." He did not say what his arrangement with the firm was, but presumably the partners did not cut back, or not far, on his share. As one partner, Timothy N. Pfeiffer, in 1967 remarked to GM on the firm's generosity to Tweed, "Well, we can't all do everything."

20. Martin (1970), 253–60.

21. "Tufters." Trollope, *Framley Parsonage*, chap. 3, third paragraph from end: "I will not degrade him by calling him a tuft-hunter"; and chap. 8, fifth paragraph from end. Martin (1970), 261–63 and 279–81.

22. "Green-goods" lawyers. GM interview with PW Jr., 9 Feb. 2000. "The Obligations of the Lawyer to His Profession" by Whitney North Seymour, the 25th Annual Benjamin Cardozo Lecture delivered before the Association of the Bar of the City of New York, 19 Mar. 1968 (New York: ABCNY, 1968). For introduction of advertising into the profession, see J. B. Morris (1997), 67, 78–80. Herbert Brownell, interview with GM, 5 Aug. 1992, strongly regretted the introduction of business positions and business ethics into the legal profession.

23. The alleged complacency recently appeared, for example, in the "President's Report" by president Barbara Paul Robinson, ABCNY, *Record* 50:5 (June 1995): 485: "Those who put this Association together 125 years ago did so because they thought they could make a difference in the New York community. And they did. They fought to wipe out corruption in the city government and its courts and they succeeded." Succeeded? After Boss Tweed, no Boss Croker, or Murphy, or Curran? No Mayor Walker? No corruption in the courts? Surely a skewed view of history.

Note: On the decline in competence of judges and lawyers. The decline may be in the eye of the beholder, but some who have studied it have left statements: E.g., Stanley M. Isaacs, SMI-COH, 204–5: After Tammany's return to City Hall, "in the Corporation Counsel's office there was a shocking change . . . When O'Dwyer came in, the office degenerated very fast, especially the rank and file who were appointed . . . Very often, their explanations showed ignorance even of the very bill they were supposed to explain and certainly no background of knowledge of city affairs or city problems or a good sound background of legal matters." Also Richard Posner, in doing research for his book on Cardozo (1990), compared the briefs of appellate lawyers in Cardozo's day to those of a later day: "They are, I am distressed to say, superior on average to the briefs I have been reading for the last eight years as a federal appellate judge." And many New York lawyers would agree that the decline in quality of the judges in, say, the New York County Surrogate's Court over the last sixty years (from the high days of Foley, Delehanty, Collins, and Frankenthaler) is indisputable.

Also, the Federal Judicial Center, in August 1978, published a book by Anthony Partridge and Gordon Bermant titled *The Quality of Advocacy in the Federal Courts: A Report to the Committee of the Judicial Conference of the United States to Consider Standards for Admission to Practice in the Federal Courts.* In a section, "Conclusion," 29–30, it states: "Based on ratings by 284 federal district judges of 1,969 actual performances, we conclude that about a twelfth of the lawyers' performances in cases that come to trial in the district courts are regarded as inadequate by the trial judge. These performances occur in about one-sixth of the trials . . . On the basis of the data from opinion questionnaires, we conclude that most federal district judges do not believe there is a serious problem of inadequate trial advocacy in their courts. A sizeable minority, however—about two-fifths of the judges—believe there is."

24. GM interview with Richard W. Palmer, 16 Dec. 1994. See SMI-COH, 205–6, on Mayor O'Dwyer's bad appointments to the Dock Department.

25. CCB-HLS, 16:12, CCB to McKee, 20 July 1944, offering resignation, which was not accepted.

26. "Why a Clinic?," published by St. George's Church, 1942. Clinic closed. Moulton (1964), 115. See CCB-HLS, 17:1, CCB to Walter Rose, 2 Aug. 1946, on the need for the clinic. For the start of the clinic, see Chapter 12.

27. McKee's example of the enemy parachutist discovered in the backyard (though CCB does not say so) is the problem posed in Kipling's disturbing story of World War I hatred "Mary Postgate" (included in Kipling's *A Diversity of Creatures*).

28. CCB-HLS, 19:14, CCB to Allen Wardwell, 22 Sept. 1940.

29. Use of church denied. Moulton (1964), 132. *Herald Tribune*, 28 June 1946, 12:2, and *Times*, 28 June 1946, 44:2.

30. TDT-YSML, 2:13, CCB to TDT, 12 Nov. 1940. Niebuhr's daughter, Elisabeth Sifton, in her article "The Serenity Prayer," *Yale Review* 86:1 (Jan. 1998): 38, states: "But beyond the college chapels where he [Neibuhr] was a hardy perennial, only two or three churches welcomed him. One was St. George's." The article became a book, *The Serenity Prayer: Faith and Politics in Times of Peace and War* (New York: Norton, 2003).

31. TDT-YSML, 2:13, CCB to TDT, 12 Nov. 1940.

32. *Christianity and Crisis.* CCB-HLS, 9:6, CCB to Frank Hirst, 12 May and 26 June 1941: "It has a circulation of nearly 10,000." Still editing. Ibid., 13:6, CCB to Niebuhr, 12 Dec. 1945. Ceases publication. *Episcopal Life*, "News Digest," May 1993. Niebuhr's statement of CCB's work—"I submitted policy statements to him for editing"—in *"C. C. B." As We Knew Him* (1959).

33. CCB-HLS, 16:12, E. M. McKee to CCB, n.d. [May 1946].

34. Miller's sermon in *"C. C. B." As We Knew Him* (1959). See Moulton (1964), 140–42. Miller accepts. CCB-HLS, 3:14, Miller to CCB, 9 Oct. 1946.

35. Women on vestry. Miller's sermon, *"C.C.B." As We Knew Him* (1959), and Moulton, (1964), 173, 181–82.

36. CCB-HLS, 17:3, CCB to Niebuhr, 28 Feb. 1957.

37. "Proposal to Billy Graham," *Christian Century*, 8 Aug. 1956; and Curtis, (1959), 162–66, republishes "nearly all" of the article. Graham, as an evangelical preacher, in many ways seems a last gasp of the frontier, preaching individual salvation, as compared, say, to Martin Luther King Jr., more urban and dealing in group responsibilities. King, in effect, presented to American white citizens the long outstanding moral debt of the Civil War: full equality for black citizens. In *The American Scholar*, Autumn 1958, C. Vann Woodward put it this way: "Then, in the middle of the twentieth century, conscience finally began to catch up with commitment. Very suddenly, relatively speaking, it became clear that the almost forgotten Civil War debt had to be paid, paid in full, and without any more stalling than was necessary." Quoted at greater length in Curtis (1959), 64.

38. GM watching from row behind, and GM interview with vestryman John N. Hazard, 10 June 1993.

39. *"C. C. B." As We Knew Him* (1959), statement of William Watts Rose Jr.

40. CCB-HLS, 7:12, Hamlen to CCB, 2 Apr. 1953; and ibid., 6:12, Hamlen to CCB, 20 Sept. 1956.

41. George W. Martin, "First Citizen of New York," HAB, 6 Apr. 1957.

42. *"C. C. B." As We Knew Him* (1959), statement of Whitney North Seymour, the lawyer who took CCB home from the dinner. It also appears on the Century Association Archives audiotapes of monthly meetings, 5 Dec. 1963. Seymour was in the chair at that meeting (substituting for the absent president) and retold the story. Dr. Russell Flinchum, Century archivist, to GM, 29 Jan. 2000.

43. GM interview with CB Jr., 14 and 15 July 1995.

44. Minutes of Vestry Meeting of St. George's, 19 May 1959, with the letter dictated the next day to the rector.

Epilogue: An American Life

1. Hamilton (1944), 208.

2. Clark. Dunne (1986), 1, 5–6.

3. Tocqueville (1946), chap. 25, "Public Associations," 388.

4. Ibid., chap. 17, "The Influence of Manners and Religion upon Democratic Institutions in the United States," 241.

5. Ibid., chap. 31, "Influence of Democracy on Public Relations," 491.

6. A grandson. CB Jr. to GM, 19 Sept. 2000. A contemporary. Barry Faulkner, a sculptor and fellow member of the Century Club, quoted by CB Jr. to GM, 30 Oct. 1992.

7. Bryce (1891), 2:274–75.

8. The first presidential election in which television played a substantial role was 1952. In that election appeared the first TV "spot," made most reluctantly by General Eisenhower. In 1954 the McCarthy hearings were on television, and in 1960, the year after CCB's death, occurred the first national TV debate between presidential candidates: Kennedy versus Nixon.

9. "Opinionated." GM phone interview with Thomas B. Fenlon, 1 Sept. 1999. Fenlon had served on the committee that in 1945 nominated Harrison Tweed for president of the bar association, one of CCB's "performances." See Martin (1970), 247–48.

10. New York's First Citizen, see Prologue, n. 16.

A SHORT BIBLIOGRAPHY

Those sources—articles, books, or unpublished materials—used only once or twice in the text are frequently listed in the headnote of sources for each chapter of Notes or in the numbered endnote, but not here.

Abbreviations explained at the start of the Notes are used here.

UNPUBLISHED MATERIAL

1. Manuscript collections primarily by or about CCB
2. Other manuscript collections with material by or about CCB
3. Unpublished studies, including theses
4. Interviews
   a) by George Martin
   b) by others
5. Reminiscences, oral histories, etc.

1. Manuscript collections primarily by or about CCB

CCB-COH: CCB's oral history on file at the Columbia University Oral History Research office.

CCB-HLS: The Charles C. Burlingham Papers at the Harvard Law School Library, Manuscripts Division. About 8,500 items. Cataloged. Twenty-three files; interior folders. The papers span the years 1876–1960, with the bulk in the period 1920–58. The collection consists mainly of correspondence, but there are also speeches, reports, government documents, genealogies, scrapbooks, newspaper clippings, and other miscellaneous items.

CCB-TFS: An uncataloged collection of letters, albums of clippings, and documents of the Burlingham family and friends, but mostly of letters by CCB, with the bulk in the period 1876–1910. Most of the letters are handwritten (terrible handwriting!) and kept in a trunk now owned by CCB's eldest great-grandchild, Timothy F. Schmiderer.

CCB-DFT: David F. Taylor (CCB's great-nephew). An uncataloged collection, chiefly of letters, 1934–56, from CCB to his nephew Lawrence Taylor.

2. Other manuscript collections in which CCB figures

BUL: Burlingham Underwood Library, the law firm's small collection of miscellanea. Some of it, however, is rarely found. Transferred in 2002 to the Harvard Law School Library.

CRB&M: Columbia University Rare Book and Manuscript Library, with collections under other names with references to CCB or his work. See James Truslow Adams, Eleanor Belmont, the Community Service Society (CSS), Irwin Edman, Robert Lee Hale, Charles Evans Hughes, Frederic Keppel, Seth Low, Frances Perkins, Calvin Plimpton, Edward M. Shepard, Lillian Wald.

GC-DCL: Grenville Clark Papers at Dartmouth College Library. Correspondence, 1929–59.

FF-LOC: Felix Frankfurter Collection, Library of Congress. Correspondence, 1912–60, with the bulk from 1936 to 1959.

Gerald Gunther Collection: two interviews with CCB, in March 1957, and some letters.

LH-HLS: Learned Hand Papers, at the Harvard Law School. Correspondence, 1904–59.

ANH-AVS: Augustus N. Hand Collection, with papers chiefly 1950–59, in possession of ANH's grandson Arthur V. Savage.

Fiorello H. La Guardia Papers: In the Municipal Archives and Record Center, New York City.

Herbert H. Lehman Papers: In the Herbert H. Lehman Suite, Columbia University. Correspondence, 1933–59.

MLA-BUL: Maritime Law Association of the United States, chiefly documents on microfiche at the Burlingham Underwood Library and since transferred to the office of the current secretary.

Charles Poletti Papers: In the Herbert H. Lehman Suite, Columbia University.

FDR-FDRL: Franklin D. Roosevelt Papers at the FDR Library, Hyde Park, New York. Correspondence, 1911–45.

St. George's Church: Records such as minutes of vestry meetings, baptisms, confirmations, etc., reports on activities, and other publications. Kept in the parish house.

HLS-YSML: Henry L. Stimson Papers, at Yale Sterling Memorial Library. Correspondence, 1911–50.

TDT-YSML: Thomas Day Thacher Papers, at Yale Sterling Memorial Library, Manuscripts and Archives, manuscript group number 757. Correspondence, 1918–50, with the bulk in the 1930s.

PW-PW Jr: Paul Windels Papers, in possession of his son Paul Windels Jr.

And of less importance: At Harvard Law School, the following collections: Mark DeWolfe Howe, James McCauley Landis, Thomas Reed Powell, Austin W. Scott, and Charles E. Wyzanski. At the Schlesinger Library, Harvard University, Elizabeth Glendower Gardiner, the Hamilton Family (Alice Hamilton), Freda Kirchway, and Frieda Miller. At the Houghton Library, Harvard University, William James Jr. Collections in private hands, Margaret Day Broussard, Michael John Burlingham, Frank Vos.

3. Unpublished studies

Shapiro, Herbert. *Reorganizations of the New York City Public School System, 1890–1910*. A thesis for a doctor's degree, Yeshiva University, New York, 1967. 231 pages.

Vos, Frank. "La Guardia and Burlingham: A Study of Political Friendship and Personal Influence." A thesis for a master's degree, Columbia University, 1983. 83 pages, including footnotes and bibliography.

Waugh, Joan. *Unsentimental Reformer: The Life of Josephine Shaw Lowell.* A thesis for a doctor's degree, University of California, Los Angeles, 1992. 645 pages.

4. Interviews

(a) Conducted by GM, 1992–2000; most in person,
several only by correspondence or telephone

Dorothy Schmiderer Baker,
  CCB's great-granddaughter
Glen W. Bowersock
Douglas V. D. Brown
Herbert Brownell
Charles Burlingham Jr.,
  CCB's grandson
Michael Burlingham,
  CCB's grandson
Michael John Burlingham,
  CCB's great-grandson
Rigmor "Mossik" Burlingham (Sheldrick),
  wife of CCB's grandson Bob
Lizabeth L. Burrell
Thomas D. Cabot
Michael A. Cardozo
Merrell E. Clark Jr.
Michael Marks Cohen
Theodore S. Cunningham
Helen Taylor Davidson
William J. Dean
Rosamond Taylor Edmondson,
  CCB's niece
Henry N. Ess III
Thomas B. Fenlon
Gerald Gunther
Charles S. Haight Jr.
John N. Hazard
Susan Hazard
John R. Hupper
Christopher P. Jones
Helen R. Kessler

Arthur Scott Long
Herbert M. Lord
Martha Urquhart Lord
Walter Lord
J. Edward Lumbard
Franklin C. Miller
Elliott B. Nixon
Daniel W. O'Connor Jr.
David Owen
Nancy Shaw Palmer
Richard W. Palmer
Gordon W. Paulsen
Thomas F. Pike
Arthur V. Savage
Caroline Fearey Schimmel
Nancy B. Schmiderer
Timothy F. Schmiderer,
  CCB's great-grandson
David F. Taylor
Philip Longley Taylor,
  CCB's nephew
Stephen H. Taylor
Thomas Thacher
Harold R. Tyler Jr.
Eugene Underwood Jr.
Katrina Burlingham Valenstein,
  CCB's granddaughter
Frank Vos
Agnes H. Whitaker
Ridley M. Whitaker
Paul Windels Jr.
John F. Woolverton

(b) Conducted by others

Tape recording of Eugene Underwood made in August 1993
by his son, Eugene Underwood Jr.

5. Reminiscences, oral histories, etc.

(a) In the Oral History Research Office at Columbia University (COH)
and individually cited by initials plus COH, e.g., CCB-COH

George W. Alger	Stanley M. Isaacs	Frances Perkins
William H. Allen	Nicholas Kelley	Justine Wise Polier
Chauncey Belknap	Reuben Lazarus	William A. Prendergast
Charles C. Burlingham	George McAneny	Clare Tousley
John W. Davis	John Lord O'Brian	Paul Windels

BOOKS

Allen, Alexander V. G. *Phillips Brooks, 1835–1893: Memories of His Life with Extracts from His Letters and Note-Books* (New York: Dutton, 1907).

Allen, Frederick Lewis. *Only Yesterday: An Informal History of the Nineteen-Twenties* (New York: Blue Ribbon Books, 1931).

———. *Since Yesterday: The Nineteen-Thirties in America, September 3, 1929–September 3, 1939* (New York: Harper, 1940).

Anstice, Henry. *History of St. George's Church in the City of New York, 1752–1811–1911* (New York: Harper, 1911).

Baker, Leonard. *Brandeis and Frankfurter: A Dual Biography* (New York: Harper, 1984).

Ballard, Robert D. *The Discovery of the Titanic* (New York: Madison, 1987; repr., New York: Warner, 1995).

Barnard, Harry. *The Forging of an American Jew: The Life and Times of Judge Julian W. Mack* (New York: Herzl, 1974).

Bailyn, Bernard, Donald Fleming, Oscar Handlin, and Stephan Thernstrom. *Glimpses of the Harvard Past* (Cambridge: Harvard University Press, 1986).

Bellush, Bernard. *Franklin D. Roosevelt as Governor of New York* (New York: Columbia University Press, 1955; repr., New York: AMS Press, 1968).

Bender, Thomas. *New York Intellect: A History of Intellectual Life in New York City, from 1750 to the Beginnings of Our Own Time* (New York: Knopf, 1987).

Bergan, Francis. *The History of the New York Court of Appeals, 1847–1932* (New York: Columbia University Press, 1985).

Bernstein, Iver. *The New York City Draft Riots: Their Significance for American Society and Politics in the Age of the Civil War* (New York: Oxford University Press, 1990).

Biddle, Francis. *In Brief Authority* (Garden City, N.Y.: Doubleday, 1962).

Biel, Steven. *Down with the Old Canoe: A Cultural History of the Titanic Disaster* (New York: Norton, 1996).

Bone, Kevin, ed. *The New York Waterfront: Evolution and Building Culture of the Port and Harbor* (New York: Monacelli, 1997).

Borkin, Joseph. *The Corrupt Judge: An Inquiry into Bribery and Other High Crimes and Misdemeanors in the Federal Courts* (New York: Clarkson N. Potter, 1962).

Botein, Bernard. *Trial Judge: The Candid, Behind-the-Bench Story of Justice Bernard Botein* (New York: Simon and Schuster, 1952).

Boyer, Paul. *Urban Masses and Moral Order in America, 1820–1920* (Cambridge: Harvard University Press, 1978).

Boyer, Richard O. *Max Steuer, Magician of the Law* (New York: Greenberg, 1932).

Bryce, James. *The American Commonwealth*, 2 vols., 2nd ed. rev. (London and New York: Macmillan, 1891).

Burlingame, Roger. *March of the Iron Men: A Social History of Union Through Invention* (New York: Scribner's, 1938).

Burlingham, Michael John. *The Last Tiffany: A Biography of Dorothy Tiffany Burlingham* (New York: Atheneum, 1989).

Burns, James MacGregor. *Roosevelt: The Lion and the Fox* (New York: Harcourt, Brace 1956).

Caro, Robert A. *The Power Broker: Robert Moses and the Fall of New York* (New York: Knopf, 1974).

Clark, Emmons. *History of the Seventh Regiment* (New York: privately printed, 1890).

Cohen, Sol. *Progressives and Urban School Reform: The Public Education Association of New York City, 1895–1954* (New York: Teachers College, Columbia University, 1964).

Coles, Robert. *Anna Freud: The Dream of Psychoanalysis* (Reading, Mass.: Addison-Wesley, 1992; one of the Radcliffe Biography Series).

Comparato, Frank E. *Chronicles of Genius and Folly: R. Hoe & Company and the Printing Press as a Service to Democracy* (Culver City, Calif.: Labyrinthos, 1979).

Cook, Adrian. *The Armies of the Streets: The New York City Draft Riots of 1863* (Lexington: University Press of Kentucky, 1974).

Cross, Whitney R. *The Burned-Over District: The Social and Intellectual History of Enthusiastic Religion in Western New York, 1800–1850* (Ithaca, N.Y.: Cornell University Press, 1950; New York: Harper, Torchbooks, 1965).

Cuneo, Ernest L. *Life with Fiorello A Memoir* (New York: Macmillan, 1955).

Curtis, Charles P. *Law as Large as Life: A Natural Law for Today and the Supreme Court as Its Prophet* (New York: Simon and Schuster, 1959).

Davis, Kenneth S. *FDR: The Beckoning of Destiny, 1882–1928, A History* (New York: Putnam, 1972).

Devine, Edward T. *When Social Work Was Young* (New York: Macmillan, 1939).

Dimond, Mary Clark, Norman Cousins, and J. Garry Clifford, eds. *Memoirs of a Man: Grenville Clark* (New York: Norton, 1975).

Douglas, William O. *Go East, Young Man: The Early Years; The Autobiography of William O. Douglas* (New York: Random House, 1974).

———. *The Court Years, 1939–1975; The Autobiography of William O. Douglas* (New York: Random House, 1980).

Dunne, Gerald T. *Grenville Clark, Public Citizen* (New York: Farrar, Straus and Giroux, 1986).

Earle, Walter K. *Mr. Shearman and Mr. Sterling and How They Grew; Being annals of their law firm, with biographical and historical highlights* (New Haven: Yale University Press, 1963).

Edwards, Ruth Dudley. *The Pursuit of Reason: The Economist, 1843–1993* (Boston: Harvard Business School, 1995).

Eisenstein, Louis, and Elliot Rosenberg. *A Stripe of Tammany's Tiger* (New York: Robert Speller, 1966).

The Encyclopedia of New York City, ed. Kenneth T. Jackson (New Haven: Yale University Press, 1995).

Farley, James A. *Jim Farley's Story: The Roosevelt Years* (New York: Whittlesey House, 1948).

Flynn, Edward J. *You're the Boss* (New York: Viking, 1947).

Fosdick, Raymond B. *Chronicle of a Generation: An Autobiography* (New York: Harper, 1958)

Fowler, Gene. *Beau James: The Life and Times of Jimmy Walker* (New York: Viking, 1949).

Frankfurter, Felix. *Felix Frankfurter Reminisces*, recorded and edited by Harlan B. Phillips (New York: Reynal, 1960).

Fredrickson, George M. *The Inner Civil War: Northern Intellectuals and the Crisis of the Union* (New York: Harper, 1965; Harper Torchbooks, 1968).

Freedman, Max, ed. *Roosevelt and Frankfurter: Their Correspondence* (Boston: Little Brown, 1967).

Freidel, Frank B. *Franklin D. Roosevelt: The Triumph* (Boston: Little, Brown, 1956).

———. *Franklin D. Roosevelt: Launching the New Deal* (Boston: Little, Brown, 1973).

Gardiner, Robin, and Dan van der Vat. *The Riddle of the Titanic* (London: Weidenfeld and Nicolson, 1995).

Garrett, Charles. *The La Guardia Years: Machine and Reform Politics in New York City* (New Brunswick, N.J.: Rutgers University Press, 1961).

Gilmartin, Gregory F. *Shaping the City: New York and the Municipal Art Society* (New York: Clarkson N. Potter, 1995).

Gilmore, Grant, and Charles L. Black Jr. *The Law of Admiralty*, 2nd ed. (Mineola, N.Y.: Foundation Press, 1975).

Goebel, Julius Jr. *A History of the School of Law, Columbia University* (New York: Columbia University Press, 1955).

Goldmark, Josephine. *Impatient Crusader: Florence Kelley's Life Story* (Urbana: University of Illinois Press, 1953).

Gould, Milton S. *The Witness Who Spoke with God and Other Tales from the Courthouse* (New York: Viking, 1979).

Greenbaum, Edward S. *A Lawyer's Job: In Court, in the Army, in the Office* (New York: Harcourt, Brace & World 1967).

Gunther, Gerald. *Learned Hand: The Man and the Judge* (New York: Knopf, 1994).

Gurstein, Rochelle. *The Repeal of Reticence: A History of America's Cultural and Legal Struggles over Free Speech, Obscenity, Sexual Liberation, and Modern Art* (New York: Hill and Wang, 1996).

Hamilton, Mary Agnes. *Remembering My Good Friends* (London: Jonathan Cape, 1944).

Hammack, David C. *Power and Society: Greater New York at the Turn of the Century* (New York: Russell Sage Foundation, 1982; repr., New York: Columbia University Press, 1987).

Hand, Learned. *The Spirit of Liberty: Papers and Addresses*, ed. Irving Dilliard, 3rd ed., enlarged (New York: Knopf, 1960).

Harbaugh, William H. *The Life and Times of Theodore Roosevelt* (New York: Collier, 1963; rev. ed., New York: Collier, 1966).

———. *Lawyer's Lawyer: The Life of John W. Davis* (New York: Oxford University Press, 1973).

Harper, J. Henry. *The House of Harper: A Century of Publishing in Franklin Square* (New York: Harper, 1912).

Heckscher, August, with Phyllis Robinson. *When La Guardia Was Mayor: New York's Legendary Years* (New York: Norton, 1978).

Hershkowitz, Leo. *Tweed's New York: Another Look* (Garden City, N.Y.: Anchor, 1977).

Hodgson, Godfrey. *The Colonel: The Life and Wars of Henry Stimson, 1867–1950* (New York: Knopf, 1990).

Hopkins, Charles Howard. *The Rise of the Social Gospel in American Protestantism, 1865–1915* (New Haven: Yale University Press, 1940).

Horwitz, Morton J. *The Transformation of American Law, 1870–1960: The Crisis of Legal Orthodoxy* (New York: Oxford University Press, 1992).

Hough, Charles M. *Reports of Cases in the Vice Admiralty of the Province of New York and in the Court of Admiralty of the State of New York, 1715–1788*, with an Historical Introduction and Appendix edited by Charles Merrill Hough, LL.D., United States Circuit Judge (New Haven: Yale University Press, 1925).

Howe, M. A. DeWolfe. *Phillips Brooks* (Boston: Small, Maynard, 1899).

Hurst, James Willard. *The Growth of American Law: The Law Makers* (Boston: Little, Brown, 1950).

Huthmacher, J. Joseph. *Senator Robert F. Wagner and the Rise of Urban Liberalism* (New York: Atheneum, 1968).

Isaacs, Edith S. *Love Affair with a City: The Story of Stanley M. Isaacs* (New York: Random House, 1967).

Jessup, Philip C. *Elihu Root*, 2 vols. (New York: Dodd, Mead, 1938).

Josephson, Matthew and Hannah. *Al Smith: Hero of the Cities* (Boston: Houghton Mifflin, 1969).

Joughin, G. Louis, and Edmund M. Morgan, *The Legacy of Sacco and Vanzetti* (New York: Harcourt, 1948; repr., 1964).

Kaufman, Andrew L. *Cardozo* (Cambridge: Harvard University Press, 1998).

Kessner, Thomas. *Fiorello H. La Guardia and the Making of New York* (New York: McGraw Hill, 1989).

Knox, John C. *A Judge Comes of Age* (New York: Scribner's, 1940).

Kronman, Anthony T. *The Lost Lawyer: Failing Ideals of the Legal Profession* (Cambridge: Harvard University Press, 1993).

La Guardia, Fiorello H. *The Making of an Insurgent: An Autobiography, 1882–1919* (Philadelphia: J. B. Lippincott, 1948).

Lash, Joseph P. *From the Diaries of Felix Frankfurter: with a Biographical Essay and Notes* (New York: Norton, 1975).

Lawrence, William. *Phillips Brooks: A Study* (Boston: Houghton, Mifflin, 1903).

———. *Life of Phillips Brooks* (New York: Harper, 1930).

Leuchtenburg, William E. *Franklin D. Roosevelt and the New Deal, 1932–1940* (New York: Harper & Row, 1963).

———. *The Supreme Court Reborn: The Constitutional Revolution in the Age of Roosevelt* (New York: Oxford University Press, 1995).

Lewinson, Edwin R. *John Purroy Mitchel, the Boy Mayor of New York* (New York: Astra Books, 1965).

Linowitz, Sol M., with Martin Mayer. *The Betrayed Profession: Lawyering at the End of the Twentieth Century* (New York: Scribner's, 1994).

Lord, Walter. *A Night to Remember* (New York: Holt, 1955).

———. *The Night Lives On* (New York: Morrow, 1986).

Mann, Arthur. *La Guardia: A Fighter Against His Times, 1882–1933* (Philadelphia: Lippincott, 1959).

———. *La Guardia Comes to Power, 1933* (Philadelphia: Lippincott, 1965).

Martin, George. *Madam Secretary, Frances Perkins* (Boston: Houghton, Mifflin, 1976).

———. *Causes and Conflicts: The Centennial History of the Association of the Bar of the City of New York, 1870–1970* (Boston: Houghton, Mifflin, 1970; repr. New York: Fordham University Press, 1997).

Mason, Alpheus Thomas. *Harlan Fiske Stone: Pillar of the Law* (New York: Viking, 1956).

Mayer, Martin. *Emory Buckner* (New York: Harper & Row, 1968).

McCague, James. *The Second Rebellion: The Story of the New York City Draft Riots of 1863* (New York: Dial Press, 1968).

McFeely, William S. *Grant: A Biography* (New York: Norton, 1981).

McShane, Clay. *Down the Asphalt Path: The Automobile and the American City* (New York: Columbia University Press, 1994).

Mendelson, Wallace, ed. *Felix Frankfurter: A Tribute* (New York: Reynal, 1964).

Miller, Nathan. *Theodore Roosevelt: A Life* (New York: Morrow, 1992).

Milne, Gordon. *George William Curtis and the Genteel Tradition* (Bloomington: Indiana University Press, 1956).

Mitgang, Herbert. *The Man Who Rode the Tiger: The Life and Times of Judge Samuel Seabury* (Philadelphia: Lippincott, 1963).

Moran, James. *Printing Presses: History and Development from the Fifteenth Century to Modern Times* (Berkeley: University of California Press, 1973).

Morison, Elting E. *Turmoil and Tradition: A Study of the Life and Times of Henry L. Stimson* (Boston: Houghton, Mifflin, 1960).

Morison, Samuel Eliot, *Three Centuries of Harvard, 1636–1936* (Cambridge: Harvard University Press, 1936).

———. ed. *The Development of Harvard University since the Inauguration of President Eliot, 1869–1929* (Cambridge: Harvard University Press, 1930).

Morison, Samuel Eliot, Henry Steele Commager, and William E. Leuchtenburg. *The Growth of the American Republic*, 7th ed., 2 vols. (New York: Oxford University Press, 1980).

Morris, Edmund. *The Rise of Theodore Roosevelt* (New York: Coward, McCann & Geoghegan, 1979).

Morris, James. *The Great Port: A Passage Through New York* (London: Faber, 1970).

Morris, Jan. *Manhattan '45* (New York: Oxford University Press, 1987).

Morris, Jeffrey B. *Federal Justice in the Second Circuit: A History of the United States Courts in New York, Connecticut and Vermont, 1787 to 1987* (New York: Federal Bar Council Foundation, 1987).

Morris, Newbold. *Let the Chips Fall: My Battles Against Corruption* (New York: Appleton-Century-Crofts, 1955).

Moscow, Warren. *Politics in the Empire State* (New York: Knopf, 1948; repr., New York: Greenwood, 1979).

Moses, Robert. *La Guardia: A Salute and a Memoir* (New York: Simon and Schuster, 1957).

Moulton, Elizabeth. *St. George's Church, New York* (New York: privately printed, 1964).

Murphy, Bruce Allen. *Wild Bill: The Legend and Life of William O. Douglas* (New York: Random House, 2003).

Nelson, Marcia, ed. *The Remarkable Hands: An Affectionate Portrait* (New York: Foundation of the Federal Bar Council, 1983).

———. "Making Sure We Are True to Our Founders": The Association of the Bar of the City of New York, 1970–95 (New York: Fordham University Press, 1977).

Nevins, Allan, and John A. Krout, eds. *The Greater City: New York, 1898–1948* (New York: Columbia University Press, 1948).

Novick, Sheldon M. *Honorable Justice: The Life of Oliver Wendell Holmes* (Boston: Little, Brown, 1989).

Pinkney, David H. *Napoleon III and the Rebuilding of Paris* (Princeton: Princeton University Press, 1958).

Polenberg, Richard. *The World of Benjamin Cardozo: Personal Values and the Judicial Process* (Cambridge: Harvard University Press, 1997).

Posner, Richard A. *Cardozo: A Study in Reputation* (Chicago: University of Chicago Press, 1990).

———. *The Federal Courts: Challenge and Reform* (Cambridge: Harvard University Press, 1996).

Pusey, Merlo J. *Charles Evans Hughes*, 2 vols. (New York: Macmillan, 1952).

Rainsford, William S. *The Story of a Varied Life: An Autobiography* (Garden City, N.Y.: Doubleday, 1922).

Ravitch, Diane. *The Great School Wars: New York City, 1805–1973* (New York: Basic Books, 1974).

Riis, Jacob A. *How the Other Half Lives: Studies among the Tenements of New York*, ed. Sam Bass Warner Jr. (Cambridge: Harvard University Press, 1970).

Riordon, William L., ed., *Plunkitt of Tammany Hall*, with an Introduction by Arthur Mann (New York: Dutton, 1963).

Rosenman, Samuel I. *Working with Roosevelt* (New York: Harper, 1952).

Schlesinger, Arthur M., Jr. *The Age of Roosevelt*, 3 vols. (Boston: Houghton, Mifflin, 1957, 1959, 1960).

Sherwood, Robert E. *Roosevelt and Hopkins: An Intimate History* (New York: Harper, 1948; rev. ed., New York: Harper, 1950).

Starr, Roger. *The Rise and Fall of New York City* (New York: Basic Books, 1985).

Steuer, Aron. *Max D. Steuer, Trial Lawyer* (New York: Random House, 1950).

Stoddard, Lothrop. *Master of Manhattan: The Life of Richard Croker* (New York: Longmans, Green 1931).

Strong, Theron G. *Landmarks of a Lawyer's Lifetime* (New York: Dodd, Mead, 1914).

Sutherland, Arthur E. *The Law at Harvard: A History of Ideas and Men, 1817–1967* (Cambridge: Harvard University Press, 1967).

Taft, Henry W. *Legal Miscellanies: Six Decades of Changes and Progress* (New York: Macmillan, 1941).

Thomas, Norman, and Paul Blanshard. *What's the Matter with New York?: A National Problem* (New York: Macmillan, 1932).

Tocqueville, Alexis de. *Democracy in America*, edited with an Introduction by Henry Steele Commager (London: Oxford University Press, 1946).

Townsend, Kim. *Manhood at Harvard: William James and Others* (New York: Norton, 1996).

United States Courts in the Second Circuit: A Collection of History Lectures Delivered by Judges of the Second Circuit (New York: Federal Bar Council Foundation, 1992).

Wade, Wyn Craig. *The Titanic: End of a Dream* (New York: Rawson, Wade, 1979).

Waldman, Louis. *Albany: The Crisis in Government* (New York: Boni & Liveright, 1920).

Welling, Richard. *As the Twig Is Bent* (New York: G. P. Putnam's Sons, 1942).

Werner, M. R. *Barnum* (New York: Harcourt, Brace, 1923).

———. *Tammany Hall* (Garden City, N.Y.: Doubleday, 1928).

White, Nelson C. *Abbott H. Thayer, Painter and Naturalist* (Connecticut Printers, 1951).

Wilson, Edmund. *Patriotic Gore* (New York: Farrar, Straus and Giroux, 1962; repr., New York: Norton, 1994).

Woolverton, John F. *The Education of Phillips Brooks* (Urbana: University of Illinois Press, 1995).

WPA (Work Projects Administration). *A Maritime History of New York* (Garden City, N.Y.: Doubleday, 1941).

———. *The WPA Guide to New York City: The Federal Writers' Project Guide to 1930s New York*, with a new Introduction by William H. Whyte (1939; repr., New York: Pantheon, 1982).

Wyzanski, Charles E., Jr. *Whereas—A Judge's Premises: Essays in Judgment, Ethics, and the Law* (Boston: Little, Brown, 1965).

Young-Bruehl, Elisabeth. *Anna Freud: A Biography* (New York: Summit Books, 1988).

ACKNOWLEDGMENTS

This biography exists chiefly because of the determination of the William Nelson Cromwell Foundation. C. C. Burlingham, for the first ninety years of his life, resisted any suggestion of a biography. But when he was ninety-one, he gave a series of interviews to Allan Nevins, of Columbia University's Oral History Research Office, and the experience evidently started a change of mind. Nevins was no doubt a persuasive advocate of preserving history, and in CCB he had a man who, in January 1949, could clearly recall Lincoln's presidency, the New York City draft riots of 1863, and Lincoln's assassination and funeral procession in New York.

Slowly, CCB came to approve the idea of a biography—but only if written and published after his death. He picked a biographer, his friend and City Court judge Samuel C. Coleman, and allowed Coleman to start collecting material. At the same time CCB dictated memorandums on his youth, love of theater, and other such subjects, leaving many dates and names blank as well as misstated facts uncorrected. Then CCB died. Coleman continued to gather material, and then he died, without a word of the book written.

CCB's son, in 1978, gave this mass of material, including a huge collection of CCB's letters (handwritten and typed) to the Harvard Law School Library, whose staff, over several years, sorted and cataloged it. Without that preparatory work, a biography would not have been possible.

Even cataloged, the amount of Burlingham material at Harvard was daunting, and still more was scattered through other collections. One scholar who had written briefly on the La Guardia-Burlingham relationship thought to undertake a longer work, chiefly on Burlingham's public activities, but decided against it: the commitment required in time and money was too great.

Early in 1992 the Cromwell Foundation, noting that the number of men and women who had known CCB was fast dwindling, commissioned a full biography, granting the author the wherewithal to sustain him through ten years of work and allowing him complete freedom. All opinions, right or wrong, are mine.

The many institutions and individuals who helped me are listed at the start of the Bibliography, where their relationship to CCB is stated. Here, besides thanking in particular the Cromwell Foundation and the Harvard Law School Library, I want to thank another institution without which this biography could not have been written: the Burlingham family. All its members were willing to talk to me, some even provided lodging overnight, and some, I discovered, had preserved many of CCB's more personal papers (one even had a trunkful of early handwritten letters). His handwriting was execrable, and he was much given to abbreviations and the use of initials, but these family letters when deciphered allowed some balance between CCB's public and private life. CCB's grandson Charles Burlingham Jr. and his great-grandson Michael John Burlingham were continually helpful.

To those three institutions I would add the New York Public Library with its exceptional collection of newspapers, journals, genealogies, and out-of-the-way books. Other libraries that opened collections to me are: the Association of the Bar of the City of New York; Baker Library, Dartmouth College; the Boston Athenaeum; Case Library, Colgate University; Cornell Law School; at Columbia University, the Archives, Law School, Low Memorial, Oral History Research Office, and the Rare Book and Manuscript Division in Butler Library; the Century Association Archives (New York); the Franklin D. Roosevelt Library (Hyde Park); Fordham Law Library; Federal Bar Council (New York); General Society of Mechanics and Tradesmen (New York); at Harvard University, the Archives, Schlesinger, and Houghton Libraries; the Hoosac School; the Harvard Club of New York City; La Guardia and Wagner Archives, La Guardia Community College (Long Island City, New York); the Library of Congress; the National Archives, Northeast Region (New York); New York County Lawyers' Association; New York Stock Exchange Archives; Peabody Essex Museum (Salem, Massachusetts); Phillips Exeter Academy; St. George's Church (New York); Seventh Regiment Fund (New York); and Sterling Memorial Library, Yale University.

I am grateful to Jonathan Hand Churchill, Learned Hand's grandson, and to Gerald Gunther, Judge Hand's biographer, for permission to use the Learned Hand Papers at the Harvard Law School Library; to Arthur V. Savage, Augustus N. Hand's grandson, for the use of his collection of his grandfather's papers; to the Century Association for the use of its archives; and to Paul Windels Jr. for the use of his collection of his father's papers.

Three people who helped me to prepare the typescript, often making editorial suggestions and solving computer problems that puzzled me, are Heather M. Quist, P. David Wilkin, and Dusan Zavasic. Those who helped with photographs are named in the Illustration Credits that follows the Index.

My editor was Elisabeth Sifton, the best editor I have ever worked with. I found it a joy to have the manuscript read with such care, and though I had thought the book was done, excited by her comments, I rewrote parts of it. Working with her (though she was in New York while I stayed in Pennsylvania's rural hills) was a rare and great experience, one I am glad to have had.

INDEX

ILLUSTRATION CREDITS

Frontispiece: CCB, c. 1930. Courtesy of Dorothy Schmiderer Baker.

CCB, by Alexander Iacovleff, signed and dated 1936. Sepia chalk on paper; image 20¼ by 14¼ inches. Photograph by Jim Strong. Courtesy of the Harvard Club of New York City.

Aaron Hale Burlingham, circa 1860. Courtesy of Michael John Burlingham.

Aaron Hale Burlingham. Oil on canvas, unsigned, undated. Photograph by Clive Russ. Courtesy of Charles Burlingham Jr.

Albert S. and his younger brother Charles C. Burlingham, circa 1863. Photograph by J. Gurney & Sons. Courtesy of Michael John Burlingham.

CCB, circa 1879, when a senior at Harvard College. Photograph by C. W. Pach. Courtesy of Michael John Burlingham.

Colonel Richard March Hoe. Courtesy of Michael John Burlingham.

Annie Corbin Hoe. Oil on canvas, approximately 11 by 13 inches, by Abbott Thayer. Unsigned, but surely the one mentioned in his biography by Nelson C. White, page 30, painted circa 1882. After ACH's death in 1886, the portrait hung in CCB's living room until his death in 1959. Photograph by Beth Ludwig. Courtesy of CCB's great-granddaughter Dorothy Schmiderer Baker.

Phillips Brooks. Drawing by "L. C. D.," 1895 (Brooks died in 1893), charcoal and white paint on brown paper, 74.4 by 54 centimeters. Courtesy of the Harvard University Portrait Collection. The portrait now hangs in Phillips Brooks House (1898), Harvard Yard, Cambridge, Massachusetts.

Adeline Hoe Lawrence and her five daughters, 1877. Courtesy of CCB's great-nephew David Fairbanks Taylor, grandson of Grace (held by her mother).

Louisa Lawrence Burlingham with her third child, Robert, in 1888, born 29 February 1888. Photograph by J. B. Luttbeg, Mount Vernon, New York. Courtesy of Michael John Burlingham.

Ellen Terry as Portia. Brown ink on paper over pencil indications, 7¼ by 3¼ inches. Inscribed *Miss Ellen Terry as Portia: / Joe Evans who drew it from a fotograf by Window & Grove / 63a Baker Street Port* [?] *Square London W. / for* [?] *AND AFTER / MANY CURIOUS JOURNEYINGS* . . . Courtesy of Charles Burlingham Jr.

Joe Evans. Courtesy of Century Association Archives Foundation.

Theron G. Strong. Courtesy of Century Association Archives Foundation.

George William Curtis. Courtesy of Century Association Archives Foundation.

Richard W. G. Welling. Courtesy of Century Association Archives Foundation.

Learned Hand, circa 1909. Courtesy of Burlingham Underwood.

The Illustrated London News, 4 May 1912. CCB at the end of the table, at Ismay's right shoulder.

CCB and Nicholas Murray Butler, walking up Fifth Avenue after morning service at St. George's Church on Easter Day, 1930. Courtesy of Charles Burlingham Jr.

Thomas D. Thacher, circa 1945. Courtesy of Mary Thacher Brown.

Paul Windels, circa 1933. Courtesy of Paul Windels Jr.

CCB and his wife, LLB, on the porch at Black Point, circa 1930. Courtesy of CCB's great-niece, Helen Taylor Davison.

CCB in his eighties, circa 1943. Photograph by and courtesy of his granddaughter Katrina Burlingham Valenstein.

The silver oar, made by Charles Le Roux, circa 1725; "Mace of the Vice Admiralty Court of the Province of New York"; Museum of the City of New York; on deposit from the United States District Court for the Southern District of New York; Photo: John Parnell.

CCB alone on the porch at Black Point, circa 1950. Courtesy of Charles Burlingham Jr.

St. George's Church, from *St. George's Church, New York*, by Elizabeth Moulton, 1964.

CCB (in the white suit) at City Hall on 19 June 1945, seconds after being introduced to General Eisenhower by Mayor La Guardia. The picture appeared in the *World-Telegram*, 19 June 1945, page 3. Courtesy of Michael Burlingham.